ALTERNATIVE INVESTMENT, PORTFOLIO MANAGEMENT, AND PRIVATE WEALTH MANAGEMENT

CFA® Program Curriculum
2023 • LEVEL III • VOLUME 4

WILEY

© 2022, 2021, 2020, 2019, 2018, 2017, 2016, 2015, 2014, 2013, 2012, 2011, 2010, 2009, 2008, 2007, 2006 by CFA Institute. All rights reserved.

This copyright covers material written expressly for this volume by the editor/s as well as the compilation itself. It does not cover the individual selections herein that first appeared elsewhere. Permission to reprint these has been obtained by CFA Institute for this edition only. Further reproductions by any means, electronic or mechanical, including photocopying and recording, or by any information storage or retrieval systems, must be arranged with the individual copyright holders noted.

CFA®, Chartered Financial Analyst®, AIMR-PPS®, and GIPS® are just a few of the trademarks owned by CFA Institute. To view a list of CFA Institute trademarks and the Guide for Use of CFA Institute Marks, please visit our website at www.cfainstitute.org.

This publication is designed to provide accurate and authoritative information in regard to the subject matter covered. It is sold with the understanding that the publisher is not engaged in rendering legal, accounting, or other professional service. If legal advice or other expert assistance is required, the services of a competent professional should be sought.

All trademarks, service marks, registered trademarks, and registered service marks are the property of their respective owners and are used herein for identification purposes only.

ISBN 978-1-953337-14-6 (paper)
ISBN 978-1-953337-38-2 (ebk)

10 9 8 7 6 5 4 3 2 1

Please visit our website at
www.WileyGlobalFinance.com.

CONTENTS

How to Use the CFA Program Curriculum ix
    Background on the CBOK ix
    Organization of the Curriculum x
    Features of the Curriculum x
    Designing Your Personal Study Program xi
    CFA Institute Learning Ecosystem (LES) xii
    Prep Providers xiii
    Feedback xiv

Portfolio Management

Study Session 9   **Alternative Investments for Portfolio Management**   3

Reading 19   **Hedge Fund Strategies**   5
    Introduction and Classification of Hedge Fund Strategies 5
        Classification of Hedge Funds and Strategies 7
    Equity Strategies: Long/Short Equity 11
        Long/Short Equity 11
    Equity Strategies: Dedicated Short Selling and Short-Biased 14
        Investment Characteristics 15
        Strategy Implementation 16
    Equity Strategies: Equity Market Neutral 18
        Investment Characteristics 19
        Strategy Implementation 21
    Event-Driven Strategies: Merger Arbitrage 22
        Merger Arbitrage 22
    Event-Driven Strategies: Distressed Securities 26
        Investment Characteristics 27
        Strategy Implementation 28
    Relative Value Strategies: Fixed Income Arbitrage 30
        Fixed-Income Arbitrage 30
    Relative Value Strategies: Convertible Bond Arbitrage 34
        Investment Characteristics 35
        Strategy Implementation 36
    Opportunistic Strategies: Global Macro Strategies 38
        Global Macro Strategies 39
    Opportunistic Strategies: Managed Futures 42
        Investment Characteristics 42
        Strategy Implementation 43
    Specialist Strategies 46
        Volatility Trading 46
        Reinsurance/Life Settlements 50
    Multi-Manager Strategies 53
        Fund-of-Funds 53
        Multi-Strategy Hedge Funds 55

◘ indicates an optional segment

Analysis of Hedge Fund Strategies using a Conditional Factor Risk Model	60
Conditional Factor Risk Model	61
Evaluating Equity Hedge Fund Strategies: Application	65
Evaluating Multi-Manager Hedge Fund Strategies: Application	70
Portfolio Contribution of Hedge Fund Strategies	73
Performance Contribution to a 60/40 Portfolio	73
Risk Metrics	76
Summary	79
Practice Problems	83
Solutions	91

Reading 20

Asset Allocation to Alternative Investments — 103

Introduction and The Role of Alternative Investments in a Multi-Asset Portfolio	103
The Role of Alternative Investments in a Multi-Asset Portfolio	104
Diversifying Equity Risk	110
Volatility Reduction over the Short Time Horizon	110
Risk of Not Meeting the Investment Goals over the Long Time Horizon	114
Traditional Approaches to Asset Classification	116
Traditional Approaches to Asset Classification	116
Risk-Based Approaches to Asset Classification and Comparing Risk-Based and Traditional Approaches	119
Illustration: Asset Allocation and Risk-Based Approaches	123
Comparing Risk-Based and Traditional Approaches	125
Risk Considerations, Return Expectations and Investment Vehicle	126
Risk Considerations	126
Return Expectations	127
Investment Vehicle	128
Liquidity	130
Liquidity Risks Associated with the Investment Vehicle	130
Liquidity Risks Associated with the Underlying Investments	132
Fees and Expenses, Tax Considerations, and Other Considerations	133
Tax Considerations	134
Other Considerations	134
Suitability Considerations	137
Investment Horizon	137
Expertise	137
Governance	138
Transparency	138
Asset Allocation Approaches and Statistical Properties and Challenges of Asset Returns	140
Statistical Properties and Challenges of Asset Returns	141
Monte Carlo Simulation	146
Simulating Skewed and Fat-Tailed Financial Variables	147
Simulation for Long-Term Horizon Risk Assessment	149
Portfolio Optimization	153
Mean–Variance Optimization without and with Constraints	154
Mean–CVaR Optimization	156

◉ indicates an optional segment

Contents

	Risk Factor-Based Optimization	160
	Liquidity Planning and Achieving and Maintaining the Strategic Asset Allocation	164
	Achieving and Maintaining the Strategic Asset Allocation	165
	Managing the Capital Calls and Preparing for the Unexpected	170
	Preparing for the Unexpected	170
	Monitoring the Investment Program	174
	Overall Investment Program Monitoring	174
	Performance Evaluation	175
	Monitoring the Firm and the Investment Process	177
	Summary	179
	Practice Problems	183
	Solutions	192
Study Session 10	**Private Wealth Management (1)**	**201**
Reading 21	**Overview of Private Wealth Management**	**203**
	Introduction and Private Clients Versus Institutional Clients	204
	Private Clients versus Institutional Clients	204
	Understanding Private Clients: Information Needed in Advising Private Clients	207
	Information Needed in Advising Private Clients	207
	Client Goals	212
	Planned Goals	212
	Unplanned Goals	213
	The Wealth Manager's Role	213
	Private Client Risk Tolerance	215
	Risk Tolerance Questionnaire	215
	Risk Tolerance Conversation	217
	Risk Tolerance with Multiple Goals	217
	Technical and Soft Skills for Wealth Managers	218
	Technical Skills	218
	Soft Skills	219
	Investment Planning, and Capital Sufficiency Analysis	220
	Capital Sufficiency Analysis	220
	Retirement Planning	223
	Retirement Stage of Life	223
	Investment Policy Statement	227
	Parts of the Investment Policy Statement	228
	Sample Investment Policy Statement	233
	Portfolio Construction and Allocation and Investments for Private Wealth Clients	237
	Portfolio Allocation and Investments for Private Wealth Clients	237
	Portfolio Reporting and Review	241
	Portfolio Reporting	241
	Portfolio Review	244
	Evaluating The Success of an Investment Program	244
	Goal Achievement	245
	Process Consistency	245

indicates an optional segment

Portfolio Performance	**245**
Definitions of Success	**246**
Ethical and Compliance Considerations in Private Wealth Management	**247**
Ethical Considerations	**247**
Compliance Considerations	**248**
Private Client Segments	**249**
Mass Affluent Segment	**250**
High-Net-Worth Segment	**250**
Ultra-High-Net-Worth Segment	**250**
Robo-Advisors	**251**
Summary	**252**
Practice Problems	**254**
Solutions	**262**

Reading 22 — Topics in Private Wealth Management — **269**

Introduction	**270**
General Principles of Taxation: Components of Return and Tax Status of the Account	**272**
Taxation of the Components of Return	**272**
The Tax Status of the Account	**275**
The Jurisdiction that Applies to the Investor	**276**
Measuring Tax Efficiency with After-Tax Returns	**283**
Tax Efficiency of Various Asset Classes and Investment Strategies	**283**
Calculating After-Tax Returns	**284**
Taxable, Tax-Exempt, and Tax-Deferred Accounts: Capital Accumulation and Asset Location	**292**
Capital Accumulation in Taxable, Tax-Deferred, and Tax-Exempt Accounts	**293**
Asset Location	**294**
Taxable, Tax-Exempt, and Tax-Deferred Accounts: Decumulation Strategies and Charitable Giving Strategies	**297**
Tax Considerations in Charitable Giving	**299**
Tax Management Strategies and Basic Tax Strategies	**300**
Basic Portfolio Tax Management Strategies	**300**
Application of Tax Management Strategies	**301**
Investment Vehicles	**301**
Tax Loss Harvesting	**304**
Quantitative Tax Management	**306**
Managing Concentrated Portfolios and Risk and Tax Considerations in Managing Concentrated Single-Asset Positions	**308**
Risk and Tax Considerations in Managing Concentrated Single-Asset Positions	**308**
Strategies for Managing Concentrated Positions in Public Equities	**310**
Staged Diversification and Completion Portfolios	**311**
Tax-Optimized Equity Strategies—Equity Monetization, Collars, and Call Writing	**312**
Tax-Free Exchanges	**315**
Charitable Remainder Trust	**316**

◎ indicates an optional segment

Contents

Strategies for Managing Concentrated Positions in Privately Owned Businesses and Strategies for Managing Concentrated Positions in Real Estate	317
Personal Line of Credit Secured by Company Shares	318
Leveraged Recapitalization	318
Employee Stock Ownership Plan	318
Strategies for Managing Concentrated Positions in Real Estate	319
Mortgage Financing	319
Real Estate Monetization for the Charitably Inclined—An Asset Location Strategy	320
Directing and Transferring Wealth and Objectives of Gift and Estate Planning	321
Objectives of Gift and Estate Planning	321
Gift and Estate Planning Strategies, Introduction to Estate Planning: Wills, Probate and Legal Systems, and Lifetime Gifts and Testamentary Bequests	325
Introduction to Estate Planning: Wills, Probate, and Legal Systems	325
Lifetime Gifts and Testamentary Bequests	326
Efficiency of Lifetime Gifts versus Testamentary Bequests	329
Estate Planning Tools: Trusts, Foundations, Life Insurance, Companies	331
Managing Wealth Across Generations, General Principles of Family Governance, Family Conflict Resolution, and Family Dynamics in the Context of Business Exit	336
General Principles of Family Governance	337
Family Conflict Resolution	338
Family Dynamics in the Context of Business Exit	339
Planning for the Unexpected	341
Divorce	342
Incapacity	342
Summary	344
Practice Problems	348
Solutions	353

Study Session 11	**Private Wealth Management (2)**	**363**
Reading 23	**Risk Management for Individuals**	**365**
	Introduction	366
	Human Capital, Financial Capital, and Economic Net Worth	366
	Human Capital	367
	Financial Capital	370
	Economic Net Worth	374
	A Framework for Individual Risk Management	375
	The Risk Management Strategy for Individuals	375
	Financial Stages of Life	376
	The Individual Balance Sheet	378
	Traditional Balance Sheet	379
	Economic (Holistic) Balance Sheet	380
	Changes in Economic Net Worth	382

◉ indicates an optional segment

Individual Risk Exposures	385
Earnings Risk	385
Premature Death Risk	386
Longevity Risk	387
Property Risk	388
Liability Risk	388
Health Risk	388
Life Insurance: Uses, Types and Elements	390
Life Insurance	391
Life Insurance - Pricing, Policy Cost Comparison and Determining Amount Needed	394
Mortality Expectations	394
Calculation of the Net Premium and Gross Premium	396
Cash Values and Policy Reserves	398
Consumer Comparisons of Life Insurance Costs	399
How Much Life Insurance Does One Need?	401
Other Types of Insurance	402
Property Insurance	404
Health/Medical Insurance	406
Liability Insurance	407
Other Types of Insurance	407
Annuities: Types, Structure and Classification	408
Parties to an Annuity Contract	409
Classification of Annuities	409
Annuities: Advantages and Disadvantages of Fixed and Variable Annuities	412
Volatility of Benefit Amount	413
Flexibility	413
Future Market Expectations	413
Fees	414
Inflation Concerns	414
Payout Methods	414
Annuity Benefit Taxation	415
Appropriateness of Annuities	415
Risk Management Implementation: Determining the Optimal Strategy and Case Analysis	417
Determining the Optimal Risk Management Strategy	418
Analyzing an Insurance Program	419
The Effect of Human Capital on Asset Allocation and Risk Reduction	426
Asset Allocation and Risk Reduction	429
Summary	432
Practice Problems	435
Solutions	441
Glossary	G-1

indicates an optional segment

How to Use the CFA Program Curriculum

Congratulations on your decision to enter the Chartered Financial Analyst (CFA®) Program. This exciting and rewarding program of study reflects your desire to become a serious investment professional. You are embarking on a program noted for its high ethical standards and the breadth of knowledge, skills, and abilities (competencies) it develops. Your commitment should be educationally and professionally rewarding.

The credential you seek is respected around the world as a mark of accomplishment and dedication. Each level of the program represents a distinct achievement in professional development. Successful completion of the program is rewarded with membership in a prestigious global community of investment professionals. CFA charterholders are dedicated to life-long learning and maintaining currency with the ever-changing dynamics of a challenging profession. CFA Program enrollment represents the first step toward a career-long commitment to professional education.

The CFA exam measures your mastery of the core knowledge, skills, and abilities required to succeed as an investment professional. These core competencies are the basis for the Candidate Body of Knowledge (CBOK™). The CBOK consists of four components:

- A broad outline that lists the major CFA Program topic areas (www.cfainstitute.org/programs/cfa/curriculum/cbok);
- Topic area weights that indicate the relative exam weightings of the top-level topic areas (www.cfainstitute.org/programs/cfa/curriculum);
- Learning outcome statements (LOS) that advise candidates about the specific knowledge, skills, and abilities they should acquire from readings covering a topic area (LOS are provided in candidate study sessions and at the beginning of each reading); and
- CFA Program curriculum that candidates receive upon exam registration.

Therefore, the key to your success on the CFA exams is studying and understanding the CBOK. The following sections provide background on the CBOK, the organization of the curriculum, features of the curriculum, and tips for designing an effective personal study program.

BACKGROUND ON THE CBOK

CFA Program is grounded in the practice of the investment profession. CFA Institute performs a continuous practice analysis with investment professionals around the world to determine the competencies that are relevant to the profession, beginning with the Global Body of Investment Knowledge (GBIK®). Regional expert panels and targeted surveys are conducted annually to verify and reinforce the continuous feedback about the GBIK. The practice analysis process ultimately defines the CBOK. The CBOK reflects the competencies that are generally accepted and applied by investment professionals. These competencies are used in practice in a generalist context and are expected to be demonstrated by a recently qualified CFA charterholder.

The CFA Institute staff—in conjunction with the Education Advisory Committee and Curriculum Level Advisors, who consist of practicing CFA charterholders—designs the CFA Program curriculum in order to deliver the CBOK to candidates. The exams, also written by CFA charterholders, are designed to allow you to demonstrate your mastery of the CBOK as set forth in the CFA Program curriculum. As you structure your personal study program, you should emphasize mastery of the CBOK and the practical application of that knowledge. For more information on the practice analysis, CBOK, and development of the CFA Program curriculum, please visit www.cfainstitute.org.

ORGANIZATION OF THE CURRICULUM

The Level III CFA Program curriculum is organized into six topic areas. Each topic area begins with a brief statement of the material and the depth of knowledge expected. It is then divided into one or more study sessions. These study sessions should form the basic structure of your reading and preparation. Each study session includes a statement of its structure and objective and is further divided into assigned readings. An outline illustrating the organization of these study sessions can be found at the front of each volume of the curriculum.

The readings are commissioned by CFA Institute and written by content experts, including investment professionals and university professors. Each reading includes LOS and the core material to be studied, often a combination of text, exhibits, and in-text examples and questions. End of Reading Questions (EORQs) followed by solutions help you understand and master the material. The LOS indicate what you should be able to accomplish after studying the material. The LOS, the core material, and the EORQs are dependent on each other, with the core material and EORQs providing context for understanding the scope of the LOS and enabling you to apply a principle or concept in a variety of scenarios.

The entire readings, including the EORQs, are the basis for all exam questions and are selected or developed specifically to teach the knowledge, skills, and abilities reflected in the CBOK.

You should use the LOS to guide and focus your study because each exam question is based on one or more LOS and the core material and practice problems associated with the LOS. As a candidate, you are responsible for the entirety of the required material in a study session.

We encourage you to review the information about the LOS on our website (www.cfainstitute.org/programs/cfa/curriculum/study-sessions), including the descriptions of LOS "command words" on the candidate resources page at www.cfainstitute.org.

FEATURES OF THE CURRICULUM

End of Reading Questions/Solutions *All End of Reading Questions (EORQs) as well as their solutions are part of the curriculum and are required material for the exam.* In addition to the in-text examples and questions, these EORQs help demonstrate practical applications and reinforce your understanding of the concepts presented. Some of these EORQs are adapted from past CFA exams and/or may serve as a basis for exam questions.

Glossary   For your convenience, each volume includes a comprehensive Glossary. Throughout the curriculum, a **bolded** word in a reading denotes a term defined in the Glossary.

Note that the digital curriculum that is included in your exam registration fee is searchable for key words, including Glossary terms.

LOS Self-Check   We have inserted checkboxes next to each LOS that you can use to track your progress in mastering the concepts in each reading.

Source Material   The CFA Institute curriculum cites textbooks, journal articles, and other publications that provide additional context or information about topics covered in the readings. As a candidate, you are not responsible for familiarity with the original source materials cited in the curriculum.

Note that some readings may contain a web address or URL. The referenced sites were live at the time the reading was written or updated but may have been deactivated since then.

Some readings in the curriculum cite articles published in the *Financial Analysts Journal®*, which is the flagship publication of CFA Institute. Since its launch in 1945, the *Financial Analysts Journal* has established itself as the leading practitioner-oriented journal in the investment management community. Over the years, it has advanced the knowledge and understanding of the practice of investment management through the publication of peer-reviewed practitioner-relevant research from leading academics and practitioners. It has also featured thought-provoking opinion pieces that advance the common level of discourse within the investment management profession. Some of the most influential research in the area of investment management has appeared in the pages of the *Financial Analysts Journal*, and several Nobel laureates have contributed articles.

Candidates are not responsible for familiarity with *Financial Analysts Journal* articles that are cited in the curriculum. But, as your time and studies allow, we strongly encourage you to begin supplementing your understanding of key investment management issues by reading this, and other, CFA Institute practice-oriented publications through the Research & Analysis webpage (www.cfainstitute.org/en/research).

Errata   The curriculum development process is rigorous and includes multiple rounds of reviews by content experts. Despite our efforts to produce a curriculum that is free of errors, there are times when we must make corrections. Curriculum errata are periodically updated and posted by exam level and test date online (www.cfainstitute.org/en/programs/submit-errata). If you believe you have found an error in the curriculum, you can submit your concerns through our curriculum errata reporting process found at the bottom of the Curriculum Errata webpage.

DESIGNING YOUR PERSONAL STUDY PROGRAM

Create a Schedule   An orderly, systematic approach to exam preparation is critical. You should dedicate a consistent block of time every week to reading and studying. Complete all assigned readings and the associated problems and solutions in each study session. Review the LOS both before and after you study each reading to ensure that you have mastered the applicable content and can demonstrate the knowledge, skills, and abilities described by the LOS and the assigned reading. Use the LOS self-check to track your progress and highlight areas of weakness for later review.

Successful candidates report an average of more than 300 hours preparing for each exam. Your preparation time will vary based on your prior education and experience, and you will probably spend more time on some study sessions than on others.

You should allow ample time for both in-depth study of all topic areas and additional concentration on those topic areas for which you feel the least prepared.

CFA INSTITUTE LEARNING ECOSYSTEM (LES)

As you prepare for your exam, we will email you important exam updates, testing policies, and study tips. Be sure to read these carefully.

Your exam registration fee includes access to the CFA Program Learning Ecosystem (LES). This digital learning platform provides access, even offline, to all of the readings and End of Reading Questions found in the print curriculum organized as a series of shorter online lessons with associated EORQs. This tool is your one-stop location for all study materials, including practice questions and mock exams.

The LES provides the following supplemental study tools:

Structured and Adaptive Study Plans The LES offers two ways to plan your study through the curriculum. The first is a structured plan that allows you to move through the material in the way that you feel best suits your learning. The second is an adaptive study plan based on the results of an assessment test that uses actual practice questions.

Regardless of your chosen study path, the LES tracks your level of proficiency in each topic area and presents you with a dashboard of where you stand in terms of proficiency so that you can allocate your study time efficiently.

Flashcards and Game Center The LES offers all the Glossary terms as Flashcards and tracks correct and incorrect answers. Flashcards can be filtered both by curriculum topic area and by action taken—for example, answered correctly, unanswered, and so on. These Flashcards provide a flexible way to study Glossary item definitions.

The Game Center provides several engaging ways to interact with the Flashcards in a game context. Each game tests your knowledge of the Glossary terms a in different way. Your results are scored and presented, along with a summary of candidates with high scores on the game, on your Dashboard.

Discussion Board The Discussion Board within the LES provides a way for you to interact with other candidates as you pursue your study plan. Discussions can happen at the level of individual lessons to raise questions about material in those lessons that you or other candidates can clarify or comment on. Discussions can also be posted at the level of topics or in the initial Welcome section to connect with other candidates in your area.

Practice Question Bank The LES offers access to a question bank of hundreds of practice questions that are in addition to the End of Reading Questions. These practice questions, only available on the LES, are intended to help you assess your mastery of individual topic areas as you progress through your studies. After each practice question, you will receive immediate feedback noting the correct response and indicating the relevant assigned reading so you can identify areas of weakness for further study.

Mock Exams The LES also includes access to three-hour Mock Exams that simulate the morning and afternoon sessions of the actual CFA exam. These Mock Exams are intended to be taken after you complete your study of the full curriculum and take practice questions so you can test your understanding of the curriculum and your readiness for the exam. If you take these Mock Exams within the LES, you will receive feedback afterward that notes the correct responses and indicates the relevant assigned readings so you can assess areas of weakness for further study. We recommend that you take Mock Exams during the final stages of your preparation for the actual CFA exam. For more information on the Mock Exams, please visit www.cfainstitute.org.

PREP PROVIDERS

You may choose to seek study support outside CFA Institute in the form of exam prep providers. After your CFA Program enrollment, you may receive numerous solicitations for exam prep courses and review materials. When considering a prep course, make sure the provider is committed to following the CFA Institute guidelines and high standards in its offerings.

Remember, however, that there are no shortcuts to success on the CFA exams; reading and studying the CFA Program curriculum *is* the key to success on the exam. The CFA Program exams reference only the CFA Institute assigned curriculum; no prep course or review course materials are consulted or referenced.

SUMMARY

Every question on the CFA exam is based on the content contained in the required readings and on one or more LOS. Frequently, an exam question is based on a specific example highlighted within a reading or on a specific practice problem and its solution. To make effective use of the CFA Program curriculum, please remember these key points:

1 All pages of the curriculum are required reading for the exam.

2 All questions, problems, and their solutions are part of the curriculum and are required study material for the exam. These questions are found at the end of the readings in the print versions of the curriculum. In the LES, these questions appear directly after the lesson with which they are associated. The LES provides immediate feedback on your answers and tracks your performance on these questions throughout your study.

3 We strongly encourage you to use the CFA Program Learning Ecosystem. In addition to providing access to all the curriculum material, including EORQs, in the form of shorter, focused lessons, the LES offers structured and adaptive study planning, a Discussion Board to communicate with other candidates, Flashcards, a Game Center for study activities, a test bank of practice questions, and online Mock Exams. Other supplemental study tools, such as eBook and PDF versions of the print curriculum, and additional candidate resources are available at www.cfainstitute.org.

4 Using the study planner, create a schedule and commit sufficient study time to cover the study sessions. You should also plan to review the materials, answer practice questions, and take Mock Exams.

5 Some of the concepts in the study sessions may be superseded by updated rulings and/or pronouncements issued after a reading was published. Candidates are expected to be familiar with the overall analytical framework contained in the assigned readings. Candidates are not responsible for changes that occur after the material was written.

FEEDBACK

At CFA Institute, we are committed to delivering a comprehensive and rigorous curriculum for the development of competent, ethically grounded investment professionals. We rely on candidate and investment professional comments and feedback as we work to improve the curriculum, supplemental study tools, and candidate resources.

Please send any comments or feedback to info@cfainstitute.org. You can be assured that we will review your suggestions carefully. Ongoing improvements in the curriculum will help you prepare for success on the upcoming exams and for a lifetime of learning as a serious investment professional.

Portfolio Management

STUDY SESSIONS

Study Session 1	Behavioral Finance
Study Session 2	Capital Market Expectations
Study Session 3	Asset Allocation and Related Decisions in Portfolio Management
Study Session 4	Derivatives and Currency Management
Study Session 5	Fixed-Income Portfolio Management (1)
Study Session 6	Fixed-Income Portfolio Management (2)
Study Session 7	Equity Portfolio Management (1)
Study Session 8	Equity Portfolio Management (2)
Study Session 9	Alternative Investments Portfolio Management
Study Session 10	Private Wealth Management (1)
Study Session 11	Private Wealth Management (2)
Study Session 12	Portfolio Management for Institutional Investors
Study Session 13	Trading, Performance Evaluation, and Manager Selection
Study Session 14	Cases in Portfolio Management and Risk Management

This volume includes Study Sessions 9–11.

© 2021 CFA Institute. All rights reserved.

TOPIC LEVEL LEARNING OUTCOME

The candidate should be able to prepare an appropriate investment policy statement and asset allocation; formulate strategies for managing, monitoring, and rebalancing investment portfolios; and evaluate portfolio performance.

PORTFOLIO MANAGEMENT
STUDY SESSION

Alternative Investments for Portfolio Management

Alternative investments comprise groups of investments with risk and return characteristics that differ from those of traditional stock and bond investments. For the purposes of this study session, private equity, hedge funds, real assets (including energy and commodity investments), commercial real estate, and private credit are included as alternative assets.

The first reading presents distinctive regulatory and investment characteristics of the major categories of hedge fund strategies. It also provides a conditional risk factor model as a unifying framework for understanding and analyzing the risk exposures of these strategies.

The second reading discusses the role alternative assets play in a multi-asset portfolio and explores how alternatives may serve to mitigate long-only equity risk. Approaches to asset allocation when incorporating alternatives in the opportunity set—whether through the traditional asset class lens or, more recently, using a risk- or factor-based lens—are examined. The reading concludes with a discussion of the need for liquidity planning in private investment alternatives and the unique monitoring requirements of an alternatives portfolio.

READING ASSIGNMENTS

Reading 19	Hedge Fund Strategies by Barclay T. Leib, CFE, CAIA, Kathryn M. Kaminski, PhD, CAIA, and Mila Getmansky Sherman, PhD
Reading 20	Asset Allocation to Alternative Investments by Adam Kobor, PhD, CFA, and Mark D. Guinney, CFA

© 2021 CFA Institute. All rights reserved.

READING 19

Hedge Fund Strategies

by Barclay T. Leib, CFE, CAIA, Kathryn M. Kaminski, PhD, CAIA, and Mila Getmansky Sherman, PhD

Barclay T. Leib, CFE, CAIA, is at Sand Spring Advisors LLC (USA). Kathryn M. Kaminski, PhD, CAIA, is at Alpha Simplex Group, LLC (USA). Mila Getmansky Sherman, PhD, is at Isenberg School of Management, UMASS Amherst (USA).

LEARNING OUTCOMES

Mastery	The candidate should be able to:
☐	a. discuss how hedge fund strategies may be classified;
☐	b. discuss investment characteristics, strategy implementation, and role in a portfolio of *equity-related* hedge fund strategies;
☐	c. discuss investment characteristics, strategy implementation, and role in a portfolio of *event-driven* hedge fund strategies;
☐	d. discuss investment characteristics, strategy implementation, and role in a portfolio of *relative value* hedge fund strategies;
☐	e. discuss investment characteristics, strategy implementation, and role in a portfolio of *opportunistic* hedge fund strategies;
☐	f. discuss investment characteristics, strategy implementation, and role in a portfolio of *specialist* hedge fund strategies;
☐	g. discuss investment characteristics, strategy implementation, and role in a portfolio of *multi-manager* hedge fund strategies;
☐	h. describe how factor models may be used to understand hedge fund risk exposures;
☐	i. evaluate the impact of an allocation to a hedge fund strategy in a traditional investment portfolio.

1. INTRODUCTION AND CLASSIFICATION OF HEDGE FUND STRATEGIES

a discuss how hedge fund strategies may be classified;

© 2019 CFA Institute. All rights reserved.

Hedge funds form an important subset of the alternative investments opportunity set, but they come with many pros and cons in their use and application across different asset classes and investment approaches. The basic tradeoff is whether the added fees typically involved with hedge fund investing result in sufficient additional alpha and portfolio diversification benefits to justify the high fee levels. This is an ongoing industry debate.

Some argue that investing in hedge funds is a key way to access the very best investment talent—those individuals who can adroitly navigate investment opportunities across a potentially wider universe of markets. Others argue that hedge funds are important because the alpha that may be produced in down markets is hard to source elsewhere.

The arguments against hedge funds are also non-trivial. In addition to the high fee levels, the complex offering memorandum documentation needs to be understood by investors (i.e., the limited partners). Other issues include lack of full underlying investment transparency/attribution, higher cost allocations associated with the establishment and maintenance of the fund investment structures, and generally longer–lived investment commitment periods with limited redemption availability.

In addition, each hedge fund strategy area tends to introduce different types of added portfolio risks. For example, to achieve meaningful return objectives, arbitrage-oriented hedge fund strategies tend to utilize significant leverage that can be dangerous to limited partner investors, especially during periods of market stress. Long/short equity and event-driven strategies may have less beta exposure than simple, long-only beta allocations, but the higher hedge fund fees effectively result in a particularly expensive form of embedded beta. Such strategies as managed futures or global macro investing may introduce natural benefits of asset class and investment approach diversification, but they come with naturally higher volatility in the return profiles typically delivered. Extreme tail risk in portfolios may be managed with the inclusion of relative value volatility or long volatility strategies, but it comes at the cost of a return drag during more normal market periods. In other words, some hedge fund strategies may have higher portfolio diversification benefits, while others may simply be return enhancers rather than true portfolio diversifiers.

Also, the hedge fund industry continues to evolve in its overall structure. Over the past decade, traditional limited partnership formats have been supplemented by offerings of liquid alternatives (liquid alts)—which are mutual fund, closed-end fund, and ETF-type vehicles that invest in various hedge fund-like strategies. Liquid alts are meant to provide daily liquidity, transparency, and lower fees while opening hedge fund investing to a wider range of investors. However, empirical evidence shows that liquid alts significantly underperform similar strategy hedge funds, which suggests that traditional hedge funds may be benefiting from an illiquidity premium phenomenon that cannot be easily transported into a mutual fund format.

Investors must understand the various subtleties involved with investing in hedge funds. Although secular bull market trends have arguably made "hedged" strategies less critical for inclusion in portfolio allocations than they were during the mid-to-late 2000s, the overall popularity of hedge funds tends to be somewhat cyclical. Notably, as demonstrated by the endowment model of investing, placing hedge funds as a core allocation can increase net returns and reduce risk.

This reading presents the investment characteristics and implementation for the major categories of hedge fund strategies. It also provides a framework for classifying and evaluating these strategies based on their risk profiles. Section 1 summarizes some distinctive regulatory and investment characteristics of hedge funds and discusses ways to classify hedge fund strategies. Sections 2 through 12 present investment characteristics and strategy implementation for each of the following hedge fund strategy categories: equity-related; event-driven; relative value; opportunistic; specialist; and multi-manager strategies. Section 13 introduces a conditional factor model as a unifying framework for understanding and analyzing the risk exposures of these strategies. Section 16 evaluates the contributions of each hedge fund strategy to the return and risk profile of a traditional portfolio of stocks and bonds. The reading concludes with a summary.

1.1 Classification of Hedge Funds and Strategies

The most important characteristics of hedge funds are summarized as follows:

1 **Legal/Regulatory Overview:** Different countries have varying requirements for investor eligibility to access hedge fund investments. These regulations are typically intended to limit access to traditional hedge funds to sophisticated investors with a minimum income or net-worth requirement, and they allow hedge fund managers to accept only a limited number of investment subscriptions. Most traditional hedge funds in the United States are offered effectively as private placement offerings. Whether the underlying fund manager must register with regulatory authorities depends on assets under management (AUM); however, regardless of AUM, all US hedge funds are subject to regulatory oversight against fraudulent conduct. Hedge funds offered in other jurisdictions—attractive, tax-neutral locales like the Cayman Islands, the British Virgin Islands, or Bermuda—are typically presented to investors as stand-alone corporate entities subject to the rules and regulations of the particular locality.

   From a regulatory perspective, the advent of liquid alts has likely caused the greatest shift in the industry over the past decade. Some of the more liquid hedge fund strategies that meet certain liquidity and diversification requirements (generally long/short equity and managed futures strategies) are offered by many fund sponsors in mutual fund-type structures in the United States and in the undertakings for collective investment in transferable securities (UCITs) format in Europe and Asia. By law, these liquid alts vehicles can be more widely marketed to retail investors. Whereas traditional hedge funds typically offer only limited periodic liquidity, liquid alts funds may be redeemed by investors on a daily basis. Also, traditional hedge funds typically involve both a management fee and an incentive fee; however, liquid alts in most countries are prohibited from charging an incentive fee.

   Finally, the overall regulatory constraints for hedge funds are far less than those for regulated investment vehicles—except for the liquid alts versions, which have much higher constraints to provide liquidity to investors.

2 **Flexible Mandates—Few Investment Constraints:** Given the relatively low legal and regulatory constraints faced by hedge funds, their mandates are flexible; thus, they are relatively unhindered in their trading and investment activities in terms of investable asset classes and securities, risk exposures, and collateral. The fund prospectus (i.e., offering memorandum) will specify the hedge fund's mandate and objectives and will include constraints, if any, on investment in certain asset classes as well as in the use of leverage, shorting, and derivatives.

3 **Large Investment Universe:** Lower regulatory constraints and flexible mandates give hedge funds access to a wide range of assets outside the normal set of traditional investments. Examples include private securities, non-investment-grade debt, distressed securities, derivatives, and more-esoteric contracts, such as life insurance contracts and even music or film royalties.

4 **Aggressive Investment Styles:** Hedge funds may use their typically flexible investment mandates to undertake strategies deemed too risky for traditional investment funds. These strategies may involve significant shorting and/or concentrated positions in domestic and foreign securities that offer exposure to credit, volatility, and liquidity risk premiums.

5 **Relatively Liberal Use of Leverage:** Hedge funds generally use leverage more extensively than regulated investment funds. Their leveraged positions are implemented either by borrowing securities from a prime broker or by using implied leverage via derivatives. In many instances, such leverage is necessary to make the return profile of the strategy meaningful. In other instances, derivatives may be used to hedge away unwanted risks (e.g., interest rate or credit risk) that may create high "notional leverage" but result in a less risky portfolio. Within long/short equity trading, leverage is most often applied to quantitative approaches in which small statistical valuation aberrations—typically over short windows of time—are identified by a manager or an algorithm. Such quant managers will typically endeavor to be market neutral but will apply high leverage levels to make the opportunities they identify meaningful from a return perspective.

6 **Hedge Fund Liquidity Constraints:** Limited partnership-format hedge funds involve initial lock-up periods, liquidity gates, and exit windows. These provide hedge fund managers with a greater ability to take and maintain positions than vehicles that allow investors to withdraw their investment essentially at will. It is thus not surprising that empirical evidence shows that such privately-placed hedge funds significantly outperform similar-strategy liquid alts products by approximately 100 bps–200 bps, on average, per year.

7 **Relatively High Fee Structures:** Hedge funds have traditionally imposed relatively high investment fees on investors, including both management fees and incentive fees. These have historically been 1% or more of AUM for management fees and 10%–20% of annual returns for incentive fees. The incentive fee structure is meant to align the interests of the hedge fund manager with those of the fund's investors.

With this background, we now address how hedge funds are classified. One distinction is between single manager hedge funds and multi-manager hedge funds. A **single-manager fund** is a fund in which one portfolio manager or team of portfolio managers invests in one strategy or style. A **multi-manager fund** can be of two types. One type is a **multi-strategy fund**, in which teams of portfolio managers trade and invest in multiple different strategies within the same fund. The second type, a fund-of-hedge funds, often simply called a **fund-of-funds** (FoF), is a fund in which the fund-of-funds manager allocates capital to separate, underlying hedge funds (e.g., single manager and/or multi-manager funds) that themselves run a range of different strategies.

At the single manager and single strategy level, hedge fund strategies can be classified in various ways. The taxonomy is often based on some combination of:

1 the instruments in which the managers invest (e.g., equities, commodities, foreign exchange, convertible bonds);

2 the trading philosophy followed by the managers (e.g., systematic, discretionary); and

3 the types of risk the managers assume (e.g., directional, event driven, relative value).

Most prominent hedge fund data vendors use a combination of these criteria to classify hedge fund strategies. For example, Hedge Fund Research, Inc. (HFR) reports manager performance statistics on more than 30 strategies and divides funds into six single strategy groupings that are widely used in the hedge fund industry. HFR's six main single strategy groupings are 1) equity hedge; 2) event driven; 3) fund-of-funds; 4) macro; 5) relative value; and 6) risk parity.

Lipper TASS, another well-known data vendor, classifies funds into the following ten categories: 1) dedicated short bias; 2) equity market neutral; 3) long/short equity hedge; 4) event driven; 5) convertible arbitrage; 6) fixed-income arbitrage; 7) global macro; 8) managed futures; 9) fund-of-funds; and 10) multi-strategy.

Morningstar CISDM goes even further and separates hedge funds in its database into finer categories, like merger arbitrage and systematic futures, among others. In addition, the Morningstar CISDM Database separates fund-of-funds strategies into several different sub-categories, such as debt, equity, event driven, macro/systematic, multi-strategy, and relative value.

Eurekahedge, an important index provider with its roots in Asia, has grown to include many smaller hedge fund managers globally. Its main strategy indexes include nine categories: 1) arbitrage; 2) commodity trading adviser (CTA)/managed futures; 3) distressed debt; 4) event driven; 5) fixed income; 6) long/short equities; 7) macro; 8) multi-strategy; and 9) relative value.

A final example of a prominent hedge fund data vendor is Credit Suisse. Its Credit Suisse Hedge Fund Index is an asset-weighted index that monitors approximately 9,000 funds and consists of funds with a minimum of US$50 million AUM, a 12-month track record, and audited financial statements. The index is calculated and rebalanced monthly, and it reflects performance net of all performance fees and expenses. Credit Suisse also subdivides managers into nine main sub-indexes for strategy areas: 1) convertible arbitrage; 2) emerging markets; 3) equity market neutral; 4) event driven; 5) fixed income; 6) global macro; 7) long/short equity; 8) managed futures; and 9) multi-strategy.

These different data providers use different methodologies for index calculation. HFR produces both the HFRX Index of equally weighted hedge funds, which includes those that are open or closed to new investment, and its HFRI index series, which tracks only hedge funds open to new investment. Because managers who have closed their funds to new investment are typically superior managers who are limited in their capacity to manage additional funds, the HFRX series regularly outperforms the HFRI series. However, the mix of managers represented by the HFRX Index would obviously not be replicable in real-time by an investor, thus limiting its usefulness. Meanwhile, the Credit Suisse Hedge Fund Index is weighted by fund size (i.e., AUM), so its overall performance is more reflective of the performance of the larger hedge funds, such as the multi-strategy managers.

Notably, less overlap exists in manager reporting to the different index providers than one might expect or is likely optimal. In fact, less than 1% of hedge fund managers self-report to all the index service providers mentioned. Clearly, no single index is all-encompassing.

Generally consistent with the above data vendor groupings and with a practice-based risk factor perspective, this reading groups single hedge fund strategies into the following six categories: 1) equity; 2) event-driven; 3) relative value; 4) opportunistic; 5) specialist; and 6) multi-manager.

- **Equity-related hedge fund strategies** focus primarily on the equity markets, and the majority of their risk profiles involve equity-oriented risk. Within this equity-related bucket, long/short equity, dedicated short bias, and equity market neutral are the main strategies that will be discussed further.

- **Event-driven hedge fund strategies** focus on corporate events, such as governance events, mergers and acquisitions, bankruptcy, and other key events for corporations. The primary risk for these strategies is event risk, the possibility that an unexpected event will negatively affect a company or security. Unexpected events include unforeseen corporate reorganization, a failed merger, credit rating downgrades, or company bankruptcy. The most common event-driven hedge fund strategies, merger arbitrage and distressed securities, will be discussed in detail.

- **Relative value hedge fund strategies** focus on the relative valuation between two or more securities. These strategies are often exposed to credit and liquidity risks because the valuation differences from which these strategies seek to benefit often are due to differences in credit quality and/or liquidity across different securities. The two common relative value hedge fund strategies to be covered further are fixed-income arbitrage and convertible bond arbitrage.

- **Opportunistic hedge fund strategies** take a top-down approach, focusing on a multi-asset (often macro-oriented) opportunity set. The risks for opportunistic hedge fund strategies depend on the opportunity set involved and can vary across time and asset classes. The two common opportunistic hedge fund strategies that are discussed in further detail are global macro and managed futures.

- **Specialist hedge fund strategies** focus on special or niche opportunities that often require a specialized skill or knowledge of a specific market. These strategies can be exposed to unique risks that stem from particular market sectors, niche securities, and/or esoteric instruments. We will explore two specialist strategies in further detail: volatility strategies involving options and reinsurance strategies.

- **Multi-manager hedge fund strategies** focus on building a portfolio of diversified hedge fund strategies. Managers in this strategy bucket use their skills to combine diverse strategies and dynamically re-allocate among them over time. The two most common types of multi-manager hedge funds are multi-strategy funds and fund-of-funds, which we will discuss in further detail.

Exhibit 1 shows the five single strategy hedge fund buckets that will be covered individually. Multi-strategy funds and fund-of funds—two types of multi-manager strategies—will also be covered. A discussion of each strategy's contributions to portfolio risk and return will follow.

Exhibit 1   Hedge Fund Strategies by Category

Equity	Event-Driven	Relative Value	Opportunistic	Specialist	Multi-Manager
• Long/Short Equity • Dedicated Short Bias • Equity Market Neutral	• Merger Arbitrage • Distressed Securitites	• Fixed Income Arbitrage • Convertible Bond Arbitrage	• Global Macro • Managed Futures	• Volatility Strategies • Reinsurance Strategies	• Multi-strategy • Fund-of-Funds

EQUITY STRATEGIES: LONG/SHORT EQUITY

b discuss investment characteristics, strategy implementation, and role in a portfolio of *equity-related* hedge fund strategies;

Equity hedge fund strategies invest primarily in equity and equity-related instruments. As mentioned previously, the alpha related to equity strategies tends to derive from the wide variety of equity investments available globally combined with astute long and short stock picking. The size and sign of equity market exposure often dictate the classification of equity hedge fund strategies. As the name suggests, long-only equity hedge fund strategies focus on holding only long positions in equities, and they sometimes use leverage. Long/short equity hedge fund strategies hold both long and short positions in equities that typically result in more-hedged, less-volatile overall portfolios. Short-biased strategies focus on strategic short selling of companies that are expected to lose value in the future (sometimes with an activist inclination, sometimes with long positions in other securities as an offset). Equity market-neutral strategies hold balanced long and short equity exposures to maintain zero (or close to zero) net exposure to the equity market and such factors as sector and size (i.e., market cap). They then focus on, for example, pairs of long and short securities whose prices are out of historical alignment and are expected to experience mean reversion. The following sections discuss long/short equity, dedicated short bias, and equity market-neutral hedge fund strategies.

2.1 Long/Short Equity

Long/short (L/S) equity managers buy equities of companies they expect will rise in value (i.e., they take long positions in undervalued companies) and sell short equities of companies they think will fall in value (i.e., they take short positions in overvalued companies). The objective of long/short equity strategies is to be flexible in finding attractive opportunities on both the long and short sides of the market and to size them within a portfolio. Depending on their specific mandates, long/short equity strategies can shift between industry sectors (e.g., from technology to consumer goods), factors (e.g., from value to growth), and geographic regions (e.g., from Europe to Asia). In practice, however, managers tend to maintain their philosophical biases and areas of focus, typically with a heavy emphasis on fundamental research.

Although market timing using "beta tilts" can play a factor in manager performance, studies have shown that most fundamental long/short equity managers offer little added alpha from such adjustments. They are typically either too net long at market highs or not net long enough at market lows. Most L/S equity managers are not known for their portfolio-level market-timing abilities, but those with such market-timing skills may be particularly valuable from a portfolio allocation perspective.

L/S equity managers also are typically able to take concentrated positions in high conviction buys or sells and can readily apply leverage to increase these positions (although higher levels of leverage are used mostly by quantitatively-oriented managers, not fundamental managers). As a result, stock selection defines manager skill for most L/S equity managers—with market-timing ability being an additive, but generally secondary, consideration. L/S equity is one of the most prevalent hedge fund strategies. It accounts for about 30% of all hedge funds.

2.1.1 *Investment Characteristics*

Because manager skill derives mainly from stock selection, it is not surprising that individual long/short equity managers tend to have a focus based on their own unique skill sets. As a result, many long/short equity managers specialize in either a specific geographic region, sector, or investment style. However, several key characteristics define long/short equity managers: their strategy focus, their flexibility in holding long and short positions over time, and their use of leverage. Given the specific mandate for a long/short equity manager, his/her exposures to various equity factors can be very different from other long/short equity managers. For example, a manager focusing on small-cap growth stocks would have a positive exposure to the size factor and a negative exposure to the value factor. Conversely, a manager with a focus on large-cap value stocks would have a negative exposure to the size factor and a positive exposure to the value factor.

Given that equity markets tend to rise over the long run, most long/short equity managers typically hold net long equity positions. Some managers maintain their short positions as a hedge against unexpected market downturns. Other managers are more opportunistic; they tend to take on more short positions after uncovering negative issues with a company's management, strategies, and/or financial statements or whenever their valuation models suggest selling opportunities in certain stocks or sectors. As a result, performance during market crisis periods is important for differentiating between hedge fund managers. Given that hedge funds typically carry high fees, it is important to avoid paying such added fees just for embedded beta exposure that could be achieved more cheaply by investing in traditional long-only strategies. The goal in long/short equity investing is generally to find more sources of idiosyncratic alpha (primarily via stock picking and secondarily by market timing) rather than embedded systematic beta. Exhibit 2 presents some key aspects of this important strategy area.

Exhibit 2   Long/Short Equity—Risk, Liquidity, Leverage, and Benchmarking

Risk Profile and Liquidity

- Diverse opportunities globally create a wide universe from which to create alpha through astute stock picking.
- Diverse investment styles include value/growth, large cap/small cap, discretionary/quantitative, and industry specialized.
- They typically have average exposures of 40%–60% net long, composed of gross exposures of 70%–90% long, vs. 20%–50% short, but they can vary widely. Return profiles are typically aimed to achieve average annual returns roughly equivalent to a long-only approach but with a standard deviation 50% lower than a long-only approach.
- Some managers use index-based short hedges to reduce market risk, but most search for single-name shorts for portfolio alpha and added absolute return.
- Some managers are able to add alpha via market timing of portfolio beta tilt, but evidence suggests that most L/S managers do this poorly.
- This strategy can typically be handled by both limited partner and mutual fund-type vehicles.
- Attractiveness: Liquid, diverse, with mark-to-market pricing driven by public market quotes; added short-side exposure typically reduces beta risk and provides an additional source of potential alpha and reduced portfolio volatility.

> **Exhibit 2 (Continued)**
>
> ### Leverage Usage
>
> - Variable: The more market-neutral or quantitative the strategy approach, the more levered the strategy application tends to be to achieve a meaningful return profile.
>
> ### Benchmarking
>
> - L/S equity benchmarks include HFRX and HFRI Equity Hedge Indices; Lipper TASS L/S Equity Hedge; Morningstar/CISDM Equity L/S Index; and Credit Suisse L/S Equity Index.

2.1.2 Strategy Implementation

When long and short stock positions are placed together into a portfolio, the market exposure is the net of the beta-adjusted long and short exposures. For example, with many strong sells and a relatively large short position, the strategy could be net short for brief periods of time. Typically, most long/short equity managers end up with modest net long exposures averaging between 40%–60% net long. Many long/short equity managers are naturally sector-specific, often designing their funds around their industry specialization. Such specialist L/S fund managers analyze fundamental situations that they know well from both a top-down and bottom-up analytical perspective. Natural areas of specialization include potentially more complex sectors, such as telecom/media/technology (TMT), financial, consumer, health care, and biotechnology sectors. Conversely, generalist L/S managers search further afield, thus having flexibility to invest across multiple industry groups. Typically, these generalists avoid complex sectors; for example, they may avoid biotechnology because corporate outcomes may be deemed too binary depending on the success or failure of drug trials. Although generalist managers do take a more balanced and flexible approach, they may miss detailed industry subtleties that are increasingly important to understand in a world where news flows 24/7 and is increasingly nuanced.

Overall, long/short equity investing in most instances is a mix of extracting alpha on the long and short sides from single-name stock selection combined with some naturally net long embedded beta.

> **EXAMPLE 1**
>
> ### Long/Short Equity Investing Dilemma
>
> The Larson family office views L/S equity investing as a significant portion of the hedge fund universe and would like to access managers talented not only at long investing but also at short selling. However, it does not want to pay high hedge fund fees just for long-biased beta because it has access to long-biased beta at lower fees elsewhere in its portfolio. But, Larson will pay hedge fund fees for strategies that can produce strong risk-adjusted performance in a unique and differentiated fashion.
>
> 1. Discuss some potential hedge fund strategies the Larson family office should consider adding to its existing portfolio.
> 2. Discuss some of the problems and risks that it may encounter.

> **Solution to 1:**
>
> The Larson family office should consider managers focused on an L/S equity strategy with a sector-specialization as opposed to a generalist fundamental L/S strategy. Generalist L/S managers can benefit from the flexibility to scan a wide universe of stocks to find investments, but they may not be able to develop a sufficient information edge in their analysis to dependably deliver sufficient alpha relative to their fees and natural long beta positioning. However, managers running specialist L/S equity strategies—especially in such complex sectors as technology, finance, and biotechnology/health care—are more likely to have the specialized capabilities to perform the "deep-dive" differentiated analysis required to develop more original views and stronger portfolio performance.
>
> **Solution to 2:**
>
> A key problem with selecting sector-specialist L/S equity hedge funds is that they are more difficult to analyze and assess. There are also fewer to choose from compared to generalist L/S hedge funds. Sectors can fall out of favor, risking an allocation to a good fund but in the wrong area given dynamic macroeconomic and financial market conditions. Moreover, generalist L/S strategies, by definition, can readily reallocate capital more efficiently as opportunities emerge in different sectors. Put another way, the Larson family office could potentially find itself with too much single sector, short-sided, or idiosyncratic exposure at the wrong time if it chooses a sector-specialist L/S equity fund.

3. EQUITY STRATEGIES: DEDICATED SHORT SELLING AND SHORT-BIASED

b discuss investment characteristics, strategy implementation, and role in a portfolio of *equity-related* hedge fund strategies;

Dedicated short-selling hedge fund managers take short-only positions in equities deemed to be expensively priced versus their deteriorating fundamental situations. Such managers may vary their short exposures only in terms of portfolio sizing by, at times, holding higher levels of cash. **Short-biased** hedge fund managers use a less extreme version of this approach. They also search for opportunities to sell expensively priced equities, but they may balance short exposure with some modest value-oriented, or possibly index-oriented, long exposure. This latter approach can potentially help short-biased hedge funds cope with long bull market periods in equities. Both types of short sellers actively aim to create an uncorrelated or negatively correlated source of return by seeking out failing business models, fraudulent accounting, corporate mismanagement, or other factors that may sour the market's perception of a given equity. Because of the overall secular up-trend in global equity markets, especially across the past several decades, it has been very difficult to be a successful short seller. As a result, fewer such managers are in existence today than in the 1990s.

One exception is the emergence of **activist short selling**, whereby managers take a short position in a given security and then publicly present their research backing the short thesis. Typically, if the hedge fund manager has a solid reputation from its past activist short-selling forays, the release of such research causes a significant stock price plunge into which the activist short seller might cover a portion of its short position. In the United States, this practice has not been deemed to be market manipulation by securities' regulators as long as the activist short seller is not publishing erroneous information, is not charging for such information (which might create potential conflicts of interest between subscribers and investors), and is acting only in the best interests of its limited partner investors.

3.1 Investment Characteristics

Short-selling managers focus on situations involving overvalued equities of companies facing deteriorating fundamentals that typically have not yet been perceived by the market. They also attempt to maximize returns during periods of market declines. If these short-selling managers can achieve success with their approaches, they can provide a unique and useful source of negatively correlated returns compared to many other strategy areas.

Short selling involves borrowing securities, selling them "high," and then after prices have declined, buying the same securities back "low" and returning them to the lender. To borrow the securities to short sell, the manager must post collateral with the securities lender to cover potential losses. The manager must also pay interest on the securities loan, which can be high if the securities are difficult for the lender to locate. One key risk is that the lender may want the securities back at an inopportune time—such as before the expected price decline has materialized, which could be disadvantageous for the hedge fund manager.

Short selling in general is a difficult investment practice to master in terms of risk management because of the natural phenomenon that positions will grow if prices advance against the short seller but will shrink if prices decline. This is the opposite of what occurs with long-only investing, and it is more difficult to manage. Additionally, access to company management for research purposes can be blocked for fund managers who become known as active short sellers.

From a regulatory perspective, many countries limit or impose stringent rules on short selling. In the United States, the "uptick rule" states that when a stock decreases by 10% or more from its prior closing price, a short sale order can be executed only at a price higher than the current best (i.e., highest) bid. This means the stock's price must be rising to execute the short sale. Although many emerging markets have allowed short selling, particularly to enhance market liquidity (e.g., the Saudi Stock Exchange allowed short sales beginning in 2016), there is always concern that limits could be placed on short selling during extreme market environments or that regulations could change. For example, for a brief period during the global financial crisis of 2007–2009, new short sales on a designated list of financial stocks were banned by the US SEC to lessen systematic market stress.

Given the difficult operational aspects of short selling, and because equity markets tend to secularly rise over time, successful short-selling managers typically have something of a short-term "attack and retreat" style. The return profile for a successful short-biased manager might best be characterized by increasingly positive returns as the market declines and the risk-free return when the market rises. In some idealized short-selling world, this would entail being short the market during down periods and investing in low-risk government debt when the market is not declining. But, the actual goal of a short seller is to pick short-sale stocks that can still generate positive returns even when the general market trend is up. Skillful, dedicated short-biased managers look for possible short-selling targets among companies that are overvalued, that are experiencing declining revenues and/or earnings, or that have internal management conflicts, weak corporate governance, or even potential accounting frauds. Other possible short-sale candidates are companies that may have single products under development that the short seller believes will ultimately either be unsuccessful or non-repeatable. Exhibit 3 shows some important aspects of this strategy area.

> **Exhibit 3 Dedicated Short Sellers and Short-Biased—Risk, Liquidity, Leverage, and Benchmarking**
>
> **Risk Profile and Liquidity**
>
> - Dedicated short sellers: They only trade with short-side exposure, although they may moderate short beta by also holding cash.
> - Short-biased managers: They are focused on good short-side stock picking, but they may moderate short beta with some value-oriented long exposure or index-oriented long exposure as well as cash.
> - Dedicated short sellers tend to be 60%–120% short at all times. Short-biased managers are typically around 30%–60% net short. The focus in both cases tends to be on single equity stock picking as opposed to index shorting.
> - Return goals are typically less than those for most other hedge fund strategies but with a negative correlation benefit. They are more volatile than a typical L/S equity hedge fund given short beta exposure.
> - Managers have some ability to add alpha via market timing of portfolio beta tilt, but it is difficult to do with consistency or added alpha.
> - This strategy is typically handled best in a limited partnership because of difficult operational aspects of short selling.
> - Attractiveness: Liquid, negatively correlated alpha to that of most other strategies, with mark-to-market pricing from public prices. Historic returns have been lumpy and generally disappointing.
>
> **Leverage Usage**
>
> - Low: There is typically sufficient natural volatility that short-selling managers do not need to add much leverage.
>
> **Benchmarking**
>
> - Short-biased indexes include Eurekahedge Equity Short Bias Hedge Fund Index and Lipper TASS Dedicated Short-Bias Index. Some investors also compare short-biased funds' returns to the inverse of returns on related stock indexes.
>
> *Note:* Each index has different methodologies for fund inclusion. Because there are fewer short-selling managers, the construction of an acceptably diverse index is particularly difficult. The Lipper TASS Dedicated Short-Bias Index, for example, includes just four managers.

3.2 Strategy Implementation

Because finding strategic selling opportunities is key to dedicated short-biased strategies, stock selection is an important part of the investment process. Short-selling managers typically take a bottom-up approach by scanning the universe of potential sell targets to uncover and sell short those companies whose shares are most likely to substantially decline in value over the relevant time horizon. Managers search for, among other factors, inherently flawed business models, unsustainable levels of corporate leverage, and indications of poor corporate governance and/or accounting gimmickry. Tools that may be helpful to dedicated short-biased managers in finding potential sell candidates include monitoring single name credit default swap spreads, corporate bond yield spreads, and/or implied volatility of exchange-traded put options. Traditional technical analysis and/or pattern recognition techniques may assist the manager in the market timing of short sales. Various accounting ratios and measures, such as the Altman Z-score for judging a company's bankruptcy potential and the Beneish M-score for identifying potentially fraudulent financial statements, may also be useful. Because of the inherent difficulty and dangers of short selling, most successful short sellers do significant "deep-dive" forensic work on their short-portfolio candidates. As such, short sellers serve as a valuable resource in creating more overall pricing efficiency in the market.

> **EXAMPLE 2**
>
> ### Candidate for Short-Biased Hedge Fund Strategy
>
> Kit Stone, a short-biased hedge fund manager, is researching Generic Inc. (GI) for possible addition to his portfolio. GI was once a drug industry leader, but for the past 10 years its R&D budgets have declined. Its drug patents have all expired, so it now operates in the competitive generic drug business. GI has staked its future on a new treatment for gastro-intestinal disease. R&D was financed by debt, so GI's leverage ratio is twice the industry average. Early clinical trials were inconclusive. Final clinical trial results for GI's new drug are to be revealed within one month. Although the market is constructive, many medical experts remain doubtful of the new drug's efficacy. Without any further insights into the trial results, Stone reviews the following information.
>
> | Generic Inc. (GI) | | | Industry Average | | |
> |---|---|---|---|---|---|
> | PE (X) | PB (X) | T12M EPS Growth | PE (X) | PB (X) | T12M EPS Growth |
> | 30 | 3.5 | 3% | 20 | 2.5 | 18% |
>
> Additionally, Stone notes that GI shares are very thinly traded, with a high short-interest ratio of 60%. Stone's broker has informed him that it is expensive to borrow GI shares for shorting; they are on "special" (i.e., difficult to borrow), with a high borrowing cost of 20% per year. Moreover, there is an active market for exchange-traded options on GI's shares. Prices of one-month GI options appear to reflect a positive view of the company.
>
> 1 Discuss whether Stone should add GI shares to his short-biased portfolio.
> 2 Discuss how Stone might instead take advantage of the situation using GI options.
>
> ### Solution to 1:
>
> Generic Inc. appears to be substantially overvalued. Its main business relies on the competitive generic drug market; it has taken on substantial debt to fund R&D; and skepticism surrounds its new drug. GI's P/Es and P/Bs are higher than industry averages by 50% and 40%, respectively, and its trailing 12-month EPS growth is meager (3% vs. 18% industry average). However, although Stone would normally decide to add GI to his short-biased portfolio, the stock's high short-interest ratio and high cost to borrow (for shorting) are very concerning. Both factors suggest significant potential that a dangerous short-squeeze situation could develop if clinical results really do show efficacy of GI's new drug. So, based on the negative demand/supply dynamics for the stock, Stone decides not to add GI to his portfolio.

> **Solution to 2:**
> Stone might instead consider expressing his negative view on GI by simply purchasing put options. Alternatively, Stone could purchase a long put calendar spread, where he would buy a put with expiry beyond and sell a put with expiry before the expected release date of the clinical trial results. In that case, the premium received from writing the shorter tenor put would finance, in part, the cost of buying the longer tenor put. As a third possibility, Stone might even consider buying GI shares and then lending them at the attractive 20% rate. In that case, he would need to hedge this long stock position with the purchase of out-of-the-money puts, thereby creating a protective put position. As a final possibility, if out-of-the-money calls are deemed to be expensive because of positive sentiment, Stone could sell such calls to finance the purchase of out-of-the-money puts, creating a short risk reversal that provides synthetic short exposure.

4. EQUITY STRATEGIES: EQUITY MARKET NEUTRAL

b discuss investment characteristics, strategy implementation, and role in a portfolio of *equity-related* hedge fund strategies;

Equity market-neutral (EMN) hedge fund strategies take opposite (i.e., long and short) positions in similar or related equities that have divergent valuations, and they also attempt to maintain a near net zero portfolio exposure to the market. EMN managers neutralize market risk by constructing their portfolios such that the expected portfolio beta is approximately equal to zero. Moreover, managers often choose to set the betas for sectors or industries as well as for such common risk factors as market size, price-to-earnings ratio, or book-to-market ratio, which are also equal to zero. Because these portfolios do not take beta risk but do attempt to neutralize so many other factor risks, they typically must apply leverage to the long and short positions to achieve a meaningful expected return from their individual stock selections. Approaches vary, but equity market-neutral portfolios are often constructed using highly quantitative methodologies; the portfolios end up being more diverse in their holdings; and the portfolios are typically modified and adjusted over shorter time horizons. The condition of zero market beta can also be achieved with the use of derivatives, including stock index futures and options. Whichever way they are constructed, the overall goal of equity market-neutral portfolios is to capture alpha while minimizing portfolio beta exposure.

Although **pairs trading** is just one subset of equity market-neutral investing, it is an intuitively easy example to consider. With this strategy, pairs are identified of similar under- and overvalued equities, divergently valued shares of a holding company and its subsidiaries, or different share classes of the same company (multi-class stocks typically having different voting rights) in which their prices are out of alignment.

In whatever manner they are created, the pairs are monitored for their typical trading patterns relative to each other—conceptually, the degree of co-integration of the two securities' prices. Positions are established when unusually divergent spread pricing between the two paired securities is observed. Underpinning such a strategy is the expectation that the differential valuations or trading relationships will revert to their long-term mean values or their fundamentally-correct trading relationships, with the long position rising and the short position declining in value. Situations will obviously vary, but strictly quantitative EMN pairs trading, while attempting to minimize overall beta exposure, may still have effective short volatility "tail risk" exposure to abnormal market situations of extreme stress. This is less the case if a fundamental pricing discrepancy is being exploited in anticipation of a possible event that would cause that discrepancy to correct.

Another type of EMN trading is **stub trading**, which entails buying and selling stock of a parent company and its subsidiaries, typically weighted by the percentage ownership of the parent company in the subsidiaries. Assume parent company A owns 90% and 75% of subsidiaries B and C, respectively, and shares of A are determined to be overvalued while shares of B and C are deemed undervalued, all relative to their historical mean valuations. Then, for each share of A sold short, the EMN fund would buy 0.90 and 0.75 shares of B and C, respectively.

Yet another type of EMN approach may involve **multi-class trading**, which involves buying and selling different classes of shares of the same company, such as voting and non-voting shares. As with pairs trading, the degree of co-integration of returns and the valuation metrics for the multi-class shares are determined. If/when prices move outside of their normal ranges, the overvalued shares are sold short while the undervalued shares are purchased. The goal is to gain on the change in relative pricing on the two securities as market pricing reverts to more normal ranges.

Fundamental trade setups—although not per se "equity market neutral" but still designed to be market neutral—may be created that are long or short equity hedged against offsetting bond exposures if relative pricing between the stocks and bonds is deemed to be out of alignment. Such pairs trading is referred to as capital structure arbitrage and will be discussed in the event-driven strategies section. In these situations, attractive expected outcomes are often created from relative security mispricings designed to exploit potential event situations (e.g., a potential merger or bankruptcy) that would have an impact on relative pricing. Moreover, when two bonds are positioned relative to each other (e.g., to exploit a misunderstood difference in bond covenants or a potential differential asset recovery), a market-neutral strategy can also be employed.

When building market-neutral portfolios, sometimes large numbers of securities are traded and positions are adjusted on a daily or even an hourly basis using algorithm-based models. Managers following this approach are referred to as **quantitative market-neutral** managers. The frequent adjustments implemented by such managers are driven by the fact that market prices change faster than company fundamental factors. This price movement triggers a rebalancing of the EMN portfolio back to a market neutrality. When the time horizon of EMN trading shrinks to even shorter intervals and mean reversion and relative momentum characteristics of market behavior are emphasized, quantitative market-neutral trading becomes what is known as statistical arbitrage trading. With EMN and statistical arbitrage trading, a natural push/pull occurs between maintaining an optimal beta-neutral portfolio and the market impacts and brokerage costs of nearly continuous adjusting of the portfolio. So, many EMN managers use trading-cost hurdle models to determine if and when they should rebalance a portfolio.

Overall, the main source of skill for an EMN manager is in security selection, with market timing being of secondary importance. Sector exposure also tends to be constrained, although this can vary by the individual manager's approach. Managers that are overall beta neutral and specialize in sector rotation exposure as their source of alpha are known as market-neutral tactical asset allocators or macro-oriented market-neutral managers.

4.1 Investment Characteristics

Equity market-neutral fund managers seek to insulate their portfolios from movements in the overall market, and they can take advantage of divergent valuations by trading specific securities. As discussed, this is often a quantitatively driven process that uses a substantial amount of leverage to generate meaningful return objectives. However, many discretionary EMN managers implement their positions with significantly less leverage.

Overall, EMN managers generally are more useful for portfolio allocation during periods of non-trending or declining markets because they typically deliver returns that are steadier and less volatile than those of many other hedge strategy areas. Over time, their conservative and constrained approach typically results in less-volatile overall returns than those of managers who accept beta exposure. The exception to this norm is when the use of significant leverage may cause forced portfolio downsizing. By using portfolio margining techniques offered by prime brokers, market-neutral managers may run portfolios with up to 300% long versus 300% short exposures. Prime broker portfolio margining rules generally allow managers to maintain such levered positioning until a portfolio loss of a specified magnitude (i.e., excess drawdown) is incurred. At the time of such excess drawdown, the prime broker can force the manager to downsize his/her overall portfolio exposure. This is a key strategy risk, particularly for quantitative market-neutral managers.

Despite the use of substantial leverage and because of their more standard and overall steady risk/return profiles, equity market-neutral managers are often considered as preferred replacements for (or at least a complement to) fixed-income managers during periods when fixed-income returns are unattractively low/and or the yield curve is flat. EMN managers are, of course, sourcing a very different type of alpha with very different risks than in fixed-income investing. EMN managers must deal with leverage risk, including the issues of availability of leverage and at what cost, and tail risk, particularly the performance of levered portfolios during periods of market stress. Exhibit 4 presents important aspects of this strategy area.

Exhibit 4   Equity Market Neutral—Risk, Liquidity, Leverage, and Benchmarking

Risk Profile and Liquidity

- They have relatively modest return profiles, with portfolios aimed to be market neutral, and differing constraints to other factors and sector exposures are allowed.
- They generally have high levels of diversification and liquidity and lower standard deviation of returns than many other strategies across normal market conditions.
- Many different types of EMN managers exist, but many are purely quantitative managers (vs. discretionary managers).
- Time horizons vary, but EMN strategies are typically oriented toward mean reversion, with shorter horizons than other strategies and more active trading.
- Because of often high leverage, EMN strategies typically do not meet regulatory leverage limits for mutual fund vehicles. So, limited partnerships are the preferred vehicle.
- Attractiveness: EMN strategies typically take advantage of idiosyncratic short-term mispricing between securities whose prices should otherwise be co-integrated. Their sources of return and alpha, unlike those of many other strategies, do not require accepting beta risk. So, EMN strategies are especially attractive during periods of market vulnerability and weakness.

> **Exhibit 4   (Continued)**
>
> ### Leverage Usage
>
> - High: As many beta risks (e.g., market, sector) are hedged away, it is generally deemed acceptable for EMN managers to apply higher levels of leverage while striving for meaningful return targets.
>
> ### Benchmarking
>
> - Market-neutral indexes include HFRX and HFRI Equity Market Neutral Indices; Lipper TASS Equity Market Neutral Index; Morningstar/CISDM Equity Market Neutral Index; and Credit Suisse Equity Market Neutral Index.

4.2 Strategy Implementation

Equity market-neutral portfolios are constructed in four main steps. First, the investment universe is evaluated to include only tradable securities with sufficient liquidity and adequate short-selling potential. Second, securities are analyzed for buy and sell opportunities using fundamental models (which use company, industry, and economic data as inputs for valuation) and/or statistical and momentum-based models. Third, a portfolio is constructed with constraints to maintain market risk neutrality, whereby the portfolio's market value-weighted beta is approximately zero and there is often dollar (i.e., money), sector, or other factor risk neutrality. Fourth, the availability and cost of leverage are considered in terms of desired return profile and acceptable potential portfolio drawdown risk. The execution costs of the strategy rebalancing are also introduced as a filter for decision making as to how often the portfolio should be rebalanced. Markets are dynamic because volatility and leverage are always changing; therefore, the exposure to the market is always changing. Consequently, EMN managers must actively manage their funds' exposures to remain neutral over time. However, costs are incurred every time the portfolio is rebalanced. So, EMN managers must be very careful to not allow such costs to overwhelm the security-selection alpha that they are attempting to capture.

Note that the following is a simplified example. In reality, most EMN managers would likely not hedge beta on a stock-by-stock basis but rather would hedge beta on an overall portfolio basis. They would also likely consider other security factor attributes.

> **EXAMPLE 3**
>
> ### Equity Market-Neutral Pairs Trading:
>
> Ling Chang, a Hong Kong-based EMN manager, has been monitoring PepsiCo Inc. (PEP) and Coca-Cola Co. (KO), two global beverage industry giants. After examining the Asia marketing strategy for a new PEP drink, Chang feels the marketing campaign is too controversial and the overall market is too narrow. Although PEP has relatively weak earnings prospects compared to KO, 3-month valuation metrics show PEP shares are substantially overvalued versus KO shares (relative valuations have moved beyond their historical ranges). As part of a larger portfolio, Chang wants to allocate $1 million to the PEP versus KO trade and notes the historical betas and S&P 500 Index weights, as shown in the following table.

Stock	Beta	S&P 500 Index Weight
PEP	0.65	0.663
KO	0.55	0.718

Discuss how Chang might implement an EMN pairs trading strategy.

Solution:

Chang should take a short position in PEP and a long position in KO with equal beta-weighted exposures. Given Chang wants to allocate $1 million to the trade, she would take on a long KO position of $1 million. Assuming realized betas will be similar to historical betas, to achieve an equal beta-weighted exposure for the short PEP position, Chang needs to short $846,154 worth of PEP shares [= –$1,000,000 / (0.65/0.55)]. Only the overall difference in performance between PEP and KO shares would affect the performance of the strategy because it will be insulated from the effect of market fluctuations. If over the next 3 months the valuations of PEP and KO revert to within normal ranges, then this pairs trading EMN strategy should reap profits.

Note: The S&P 500 Index weights are not needed to answer this question.

5. EVENT-DRIVEN STRATEGIES: MERGER ARBITRAGE

c   discuss investment characteristics, strategy implementation, and role in a portfolio of *event-driven* hedge fund strategies;

Event-driven (ED) hedge fund strategies take positions in corporate securities and derivatives that are attempting to profit from the outcome of mergers and acquisitions, bankruptcies, share issuances, buybacks, capital restructurings, re-organizations, accounting changes, and similar events. ED hedge fund managers analyze companies' financial statements and regulatory filings and closely examine corporate governance issues (e.g., management structure, board composition, issues for shareholder consideration, proxy voting) as well as firms' strategic objectives, competitive position, and other firm-specific issues. Investments can be made either proactively in anticipation of an event that has yet to occur (i.e., a **soft-catalyst event-driven approach**), or investments can be made in reaction to an already announced corporate event in which security prices related to the event have yet to fully converge (i.e., a **hard-catalyst event-driven approach**). The hard approach is generally less volatile and less risky than soft-catalyst investing. Merger arbitrage and distressed securities are among the most common ED strategies.

5.1 Merger Arbitrage

Mergers and acquisitions can be classified by the method of purchase: cash-for-stock or stock-for-stock. In a cash-for-stock acquisition, the acquiring company (A) offers the target company (T) a cash price per share to acquire T. For example, assume T's share price is $30 and A decides to purchase T for $40 per share (i.e., A is offering a 33% premium to purchase T's shares). In a stock-for-stock acquisition, A offers a specific number of its shares in exchange for 1 T share. So, if A's share price is $20 and it offers 2 of its shares in exchange for 1 T share, then T's shareholders would receive a value of $40 per T share, assuming A's share price is constant until the merger is completed. Although merger deals are structured in different ways for many reasons (e.g., tax implications, corporate structure, or provisions to dissuade a merger, such as a "poison pill"[1]), acquiring companies are generally more likely to offer cash for their target companies when cash surpluses are high. However, if the stock prices are high and acquiring companies' shares are considered richly valued by management, then stock-for-stock acquisitions can take advantage of potentially overvalued shares as a "currency" to acquire target companies.

5.1.1 *Investment Characteristics*

In a cash-for-stock acquisition, the merger-arb manager may choose to buy just the target company (T), expecting it to increase in value once the acquisition is completed. In a stock-for-stock deal, the fund manager typically buys T and sells the acquiring company (A) in the same ratio as the offer, hoping to earn the spread on successful deal completion. If the acquisition is unsuccessful, the manager faces losses if the price of T (A) has already risen (fallen) in anticipation of the acquisition. Less often, managers take the view that the acquisition will fail—usually due to anti-competition or other regulatory concerns. In this case, he/she would sell T and buy A.

For most acquisitions, the initial announcement of a deal will cause the target company's stock price to rise toward the acquisition price and the acquirer's stock price to fall (either because of the potential dilution of its outstanding shares or the use of cash for purposes other than a dividend payment). The considerable lag time between deal announcement and closing means that proposed merger deals can always fail for any variety of reasons, including lack of financing, regulatory hurdles, and not passing financial due diligence. Hostile takeover bids, where the target company's management has not already agreed to the terms of a merger, are typically less likely to be successfully completed than friendly takeovers, where the target's management has already agreed to merger terms.

Approximately 70%–90% of announced mergers in the United States eventually close successfully. Given the probability that some mergers will not close for whatever reason as well as the costs of establishing a merger arbitrage position (e.g., borrowing the acquiring stock, commissions) and the risk that merger terms might be changed because of market conditions (especially in stressed market environments), merger arbitrage typically offers a 3%–7% return spread depending on the deal-specific risks. Of course, a particularly risky deal might carry an even larger spread. If the average time for merger deal completion is 3-4 months—with managers recycling capital into new deals several times a year and typically applying some leverage to their portfolio positions—then attractive return/risk profiles can be created, earning net annualized returns in the range of 7%–12%, with little correlation to non-deal-specific factors. Diversifying across a variety of mergers, deals, and industries can further help hedge the risk of any one deal failing. So overall, this strategy can be a good uncorrelated source of alpha.

When merger deals do fail, the initial price rise (fall) of the target (acquirer) company is typically reversed. Arbitrageurs who jumped into the merger situation after its initial announcement stand to incur substantial losses on their long (short) position in the target (acquirer)—often as large as negative 20% to 40%. So, the strategy thus does have left-tail risk associated with it.

Corporate events are typically binary: An acquisition either succeeds or fails. The merger arbitrage strategy can be viewed as selling insurance on the acquisition. If the acquisition succeeds (no adverse event occurs), then the hedge fund manager collects the spread (like the premium an insurance company receives for selling insurance) for

---

[1] A poison pill is a pre-offer takeover defense mechanism that gives target company bondholders the right to sell their bonds back to the target at a pre-specified redemption price, typically at or above par; this defense increases the acquirer's need for cash and raises the cost of the acquisition.

taking on event risk. If the acquisition fails (an adverse event occurs), then he/she faces the losses on the long and short positions (similar to an insurance company paying out a policy benefit after an insured event has occurred). Thus, the payoff profile of the merger arbitrage strategy resembles that of a riskless bond and a short put option. The merger arbitrage investor also can be viewed as owning an additional call option that becomes valuable if/when another interested acquirer (i.e., White Knight) makes a higher bid for the target company before the initial merger proposal is completed. Exhibit 5 shows risk and return attributes of merger arbitrage investing.

Exhibit 5 Event-Driven Merger Arbitrage—Risk, Liquidity, Leverage, and Benchmarking

Risk Profile and Liquidity

- Merger arbitrage is a relatively liquid strategy—with defined gains from idiosyncratic single security takeover situations but occasional downside shocks when merger deals unexpectedly fail.

- To the extent that deals are more likely to fail in market stress periods, this strategy has market sensitivity and left-tail risk attributes. Its return profile is insurance-like plus a short put option.

- Because cross-border merger and acquisition (M&A) usually involves two sets of governmental approvals and M&A deals involving vertical integration often face anti-trust scrutiny, these situations carry higher risks and offer wider merger spread returns.

- Some merger arbitrage managers invest only in friendly deals trading at relatively tight spreads, while others embrace riskier hostile takeovers trading at wider spreads. In the latter case, there may be expectations of a higher bid from a White Knight.

- The preferred vehicle is limited partnership because of merger arbitrage's use of significant leverage, but some low-leverage, low-volatility liquid alts merger arbitrage funds do exist.

- Attractiveness: Relatively high Sharpe ratios with typically low double-digit returns and mid–single digit standard deviation (depending on specific levels of leverage applied), but left-tail risk is associated with an otherwise steady return profile.

Leverage Usage

- Moderate to high: Managers typically apply 3 to 5 times leverage to this strategy to generate meaningful target return levels.

Benchmarking

- Sub-indexes include HFRX or HFRI Merger Arbitrage Index; CISDM Hedge Fund Merger Arbitrage Index; and Credit Suisse Merger Arbitrage Index.

5.1.2 *Strategy Implementation*

Merger arbitrage strategies are typically established using common equities; however, a range of other corporate securities, including preferred stock, senior and junior debt, convertible securities, options, and other derivatives, may also be used for positioning and hedging purposes. Often for a cash-for-stock acquisition, a hedge fund manager may choose to use leverage to buy the target firm. For a stock-for-stock acquisition, leverage may also often be used, but short selling the acquiring firm may be difficult due to liquidity issues or short-selling constraints, especially in emerging markets. Merger arbitrage strategies can utilize derivatives to overcome some short-sale constraints or to manage risks if the deal were to fail. For example, the manager could buy out-of-the money (O-T-M) puts on T and/or buy O-T-M call options on A (to cover the short position).

Convertible securities also provide exposure with asymmetrical payoffs. For example, the convertible bonds of T would also rise in value as T's shares rise because of the acquisition; the convertibles' bond value would provide a cushion if the deal fails and T's shares fall. When the acquiring company's credit is superior to the target company's credit, trades may be implemented using credit default swaps (CDS). In this case, protection would be sold (i.e., shorting the CDS) on the target company to benefit from its improved credit quality (and decline in price of protection and the CDS) once a merger is completed. If the pricing is sufficiently cheap, buying protection (i.e., going long the CDS) on the target may also be used as a partial hedge against a merger deal failing. Overall market risk (that could potentially disrupt a merger's consummation) might also be hedged by using added short equity index ETFs/futures or long equity index put positions.

In sum, the true source of return alpha for a merger arbitrage hedge fund manager is in the initial decision as to which deals to embrace and which to avoid. However, once involved with a given merger situation, there may be multiple ways to implement a position depending on the manager's deal-specific perspectives.

EXAMPLE 4

Merger Arbitrage Strategy Payoffs

An acquiring firm (A) is trading at $45/share and has offered to buy target firm (T) in a stock-for-stock deal. The offer ratio is 1 share of A in exchange for 2 shares of T. Target firm T was trading at $15 per share just prior to the announcement of the offer. Shortly thereafter, T's share price jumps up to $19 while A's share price falls to $42 in anticipation of the merger receiving required approvals and the deal closing successfully. A hedge fund manager is confident this deal will be completed, so he buys 20,000 shares of T and sells short 10,000 shares of A.

What are the payoffs of the merger arbitrage strategy if the deal is successfully completed or if the merger fails?

Solution:

At current prices it costs $380,000 to buy 20,000 shares of T, and $420,000 would be received for short selling 10,000 shares of A. This provides a net spread of $40,000 to the hedge fund manager if the merger is successfully completed. If the merger fails, then prices should revert to their pre-merger announcement levels. The manager would need to buy back 10,000 shares of A at $45 (costing $450,000) to close the short position, while the long position in 20,000 shares of T would fall to $15 per share (value at $300,000). This would cause a total loss of $110,000 [= (A: +$420,000 − $450,000) + (T: −$380,000 + $300,000)]. In sum, this merger strategy is equivalent to holding a riskless bond with a face value of $40,000 (the payoff for a successful deal) and a short binary put option, which expires worthless if the merger succeeds but pays out $110,000 if the merger fails.

6 EVENT-DRIVEN STRATEGIES: DISTRESSED SECURITIES

c discuss investment characteristics, strategy implementation, and role in a portfolio of *event-driven* hedge fund strategies;

Distressed securities strategies focus on firms that either are in bankruptcy, facing potential bankruptcy, or under financial stress. Firms face these circumstances for a wide variety of reasons, including waning competitiveness, excessive leverage, poor governance, accounting irregularities, or outright fraud. Often the securities of such companies have been sold out of long-only portfolios and may be trading at a significant discount to their eventual work-out value under proper stewardship and guidance. Because hedge funds are not constrained by institutional requirements on minimum credit quality, hedge fund managers are often natural candidates to take positions in such situations. Hedge funds, generally, also provide their investors only periodic liquidity (typically quarterly or sometimes only annually), making the illiquid nature of such securities less problematic than if such positions were held within a mutual fund. Hedge fund managers may find inefficiently priced securities before, during, or after the bankruptcy process, but typically they will be looking to realize their returns somewhat faster than the longer-term orientation of private equity firms. However, this is not always the case; for example, managers that invest in some distressed sovereign debt (e.g., Puerto Rico, Venezuela) often must face long time horizons to collect their payouts.

At times, distressed hedge fund managers may seek to own the majority or all of a certain class of securities within the capital structure, which enables them to exert creditor control in the corporate bankruptcy or reorganization process. Such securities will vary by country depending on individual bankruptcy laws and procedures. Some managers are active in their distressed investing by building concentrated positions and placing representatives on the boards of the companies they are seeking to turn around. Other distressed managers may be more "passive" in their orientation, relying on others to bear the often substantial legal costs of a corporate capital structure reorganization that may at times involve expensive proxy contests.

By nature, distressed debt and other illiquid assets may take several years to resolve, and they are generally difficult to value. Therefore, hedge fund managers running portfolios of distressed securities typically require relatively long initial lock-up periods (e.g., no redemptions allowed for the first two years) from their investors. Distressed investment managers may also impose fund-level or investor-level redemption gates that are meant to limit the amount of money that investors (i.e., limited partners) may withdraw from a partnership during any given quarter. As for valuing distressed securities, external valuation specialists may be needed to provide an independent estimate of fair value. Valuations of distressed securities with little or no liquidity (e.g., those deemed Level 3 assets for US accounting purposes) are subject to the smoothing effect of "mark-to-model" price determination.

The bankruptcy process typically results in one or two outcomes: liquidation or firm re-organization. In a liquidation, the firm's assets are sold off over some time period; then, based on the priority of their claim, debt- and equity-holders are paid off sequentially. In this case, claimants on the firm's assets are paid in order of priority from senior secured debt, junior secured debt, unsecured debt, convertible debt, preferred stock, and finally common stock. In a re-organization, a firm's capital structure is re-organized and the terms for current claims are negotiated and revised. Current debtholders may agree to extend the maturity of their debt contracts or even to exchange their debt for new equity shares. In this case, existing equity would be canceled (so existing shareholders would be left with nothing) and new equity issued, which would also be sold to new investors to raise funds to improve the firm's financial condition.

6.1 Investment Characteristics

Distressed securities present new sets of risks and opportunities and thus require special skills and increased monitoring. As previously mentioned, many institutional investors, like banks and insurance companies, by their mandates cannot hold non-investment-grade securities in their portfolios. As a result, many such investors must sell off investments in firms facing financial distress. This situation may result in illiquidity and significant price discounting when trades do occur, but it also creates potentially attractive opportunities for hedge funds. Moreover, the movement from financial distress to bankruptcy can unfold over long periods and because of the complexities of legal proceedings, informational inefficiencies cause securities to be improperly valued.

To successfully invest in distressed securities, hedge fund managers require specific skills for analyzing complicated legal proceedings, bankruptcy processes, creditor committee discussions, and re-organization scenarios. They also must be able to anticipate market reactions to these actions. At times, and depending on relative pricing, managers may establish "capital structure arbitrage" positions: For the same distressed entity, they may be long securities where they expect to receive acceptable recoveries but short other securities (including equity) where the value-recovery prospects are dim.

Current market conditions also affect the success of distressed securities strategies. In liquidation, assets may need to be sold quickly, and discounted selling prices will lower the total recovery rate. When illiquid assets must be sold quickly, forced sales and liquidity spirals may lead to fire-sale prices. For re-organizations, current market conditions partly determine whether (and how much) a firm can raise capital from asset sales and/or from the issuance of new equity. Exhibit 6 provides some key attributes of distressed securities investing.

Exhibit 6   Distressed Securities—Risk, Liquidity, Leverage, and Benchmarking

Risk Profile and Liquidity

- The return profile for distressed securities investing is typically at the higher end of event-driven strategies but with more variability.
- Outright shorts or hedged positions are possible, but distressed securities investing is usually long-biased. It is subject to security-specific outcomes but still impacted by the health of the macro-economy.
- Distressed securities investing typically entails relatively high levels of illiquidity, especially if using a concentrated activist approach. Pricing may involve "mark-to-model" with return smoothing. Ultimate results are generally binary: either very good or very bad.
- Attractiveness: Returns tend to be "lumpy" and somewhat cyclical. Distressed investing is particularly attractive in the early stages of an economic recovery after a period of market dislocation.

Leverage Usage

- Moderate to low: Because of the inherent volatility and long-biased nature of distressed securities investing, hedge fund managers utilize modest levels of leverage, typically with 1.2 to 1.7 times NAV invested, and with some of the nominal leverage from derivatives hedging.

(continued)

Exhibit 6 (Continued)

Benchmarking

- Hedge fund sub-indexes include HFRX and HFRI Distressed Indices; CISDM Distressed Securities Index; Lipper TASS Event-Driven Index; and Credit Suisse Event Driven Distressed Hedge Fund Index.

Note: Alpha produced by distressed securities managers tends to be idiosyncratic. Also, the strategy capitalizes on information inefficiencies and structural inabilities of traditional managers to hold such securities.

6.2 Strategy Implementation

Hedge fund managers take several approaches when investing in distressed securities. In a liquidation situation, the focus is on determining the recovery value for different classes of claimants. If the fund manager's estimate of recovery value is higher than market expectations, perhaps due to illiquidity issues, then he/she can buy the undervalued debt securities in hopes of realizing the higher recovery rate. For example, assume bankrupt company X's senior secured debt is priced at 50% of par. By conducting research on the quality of the collateral and by estimating potential cash flows (and their timing) in liquidation, the hedge fund manager estimates a recovery rate of 75%. He/she can buy the senior secured debt and expect to realize the positive difference in recovery rates. However, even assuming the manager is correct, if the liquidation process drags on and/or market conditions deteriorate, then this premium may be only partly realized, if at all.

In a reorganization situation, the hedge fund manager's focus is on how the firm's finances will be restructured and on assessing the value of the business enterprise and the future value of different classes of claims. There are various avenues for investing in a re-organization. The manager will evaluate the different securities of the company in question and purchase those deemed to be undervalued given the likely re-organization outcome. The selection of security will also depend on whether the manager seeks a control position or not. If so, he/she will be active in the negotiating process and will seek to identify fulcrum securities that provide leverage (or even liquidation) in the reorganization. **Fulcrum securities** are partially-in-the-money claims (not expected to be repaid in full) whose holders end up owning the reorganized company. Assuming the re-organization is caused by excessive financial leverage but the company's operating prospects are still good, a financial restructuring may be implemented whereby senior unsecured debt purchased by the hedge fund manager is swapped for new shares (existing debt and equity are cancelled) and new equity investors inject fresh capital into the company. As financial distress passes and the intrinsic value of the reorganized company rises, an initial public offering (IPO) would likely be undertaken. The hedge fund manager could then exit and earn the difference between what was paid for the undervalued senior unsecured debt and the proceeds received from selling the new shares of the revitalized company in the IPO.

> **EXAMPLE 5**
>
> ### Capital Structure Arbitrage in the Energy Crisis of 2015–2016
>
> With a sudden structural increase in US energy reserves caused by modern fracking techniques, oil prices tumbled dramatically from more than $60/barrel in mid-2015 to less than $30/barrel in early 2016. Debt investors suddenly became concerned about the very survivability of the smaller, highly levered exploration and production (E&P) companies if such low energy prices were to persist. Prices of many energy-related, junior, unsecured, non-investment-grade debt securities fell dramatically. However, retail equity investors generally reacted more benignly. As a result, the shares of several such E&P companies still carried significant implied enterprise value while their debt securities traded as if bankruptcy was imminent.
>
> 1 Discuss why such a divergence in the valuation of the debt and equity securities of these E&P companies might have occurred.
>
> 2 Discuss how a hedge fund manager specializing in distressed securities might take advantage of this situation.
>
> **Solution to 1:**
>
> This divergence in valuation occurred because of structural differences between the natural holders of debt and equity securities. Institutional holders of the debt likely felt more compelled, or in some cases were required by investment policy, to sell these securities as credit ratings on these bonds were slashed. Retail equity investors were likely less informed as to the potential seriousness of the impact of such a sharp energy price decline on corporate survivability. With equity markets overall still moving broadly higher, retail equityholders may have been expressing a "buy the dip" mentality. Such cross-asset arbitrage situations represent a significant opportunity for nimble and flexible hedge fund managers that are unrestrained by a single asset class perspective or other institutional constraints.
>
> **Solution to 2:**
>
> An astute hedge fund manager would have realized three key points: 1) the junior unsecured debt securities were temporarily undervalued; 2) although bankruptcy in certain specific companies was indeed possible (depending on how long energy prices stayed low), detailed research could uncover those E&P companies for which bankruptcy was less likely; and 3) the unsecured debt securities could be purchased with some safety by shorting the still overvalued equities (or buying put options on those equities) as a hedge.
>
> If energy prices subsequently remained low for too long and bankruptcy was indeed encountered, the equities would become worthless. However, the unsecured debt might still have some recovery value from corporate asset sales, or these securities might become the fulcrum securities that would be converted in a bankruptcy reorganization into new equity in an ongoing enterprise. Alternatively, if oil prices were to recover (as indeed transpired; oil prices closed 2017 at more than $60/barrel), the unsecured debt securities of many of these companies would rebound far more substantially than their equity shares would rise.

> In sum, a distressed securities hedge fund arbitrageur willing to take a position in the unsecured debt hedged against short equity (or long puts on the equity) could make money under a variety of possible outcomes.

7. RELATIVE VALUE STRATEGIES: FIXED INCOME ARBITRAGE

d discuss investment characteristics, strategy implementation, and role in a portfolio of *relative value* hedge fund strategies;

We have previously described equity market-neutral investing as one specific equity-oriented relative value hedge fund approach, but other types of relative value strategies are common for hedge funds involving fixed-income securities and hybrid convertible debt. Like equity market-neutral trading, many of these strategies involve the significant use of leverage. Changes in credit quality, liquidity, and implied volatility (for securities with embedded options) are some of the causes of relative valuation differences. During normal market conditions, successful relative value strategies can earn credit, liquidity, or volatility premiums over time. But, in crisis periods—when excessive leverage, deteriorating credit quality, illiquidity, and volatility spikes come to the fore—relative value strategies can result in losses. Fixed-income arbitrage and convertible bond arbitrage are among the most common relative value strategies.

7.1 Fixed-Income Arbitrage

Fixed-income arbitrage strategies attempt to exploit pricing inefficiencies by taking long and short positions across a range of debt securities, including sovereign and corporate bonds, bank loans, and consumer debt (e.g., credit card loans, student loans, mortgage-backed securities). Arbitrage opportunities between fixed-income instruments may develop because of variations in duration, credit quality, liquidity, and optionality.

7.1.1 Investment Characteristics

In its simplest form, fixed-income arbitrage involves buying the relatively undervalued securities and short selling the relatively overvalued securities with the expectation that the mispricing will resolve itself (reversion back to normal valuations) within the specified investment horizon. Valuation differences beyond normal historical ranges can result from differences in credit quality (investment-grade versus non-investment-grade securities), differences in liquidity (on-the-run versus off-the-run securities), differences in volatility expectations (especially for securities with embedded options), and even differences in issue sizes. More generally, fixed-income arbitrage can be characterized as exploiting price differences relative to expected future price relationships, with mean reversion being one important aspect. In many instances, realizing a net positive relative carry over time may also be the goal of the relative security positioning, which may involve exploiting kinks in a yield curve or an expected shift in the shape of a yield curve.

Where positioning may involve the acceptance of certain relative credit risks across different security issuers, fixed-income arbitrage morphs into what is more broadly referred to as L/S credit trading. This version of trading tends to be naturally more volatile than the exploitation of small pricing differences within sovereign debt alone.

Unless trading a price discrepancy directly involves establishing a desired yield curve exposure, fixed-income arbitrageurs will typically immunize their strategies, which involve both long and short positions, from interest rate risk by taking duration-neutral positions. However, duration neutrality provides a hedge against only small shifts in the yield curve. To hedge against large yield changes and/or non-parallel yield curve movements (i.e., steepening or flattening), the manager might employ a range of fixed-income derivatives, including futures, forwards, swaps, and swaptions (i.e., options on a swap). Moreover, fixed-income securities also vary in their complexity. For example, in addition to interest rate risk, straight government debt is exposed to sovereign risk (and potentially currency risk), which can be substantial in many countries, while asset-backed and mortgaged-backed securities are subject to credit risk and pre-payment risk. Derivatives are also useful for hedging such risks.

Fixed-income security pricing inefficiencies are often quite small, especially in the more-efficient developed capital markets, but the correlation aspects across different securities is typically quite high. Consequently, it may be necessary and acceptable to utilize substantial amounts of leverage to exploit these inefficiencies. Typical leverage ratios in fixed-income arbitrage strategies can be 4 to 5 times (assets to equity). In the case of some market-neutral multi-strategy funds, where fixed-income arbitrage may form just a portion of total risk, fixed-income arbitrage leverage levels can sometimes be as high as 12 to 15 times assets to equity. Of course, leverage will magnify the myriad risks to which fixed-income strategies are exposed, especially during stressed market conditions.

Another factor that has compounded the risks of fixed-income arbitrage strategies has been the inclination of financial engineers to create tranched, structured products around certain fixed-income cash flows—particularly involving residential mortgages—to isolate certain aspects of credit risk and prepayment risk. For example, within a pool of mortgages, cash flows may be divided such that some credit tranche holders have seniority over others or so that interest-only income payments flow to one set of holders and principal-only payoffs flow to another set of holders. The risks of relative value strategies involving mortgage-related securities, which are especially relevant during periods of market stress, include negative convexity aspects of many mortgage-backed securities and some of the structured products built around them; underlying default rates potentially exceeding expectations and resulting in a high-volatility environment; balance sheet leverage of hedge funds; and hedge fund investor redemption pressures.

Globally, fixed-income markets are substantially larger in total issuance size and scale than equity markets and come in a myriad of different securities types. Away from on-the-run government securities and other sovereign-backed debt securities, which in most developed financial markets are generally very liquid, the liquidity aspects of many fixed-income securities are typically poor. This creates relative value arbitrage opportunities for hedge fund managers, but it also entails positioning and liquidity risks in portfolio management. Natural price opaqueness must often be overcome—particularly for "off-the-run" securities that may trade only occasionally. Liquidity in certain municipal bond markets and corporate debt markets, for example, can be particularly thin. Some key points of fixed-income arbitrage appear in Exhibit 7.

> **Exhibit 7   Fixed-Income Arbitrage—Risk, Liquidity, Leverage, and Benchmarking**
>
> ### Risk Profile and Liquidity
>
> - The risk/return profile of fixed-income arbitrage trading derives from the high correlations found across different securities, the yield spread pick-up to be captured, and the sheer number of different types of debt securities across different markets with different credit quality and convexity aspects in their pricing. Structured products built around debt securities introduce added complexity that may result in mispricing opportunities.
> - Yield curve and carry trades within the US government universe tend to be very liquid but typically have the fewest mispricing opportunities. Liquidity for relative value positions generally decreases in other sovereign markets, mortgage-related markets, and especially across corporate debt markets.
> - Attractiveness: A function of correlations between different securities, the yield spread available, and the high number and wide diversity of debt securities across different markets.
>
> ### Leverage Usage
>
> - High: This strategy has high leverage usage, but leverage availability typically diminishes with product complexity. To achieve the desired leverage, prime brokers offer collateralized repurchase agreements with associated leverage "haircuts" depending on the types of securities being traded. The haircut is the prime broker's cushion against market volatility and illiquidity if posted collateral ever needs to be liquidated.
>
> ### Benchmarking
>
> - This is a broad category that encompasses the following sub-indexes: HFRX and HFRI Fixed Income Relative Value Indices; Lipper TASS Fixed Income Arbitrage Index; CISDM Debt Arbitrage Index; and Credit Suisse Fixed Income Arbitrage Index.
>
> *Note*: HFRX and HFRI also offer more granular hedge fund fixed-income, relative value indexes related to sovereign bonds trading, credit trading, and asset-backed trading.

7.1.2 *Strategy Implementation*

The most common types of fixed-income arbitrage strategies include yield curve trades and carry trades. Considering yield curve trades, the prevalent calendar spread strategy involves taking long and short positions at different points on the yield curve where the relative mispricing of securities offers the best opportunities, such as in a curve flattening or steepening, to profit. Perceptions and forecasts of macroeconomic conditions are the backdrop for these types of trades. The positions can be in fixed-income securities of the same issuer; in that case, most credit and liquidity risks would likely be hedged, making interest rate risk the main concern. Alternatively, longs and shorts can be taken in the securities of different issuers—but typically ones operating in the same industry or sector. In this case, differences in credit quality, liquidity, volatility, and issue-specific characteristics would likely drive the relative mispricing. In either case, the hedge fund manager aims to profit as the mispricing reverses (mean reversion occurs) and the longs rise and shorts fall in value within the targeted time frame.

Carry trades involve going long a higher yielding security and shorting a lower yielding security with the expectation of receiving the positive carry and of profiting on long and short sides of the trade when the temporary relative mispricing reverts to normal. A classic example of a fixed-income arbitrage trade involves buying lower liquidity, off-the-run government securities and selling higher liquidity, duration matched, on-the-run government securities. Interest rate and credit risks are hedged because long and short positions have the same duration and credit exposure. So, the key concern is liquidity risk. Under normal conditions, as time passes the more (less) expensive on- (off-) the-run securities will decrease (increase) in price as the current on-the-runs are replaced by a more liquid issue of new on-the-run bonds that then become off-the-run bonds.

The payoff profile of this fixed-income arbitrage strategy resembles a short put option. If the strategy unfolds as expected, it returns a positive carry plus a profit from spread narrowing. But, if the spread unexpectedly widens, then the payoff becomes negative. Mispricing of government securities is generally small, so substantial leverage would typically be used to magnify potential profits. But, with highly levered positions, even a temporary negative price shock can be sufficient to set off a wave of margin calls that force fund managers to sell at significant losses. Such a scenario in the wake of the 1997 Asian Financial Crisis and the 1998 Russian Ruble Crisis led to the collapse and subsequent US Federal Reserve-supervised bailout of legendary hedge fund Long-Term Capital Management. It is important to note that there are far more complex relative value fixed-income strategies beyond just yield curve trades, carry trades, or relative credit trades.

EXAMPLE 6

Fixed-Income Arbitrage: Treasuries vs. Inflation Swap + TIPS

Guernsey Shore Hedge Fund closely monitors government bond markets and looks for valuation discrepancies among the different issues.

Portfolio manager Nick Landers knows that Treasury Inflation-Protected Securities (TIPS) pay a coupon (i.e., real yield) while accruing inflation into the principal, which is paid at maturity. This insulates the TIPS owner from inflation risk.

Landers also understands that because the US government issues both TIPS and Treasuries that have the same maturity, they should trade at similar yields after adjusting for inflation. Landers knows that by using OTC inflation swaps, the inflation-linked components of TIPS can be locked in, thereby fixing all payments to be similar to those of a Treasury bond.

After accounting for expected inflation in normal periods, global investors often prefer Treasuries to inflation-indexed bonds. This may be because market participants do not fully trust the way inflation may be measured over time. As such, inflation-hedged TIPS (as a package with the associated offsetting inflation swap) have typically yielded about 25 bps to 35 bps more than similar maturity Treasuries.

During a period of extreme market distress, in November 2XXX, Landers keenly observed that TIPS were particularly mispriced. Their yields, adjusted for inflation, were substantially higher than straight Treasuries, while inflation swaps were priced as if outright deflation was imminent. Landers notes the information on the relative pricing of these different products and considers whether to implement the follow trade:

November 2XXX	Fixed Rate	Inflation Rate	Cost
Buy 5-year TIPS	Receive 3.74%	Receive inflation	−1,000,000
Short 5-year Treasuries	Pay 2.56%	—	+1,000,000
Inflation swap: receive fixed rate and pay inflation index	Receive 1.36%	Pay inflation	0
Net of three trades	Receive 2.54%	—	0

Discuss whether Landers has uncovered a risk-free arbitrage, and if so, discuss some of the risks he may still face with its execution.

Solution:

The situation observed by Landers occurred during a period of extreme market stress. In such turbulent times, instances of very attractive, near risk-free arbitrage can occur, as in this case. Often these periods are characterized by a fear of deflation, so straight Treasury bonds are in high demand for flight-to-quality reasons. But there would be some operational hurdles to overcome. For Landers to short the expensive Treasuries and buy the more attractive TIPS, Guernsey Shore would need access as a counterparty to the interbank repurchase market to borrow the Treasury bonds. Bank credit approval [via an International Swaps and Derivatives Association (ISDA) relationship] would also be required for accessing the inflation swap market for yield enhancement and to lock in the inflation hedge. Unfortunately, during periods of extreme market distress, credit lines to hedge funds typically shrink (or are withdrawn), not expanded. Moreover, there is potential for "losing the borrow" on the short Treasuries (i.e., the lender demanding return of his/her Treasuries), which makes the trade potentially difficult to maintain. Assuming Guernsey Shore met these operational requirements, Landers would need to act quickly to capture the fixed-income arbitrage profit of 2.54%. Such extreme levels of arbitrage rarely persist for very long.

8. RELATIVE VALUE STRATEGIES: CONVERTIBLE BOND ARBITRAGE

d discuss investment characteristics, strategy implementation, and role in a portfolio of *relative value* hedge fund strategies;

Convertible bonds are hybrid securities that can be viewed as a combination of straight debt plus a long equity call option with an exercise price equal to the strike price times the conversion ratio. The conversion ratio is the number of shares for which the bond can be exchanged. The bond's conversion value is the current stock price times the conversion ratio. The conversion price is the current convertible bond price divided by the conversion ratio. If the current conversion value is significantly below the convertible bond price (or equivalently, the current share price is significantly below the conversion price), the call is out-of-the-money and the convertible bond will behave more like a straight bond. Conversely, if the conversion value is significantly above the convertible bond price (or equivalently, the current share price is significantly above the conversion price), the call is in-the-money and the convertible bond will behave more like the underlying equity.

8.1 Investment Characteristics

Convertible securities are naturally complex and thus generally not well understood. They are impacted by numerous factors, including overall interest rate levels, corporate credit spreads, bond coupon and principal cash flows, and the value of the embedded stock option (which itself is influenced by dividend payments, stock price movements, and equity volatility). Convertibles are often issued sporadically by companies in relatively small sizes compared to straight debt issuances, and thus they are typically thinly-traded securities. Moreover, most convertibles are non-rated and typically have fewer covenants than straight bonds. Because the equity option value is embedded within such thinly-traded, complex securities, the embedded options within convertibles tend to trade at relatively low implied volatility levels compared to the historical volatility level of the underlying equity. Convertibles also trade cyclically relative to the amount of new issuance of such securities in the overall market. The higher the new convertible issuance that the market must absorb, the cheaper their pricing and the more attractive the arbitrage opportunities for a hedge fund manager.

The key problem for the convertible arbitrage manager is that to access and extract the relatively cheap embedded optionality of the convertible, he/she must accept or hedge away other risks that are embedded in the convertible security. These include interest rate risk, credit risk of the corporate issuer, and market risk (i.e., the risk that the stock price will decline and thus render the embedded call option less valuable). Should the convertible manager desire, all these risks can be hedged using a combination of interest rate derivatives, credit default swaps, and short sales of an appropriate delta-adjusted amount of the underlying stock. The purchase of put options can also be a stock-sale substitute. The use of any such hedging tools may also erode the very attractiveness of the targeted convertible holding.

Convertible managers who are more willing to accept credit risk may choose to not hedge the credit default risk of the corporate issuer; instead, they will take on the convertible position more from a credit risk perspective. Such managers are known as credit-oriented convertible managers. Other managers may hedge the credit risk but will take a more long-biased, directional view of the underlying stock and then underhedge the convertible's equity exposure. Yet other managers may overhedge the equity risk to create a bearish tilt with respect to the underlying stock, thus providing a more focused exposure to increased volatility. These managers are referred to as volatility-oriented convertible managers. In sum, several different ways and styles can be utilized to set up convertible arbitrage exposures. Exhibit 8 presents some key aspects of convertible bond arbitrage.

Exhibit 8   Convertible Bond Arbitrage—Risk, Liquidity, Leverage, and Benchmarking

Risk Profile and Liquidity

- Convertible arbitrage managers strive to extract and benefit from this structurally cheap source of implied volatility by delta hedging and gamma trading short equity hedges against their long convertible holdings.

(continued)

> **Exhibit 8   (Continued)**
>
> - Liquidity issues surface for convertible arbitrage strategies in two ways: 1) naturally less-liquid securities because of their relatively small issue sizes and inherent complexities; 2) availability and cost to borrow underlying equity for short selling.
> - Attractiveness: Convertible arbitrage works best during periods of high convertible issuance, moderate volatility, and reasonable market liquidity. It fares less well in periods of acute credit weakness and general illiquidity, when the pricing of convertible securities is unduly impacted by supply/demand imbalances.
>
> **Leverage Usage**
>
> - High: Because of many legs needed to implement convertible arbitrage trades (e.g., short sale, CDS transaction, interest rate hedge), relatively high levels of leverage are used to extract a modest ultimate gain from delta hedging. Managers typically run convertible portfolios at 300% long vs. 200% short, the lower short exposure being a function of the delta-adjusted equity exposure needed from short sales to balance the long convertible.
>
> **Benchmarking**
>
> - Sub-indexes include HFRX and HFRI FI-Convertible Arbitrage Indices; Lipper TASS Convertible Arbitrage Index; CISDM Convertible Arbitrage Index; and Credit Suisse Convertible Arbitrage Index.
>
> *Note*: Convertible bond arbitrage is a core hedge fund strategy area that is run within many multi-strategy hedge funds together with L/S equity, merger arbitrage, and other event-driven distressed strategies.

8.2 Strategy Implementation

A classic convertible bond arbitrage strategy is to buy the relatively undervalued convertible bond and take a short position in the relatively overvalued underlying stock. The number of shares to sell short to achieve a delta neutral overall position is determined by the delta of the convertible bond. For convertible bonds with low conversion prices relative to the current stock price (i.e., the long call is I-T-M), the delta will be close to 1. For convertibles with high conversion prices relative to the current stock price (i.e., the long call is O-T-M), the delta will be closer to 0. The combination of a long convertible and short equity delta exposure would create a situation where for small changes in the equity price, the portfolio will remain essentially balanced. As the underlying stock price moves further, however, the delta hedge of the convertible will change because the convertible is an instrument with the natural positive convexity attributes of positive gamma. Because stock gamma is always zero, the convertible arbitrage strategy will leave the convertible arbitrageur "synthetically" longer in total equity exposure as the underlying security price rises and synthetically less long as the equity price falls. This added gamma-driven exposure can then be hedged at favorable levels with appropriate sizing adjustments of the underlying short stock hedge—selling more stock at higher levels and buying more stock at lower levels. The convertible arbitrage strategy will be profitable given sufficiently large stock price swings and proper periodic rebalancing (assuming all else equal). If realized equity volatility exceeds the implied volatility of the convertible's embedded option (net of hedging costs), an overall gain is achieved by the arbitrageur.

Several circumstances can create concerns for a convertible arbitrage strategy. First, when short selling, shares must be located and borrowed; as a result, the stock owner may subsequently want his/her shares returned at a potentially inopportune time, such as during stock price run-ups or more generally when supply for the stock is low or demand for the stock is high. This situation, particularly a short squeeze, can lead to substantial losses and a suddenly unbalanced exposure if borrowing the underlying equity shares becomes too difficult or too costly for the arbitrageur (of course, initially locking in a "borrow" over a "term period" can help the arbitrageur avoid short squeezes, but this may be costly to execute). Second, credit issues may complicate valuation given that bonds have exposure to credit risk; so when credit spreads widen or narrow, there would be a mismatch in the values of the stock and convertible bond positions that the convertible manager may or may not have attempted to hedge away. Third, the strategy can lose money because of time decay of the convertible bond's embedded call option during periods of reduced realized equity volatility and/or from a general compression of market implied volatility levels.

Convertible arbitrage strategies have performed best when convertible issuance is high (implying a wider choice among convertible securities and generally cheaper prices), general market volatility levels are moderate, and the liquidity to trade and adjust positions is ample. On the other hand, extreme market volatility also typically implies heightened credit risks; given that convertibles are naturally less-liquid securities, convertible managers generally do not fare well during such periods. The fact that hedge funds have become the natural market makers for convertibles and they typically face significant redemption pressures from investors during crises implies further unattractive left-tail risk attributes to the strategy during periods of market stress.

EXAMPLE 7

Convertible Arbitrage Strategy

Cleopatra Partners is a Dubai-based hedge fund engaging in convertible bond arbitrage. Portfolio manager Shamsa Khan is considering a trade involving the euro-denominated convertible bonds and stock of QXR Corporation. She has assembled the following information:

QXR Convertible Bond		
Price (% of par)	120	—
Coupon (%)	5.0	—
Remaining maturity (years)	1.0	—
Conversion ratio	50	—
S&P Rating	BBB	—

QXR Inc.		Industry Average
Price (per share)	30	--
P/E (x)	30	20
P/BV (x)	2.25	1.5
P/CF (x)	15	10

Additional Information:

- It costs €2 to borrow each QXR share (paid to the stock lender) to carry the short position for a year.
- The stock pays a €1 dividend.

1. Discuss (using only the information in the table) the basic trade setup that Khan should implement.
2. Demonstrate (without using the additional information) that potential profits earned are the same whether QXR's share price falls to €24, rises to €36, or remains flat at €30.
3. Discuss (using also the additional information) how the results of the trade will change.

Solution to 1:

QXR's convertible bond price is €1,200 [= €1,000 × (120/100)], and its conversion ratio is 50; so, the conversion price is €24 (€1,200/50). This compares with QXR's current share price of €30. QXR's share valuation metrics are all 50% higher than its industry's averages. It can be concluded that in relative terms, QXR's shares are overvalued and its convertible bonds are undervalued. Thus, Khan should buy the convertibles and short sell the shares.

Solution to 2:

By implementing this trade and buying the bond at €1,200, exercising the bond's conversion option, and selling her shares at the current market price, Khan can lock in a profit of €6 per share under any of the scenarios mentioned, as shown in the following table:

	Profit on:		
QXR Share Price	Long Stock via Convertible Bond	Short Stock	Total Profit
24	0	6	6
36	12	−6	6
30	6	0	6

Solution to 3:

The €2 per share borrowing costs and the €1 dividend payable to the lender together represent a €3 per share outflow that Khan must pay. But, the convertible bond pays a 5% coupon or €50, which equates to an inflow of €1 per share equivalent (€50 coupon/50 shares per bond). Therefore, the total profit outcomes, as indicated in the table, would each be reduced by €2. In sum, Khan would realize a total profit of €4 per each QXR share.

9. OPPORTUNISTIC STRATEGIES: GLOBAL MACRO STRATEGIES

e discuss investment characteristics, strategy implementation, and role in a portfolio of *opportunistic* hedge fund strategies;

Opportunistic Strategies: Global Macro Strategies

Opportunistic hedge fund strategies seek to profit from investment opportunities across a wide range of markets and securities using a variety of techniques. They invest primarily in asset classes, sectors, regions, and across macro themes and multi-asset relationships on a global basis (as opposed to focusing on the individual security level). So, broad themes, global relationships, market trends, and cycles affect their returns.

Although opportunistic hedge funds can sometimes be difficult to categorize and may use a variety of techniques, they can generally be divided by 1) the type of analysis and approach that drives the trading strategy (technical or fundamental), 2) how trading decisions are implemented (discretionary or systematic), and 3) the types of instruments and/markets in which they trade. Fundamental-based strategies use economic data as inputs and focus on fair valuation of securities, sectors, markets, and intra-market relationships. Technical analysis utilizes statistical methods to predict relative price movements based on past price trends.

Discretionary implementation relies on manager skills to interpret new information and make investment decisions, and it may be subject to such behavioral biases as overconfidence and loss aversion. Systematic implementation is rules-based and executed by computer algorithms with little or no human intervention; however, it may encounter difficulty coping with new, complex situations (not seen historically). As the absolute size of systematic trend-following funds has increased in significance, so too has the issue of negative execution slippage caused by the simultaneous reversal of multiple trend-following models that sometimes create a "herding effect." Such effects can temporarily overwhelm normal market liquidity and at times temporarily distort fundamental market pricing of assets (i.e., trend-following "overshoots" caused by momentum-signal triggers). We now discuss the two most common hedge fund strategies: global macro and managed futures.

9.1 Global Macro Strategies

Global macro strategies focus on global relationships across a wide range of asset classes and investment instruments, including derivative contracts (e.g., futures, forwards, swaps, and options) on commodities, currencies, precious and base metals, and fixed-income and equity indexes—as well as on sovereign debt securities, corporate bonds, and individual stocks. Given the wide range of possibilities to express a global macro view, these strategies tend to focus on certain themes (e.g., trading undervalued emerging market currencies versus overvalued US dollar using OTC currency swaps), regions (e.g., trading stock index futures on Italy's FTSE MIB versus Germany's DAX to capitalize on differences in eurozone equity valuations), or styles (e.g., systematic versus discretionary spread trading in energy futures). Global macro managers typically hold views on the relative economic health and central bank policies of different countries, global yield curve relationships, trends in inflation and relative purchasing power parity, and capital trade flow aspects of different countries (typically expressed through relative currency or rate-curve positioning).

Global macro managers tend to be anticipatory and sometimes contrarian in setting their strategies. Some macro managers may try to extract carry gains or ride momentum waves, but most have a tendency to be early in their positioning and then benefit when some rationality eventually returns to relative market pricing. This can make an allocation to global macro strategies particularly useful when a sudden potential reversal in markets is feared. For example, many global macro managers sensed the developing sub-prime mortgage crisis in the United States as early as 2006. They took on long positions in credit default swaps (CDS) (i.e., they purchased protection) on mortgage bonds, on tranches of mortgage structured products, or simply on broader credit indexes that they deemed particularly vulnerable to weakening credit conditions. Although they had to wait until 2007–2008 for these CDS positions to pay off, some global macro managers performed spectacularly well as market conditions morphed into the global financial crisis. Including global macro managers with significant subprime mortgage-focused CDS positions within a larger portfolio turned out to be a very valuable allocation.

It is important to note that because global macro managers trade a wide variety of instruments and markets and typically do so by different methods, these managers are fairly heterogeneous as a group. Thus, global macro funds are not as consistently dependable as a source of short alpha when compared to pure systematic, trend-following managed futures funds that typically attempt to capture any significant market trend. But, as noted earlier, global macro managers tend to be more anticipatory (compared to managed futures managers), which can be a useful attribute.

9.1.1 Investment Characteristics

Global macro managers use fundamental and technical analysis to value markets, and they use discretionary and systematic modes of implementation. The view taken by global macro portfolio managers can be directional (e.g., buy bonds of banks expected to benefit from "normalization" of US interest rates) or thematic (e.g., buy the "winning" companies and short sell the "losing" companies from Brexit). Because of their heterogeneity, added due diligence and close attention to the current portfolio of a macro manager may be required by an allocator to correctly anticipate the factor risks that a given global macro manager will deliver.

Despite their heterogeneity, a common feature among most global macro managers is the use of leverage, often obtained through the use of derivatives, to magnify potential profits. A margin-to-equity ratio typically of 15% to 25% posted against futures or forward positions allows a manager to control face amounts of assets up to 6 to 7 times a fund's assets. The use of such embedded leverage naturally allows the global macro manager ease and flexibility in relative value and directional positioning.

Generally, the key source of returns in global macro strategies revolves around correctly discerning and capitalizing on trends in global markets. As such, mean-reverting low volatility markets are the natural bane of this strategy area. Conversely, steep equity market sell-offs, interest rate regime changes, currency devaluations, volatility spikes, and geopolitical shocks caused by such events as trade wars and terrorism are examples of global macro risks; however, they can also provide some of the opportunities that global macro managers often attempt to exploit. Of course, the exposures selected in any global macro strategy may not react to the global risks as expected because of either unforeseen contrary factors or global risks that simply do not materialize. Thus, macro managers tend to produce somewhat lumpier and uneven return streams than other hedge fund strategies, and generally higher levels of volatility are associated with their returns.

Notably, the prevalence of quantitative easing since the global financial crisis of 2007–2009 resulted in generally benign market conditions for most of the subsequent decade, which was an especially imperfect environment for global macro managers. Although equity and fixed-income markets generally trended higher during this period, overall volatility levels across these and many other markets, such as currencies and commodities, were relatively low. In some cases, central bankers intervened to curtail undesirable market outcomes, thereby preventing certain global macro trends from fully materializing. Because such intervention substantially moderates the trendiness and the volatility of markets, which are the lifeblood of global macro strategies, some hedge fund allocators began avoiding these strategies. This may be shortsighted, however, because such opportunistic strategies as global macro can be very useful over a full market cycle in terms of portfolio diversification and alpha generation.

9.1.2 Strategy Implementation

Global macro strategies are typically top-down and employ a range of macroeconomic and fundamental models to express a view regarding the direction or relative value of an asset or asset class. Positions may comprise a mix of individual securities, baskets of securities, index futures, foreign exchange futures/forwards, precious or base metals futures, agricultural futures, fixed-income products or futures, and derivatives or options on any of these. If the hedge fund manager is making a directional bet, then directional models will use fundamental data regarding a specific market or asset to determine if it is undervalued or overvalued relative to history and the expected macro trend. Conversely, if the manager's proclivity is toward relative value positioning, then that manager will consider which assets are under- or overvalued relative to each other given historical and expected macro conditions.

For example, if currencies of the major ASEAN block countries (i.e., Indonesia, Malaysia, Philippines, Singapore, and Thailand) are depreciating against the US dollar, a directional model might conclude that the shares of their key exporting companies are undervalued and thus should be purchased. However, further investigation might signal that the public bonds of these exporters are cheap relative to their shares, so the bonds should be bought and the shares sold short. This situation might occur in the likely scenario that the share prices react quickly to the currency depreciation and bond prices take longer to react to the trend.

Successful global macro trading requires the manager to have both a correct fundamental view of the selected market(s) and the proper methodology and timing to express tactical views. Managers who repeatedly implement a position too early/unwind one too late or who choose an inappropriate method for implementation will likely face redemptions from their investors. Given the natural leverage used in global macro strategies, managers may be tempted to carry many (possibly too many) positions simultaneously; however, the diversification benefits of doing so are typically less than those derived from more idiosyncratic long/short equity strategies. This is because of the nature of "risk-on" or "risk-off" market conditions (often caused by central bank policies) that impact a variety of asset classes in a correlated manner.

EXAMPLE 8

Global Macro Strategy

Consider the following (hypothetical) macroeconomic scenario: Emerging market (EM) countries have been growing rapidly (in fact, overheating) and accumulating both historically large government budget deficits and trade deficits as expanding populations demand more public services and foreign goods. EM central banks have been intervening to support their currencies for some time, and electoral support for candidates promoting exorbitant business taxes and vast social welfare schemes in many EM countries has risen dramatically. These trends are expected to continue.

Melvin Chu, portfolio manager at Bermuda-based Global Macro Advisers (GMA), has been considering how to position his global macro hedge fund. After meeting with a senior central banker of a leading EM country, GMA's research director informs Chu that it appears this central bank may run out of foreign exchange reserves soon and thus may be unable to continue its supportive currency intervention.

Discuss a global macro strategy Chu might implement to profit from these trends by using options.

> **Solution:**
>
> Assuming this key EM country runs out of foreign currency reserves, then it is likely its currency will need to be devalued. This initial devaluation might reasonably be expected to trigger a wave of devaluations and economic and financial market turbulence in other EM countries in similar circumstances. So, Chu should consider trades based on anticipated EM currency depreciation (maybe even devaluation) as well as trades benefitting from rising interest rates, downward pressure on equities, and spikes in volatility in the EM space.
>
> A reasonable way for Chu to proceed would be to buy put options. If his expectations fail to materialize, his losses would then be capped at the total of the premiums paid for the options. Chu should consider buying puts on the following: a variety of EM currencies, EM government bond futures, and EM equity market indexes. He should buy in-the-money puts to implement his high conviction trades and out-of-the money puts for trades where he has a lower degree of confidence. Moreover, to take advantage of a possible flight-to-safety, Chu should consider buying call options on developed market (DM) reserve currencies as well as call options on bond futures for highly-rated DM government issuers.

10. OPPORTUNISTIC STRATEGIES: MANAGED FUTURES

e discuss investment characteristics, strategy implementation, and role in a portfolio of *opportunistic* hedge fund strategies;

Managed futures, which gained its first major academic backing in a classic paper by John Lintner in 1983, is a hedge fund strategy that focuses on investments using futures, options on futures, and sometimes forwards and swaps (primarily on stock and fixed-income indexes) and commodities and currencies. As futures markets have evolved over time and in different countries—gaining in size (i.e., open interest) and liquidity—some managers have also engaged in trading sector and industry index futures as well as more exotic contracts, such as futures on weather (e.g., temperature, rainfall) and derivatives contracts on carbon emissions.

10.1 Investment Characteristics

The uncorrelated nature of managed futures with stocks and bonds generally makes them a potentially attractive addition to traditional portfolios for improved risk-adjusted return profiles (i.e., improved efficient frontiers in a mean–variance framework). The value added from managed futures has typically been demonstrated during periods of market stress; for example, in 2007–2009 managers using this strategy benefitted from short positions in equity futures and long positions in fixed-income futures at a time when equity indexes were falling and fixed-income indexes were rising. Put another way, managed futures demonstrated natural positive skewness that has been useful in balancing negatively-skewed strategies.

The return profile of managed futures tends to be very cyclical. Between 2011 and 2018, the trendiness (i.e., directionality) of foreign exchange and fixed-income markets deteriorated, volatility levels in many markets dissipated, and periods of acute market stress temporarily disappeared. Except for equity markets in some developed countries, many markets became range-bound or mean-reverting, which hurt managed futures performance. The diversification benefit of trend following strong equity markets is also (by definition) less diversifying to traditional portfolios than if such trends existed in other non-equity markets.

In a world where sovereign bonds have approached the zero-yield boundary, the correlation benefit of managed futures has also changed. The past practice of trend following the fixed-income markets as they get higher may likely not be as repeatable going forward. Assuming managed futures managers begin to trend follow fixed-income markets as they get lower (i.e., as developed market interest rates "normalize"), then positive returns may still be realized—although with a very different type of correlation behavior to equity markets (i.e., not as valuable). Also, given the upward sloping nature of most global yield curves, less natural fixed-income "carry" contribution may occur from trend following the fixed-income markets to the downside (i.e., higher interest rates and lower prices).

Managed futures strategies are typically characterized as highly liquid, active across a wide range of asset classes, and able to go long or short with relative ease. High liquidity results from futures markets being among the most actively traded markets in the world. For example, the E-mini S&P 500 futures contract on the Chicago Mercantile Exchange has 3 to 4 times the daily dollar volume of the SPDR S&P 500 ETF (SPY), the world's most actively traded equity index fund. Futures contracts also provide highly liquid exposures to a wide range of asset classes that can be traded across the globe 24 hours a day. Because futures contracts require relatively little collateral to take positions as a result of the exchanges' central clearinghouse management of margin and risk, it is easier to take long and short positions with higher leverage than traditional instruments.

For example, futures contracts require margin from 0.1% to 10% of notional value for both long and short positions, as compared to standard equity market margin levels in the United States of 50%. Thus, the capital efficiency of futures contracts makes it easier for managed futures managers to be dynamic in both their long and short exposures. A traditional long-only portfolio is levered by borrowing funds to purchase additional assets. Futures portfolios do not own assets; they acquire asset exposures based on the notional value of the futures contracts held. The majority (typically 85% to 90%) of capital in a managed futures account is invested in short-term government debt (or other highly liquid collateral acceptable to the futures clearing house). The remainder (10% to 15%) is used to collateralize long and short futures contracts.

10.2 Strategy Implementation

Highly liquid contracts allow managed futures funds the flexibility to incorporate a wide range of investment strategies. Most managed futures strategies involve some "pattern recognition" trigger that is either momentum/trend driven or based on a volatility signal. Managers trade these signals across different time horizons, often with short-term mean reversion filters imposed on top of their core longer-term models. For example, a manager might have traded using a long-term horizon model that suggested gold prices would trend lower; as a result, the manager established a short position in gold futures some time ago. A short-term moving average of gold prices crossing below a longer-term moving average could have triggered this view. But later, that manager might also trade using a second, shorter time horizon model, which suggests that the downside momentum in gold prices has temporarily subsided and a mean-reverting bounce is likely. The results of these two models would be weighted and combined into an adjusted net position, typically with the longer-term model weighted more heavily than the shorter-term filter.

Such fundamental factors as carry relationships or volatility factors are often added to the core momentum and breakout signal methodologies, and they can be particularly useful regarding position sizing. Many managed futures managers implement their portfolios' relative position sizing by assessing both the volatility of each underlying futures position as well as the correlation of their return behaviors against one another. Generally, the greater the volatility of an asset, the smaller its portfolio sizing; and the greater its correlation to other futures being positioned, the smaller its portfolio sizing. Being attentive to correlation aspects between different futures contracts would then become a second step of analysis for most managed futures traders as a portfolio sizing risk constraint.

Besides core position sizing and sizing adjustments for volatility and correlation, managed futures managers will have either a price target exit methodology, a momentum reversal exit methodology, a time-based exit methodology, a trailing stop-loss exit methodology, or some combination thereof. A key to successful managed futures strategies is to have a consistent approach and to avoid overfitting of a model when backtesting performance across different markets and time periods. The goal is to have a model that performs well in a future "out of sample" period. Of course, trading models have a natural tendency to degrade in effectiveness over time as more and more managers use similar signals and the market opportunity being exploited consequently diminishes. Managed futures traders are thus constantly searching for new and differentiated trading signals. In today's world, many new signals are increasingly being developed using nontraditional, unstructured data and other types of "big data" analysis.

Apart from this accelerating search for more unique nonprice signals, the most common type of managed futures approach is typically referred to as **time-series momentum** (TSM) trend following. Momentum trading strategies are driven by the past returns of the individual assets. Simply put, managers go long assets that are rising in price and go short assets that are falling in price. TSM strategies are traded on an absolute basis, meaning the manager can be net long or net short depending on the current price trend of an asset. Such TSM strategies work best when an asset's (or market's) own past returns are a good predictor of its future returns.

A second, less common approach is using **cross-sectional momentum** (CSM) strategies, which are implemented with a cross-section of assets (generally within an asset class) by going long those that are rising in price the most and by shorting those that are falling the most. Such CSM strategies generally result in holding a net zero or market-neutral position. CSM strategies work well when a market's out- or underperformance relative to other markets is a reliable predictor of its future performance. However, CSM may be constrained by limited futures contracts available for a cross section of assets at the asset class level.

Global macro strategies and managed futures strategies often involve trading the same subset of markets but in different ways. It is important to understand the respective attributes of these two strategies. Exhibit 9 provides such a comparison.

Exhibit 9 Managed Futures and Global Macro Strategies—Comparison of Risk, Liquidity, Leverage, and Benchmarking

Risk Profile and Liquidity

- Both global macro and managed futures strategies are highly liquid but with some crowding aspects and execution slippage in managed futures as AUM have grown rapidly. Being more heterogeneous in approaches used, global macro strategies face less significant execution crowding effects.

- Typically, managed futures managers tend to take a more systematic approach to implementation than global macro managers, who are generally more discretionary in their application of models and tools.

Opportunistic Strategies: Managed Futures

Exhibit 9 (Continued)

- Returns of managed futures strategies typically exhibit positive right-tail skewness in periods of market stress, which is very useful for portfolio diversification. Global macro strategies have delivered similar diversification in such stress periods but with more heterogeneous outcomes.
- Despite positive skewness, managed futures and global macro managers are somewhat cyclical and at the more volatile end of the spectrum of hedge fund strategies (with volatility positively related to the strategy's time horizon). In addition, macro managers can also be early and overly anticipatory in their positioning.

Leverage Usage

- High: High leverage is embedded in futures contracts. Notional amounts up to 6 to 7 times fund assets can be controlled with initial margin-to-equity of just 10%–20% (with individual futures margin levels being a function of the volatility of the underlying assets). Active use of options by many global macro managers adds natural elements of leverage and positive convexity.

Benchmarking

- Managed futures are best tracked by such sub-indexes as HFRX and HFRI Macro Systematic Indices; CISDM CTA Equal-Weighted Index; Lipper TASS Managed Futures Index; and Credit Suisse Managed Futures Index.
- Global macro strategies are best tracked by HFRX and HFRI Macro Discretionary Indices; CISDM Hedge Fund Global Macro Index; Lipper TASS Global Macro Index; and Credit Suisse Global Macro Index.

EXAMPLE 9

Cross-Sectional and Time-Series Momentum

An institutional investor is considering adding an allocation to a managed futures strategy that focuses on medium-term momentum trading involving precious metals. This investor is evaluating two different managed futures funds that both trade precious metals futures, including gold, silver, platinum, and palladium futures. Of the two funds being considered, one is run using a cross-sectional momentum (CSM) strategy, and the other is managed using a time-series momentum (TSM) strategy. Both funds use trailing 6-month returns for developing their buy/sell signals, and they both volatility-weight their futures positions to have equal impact on their overall portfolios.

Explain how the CSM and TSM strategies would work and compare their risk profiles.

Solution:

For the CSM strategy, each day the manager will examine the returns for the four metals in question and then take a long position in the two metals futures with the best performance (i.e., the top 50%) in terms of trailing 6-month risk-adjusted returns and a short position in the two metals contracts with the worst performance (i.e., the bottom 50%) of returns. According to this strategy, the top (bottom) 50% will continue their relative value out- (under-) performance. Note that it is possible for metals contracts (or markets more generally) in the top (bottom) 50% to have negative (positive) absolute returns—for example, during bear (bull) markets. The CSM strategy is very much a relative momentum strategy, with the established positions acting as a quasi-hedge relative to each other in terms of total sector exposure. This CSM-run fund would likely deliver an overall return profile with somewhat less volatility than the TSM strategy.

For the TSM strategy, each day the manager will take a long position in the precious metals futures with positive trailing 6-month returns and sell short those metals contracts with negative trailing 6-month returns. According to this TSM strategy, the metals futures (or markets, more generally) with positive (negative) returns will continue to rise (fall) in absolute value, resulting in an expected profit on both long and short positions. However, by utilizing a TSM strategy, the fund might potentially end up with long positions in all four metals contracts or short positions in all these precious metals futures at the same time.

Consequently, the CSM strategy typically results in a net zero market exposure during normal periods, while the TSM strategy can be net long or net short depending on how many metal (or markets, generally) have positive and negative absolute returns. The return profile of the TSM managed fund is thus likely to be more volatile than that of the CSM managed fund and also far more sensitive to periods when the precious metals sector is experiencing strong trends (i.e., directionality).

11. SPECIALIST STRATEGIES

f   discuss investment characteristics, strategy implementation, and role in a portfolio of *specialist* hedge fund strategies;

Specialist hedge fund strategies require highly specialized skill sets for trading in niche markets. Two such typical specialist strategies are volatility trading and reinsurance/life settlements.

11.1 Volatility Trading

Over the past several decades, volatility trading has become an asset class unto itself. Niche hedge fund managers specialize in trading relative volatility strategies globally across different geographies and asset classes. For example, given the plethora of structured product offerings in Asia with inexpensive embedded options that can be stripped out and resold (usually by investment banks), volatility pricing in Asia is often relatively cheap compared to the more expensive implied volatility of options traded in North American and European markets. In these latter markets, there is a proclivity to buy out-of-the-money options as a protective hedge (i.e., insurance). The goal of **relative value volatility arbitrage** strategies is to source and buy cheap volatility and sell more expensive volatility while netting out the time decay aspects normally associated with options portfolios. Depending on the instruments used (e.g., puts and calls or variance swaps), these strategies may also attempt to extract value from active gamma trading adjustments when markets move.

11.1.1 *Investment Characteristics and Strategy Implementation*

The easiest way to understand relative value volatility trading is through a few examples. Throughout the 1980s and 1990s, options on the Japanese yen consistently traded at lower volatility levels within Asian time zones than similar options were traded in London, New York, or Chicago (i.e., IMM futures market). Capturing the volatility spread between these options is a type of relative value volatility trading known as time-zone arbitrage—in this case of a single underlying fungible global asset, the Japanese yen. As a second arbitrage example, managers in today's markets may periodically source Nikkei 225 implied volatility in Asia at cheaper levels than S&P 500 implied volatility is being traded in New York, even though the Nikkei 225 typically has realized volatility higher than that of the S&P 500. This type of relative value volatility trading is known as cross-asset volatility trading, which may often involve idiosyncratic, macro-oriented risks.

Of course, another simpler type of volatility trading involves outright long volatility traders who may trade against consistent volatility sellers. Equity volatility is approximately 80% *negatively* correlated with equity market returns. Otherwise stated, volatility levels tend to go up when equity markets fall, with options pricing skew reflecting such a tendency. Clearly, this makes the long volatility strategy a useful potential diversifier for long equity investments, albeit at the cost to the option premium paid by the volatility buyer. Selling volatility provides a volatility risk premium or compensation for taking on the risk of providing insurance against crises for holders of equities and other securities.

In the United States, the most liquid volatility contracts are short-term VIX Index futures contracts, which track the 30-day implied volatility of S&P 500 Index options as traded on the Chicago Board Options Exchange (CBOE). Because volatility is nonconstant but high levels of volatility are difficult to perpetuate over long periods of time (markets eventually calm down after sudden jump shifts), VIX futures are often prone to mean reversion. Given this fact and the fact that VIX futures prices typically slide down a positively sloped implied volatility curve as expiration approaches, many practitioners prefer trading simple exchange-traded options, over-the-counter (OTC) options, variance swaps, and volatility swaps. The general mean-reverting nature of volatility still impacts these products, but it does so in a less explicit fashion than with the futures.

Multiple paths can be taken to implement a volatility trading strategy. If a trader uses simple exchange-traded options, then the maturity of such options typically extends out to no more than approximately two years. In terms of expiry, the longer-dated options will have more absolute exposure to volatility levels (i.e., vega exposure) than shorter-dated options, but the shorter-dated options will exhibit more delta sensitivity to price changes (i.e., gamma exposure). Traders need to monitor the following: the term structure of volatility, which is typically upward sloping but can invert during periods of crisis; the volatility smile across different strike prices, whereby out-of-the-money options will typically trade at higher implied volatility levels than at-the-money options; and the volatility skew, whereby out-of-the-money puts may trade at higher volatility levels than out-of-the-money calls. Volatility traders strive to capture relative timing and strike pricing opportunities using various types of option spreads, such as bull and bear spreads, straddles, and calendar spreads.

To extract an outright long volatility view, options are purchased and delta hedging of the gamma exposure is required. How the embedded gamma of the long options position is managed is also important. For example, one could have a positive view of a volatility expansion but then fail to capture gains in a volatility spike during an adverse market move by poorly managing gamma exposure. Conversely, some managers may use options to extract a more intermediate-term, directional insurance protection-type view of both price and volatility and not engage in active delta hedging.

A second, similar path might be to implement the volatility trading strategy using OTC options. Then the tenor and strike prices of the options can be customized, and the tenor of expiry dates can be extended beyond what is available with exchange-traded options. However, by utilizing OTC options, the strategy is subject to counterparty credit risk as well as added illiquidity risk.

Migrating to the use of VIX Index futures (or options on VIX futures) can more explicitly express a pure volatility view without the need for constant delta hedging of an equity put or call for isolating the volatility exposure. However, as just mentioned, volatility pricing tends to be notoriously mean reverting. Also, an abundant supply of traders and investors typically are looking to sell volatility to capture the volatility premium and the volatility roll down payoff. Roll down refers to the fact that the term structure of volatility tends to be positively sloped, so the passage of time causes added option price decay. In other words, the theta of a long option position is always negative, and if shorter-dated options have a lower implied volatility, then the passage of time increases the rate of natural theta decay.

A fourth path for implementing a volatility trading strategy would be to purchase an OTC volatility swap or a variance swap from a creditworthy counterparty. A volatility swap is a forward contract on future realized price volatility. Similarly, a variance swap is a forward contract on future realized price variance, where variance is the square of volatility. In both cases, at inception of the trade the strike is typically chosen such that the fair value of the swap is zero. This strike is then referred to as fair volatility or fair variance, respectively. At expiry of the swaps, the receiver of the floating leg pays the difference between the realized volatility (or variance) and the agreed-on strike times some prespecified notional amount that is not initially exchanged. Both volatility and variance swaps provide "pure" exposure to volatility alone—unlike standardized options in which the volatility exposure depends on the price of the underlying asset and must be isolated and extracted via delta hedging. These swaps can thus be used to take a view on future realized volatility, to trade the spread between realized and implied volatility, or to hedge the volatility exposure of other positions. These OTC products also offer the advantage of longer-dated, tailored maturities and strikes.

A long volatility strategy utilizing OTC volatility or variance swaps, options, or swaptions requires finding undervalued instruments. This is accomplished by being in frequent contact with options dealers around the world in a variety of asset classes. Once implemented, positions are held until they are either exercised, sold during a volatility event, actively delta hedged (in the case of a long options position), or expire. A long volatility strategy is a convex strategy because the movement of volatility pricing is typically asymmetric and skewed to the right. Also, strike prices of options may be set such that the cost of the options is small, but their potential payoffs are often many multiples of the premiums paid for the options.

Long volatility strategies are potentially attractive but also come with key challenges and risks for implementation. Given that OTC options, as well as volatility and variance swaps, are not exchange-traded, they must be negotiated. These contracts are typically structured under ISDA documentation; they are subject to bilateral margin agreements (as negotiated within an ISDA Credit Support Annex document), but they still carry more counterparty risk and liquidity risk to both establish and liquidate than instruments traded on an exchange. Also, smaller hedge funds may not even be able to access ISDA-backed OTC derivatives with banking counterparts until surpassing a minimum AUM threshold, generally $100 million. Above all, although the purchase of volatility assets provides positively convex outcomes, it almost always involves some volatility curve roll down risk and premium expense. Key aspects of volatility trading are presented in Exhibit 10.

Specialist Strategies

> **Exhibit 10** Volatility Trading Strategies—Risk, Liquidity, Leverage, and Benchmarking

Risk Profile and Liquidity

- Long volatility positioning exhibits positive convexity, which can be particularly useful for hedging purposes. On the short side, option premium sellers generally extract steadier returns in normal market environments.
- Relative value volatility trading may be a useful source of portfolio return alpha across different geographies and asset classes.
- Liquidity varies across the different instruments used for implementation. VIX Index futures and options are very liquid; exchange-traded index options are generally liquid, but with the longest tenors of about two years (with liquidity decreasing as tenor increases); OTC contracts can be customized with longer maturities but are less liquid and less fungible between different counterparties.

Leverage Usage

- The natural convexity of volatility instruments typically means that outsized gains may be earned at times with very little up-front risk. Although notional values appear nominally levered, the asymmetric nature of long optionality is an attractive aspect of this strategy.

Benchmarking

- Volatility trading is a niche strategy that is difficult to benchmark.
- CBOE Eurekahedge has the following indexes:

    Long (and Short) Volatility Index, composed of 11 managers with a generally long (short) volatility stance; Relative Value Volatility Index (composed of 35 managers); and Tail Risk Index (composed of 8 managers), designed to perform best during periods of market stress.

EXAMPLE 10

Long Volatility Strategy Payoff

Consider the following scenario: Economic growth has been good, equity markets have been rising, and interest rates have been low. However, consumer debt (e.g., subprime mortgages, credit card debt, personal loans) has been rising rapidly, surpassing historic levels. In mid-January, Serena Ortiz, a long volatility hedge fund manager, purchased a basket of long-dated (one-year), 10% out-of-the money put options on a major stock index for $100 per contract at an implied volatility level of 12%.

As of mid-April, consumer debt is still at seemingly dangerous levels and financial markets appear ripe for a major correction. However, the stock index has risen another 20% above its mid-January levels, and volatility is low. So, Ortiz's options are priced even more cheaply than before, at $50 per contract.

> Now jump forward in time by another three months to mid-July, when a crisis—unexpected by many participants—has finally occurred. Volatility has spiked, and the stock index has fallen to 25% below its April level and 10% below its starting January level. Ortiz's put options are now trading at an implied volatility pricing of 30%.
>
> 1. Discuss the time, volatility, and price impact on Ortiz's long volatility exposure in put options as of mid-July.
> 2. Discuss what happens if the market subsequently moves broadly sideways between July and the January of the next year.
>
> **Solution to 1:**
>
> Despite an initial 50% mark-to-market loss on her put exposure as of mid-April, Ortiz likely has substantial unrealized profits by mid-July. As six months passed (other things being equal), Ortiz would have suffered some time decay loss in her long put position, but her options have also gone from being 10% out-of-the-money to now being at-the-money. Implied volatility has increased 2.5 times (from 12% to 30%), which on a six-month, at-the-money put will have a significant positive impact on the option's pricing (the closer an option is to being at-the-money, the greater the impact that changes in implied volatility will have on its price). So, as of mid-July, Ortiz will likely have a significant mark-to-market gain.
>
> **Solution to 2:**
>
> If the market subsequently moves broadly sideways until January of the next year, Ortiz's at-the-money option premium will slowly erode because of time decay. Assuming the puts remain at-the-money, their volatility value will eventually dissipate; Ortiz will ultimately lose all of her original $100 investment per contract unless she has nimbly traded against the position with active delta hedging of the underlying stock index futures. This would entail buying and selling the index futures over time to capture small profitable movements to offset the time decay and volatility erosion in the puts.

11.2 Reinsurance/Life Settlements

Although still somewhat nascent, hedge funds have also entered the world of insurance, reinsurance, life settlements, and catastrophe reinsurance. Underlying insurance contracts provide a payout to the policyholder (or their beneficiaries) on the occurrence of a specific insured event in exchange for a stream of cash flows (periodic premiums) paid by the policyholder. Common types of insurance contracts sold by insurance providers include vehicle and home insurance, life insurance, and catastrophe insurance, which covers damage from such events as floods, hurricanes, or earthquakes. The insurance market encompasses a wide range of often highly specific and detailed contracts that are less standardized than other financial contracts. As a result, insurance contracts are generally not liquid and are difficult to sell or purchase after contract initiation.

Although the primary market for insurance has existed for centuries, the secondary market for insurance has grown substantially in the last several decades. Individuals who purchased whole or universal life policies and who no longer want or need the insurance can surrender their policies to the original insurance issuer. However, such policyholders are increasingly finding that higher cash values (i.e., significantly above surrender value) are being paid for their policies by third-party brokers, who, in turn, offer these policies as investments to hedge funds. Hedge funds may formulate a differentiated view of individual or group life expectancy; if correct, investment in such life policies can provide attractive uncorrelated returns.

Specialist Strategies

Reinsurance of catastrophe risk has also increasingly attracted hedge fund capital. These new secondary markets have improved liquidity and enhanced the value of existing insurance contracts. For insurance companies, the reinsurance market allows for risk transfer, capital management, and solvency management. For hedge funds, the reinsurance market offers a source of uncorrelated return alpha.

11.2.1 *Investment Characteristics and Strategy Implementation*

Life insurance protects the policyholder's dependents in the case of his/her death. The secondary market for life insurance involves the sale of a life insurance contract to a third party—a **life settlement**. The valuation of a life settlement typically requires detailed biometric analysis of the individual policyholder and an understanding of actuarial analysis. So, a hedge fund manager specialized in investing in life settlements would require such expert knowledge and skills or would need to source such knowledge from a trusted partner/actuarial adviser.

A hedge fund strategy focusing on life settlements involves analyzing pools of life insurance contracts being offered for sale, typically being sold by a third-party broker who purchased the insurance contracts from the original policyholders. The hedge fund would look for the following policy characteristics: 1) the surrender value being offered to an insured individual is relatively low; 2) the ongoing premium payments to keep the policy active are also relatively low; and, yet, 3) the probability is relatively high that the designated insured person is indeed likely to die within a certain period of time (i.e., earlier than predicted by standard actuarial methods).

On finding the appropriate policy (or, more typically, a pool of policies), the hedge fund manager pays a lump sum (via a broker) to the policyholder(s), who transfers the right to the eventual policy benefit to the hedge fund. The hedge fund is then responsible for making ongoing premium payments on the policy in return for receiving the future death benefit. This strategy is successful when the present value of the future benefit payment received by the hedge fund exceeds the present value of intervening payments made by the hedge fund. The two key inputs in the hedge fund manager's analysis are the expected policy cash flows (i.e., up-front, lump-sum payment to buy the policy; ongoing premium payments to the insurance company; and the eventual death benefit to be received) and the time to mortality. Neither of these factors has anything to do with the overall behavior of financial markets. Thus, this strategy area is unrelated and uncorrelated with other hedge fund strategies.

Catastrophe insurance protects the policyholder in case of such events as floods, hurricanes, and earthquakes, which are highly idiosyncratic and also unrelated and uncorrelated with financial market behavior. Insurance companies effectively reinsure portions of their exposure (typically above a given threshold and for a limited amount) with reinsurance companies, who, in turn, deal with hedge funds as a source of capital. An attractive and uncorrelated return profile may be achieved if by making such reinsurance investments a hedge fund can do the following: 1) obtain sufficient policy diversity in terms of geographic exposure and type of insurance being offered; 2) receive a sufficient buffer in terms of loan loss reserves from the insurance company; and 3) receive enough premium income.

Valuation methods for catastrophe insurance may require the hedge fund manager to consider global weather patterns and make forecasts using sophisticated prediction models that involve a wide range of geophysical inputs. But, more generally, assumptions are made as to typical weather patterns; the worst-case loss potentials are made from different reinsurance structures. These assumptions are then weighed against the reinsurance income to be received. If a catastrophic event does occur, then hedge fund managers hope to have enough geographic diversity that they are not financially harmed by a single event, thereby continuing to benefit when insurance premiums are inevitably increased to cover future catastrophic events.

Organized markets for catastrophe bonds and catastrophe risk futures continue to develop. These bonds and financial futures can be used to take long positions or to hedge catastrophe risk in a portfolio of insurance contracts. Their issuance and performance tend to be seasonal. Many such catastrophe bonds are issued before the annual North American hurricane season begins (May/June) and may perform particularly well if a given hurricane season is benign.

> **EXAMPLE 11**
>
> ### Investing in Life Settlements
>
> Mikki Tan runs specialty hedge fund SingStar Pte. Ltd. (SingStar), based in Singapore, that focuses on life settlements. SingStar is staffed with biometric and actuarial science experts who perform valuation analysis on pools of life insurance policies offered for sale by insurance broker firms. These intermediaries buy the policies from individuals who no longer need the insurance and who want an up-front cash payment that is higher than the surrender value offered by their insurance companies.
>
> Tan knows that Warwick Direct has been buying many individuals' life insurance policies that were underwritten by NextLife, an insurance company with a reputation in industry circles for relatively weak underwriting procedures (i.e., charging low premiums for insuring its many relatively unhealthy policyholders) and for paying low surrender values. Tan is notified that Warwick Direct is selling a pool of life settlements heavily weighted with policies that were originated by NextLife. Parties wishing to bid will be provided with data covering a random sample of the life insurance policies in the pool.
>
> Tan asks SingStar's experts to analyze the data, and they report that many of the policies in the pool were written on individuals who have now developed early-onset Alzheimer's and other debilitating diseases and thus required the up-front cash for assisted living facilities and other special care. Moreover, the analysts indicate that early-onset Alzheimer's patients have a life expectancy, on average, that is 10 years shorter than persons without the disease.
>
> Discuss how Tan and SingStar's team might proceed given this potential investment.
>
> ### Solution:
>
> SingStar's financial, biometric, and actuarial experts need to work together to forecast expected cash flows from this potential investment and then value it using an appropriate risk-adjusted discount rate. The cash flows would include the following:
>
> - The ongoing premium payments that SingStar would need to make to the originating insurance companies (in this case, mainly to NextLife) to keep the policies active. The low premiums NextLife is known to charge as well as the shorter average life expectancy of many individuals represented in the pool are important factors to consider in making this forecast.
>
> - The timing of future benefit payments to be received by SingStar on the demise of the individuals (the formerly insured). The prevalence of early-onset Alzheimer's disease and other debilitating diseases as well as the shorter average life expectancy of many individuals in the pool are key factors to consider in formulating this forecast.
>
> Once an appropriate discount rate is decided on—one that compensates for the risks of the investment—then its present value can be determined. The difference between the PV and any minimum bid price set by Warwick Direct,

as well as Tan's perceptions of the competition in bidding, will determine Tan's proposed purchase price. If SingStar ultimately buys the pool of life settlement policies and the forecasts (e.g., biometric, actuarial, and financial) of Tan's team are met or exceeded, then this investment should yield attractive returns to SingStar that are uncorrelated to other financial markets.

MULTI-MANAGER STRATEGIES

g discuss investment characteristics, strategy implementation, and role in a portfolio of *multi-manager* hedge fund strategies;

The previous sections examined individual hedge fund strategies. In practice, most investors invest in a range of hedge fund strategies. Three main approaches are used to combine individual hedge fund strategies into a portfolio: 1) *creating one's own mix of managers* by investing directly into individual hedge funds running different strategies; 2) *fund-of-funds*, which involves investing in a single fund-of-funds manager who then allocates across a set of individual hedge fund managers running different strategies; and 3) *multi-strategy funds*, which entails investing in a single fund that includes multiple internal management teams running different strategies under the same roof. Of course, approaches (1) and (2) are not specific to combinations of strategies; they apply to individual strategies too.

12.1 Fund-of-Funds

Fund-of-funds (FoF) managers aggregate investors' capital and allocate it to a portfolio of separate, individual hedge funds following different, less correlated strategies. The main roles of the FoF manager are to provide diversification across hedge fund strategies; to make occasional tactical, sector-based reallocation decisions; to engage in underlying manager selection and due diligence; and to perform ongoing portfolio management, risk assessment, and consolidated reporting. FoF managers can provide investors with access to certain closed hedge funds, economies of scale for monitoring, currency hedging capabilities, the ability to obtain and manage leverage at the portfolio level, and such other practical advantages as better liquidity terms than would be offered by an individual hedge fund manager.

Disadvantages of the FoF approach include a double layer of fees the investor must pay; a lack of transparency into individual hedge fund manager processes and returns; the inability to net performance fees on individual managers; and an additional principal–agent relationship. Regarding fees, in addition to management and incentive fees charged by the individual hedge funds (with historical norms of 1%–2% and 10%–20%, respectively) in which the FoF invests, investors in a fund-of-funds historically paid an additional 1% management fee and 10% incentive fee (again, historical norms) on the performance of the total FoF portfolio. As the performance of funds of funds has generally waned, fees have become more negotiable; management fees of 50 bps and incentive fees of 5% (or simply just a 1% flat total management fee) are becoming increasingly prevalent.

Occasionally, liquidity management of FoF can result in liquidity squeezes for FoF managers. Most FoFs require an initial one-year lock-up period, and then they offer investors monthly or quarterly liquidity thereafter, typically with a 30- to 60-day redemption notice also being required. However, the underlying investments made by the FoF may not fit well with such liquidity needs. Some underlying managers or newer underlying investments may have their own lock-up provisions or liquidity (i.e., redemption) gates. So, the FoF manager must stagger his/her underlying portfolio investments to create a conservative liquidity profile while carefully assessing the probability and potential magnitude of any FoF-level redemptions that he/she might face. FoFs may also arrange a reserve line of credit as an added liquidity backstop to deal with the potential mismatch between cash flows available from underlying investments and cash flows required to meet redemptions.

12.1.1 *Investment Characteristics*

FoFs are important hedge fund "access vehicles" for smaller high-net-worth investors and smaller institutions. Most hedge funds require minimum initial investments that range from $500,000 to $5,000,000 (with $1,000,000 being the most typical threshold). To create a reasonably diversified portfolio of 15–20 managers, $15–20 million would be required, which is a large amount even for most wealthy families and many small institutions. Selecting the 15–20 different hedge fund managers would itself require substantial time and resources that most such investors may lack. In addition, investors may potentially face substantial tax reporting requirements for each separate hedge fund investment owned. By comparison, a high-net-worth investor or small institution can typically start FoF investments with just $100,000, effectively achieving a portfolio that includes a diversified mix of talented hedge fund managers. Through their network of relationships and their large scale, FoFs may also provide access to successful managers whose funds are otherwise closed to new investment. Overall, FoFs may thus be considered convenient for access, diversification, liquidity, and operational tax reporting reasons.

But FoFs are also designed to provide other attractive features, even for such institutional investors as endowments, foundations, and pension plans. Such institutional clients may initially turn to FoFs as their preferred path to navigate their way into the hedge fund space. FoFs offer expertise not only in individual manager selection and due diligence but also in strategic allocation, tactical allocation, and style allocation into individual hedge fund strategies. The FoF strategic allocation is the long-term allocation to different hedge fund styles. For example, a FoF may have a strategic allocation of 20% to long/short equity strategies, 30% to event-driven strategies, 30% to relative value strategies, and 20% to global macro strategies. Tactical allocations include periodically overweighting and underweighting different hedge fund styles across different market environments depending on the level of conviction of the FoF manager. The overall capital or risk exposure can also be geared up or down to reflect the opportunity set in different market conditions.

Through their prime brokerage services, commercial banks provide levered capital to FoFs. Such leverage is typically collateralized by the existing hedge fund assets held in custody by these banks. Because hedge funds often deliver full funds back to redeeming investors with some substantial time lag (a 10% holdback of the total redemption amount until audit completion is typical), access to leverage can often be useful from a bridge loan point of view. In this way, capital not yet returned can be efficiently redeployed for the benefit of remaining investors.

Another attractive aspect of larger FoFs is that by pooling smaller investor assets into a larger single investment commitment, the FoF may be able to extract certain fee breaks, improved liquidity terms, future capacity rights, and/or added transparency provisions from an underlying hedge fund. The FoF may also be able to secure a commitment from the underlying fund to receive the best terms that might subsequently be offered to any future investor. These can all be valuable concessions that a smaller investor would most likely be unable to obtain by investing directly. Some FoFs have argued that these concessions made at the underlying fund manager level can be worth more than the added layering of fees by the FoF.

Overall, by combining different and ideally less correlated strategies, a FoF portfolio should provide more diversification, less extreme risk exposures, lower realized volatility, and generally less single manager tail risk than direct investing in individual hedge fund strategies. FoFs may also achieve economies of scale, manager access, research expertise, potential liquidity efficiencies, useful portfolio leverage opportunities, and potentially valuable concessions from the underlying funds.

12.1.2 Strategy Implementation

Implementing a FoF portfolio is typically a multi-step process that transpires over several months. First, FoF managers will become acquainted with different hedge fund managers via the use of various databases and introductions at prime broker-sponsored capital introduction events, where hedge fund managers present their perceived opportunity sets and qualifications to potential investors. Then, the FoF manager must decide the desired strategic allocation of the portfolio across the different hedge fund strategy groupings.

Next, with both quantitative and qualitative top-down and bottom-up approaches, the formal manager selection process is initiated. For each strategy grouping, the FoF manager screens the available universe of hedge funds with the goal to formulate a select "peer group" of potential investment candidates. This is followed by direct interviews of each hedge fund manager as well as a review of their relevant materials, such as presentation booklets, Alternative Investment Management Association Due Diligence Questionnaires (AIMA DDQs), recent quarterly letters and risk reports, as well as past audits. Typically, FoF managers will meet with prospective hedge fund managers on several different occasions (with at least one onsite visit at their offices). FoF managers will have an increasingly granular focus not only on the hedge fund managers' investment philosophy and portfolio construction but also on the firms' personnel, operational, and risk management processes.

Once an individual hedge fund is deemed a true candidate for investment, the fund's Offering Memorandum and Limited Partnership Agreement will be fully reviewed. The fund's service providers (e.g., auditor, legal adviser, custodian bank, prime broker) will be verified and other background checks and references obtained. At some larger FoF firms, these more operational aspects of the due diligence process will be performed by a dedicated team of specialists who validate the original FoF team's investment conclusions or cite concerns that may need to be addressed prior to an allocation. At this point, the FoF manager may endeavor to obtain certain concessions, agreed to in "side letters," from the hedge fund manager entitling the FoF to reduced fees, added transparency provisions, capacity rights to build an investment in the future, and/or improved redemption liquidity provisions. The larger the potential investment, the greater the FoF's negotiation advantage.

After a hedge fund is approved and the strategy is included in the FoF portfolio, then the process moves into the ongoing monitoring and review phases. The main concerns are monitoring for performance consistency with investment objectives and for any style drift, personnel changes, regulatory issues, or other correlation/return shifts that may transpire when compared to other managers both within the portfolio and when compared to similar hedge fund peers.

12.2 Multi-Strategy Hedge Funds

Multi-strategy hedge funds combine multiple hedge fund strategies under the same hedge fund structure. Teams of managers dedicated to running different hedge fund strategies share operational and risk management systems under the same roof.

12.2.1 *Investment Characteristics*

A key advantage to this approach is that the multi-strategy manager can reallocate capital into different strategy areas more quickly and efficiently than would be possible by the FoF manager. The multi-strategy manager has full transparency and a better picture of the interactions of the different teams' portfolio risks than would ever be possible for the FoF manager to achieve. Consequently, the multi-strategy manager can react faster to different real-time market impacts—for example, by rapidly increasing or decreasing leverage within different strategies depending on the perceived riskiness of available opportunities. Teams within a multi-strategy manager also can be fully focused on their respective portfolios because the business, operational, and regulatory aspects of running the hedge fund are handled by other administrative professionals. Many talented portfolio managers decide to join a multi-strategy firm for this reason.

The fees paid by investors in a multi-strategy fund can be structured in many ways, some of which can be very attractive when compared to the FoF added fee layering and netting risk attributes. Conceptually, the FoF investor always faces netting risk, whereby he/she is responsible for paying performance (i.e., incentive) fees due to winning underlying funds while suffering return drag from the performance of losing underlying funds. Even if the FoF's overall performance (aggregated across all funds) is flat or down, FoF investors must still pay incentive fees due to the managers of the winning underlying funds.

The fee structure is more investor-friendly at multi-strategy hedge funds where the general partner absorbs the netting risk arising from the divergent performances of his/her fund's different strategy teams. This is an attractive outcome for the multi-strategy fund investor because 1) the GP is responsible for netting risk; and 2) the only investor-level incentive fees paid are those due on the total fund performance after netting the positive and negative performances of the various strategy teams. Although beneficial to investors, this structure can at times cause discord within a multi-strategy fund. Because the GP is responsible for netting risk, the multi-strategy fund's overall bonus pool may shrink; thus, high-performing strategy teams will be disaffected if they do not receive their full incentive amounts, which ultimately results in personnel losses.

However, some multi-strategy hedge fund firms operate with a "pass-through" fee model. Using this model, they may charge no management fee but instead pass through the costs of paying individual teams (inclusive of salary and incentive fees earned by each team) before an added manager level incentive fee is charged to the investor on total fund performance. In this instance, the investor does implicitly pay for a portion of netting risk between the different teams (in place of a management fee), while the multi-strategy fund's GP bears a portion of that netting risk (via the risk that the total fund-level incentive fee may not cover contractual obligations that the GP is required to pay individual teams).

The main risk of multi-strategy funds is that they are generally quite levered: Position transparency is closely monitored in-house, and fee structures are typically tilted toward performance (due to high costs of the infrastructure requirements). Leverage applied to tight risk management is usually benign, but in market stress periods, risk management miscalibrations can certainly matter. The left-tail, risk-induced implosions of prominent multi-strategy funds, such as Ritchie Capital (2005) and Amaranth Advisors (2006), are somewhat legendary. Moreover, the operational risks of a multi-strategy firm, by definition, are not well diversified because all operational processes are performed under the same fund structure. Finally, multi-strategy funds can be somewhat limited in the scope of strategies offered because they are constrained by the available pool of in-house manager talent and skills (and are often staffed by managers with similar investment styles and philosophies).

12.2.2 Strategy Implementation

Multi-strategy funds invest in a range of individual hedge fund strategies. As mentioned, the breadth of strategies they can access is a function of the portfolio management skills available within the particular multi-strategy fund. Similar to a FoF manager, a multi-strategy fund will engage in both strategic and tactical allocations to individual hedge fund strategies. Given that multi-strategy fund teams manage each strategy directly and operate under the same fund roof, compared FoF managers, they are more likely to be well informed about when to tactically reallocate to a particular strategy and more capable of shifting capital between strategies quickly. Conversely, multi-strategy funds may also be less willing to exit strategies in which core expertise is in-house. Common risk management systems and processes are also more likely to reveal interactions and correlations between the different strategies run by the various portfolio management teams. Such nuanced aspects of risk might be far harder to detect within a FoF structure.

Exhibit 11 compares some key attributes of fund-of-funds and multi-strategy funds that investors must consider when deciding which of these two multi-manager types best fits their needs.

Exhibit 11 Fund-of-Funds and Multi-Strategy Funds—Comparison of Risk, Liquidity, Leverage, and Benchmarking

Risk Profile and Liquidity

- FoF and multi-strategy funds are designed to offer steady, low-volatility returns via their strategy diversification. Multi-strategy funds have generally outperformed FoFs but with more variance and occasional large losses often related to their higher leverage.
- Multi-strategy funds offer potentially faster tactical asset allocation and improved fee structure (netting risk handled at strategy level) but with higher manager-specific operational risks. FoFs offer a potentially more diverse strategy mix but with less transparency and slower tactical reaction time.
- Both groups typically have similar initial lock-up and redemption periods, but multi-strategy funds also often impose investor-level or fund-level gates on maximum redemptions allowed per quarter.

Leverage Usage

- Multi-strategy funds tend to use significantly more leverage than most FoFs, which gravitate to modest leverage usage. Thus, multi-strategy funds are somewhat more prone to left-tail blow-up risk in stress periods. Still, better strategy transparency and shorter tactical reaction time make multi-strategy funds overall more resilient than FoFs in preserving capital.

(continued)

Exhibit 11 (Continued)

Benchmarking

- FoFs can be tracked using such sub-indexes as HFRX and HFRI Fund of Funds Composite Indices; Lipper/TASS Fund-of-Funds Index; CISDM Fund-of-Funds Multi-Strategy Index; and the broad Credit Suisse Hedge Fund Index as a general proxy for a diversified pool of managers.
- Multi-strategy managers can be tracked via HFRX and HFRI Multi-Strategy Indices; Lipper/TASS Multi-Strategy Index; CISDM Multi-Strategy Index; and CS Multi-Strategy Hedge Fund Index.

Note: The FoF business model has been under significant pressure since 2008 because of fee compression and increased investor interest in passive, long-only investing and the advent of liquid alternatives for retail investors. Conversely, multi-strategy funds have grown as many institutional investors prefer to invest directly in such funds and avoid FoF fee layering.

EXAMPLE 12

Fund-of-Funds: Net-of-Fee Returns

Squaw Valley Fund of Funds (SVFOF) charges a 1% management fee and 10% incentive fee and invests an equal amount of its assets into two individual hedge funds: Pyrenees Fund (PF) and Ural Fund (UF), each charging a 2% management fee and a 20% incentive fee. For simplicity in answering the following questions, please ignore fee compounding and assume that all fees are paid at year-end.

1. If the managers of both PF and UF generate 20% gross annual returns, what is the net-of-fee return for an investor in SVFOF?
2. If PF's manager earns a gross return of 20% but UF's manager loses 5%, what is the net-of-fee return for an investor in SVFOF?

Solution to 1:

Incentive fees are deducted only from gross gains net of management fees and expenses. Thus, the answer becomes:

Net of Fees Return for PF and UF Investor = (20% − 2% − 3.6%) = 14.4%, where 3.6% = 20% x (20% − 2%);

Net of Fees Return for SVFOF Investor = (14.4% − 1% − 1.34%) = **12.06%**, where 1.34% = 10% x (14.4% − 1%).

Solution to 2:

Net of Fees Return for PF Investor = (20% − 2% − 3.6%) = 14.4%;

Net of Fees Return for UF Investor = (−5% − 2% − 0%) = −7.0%;

Gross Return for SVFOF Investor = (0.5 x 14.4% + 0.5 x −7.0%) = 3.7%;

Net of Fees Return for SVFOF Investor = (3.7% − 1% − 0.27%) = **2.43%**, where 0.27% = 10% x (3.7% − 1%).

In conclusion, if both PF and UF managers generate gross returns of 20%, then the net-of-fee return for SVFOF's investor is 12.06%, with fees taking up 39.7% of the total gross investment return [(2% + 3.6% + 1% + 1.34%)/20% = 39.7%] and the remainder going to the SVFOF investor.

But, if PF's manager earns a 20% gross return and UF's manager loses 5%, then the net-of-fee return for the SVFOF investor is a meager 2.43%. In this case, most (67.6%) of the original gross return of 7.5% [= 20% x 0.50 + (−5% x 0.50)] goes to PF, UF, and SVFOF managers as fees. Note that {[0.50 x (2% + 3.6% + 2% + 0%)] + (1% + 0.27%)}/7.5% equals 67.6%. This is an example of fee netting risk that comes with investing in FoFs.

EXAMPLE 13

Fund-of-Funds or Multi-Strategy Funds—Which to Choose?

The Leonardo family office in Milan manages the €435 million fortune of the Da Vinci family. Mona, the family's matriarch, trained as an economist and worked at Banca d'Italia for many years. She is now retired but still monitors global financial markets. The portfolio that Leonardo manages for the Da Vinci family consists of traditional long-only stocks and bonds, real estate, private equity, and single manager hedge funds following distressed securities and merger arbitrage strategies.

Mona believes global financial markets are about to enter a prolonged period of heightened volatility, so she asks Leonardo's senior portfolio manager to sell some long-only stocks and the merger arbitrage hedge fund and then buy a multi-manager hedge fund. Mona's objectives are to increase the portfolio's diversification, flexibility, and transparency while maximizing net-of-fees returns during the volatile period ahead.

Discuss advantages and disadvantages that Leonardo's portfolio manager should consider in choosing between a FoF and a multi-strategy fund.

Solution:

Leonardo's portfolio manager understands that both multi-strategy funds and FoFs are designed to offer steady, low-volatility returns via their strategy diversification.

However, digging deeper he sees that multi-strategy funds have generally outperformed FoFs. This may be because of such key advantages as their enhanced flexibility and the fast pace of tactical asset allocation (important in dynamic, volatile markets) given that the different strategies are executed within the same fund structure. Another advantage of this set-up of multi-strategy funds is increased transparency regarding overall positions and exposures being carried. Moreover, many multi-strategy funds have an investor-friendly fee structure, in which fee netting risk is handled at the strategy level and absorbed (or partially absorbed) by the general partner of the multi-strategy fund. As for disadvantages, Leonardo's portfolio manager should consider that multi-strategy funds entail higher manager-specific operational risks, so detailed due diligence is important; moreover, they tend to use relatively high leverage, which may increase the variance of returns.

The main advantages of FoFs are that they offer a potentially more diverse strategy mix with lower leverage (and somewhat less return variance), and they have less operational risk (i.e., each separate underlying hedge fund is responsible for its own risk management). Leonardo's portfolio manager realizes that FoFs also entail reduced transparency into the portfolio decisions made at the

> underlying hedge funds as well as a slower tactical reaction time. Another key disadvantage is that FoFs require a double layer of fees to be paid, with netting risk borne by the investor, which imposes a substantial drag on net-of-fees returns.

13. ANALYSIS OF HEDGE FUND STRATEGIES USING A CONDITIONAL FACTOR RISK MODEL

h   describe how factor models may be used to understand hedge fund risk exposures;

From the foregoing discussion, it is reasonable to conclude the following: L/S equity and event-driven managers tend to be exposed to some natural equity market beta risk; arbitrage managers often are exposed to credit spread risk and market volatility tail risk; opportunistic managers tend to have risk exposures to the trendiness (or directionality) of markets; and relative value managers do not expect trendiness but are typically counting on mean reversion. Each strategy has unique sources of factor exposures and resulting vulnerabilities. Moreover, risk factor exposures in many strategies arise from simply holding financial instruments whose prices are directly impacted by those risk factors. That is, long and short exposures to a given risk factor in different securities are not equal, thereby giving rise to a non-zero *net* exposure. Following a practice-based risk factor perspective, this reading uses a conditional linear factor model to uncover and analyze hedge fund strategy risk exposures. While this is just one way to go about explaining hedge fund strategies' risks and returns, it is representative of the widely used risk factor approach.

One may ask why it is necessary to use such a model to investigate hedge fund strategies. It is because a linear factor model can provide insights into the intrinsic characteristics and risks in a hedge fund investment. Moreover, given the dynamic nature of hedge fund strategies, a conditional model allows for the analysis in a specific market environment to determine, for example, whether hedge fund strategies are exposed to certain risks under abnormal market conditions. A conditional model can show whether hedge fund risk exposures (e.g., to credit or volatility) that are insignificant during calm market periods may become significant during turbulent market periods. The importance of using a conditional factor model is underscored by the fact that the hedge fund industry is dynamic; for example, it experienced a huge decline in AUM during the global financial crisis. Specifically, after recording more than a 25% CAGR (compound annual growth rate) in assets between 2000 and 2007, the global hedge fund industry's aggregate AUM declined by 17% CAGR between 2007 and 2009 (the period of the global financial crisis) from a high of more than $2.6 trillion. Moreover, global AUM did not surpass the 2007 high until 2014. In short, thousands of hedge funds were shuttered during this time as performance plunged when many managers were caught off guard by their funds' actual risk exposures during the crisis period and in its aftermath.

13.1 Conditional Factor Risk Model

A simple conditional linear factor model applied to a hedge fund strategy's returns can be represented as:

$$(\text{Return on HF}_i)_t = \alpha_i + \beta_{i,1}(\text{Factor 1})_t + \beta_{i,2}(\text{Factor 2})_t + \ldots + \beta_{i,K}(\text{Factor } K)_t +$$
$$D_t\beta_{i,1}(\text{Factor 1})_t + D_t\beta_{i,2}(\text{Factor 2})_t + \ldots + D_t\beta_{i,K}(\text{Factor } K)_t +$$
$$(\text{error})_{i,t}, \text{where}$$

- $(\text{Return on HF}_i)_t$ is the return of hedge fund i in period t;
- $\beta_{i,1}(\text{Factor 1})_t$ represents the exposure to risk factor 1 (up to risk factor K) for hedge fund i in period t during normal times;
- $D_t\beta_{i,1}(\text{Factor 1})_t$ represents the *incremental* exposure to risk factor 1 (up to risk factor K) for hedge fund i in period t during financial crisis periods, where D_t is a dummy variable that equals 1 during financial crisis periods (i.e., June 2007 to February 2009) and 0 otherwise;
- α_i is the intercept for hedge fund i; and
- $(\text{error})_{i,t}$ is random error with zero mean and standard deviation of σ_i.

Each factor beta represents the expected change in hedge fund returns for a one-unit increase in the specific risk factor, holding all other factors (independent variables) constant. The portion of hedge fund returns not explained by the risk factors is attributable to three sources: 1) alpha, the hedge fund manager's unique investment skills; 2) omitted factors; and 3) random errors. The starting point for building this model is the identification of a comprehensive set of asset class and macro-oriented, market-based risks, including the behavior of stocks, bonds, currencies, commodities, credit spreads, and volatility. Following Hasanhodzic and Lo (2007) and practice, the model starts with the following six factors:

- **Equity risk (SNP500):** monthly total return of the S&P 500 Index, including dividends.
- **Interest rate risk (BOND):** monthly return of the Bloomberg Barclays Corporate AA Intermediate Bond Index.
- **Currency risk (USD):** monthly return of the US Dollar Index.
- **Commodity risk (CMDTY):** monthly total return of the Goldman Sachs Commodity Index (GSCI).
- **Credit risk (CREDIT):** difference between monthly seasoned Baa and Aaa corporate bond yields provided by Moody's.
- **Volatility risk (VIX):** first-difference of the end-of-month value of the CBOE Volatility Index (VIX).

Once these potentially relevant macro risk factors were identified for analysis, the next consideration was the appropriateness of using them together in the model. To address the issue of highly correlated risk factors and to avoid potential multicollinearity problems, a four-step "stepwise regression" process was used to build a conditional linear factor model that is less likely to include highly correlated risk factors. This process is described briefly in the accompanying sidebar.

Practical Steps for Building Hedge Fund Risk Factor Models

The following four-step procedure describes a stepwise regression process that can help build linear conditional factor models that are less likely to include highly correlated risk factors, thereby avoiding multi-collinearity issues.

Step 1: Identify potentially important risk factors.

Step 2: Calculate pairwise correlations across all risk factors. If two-state conditional models are used, calculate correlations across all risk factors for both states—for example, during normal market conditions (state 1) and during market crisis conditions (state 2). For illustration purposes, risk factors A and B can be assumed to be highly correlated if the correlation coefficient between them exceeds 60%.

Step 3: For highly correlated risk factors A and B, regress the return series of interest (e.g., hedge fund returns) on all risk factors excluding factor A. Then, regress the same returns on the all risk factors, but this time exclude factor B. Given the adjusted R^2 for regressions without A and without B, keep the risk factor that results in the highest adjusted R^2.

Step 4: Repeat step 3 for all other highly correlated factor pairs, with the aim of eliminating the least useful (in terms of explanatory power) factors and thereby avoiding multi-collinearity issues.

To address the multi-collinearity problem, the stepwise regression procedure was implemented using two of the hedge fund databases mentioned previously: Lipper TASS (TASS) and Morningstar Hedge/CISDM (CISDM). The accompanying sidebar provides useful background for practitioners on these two important sources of hedge fund information.

Hedge Fund Databases

The analysis in this reading uses two well-known hedge fund databases to evaluate hedge fund strategies: Lipper TASS (TASS) and Morningstar Hedge/CISDM (CISDM) databases. These databases are among the ones most widely used for hedge fund research.

The analysis covers the period of 2000–2016. Each database is separated into "live" (operating/open), "defunct" (non-operating/shut down or operating/closed to new investment or operating/delisted and relisted with another database), and "all" funds (live + defunct) groups. Hedge fund return data are filtered to exclude funds that 1) do not report net-of-fee returns; 2) report returns in currencies other than US dollar; 3) report returns less frequently than monthly; 4) do not provide AUM or estimates; and 5) have less than 36 months of return data. TASS and CISDM databases have a total of 6,352 and 7,756 funds, respectively. Importantly, 82% (18%) and 80% (20%) of all TASS and CISDM funds, respectively, are defunct (live). This is consistent with the relatively high attrition rate of hedge funds and the relatively short life of a typical hedge fund.

Databases that include defunct funds can be highly useful for asset allocators because the historical track record of managers that may be starting new funds might be found to include defunct funds. Then, further analysis could be conducted to determine if such funds became defunct because of the managers' poor performance and/or excessive redemptions, so they were shut down, or because of the managers' initial success, such that an overabundance of inflows caused subsequent investment capacity issues. From a data analysis point of view, including defunct funds also helps to appropriately adjust for database survivorship bias that might otherwise yield incorrect analytical conclusions.

Live, Defunct, and All Funds in TASS Database from 2000–2016

Grouping	TASS Primary Categories	Number of Live Funds	Number of Defunct Funds	Total Number of Funds
Equity	Dedicated short bias	4	38	42
Equity	Equity market neutral	38	270	308
Equity	Long/short equity hedge	350	1,705	2,055
Event driven	Event driven	87	465	552
Relative value	Convertible arbitrage	17	162	179
Relative value	Fixed income arbitrage	42	167	209
Opportunistic	Global macro	59	266	325
Opportunistic	Managed futures	1	2	3
Multi-manager	Fund of funds	454	1,711	2,165
Multi-manager	Multi-strategy	100	414	514
Total		1,152	5,200	6,352

Live, Defunct, and All Funds in CISDM Database from 2000–2016

Grouping	CISDM Categories	Number of Live Funds	Number of Defunct Funds	Total Number of Funds
Equity	Asia/Pacific long/short equity	31	203	234
Equity	Bear market equity	2	36	38
Equity	Equity market neutral	40	272	312
Equity	Europe long/short equity	47	161	208
Equity	Global long/short equity	86	406	492
Equity	US long/short equity	218	849	1,067
Equity	US small-cap long/short equity	67	171	238
Event driven	Merger arbitrage	22	16	38
Event driven	Distressed securities	46	159	205
Event driven	Event driven	63	228	291
Relative value	Convertible arbitrage	25	125	150
Relative value	Debt arbitrage	32	141	173
Opportunistic	Global macro	84	380	464
Opportunistic	Systematic futures	182	518	700
Multi-manager	Fund of funds – debt	20	97	117
Multi-manager	Fund of funds – equity	104	592	696
Multi-manager	Fund of funds – event	10	124	134
Multi-manager	Fund of funds – macro/systematic	30	163	193

(continued)

Grouping	CISDM Categories	Number of Live Funds	Number of Defunct Funds	Total Number of Funds
Multi-manager	Fund of funds – multi-strategy	164	789	953
Multi-manager	Fund of funds – relative value	12	83	95
Multi-manager	Multi-strategy	111	395	506
Specialist	Volatility	28	30	58
Specialist	Long/short debt	115	279	394
Total		1,539	6,217	7,756

Using TASS and CISDM datasets, the stepwise regression procedure resulted in both BOND and CMDTY factors being dropped from the final conditional linear risk model because of multi-collinearity issues. This is because retaining CREDIT and SNP500 factors produced higher adjusted R^2s compared to retaining BOND and CMDTY factors.

Exhibit 12 provides useful information for interpreting the effects of the factor exposures included in the conditional risk model on hedge fund strategy returns. For both normal and crisis periods, it shows the four risk factors, the typical market trend during these periods, the hedge fund manager's desired position (long or short), and the desired factor exposure for benefitting from a particular market trend.

Exhibit 12 Interpretation of Conditional Risk Factor Exposures

Period/Risk Factor	Typical Market Trend	Desired Position	Desired Factor Exposure	Comments
Normal				
SNP500	Equities Rising	Long	Positive	Aims to add risk, increase return
CREDIT	Spreads Flat/Narrowing	Long	Positive	Aims to add risk, increase return
USD	USD Flat/Depreciating	Short	Negative	Sells USD to boost returns
VIX	Volatility Falling	Short	Negative	Sells volatility to boost returns
Crisis				
DSNP500	Equities Falling Sharply	Short	Negative	Aims to reduce risk
DCREDIT	Spreads Widening	Short	Negative	Aims to reduce risk
DUSD	USD Appreciating	Long	Positive	USD is haven in crisis periods
DVIX	Volatility Rising	Long	Positive	Negative correlation with equities

EVALUATING EQUITY HEDGE FUND STRATEGIES: APPLICATION

h describe how factor models may be used to understand hedge fund risk exposures;

Using data from the CISDM and TASS databases from 2000 to 2016, this section discusses key return and risk characteristics for hedge funds pursuing equity-related strategies. More specifically, the conditional factor model is used to assess average risk exposures (during both normal and crisis market periods) for all "live" funds in each of the equity-related categories in these databases. Finally, the heterogeneity among funds, which is masked in the average exposures, is then revealed in an analysis showing the percentage of all hedge funds in each category that have significant factor exposures (positive and negative) during normal and crisis periods.

Note that the results of such a risk factor analysis may vary somewhat based on the hedge fund database used, the time period examined, and the specification of the factor model. However, the key takeaway is that such an analysis can uncover unintended adverse risk exposures to a hedge fund—stemming from the strategy it pursues—that may assert themselves only during turbulent market periods. As mentioned previously, unintended adverse risk exposures that revealed themselves during the global financial crisis resulted in the demise of literally thousands of hedge funds worldwide. Thus, understanding how to interpret the results of such a risk factor analysis is a key practical competency for any practitioner involved in advising on the strategies followed by hedge funds or in managing or owning the hedge funds themselves. First, we describe how the factor model can be used to understand risk exposures of equity-related hedge fund strategies. Then, we turn to understanding risks of multi-manager strategies.

The key return characteristics are shown for equity-related hedge fund strategies by category in Exhibit 13. In addition to the Sharpe ratio, we calculate the Sortino ratio.[2] The Sortino ratio replaces standard deviation in the Sharpe ratio with downside deviation, so it concentrates on returns below a specified threshold. For example, if the threshold return is zero, then the Sortino ratio uses downside deviation based on losses. Because hedge funds potentially invest in illiquid securities (which artificially smooth returns, thus lowering the measured standard deviation), besides measuring risk and return one should also investigate the autocorrelation of returns. Rho is a measure of first order serial autocorrelation, the correlation between a fund's return and its own lagged returns. High Rho signals smoothed returns and thus is an indicator of potential liquidity issues (specifically, illiquidity and infrequent trading) in the underlying securities.

Exhibit 13 shows that L/S Equity Hedge (TASS) has the highest mean return (11.30%) but also the highest standard deviation (22.86%). Among categories with more than four funds, EMN (TASS) has the highest Sharpe ratio; notably, despite having the highest standard deviation, L/S Equity Hedge (TASS) also has the highest Sortino ratio; and Global L/S Equity (CISDM) shows the largest Rho. Overall, these results indicate that by accepting some beta and illiquidity exposure, L/S equity managers generally outperform equity market-neutral managers in terms of total returns delivered. Returns of L/S equity managers, however, are also more volatile than those of EMN managers and so produce lower Sharpe ratios. Intuitively, these results are in line with expectations.

---

[2] In addition to Sharpe and Sortino ratios, other performance measures can be used, such as the Treynor ratio, information ratio, return on VaR, Jensen's alpha, M^2, maximum drawdown, and gain-to-loss ratio.

Exhibit 13   Key Return Characteristics for Equity Hedge Fund Strategies (2000–2016)

Database	Category	Sample Size	Annualized Mean (%)		Annualized Sharpe Ratio		Annualized Sortino Ratio		Rho (%)	
			Mean	SD	Mean	SD	Mean	SD	Mean	SD
TASS	Dedicated short bias	4	2.91	14.75	2.27	4.36	1.35	1.07	20.0	45.7
CISDM	Bear market equity	2	2.04	7.37	0.29	1.18	0.70	1.47	9.15	1.79
TASS	Equity market neutral	38	7.81	10.20	0.83	0.56	0.80	0.53	9.3	15.8
CISDM	Equity market neutral	40	7.48	8.82	0.79	0.81	0.65	0.92	16.29	8.88
TASS	Long/short equity hedge	350	11.30	22.86	0.62	0.64	1.33	1.04	11.0	13.5
CISDM	Global long/short equity	86	8.83	16.93	0.44	0.57	0.76	1.09	17.43	15.63
CISDM	Asia/Pacific long/short equity	31	8.87	20.27	0.45	0.36	0.73	0.57	16.72	10.49
CISDM	Europe long/short equity	47	7.05	11.59	0.56	0.37	0.69	1.08	13.92	10.53
CISDM	US long/short equity	218	9.41	17.50	0.62	0.46	0.60	0.55	12.76	8.98
CISDM	US small cap long/short equity	67	9.88	19.60	0.65	0.48	1.14	0.86	11.71	7.44

Taking a more granular view of factor risks, Exhibit 14 presents average risk exposures (equity, credit, currency, and volatility) for equity-related hedge fund strategies using the conditional risk factor model from 2000 to 2016. The crisis period is from June 2007 to February 2009, and crisis period factors are preceded by the letter "D" (e.g., the crisis period equity factor is DSNP500). Light (dark) shaded coefficients have t-statistics greater than 1.96 (1.67) and are significant at the 5% (10%) level.

Exhibit 14 Risk Exposures for Equity Hedge Funds Using the Conditional Risk Factor Model (2000–2016)

Strategy	Dedicated Short Bias	Bear Market Equity	Equity Market Neutral	Equity Market Neutral	Asia/Pacific Long/Short Equity	Europe Long/Short Equity	Global Long/Short Equity	US Long/Short Equity	US Small Cap Long/Short Equity	Long/Short Equity Hedge
Database	TASS	CISDM	TASS	CISDM	CISDM	CISDM	CISDM	CISDM	CISDM	TASS
Sample Size	4	2	38	40	31	47	86	218	67	350
Normal Times Exposures										
Intercept	−0.02	0.00	0.01	0.01	0.01	0.01	0.02	−0.01	0.01	0.01
SNP500	−0.28	−0.46	0.11	0.09	0.42	0.24	0.52	0.58	0.58	0.41
USD	−0.13	−0.07	−0.02	0.00	−0.02	0.06	−0.01	−0.03	−0.01	−0.04
CREDIT	1.24	0.22	−0.12	−0.07	−0.26	−0.23	−0.77	0.63	−0.09	−0.20
VIX	0.04	−0.05	0.01	0.00	−0.01	0.02	−0.01	−0.03	0.03	0.07
Crisis Times Exposures (Incremental)										
DSNP500	0.04	0.11	0.04	0.05	−0.02	−0.14	−0.04	0.03	−0.02	−0.03
DUSD	−0.08	−0.06	−0.17	−0.02	0.15	−0.42	−0.07	−0.07	−0.09	−0.17
DCREDIT	0.02	0.05	0.06	0.10	−0.01	0.07	0.16	0.03	−0.20	0.07
DVIX	0.00	−0.02	−0.06	−0.04	−0.04	−0.09	−0.04	0.02	−0.02	−0.02

On average, funds following EMN strategies maintain low exposure to equity market risk (0.11, significant at 10%) as well as a neutral exposure to the other risk factors in the model in both normal and crisis periods. L/S equity strategies maintain significant (at the 5% level) average beta loadings to equity risk during normal periods. The equity risk betas range from 0.24 for Europe L/S Equity to 0.58 for both US and US Small Cap L/S Equity strategies. Although there are no significant incremental (i.e., additional) exposures to equity risk (DSNP500) during crisis periods, total exposures during crisis periods (normal + crisis) are positive and significant for all L/S equity strategies. For example, the total equity exposure in crisis times for US L/S Equity is 0.61 (= 0.58 + 0.03). Because they show average exposures across all live funds in the given strategy category, these results mask significant heterogeneity between funds in their exposures to the four risk factors.

Exhibit 15 highlights this heterogeneity by presenting the percentage of funds experiencing significant (at the 10% level or better) factor exposures within each strategy category. The (T) indicates funds from the TASS database, and all other funds are from CISDM; gray (white) bars signify positive (negative) factor exposures. The y-axis indicates the percentage of funds within each strategy category that experienced the significant risk exposures.

Exhibit 15 Significant Positive and Negative Factor Exposures for Funds by Equity Hedge Strategy During Normal and Crisis Periods (2000–2016)

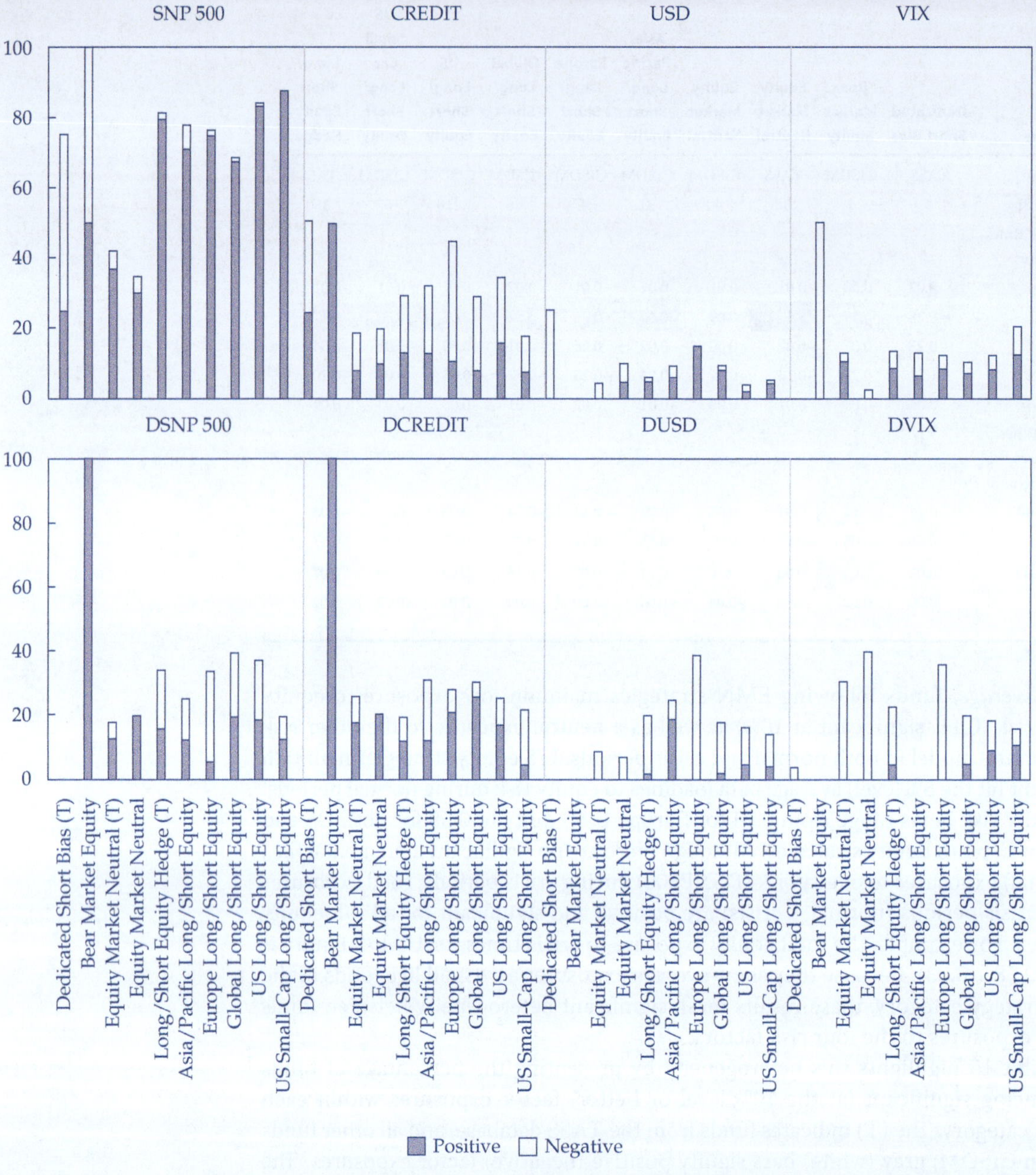

For example, with the exception of dedicated short-biased funds, most equity-related hedge funds have significant positive exposure to equity risk during normal market periods (30%+ for EMN funds and 70%+ for L/S equity funds). However, during crisis periods, less than 40% of L/S equity funds have any significant incremental equity exposure; for those that do, their added exposure is mixed (negative and positive). This suggests that managers were able to decrease adverse crisis period effects on their returns—likely by deleveraging, outright selling of stock (short sales, too) and equity index futures, and/or by buying index put options. This also indicates that although they did not reduce long beta tilting by much, on average L/S equity managers did not make things worse by trying to aggressively "bottom pick" the market. Finally, these results are consistent with the average incremental equity exposure during crisis periods of approximately zero, as seen in the previous exhibit.

Evaluating Equity Hedge Fund Strategies: Application

As one might intuitively expect, most L/S equity managers do not have significant exposure to CREDIT. Only about one-third of L/S equity funds have significant exposure to CREDIT—mainly negative exposure, indicating that they are unlikely to benefit from moderating credit risk (spreads narrowing, credit upgrades). Interestingly, for the 25% of funds with significant incremental crisis period CREDIT exposure, these exposures become more positive, which would tend to hurt returns as spreads widen and credit downgrades accelerate during market sell-offs. Similarly, exposures to USD and VIX for L/S equity funds are marginal during normal times, with few funds having any significant exposures. However, in most cases during crisis periods, any significant additional exposures are mainly negative. For example, about 40% of Europe L/S Equity funds show significant negative exposure to USD—perhaps expecting a crisis-induced flight to quality into the euro or Japanese yen as opposed to USD. Again, nearly 40% of these funds show negative added VIX exposure (i.e., short volatility) during crisis times. Returns of some high-profile hedge funds have been hurt by being unexpectedly short volatility during crisis periods, which underscores why understanding the heterogeneity of factor exposures is important to understanding risk profiles of hedge funds.

EXAMPLE 14

Dedicated Short-Biased Hedge Fund

Bearish Asset Management (BAM) manages a short-biased hedge fund that varies its portfolio's short tilt depending on perceived opportunities. Using the fund's monthly returns for the past 10 years, which include periods of financial market crisis, a conditional risk factor model was estimated. The following table provides factor beta estimates with corresponding t-statistics [dark (light) shaded are significant at the 5% (10%) level].

Interpret the factor loadings. Also, what can you infer about BAM's overall risk exposure during crisis periods?

Coefficient	Estimate	t-Statistic
Normal Times Exposures		
Intercept	0.005	1.10
USD	0.072	0.72
CREDIT	−0.017	−0.07
SNP500	−0.572	−9.65
VIX	−0.164	−2.19
Crisis Times Exposures (Incremental)		
DUSD	0.456	1.31
DCREDIT	−0.099	−0.40
DSNP500	0.236	1.74
DVIX	0.105	1.03

Solution:

BAM's fund has highly significant negative loadings on equity risk (SNP500) and volatility risk (VIX). The negative equity risk exposure is as expected for a short-biased strategy. But the negative VIX loading is consistent with short volatility exposure. This suggests that BAM's manager may be selling puts against some of its short exposures, thereby attempting to also capture a volatility premium. During crisis periods, the equity beta rises from −0.572 to −0.336 (= −0.572 + 0.236 = −0.336). This negative exposure is still significant and suggests that

> despite being a short-biased fund, BAM had less negative equity risk exposure during crisis periods. In this case, the manager may be purposefully harvesting some of its short exposure into market weakness.

15. EVALUATING MULTI-MANAGER HEDGE FUND STRATEGIES: APPLICATION

h describe how factor models may be used to understand hedge fund risk exposures;

It is important to understand the risks of multi-manager hedge fund strategies. Exhibit 16 shows that multi-strategy hedge funds outperform funds-of-funds: They have higher mean returns (7.85%/TASS and 8.52%/CISDM) and among the highest Sharpe ratios and Sortino ratios. Multi-strategy funds have higher Rho (more than 20%) compared to FoF, indicating relatively high serial autocorrelation. This is reasonable because multi-strategy funds may be simultaneously running strategies using less liquid instruments, such as convertible arbitrage, fixed-income arbitrage, and other relative value strategies. That is why, unlike FoFs, they often impose investor-level or fund-level gates on maximum quarterly redemptions.

Exhibit 16 Key Return Characteristics for Multi-Manager Hedge Fund Strategies (2000–2016)

Database	Category	Sample Size	Annualized Mean (%)		Annualized Sharpe Ratio		Annualized Sortino Ratio		Rho (%)	
			Mean	SD	Mean	SD	Mean	SD	Mean	SD
CISDM	Fund of funds – debt	20	6.52	7.94	0.89	0.66	0.68	1.17	13.89	4.24
CISDM	Fund of funds – equity	104	4.69	9.15	0.41	0.28	0.44	0.91	12.27	10.61
CISDM	Fund of funds – event	10	4.59	4.99	0.75	0.51	0.56	1.19	13.76	6.71
CISDM	Fund of funds – macro/systematic	30	5.09	10.16	0.39	0.39	0.57	0.60	8.15	3.52
CISDM	Fund of funds – multi-strategy	164	4.47	7.18	0.54	1.84	1.34	1.43	12.43	9.31
CISDM	Fund of funds – relative value	12	5.31	8.58	0.70	0.42	1.31	0.63	15.86	13.77
TASS	Fund of funds	454	5.73	10.03	0.38	0.71	0.52	0.62	19.9	18.1
CISDM	Multi-strategy	111	8.52	11.01	0.89	1.36	1.32	1.58	20.09	16.24
TASS	Multi-strategy	100	7.85	11.51	0.86	1.40	1.00	1.05	22.7	24.3

Exhibit 17 presents average risk exposures for multi-manager hedge fund strategies using the conditional risk factor model. The crisis period is from June 2007 to February 2009, and light (dark) shaded betas have *t*-statistics of more than 1.96 (1.67).

Exhibit 17 Risk Exposures for Multi-Manager Hedge Funds Using the Conditional Risk Factor Model (2000–2016)

Strategy	Fund of Funds – Debt	Fund of Funds – Equity	Fund of Funds – Event	Fund of Funds – Macro/ Systematic	Fund of Funds – Multi- Strategy	Fund of Funds – Relative Value	Fund of Funds	Multi- Strategy	Multi- Strategy
Database	CISDM	CISDM	CISDM	CISDM	CISDM	CISDM	TASS	CISDM	TASS
Sample Size	20	104	10	30	163	12	454	111	100
Normal Times Exposures									
Intercept	0.01	0.01	0.01	0.01	0.01	0.01	0.01	0.10	0.01
SNP500	0.16	0.33	0.14	−0.02	0.21	0.12	0.24	−0.14	0.22
USD	−0.01	0.01	0.01	−0.07	0.00	0.01	0.01	−0.41	−0.01
CREDIT	−0.36	−0.43	−0.22	−0.10	−0.28	−0.14	−0.45	−5.71	−0.03
VIX	0.00	0.03	0.00	0.04	0.01	0.02	0.01	−0.03	0.01
Crisis Times Exposures (Incremental)									
DSNP500	−0.02	0.02	−0.01	−0.01	0.00	0.02	0.00	0.05	0.06
DUSD	0.03	−0.09	−0.19	−0.21	−0.20	−0.27	−0.05	−0.05	−0.05
DCREDIT	−0.10	0.09	−0.13	0.01	0.03	−0.10	0.09	0.07	−0.05
DVIX	0.03	−0.09	−0.03	−0.05	−0.07	−0.06	−0.05	−0.02	−0.05

Results show that all FoF strategies (except macro/systematic) have significant positive exposure to equity risk (ranging from 0.14 to 0.33) for the full period. The finding for macro/systematic is consistent with results presented earlier for opportunistic hedge funds, which show they tend not to be exposed to equity risks in aggregate. Interestingly, multi-strategy funds have significant equity exposure but differing signs—negative (positive) for CISDM (TASS)—which highlights the heterogeneity between the two databases.

Multi-manager funds as a group do not appear to provide significant hedging benefits (via diversification) in crisis times. If they did, then significant negative exposures to DSNP500 would be observed. This is consistent with the research findings that in the 2007–2009 global financial crisis, diversification across hedge fund strategies did not decrease total portfolio risk. These researchers conclude that during crises, simple diversification is insufficient; rather, it is important to focus on such other risks as liquidity, volatility, and credit—particularly because these risks may be magnified by the application of leverage.

Exhibit 18 tells a different story when individual funds are studied. The majority of multi-manager funds have significant positive exposure to the equity factor, but around 30% of funds show a mix of negative and positive incremental exposures (DSNP 500) to equities during the crisis period. This suggests that at least some funds (ones with negative loadings) were able to shield their investors from substantial market declines by either deleveraging, selling equity pre-crisis, and/or short selling. About 40% of all multi-manager funds have significant, mostly negative, exposure to CREDIT, indicating that they generally were not positioned to benefit from improving credit spreads. In crisis times, they took on additional (mostly negative) CREDIT exposure. For example, about 50% of FoF-Debt and FoF-Relative Value funds experienced incremental negative CREDIT exposure during turbulent periods, which hedged them from deteriorating credit conditions.

Exhibit 18　Significant Positive and Negative Factor Exposures for Multi-Manager Hedge Funds During Normal and Crisis Periods (2000–2016)

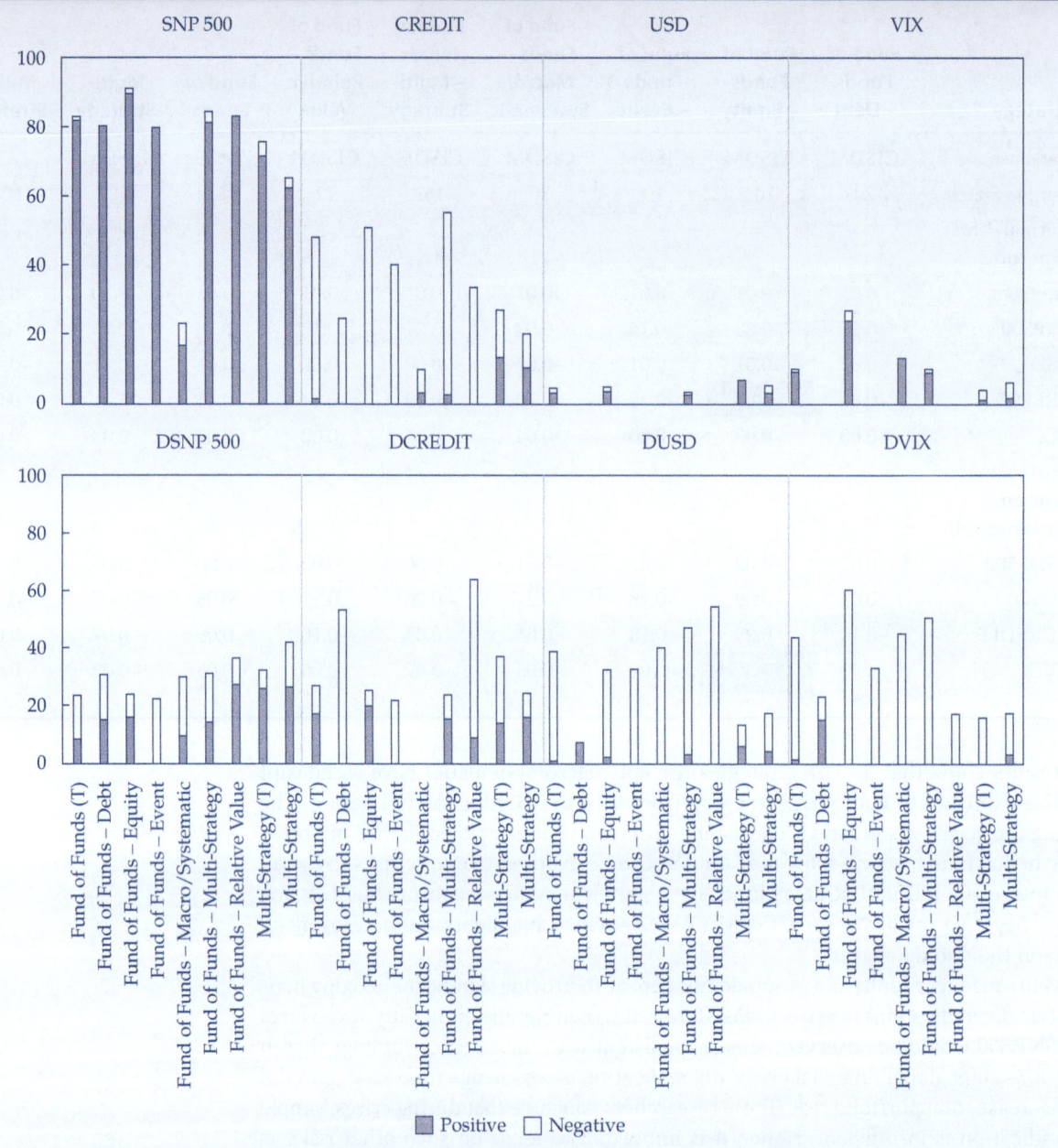

For the full period, multi-manager funds have minimal exposures to USD and VIX. Notably, these exposures increase dramatically, becoming significantly negative during financial crises. For example, only 2% of FoF-Equity have negative exposure to VIX overall. But, 60% of these funds show additional significant negative VIX exposure in crisis times. A similar pattern is revealed for USD exposure. Such negative exposures would seem undesirable during times when volatility is spiking and the USD is likely appreciating. Natural embedded leverage may be a partial explanation for these seemingly undesirable exposures during crisis times. In sum, as crisis periods generate potentially unexpected exposures to systematic risks, it is essential to use conditional factor models to understand risks of hedge fund strategies.

PORTFOLIO CONTRIBUTION OF HEDGE FUND STRATEGIES

i. evaluate the impact of an allocation to a hedge fund strategy in a traditional investment portfolio.

This section examines the return and risk contributions of the hedge fund strategies previously covered when added to a traditional 60% stock/40% bond investment portfolio.

16.1 Performance Contribution to a 60/40 Portfolio

For each hedge fund strategy category that has been discussed, we now consider an equal-weighted portfolio of the individual funds in that category. We examine the impact of a 20% allocation to such a hedge fund strategy portfolio when combined with a traditional investment portfolio consisting of 60% stocks and 40% bonds. The S&P500 Total Return Index and the Bloomberg Barclays Corporate AA Intermediate Bond Index are used to proxy the 60%/40% portfolio. When the hedge fund strategy portfolio is added to the traditional portfolio, the resulting allocations for the combined portfolio are 48% stocks, 32% bonds, and 20% in the particular hedge fund strategy portfolio. Please note this exercise is for illustrating the portfolio performance contribution of hedge fund strategies; practically speaking, it is unlikely an investor would hold an allocation (here 20%) that included an equal weighting of all live funds in one particular hedge fund strategy category.

Exhibit 19 provides performance and risk metrics for the combined portfolios from 2000 to 2016. It shows that when added to a traditional 60%/40% portfolio (with a mean return of 6.96%), a 20% allocation to the US Small Cap L/S Equity strategy generates the highest mean return (7.53%) of all the combined portfolios—an improvement of 57 bps. Adding a 20% allocation of an equal-weighted portfolio of funds in any of the following hedge fund categories to the traditional portfolio produces average annual returns of more than 7.30%: fixed-income arbitrage, distressed securities, or systematic futures. Adding a 20% allocation of any of the hedge fund strategies shown in Exhibit 19 to the traditional portfolio almost always decreases total portfolio standard deviation while increasing Sharpe and Sortino ratios (and also decreasing maximum drawdown in about one-third of the combined portfolios). These results demonstrate that hedge funds act as both risk-adjusted return enhancers and diversifiers for the traditional stock/bond portfolio.

Exhibit 19 Performance and Risk of 48/32/20 Portfolio, Where 20% Allocation Is to an Equal-Weighted Portfolio for Each Hedge Fund Strategy Category (2000–2016)

Category	Type	Database	Mean Return (%)	SD (%)	Sharpe Ratio	Sortino Ratio	Maximum Drawdown (%)
60% Stocks/40% Bonds	*Traditional Portfolio*	—	**6.96**	**8.66**	**0.62**	**1.13**	**14.42**
Long/Short Equity Hedge	Equity	TASS	7.22	8.29	0.68	1.45	21.34
Global Long/Short Equity	Equity	CISDM	7.06	8.17	0.67	1.22	22.51
U.S. Long/Short Equity	Equity	CISDM	7.17	8.22	0.68	1.24	16.77

(continued)

Exhibit 19 (Continued)

Category	Type	Database	Mean Return (%)	SD (%)	Sharpe Ratio	Sortino Ratio	Maximum Drawdown (%)
U.S. Small Cap Long/Short Equity	Equity	CISDM	7.53	8.75	0.68	1.23	27.02
Asia/Pacific Long/Short Equity	Equity	CISDM	6.44	8.12	0.60	1.07	21.74
Europe Long/Short Equity	Equity	CISDM	6.79	7.69	0.67	1.24	15.20
Dedicated Short Bias	Equity	TASS	6.02	5.59	0.79	1.02	16.06
Bear Market Equity	Equity	CISDM	5.97	5.68	0.77	1.43	16.62
Equity Market Neutral	Equity	TASS	6.81	7.17	0.73	1.80	10.72
Equity Market Neutral	Equity	CISDM	6.79	7.13	0.73	1.36	4.99
Event Driven	Event Driven	TASS	7.13	7.76	0.71	1.44	20.96
Event Driven	Event Driven	CISDM	7.19	7.83	0.71	1.31	20.57
Distressed Securities	Event Driven	CISDM	7.40	7.67	0.75	1.38	20.00
Merger Arbitrage	Event Driven	CISDM	6.85	7.22	0.73	1.35	5.60
Convertible Arbitrage	Relative Value	TASS	6.76	7.75	0.66	1.27	31.81
Fixed-Income Arbitrage	Relative Value	TASS	7.50	7.82	0.75	1.39	12.68
Convertible Arbitrage	Relative Value	CISDM	6.91	7.68	0.69	1.25	27.91
Global Macro	Opportunistic	TASS	6.96	7.36	0.73	1.29	5.14
Global Macro	Opportunistic	CISDM	6.97	7.29	0.74	1.38	5.19
Systematic Futures	Opportunistic	CISDM	7.34	6.94	0.83	1.68	8.04
Fund of Funds	Multi-Manager	TASS	6.43	7.53	0.64	1.23	18.92
Multi-Strategy	Multi-Manager	TASS	6.98	7.57	0.71	1.13	17.35
Fund of Funds – Debt	Multi-Manager	CISDM	6.56	7.40	0.67	1.22	17.77
Fund of Funds – Equity	Multi-Manager	CISDM	6.39	7.76	0.62	1.11	21.63
Fund of Funds – Event	Multi-Manager	CISDM	6.35	7.48	0.63	1.15	21.37
Fund of Funds - Macro/Systematic	Multi-Manager	CISDM	6.47	7.05	0.69	1.31	10.65
Fund of Funds – Multi-Strategy	Multi-Manager	CISDM	6.36	7.41	0.64	1.17	18.17
Fund of Funds - Relative Value	Multi-Manager	CISDM	6.46	7.22	0.67	1.23	17.16
Multi-Strategy	Multi-Manager	CISDM	7.00	7.47	0.72	1.34	13.83

The Sharpe ratio measures risk-adjusted performance, where risk is defined as standard deviation, so it penalizes both upside and downside variability. The Sortino ratio measures risk-adjusted performance, where risk is defined as downside deviation, so it penalizes only downside variability below a minimum target return. For hedge fund strategies with large negative events, the Sortino ratio is considered a better performance measure. The combined portfolio with the highest Sharpe ratio (0.83) includes a 20% allocation to systematic futures hedge funds. High Sharpe ratios are also achieved from allocations to distressed securities, fixed-income arbitrage, and global macro or equity market-neutral strategies. Adding allocations of 20% consisting of hedge funds from equity market-neutral (TASS), systematic futures, L/S equity hedge, or event-driven (TASS) categories to the traditional portfolio produces combined portfolios with by far the best Sortino ratios.

Exhibit 20 plots the Sharpe and Sortino ratios for 48/32/20 portfolios, where the 20% allocation is to an equal-weighted portfolio of the funds in each hedge fund strategy category. As a point of reference, the Sharpe and Sortino ratios for the 60/40 portfolio are 0.62 and 1.13, respectively. This graphic visually demonstrates that adding allocations of systematic futures, equity market-neutral, global macro, or event-driven hedge fund strategies, among others, to the traditional portfolio is effective in generating superior risk-adjusted performance—as evidenced by their relatively high Sharpe and Sortino ratios. Moreover, the implication is that despite the flexibility to invest in a wide range of strategies, fund-of-funds and multi-manager funds do not enhance risk-adjusted performance very much.

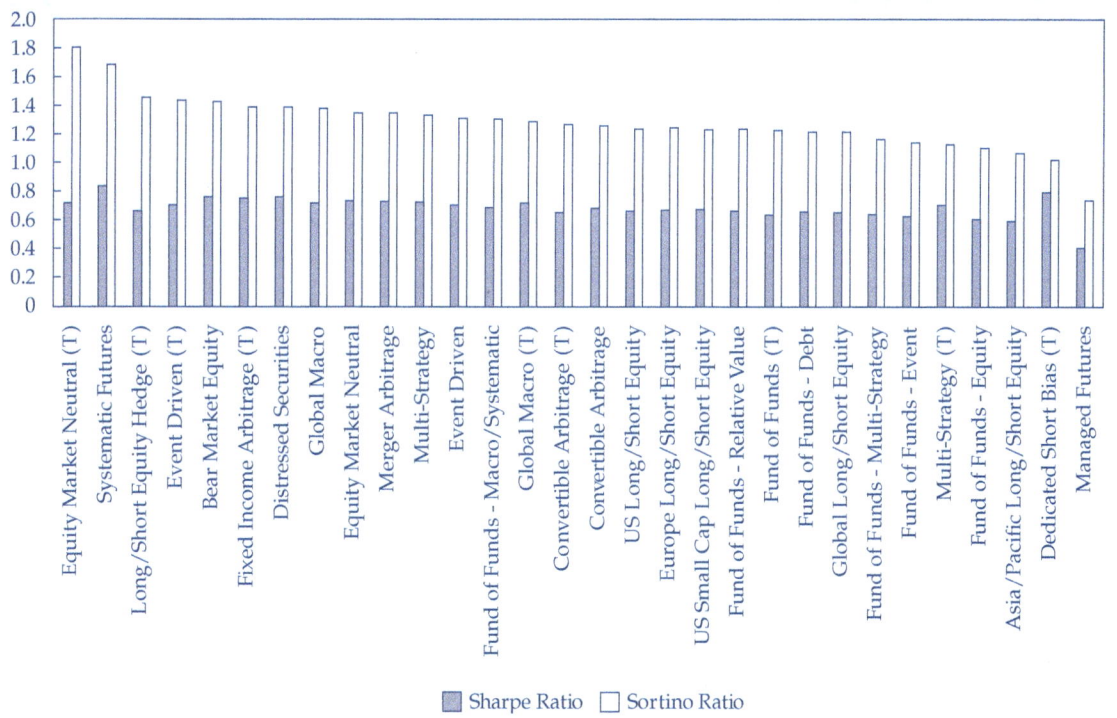

Exhibit 20 Sharpe and Sortino Ratios for 48/32/20 Portfolios, Where 20% Allocation Is to an Equal-Weighted Portfolio for Each Hedge Fund Strategy Category

16.2 Risk Metrics

Considering the different risk exposures and investments that hedge fund strategies entail, many investors consider these strategies for portfolio risk reduction or risk mitigation. Exhibit 21 illustrates which strategies may be most effective in reducing risk in a traditional portfolio (with standard deviation of 8.66%). The exhibit presents the standard deviation of returns for 48/32/20 portfolios, where the 20% allocation is to an equal-weighted portfolio for each hedge fund strategy category.

Exhibit 21 Standard Deviations for 48/32/20 Portfolios, Where 20% Allocation Is to an Equal-Weighted Portfolio for Each Hedge Fund Strategy Category

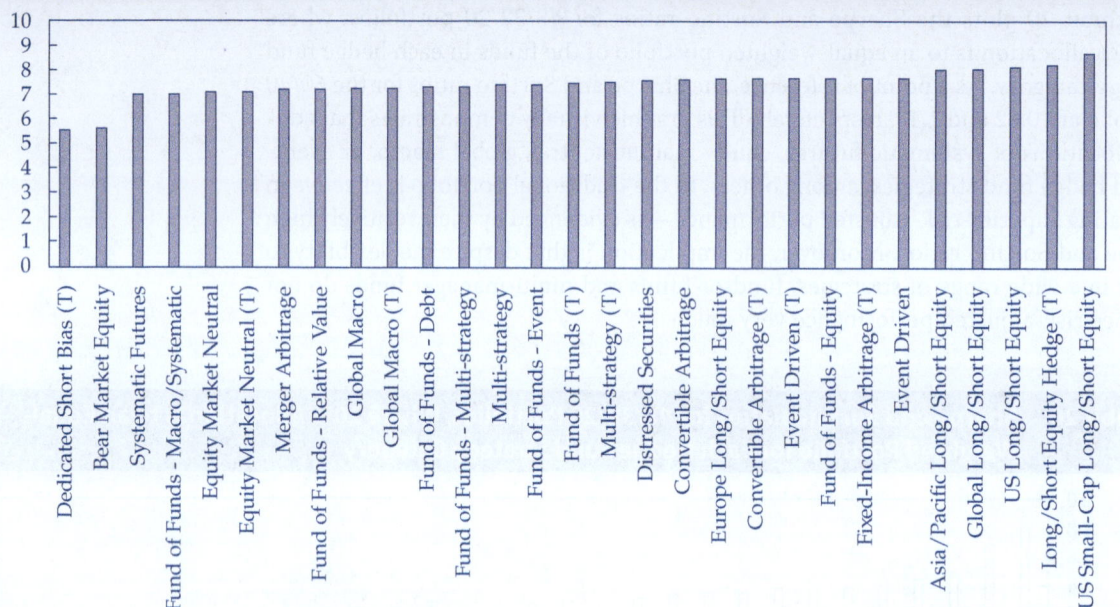

Besides dedicated short-biased and bear market-neutral strategies—for which there are only 6 live funds in total—it can be seen that among the hedge fund strategies that produce the lowest standard deviations of returns in the combined portfolios are systematic futures (6.94%) and FoF-macro/systematic and equity market neutral (a little more than 7.0%). These strategies appear to provide significant risk-reducing diversification benefits; and as discussed previously, they are also the same categories of hedge funds that enhance risk-adjusted returns when added to the traditional 60/40 portfolio. It is evident that standard deviations are relatively high for combined portfolios with event-driven/distressed securities and relative value/convertible arbitrage strategies, indicating they provide little in the way of risk-reduction benefits. This may be attributed to the binary, long-biased nature of most event-driven/distressed securities investing and the typical leverage downsizing/liquidity issues of relative value/convertible arbitrage during periods of market stress.

A drawdown is the difference between a portfolios' highest value (i.e., high-water mark) for a period and any subsequent low point until a new high-water mark is reached. Maximum drawdown is the *largest* difference between a high-water mark and a subsequent low point. The results for maximum drawdown for the 48/32/20 portfolios are shown in Exhibit 22.

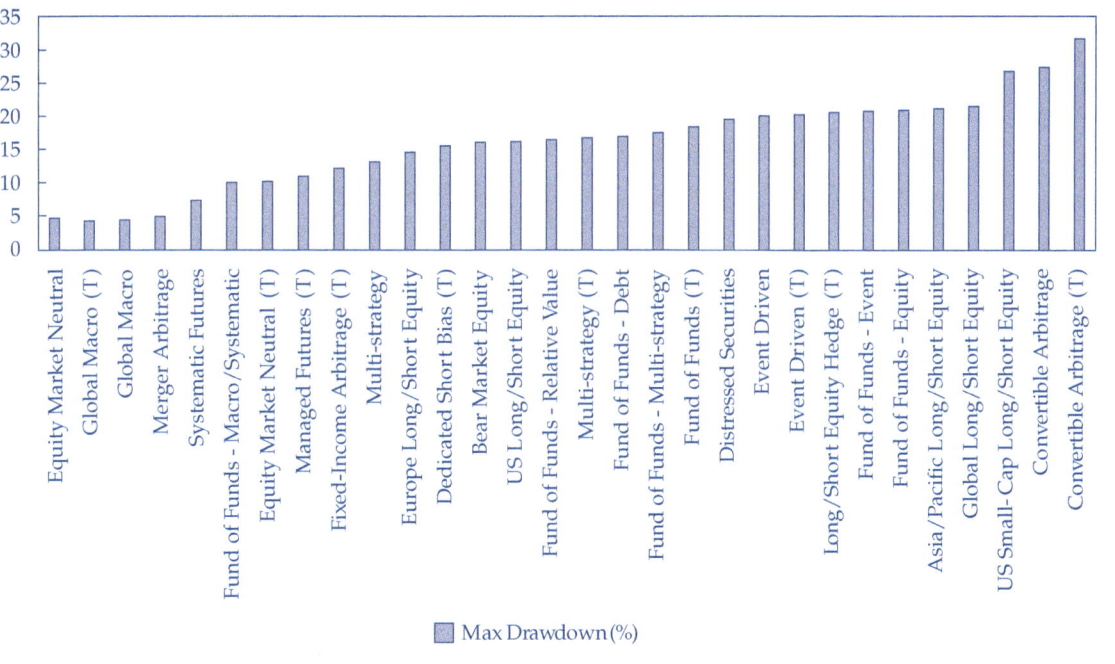

Exhibit 22. Maximum Drawdowns for 48/32/20 Portfolios, Where 20% Allocation Is to an Equal-Weighted Portfolio for Each Hedge Fund Strategy Category

The graphic shows that when combined with the traditional stock and bond portfolio (with a maximum drawdown of 14.42%), the hedge fund strategy portfolios that generate the smallest maximum drawdowns are the opportunistic strategies—specifically, global macro and systematic futures as well as merger arbitrage and equity market-neutral strategies. Notably, the conditional risk model showed that these strategies did not have much exposure to high equity or credit risk during crisis periods. In addition, they also tend to be the strategies with the lowest serial autocorrelation, signaling good liquidity. This suggests that these types of strategies provide risk mitigation for traditional assets because they are not exposed to the same risks, are relatively opportunistic, and are liquid even during periods of market stress. On the other side of the spectrum, L/S equity strategies, event-driven/distressed securities strategies, and relative value/convertible arbitrage strategies show high maximum drawdowns when combined with the traditional portfolio. This is unsurprising because the conditional risk model showed that these event-driven and relative value strategies tended to hold equity risk and that their credit risk also became significant during crisis periods.

EXAMPLE 15

Combining a Hedge Fund Strategy with a Traditional Portfolio

DIY Investment Advisors is a "CIO in a box." Its clients are mainly small institutions and local college endowments. Evergreen Tech, a private 4-year college, is a client with a $150 million endowment and an enrollment of 3,000 students. The endowment's portfolio, which supports 5% of Evergreen's current annual spending needs, has a traditional asset allocation of 60% stocks/40% bonds. Evergreen plans to dramatically increase enrollment to 4,000 students over the next 5 years.

Patricia Chong, principal of DIY, wants to recommend to Evergreen's investment committee (IC) that it add alternative investments to the endowment's portfolio, specifically a 20% allocation to a hedge fund strategy. The IC has indicated to Chong that Evergreen's main considerations for the combined portfolio are that any hedge fund strategy allocation should a) maximize risk-adjusted returns; b) limit downside risk; and c) not impair portfolio liquidity. The IC is also sensitive to fees and considers it important to avoid layering of fees for any hedge fund allocation.

At Chong's request, DIY's hedge fund analysts perform due diligence on numerous hedge funds and assemble the following information on several short-listed funds, showing their past performance contribution to a 48% stocks/32% bonds/20% hedge fund strategy portfolio. Finally, Chong believes historical returns are good proxies for future returns.

Category	Type	Mean Return (%)	SD (%)	Sharpe Ratio	Sortino Ratio	Maximum Drawdown (%)
60% Stocks/40% Bonds	Traditional Portfolio	6.96	8.66	0.62	1.13	14.42
US small-cap long/short equity	Equity	7.53	8.75	0.68	1.23	27.02
Event driven	Event driven	7.19	7.83	0.71	1.31	20.57
Sovereign debt fixed-income arbitrage	Relative value	7.50	7.82	0.75	1.39	12.68
Fund-of-funds – equity	Multi-manager	6.39	7.76	0.62	1.11	21.63

Use the information provided to answer the following questions.

1. Discuss which hedge fund strategy Chong should view as *least* suitable for meeting the considerations expressed by Evergreen's IC.

2. Discuss which hedge fund strategy Chong should view as *most* suitable for meeting the considerations expressed by Evergreen's IC.

Solution to 1:

Based on the IC's considerations, Chong should view a 20% allocation to the fund-of-funds equity hedge fund strategy as least suitable for Evergreen's endowment portfolio. Such an allocation offers no improvements in the combined portfolio's Sharpe and Sortino ratios (to 0.62 and 1.11, respectively). The substantially higher maximum drawdown (50% higher at 21.63%) indicates much more downside risk would be in the combined portfolio. Portfolio liquidity may also be impaired due to two levels of redemption lock-ups and liquidity gates. Finally, given the FoF structure for this strategy allocation, Evergreen would need to pay two layers of fees and would also likely face fee netting risk.

Solution to 2:

Based on the IC's considerations, Chong should view a 20% allocation to the sovereign debt fixed-income arbitrage hedge fund strategy as most suitable for Evergreen's endowment portfolio. Such an allocation would result in significant increases in the combined portfolio's Sharpe and Sortino ratios (to 0.75 and 1.39, respectively), the highest such ratios among the strategies presented. Besides the improvement in Sortino ratio, the lower maximum drawdown (12.68%) indicates less downside risk in the combined portfolio than with any of the other strategy choices. Portfolio liquidity would also likely not be impaired as this strategy focuses on sovereign debt, which typically has good liquidity for most developed market issuers. Finally, similar to the other non-FoF strategies shown, Evergreen would pay only one layer of fees and would also not face any fee netting risk.

SUMMARY

- Hedge funds are an important subset of the alternative investments space. Key characteristics distinguishing hedge funds and their strategies from traditional investments include the following: 1) lower legal and regulatory constraints; 2) flexible mandates permitting use of shorting and derivatives; 3) a larger investment universe on which to focus; 4) aggressive investment styles that allow concentrated positions in securities offering exposure to credit, volatility, and liquidity risk premiums; 5) relatively liberal use of leverage; 6) liquidity constraints that include lock-ups and liquidity gates; and 7) relatively high fee structures involving management and incentive fees.

- Hedge fund strategies are classified by a combination of the instruments in which they are invested, the trading philosophy followed, and the types of risks assumed. Some leading hedge fund strategy index providers are Hedge Fund Research; Lipper TASS; Morningstar Hedge/CISDM; Eurekahedge; and Credit Suisse. There is much heterogeneity in the classification and indexes they provide, so no one index group is all-encompassing.

- This reading classifies hedge fund strategies by the following categories: equity-related strategies; event-driven strategies; relative value strategies; opportunistic strategies; specialist strategies; and multi-manager strategies.

- Equity L/S strategies take advantage of diverse opportunities globally to create alpha via managers' skillful stock picking. Diverse investment styles include value/growth, large cap/small cap, discretionary/quantitative, and industry specialization. Some equity L/S strategies may use index-based short hedges to reduce market risk, but most involve single name shorts for portfolio alpha and added absolute return.

- Equity L/S strategies are typically liquid and generally net long, with gross exposures at 70%–90% long vs. 20%–50% short (but they can vary).

- Equity L/S return profiles are typically aimed to achieve average annual returns roughly equivalent to a long-only approach but with standard deviations that are 50% lower. The more market-neutral or quantitative the strategy approach, the more levered the strategy application to achieve a meaningful return profile.

- Dedicated short sellers only trade with short-side exposure, but they may moderate short beta by also holding cash. Short-biased managers are focused on short-side stock picking, but they typically moderate short beta with some value-oriented long exposure and cash.

- Dedicated short strategies tend to be 60%–120% short at all times, while short-biased strategies are typically around 30%–60% net short. The focus in both cases is usually on single equity stock picking, as opposed to index shorting, and using little if any leverage.

- Dedicated short-selling and short-biased strategies have return goals that are typically less than most other hedge fund strategies but with a negative correlation benefit. Returns are more volatile than a typical L/S equity hedge fund given short beta exposure.
- Equity market-neutral (EMN) strategies take advantage of idiosyncratic short-term mispricing between securities. Their sources of return and alpha do not require accepting beta risk, so EMN strategies are especially attractive in periods of market vulnerability/weakness. There are many types of EMN managers, but most are purely quantitative managers (vs. discretionary managers).
- As many beta risks (e.g., market, sector) are hedged away, EMN strategies generally apply relatively high levels of leverage in striving for meaningful return targets.
- Equity market-neutral strategies exhibit relatively modest return profiles. Portfolios are aimed at market neutrality and with differing constraints to other factor/sector exposures. Generally high levels of diversification and liquidity with lower standard deviation of returns are typical due to an orientation toward mean reversion.
- Merger arbitrage is a relatively liquid strategy. Defined gains come from idiosyncratic, single security takeover situations, but occasional downside shocks can occur when merger deals unexpectedly fail.
- Cross-border M&A usually involves two sets of governmental approvals. M&A deals involving vertical integration often face antitrust scrutiny and thus carry higher risks and offer wider merger spread returns.
- Merger arbitrage strategies have return profiles that are insurance-like, plus a short put option, with relatively high Sharpe ratios; however, left-tail risk is associated with otherwise steady returns. Merger arbitrage managers typically apply moderate to high leverage to generate meaningful target return levels.
- Distressed securities strategies focus on firms in bankruptcy, facing potential bankruptcy, or under financial stress. Hedge fund managers seek inefficiently priced securities before, during, or after the bankruptcy process, which results in either liquidation or reorganization.
- In liquidation, the firm's assets are sold off and securities holders are paid sequentially based on priority of their claims—from senior secured debt, junior secured debt, unsecured debt, convertible debt, preferred stock, and finally common stock.
- In re-organization, a firm's capital structure is re-organized and terms for current claims are negotiated and revised. Debtholders either may agree to maturity extensions or to exchanging their debt for new equity shares (existing shares are canceled) that are sold to new investors to improve the firm's financial condition.
- Outright shorts or hedged positions are possible, but distressed securities investing is usually long-biased, entails relatively high levels of illiquidity, and has moderate to low leverage. The return profile is typically at the higher end of event-driven strategies, but it is more discrete and cyclical.
- For fixed-income arbitrage, the attractiveness of returns is a function of the correlations between different securities, the yield spread pick-up available, and the high number and wide diversity of debt securities across different markets, each having different credit quality and convexity aspects in their pricing.

Summary

- Yield curve and carry trades within the US government space are very liquid but have the fewest mispricing opportunities. Liquidity for relative value positions generally decreases in other sovereign markets, mortgage-related markets, and across corporate debt markets.
- Fixed-income arbitrage involves high leverage usage, but leverage availability diminishes with trade and underlying instrument complexity.
- Convertible arbitrage strategies strive to extract "underpriced" implied volatility from long convertible bond holdings. To do this, managers will delta hedge and gamma trade short equity positions against their convertible positions. Convertible arbitrage works best in periods of high convertible issuance, moderate volatility, and reasonable market liquidity.
- Liquidity issues may arise from convertible bonds being naturally less-liquid securities due to their relatively small issue sizes and inherent complexities as well as the availability and cost to borrow underlying equity for short selling.
- Convertible arbitrage managers typically run convertible portfolios at 300% long vs. 200% short. The lower short exposure is a function of the delta-adjusted exposure needed from short sales to balance the long convertibles.
- Global macro strategies focus on correctly discerning and capitalizing on trends in global financial markets using a wide range of instruments. Managed futures strategies have a similar aim but focus on investments using mainly futures and options on futures, on stock and fixed-income indexes, as well as on commodities and currencies.
- Managed futures strategies typically are implemented via more systematic approaches, while global macro strategies tend to use more discretionary approaches. Both strategies are highly liquid and use high leverage.
- Returns of managed futures strategies typically exhibit positive right-tail skewness during market stress. Global macro strategies generally deliver similar diversification in stress periods but with more heterogeneous outcomes.
- Specialist hedge fund strategies require highly specialized skill sets for trading in niche markets. Two such typical specialist strategies—which are aimed at generating uncorrelated, attractive risk-adjusted returns—are volatility trading and reinsurance/life settlements.
- Volatility traders strive to capture relative timing and strike pricing opportunities due to changes in the term structure of volatility. They try to capture volatility smile and skew by using various types of option spreads, such as bull and bear spreads, straddles, and calendar spreads. In addition to using exchange-listed and OTC options, VIX futures, volatility swaps, and variance swaps can be used to implement volatility trading strategies.
- Life settlements strategies involve analyzing pools of life insurance contracts offered by third-party brokers, where the hedge fund purchases the pool and effectively becomes the beneficiary. The hedge fund manager looks for policies with the following traits: 1) The surrender value being offered to the insured individual is relatively low; 2) the ongoing premium payments are also relatively low; and 3) the probability is relatively high that the insured person will die sooner than predicted by standard actuarial methods.
- Funds-of-funds and multi-strategy funds typically offer steady, low-volatility returns via their strategy diversification. Multi-strategy funds have generally outperformed FoFs, but they have more variance due to using relatively high leverage.

- Multi-strategy funds offer potentially faster tactical asset allocation and generally improved fee structure (netting risk between strategies is often at least partially absorbed by the general partner), but they have higher manager-specific operational risks. FoFs offer a potentially more diverse strategy mix, but they have less transparency, slower tactical reaction time, and contribute netting risk to the FoF investor.

- Conditional linear factor models can be useful for uncovering and analyzing hedge fund strategy risk exposures. This reading uses such a model that incorporates four factors for assessing risk exposures in both normal periods and market stress/crisis periods: equity risk, credit risk, currency risk, and volatility risk.

- Adding a 20% allocation of a hedge fund strategy group to a traditional 60%/40% portfolio (for a 48% stocks/32% bonds/20% hedge funds portfolio) typically decreases total portfolio standard deviation while it increases Sharpe and Sortino ratios (and also often decreases maximum drawdown) in the combined portfolios. This demonstrates that hedge funds act as both risk-adjusted return enhancers and diversifiers for the traditional stock/bond portfolio.

REFERENCES

Hasanhodzic, Jasmina, and Andrew Lo. 2007. "Can Hedge-Fund Returns Be Replicated?: The Linear Case." *Journal of Investment Management* 5 (2): 5–45.

Lintner, John. 1983. "*The Potential Role of Managed Commodity-Financial Futures Accounts (and/or Funds) in Portfolios of Stocks and Bonds.*" Working paper, Division of Research, Graduate School of Business Administration, Harvard University.

PRACTICE PROBLEMS

1. Bern Zang is the chief investment officer of the Janson University Endowment Investment Office. The Janson University Endowment Fund (the "Fund") is based in the United States and has current assets under management of $10 billion, with minimal exposure to alternative investments. Zang currently seeks to increase the Fund's allocation to hedge funds and considers four strategies: dedicated short bias, merger arbitrage, convertible bond arbitrage, and global macro.

   At a meeting with the Fund's board of directors, the board mandates Zang to invest only in event-driven and relative value hedge fund strategies.

   Determine, among the four strategies under consideration by Zang, the two that are permitted given the board's mandate. **Justify** your response.

   i. Dedicated short bias
   ii. Merger arbitrage
   iii. Convertible bond arbitrage
   iv. Global macro

Determine, among the four strategies under consideration by Zang, the two that are permitted given the board's mandate. (circle two)	Justify your response.
Dedicated short bias	
Merger arbitrage	
Convertible bond arbitrage	
Global macro strategies	

The following information relates to Questions 2 and 3

Jane Shaindy is the chief investment officer of a large pension fund. The pension fund is based in the United States and currently has minimal exposure to hedge funds. The pension fund's board has recently approved an additional investment in a long/short equity strategy. As part of Shaindy's due diligence on a hedge fund that implements a long/short equity strategy, she uses a conditional linear factor model to uncover and analyze the hedge fund's risk exposures. She is interested in analyzing several risk factors, but she is specifically concerned about whether the hedge fund's long (positive) exposure to equities increases during turbulent market periods.

2. **Describe** how the conditional linear factor model can be used to address Shaindy's concern.

   During a monthly board meeting, Shaindy discusses her updated market forecast for equity markets. Due to a recent large increase in interest rates and geopolitical tensions, her forecast has changed from one of modestly rising equities to several periods of non-trending markets. Given this new market view, Shaindy concludes that a long/short strategy will not be optimal at this time and seeks another equity-related strategy. The Fund has the capacity to use a substantial amount of leverage.

3. **Determine** the *most appropriate* equity-related hedge fund strategy that Shaindy should employ. **Justify** your response.

---

4. Gunnar Patel is an event-driven hedge fund manager for Senson Fund, which focuses on merger arbitrage strategies. Patel has been monitoring the potential acquisition of Meura Inc. by Sellshom, Inc. Sellshom has offered to buy Meura in a stock-for-stock deal. Sellshom was trading at $60 per share just prior to the announcement of the acquisition, and Meura was trading at $18 per share.

   The offer ratio is 1 share of Sellshom in exchange for 2 shares of Meura. Soon after the announcement, Meura's share price jumps to $22 while Sellshom's falls to $55 in anticipation of the merger receiving required approvals and the deal closing successfully.

   At the current share prices of $55 for Sellshom and $22 for Meura, Patel attempts to profit from the merger announcement. He buys 40,000 shares of Meura and sells short 20,000 shares of Sellshom.

   Calculate the payoffs of the merger arbitrage under the following two scenarios:

   i. The merger is successfully completed.

   ii. The merger fails.

5. John Puten is the chief investment officer of the Markus University Endowment Investment Office. Puten seeks to increase the diversification of the endowment by investing in hedge funds. He recently met with several hedge fund managers that employ different investment strategies. In selecting a hedge fund manager, Puten prefers to hire a manager that uses the following:

   - Fundamental and technical analysis to value markets
   - Discretionary and systematic modes of implementation
   - Top-down strategies
   - A range of macroeconomic and fundamental models to express a view regarding the direction or relative value of a particular asset

   Puten's staff prepares a brief summary of two potential hedge fund investments:

   Hedge Fund 1: A relative value strategy fund focusing only on convertible arbitrage.

   Hedge Fund 2: An opportunistic strategy fund focusing only on global macro strategies.

   Determine which hedge fund would be *most appropriate* for Puten. **Justify** your response.

6. Yankel Stein is the chief investment officer of a large charitable foundation based in the United States. Although the foundation has significant exposure to alternative investments and hedge funds, Stein proposes to increase the foundation's exposure to relative value hedge fund strategies. As part of Stein's due diligence on a hedge fund engaging in convertible bond arbitrage, Stein asks his investment analyst to summarize different risks associated with the strategy.

   Describe how each of the following circumstances can create concerns for Stein's proposed hedge fund strategy:

   i. Short selling

   ii. Credit issues

Practice Problems

    iii. Time decay of call option

    iv. Extreme market volatility

	Describe how each of the following circumstances can create concerns for Stein's proposed hedge fund strategy:
Short selling	
Credit issues	
Time decay of call option	
Extreme market volatility	

The following information relates to Questions 7 and 8

Sushil Wallace is the chief investment officer of a large pension fund. Wallace wants to increase the pension fund's allocation to hedge funds and recently met with three hedge fund managers. These hedge funds focus on the following strategies:

    Hedge Fund A: Specialist—Follows relative value volatility arbitrage

    Hedge Fund B: Multi-Manager—Multi-strategy fund

    Hedge Fund C: Multi-Manager—Fund-of-funds

7 **Describe** three paths for implementing the strategy of Hedge Fund A.

After a significant amount of internal discussion, Wallace concludes that the pension fund should invest in either Hedge Fund B or C for the diversification benefits from the different strategies employed. However, after final due diligence is completed, Wallace recommends investing only in Hedge Fund B, noting its many advantages over Hedge Fund C.

8 **Discuss** *two* advantages of Hedge Fund B relative to Hedge Fund C with respect to investment characteristics.

---

9 Kloss Investments is an investment adviser whose clients are small institutional investors. Muskogh Charitable Foundation (the "Foundation") is a client with $70 million of assets under management. The Foundation has a traditional asset allocation of 65% stocks/35% bonds. Risk and return characteristics for the Foundation's current portfolio are presented in Panel A of Exhibit 1.

Kloss' CIO, Christine Singh, recommends to Muskogh's investment committee that it should add a 10% allocation to hedge funds. The investment committee indicates to Singh that Muskogh's primary considerations for the Foundation's portfolio are that any hedge fund strategy allocation should: a) limit volatility, b) maximize risk-adjusted returns, and c) limit downside risk.

Singh's associate prepares expected risk and return characteristics for three portfolios that have allocations of 60% stocks, 30% bonds, and 10% hedge funds, where the 10% hedge fund allocation follows either an equity market-neutral, global macro, or convertible arbitrage strategy. The risk and return characteristics of the three portfolios are presented in Panel B of Exhibit 1.

Exhibit 1

Hedge Fund Strategy	SD (%)	Sharpe Ratio	Sortino Ratio	Maximum Drawdown (%)
Panel A: Current Portfolio				
N/A	8.75	0.82	1.25	16.2
Panel B: Three Potential Portfolios with a 10% Hedge Fund Allocation				
Equity market neutral	8.72	0.80	1.21	15.1
Global macro	8.55	0.95	1.35	15.0
Convertible arbitrage	8.98	0.83	1.27	20.2

Discuss which hedge fund strategy Singh should view as most suitable for meeting the considerations expressed by Muskogh's investment committee.

The following information relates to Questions 10–17

Snohomish Mukilteo is a portfolio analyst for the Puyallup-Wenatchee Pension Fund (PWPF). PWPF's investment committee (IC) asks Mukilteo to research adding hedge funds to the PWPF portfolio.

A member of the IC meets with Mukilteo to discuss hedge fund strategies. During the meeting, the IC member admits that her knowledge of hedge fund strategies is fairly limited but tells Mukilteo she believes the following:

Statement 1   Equity market-neutral strategies use a relative value approach.

Statement 2   Event-driven strategies are not exposed to equity market beta risk.

Statement 3   Opportunistic strategies have risk exposure to market directionality.

The IC member also informs Mukilteo that for equity-related strategies, the IC considers low volatility to be more important than negative correlation.

Mukilteo researches various hedge fund strategies. First, Mukilteo analyzes an event-driven strategy involving two companies, Algona Applications (AA) and Tukwila Technologies (TT). AA's management, believing that its own shares are overvalued, uses its shares to acquire TT. The IC has expressed concern about this type of strategy because of the potential for loss if the acquisition unexpectedly fails. Mukilteo's research reveals a way to use derivatives to protect against this loss, and he believes that such protection will satisfy the IC's concern.

Next, while researching relative value strategies, Mukilteo considers a government bond strategy that involves buying lower-liquidity, off-the-run bonds and selling higher-liquidity, duration-matched, on-the-run bonds.

Mukilteo examines an opportunistic strategy implemented by one of the hedge funds under consideration. The hedge fund manager selects 12 AAA rated corporate bonds with actively traded futures contracts and approximately equal durations. For

Practice Problems

each corporate bond, the manager calculates the 30-day change in the yield spread over a constant risk-free rate. He then ranks the bonds according to this spread change. For the bonds that show the greatest spread narrowing (widening), the hedge fund will take long (short) positions in their futures contracts. The net holding for this strategy is market neutral.

Mukilteo also plans to recommend a specialist hedge fund strategy that would allow PWPF to maintain a high Sharpe ratio even during a financial crisis when equity markets fall.

The IC has been considering the benefits of allocating to a fund of funds (FoF) or to a multi-strategy fund (MSF). Mukilteo receives the following email from a member of the IC:

> "From my perspective, an FoF is superior even though it entails higher manager-specific operational risk and will require us to pay a double layer of fees without being able to net performance fees on individual managers. I especially like the tactical allocation advantage of FoFs—that they are more likely to be well informed about when to tactically reallocate to a particular strategy and more capable of shifting capital between strategies quickly."

Finally, Mukilteo creates a model to simulate adding selected individual hedge fund strategies to the current portfolio with a 20% allocation. The IC's primary considerations for a combined portfolio are (1) that the variance of the combined portfolio must be less than 90% of that of the current portfolio and (2) that the combined portfolio maximize the risk-adjusted return with the expectation of large negative events. Exhibit 1 provides historical performance and risk metrics for three simulated portfolios.

Exhibit 1 Performance of Various Combined Portfolios

Hedge Fund Strategy	Standard Deviation (%)	Sharpe Ratio	Sortino Ratio	Maximum Drawdown (%)
Current Portfolio				
NA	7.95	0.58	1.24	14.18
Three Potential Portfolios with a 20% Hedge Fund Allocation				
Merger arbitrage	7.22	0.73	1.35	5.60
Systematic futures	6.94	0.83	1.68	8.04
Equity market neutral	7.17	0.73	1.80	10.72

10 Which of the IC member's statements regarding hedge fund strategies is *incorrect*?
   A Statement 1
   B Statement 2
   C Statement 3

11 Based on what the IC considers important for equity-related strategies, which strategy should Mukilteo *most likely* avoid?
   A Long/short equity
   B Equity market neutral
   C Dedicated short selling and short biased

12 Which of the following set of derivative positions will *most likely* satisfy the IC's concern about the event-driven strategy involving AA and TT?
   A Long out-of-the-money puts on AA shares and long out-of-the-money calls on TT shares
   B Long out-of-the-money calls on AA shares and long out-of-the-money puts on TT shares
   C Long risk-free bonds, short out-of-the-money puts on AA shares, and long out-of-the-money calls on TT shares

13 The government bond strategy that Mukilteo considers is *best* described as a:
   A carry trade.
   B yield curve trade.
   C long/short credit trade.

14 The opportunistic strategy that Mukilteo considers is *most likely* to be described as a:
   A global macro strategy.
   B time-series momentum strategy.
   C cross-sectional momentum strategy.

15 The specialist hedge fund strategy that Mukilteo plans to recommend is *most likely*:
   A cross-asset volatility trading between the US and Japanese markets.
   B selling equity volatility and collecting the volatility risk premium.
   C buying longer-dated out-of-the-money options on VIX index futures.

16 Based on the email that Mukilteo received, the IC member's perspective is correct with regard to:
   A layering and netting of fees.
   B tactical allocation capabilities.
   C manager-specific operational risks.

17 Based on the IC's primary considerations for a combined portfolio, which simulated hedge fund strategy portfolio in Exhibit 1 creates the *most suitable* combined portfolio?
   A Merger arbitrage
   B Systematic futures
   C Equity market neutral

The following information relates to Questions 18–23

Lynet Xu is the Chief Investment Officer for the North University Endowment Fund (the Fund), which is based in Europe. The Fund's investment committee recently made the decision to add hedge funds to the Fund's portfolio to increase diversification. Xu meets with Yolanda Anderson, a junior analyst, to discuss various hedge fund strategies that might be suitable for the Fund. Anderson tells Xu the following:

Statement 1   Relative value strategies tend to use minimal leverage.

Practice Problems

Statement 2   Long/short equity strategies are typically not exposed to equity market beta risk.

Statement 3   Global macro strategies come with naturally higher volatility in the return profiles typically delivered.

Xu tells Anderson that while she is open to using all hedge fund strategies, she is particularly interested in opportunistic hedge fund strategies. Xu states that she prefers opportunistic hedge fund strategies that use high leverage, have high liquidity, and exhibit right-tail skewness.

Xu asks Anderson to research an event-driven strategy involving a potential merger between Aqua Company and Taurus, Inc. Aqua has offered to buy Taurus in a stock-for-stock deal: The offer ratio is two shares of Aqua for three shares of Taurus. Aqua was trading at €50 per share prior to the merger announcement, and it fell to €45 per share after the merger announcement. Taurus was trading at €15 per share prior to the announcement, and it rose to €20 per share in anticipation of the merger deal receiving required approvals and closing successfully. Xu decides to enter into a merger arbitrage trade: She buys 22,500 shares of Taurus at €20 per share and sells short 15,000 shares of Aqua at €45 per share.

Xu and Anderson discuss an equity strategy involving two large European car companies, ZMD and Tarreras. Anderson recently attended a trade show where she inspected ZMD's newest model car. Based on information from the trade show and other analysis conducted by Anderson, Xu concludes that ZMD will not meet its revenue expectations. Current valuation metrics indicate that ZMD shares are overvalued relative to shares of Tarreras. Xu decides to take a short position in ZMD and a long position in Tarreras with equal beta-weighted exposure.

Xu next reviews a convertible arbitrage strategy and analyzes a trade involving the euro-denominated stock and convertible bonds of AVC Corporation, a European utility company. Anderson gathers selected data for AVC Corporation, which is presented in Exhibit 1.

Exhibit 1   Selected Data for AVC Corporation

AVC Convertible Bond		AVC Stock	
Price (% of par)	115	Current price (per share)	€28
Coupon (%)	6	P/E	25
Remaining maturity (years)	2	P/BV	2.25
Conversion ratio	50	P/CF	15

Based on comparisons with industry ratios, Xu believes that AVC's shares are overvalued in relative terms and the convertible bonds are undervalued. Anderson analyzes the potential profit outcomes of a long position in the convertible bond combined with a short stock position, assuming small changes in the share price and ignoring dividends and borrowing costs. She offers the following conclusion to Xu:

"The profit earned on the convertible arbitrage trade will be the same regardless of whether the share price of AVC decreases or increases."

Finally, Xu and Anderson consider a hedge fund that specializes in reinsurance and life settlements. Xu tells Anderson about three characteristics that hedge fund managers look for when investing in life settlements:

Characteristic 1   The surrender value offered to the insured individual is relatively high.

Characteristic 2   The ongoing premium payments to keep the policy active are relatively low.

Characteristic 3   There is a high probability that the designated insured person is likely to die within the period predicted by standard actuarial methods.

---

18 Which of Anderson's three statements regarding hedge fund strategies is correct?
    A   Statement 1
    B   Statement 2
    C   Statement 3

19 Which opportunistic hedge fund strategy meets Xu's preferences?
    A   Only global macro
    B   Only managed futures
    C   Both global macro and managed futures

20 Assuming the merger between Aqua and Taurus successfully closes, the payoff on Xu's merger arbitrage trade will be:
    A   −€187,500.
    B   €225,000.
    C   €412,500.

21 Which equity hedge fund strategy *best* describes the ZMD and Tarreras positions taken by Xu?
    A   Short bias
    B   Long/short equity
    C   Equity market neutral

22 Anderson's conclusion about the profitability of the AVC convertible arbitrage trade is:
    A   correct.
    B   incorrect, because the profit will be higher if the share price decreases.
    C   incorrect, because the profit will be higher if the share price increases.

23 Which of the three characteristics of life settlements noted by Anderson is correct?
    A   Characteristic 1
    B   Characteristic 2
    C   Characteristic 3

SOLUTIONS

1

Determine, among the four strategies under consideration by Zang, the two that are permitted given the board's mandate. (circle two)	Justify your response.
Dedicated short bias	A dedicated short bias hedge fund strategy is an example of an equity hedge fund strategy, not an event-driven or relative value strategy. Equity hedge fund strategies focus primarily on the equity markets, and the majority of their risk profiles contain equity-oriented risk. Dedicated short bias managers look for possible short selling targets among companies that are overvalued, that are experiencing declining revenues and/or earnings, or that have internal management conflicts, weak corporate governance, or even potential accounting frauds.
Merger arbitrage	A merger arbitrage hedge fund strategy is an example of an event-driven strategy, which is permitted under the board's mandate. Event-driven hedge fund strategies focus on corporate events, such as governance events, mergers and acquisitions, bankruptcy, and other key events for corporations. Merger arbitrage involves simultaneously purchasing and selling the stocks of two merging companies to create "riskless" profits.
Convertible bond arbitrage	A convertible bond arbitrage hedge fund strategy is an example of a relative value strategy, which is permitted under the board's mandate. Relative value hedge fund strategies focus on the relative valuation between two or more securities. Relative value strategies are often exposed to credit and liquidity risks because the valuation differences from which these strategies seek to benefit are often due to differences in credit quality and/or liquidity across different securities. A classic convertible bond arbitrage strategy is to buy the relatively undervalued convertible bond and take a short position in the relatively overvalued underlying stock.
Global macro	A global macro hedge fund strategy is an example of an opportunistic hedge fund strategy, not an event-driven or relative value strategy. Opportunistic hedge fund strategies take a top-down approach, focus on a multi-asset opportunity set, and include global macro strategies. Global macro managers use both fundamental and technical analysis to value markets as well as discretionary and systematic modes of implementation.

2 A linear factor model can provide insights into the intrinsic characteristics and risks in a hedge fund investment. Since hedge fund strategies are dynamic, a conditional model allows for the analysis in a specific market environment to determine whether hedge fund strategies are exposed to certain risks under abnormal market conditions. A conditional model can show whether hedge fund risk exposures to equities that are insignificant during calm periods become significant during turbulent market periods. During normal periods when equities are rising, the desired exposure to equities (S&P 500 Index) should be long (positive) to benefit from higher expected returns. However, during crisis periods when equities are falling sharply, the desired exposure to equities should be short (negative).

3 Shaindy should employ an equity market-neutral (EMN) equity strategy. Overall, EMN managers are more useful for portfolio allocation during periods of non-trending or declining markets. EMN hedge fund strategies take opposite (long and short) positions in similar or related equities having divergent valuations while attempting to maintain a near net zero portfolio exposure to the market. EMN managers neutralize market risk by constructing their portfolios such that the expected portfolio beta is approximately equal to zero. Moreover, EMN managers often choose to set the betas for sectors or industries as well as for common risk factors (e.g., market size, price-to-earnings ratio, and book-to-market ratio) equal to zero. Since these portfolios do not take beta risk and attempt to neutralize many other factor risks, they typically must apply leverage to the long and short positions to achieve a meaningful return profile from their individual stock selections.

EMN strategies typically deliver return profiles that are steadier and less volatile than those of many other hedge strategy areas. Over time, their conservative and constrained approach typically results in a less dynamic overall return profile than those of managers who accept beta exposure. Despite the use of substantial leverage and because of their more standard and overall steady risk/return profiles, equity market-neutral managers are often a preferred replacement for fixed-income managers during periods when fixed-income returns are unattractively low.

4 i. At the current share prices of $55 for Sellshom and $22 for Meura, Patel would receive $1,100,000 from short selling 20,000 shares of Sellshom and would pay $880,000 to buy 40,000 shares of Meura. This provides a net spread of $220,000 to Patel if the merger is successfully completed.

ii. If the merger fails, then prices should revert back to their pre-merger announcement levels of $18 per share for Meura and $60 per share for Sellshom. The manager would need to buy back 20,000 shares of Sellshom at $60 per share, for a total of $1,200,000, to close the short position. Patel would then sell the long position of 40,000 shares of Meura at $18 per share for a total of $720,000. This net loss would be $260,000, calculated as: (Sellshom: $1,100,000 − $1,200,000 = −$100,000) + (Meura: −$880,000 + $720,000 = −$160,000).

5 Hedge Fund 2 would be most appropriate for Puten because it follows a global macro strategy, which is consistent with Puten's preferences. Global macro managers use both fundamental and technical analysis to value markets, and they use discretionary and systematic modes of implementation. The key source of returns in global macro strategies revolves around correctly discerning and capitalizing on trends in global markets.

Global macro strategies are typically top-down and employ a range of macroeconomic and fundamental models to express a view regarding the direction or relative value of a particular asset or asset class. Positions may comprise a mix of individual securities, baskets of securities, index futures, foreign exchange futures/forwards, fixed-income products or futures, and derivatives or options on any of the above. If the hedge fund manager is making a directional bet, then directional models will use fundamental data regarding a specific market or asset to determine if it is undervalued or overvalued relative to history and the expected macro-trend.

Hedge Fund 1 follows a relative value strategy with a focus on convertible arbitrage, which is not aligned with Puten's preferences. In a convertible bond arbitrage strategy, the manager strives to extract "cheap" implied volatility by buying the relatively undervalued convertible bond and taking a short position

Solutions

in the relatively overvalued common stock. Convertible arbitrage managers are typically neither using fundamental and technical analysis to value markets nor employing top-down strategies to express a view regarding the direction or relative value of an asset.

6.

	Describe how each of the following circumstances can create concerns for Stein's proposed hedge fund strategy:
Short selling	Since Hedge Fund 1 employs a convertible arbitrage strategy, the fund buys the convertible bond and takes a short position in the underlying security. When short selling, shares must be located and borrowed; as a result, the stock owner may want his/her shares returned at a potentially inopportune time, such as during stock price run-ups or when supply for the stock is low or demand for the stock is high. This situation, particularly a short squeeze, can lead to substantial losses and a suddenly unbalanced exposure if borrowing the underlying equity shares becomes too difficult or too costly for the arbitrageur.
Credit issues	Credit issues may complicate valuation since bonds have exposure to credit risk. When credit spreads widen or narrow, there would be a mismatch in the values of the stock and convertible bond positions that the convertible manager may or may not have attempted to hedge away.
Time decay of call option	The convertible bond arbitrage strategy can lose money due to time decay of the convertible bond's embedded call option during periods of reduced realized equity volatility and/or due to a general compression of market implied volatility levels.
Extreme market volatility	Convertible arbitrage strategies have performed best when convertible issuance is high (implying a wider choice among convertible securities as well as downward price pressure and cheaper prices), general market volatility levels are moderate, and the liquidity to trade and adjust positions is sufficient. Extreme market volatility typically implies heightened credit risks. Convertibles are naturally less-liquid securities, so convertible managers generally do not fare well during such periods. Because hedge funds have become the natural market makers for convertibles and typically face significant redemption pressures from investors during crises, the strategy may have further unattractive left-tail risk attributes during periods of market stress.

7. Hedge Fund A's volatility trading strategy can be implemented by following multiple paths. One path is through simple exchange-traded options. The maturity of such options typically extends to no more than two years. In terms of expiry, the longer-dated options will have more absolute exposure to volatility levels than shorter-dated options, but the shorter-dated options will exhibit more delta sensitivity to price changes.

A second, similar path is to implement the volatility trading strategy using OTC options. In this case, the tenor and strike prices of the options can be customized. The tenor of expiry dates can then be extended beyond what is available with exchange-traded options.

A third path is to use VIX futures or options on VIX futures as a way to more explicitly express a pure volatility view without the need for constant delta hedging of an equity put or call for isolating the volatility exposure.

A fourth path for implementing a volatility trading strategy would be to purchase an OTC volatility swap or a variance swap from a creditworthy counterparty. A volatility swap is a forward contract on future realized price volatility. Similarly, a variance swap is a forward contract on future realized price variance, where variance is the square of volatility. Both volatility and variance swaps provide "pure" exposure to volatility alone, unlike standardized options in which the volatility exposure depends on the price of the underlying asset and must be isolated and extracted via delta hedging.

8   a   Multi-strategy managers like Hedge Fund B can reallocate capital into different strategy areas more quickly and efficiently than would be possible by a fund-of-funds (FoF) manager like Hedge Fund C. The multi-strategy manager has full transparency and a better picture of the interactions of the different teams' portfolio risks than would ever be possible for FoF managers to achieve. Consequently, the multi-strategy manager can react faster to different real-time market impacts—for example, by rapidly increasing or decreasing leverage within different strategies depending upon the perceived riskiness of available opportunities.

   b   The fees paid by investors in a multi-strategy fund can be structured in a number of ways, some of which can be very attractive when compared to the FoFs' added fee layering and netting risk attributes. Conceptually, FoF investors always face netting risk, whereby they are responsible for paying performance fees due to winning underlying funds while suffering return drag from the performance of losing underlying funds. Even if the FoF's overall performance is flat or down, FoF investors must still pay incentive fees due to the managers of winning funds.

9   Based on the investment committee's considerations, Singh should view a 10% allocation to the global macro hedge fund strategy as most suitable for the Foundation. Such an allocation would result in a decrease in standard deviation (volatility) and significant increases in the combined portfolio's Sharpe and Sortino ratios (these are the highest such ratios among the strategies presented). In addition, the lower maximum drawdown (15.0%) indicates less downside risk in the combined portfolio than with any of the other strategy choices.

10 B is correct. Statement 2 is incorrect: Event-driven strategies, such as merger arbitrage, tend to be exposed to some natural equity market beta risk. Overall market risk can potentially disrupt a merger's consummation (though hedging may be possible). To the extent that deals are more likely to fail in market stress periods, event-driven merger arbitrage strategies have market sensitivity and left-tail risk attributes. Also, while event-driven strategies may have less beta exposure than simple, long-only beta allocations, the higher hedge fund fees effectively result in a particularly expensive form of embedded beta. Equity market-neutral strategies do use a relative value approach, because such strategies hold balanced long and short equity exposures to maintain zero (or close to zero) net exposure to the equity market and such factors as sector and size. Also, opportunistic strategies do have risk exposure to market directionality, also called trendiness.

A is incorrect because equity market-neutral strategies do use a relative value approach. Equity market-neutral strategies hold balanced long and short equity exposures to maintain zero (or close to zero) net exposure to the equity market and such factors as sector and size (i.e., market cap). They then focus on, for example, pairs of long and short securities whose prices are out of historical alignment and are expected to experience mean reversion. To take advantage of idiosyncratic short-term mispricing between securities whose prices should otherwise be co-integrated, equity market-neutral hedge fund strategies take opposite (i.e., long and short) positions in similar or related equities that have divergent valuations, while also attempting to maintain a near net zero portfolio exposure to the market.

C is incorrect because opportunistic strategies do have risk exposure to market directionality, also called trendiness. Opportunistic strategies are based on macro themes and multi-asset relationships on a global basis; therefore, broad themes, global relationships, market trends, and cycles affect their returns. Generally, the key source of returns in global macro strategies revolves around

Solutions

correctly discerning and capitalizing on trends in global markets. For example, global macro managers typically hold views on trends in inflation (among other things). Global macro strategies are typically top down and use a range of macroeconomic and fundamental models to express a view regarding the direction or relative value of an asset or asset class. If the hedge fund manager is making a directional bet, then directional models will use fundamental data regarding a specific market or asset to determine whether it is undervalued or overvalued relative to history and the expected macro trend.

11 C is correct. For equity-related strategies, the IC considers low volatility to be more important than negative correlation. Dedicated short selling and short-biased strategies have return goals that are typically less than those for most other hedge fund strategies but with a negative correlation benefit. In addition, they are more volatile than a typical long/short equity hedge fund because of their short beta exposure. As a result, Mukilteo should avoid dedicated short selling and short-biased strategies.

A is incorrect because long/short equity is a lower-volatility strategy. A long/short equity manager aims to achieve a standard deviation that is 50% lower than a long-only approach while achieving average annual returns roughly equivalent to a long-only approach. Since the IC considers low volatility important, this is not a strategy that Mukilteo should necessarily avoid.

B is incorrect because equity market-neutral strategies generally have high levels of diversification and lower standard deviations of returns than many other strategies across normal market conditions. Because they typically deliver returns that are steadier and less volatile than those of many other hedge strategy areas, equity market-neutral managers generally are more useful for portfolio allocation during periods of non-trending or declining markets. Equity market-neutral managers neutralize market risk by constructing their portfolios such that the expected portfolio beta is approximately equal to zero. Over time, their conservative and constrained approach typically results in less volatile overall returns than those of managers who accept beta exposure. (The exception to this norm is when the use of significant leverage may cause forced portfolio downsizing.) Since the IC considers low volatility important, this is not a strategy that Mukilteo should necessarily avoid.

12 B is correct. The event-driven strategy that Mukilteo researches is a stock-for-stock merger arbitrage strategy. In this strategy, because the management of the acquiring company (AA) believes its shares to be overvalued, it will offer AA shares in exchange for target company (TT) shares in a specified ratio. The merger arbitrage fund manager will then buy TT shares and sell AA shares in the same ratio as the offer, hoping to earn the spread on successful deal completion.

For most acquisitions, the initial announcement of a deal will cause the target's share price to rise toward the acquisition price and the acquirer's share price to fall (either because of the potential dilution of its outstanding shares or the use of cash for purposes other than a dividend payment). If the acquisition is unsuccessful, the manager faces losses if the target's share price has already risen and/or the acquirer's share price has already fallen in anticipation of the acquisition. When merger deals do fail, the initial price rise of the target's shares and the initial price fall of the acquirer's shares are typically reversed. Arbitrageurs who jumped into the merger situation after its initial announcement stand to incur substantial losses on their long positions in the target's shares and their short positions in the acquirer's shares.

To manage the risk of the acquisition failing, the manager can buy out-of-the-money calls on AA shares (to cover the short position) and buy out-of-the-money puts on TT shares (to protect against loss in value). Such a position will provide protection that would likely satisfy the IC's concern about losses with this strategy.

A is incorrect because protecting against loss with this strategy requires buying out-of-the-money calls (not puts) on AA and buying out-of-the-money puts (not calls) on TT.

C is incorrect because it represents the payoff profile of this merger arbitrage strategy, not a way to protect the strategy against loss should the acquisition fail. The payoff profile of this merger arbitrage strategy resembles that of a riskless bond combined with a short put option on AA shares and a long call option on TT shares. The short put on the AA shares reflects the need to cover the short position in AA when the share price rises. The long call on TT shares becomes valuable if and when another interested acquirer (i.e., White Knight) makes a higher bid for TT before the initial merger proposal is completed.

13. A is correct. Carry trades involve going long a higher-yielding security and shorting a lower-yielding security with the expectation of receiving the positive carry and of profiting on long and short sides of the trade when the temporary relative mispricing reverts to normal. A classic example of a fixed-income arbitrage trade involves buying lower-liquidity, off-the-run government securities and selling higher-liquidity, duration-matched, on-the-run government securities. Interest rate and credit risks are hedged because long and short positions have the same duration and credit exposure. So, the key concern is liquidity risk. Under normal conditions, as time passes, the more (less) expensive on-the-run (off-the-run) securities will decrease (increase) in price as the current on-the-runs are replaced by a more liquid issue of new on-the-run bonds that then become off-the-run bonds.

B is incorrect because Mukilteo considers a carry trade, not a yield curve trade. For yield curve trades, the prevalent calendar spread strategy involves taking long and short positions at different points on the yield curve where the relative mispricing of securities offers the best opportunities, such as in a curve flattening or steepening, to profit. Perceptions and forecasts of macroeconomic conditions are the backdrop for these types of trades. The positions can be in fixed-income securities of the same issuer; in that case, most credit and liquidity risks would likely be hedged, making interest rate risk the main concern. Alternatively, longs and shorts can be taken in the securities of different issuers—but typically ones operating in the same industry or sector. In this case, differences in credit quality, liquidity, volatility, and issue-specific characteristics would likely drive the relative mispricing. In either case, the hedge fund manager aims to profit as the mispricing reverses (mean reversion occurs) and the longs rise and shorts fall in value within the targeted time frame.

C is incorrect because Mukilteo considers a carry trade, not a long/short credit trade. In a long/short credit trade, valuation differences result from differences in credit quality—for example, investment-grade versus non-investment-grade securities. It involves the relative credit risks across different security issuers and tends to be naturally more volatile than the exploitation of small pricing differences within sovereign debt alone.

14. C is correct. The strategy under consideration is a managed futures strategy—specifically, a cross-sectional momentum approach. Such an approach is generally implemented with securities in the same asset class, which is corporate bonds in this case. The strategy is to take long positions in contracts for bonds

that have risen the most in value relative to the others (the bonds with the narrowing spreads) and short positions in contracts for bonds that have fallen the most in value relative to the others (the bonds with the widening spreads). Cross-sectional momentum strategies generally result in holding a net zero or market-neutral position. In contrast, positions for assets in time-series momentum strategies are determined in isolation, independent of the performance of the other assets in the strategy and can be net long or net short depending on the current price trend of an asset.

A is incorrect because the opportunistic strategy under consideration is more likely to be described as a managed futures strategy—specifically, a cross-sectional momentum approach—rather than a global macro strategy. Global macro strategies are typically top down and generally focus on correctly discerning and capitalizing on trends in global financial markets, which does not describe the strategy under consideration. In contrast, managed futures strategies that use a cross-sectional momentum approach are implemented with a cross-section of assets (generally within an asset class, which in this case is highly rated corporate bonds) by going long those that are rising in price the most and by shorting those that are falling the most.

B is incorrect because the strategy under consideration is a managed futures strategy—specifically, a cross-sectional (not time-series) momentum approach. Time-series trading strategies are driven by the past performance of the individual assets. The manager will take long positions for assets that are rising in value and short positions for assets that are falling in value. Positions are taken on an absolute basis, and individual positions are determined independent of the performance of the other assets in the strategy. This approach is in contrast to cross-sectional strategies, where the position taken in an asset depends on that asset's performance relative to the other assets. With time-series momentum strategies, the manager can be net long or net short depending on the current price trend of an asset.

15. C is correct. Mukilteo needs to recommend a specialist hedge fund strategy that can help PWPF maintain a high Sharpe ratio even in a crisis when equity markets fall. Buying longer-dated out-of-the-money options on VIX index futures is a long equity volatility position that works as a protective hedge, particularly in an equity market crisis when volatility spikes and equity prices fall. A long volatility strategy is a useful potential diversifier for long equity investments (albeit at the cost of the option premium paid by the volatility buyer). Because equity volatility is approximately 80% negatively correlated with equity market returns, a long position in equity volatility can substantially reduce the portfolio's standard deviation, which would serve to increase its Sharpe ratio. Longer-dated options will have more absolute exposure to volatility levels (i.e., vega exposure) than shorter-dated options, and out-of-the-money options will typically trade at higher implied volatility levels than at-the-money options.

A is incorrect because cross-asset volatility trading, a type of relative value volatility trading, may often involve idiosyncratic, macro-oriented risks that may have adverse effects during an equity market crisis.

B is incorrect because the volatility seller is the provider of insurance during crises, not the beneficiary of it. Selling volatility provides a volatility risk premium or compensation for taking on the risk of providing insurance against crises for holders of equities and other securities. On the short side, option premium sellers generally extract steadier returns in normal market environments.

16 A is correct. FoFs have double layers of fees without being able to net performance fees on individual managers. The FoF investor always faces netting risk and is responsible for paying performance fees that are due to winning underlying funds while suffering return drag from the performance of losing underlying funds. Even if the FoF's overall performance (aggregated across all funds) is flat or down, FoF investors must still pay incentive fees that are due to the managers of the winning underlying funds.

The fee structure is more investor friendly at MSFs, where the general partner absorbs the netting risk arising from the divergent performance of the fund's different strategy teams. This is an attractive outcome for the MSF investor because (1) the GP is responsible for netting risk and (2) the only investor-level incentive fees paid are those due on the total fund performance after netting the positive and negative performances of the various strategy teams.

However, if the MSF operates with a pass-through fee model, the investor will pay for a portion of the netting risk. Using this model, the MSF may charge no management fee but instead pass through the costs of paying individual teams (inclusive of salary and incentives fees earned by each team) before an added manager-level incentive fee is charged to the investor on total fund performance. In this instance, the investor does implicitly pay for a portion of netting risk.

B is incorrect because MSFs have a tactical allocation advantage over FoFs. MSFs can reallocate capital into different strategy areas more quickly and efficiently than is possible in FoFs, allowing MSFs to react faster to real-time market impacts. This shorter tactical reaction time, combined with MSFs' better strategy transparency, makes MSFs more resilient than FoFs in preserving capital.

C is incorrect because MSFs have higher manager-specific operational risks than FoFs. In MSFs, teams of managers dedicated to running different hedge fund strategies share operational and risk management systems under the same roof. This means that the MSF's operational risks are not well diversified because all operational processes are performed under the same fund structure. FoFs, in contrast, have less operational risk because each separate underlying hedge fund is responsible for its own risk management.

17 C is correct. The equity market-neutral strategy makes for a combined portfolio that has a standard deviation below the maximum specified and has the highest Sortino ratio.

The primary consideration is that the variance of the combined portfolio must be less than 90% of that of the current portfolio. Since variance is the square of standard deviation, the maximum variance allowed is

$$\sigma^2_{max} = (\sigma_{current})^2 \times 90\%$$

$$\sigma^2_{max} = (7.95)^2 \times 90\% = 63.20 \times 0.9 = 56.88$$

And standard deviation is the square root of variance, so the maximum standard deviation allowed is

$$\sigma_{max} = \sqrt{\sigma^2_{max}}$$

$$\sigma_{max} = \sqrt{56.88} = 7.54$$

All three portfolios are below the maximum specified variance.

Solutions

The next consideration is that the portfolio should maximize the risk-adjusted return with the expectation of large negative events. For hedge fund strategies with large negative events, the Sortino ratio is a more appropriate measure of risk-adjusted return than the Sharpe ratio. The Sharpe ratio measures risk-adjusted performance, where risk is defined as standard deviation, so it penalizes both upside and downside variability. The Sortino ratio measures risk-adjusted performance, where risk is defined as downside deviation, so it penalizes only downside variability below a minimum target return. Of the portfolios that meet the variance requirement, the one with the highest Sortino ratio is the portfolio with the equity market-neutral allocation, with a Sortino ratio of 1.80. Therefore, the portfolio with the equity market-neutral allocation is the most suitable portfolio for the considerations specified by the IC.

A is incorrect because the portfolio with an allocation to the merger arbitrage hedge fund strategy, while meeting the variance requirement, has a lower Sortino ratio (1.35) than the portfolio with an allocation to the equity market-neutral hedge fund strategy (1.80). Although the portfolio with the merger arbitrage allocation has the lowest value of maximum drawdown (5.60), the relevant measure of downside risk is the Sortino ratio. As a result, the portfolio with the equity market-neutral allocation is the most suitable portfolio given the considerations specified by the IC.

B is incorrect because the portfolio with an allocation to the systematic futures hedge fund strategy, while meeting the variance requirement, has a lower Sortino ratio (1.68) than the portfolio with an allocation to the equity market-neutral hedge fund strategy. As a result, the portfolio with the equity market-neutral allocation is the most suitable portfolio given the considerations specified by the IC.

18. C is correct. Global macro investing may introduce natural benefits of asset class and investment approach diversification, but they come with naturally higher volatility in the return profiles typically delivered. The exposures selected in any global macro strategy may not react to the global risks as expected because of either unforeseen contrary factors or global risks that simply do not materialize; thus, macro managers tend to produce somewhat lumpier and more uneven return streams than other hedge fund strategies.

A is incorrect because relative value hedge fund strategies tend to use significant leverage that can be dangerous to limited partner investors, especially during periods of market stress. During normal market conditions, successful relative value strategies can earn credit, liquidity, or volatility premiums over time. However, in crisis periods when excessive leverage, deteriorating credit quality, illiquidity, and volatility spikes come to fruition, relative value strategies can result in losses.

B is incorrect because long/short equity strategies tend to be exposed to some natural equity market beta risk but have less beta exposure than simple long-only beta allocations. Given that equity markets tend to rise over the long run, most long/short equity managers typically hold net long equity positions with some managers maintaining their short positions as a hedge against unexpected market downturns.

19. C is correct. Xu states that she prefers opportunistic hedge fund strategies that use high leverage, have high liquidity, and exhibit right-tail skewness. The two most common opportunistic hedge fund strategies are global macro and managed futures. Both global macro and managed futures are highly liquid. Further, returns of managed futures strategies typically exhibit positive right-tail skewness in periods of market stress, whereas global macro strategies have delivered

similar diversification in such stress periods but with more heterogeneous outcomes. Global macro and managed futures strategies can also use high leverage, either through the use of futures contracts, in which high leverage is embedded, or through the active use of options, which adds natural elements of leverage and positive convexity.

A and B are incorrect because both global macro and managed futures strategies can offer the three characteristics that Xu seeks in an opportunistic hedge fund strategy.

20 B is correct. Xu bought 22,500 shares of Taurus at €20 per share for a total cost of €450,000 and sold short 15,000 shares of Aqua at €45 per share for a total cost of €675,000. Given the offer ratio of two shares of Aqua for three shares of Taurus, the 22,500 shares of Taurus are economically equivalent to 15,000 shares of Aqua. Thus, assuming the deal closes, the payoff to Xu's trade is €675,000 − €450,000 = €225,000.

A is incorrect because −€187,500 is the payoff if the merger fails and both companies' share prices revert back to their pre-merger prices. Xu bought 22,500 shares of Taurus at €20 per share for a total cost of €450,000 and sold short 15,000 shares of Aqua at €45 per share for a total cost of €675,000. If the merger fails and the share prices revert back to pre-announcement levels, Xu will have to sell 22,500 shares of Taurus at €15 per share for proceeds of €337,500, resulting in a loss on the Taurus stock of −€112,500 (€337,500 − €450,000). Xu will also have to close the short position by purchasing 15,000 shares of Aqua at €50 per share for a total cost of €750,000. This will result in a loss on Aqua of −€75,000 (€675,000 − €750,000). The total loss is −€112,500 + −€75,000 = −€187,500.

C is incorrect because the initial pre-merger prices are used to compute the payoff: 22,500 shares of Taurus are bought for €15 per share for a total of €337,500, and 15,000 shares of Aqua are sold short at €50 per share for a total of €750,000. The payoff is €750,000 − €337,500 = €412,500.

21 C is correct. Xu's decision to short ZMD and take a long position in Tarreras with equal beta-weighted exposure is an example of a pairs trade or an equity-market-neutral strategy. Xu is neutralizing market risk by constructing a strategy where the expected portfolio beta is zero. Since her strategy does not take beta risk and attempts to neutralize many other factor risks, Xu must apply leverage to the long and short positions to achieve a meaningful expected return from the stock selection.

A is incorrect because in a short-biased hedge fund strategy, the manager aims to sell expensively priced equities but may balance the short exposure with some modest long exposure. Xu, however, has entered into an equity-market-neutral pairs trade that takes opposite long and short positions in an attempt to eliminate market exposure. Her positions do not have a short bias.

B is incorrect because long/short equity managers buy equities of companies they expect will rise and sell short equities of companies they believe will fall in value. When long and short positions are placed together into a portfolio, the market exposure is the net of the beta-adjusted long and short exposures; however, the target beta is typically not zero. Xu is neutralizing market risk by constructing a strategy where the expected portfolio beta is zero.

22 A is correct. The classic convertible bond arbitrage strategy is to buy the relatively undervalued convertible bond and take a short position in the relatively overvalued underlying stock. If the convertible bond's current price is near the conversion value, then the combination of a long convertible and short equity delta exposure will create a situation where for small changes in the share price and ignoring dividends and borrowing costs, the profit/loss will be the same.

The current conversion price of the AVC convertible bond is €1,000 × (115/100)/50 = €23, and the current AVC share price is €28. Thus, by purchasing the convertible bond, selling short the shares, exercising the conversion option, and selling the shares at the current market price, a profit of €5 can be locked in regardless of changes in the share price. The following table demonstrates this result by showing the same trade profit of €5 for three different stock prices:

	Profit on:		Total Profit
AVC New Share Price	Long Stock via Convertible Bond at $23/Sh.	Short Stock at $28/Sh.	
€26	€3	€2	€5
€28	€5	€0	€5
€34	€11	–€6	€5

where

Long stock via convertible bond profit = New share price − Current conversion price

Short stock profit = Current share price − New share price

Total profit = Long stock via convertible bond profit + Short stock profit

Thus, regardless of the share price, the total profit on the convertible arbitrage trade is €5.

B is incorrect because if the convertible bond's current price is near the conversion value, then the combination of a long convertible and short equity delta exposure will create a situation where the profit/loss will be the same (not higher if the share price decreases).

C is incorrect because if the convertible bond's current price is near the conversion value, then the combination of a long convertible and short equity delta exposure will create a situation where for small changes in equity price, the profit/loss will be the same (not higher if the share price increases).

23. B is correct. Hedge funds look for policies in which the ongoing premium payments to keep the policy active are relatively low, so Characteristic 2 is correct. Hedge funds also look for life settlements where the surrender value offered to the insured individual is also relatively low and the probability that the designated insured person is likely to die earlier than predicted by standard actuarial methods is relatively high.

A is incorrect because hedge funds look for policies in which the surrender value offered to the insured individual is relatively low (not high) in order to enhance return by purchasing at a lower price.

C is incorrect because hedge funds look for settlements in which the probability that the designated insured person is likely to die *earlier* than predicted by standard actuarial methods is relatively high. This means the hedge fund's cash outflows to pay the ongoing premium will be less than predicted, which will enhance return.

READING 20

Asset Allocation to Alternative Investments

by Adam Kobor, PhD, CFA, and Mark D. Guinney, CFA

Adam Kobor, PhD, CFA, is at New York University (USA). Mark D. Guinney, CFA (USA).

LEARNING OUTCOMES

Mastery	The candidate should be able to:
☐	a. explain the roles that alternative investments play in multi-asset portfolios;
☐	b. compare alternative investments and bonds as risk mitigators in relation to a long equity position;
☐	c. compare traditional and risk-based approaches to defining the investment opportunity set, including alternative investments;
☐	d. discuss investment considerations that are important in allocating to different types of alternative investments;
☐	e. discuss suitability considerations in allocating to alternative investments;
☐	f. discuss approaches to asset allocation to alternative investments;
☐	g. discuss the importance of liquidity planning in allocating to alternative investments;
☐	h. discuss considerations in monitoring alternative investment programs.

1. INTRODUCTION AND THE ROLE OF ALTERNATIVE INVESTMENTS IN A MULTI-ASSET PORTFOLIO

a explain the roles that alternative investments play in multi-asset portfolios;

Asset allocation is a critical decision in the investment process. The mathematical and analytical processes inherent in contemporary asset allocation techniques are complicated by the idiosyncrasies of alternative investments. Approaches to incorporating alternative assets into the strategic asset allocation have developed rapidly as allocations to assets other than stocks and bonds have accelerated in the aftermath of the 2008 Global Financial Crisis. The term "alternative" understates the prominence of alternative investment allocations in many investment programs, because institutional and private clients have been increasingly turning to these investments not just to supplement traditional long-only stocks and bonds but also sometimes to replace them altogether. For example, the Yale Endowment and the Canada Pension Plan Investment Board both have close to 50% of their assets allocated to alternatives.[1] Although these two funds are admittedly outliers, between 2008 and 2017 most of the pension funds around the world substantially expanded their allocations to alternative asset classes. On average, pension funds in developed markets increased their allocation from 7.2% to 11.8% of assets under management (AUM) in 2017, a 63% increase.[2]

"Alternative" investment has no universally accepted definition. For the purposes of this reading, alternative investments include private equity, hedge funds, real assets (including energy and commodity investments), commercial real estate, and private credit.

The reading begins with a discussion of the role alternative assets play in a multi-asset portfolio and explores how alternatives may serve to mitigate long-only equity risk, a role traditionally held by bonds. We then consider different ways investors may define the opportunity set—through the traditional asset class lens or, more recently, using a risk- or factor-based lens. An allocation to alternatives is not for all investors, so the reading describes issues that should be addressed when considering an allocation to alternatives. We then discuss approaches to asset allocation when incorporating alternatives in the opportunity set and the need for liquidity planning in private investment alternatives. Finally, the reading discusses the unique monitoring requirements for an alternatives portfolio.

1.1 The Role of Alternative Investments in a Multi-Asset Portfolio

Allocations to alternatives are playing an increasing role in investor portfolios largely driven by the belief that these investments increase the risk-adjusted return expectations for their programs. Some allocations are driven by expectations of higher returns, while others are driven by the expected diversification (risk-reduction) benefits. In the aggregate, the portfolio's *risk-adjusted* return is expected to improve. Exhibit 1 provides a framework for how the common alternative strategies are generally perceived to affect the risk/return profile of a "typical" 60/40 portfolio of public stocks and bonds.

---

1 Boston Consulting Group (BCG), "The Rise of Alternative Assets and Long-Term Investing (March 2017).
2 See Ivashina and Lerner 2018.

Introduction and The Role of Alternative Investments in a Multi-Asset Portfolio

Exhibit 1 Alternative Investments in the Risk/Reward Continuum

Although we present a simplified view, real assets are generally believed to mitigate the risks to the portfolio arising from unexpected inflation. At the other end of the spectrum, venture capital investments (private equity) are expected to provide a sufficient return premium over public equities to compensate for their illiquidity risk and heightened operational complexity. Hedge funds, the least homogenous of strategies, span the spectrum from "risk reducing" or diversifying (many arbitrage strategies) to "return enhancing" (e.g., an activist fund that takes significant positions in public companies with the goal of improving performance through management changes, capital allocation policies, and/or company strategy).

Risk reduction can mean different things to different investors. Institutions may choose to add non-correlated strategies to their portfolios to reduce the volatility of the overall investment program. Private clients are frequently concerned with reducing only downside volatility—the "left tail" risk associated with significant public equity market drawdowns. An insurance pool whose liabilities are sensitive to inflation might benefit from real assets that could reduce its asset–liability mismatch. Exhibit 2 provides some guidance as to how an allocator might view alternative assets vis-à-vis traditional asset classes.

Exhibit 2 Illustrative Capital Market Assumptions

	Traditional Assets				Alternative Assets					
	Public Equities	Cash	Govt Bonds	Broad Fixed Income	Private Credit	Hedge Funds	Commodities	Public Real Estate	Private Real Estate	Private Equity
Expected Return (Geometric Average)	6.5%	2.0%	2.3%	2.8%	6.5%	5.0%	4.5%	6.0%	5.5%	8.5%
Volatility	17.0%	1.1%	4.9%	3.4%	10.0%	8.1%	25.2%	20.4%	13.8%	15.7%
Correlation with Equities	1.00	−0.12	−0.60	−0.41	0.70	0.83	0.21	0.60	0.37	0.81
Equity Beta	1.00	−0.01	−0.17	−0.08	0.40	0.40	0.31	0.72	0.30	0.74

Source: Authors' own data.

In the context of asset allocation, investors may categorize an asset class based on the role it is expected to play in the overall portfolio. The roles and their relative importance will vary among investors, but it is common to identify the following functional roles:

- *Capital growth*: This role may be a top priority for portfolios with a long-term time horizon and relatively high-return target. Usually, public and private equity investments would be the most obvious choices for this role.
- *Income generation*: Certain asset classes, like fixed income or real estate, are capable of generating reasonably steady cash flow stream for investors.
- *Risk diversification*: In the case of an equity-oriented portfolio, investors may seek assets that diversify the dominant equity risk. Real assets and several hedge fund strategies may fit here. Similarly, fixed-income investors may be interested in diversifying pure yield curve risk via private credit.
- *Safety*: Certain asset classes may play the role of safe haven when most of the risky asset classes suffer. Government bonds or gold may potentially play such roles in a well-diversified portfolio.

Exhibit 3 illustrates how each of the alternative assets is generally perceived to fulfill these functional roles.

Exhibit 3 The Role of Asset Classes in a Multi-Asset Portfolio

Asset Class		Capital Growth	Income	Diversifying Public Equities	Safety
Fixed Income and Credit	Governments		M	H	H
	Inflation-Linked		M	H	H/M
	Inv.-Grade Credit		M	H	M
	High-Yield Credit		H	M	
	Private Credit		H	M	
Equities	Public Equity	H	M		
	Private Equity	H	M	M	
Real Estate	Public Real Estate	M	H	M	
	Private Real Estate	M	H	M	
Real Assets	Public Real Assets (Energy, Metal, etc.)			H	
	Private Real Assets (Timber, etc.)	H	H	H	
Hedge Funds	Absolute Return		M	H	
	Equity Long/Short			M	

Notes: H = high/strong potential to fulfill the indicated role; M = moderate potential to fulfill the indicated role.

Introduction and The Role of Alternative Investments in a Multi-Asset Portfolio

Exhibit 4 illustrates the potential contributions the various alternative strategies might make to a portfolio dominated by equity risk. Note that the graph illustrates the *average* investment characteristics of each asset class over some extended period of time. Some assets—gold, for example—may not consistently exhibit attractive *aggregate* characteristics compared to other strategies but may serve the portfolio well during many major market shocks.

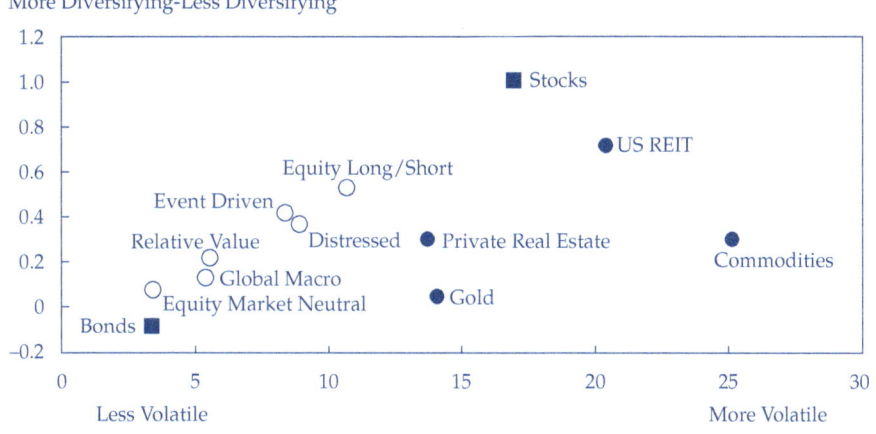

Exhibit 4 Diversification Potential of Various Alternative Asset Classes

Sources: Bloomberg and authors' own data and calculations.

1.1.1 *The Role of Private Equity in a Multi-Asset Portfolio*

Private equity investments are generally viewed as a return enhancer in a portfolio of traditional assets. The expectation for a return premium over public equities stems from the illiquidity risk that comes with most forms of private equity investment. Because of the strong link between the fundamentals of private and public companies, there are limited diversification benefits when added to a portfolio that otherwise contains significant public equity exposure. Private equity volatility is not directly observable because holdings are not publicly traded. Assets tend to be valued at the lower of cost or the value at which the company raises additional capital or when ownership changes hands (e.g., through an initial public offering or a sale to a strategic buyer or to another private equity sponsor). Consequently, private equity indexes do not provide a true picture of the strategy's risk. For asset allocation exercises, volatility is often estimated using a public equity proxy with an adjustment to better represent the nature of the private equity program. For example, a proxy for early stage venture capital might be microcap technology companies. A proxy for buyout funds might start with the volatility of a geographically relevant large-cap equity index (e.g., S&P 500, Nikkei), which is then adjusted for relative financial leverage.

1.1.2 *The Role of Hedge Funds in a Multi-Asset Portfolio*

As illustrated in Exhibit 1, hedge funds span the spectrum from being risk reducers to return enhancers. Generally speaking, long/short equity strategies are believed to deliver equity-like returns with less than full exposure to the equity premium but with an additional source of return that might come from the manager's shorting of individual stocks. Short-biased equity strategies are expected to lower a portfolio's overall equity beta while producing some measure of alpha. Arbitrage and event-driven strategies, executed properly, look to exploit small inefficiencies in the public markets while exhibiting low to no correlation with traditional asset classes. However, most hedge fund arbitrage strategies involve some degree of "short volatility" risk. Because of this "short volatility" risk, the volatility in an arbitrage strategy is non-symmetrical; the aggregate volatility may look muted if the period from which the data are drawn does not include a market stress period. "Opportunistic" strategies (e.g., global macro and managed futures), although very volatile as stand-alone strategies, provide exposures not otherwise readily accessible in traditional stock and bond strategies.

1.1.3 The Role of Real Assets in a Multi-Asset Portfolio

This category includes timber, commodities, farmland, energy, and infrastructure assets. The common thread for these investments is that the underlying investment is a physical asset with a relatively high degree of correlation with inflation broadly or with a sub-component of inflation, such as oil (energy funds), agricultural products (farmland), or pulp and wood products (timber).

Timber investments provide both growth and inflation-hedging properties in a multi-asset portfolio. Growth is provided through the biological growth of the tree itself as well as through the appreciation in the underlying land value. Timber's inflation-hedging characteristics are derived from the unique nature in which the value of the asset is realized: If the market for timber products is weak, the owner of the asset can leave it "on the stump" waiting for prices to rise. While waiting, the volume of the asset increases—the tree continues to grow—and there is ultimately more of the asset to sell when prices recover. At the same time, the volatility of the timber asset rises; the market for more mature timber is more volatile, and the potential loss from pests and natural disasters rises.

Commodities investments (i.e., tradable commodities) fall into the following four categories:

- Metals (gold, silver, platinum, copper)
- Energy (crude oil, natural gas, heating oil, gasoline)
- Livestock and Meat (hogs, pork bellies, live cattle)
- Agricultural (corn, soybeans, wheat, rice, cocoa, coffee, cotton, sugar)

Although it is possible to own the commodity asset directly (e.g., corn, wheat, barrel of oil), most investors will invest in commodity derivatives (i.e., futures contracts) whose price is directly related to the price of the physical commodity. Investors generally own commodities as a hedge against a core constituent of inflation measures as well as a differentiated source of alpha. Gold and other precious metals are frequently owned directly because they are thought to be a good store of value in the face of a depreciating currency. Storage and insurance costs come with owning commodities directly.

Farmland investing involves two primary approaches. The higher return/risk strategy involves owning the farmland while providing the farmer a salary for tending and selling the crops. The investor retains the commodity risk and the execution risk. This approach requires a long time horizon and has high sensitivity to natural disasters and regulatory risk, such as trade disputes. In the other main approach, the investor owns the farmland but leases the property to the farmer. The farmer retains the risk for execution and commodity prices. If an investor pursues this second strategy, farmland is more like core commercial real estate investing than a real asset (commodity) strategy.

Energy investments consist of strategies that focus on the exploration, development, transportation, and delivery of energy (primarily oil and natural gas-based energy sources but also increasingly wind, hydroelectric, and solar) as well as all the ancillary services that facilitate energy production. Investors usually do not own the land that holds the minerals. Most energy investments are executed through call-down, private equity-style funds and are usually long-dated, illiquid holdings. Energy assets are generally considered real assets because the investor owns the mineral rights to certain commodities (e.g., natural gas, oil, methane) that can be correlated with certain inflationary factors. Master limited partnerships (MLPs) are another frequently used vehicle for energy investments. MLPs generally construct and own the pipelines that carry oil or natural gas from the wellhead to the storage facility. MLPs rarely take ownership of the energy assets. The companies charge a fee based on the volume of oil/natural gas they transport. This fee is often pegged to the Producer Price Index.

Infrastructure is a strategy that typically involves the construction and maintenance of public-use projects, such as building bridges, toll roads, or airports. Because of the illiquid nature of these assets, the holding period associated with these funds can be even longer than the typical illiquid strategy, with some lasting 20 years or longer. These assets tend to generate stable or modestly growing income, and the asset itself often requires minimal upkeep or capital expenditures once built. The revenue generated by the assets tends to have high correlation with overall inflation, though it is often subject to regulatory risks because governmental agencies may be involved in price setting with certain jurisdictions and assets.

1.1.4 The Role of Commercial Real Estate in a Multi-Asset Portfolio

Real estate investing involves the development, acquisition, management, and disposition of commercial properties, including retail, office, industrial, housing (including apartments), and hotels. Strategies range from *core*, the ownership of fully occupied properties and collecting rents, to *opportunistic*, ground-up property development (land acquisition, construction, and sale) and/or the purchase of distressed assets with the intent to rehabilitate them.

Real estate investments are believed to provide protection against unanticipated increases in inflation. Two fundamental attributes of real estate investment contribute to this inflation protection. Well-positioned properties frequently have the ability to increase rents in response to inflationary pressures, and the value of the physical buildings may increase with inflation (properties are often valued as a function of replacement cost). In this way, real estate contributes both income and capital gain potential to a portfolio. Building a diversified private commercial real estate program can be challenging for all but the largest and most sophisticated allocators. The public real estate market is a fraction of the size of the private real estate market, but it may be easier and cheaper to build a diversified real estate investment program in some geographies (e.g., United States, Europe) via the public markets. However, private real estate can offer exposures that are difficult if not impossible to achieve through publicly-traded real estate securities. Investing directly (or in a private fund) offers customization by geography, property type, and strategy (e.g., distressed, core, development).

1.1.5 The Role of Private Credit in a Multi-Asset Portfolio

Private credit includes distressed investment and direct lending. Although both strategies involve the ownership of fixed-income assets, their roles in an investment program are quite different. Direct-lending assets are income-producing, and the asset owner assumes any default or recovery risks. Direct-lending assets generally behave like their public market counterparts with similar credit profiles (i.e., high-quality, direct-lending assets behave like investment-grade bonds, and low-quality, direct-lending assets behave like high-yield bonds). Distressed debt assets have a more equity-like profile. The expected return is derived from the value of a company's assets relative to its debt. Illiquidity risks are high with both strategies. Direct-lending assets have no secondary market.

Direct-lending funds provide capital to individuals and small businesses that generally cannot access more traditional lending channels. Some loans are unsecured while others might be backed by an asset, such as a house or car. Direct lending is one of the least liquid debt strategies because there is typically no secondary market for these instruments. Investors in direct-lending strategies gain access to a high-yielding but riskier segment of the debt market that is not available via the traditional public markets.

Distressed funds typically purchase the securities of an entity that is under stress and where the stress is relieved through legal restructuring or bankruptcy. The investment can take the form of debt or equity, and in many strategies, the manager often takes an active role throughout the restructuring or bankruptcy. Because many investors are precluded from owning companies or entities that are in bankruptcy or default, managers of distressed funds are often able to purchase assets (usually the debt) at a significant discount. Experience with the bankruptcy process frequently distinguishes these managers from others. Although the asset is usually a bond, distressed investments typically have low sensitivity to traditional bond risks (i.e., interest rate changes or changes in spreads) because the idiosyncratic risk of the company itself dominates all other risks.

2 DIVERSIFYING EQUITY RISK

b compare alternative investments and bonds as risk mitigators in relation to a long equity position;

In this section, we examine the claim that alternative assets may be better risk mitigators than government bonds. To address this question, we must agree on *which* risks alternatives are said to mitigate and on *what* time horizon is relevant. If your investment horizon is short term, volatility may be the most important risk measure. If you are a long-term investor, not achieving the long-horizon return objective may be the most relevant concern.

2.1 Volatility Reduction over the Short Time Horizon

Let's look first at the short horizon investor and consider how alternative asset classes compare to bonds as a volatility reducer in an equity-dominated portfolio. Advocates of alternative investments as risk reducers sometimes argue that alternative investments' volatilities calculated based on reported returns are significantly lower than the volatility of public equities. An immediate technical challenge is that reported returns of many alternative asset classes need an adjustment called **unsmoothing** for proper risk estimation. (Various approaches have been developed to unsmooth a return series that demonstrates serial correlation. The specifics of those approaches are beyond the scope of this reading.) In the case of private investments, reported returns are calculated from appraisal-based valuations that may result in volatility and correlation estimates that are too low. (The underlying assumptions in most appraisal models tend to lead to gradual and incremental changes in appraised value that may not accurately capture the asset's true price realized in an actual transaction. The low volatility of the return stream may also dampen the reported correlation between the appraisal-based asset and the more volatile market-based asset.) Other factors may also contribute to underestimated risk across alternatives. For example, **survivorship bias** and **back-fill bias** (reporting returns to a database only after they are known to be good returns) in hedge fund databases can potentially lead to an understatement of downside risk. Additionally, a hedge fund "index" includes many managers whose returns exhibit low correlation; in the same way that combining stocks and bonds in a portfolio can be expected to lower overall portfolio volatility, so too does combining several hedge funds into an "index."

As an example, we build a hypothetical, equally-weighted index of long/short equity hedge funds with volatilities ranging from 6% to 11%. As shown in Exhibit 5, given the less-than-perfect correlation among the constituents of our index, the index volatility is only 4.9%:

Exhibit 5 Volatility Is Less Than the Sum of Its Parts

	Fund 1	Fund 2	Fund 3	Fund 4	Fund 5	Combined
Volatility	10.9%	6.5%	8.5%	9.7%	8.1%	**4.9%**
Correlation						
Fund 1		−0.02	0.14	0.00	0.15	
Fund 2			0.27	0.39	0.29	
Fund 3				0.25	−0.03	
Fund 4					0.14	

Exhibit 6 shows the correlations of fixed-income and alternative asset classes to public equities based on observed market data over 1997–2017. We also show each asset class's estimated equity beta. To estimate correlations and betas, we used unsmoothed return data for alternative asset classes. We discuss unsmoothing of returns in more detail in a later section.

Exhibit 6 Fixed-Income's and Alternative's Equity Beta and Correlation with Equities

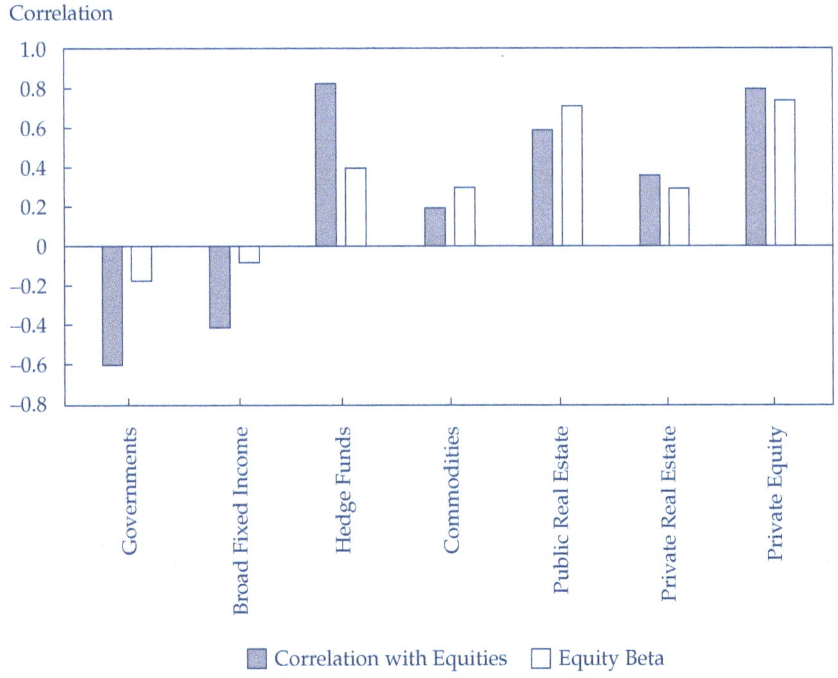

Sources: Bloomberg and authors' own data and calculations.

Most of the alternative investment categories had positive, but less than perfect, correlation with equities. Although certain alternatives (e.g., commodities, particularly gold) may rally during a public equity market downturn, other alternative investments—like hedge funds, private credit, or private equities—also experience drawdowns at the same time the equity market falls. Hedge funds and private equities have a correlation co-efficient with equities over +0.8, and this indicates a fairly strong positive relationship between public equities and these alternative investments.

Government bonds, however, have a −0.6 estimated correlation with equities, which indicates a negative relationship of moderate strength. This is consistent with the tendency for government bonds to serve as a risk haven during "risk-off" or "flight to quality" episodes.

Although correlation and beta have the same sign and are statistically interrelated, we have to remember that they quantify two different things. The correlation coefficient quantifies the strength of a linear relationship between two variables, thus playing a crucial role in portfolio diversification: The lower the correlation, the stronger the asset's diversification power. Beta, however, measures the response of an asset to a unit change in a reference index; for example, equity beta measures how various assets would respond to a 1% rise of public equities. Hedge funds' beta is estimated at around 0.4; thus, we would expect a 0.4% return (excluding manager alpha) from hedge funds if equities rose by 1%. Hedge funds' relatively low beta (0.4) and high correlation (+0.8) means that hedge funds' rise or fall is milder than those of public equities in magnitude, but this directional relationship is fairly strong in a statistical sense. Commodities also have an equity beta of similar positive magnitude (0.3), but their correlation with equities is much weaker (+0.2); so, we can expect that a much bigger portion of commodity price changes would be driven by factors unrelated to the equity markets.

In Exhibit 7, we compare the total return volatility of public equities (black bar) with volatilities of portfolios comprised of 70% equity and 30% other asset classes. Using 20 years of data, the volatility of public equities is estimated at approximately 17%. A portfolio allocated 70% to equity and 30% to cash would imply a portfolio volatility of 11.9% (70% × 17%). Portfolios of 70% equities and 30% any of the alternative asset classes also reduces portfolio volatility relative to an all-equity portfolio, but the lowest volatility of 11.1% could be achieved by combining equities with government bonds because of the negative correlation between these two asset classes.

Diversifying Equity Risk

Exhibit 7 Volatility of Portfolios Comprised of 70% Equities and 30% Other Asset Class

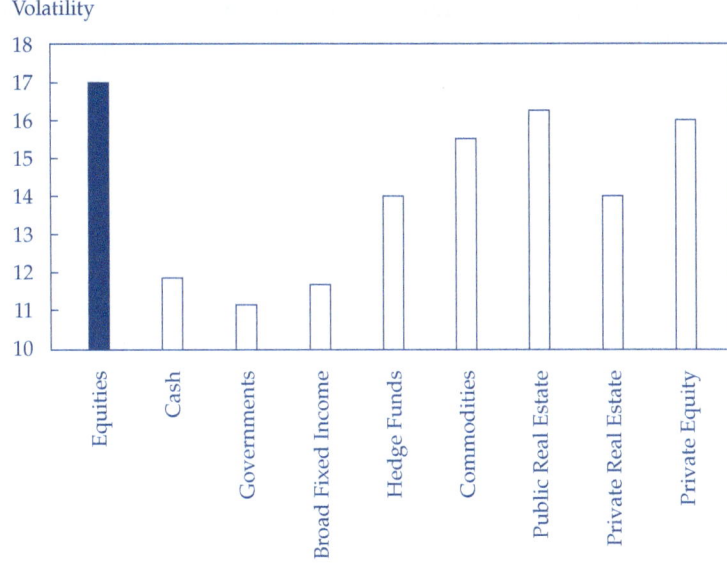

Sources: Bloomberg and authors' own data and calculations.

Bear in mind, however, that this analysis is based on 20 years of returns ending in 2017, a period that was characterized by a persistent negative equity–bond correlation. Because there was limited inflation in developed markets over this period, economic growth prospects were the dominant influence on asset prices. Positive growth surprises are good for equities (better earnings outlook) and negative for bonds (potential central bank rate increases). If inflation becomes a threat, bonds' risk mitigation power could erode. Exhibit 8 looks at the US equity–bond correlation since the 1950s. As the chart suggests, the correlation between US equities and government bonds was, in fact, positive in the 1970s through the 1990s when inflation was also more elevated.

Exhibit 8 Long-Term Historical Equity–Bond Correlation and Inflation

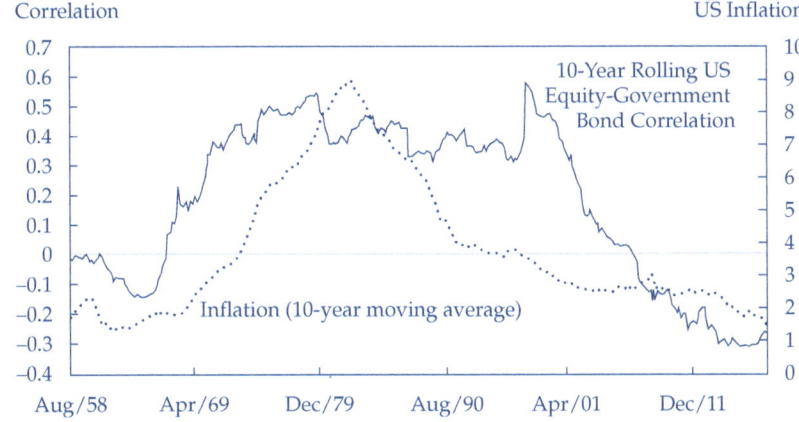

Sources: Bloomberg and the authors' own data and calculations.

2.2 Risk of Not Meeting the Investment Goals over the Long Time Horizon

Volatility is not always the most relevant risk measure. An endowment portfolio is often focused on generating a total return equal to at least the spending rate, say 5%, plus inflation to preserve real value of capital over a long time horizon. When bond yields are very low, the likelihood of meeting the investment objective would be reduced given a heavy allocation to bonds, simply because the portfolio's value would likely grow more slowly than the rate implied by the spending rate and inflation. Exhibit 9 illustrates this point: We show the probability of achieving a 5% real (7.1% nominal[3]) return over various horizons up to 10-years for three 70% equity/30% other asset class portfolios. We used quarterly rebalancing. Although allocating the 30% "other" to government bonds would lead to the greatest reduction in portfolio volatility, government bonds also have lower expected return compared to hedge funds and private equity (see Exhibit 2).

Exhibit 9 The Probability of Achieving Investment Objectives over the Longer Time Horizon

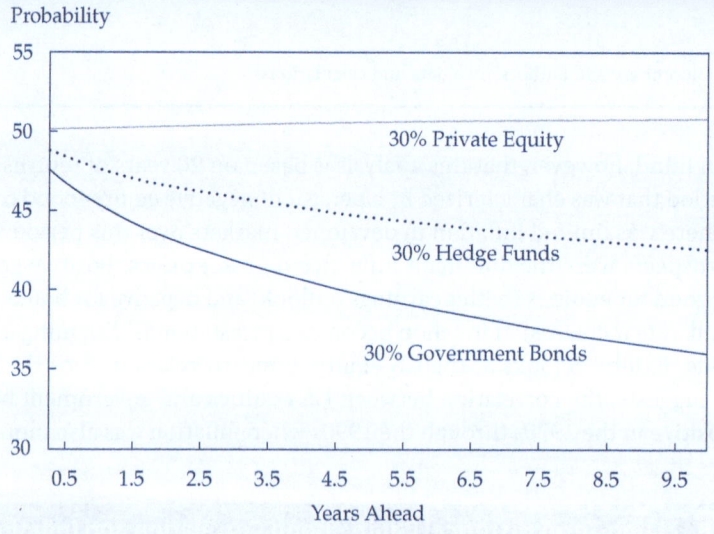

Note: Portfolios comprised of 70% equities and 30% other asset classes.
Source: Authors' calculations.

The 70% public equities/30% government bond portfolio has an expected return of 5.7%[4], below the nominal return target of 7.1%. The 70% public equities/30% private equities portfolio has an expected geometric return of 7.2%, slightly over the return target. Both portfolios' expected returns are 50th percentile returns; there is a 50% probability that this is the return that would be realized over time. Thus, the 70% public equities/30% private equities portfolio, with a nominal expected return of 7.2%, has slightly better than a 50% probability of meeting the 7.1% nominal return target. The 70% public equities/30% government bond portfolio, with an expected return less than the nominal return target, therefore has less than a 50% probability of

---

[3] By using the Fisher equation to combine the 5% real return and 2% inflation: $(1 + 5\%) * (1 + 2\%) - 1 = 7.1\%$.
[4] Note that geometric expected return is approximated as the expected arithmetic return minus half of the investment's variance. Thus, portfolio expected geometric return is not simply the weighted average of the asset classes' expected geometric returns because portfolio variance benefits from diversification.

meeting the required return. Why does the 70% public equities/30% private equities portfolio maintain its 50%+ probability of meeting the return target over time while the probability that the 70% public equities/30% government bond portfolio meets the return target declines over time? As the time horizon lengthens, return accumulation (compounding) becomes more and more important. In a simplified way, return accumulates proportionally with time, whereas volatility scales with the square root of time. Thus, as we lengthen the time horizon, the gap between the cumulative return target and the expected return accumulation widens faster than the range of possible portfolio return outcomes. As a result, the likelihood of a low-returning portfolio catching up to the target return declines over time.

To summarize, bonds have been a more effective volatility mitigator than alternatives over shorter time horizons, but over long horizons, a heavy allocation to bonds would reduce the probability of achieving the investment goal. It is important to emphasize that volatility and the probability of achieving the target return are two very different dimensions of risk. Volatility addresses interim fluctuations in portfolio return, whereas achieving a return target takes on increasing importance as we expand the time horizon over multiple years. Both risks are important, especially for a program that is distributing 7% of assets per year as in this example. Although the 30% allocation to private equity increases the chance of meeting the expected return, a severe and sustained short-term drawdown in the public equity markets could significantly handicap the fund's ability to achieve its long-term return objectives. This is why drawdowns (related to volatility) need to be considered and managed.

EXAMPLE 1

Mitigating Equity Risk by Allocating to Hedge Funds or Bonds

The investment committee of a major foundation is concerned about high equity valuations and would like to increase the allocation either to hedge funds or to high-grade, fixed-income assets to diversify equity risk. As the risk manager of this foundation:

1. Discuss the justifications and the limitations of using bonds to mitigate equity risk.
2. Discuss the justifications and the limitations of using hedge funds to mitigate equity risk.

Solution to 1:

- Supporting argument: Bonds have exhibited negative correlation and beta to equities in a low inflation environment, so as long as inflation stays at or below average historical levels, this negative equity–bond correlation should lead to the highest reduction in portfolio volatility.
- Limitations: The negative stock/bond correlation may be temporary, and amid high inflation the stock/bond correlation could turn positive. Furthermore, if bonds' expected return is low, a heavy allocation to bonds may reduce the probability of achieving the foundation's long-term return objectives.

> **Solution to 2:**
>
> - Supporting argument: With an equity beta of around 0.4 (see Exhibit 2), hedge funds would reduce an equity-dominated portfolio's overall beta. With higher expected returns than bonds, an allocation to hedge funds would make achieving the long-term return target more feasible.
> - Limitations: Although a well-constructed hedge fund portfolio may reduce portfolio volatility and beta, hedge funds are often highly actively managed, levered investment strategies, and individual hedge funds may suffer significant and permanent losses during turbulent times.

3. TRADITIONAL APPROACHES TO ASSET CLASSIFICATION

c compare traditional and risk-based approaches to defining the investment opportunity set, including alternative investments;

In this section, we consider how traditional approaches to asset allocation can be adapted to include alternative investments and how investors can apply risk-based approaches to incorporate alternatives in their asset allocation. This reading extends the asset allocation framework introduced in earlier readings on asset allocation. Although the ultimate goal of meeting the investment objectives subject to the relevant constraints remains the same, investors often face several analytical and operational challenges when introducing alternative asset classes.

3.1 Traditional Approaches to Asset Classification

When defining asset classes for the traditional approaches to asset allocation, investors may group and classify alternative assets along several dimensions. Two common approaches (in addition to the growth–income–diversification–safety roles described earlier) are with respect to the liquidity of the asset class and with respect to asset behavior under various economic conditions.

3.1.1 A Liquidity-Based Approach to Defining the Opportunity Set

Certain alternative investments, like REITs or commodity futures, are highly liquid and can be easily traded in public markets. Private investments, however, are highly illiquid and usually require long-term commitments (more than 10 years) from the investors. Of course, there are differences among various private asset classes in this respect as well: Private equity investments may require longer than a 10-year commitment, while the term of a private credit fund can be shorter, say 5 to 8 years. Although public equity and private equity may be similar asset classes from the fundamental economic point of view, they differ significantly in their liquidity characteristics.

The long investment horizon and the lack of liquidity in many of the alternative asset classes make it difficult to accurately characterize their risk characteristics for purposes of the asset allocation exercise. One approach to dealing with this issue is to make the initial asset allocation decision using only the broad, liquid asset classes in which the underlying data that drive risk, return, and correlation assumptions are robust (e.g., stocks, bonds, and real estate). A second iteration of the asset allocation exercise would break the equity/fixed-income/real estate asset allocation further by using the asset groupings as shown in Exhibit 10, which illustrates a possible categorization of asset classes that incorporates their broad liquidity profile.

Exhibit 10 Major Asset Class Categories

	Equity & Equity-Like	Fixed Income & Fixed Income-Like	Real Estate
Marketable/Liquid	Public Equity Long/Short Equity Hedge Funds	Fixed Income Cash	Public Real Estate Commodities
Private/Illiquid	Private Equity	Private Credit	Private Real Estate Private Real Assets

3.1.2 An Approach Based on Expected Performance under Distinct Macroeconomic Regimes

Investors may also categorize asset classes based on how they are expected to behave under different macroeconomic environments, and investors may assign roles to them in a broad macroeconomic context:

- *Capital growth assets* would be expected to benefit from healthy economic growth. Public and private equities would belong to this category.
- *Inflation-hedging assets*—so-called "real assets" such as real estate, commodities, and natural resources but also inflation-linked bonds—would be expected to outperform other asset classes when inflation expectations rise or actual inflation exceeds expectations.
- *Deflation-hedging assets* (e.g., nominal government bonds) would be expected to outperform most of the other asset classes when the economy slows and inflation becomes very low or negative.

In Exhibit 11, we illustrate how investors may think about the expected performance of various asset classes in a broad macroeconomic context. Each asset class is positioned along the continuum to illustrate the macroeconomic environment in which we would expect it to generate strong performance. Such mapping is usually based on both historical experience and qualitative judgment. Considering the fundamental economic drivers of asset classes could help investors construct portfolios that are better diversified and more robust under various economic conditions and scenarios.

Exhibit 11 Asset Classes Grouped by the Macroeconomic Environment under Which They Would Be Expected to Generate Strong Performance

		Inflation Environment		
		Deflation	Moderate Inflation	High Inflation
Economic Environment	High Growth		Public Equity Private Equity High-Yield Bonds Private Credit	Real Estate Commodities
	Low Growth/ Recession	Government Bonds		Inflation-Linked Bonds Gold

Source: Authors' data.

Exhibit 12 illustrates the average quarterly total return of various asset classes and alternative strategies under stronger and weaker economic growth environments between 1997 and 2017, a period of low to moderate inflation in developed markets.

Exhibit 12 Historical Asset Class Performance under Stronger and Weaker Economic Growth Periods (1997–2017)

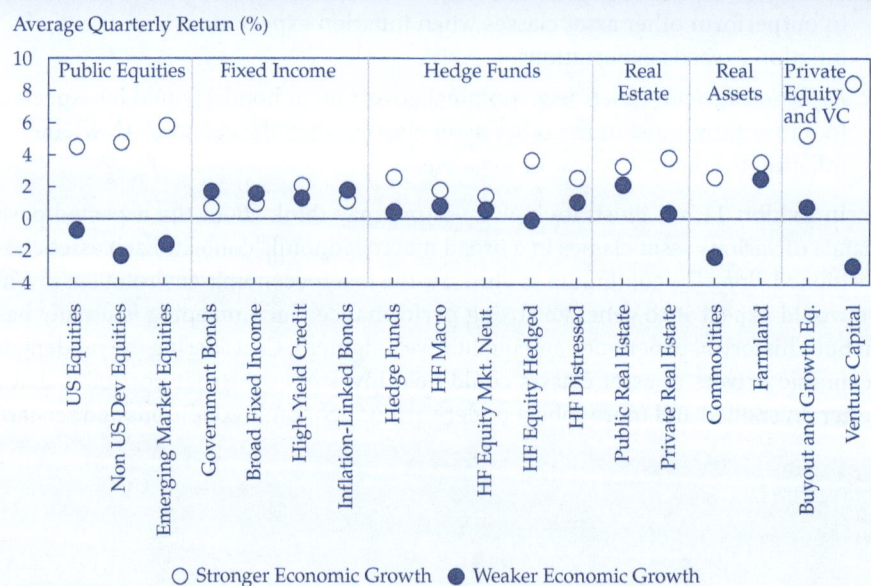

Notes: Strong and weak economic periods were determined using quarterly GDP data. Strong growth periods were those quarters when GDP growth exceeded the average GDP growth through the full historical sample.

Exhibit 12   (Continued)

Sources: The exhibit is based on the authors' calculations. Index data is based on the following. US Equities: Russell 3000; Non-US Developed Market Equities: MSCI EAFE USD Net unhedged; Emerging Market Equities: MSCI Emerging Markets Net USD unhedged; Governments: Bloomberg Barclays US Treasury Index; Broad Fixed Income: Bloomberg Barclays US Aggregate; High Yield: Bloomberg Barclays US Corporate High Yield; Inflation-Linked Bonds: Bloomberg Barclays US Government Inflation-Linked Bonds Index; Hedge Funds: HFRI; Public Real Estate: Dow Jones Equity REIT Index; Private Real Estate: NCREIF Property Index; Commodities: S&P GSCI Total Return Index; Farmland: NCREIF Farmland Index; Buyout and Growth Equities: Cambridge Associates US Private Equity Index; Venture Capital: Cambridge Associates US Venture Capital Index.

Public and private equities, hedge funds, and commodities posted strong returns amid strong economic growth conditions and weaker returns amid weaker economic conditions. Commodities exhibit a bigger disparity between returns in periods of stronger and weaker growth than does the hedge fund category.

Within fixed income, government bonds posted higher returns during periods of weaker economic growth—when investors likely reallocated from risky assets to safer assets. On the other hand, high-yield bonds (and potentially private credit, if we assume a behavior pattern similar to that of high-yield bonds) performed well during periods of stronger economic growth but posted lower returns during weaker economic periods, likely because of concerns about weakening credit quality.

Understanding how various asset classes behave under distinct macroeconomic regimes enables investors to tailor the asset allocation to align with their fundamental goals or to mitigate their fundamental risks. If the investment portfolio has a specific goal, such as hedging inflation risk, then it would be logical to build a portfolio that is dominated by asset classes that are expected to perform best amid rising inflation. Even if the portfolio's goal is to generate high return over the long run, combining "growth" asset classes with "inflation-hedging" or "deflation-hedging" asset classes could make the asset allocation more resilient to changing economic and market conditions. This approach can be extended to macroeconomic scenario analysis and stress testing when the analyst evaluates how various asset allocation options would perform under conditions of high or low economic growth and/or inflation, and it can identify which economic conditions would hurt the investment portfolio the most.

RISK-BASED APPROACHES TO ASSET CLASSIFICATION AND COMPARING RISK-BASED AND TRADITIONAL APPROACHES

4

c   compare traditional and risk-based approaches to defining the investment opportunity set, including alternative investments;

When we assign traditional and alternative asset classes to certain functional roles in the portfolio, or when we assess how different asset classes would perform under distinct macroeconomic regimes, we can also easily realize that many traditional and alternative asset classes share similar characteristics that can result in high correlations. We may put public equities in the same functional bucket as private equity, and we may expect elevated default rates from high-yield bonds and private credit during recessionary environments.

Exhibit 13 compares the betas of various traditional and alternative asset classes to global equities. The chart clearly shows that private equity and venture capital asset classes have global equity betas similar to public equites. On the other hand, betas of various hedge fund strategies differ significantly. Hedge fund returns, in aggregate, had a beta of 0.4. However, global macro or equity market-neutral strategies had betas as low as 0.1. The long/short "equity hedged" strategy's beta is estimated to be much higher, around 0.5, which is consistent with its long equity bias.

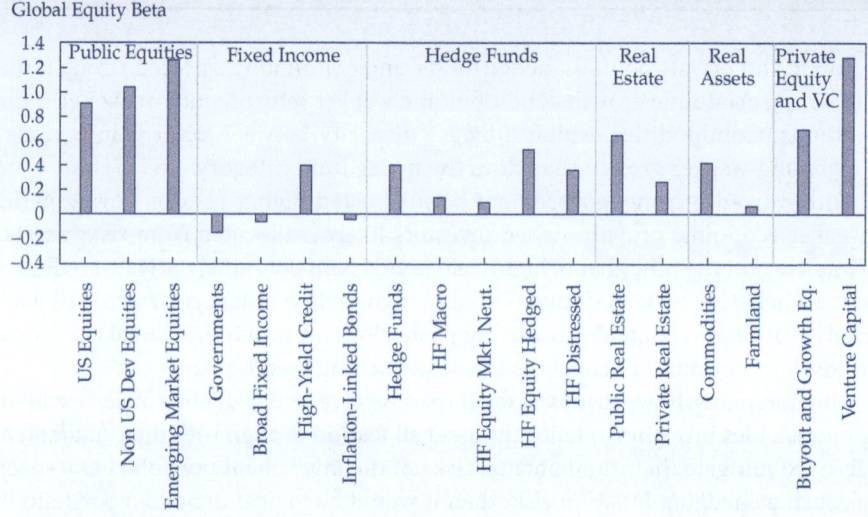

Exhibit 13 Global Equity Beta of Various Asset Classes, 1997–2017

Note: Betas were estimated as a regression slope of representative index returns relative to the global equity return stream over the time period 1997–2017.
Sources: Authors' calculations; index data sources are the same as those in Exhibit 12.

Many investors have begun to view asset allocation through a risk factor lens to capture these similarities. In this section, we extend the risk factor asset allocation framework introduced in earlier readings to alternative investments using the following risk factors:

- *Equity market return*: representative of the general direction of global equity markets, and investors may also refer to this as the best market proxy for "growth."
- *Size*: excess return of small-cap equities over large-cap equities.
- *Value*: excess return of value versus growth stocks (*negative* factor sensitivity = *growth* bias.
- *Liquidity*: the Pastor–Stambaugh liquidity factor[5]—a market-wide liquidity measure based on the excess returns of stocks with large sensitivity to changes in aggregate liquidity (less-liquid stocks) versus stocks with less sensitivity to changing liquidity (more-liquid stocks).
- *Duration*: sensitivity to 10-year government yield changes.
- *Inflation*: sensitivity to 10-year breakeven inflation changes obtained from the inflation-linked bond markets.

---

[5] For more details on Pastor–Stambaugh liquidity factors, see Naik et al. (2016).

- *Credit spread*: sensitivity to changes in high-yield spread.
- *Currency*: sensitivity to changes in the domestic currency versus a basket of foreign currencies.

This framework can easily be extended further to other risk factors, like momentum or volatility.

Exhibit 14 illustrates risk factor sensitivities of various traditional and alternative investment strategies using a construct as discussed by Naik, Devarajan, Nowobilski, Page, and Pedersen (2016). The parameters in the table are regression coefficients based on 20 years of historical data. Quarterly index returns representing each asset class were regressed on the risk factors listed previously. Note that for conventional reasons we changed the signs of the "nominal duration" and "credit spread" sensitivities: The 4.2 duration of broad fixed income, for example, means that this asset class would experience an approximate 4.2% decline in response to a 100 bps increase in the nominal interest rates.

Exhibit 14 Factor Sensitivity Estimates across Various Asset Classes

Asset Classes	Equity	Size	Value	Liquidity	Nominal Duration	Inflation	Credit Spread	Currency	R-squared
US Equities	1.0								1.00
Non-US Dev Equities	0.9							0.7	0.86
Emerging Mkt Equities	1.1	0.5						0.5	0.66
Government Bonds					4.8				0.96
Broad Fixed Income					4.2		0.6		0.89
High-Yield Credit					4.1		4.2		0.95
Inflation-Linked Bonds					6.6	7.0			0.82
Hedge Funds	0.3	0.1					0.6		0.74
HF Macro	0.2	0.2			1.9	3.1	−0.9	0.1	0.28
HF Equity Mkt. Neut.	0.1								0.14
HF Equity Hedged	0.5								0.72
HF Distressed	0.1	0.2					1.8		0.72
Commodities						18.0		0.8	0.36
Public Real Estate	0.9				4.6	0.9			0.38
Private Real Estate	0.2			0.1		2.4			0.20
Buyout & Growth Equities	0.6	0.2	−0.3	0.1					0.70
Venture Capital	0.8	0.6	−1.8	0.2					0.38

Note: Only statistically significant slopes are displayed in the exhibit. Sources are the same as those for Exhibit 12.

In a risk factor-based asset allocation framework, the factors represent the systematic risks embedded in the selected asset classes and investment strategies. The primary systematic risk factors would fully, or almost fully, explain the behavior of broad, passive traditional public asset classes. There should be a relatively larger portion of unexplained risk in the alternative asset classes. This arises from such issues as the appraisal-based valuation in real estate, the idiosyncratic risks in the portfolio companies of private equity funds, or the idiosyncratic risks in hedge funds resulting from active management. (This last one is logically intuitive if you subscribe to the belief that returns generated by hedge fund strategies should be primarily driven by *alpha* rather than systematic risk factors.)

The extension of the risk factor framework to alternative asset classes allows every asset class to be described using the same framework. Investors can therefore more clearly understand their sources of investment risk and identify the intended and unintended tilts and biases they have in the portfolio. Furthermore, a risk factor framework enables investors to more efficiently allocate capital and risk in a multi-dimensional framework (i.e., a framework that seeks to do more than simply achieve the highest return at a given level of volatility). If an investor, for example, would like to increase the portfolio's inflation risk-mitigating exposure, decomposing this specific risk factor from inflation-linked bonds, real estate, or commodity asset classes could help the investor to identify the asset classes and exposures that are most likely to facilitate that goal.

Risk factor-based approaches improve upon the traditional approaches in identifying the investment opportunity set but do have certain limitations. As mentioned earlier, a small set of systematic risk factors is insufficient to describe the historical return stream of alternative asset classes. Note that all non-zero-risk factor coefficients displayed in the table are statistically significant based on their *t*-statistics. Although our eight illustrative factors fit the total return history of traditional asset classes with *r*-squared statistics of 0.8–1.0, the *r*-squared ratios for alternative investments are lower, ranging between 0.3 and 0.7. Increasing the number of risk factors would certainly improve the goodness of fit, but too many factors could make the risk factor-based asset allocation framework difficult to handle and interpret. In addition, certain risk factor sensitivities can be quite volatile, making a "point in time" factor-based definition of an asset class a poor descriptor of the class's expected behavior. For example, the aggregate hedge fund inflation beta typically fluctuates in the range of 0.3 to 0.4, while the inflation beta of commodities fluctuates much more widely.[6]

EXAMPLE 2

Applying Risk Factors for Inflation Hedging

1. The CIO (chief investment officer) of the United Retired Workers Plan would like to reduce inflation risk in the portfolio. Based on the data displayed in Exhibit 14, which asset classes would you recommend as potential inflation-hedging tools?

2. The CIO is not only concerned about inflation but also rising interest rates. Which alternative asset classes would you recommend for consideration?

Solution to 1:

Commodities and inflation-linked bonds have the highest factor sensitivity to inflation, so they are the most obvious candidates. Real estate (both public and private) also has some potential to protect against inflation. Based on the data

---

[6] For further detail on expanding asset allocation to risk allocation, we refer to Naik et al. (2016) and Cambridge Associates LLC (2013).

presented, macro hedge fund strategies also exhibited a positive inflation beta, but given their active nature, further analysis may be needed before choosing them as inflation-hedging vehicles.

Solution to 2:

Commodities and private real estate would be the likely asset classes to hedge against rising interest rates, given their zero-factor sensitivity to nominal duration. Some of the hedge fund strategies also show zero-factor sensitivity to duration, but the relationship may not hold true in the future given the actively managed nature of hedge funds. Although Exhibit 14 indicates equity strategies (both public and private) also show little to no sensitivity to rising interest rates (duration) bonds and equities have been more highly correlated in the past.

4.1 Illustration: Asset Allocation and Risk-Based Approaches

Let's look at an example of how a risk-based approach may enhance traditional asset allocation. In Exhibit 15, we show two investment portfolios, Portfolio A and Portfolio B, that have exactly the same high-level asset allocations. However, the underlying investments in the two portfolios are quite different. The fixed-income assets in Portfolio A are government bonds, while the fixed-income assets in Portfolio B are high-yield bonds. Hedge fund investments in Portfolio A are represented by very low equity beta market neutral strategies, while Portfolio B is invested in the higher beta long/short equity hedge funds. Similarly, Portfolio B's investments in real assets and private equity have higher risk than those in Portfolio A.

Exhibit 15   Traditional Asset Allocation and Risk Contribution Comparison

Broad Asset Classes	Asset Allocation		Underlying Investments		% Contribution to Risk	
	Portfolio A	Portfolio B	Portfolio A	Portfolio B	Portfolio A	Portfolio B
Fixed Income	20%	20%	Government Bonds	High-Yield Bonds	−6.5%	7.6%
Public Equities	20%	20%	US Equities	Non-US Developed Equities	51.4%	18.2%
Hedge Funds	20%	20%	Equity Market Neutral	Long/Short Equity	5.4%	11.1%
Real Assets	20%	20%	Inflation-linked bonds	REITs	0.7%	13.2%
Private Equity	20%	20%	Buyout	Venture Capital	48.9%	49.8%
Total	**100%**	**100%**				
				Expected Return	5.3%	8.8%
				Volatility	5.9%	16.5%
				Equity Beta	0.30	0.79

Notes: The percentage contribution to risk is a result of three components: the asset allocation to a specific asset, its volatility, and its correlation with the other assets. For fixed income, the contribution to total risk is negative in the case of Portfolio A because government bonds have negative correlations with other asset classes; however, it is positive in the case of Portfolio B because high-yield bonds have positive correlations with the other asset classes.
Source: Authors' calculations.

As a result of these major differences between nominally similar broad asset allocations, it is not surprising that Portfolio B has higher volatility, beta, and expected return compared to Portfolio A. Let's look more closely at the risk contribution of each of the asset classes:

Portfolio A.

The majority of the risk in Portfolio A comes from public and private equity. Hedge funds contribute approximately 5% to the total risk, and fixed income actually reduces risk because government bonds had negative correlations with public equities in our historical data sample.

Portfolio B.

Private equity explains about half of the total portfolio risk of Portfolio B. (In this portfolio, the private equity allocation is represented by the higher risk venture capital.) Public equities, hedge funds, and real assets each contribute roughly the same to the total risk of the portfolio. This is consistent with the equity-like characteristics of the underlying assets in the portfolio. The long/short equity hedged strategy has an equity beta of around 0.5, and REITs have an equity beta of 0.9. In Portfolio B, fixed income contributes positively to total risk, consistent with high-yield bonds' positive correlation with equities over the time series.

Although the nominal asset allocations of the two portfolios are the same, the risk profile and the risk allocation among asset classes are significantly different. Let's go one step further and apply the risk factor sensitivities of Exhibit 14 to our hypothetical portfolios. Exhibit 16 shows the absolute contribution to total portfolio risk by risk factor. This approach moves beyond the borders of asset classes and aggregates the equity risk factor embedded in public equities, private equities, venture capital, and REITs into a single-factor contribution. Both portfolios are highly dominated by exposure to equity risk. Portfolio A's total risk is almost fully explained by the exposure to the equity factor, while about 70% of Portfolio B's total risk comes from the equity risk factor alone. Portfolio B also has exposure to the size and value factors, driven by the allocation to venture capital. Finally, we can also see that although Portfolio B is not directly investing in government bonds, some risk mitigation benefit still arises from the low "duration" component of high-yield bonds and REITs.

Exhibit 16   Absolute Contribution to Total Risk by Risk Factors

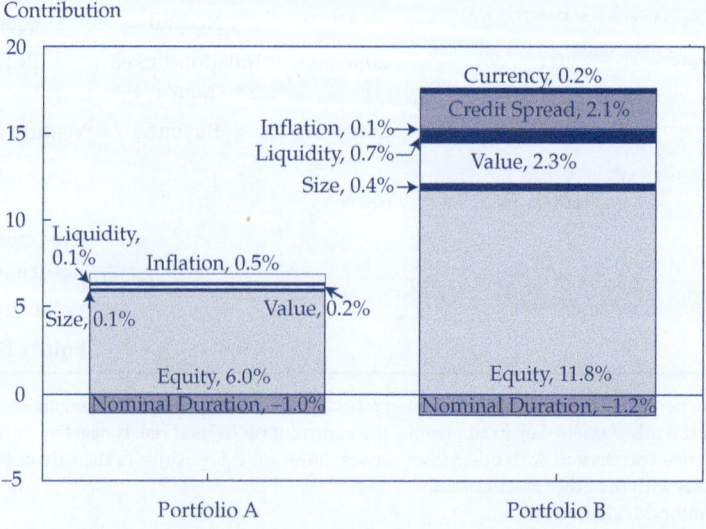

This is an extreme example (the two portfolios have vastly different expected returns), but it is useful to illustrate how factor sensitivities can be used to explore the underlying risk exposures in seemingly similar asset allocations.

4.2 Comparing Risk-Based and Traditional Approaches

Investors often employ multiple approaches in setting their asset allocation for a portfolio that includes alternative investments. When applying these various approaches, investors must consider their strengths and limitations.

Main strengths of traditional approaches:

- *Easy to communicate.* Listing the roles of various asset classes is intuitive and easy to explain to the decision makers, who often have familiarity with the traditional asset class-based approach. Scenario analyses based on historical or expected behavior of various asset classes under different macroeconomic conditions can help to introduce quantitative aspects of the portfolio's expected performance and risk and substantiate the asset allocation proposal.
- *Relevance for liquidity management and operational considerations.* Public and private asset class mandates have vastly distinct liquidity profiles. Thus, although private and public equity would have a lot of commonality in their risk factor exposures, they would be positioned very differently from a liquidity management perspective. Similarly, investors must implement the target asset allocation by allocating to investment managers. The traditional categorization of asset classes may be necessary to identify the relevant mandates—what portion of the equity portfolio she would like to allocate to equity-oriented hedge funds rather than to long-only equity managers.

Main limitations of traditional approaches:

- *Over-estimation of portfolio diversification.* Without a proper analytical framework for assessing risk, investors may have a false sense of diversification. An allocation spread across a large number of different asset classes may appear to be very well diversified, when, in fact, the underlying investments may be subject to the same underlying risks.
- *Obscured primary drivers of risk.* Investments with very different risk characteristics may be commingled under the same asset class category. For example, government bonds and high-yield bonds may both be classified as "fixed income," but each has distinct risk characteristics.

Risk-based approaches are designed to overcome some of these limitations.

Key benefits of risk-based approaches:

- *Common risk factor identification.* Investors are able to identify common risk factors across all investments, whether public or private, passive or active.
- *Integrated risk framework.* Investors are able to build an integrated risk management framework, leading to more reliable portfolio-level risk quantification.

Key limitations of risk-based approaches:

- *Sensitivity to the historical look-back period.* Empirical risk factor exposure estimations may be sensitive to the historical sample. For example, the duration of a bond portfolio or the beta of a diversified equity portfolio could be reasonably stable, but the estimated inflation sensitivity of real assets can change rapidly over time. Thus, the analyst has to be cautious when interpreting some of the risk factor sensitivities, such as the "inflation beta" of commodities.

- *Implementation hurdles.* Establishing a strategic target to different risk factors is a very important high-level decision, but converting these risk factor targets to actual investment mandates requires additional considerations, including liquidity planning, time and effort for manager selection, and rebalancing policy.

- *Determining which risk factors should be used and how to measure them in different asset classes.* One drawback with risk-based approaches is the decision on which risk factors to use is somewhat subjective and how these factors are measured can also be subjective. For example, if using a liquidity factor, should it be measured by the Pastor-Stambaugh metric or by some other metric?

This issue is highlighted by noting that in Level III *Hedge Fund Strategies*, hedge fund returns are analyzed via a conditional factor model using just four risk factors: equities, credit, currencies, and volatility. These risk factors were selected as they are deemed to provide a reasonably broad cross-section of risk exposures for the typical hedge fund, and each of the factor returns can be realized through relatively liquid instruments.

In sum, a limitation of risk-based approaches is the potential subjectivity embedded in their implementation.

5. RISK CONSIDERATIONS, RETURN EXPECTATIONS AND INVESTMENT VEHICLE

d   discuss investment considerations that are important in allocating to different types of alternative investments;

In addition to the risk, return, and correlation characteristics relevant to the decision to invest in the alternative asset classes, many operational and practical complexities must be considered before finalizing a decision to invest. It is essential that the investor be fully aware of these complexities: Failure to grasp these differences between traditional and alternative investments can derail an investment program. The primary factors to consider include:

- properly defining risk characteristics;
- establishing return expectations;
- selection of the appropriate investment vehicle;
- operational liquidity issues;
- expense and fee considerations;
- tax considerations (applicable for taxable entities); and
- build vs. buy.

5.1 Risk Considerations

Mean–variance optimization (MVO), widely used in modeling asset allocation choices, cannot easily accommodate the characteristics of most alternative investments. MVO characterizes an asset's risk using standard deviation. Standard deviation is a one-dimensional view of risk and an especially poor representation of the risk characteristics of alternative investments—where assets suffer some degree of illiquidity, valuations may be subjective, and returns may be "chunky" and not normally distributed. The non-standard deviation risks are usually accommodated in an MVO framework by assigning a higher standard deviation than might be derived solely by looking at the historical returns of the asset class.

Most approaches to asset allocation assume that the portfolio's allocation to an asset class is always fully invested. Although this is not an assumption that is limited to alternatives, the problem is exaggerated with the private alternative strategies where it could take several years for capital to be invested and where capital is returned to the investor as investments are sold. Thus, it is rare that the *actual* asset allocation of a program with a significant exposure to alternatives will mirror the *modeled* asset allocation. This suggests that the investor must carefully (and continually) monitor the program's aggregate exposures to ensure that the risks are in line with the strategic asset allocation. A case in point: Some investors over-allocated to private equity, real-estate, and other call-down funds prior to 2008 in order to more quickly reach their asset allocation targets. Many of these investors then found themselves in a situation where they were receiving capital calls for these commitments during 2008 and 2009, a period where their public assets had lost considerable value and liquidity and cash were scarce. Some investors had to reduce distributions, sell illiquid investments in the secondary market at severely discounted prices, and/or walk away from their fund commitments, thereby forfeiting earlier investments.

Although every strategy (and, by extension, each individual fund) will have its own unique risk profile, we provide two examples of the complications that might be encountered when modelling an allocation to alternative investments.

Short-only strategy:

A short-biased fund can provide strong diversification benefits, lowering a portfolio's aggregate exposure to the equity risk factor; however, a short-only fund has a risk profile quite unlike a long-only equity fund. Most investors understand that a long-only equity fund has theoretically infinite upside potential and a downside loss bounded by zero (assuming no leverage). A short-biased or short-only fund has the opposite distribution. A short-selling strategy is capped on its upside but has unlimited downside risk.

Option payouts:

Some hedge fund strategies will structure their trades as call options either by owning call options outright or by synthetically replicating a call option (e.g., convertible bond arbitrage in which the manager goes long the convertible bond, short the equity for the same underlying, and hedges the interest rate risk). If executed properly, the fund would have limited downside but unlimited upside. It is difficult, if not impossible, to accurately model such a return profile by looking simply at a fund's historical standard deviation or other risk metrics, especially if the fund's track record does not encompass a full market cycle.

5.2 Return Expectations

Given the limited return history of alternative investments (relative to stocks and bonds) and the idiosyncratic nature of alternative investment returns, no single accepted approach to developing the return expectations required in an asset allocation exercise exists. One approach that can be applied with some consistency across asset classes is a "building blocks" approach: Begin with the risk-free rate, estimate the return associated with the factor exposures relevant to the asset class (e.g., credit spreads, level and shape of the yield curve, equity, leverage, liquidity), apply an assumption for manager alpha, and deduct appropriate fees (management and incentive) and taxes. Where the portfolio already contains an allocation to alternative investments, the underlying money managers can be helpful in estimating exposures and return potential. The portfolio's current positions can be characterized by their known exposures, rather than through a generic set of exposures that may not be truly representative of the program's objectives for the asset class exposure. Say, for example, that the investor's hedge fund program deliberately excludes long/short equity hedge funds because the investor chooses to take equity risk in the long-only portion of the portfolio. The return (and risk) characteristics of this hedge fund allocation would be very different from those of a broad-based allocation to hedge funds, which typically has a significant weight to long/short equity funds.

5.3 Investment Vehicle

Most alternative investments are implemented through a private (limited) partnership that is controlled by a general partner (GP), the organization and individuals that manage the investments. The asset owner becomes a limited partner (LP) in the private partnership. The main rationale for using the limited partnership format is that it limits the investor's liability to the amount of capital that she has contributed; she is not responsible for the actions of or the debts incurred by the GP. The investor may invest directly into a manager's fund or through a fund of funds, a private partnership that invests in multiple underlying partnerships. Larger investors may also consider making co-investments alongside a manager into a portfolio company, or they may make direct private equity investments on their own.

Private limited partnerships are the dominant investment vehicle for most alternative investments in private equity, real estate, private credit, and real assets. In the United States, hedge funds will tend to employ two structures: a limited partnership (typically Delaware-based) or an offshore corporation or feeder fund (possibly based in the Cayman Islands, Bermuda, or the British Virgin Islands) that usually feeds into an underlying limited partnership (i.e., feeder fund). European hedge funds tend to register their vehicles in Ireland or Luxembourg[7] as a public limited company, a partnership limited by shares, or a special limited partnership.

There are growing opportunities to invest in alternatives using mutual funds, undertakings for collective investment in transferable securities (UCITS), and/or separately managed accounts (SMAs), although the strategies implemented through these more-liquid vehicles are unlikely to have the same risk/return profile as their less-liquid counterparts. The requirements and demands of a broader investor base have made mutual funds, UCITS, and SMAs increasingly popular. We describe the structure, benefits, and drawbacks of each of these vehicles.

Direct investment in a limited partnership:

An investor with the necessary scale and expertise can purchase limited partnership interests directly from the GP. GPs have broad discretion to select and manage the underlying investments and will typically invest a portion of their capital in the fund alongside the limited partners. Because each limited partnership follows its own distinct investment strategy, the investor must often invest in multiple partnerships to diversify idiosyncratic risk. In order to maintain the limited liability shield afforded by the limited partnership structure, the investor must not become too involved in the operation of the fund itself.

---

[7] See Eurekahedge, "2016 Key Trends in Global Hedge Funds" (August 2016).

Funds of funds (FOFs):

Many investors lack the necessary scale and investment/operational expertise to access, evaluate, and develop a diversified alternative investment program. An FOF pools the capital of these investors, allowing them to achieve an allocation to an asset class that would otherwise be unobtainable. An FOF manager will typically specialize in a certain alternative strategy, such as Asian private equity funds, and may invest in either many or just a handful of underlying funds. The FOF manager is responsible for sourcing, conducting due diligence on, and monitoring the underlying managers. Using an FOF simplifies the investor's accounting and reporting: Capital calls from the underlying funds are frequently consolidated into a single capital call by the FOF, and investors receive a single report consolidating the accounting and investment results of all the underlying funds. The FOF manager does charge additional fees for these services. Investors in an FOF also lose a degree of flexibility to customize their exposures.

SMAs/funds of one:

As large institutions and family offices increased capital allocated to the alternative investment space, many of them demanded more-favorable investment terms and conditions than those offered to smaller investors. Some alternative investment managers, interested in accessing these large pools of capital, have agreed to offer investment management services to these clients through a highly customizable SMA. SMAs have very high minimum investments and pose greater operational challenges for both the manager and the investor. In instances where an SMA is impractical, fund managers have created a "fund of one"—a limited partnership with a single client. These funds have many of the same benefits as an SMA but can be easier to implement. (For example, an SMA requires that the *investor* must be approved by each of the counterparties to any derivatives contracts. In a fund of one, GPs must obtain and maintain these approvals, which is something that they do in the ordinary course of running their investment businesses.)

SMAs and funds of one cannot generally avail themselves of the alignment of interests that arises from the investment of GP capital alongside that of the LPs. When other clients are invested in the GP's primary investment vehicles at the GP's standard fees and to which the GP has committed some of its own capital, there is a risk that the GP favors these other funds in allocating capital-constrained investment opportunities.

Mutual funds/UCITS/publicly traded funds:

A number of open-ended mutual funds and UCITS seek to replicate some alternative investment strategies, particularly hedge funds. Nominally, these allow smaller investors to access asset classes that would otherwise be unavailable to them. It should be noted, however, that these vehicles often operate with regulatory restrictions that limit the fund manager's ability to implement the investment strategy offered via their primary investment vehicle. Accordingly, the investor must be cautious in considering whether the track record achieved in the manager's primary investment vehicle is representative of what might be achieved in a mutual fund, UCIT, or other publicly-traded vehicle. For example, a mutual fund that offers daily liquidity is unlikely to be a suitable investment vehicle for a distressed or activist investment fund, where the time horizon to realize investment returns may be one to two years. This "liquid-alt" space grew significantly following the Global Financial Crisis.

6 LIQUIDITY

d discuss investment considerations that are important in allocating to different types of alternative investments;

Traditional assets are generally highly liquid, and the vehicles that are typically used by investors to access the asset class (e.g., separate accounts or daily valued commingled funds, such as mutual funds and UCITS) typically do not impose additional liquidity constraints. That is not the case with many alternative assets, where both the vehicle and the underlying instruments may expose the investor to some degree of liquidity risk. We address liquidity risks at the fund and security level separately.

6.1 Liquidity Risks Associated with the Investment Vehicle

The most common vehicle employed by alternative asset managers is the private limited partnership previously described. (Some investors will invest via an offshore corporate structure used for certain tax and regulatory reasons. This offshore corporation is typically a "feeder" fund—a vehicle that channels investors' assets to the master limited partnership.) The private placement memorandum (PPM) details the subscription and redemption features of the partnership. Liquidity provisions differ across asset classes but are substantially similar within asset classes. Exhibit 17 details the typical liquidity considerations associated with investing in a private limited partnership. SMA liquidity provisions may be negotiated directly with the manager.

Exhibit 17 Typical Liquidity Provisions for Alternative Investment Vehicles

	Subscription	Redemption	Lock-Up
Hedge Funds	▪ Typically accept capital on a monthly or quarterly basis.	▪ Quarterly or annual redemptions with 30 to 90 days' notice required. ▪ May be subject to a gate limiting the amount of fund or investor assets that can be redeemed at any one redemption date. ▪ 10% holdback of the redemption amount pending completion of the annual audit.	▪ Typically one year in the US; shorter in Europe. ▪ Redemptions prior to the lock-up period may be permitted but are subject to a penalty, typically 10%.
Private Equity, Private Credit, Real Estate, and Real Asset Funds	▪ Funds typically have multiple "closes." The final close for new investors is usually one year after the first close. Committed capital is called for investment in stages over a 3-year investment period.	▪ No redemption provisions. Fund interests may be sold on the secondary market, subject to GP approval. ▪ Distributions paid as investments are realized over the life of the fund. Unrealized assets may be distributed in kind to the LP at fund termination.	▪ Typical 10-year life, with GP option to extend fund term 1 to 2 years.

Liquidity

Secondary markets:

Although fund terms may prevent investors from redeeming early, a small but growing secondary market for many alternative funds exists. Some brokers will match sellers and buyers of limited partnership interests, and some secondary funds' main objective is to buy limited partnership interests from the original investor. These transactions typically occur at a significant discount to the net asset value (NAV) of the fund and usually require the GP to approve the transaction.

Understanding a drawdown structure:

Private equity/credit, private real estate, and real asset funds typically call investors' capital in stages as fund investments are identified. This investment period is specified in the PPM and typically ranges from three to five years from the initial capital call. Thus, although an investor may have committed a specified percentage of the portfolio to an asset class, the allocation may not be fully funded until some point well into the future. We will illustrate the drawdown structure for a single fund using a hypothetical commitment to a real estate fund:

The Chan Family Partnership commits €5,000,000 to Uptown Real Estate LP. The fund has a three-year investment period. When fully invested, Uptown expects to hold 12 to 15 properties. The capital call schedule for Uptown may look something like this:

- Year 1: €1,500,000 of the €5,000,000 committed is called, covering three investments
- Year 2: €2,500,000 is called, covering six investments
- Year 3: €500,000 is called, covering two investments
- Year 6: €2,000,000 is distributed by Uptown Real Estate
- More distributions in subsequent years

Expanding on this example, Exhibit 18 shows how the cash flows for our hypothetical fund might operate throughout the fund's life.

Exhibit 18: Hypothetical Capital Call—Distribution Schedule

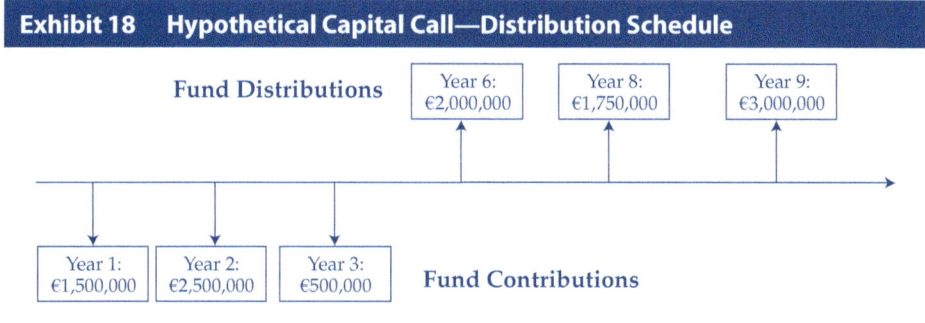

In reality, most funds will have several capital calls in a year. It is also possible that a fund may make a distribution before the final capital call occurs. Because of the highly uncertain liquidity profile of call down (or drawdown) funds (private equity/credit, real estate/real assets), it is incumbent on the investor to plan for multiple contingencies. Funds may end up calling significantly less capital than the investor assumed or may call capital at a faster pace than planned. Capital may be returned to the investor more quickly or more slowly than originally anticipated. Each of these scenarios could result in investors being under or over their target allocations. Critically, investors will want to verify that they have suitable liquidity, such that even under adverse conditions they are able to meet their capital calls. Investors who are unable to meet their capital calls may be required to forfeit their entire investment in the fund (or such other penalties as may be specified in the PPM).

The capital commitment/drawdown structure also presents potential opportunity costs for the investor. Returning to Exhibit 18, having committed €5,000,000 to Uptown Real Estate LP, the Chan Family Partnership is obligated to meet the GP's capital calls but must address the opportunity cost of having the committed capital invested in lower-returning liquid (cash) assets pending the capital call—or face the risk of having insufficient assets available to meet the capital call if the funds were invested in another asset class that has experienced a loss in the interim. Also note that only €4,500,000 of the €5,000,000 commitment was called before distributions began.

6.2 Liquidity Risks Associated with the Underlying Investments

The investor must be aware of any potential mismatch between the fund terms and the liquidity profile of the underlying instruments held by the fund. This is particularly important if the investor is negotiating fund terms or if other investors have terms that may be different from his own. Because the private market funds rarely offer interim liquidity, this problem most often arises in hedge funds. We provide a few examples of the issues an investor may encounter.

Equity-oriented hedge funds:

The majority of assets in a typical equity-oriented hedge fund are liquid, marketable securities compatible with monthly or quarterly fund-level liquidity terms. Short positions may be notably less liquid than long positions, so funds that make greater use of short selling will have correspondingly lower overall liquidity. This should be taken into consideration when evaluating the potential for a liquidity mismatch between the fund's terms and the underlying holdings. Some otherwise liquid hedge fund strategies may own a portion of their holdings in illiquid or relatively illiquid securities. The GP may designate these securities as being held in a "side pocket." Such "side-pocketed" securities are not subject to the fund's general liquidity terms. The redeeming investor's pro rata share of the side pocket would remain in the fund and be distributed at such time as the fund manager liquidates these assets, which could take quarters or even years to accomplish. If the percentage of assets held in side pockets is large, this could render the fund's liquidity terms irrelevant. The investor must evaluate the illiquidity challenges inherent in the underlying holdings, including side pockets, in order to estimate a liquidity profile for the total portfolio.

Event-driven hedge funds:

Event-driven strategies, by their nature, tend to have longer investment horizons. The underlying investments in a merger arbitrage strategy, for example, are generally liquid, but the nature of the strategy is such that returns are realized in "chunks." It is in the manager's and the investor's interests to ensure that the liquidity terms provide the necessary flexibility to execute the investment thesis. A hedge fund focused on distressed investing is dealing with both the "workout" horizon (the time frame over which the negotiations between the creditors and the company are being conducted) and the lesser liquidity of the distressed assets. The fund terms for a distressed strategy are likely to be much longer than other hedge fund strategies. (In fact, many distressed funds choose to organize in a private equity fund structure.)

Relative value hedge funds:

Many relative value hedge funds will invest in various forms of credit, convertibles, derivatives, or equities that have limited or at least uncertain liquidity characteristics. Many funds will include provisions in the fund documents to restrict redemptions under certain scenarios so that they are not forced to sell illiquid securities at inopportune moments. Without such provisions, the fund manager may be forced to sell what securities they *can* (i.e., the more liquid holdings) rather than the securities that they *want.* This could have the unfortunate consequence of leaving remaining investors in the fund holding a sub-optimally illiquid portfolio. On the other hand, funds that deal in managed futures or similar instruments may have very flexible terms (daily or weekly liquidity, only a few days notification, etc.). This was a scenario many hedge fund managers faced during the Global Financial Crisis as investors made significant redemption requests to meet their own cash needs. The liquid funds were disproportionately affected as investors sought to raise cash wherever they could find it.

Leverage:

A fund's use of leverage and its agreements with counterparties providing the leverage can also affect the alignment between fund terms and the investment strategy. If a strategy is levered, lenders have a first claim on the assets. The lenders' claims are superior to those of the LPs, and the lenders have preferential liquidity terms; most lenders can make a margin call on stocks, bonds, or derivatives positions with just two days' notice. Given that margin calls are most likely to happen when the markets (and/or the fund) are stressed, the LPs' liquidity can evaporate as the most-liquid positions in the portfolio are sold to meet margin calls. The need to de-lever and sell assets to meet margin calls will typically result in a lower return when the market eventually recovers.

FEES AND EXPENSES, TAX CONSIDERATIONS, AND OTHER CONSIDERATIONS

d discuss investment considerations that are important in allocating to different types of alternative investments;

In addition to management fees of 0.5% to 2.5% of assets and incentive fees of 10% to 20% of returns, investments in alternative assets often entail higher expenses passed through to or paid directly by the investor. These fees can result in a significant variation between the gross and net of fee returns. Consider a hedge fund that was earning a 3% gross quarterly return (12.6% annualized). After deducting a 2% management and a 20% incentive fee, accrued quarterly, the net return at year-end is just 8.2%.

Fees can have a larger impact on the difference between gross and net returns for such call-down-type fund structures as private equity funds, where the management fee is charged on *committed* capital, not invested capital. If the manager is slow to deploy capital, there can be a pronounced J-curve effect (negative IRRs in the early years) that can be difficult to overcome (the adage 'it takes a 100% return to recover from a 50% loss').

In addition, most alternative investment funds will pass through normal fund expenses, including legal, custodial, audit, administration, and accounting fees. For smaller funds, these additional costs can add up to another 0.5%. Larger funds can spread these same costs out over the larger asset base, and the pass-through to investors is likely to be in the range of 0.05% to 0.20% of assets. Some of these expenses have a limited life (e.g., the capitalized organizational expenses), so the impact can vary over time. Funds may also pass through to investors costs associated with acquiring an asset, including the due diligence costs and any brokerage commissions paid. A careful evaluation of the fund's offering documents is essential to understanding the all-in cost of an investment in alternatives.

7.1 Tax Considerations

For taxable investors, the tax implications associated with many alternatives can have a significant impact on their relative attractiveness. In many instances, a tax inefficient strategy, one that generates substantial short-term gains or taxable income, can significantly erode the anticipated return benefits. This arises frequently with many hedge fund strategies, especially those funds and fund companies where tax-exempt investors dominate the client base and the fund manager may be insensitive to tax efficiency. Vehicle selection becomes an important tool to mitigate potential tax consequences. For example, certain Asia-based investors may use European or other offshore vehicles that feed into US strategies in order to mitigate US tax withholding. Conversely, some funds benefit from preferential tax treatment that might add to its relative attractiveness.

Here are a few examples of these tax considerations:

- The US tax code has provisions that favor real estate, timber, and energy investments. Timber sales, for example, are taxed at lower capital gains rates rather than as ordinary income and may benefit from a depletion deduction. Commercial and residential building assets can be depreciated according to various schedules, with the depreciation offsetting income received on those assets. Some oil and natural gas royalty owners may benefit from a depletion deduction, offsetting income generated from the sale of the oil or gas.

- Some alternative investment strategies can generate unrelated business income tax (UBIT). UBIT arises when a US tax-exempt organization engages in activities that are not related to the tax-exempt purpose of that organization. Since most tax-exempt entities seek to mitigate (if not avoid) taxes, they will want to verify whether such a fund might generate UBIT and, if so, whether the fund manager has an offshore vehicle that may shield the investor from such income.

- The taxable investor faces additional costs and operational hurdles because of the more complex tax filings. Some taxable investors must estimate their expected annual income, including income that is derived from investments. Deriving an accurate estimate can be a challenge. Unfortunately, if the misestimation is large enough it might result in tax penalties.

Tax considerations, like fees, will affect the return assumptions used in the asset allocation exercise.

7.2 Other Considerations

Although smaller investors seeking to build a diversified alternative investment program are generally constrained to use an intermediary, such as a fund of funds, large investors have the opportunity to build a program in-house and must decide whether this approach is appropriate given their governance structure. Key questions to explore in evaluating the options include the following:

- What is the likelihood that the investor can identify and gain access to the top-tier managers in the investment strategy?

  Truly differentiated strategies and top-tier managers are notoriously capacity constrained, which tends to limit the amount of assets they can reasonably manage without negatively affecting investment returns. Fund managers who recognize this problem frequently limit the number of investors that they allow into their fund and may close their doors to new clients or capital. This can make it extremely difficult for investors to find and access top-tier managers. Investors who are subject to public disclosure requirements may be rejected by a manager who believes that success is based on a proprietary informational edge that could be eroded through these required public disclosures. Many studies on alternative assets have concluded that it may not be worth the costs and resources required to be successful in this space if investors do not have access to top-tier funds.

- What is the likelihood that the investor will be accorded the access needed to conduct effective due diligence on an investment strategy?

   It is not enough to know when or if to invest with a fund manager; it is equally, if not more, important to be able to determine when to terminate the relationship. Having poor to no access to the key decision makers within the organization could make it difficult to ascertain if the conditions have changed such that a redemption is warranted. The situation could be even worse if other clients have good (or preferential) access to the fund manager, which might result in their redeeming early, leaving other, less-informed investors subject to gates or other more-restrictive redemption terms that could be triggered.

- What skills and resources does the investor have in-house to evaluate and monitor an alternative investment program?

   This question is evaluated through a consideration of the cost tradeoffs, the investment expertise of in-house staff, the desire to tailor an investment program to investor-specific wants and needs, and the degree of control.

   - Cost is typically the overriding factor in the decision to build a program in-house or buy an existing off-the-shelf product. The all-in costs of compensation, benefits, rent, technology, reporting, travel, overhead, and other miscellaneous expenses associated with managing an alternative investments program can far exceed the costs associated with running a traditional asset portfolio. However, very large organizations may be able to justify the costs of building in-house teams.
   - Investors seeking to leverage a manager's expertise through co-investments and other direct investment opportunities must build an in-house team with the expertise to evaluate specific securities and deals and must provide the infrastructure needed to support those efforts.
   - Investors who require highly customized investment programs might be poorly served by consultants or FOFs who typically gain scale and margin by providing solutions that can be broadly applied to a large number of clients. For example, an endowment that wants their alternative investment program to consider environmental, social, and governance (ESG) factors (i.e., socially responsible investing) may have a difficult time finding an investment consultant who can deliver on the client's specific ESG requirements. Or, a family office that wants to emphasize tax-efficient angel investments might need to hire in-house resources in order to find and supervise these more specialized investments.
   - Those investors who desire a high degree of control and/or influence over the implementation of the investment program are more likely to have this need met through an in-house program.

EXAMPLE 3

Considerations in Allocating to Alternative Investments

The investment committee (IC) for a small endowment has decided to invest in private equity for the first time and has agreed upon a 10% strategic target. The internal investment team comprises the CIO (chief investment officer) and two analysts. The IC asks the CIO to recommend an implementation plan at the next meeting.

1. What are the options the CIO should include in her report as it relates to vehicles, and what factors might influence the recommendation?
2. The IC provided no guidance as to expectations for when the investment program should reach its 10% target weight. What additional information should the CIO gather before presenting her plan of action?

Solution to 1:

The primary considerations for the CIO include the size of the private equity allocation, the team's expertise with private equity, and the available resources. Because this is a small endowment, it may be difficult to commit enough capital to achieve an adequate level of diversification. The size of the fund's investment team is also likely to be a concern. Unless there are financial resources to add a private equity specialist and/or employ an outside consultant, the fund-of-funds route would likely be the optimal vehicle(s) to implement a diversified private equity program.

Solution to 2:

The CIO should factor in the cash flows and anticipated liquidity profile of the overall endowment in considering the speed with which they would commit to a significant PE program. If, for example, the foundation is embarking on a capital campaign and anticipated distributions are small over the next few years, then commitments may be accelerated after factoring in an appropriate vintage year diversification. (Because private investment returns are very sensitive to the fund's vintage year, it is common for investors to build up to a full allocation over a period of years, called vintage year diversification.) However, if the rest of the investment program is heavily exposed to illiquid investments (e.g., real estate, certain hedge fund strategies) and anticipated distributions to fund operating expenses are high, the CIO may want to commit at a slower pace.

EXAMPLE 4

Considerations in Allocating to Alternative Investments

A $100 million client of a family office firm has requested that all public securities investments meet certain ESG criteria. The ESG ratings will be provided by an independent third-party firm that provides a rating for most public equities and some fixed-income issuers. Moreover, the family would like to dedicate a percentage of assets to support an "environmental sustainability" impact theme.

1. Which alternative investment strategies may not be suitable for this client given the ESG requirements?
2. What additional information might the family office firm require from the client in order to meet the environmental sustainability threshold?

Solution to 1:

Because the ESG criteria apply to all public securities, most hedge fund strategies would be precluded because they are typically owned in a commingled vehicle, such as a limited partnership or a mutual fund where transparency of holdings is limited and the investor has no influence over the composition of the underlying portfolio. Separate account strategies are available for certain large portfolios, but it is unlikely that a $100 million client would be eligible for a custom portfolio that would be allocating only a small asset base to any particular fund.

Solution to 2:

The client and the manager would need to agree on a clear definition of environmental sustainability and the types of investments that might qualify for this theme. It is unlikely that most hedge funds, private credit, energy, or infrastructure strategies would be considered to positively impact environmental sustainability. The most likely candidates for consideration could be timber, sustainable farmland, and clean-tech funds under the venture capital category.

SUITABILITY CONSIDERATIONS

e   discuss suitability considerations in allocating to alternative investments;

Alternative investments are not appropriate for all investors. We discuss briefly several *investor* characteristics that are important to a successful alternative investment program.

8.1 Investment Horizon

Investors with less than a 15-year investment horizon should generally avoid investments in private real estate, private real assets, and private equity funds. An alternative investment program in private markets may take 5 to 7 years to fully develop and another 10 to 12 years to unwind, assuming no new investments are made after the 7-year mark. Even a 10-year horizon may be too short to develop a robust private alternative investment program.

Other strategies can tolerate a shorter investment focus. Many hedge fund strategies that focus on public equities or managed futures have much shorter lock-ups (on the order of months or not at all). Some strategies can be entered and exited in shorter time frames, and the purchase or sale of limited partnership interests on the secondary market may be used to shorten the entry and exit phases of the process. However, the alternative investment program has a higher likelihood of success if the investor adopts a long-horizon approach coupled with an understanding of the underlying investment processes.

8.2 Expertise

A successful alternative investment program requires that the investor understand the risks entailed and the market environments that drive success or failure of each of the strategies. Understanding the breadth of the alternative investment opportunities and the complexity of strategies within each alternative class requires a relatively high level of investment expertise. Even if the investor is highly experienced, the risk of information asymmetry between the limited partner (LP) and the general partner (GP) is always there. A pension fund without full-time investment staff, or an individual without the resources to hire an adviser with a dedicated alternative investments team, is unlikely to have the investment expertise necessary to implement a successful alternative investment program.

Additionally, the investment philosophy of the asset owner (or its overseers) must be consistent with the principles of alternative investments. An investor whose investment philosophy is rooted in a belief that markets are fundamentally efficient may struggle to embrace an alternative investment program, where success is predicated on active management. A mismatch in philosophy could very well be a set up for failure when the alternative investments underperform traditional asset classes.

8.3 Governance

A robust investment governance framework ensures that an alternative investment program is structured to meet the needs of the investor. The following are hallmarks of a strong governance framework suitable to an alternative investment program:

- The long- and short-term objectives of the investment program are clearly articulated.
- Decision rights and responsibilities are allocated to those individuals with the knowledge, capacity, and time required to critically evaluate possible courses of action.
- A formal investment policy has been adopted to govern the day-to-day operations of the investment program.
- A reporting framework is in place to monitor the program's progress toward the agreed-on goals and objectives.

Investors without a strong governance program are less likely to develop a successful alternative investment program.

8.4 Transparency

Investors must be comfortable with less than 100% transparency into the underlying holdings of their alternative investment managers. In real estate, private equity, and real asset funds, the investor is typically buying into a "blind pool"—committing capital for investment in a portfolio of as-yet-unidentified assets. During the course of investment due diligence, the investor may have looked at the assets acquired in the manager's previous funds, but there is no assurance that the new fund will look anything like the prior funds. Hedge fund managers are generally reluctant to disclose the full portfolio to investors on an ongoing basis. Even if you were to have access to the full underlying portfolio, it is rarely apparent where the true risk exposures lie without a detailed understanding of the investment themes the manager is pursuing.

Reporting for alternative funds is often less transparent than investors are accustomed to seeing on their stock and bond portfolios. Generally, no legal requirements mandate the frequency, timing, and details of fund reporting for private investment partnerships. For many illiquid strategies (real estate/assets, private equity/credit), reporting is often received well past month- or quarter-end deadlines that investors are accustomed to with their traditional investments.

A typical hedge fund report, usually available on a quarterly basis, may detail performance, top 10 holdings, and some general commentary on the capital markets as well as some factors that influenced fund performance. The hedge fund manager may also provide a risk report that broadly outlines the major risk exposures of the fund. There is no commonality among the risk reports provided from fund to fund. This

Suitability Considerations

hampers an investor's efforts to develop a picture of aggregate risk exposure. Clients with separately managed accounts have access to portfolio holdings and may be able to produce their own risk reporting with a common set of risk metrics.

Private equity funds will provide more transparency into portfolio holdings, but the private equity fund report is unlikely to "slice-and-dice" the exposures by geography, sector, or industry. The investor must gather the additional information needed to develop a fuller exposure of the portfolio's risk exposures and progress toward meeting expectations. Private equity managers typically provide an abbreviated quarterly report with a more detailed annual report following the completion of the fund's annual audit.

This lack of transparency can shield questionable actions by GPs. In 2014, the US Securities and Exchange Commission found that more than 50% of private equity firms had collected or misallocated fees without proper disclosure to their clients.[8] This study and subsequent lawsuits have increased transparency within the industry, although the industry remains opaque at many levels.

Reporting for private real estate funds commonly consists of a quarterly report with details on the fund's size, progress in drawdowns, realizations to date, and valuations of unrealized investments as well as market commentary relevant to the fund's strategy. Reports typically include details on each investment such as the original acquisition cost(s), square footage, borrowing details (e.g., cost of debt, leverage ratios, and debt maturity dates), and fundamental metrics regarding the health of the properties (e.g., occupancy rates and, if appropriate, the estimated credit health of tenants). Often there is qualitative commentary on the health of the property's submarket, on anticipated next steps, and on the timing of realization(s). Reports are typically issued with a one-quarter lag to allow sufficient time to update property valuations. Annual reports, which frequently require updated third-party appraisals, may not be available until the second quarter following year end.

Investors should ensure that funds use independent administrators to calculate the fund and LPs' NAV. These administrators are also responsible for processing cash flows, including contributions, fee payments, and distributions that are consistent with the fund documents. The use of independent administrators is common practice among hedge funds. It is relatively uncommon for a fund investing in illiquid strategies (e.g., private equity/credit, real estate/natural resources) to use an independent administrator. Funds that do not use third-party administrators have wide discretion in valuing assets. In the midst of the Great Financial Crisis, it was not uncommon for two different private equity firms with ownership interests in the same company to provide very different estimates of the company's value.

The lack of transparency common with many alternative investments can challenge risk management and performance evaluation. High-quality alternative investment managers will engage an independent and respected accounting firm to perform an annual audit of the fund; the audit report should be available to the LPs.

Regulatory requirements for mutual funds and UCITS funds require such standardized information as costs, expected risks, and performance data. Additional information may also be available on a periodic basis. Information provided to one investor should be available to all shareholders. These rules have been interpreted by some mutual fund/UCITS managers to mean that they cannot provide more-detailed, non-standardized information given the complexity of sharing it with a broad audience. This can possibly restrict the level of transparency certain shareholders can obtain for these vehicles.

---

[8] Andrew Ceresney, "Keynote Address: Private Equity Enforcement," Securities Enforcement Forum West (12 May 2016).

> **EXAMPLE 5**
>
> ### Suitability Considerations in Allocating to Alternative Investments
>
> The Christian family office is concerned with investor or manager fraud and so will invest only in separately managed accounts (SMAs).
>
> 1. What are the benefits and drawbacks to the use of SMAs?
> 2. The 75-year-old patriarch of the Christian family would like to consider a significant private equity allocation in a trust that he oversees on behalf of his youngest daughter. This would be the first alternative investment commitment made with any of the family's assets. The daughter is 40 years old. She will receive one-half of the assets outright upon his death. The remainder of the assets will be held in trust subject to the terms of the trust agreement. List some of the reasons why private equity may or may not be appropriate for this trust.
>
> ### Solution to 1:
>
> Although an SMA allows for greater transparency and control of capital flows (the manager does not generally have the authority to distribute capital from the client account), it has several potential disadvantages: 1) SMAs are not available or appropriate for many alternative strategies; thus, the requirement to invest via an SMA may limit the ability to develop an optimal alternative investment program. 2) A manager cannot invest alongside the client in the client's SMA. This may reduce the alignment of interest between the manager and the client and may give rise to conflicts of interest as trades are allocated between the SMA and the manager's other funds.
>
> ### Solution to 2:
>
> - Successful private equity investment requires a long time horizon. Given the patriarch's age, it is likely that half of the trust's assets will be distributed before the private equity program has had time to mature. This may lead to an unintended doubling in the size of the private equity allocation.
> - The patriarch has no experience investing in alternative assets. Unless he is willing to commit the time, money, and effort and engage an outside adviser with the relevant expertise and access to top-tier funds, the likelihood of a successful private equity investment program would be low.
> - Because the beneficiary of the trust is relatively young, the time horizon of the investment likely matches the profile of the underlying investor. It may be appropriate for the trust to invest in long-dated private equity assets, provided the investment is sized appropriately and the necessary expertise has been retained.

9. ASSET ALLOCATION APPROACHES AND STATISTICAL PROPERTIES AND CHALLENGES OF ASSET RETURNS

f discuss approaches to asset allocation to alternative investments;

We mentioned earlier that one approach to determining the desired allocation to the alternative asset classes is to make the initial asset allocation decision using only the broad, liquid asset classes and do a second iteration of the asset allocation exercise incorporating alternative assets. After first addressing the challenges in developing risk and return assumptions for alternative asset classes, we then discuss three primary approaches that investors use to approach this second iteration.

1 *Monte Carlo simulation.* We discuss how Monte Carlo simulation may be used to generate return scenarios that relax the assumption of normally distributed returns. We illustrate how simulation can be applied to estimate the long-term risk profile and return potential of various asset allocation alternatives, and, in particular, we evaluate whether various asset allocation alternatives would satisfy the investor's ultimate investment objectives.

2 *Optimization techniques.* Mean–variance optimization (MVO) typically over-allocates to alternative asset classes, partly because risk is underestimated because of stale or infrequent pricing and the underlying assumption that returns are normally distributed. Practitioners usually address this bias towards alternatives by establishing limits on the allocations to alternatives. Optimization methods that incorporate downside risk (mean–CVaR optimization) or take into account skew may be used to enhance the asset allocation process.

3 *Risk factor-based approaches.* Risk factor-based approaches to alternative asset allocation can be applied to develop more robust asset allocation proposals.

These analytical techniques complement each other, and investors frequently rely on all of them rather than just using one or the other. Monte Carlo simulation can provide simulated non-normal (fat-tailed) data for a mean–CVaR optimization, but simulation can also be applied to analyze the long-term behavior of various asset allocation alternatives that are the results of portfolio optimization.

9.1 Statistical Properties and Challenges of Asset Returns

Alternative investments present the modeler with a number of analytical challenges. These two are particularly relevant in the asset allocation process:

1 Appraisal-based valuations used in private alternative investments often lead to stale and/or artificially smoothed returns. Volatility and other risk measures estimated based on these smoothed time series would potentially understate the actual, fundamental risk.

2 Although even the public asset classes can exhibit non-normal return distributions, skewness and fat tails (excess kurtosis) are more pronounced with many of the alternative investment strategies. Leverage, sensitivity to the disappearance of liquidity, and even the asymmetric nature of performance fees all contribute to additional skewness and excess kurtosis among alternative investments. This option–payoff style quality can undermine a simplistic statistical approach.

Asset allocators use various analytical approaches to mitigate the impact of these challenges.

9.1.1 *Stale Pricing and Unsmoothing*

Appraisal-based valuation is common in private real estate and private equity. The valuation parameter assumptions in the appraisal process change quite slowly. This has a smoothing effect on reported returns and gives the illusion that illiquid assets' performance is much less volatile than that of public marketable assets with similar fundamental characteristics. This issue also affects hedge funds in which the manager invests in illiquid or less-liquid assets whose valuations are updated infrequently or are using models with static valuation assumptions. These artificially smoothed returns can be detected by testing the return stream for serial correlation. If serial correlation is detected and found statistically significant, the analyst needs to unsmooth the returns to get a more accurate representation of the risk and return characteristics of the asset class we are modelling.

To illustrate unsmoothing, we use a simple approach described by Ang (2014). Exhibit 19 illustrates the reported quarterly return history of the Cambridge Associates Private Equity Index, as well as the unsmoothed series.[9] The annualized volatility estimated using the reported quarterly return data and scaling using the square root of time convention is 9.5%.[10] The widely accepted rule of scaling by the square root of time, however, is based on the assumption of serially uncorrelated, normally-distributed returns. In our example, the serial correlation of the quarterly reported private equity returns is 0.38, which, given the number of observations, is significant with a t-statistic of 4.09. Because our returns are serially correlated, we want to unsmooth the returns to get a better estimate of volatility. The volatility calculated on the unsmoothed return series is 14.0%, significantly higher than the volatility estimated from the unsmoothed data.

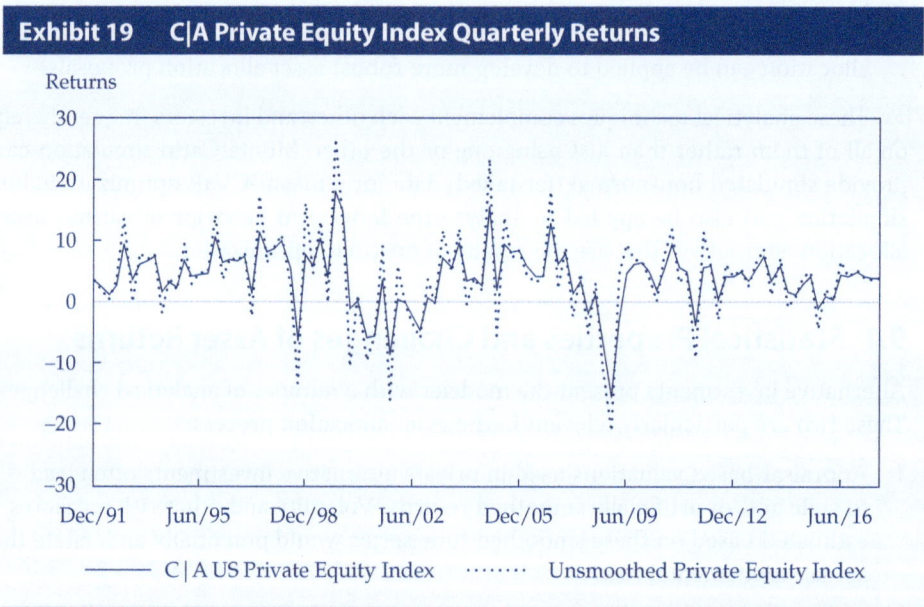

Exhibit 19   C|A Private Equity Index Quarterly Returns

Exhibit 20 illustrates serial correlation and volatility estimates based on quarterly returns of a broad range of asset classes. Although the serial correlation of public marketable asset classes is generally low, private asset classes and some hedge fund strategies have higher serial correlations that indicate stronger smoothing effects. The higher the serial correlation in the reported return series, the larger the difference between the volatility based on the unsmoothed and reported (smoothed) return data.

---

9 We used the following formula to unsmooth the report total return time series:
$r_{t,\text{unsmoothed}} = (r_{t,\text{reported}} - s \times r_{t-1,\text{reported}})/(1 - s)$,
where s denotes the estimated serial correlation of the time series.

10 To scale volatility estimates to a longer (or shorter) time horizon, the volatility can be multiplied by the square root of time. For example, if we know the quarterly volatility and want an annual volatility estimate, we would multiply the quarterly volatility estimate by the square root of 4. (This scaling convention assumes price changes are independent and returns are not serially correlated over time.)

The impact of smoothing is the highest in the case of private investments, as suggested by the serial correlation for private real estate (0.85) and private equity (0.38). The unsmoothed volatility of private real estate is, in fact, three times the volatility that we would estimate based on the reported returns. Given the serial correlation evident in private alternative strategies, it is not surprising that the distressed hedge fund strategy exhibits higher serial correlation (0.36) than other hedge fund strategies.

Exhibit 20   The Effect of Serial Correlation on Volatility

Quarterly Data Dec. 1997–Sept. 2017	Serial Correlation	Volatility (reported returns)	Volatility (unsmoothed)
US Equities	0.03	17.0%	17.7%
Non-US Developed Market Equities	0.08	19.2%	20.8%
Emerging Market Equities	0.17	26.2%	30.8%
Governments	−0.01	4.9%	4.9%
Broad Fixed Income	0.02	3.4%	3.5%
High-Yield Credit	0.34	10.0%	14.3%
Inflation-Linked Bonds	0.12	5.0%	5.7%
Hedge Funds—Aggregate	0.15	8.1%	9.5%
HF Macro	0.08	5.4%	5.9%
HF Equity Market Neutral	0.17	3.5%	4.1%
HF Equity Hedged	0.19	10.7%	13.1%
HF Distressed	0.36	8.9%	13.0%
Commodities	0.14	25.2%	28.8%
Public Real Estate	0.15	20.4%	24.0%
Private Real Estate	0.85	4.6%	13.8%
Private Equity	0.38	10.7%	15.7%

9.1.2 *Skewness and Fat Tails*

A common and convenient assumption behind asset pricing theory, as well as models applied for asset allocation and risk analytics, is that asset returns are normally distributed. Both academic researchers and practitioners are widely aware of the limitations of this assumption, but no standard quantitative method to replace this assumption of normality exists. Skewness and excess kurtosis, or so-called "fat tails," in the distributions of empirically observed asset returns may lead to underestimated downside risk measures in the case of both traditional and alternative asset classes. Non-normality of returns, however, can be more severe in private alternative asset class and certain hedge fund strategies than in most of the traditional asset classes.

In Exhibit 21, we show skewness and excess kurtosis parameters calculated based on 20 years of unsmoothed quarterly return data of various public and alternative asset classes. We also show 95% quarterly conditional value at risk (CVaR) estimates based on the assumption of normally distributed asset returns, as well as based on the observed (actual) distributions. Positive skewness indicates smaller downside risk potential, while negative skewness indicates greater downside risk potential. Excess kurtosis (i.e., a kurtosis parameter exceeding 3) similarly points toward greater downside risk than would be apparent from the numbers calculated using the assumption of normally-distributed returns. The observed (actual) CVaR estimates typically exceed the normal distribution-based CVaR figures when kurtosis is high and skewness is negative. Equity market-neutral hedge funds and private real estate have the biggest *relative* differences between the 95% normal distribution CVaR and the observed CVaR (columns C and D divided by column C). Both of these strategies have negative skewness and fairly high excess kurtosis. It's interesting to note that distressed hedge funds similarly have high kurtosis and negative skewness, but the difference in tail risk measures becomes mainly visible at the 99% confidence level, where the extreme but infrequent losses may occur.

Exhibit 21   Normal Distribution Assumption and Observed Downside Risk Measures

Unsmoothed Quarterly Data Dec. 1997–Sept. 2017	(A) Skewness	(B) Excess Kurtosis	(C) 95% CVaR (Normal Distribution)	(D) 95% CVaR (Observed)	(E) 99% CVaR (Normal Distribution)	(F) 99% CVaR (Observed)
US Equities	−0.51	0.43	−15.3%	−17.7%	−20.3%	−23.9%
Non-US Dev Equities	−0.19	0.29	−18.9%	−19.8%	−24.8%	−20.7%
Emerging Mkt Equities	−0.23	−0.03	−28.2%	−25.4%	−37.0%	−27.7%
Governments	0.59	0.39	−3.5%	−3.2%	−4.9%	−4.0%
Broad Fixed Income	−0.05	−0.41	−2.1%	−2.4%	−3.1%	−3.1%
High-Yield Credit	0.18	6.14	−7.9%	−9.8%	−10.8%	−19.7%
Inflation-Linked Bonds	−0.32	1.08	−4.2%	−4.2%	−5.8%	−8.1%
Hedge Funds	−0.17	1.69	−7.6%	−8.6%	−10.3%	−9.7%
HF Macro	0.36	0.85	−4.3%	−4.1%	−6.0%	−5.1%
HF Equity Market Neutral	−1.17	3.55	−2.9%	−3.9%	−4.1%	−5.4%
HF Equity Hedged	0.08	2.24	−10.8%	−10.6%	−14.5%	−12.7%
HF Distressed	−1.25	3.52	−10.8%	−11.1%	−14.5%	−16.9%
Commodities	−0.71	1.62	−28.4%	−30.6%	−36.6%	−50.6%
Public Real Estate	−0.88	4.60	−20.9%	−24.5%	−27.7%	−40.2%
Private Real Estate	−2.80	9.62	−11.3%	−15.4%	−15.3%	−27.9%
Private Equity	−0.46	2.05	−12.2%	−15.7%	−16.7%	−22.6%

Source: Authors' calculations.

To further illustrate the impact of non-normality on the downside risk, in Exhibit 22 we compare the ratio of observed to normal CVaR measures with the skewness and excess kurtosis. Although the skewness or excess kurtosis alone doesn't fully explain the relative difference between observed and normal 95% CVaR (positive skewness may compensate high excess kurtosis or vice versa), we can see the evidence that higher kurtosis or more negative skewness usually increases the likely severity of any tail risk.

Exhibit 22   The Impact of Skewness and Kurtosis on Tail Risk

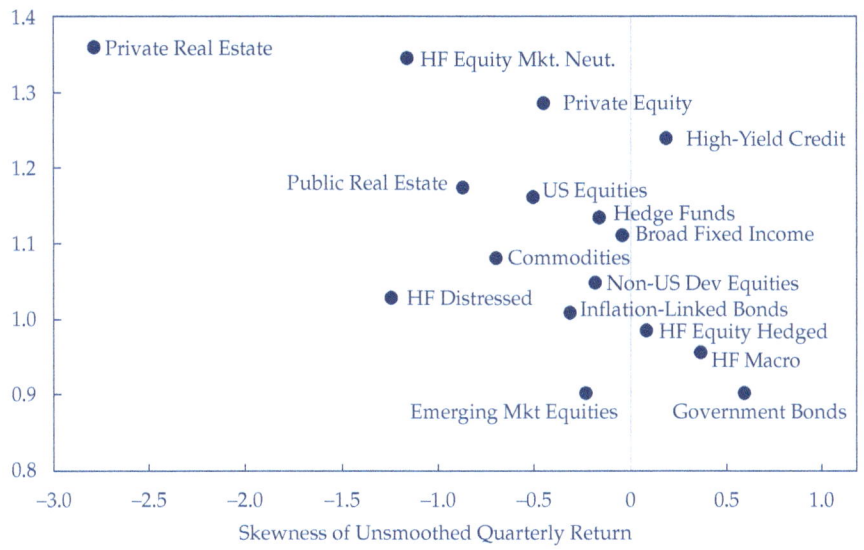

Source: Authors' calculations.

Analysts can choose to incorporate non-normality into their analyses in a few different ways. The most obvious and straightforward choice is to use empirically observed asset returns instead of working with the normal distribution. Still, in private investments where we typically have only quarterly return data, the analyses may be subject to serious limitations. Even with 20 years of quarterly return data, we have only 80 data points (and the industry has changed significantly over this time, further straining the validity of the data).

With sufficient data, analysts and researchers can capture the effects of fat tails by using advanced mathematical or statistical models:

- Time-varying volatility models (e.g., stochastic volatility), which assume that volatility is not constant over time but changes dynamically, can be used.
- Regime-switching models capture return, volatility, and correlation characteristics in different market environments (bull/bear or low volatility and moderate correlation vs. high volatility and elevated correlation). The combination of two or more normal distributions with different average returns, volatilities, and correlations could capture skewed and fat-tailed distributions.
- Extreme value theory and other fat-tailed distributions can be used when the analyst wants to focus on the behavior in the tails.

Although no single and uniformly accepted approach exists to address all of these quantitative challenges to the asset allocation exercise, a sound asset allocation process will do the following:

1   Adjust the observed asset class return data by unsmoothing the return series if the autocorrelation is significant.

2 Determine whether it is reasonable to accept an assumption of normal return distributions, in which case mean–variance optimization is appropriate to use.

3 Allow you to choose an optimization approach that takes the tail risk into account if the time series exhibits fat tails and skewness and if the potential downside risk would exceed the levels that would be observed with a normal distribution.

10 MONTE CARLO SIMULATION

f discuss approaches to asset allocation to alternative investments;

Monte Carlo simulation can be a very useful tool in asset allocation to alternative investments. In this section, we discuss two applications of this modeling approach. First, we discuss how we can simulate risk factor or asset return scenarios that exhibit the skewness and kurtosis commonly seen in alternative investments. Second, we illustrate simulation-based risk and return analytics over a long time horizon in a broad asset allocation context.

At a very high level, we can summarize the model construction process in the following steps:

1 Identify those variables that we would like to randomly generate in our simulation. These variables may be asset class total returns directly, or risk factors, depending on the model.

2 Establish the quantitative framework to generate realistic random scenarios for the selected asset class returns or risk factors. Here, the analyst faces several choices, including the following:

   a What kind of time-series model are we using? Will it be a random walk? Or will it incorporate serial correlations and mean-reversion-like characteristics?

   b What kind of distribution should we assume for the shocks or innovations to the variables? Is normal distribution reasonable? Or, will we use some fat-tailed distribution model instead?

   c Are volatilities and correlations stable over time? Or, do they vary across time?

3 If using a risk factor approach, convert the risk factors to asset or asset class returns using a factor-based model. In this reading, all our illustrations are based on linear factor models, but certain asset types with optionality need more-sophisticated models to incorporate non-linear characteristics as well.

4 Further translate realistic asset class return scenarios into meaningful indicators. We can simultaneously model, for example, the investment portfolio and the liability of a pension fund, enabling us to assess how the funding ratio is expected to evolve over time. Or, in the case of an endowment fund, we can assess whether certain asset allocation choices would improve the probability of meeting the spending rate target while preserving the purchasing power of the asset base.

10.1 Simulating Skewed and Fat-Tailed Financial Variables

A fairly intuitive way of incorporating non-normal returns into the analysis is to assume that there are two (or more) possible states of the world. Individually, each state can be described by using a normal distribution (*conditional normality*), but the combination of these two distributions will not be normally distributed.[11] Next, we show a fairly simplified application for the public equities and government bonds. Note that the same approach can be applied to more asset classes as well, or it can be applied to risk factor changes rather than asset class returns.

For this illustration, we assume that the capital markets can be described by two distinct regimes—a "quiet period" (Regime 1) and a high-volatility state (Regime 2). Exhibit 23 shows the quarterly return history of the US equities and government bonds as well as the model's more volatile regimes (the gray-shaded periods). It is easy to see that the Global Financial Crisis—and such earlier crisis periods as the 1997 Asian currency contagion, the 1998 Russian ruble crisis and LTCM meltdown, and the 2002 tech bubble burst—all belong to the high-volatility regimes. The mean return and volatility statistics for the full period as well as each of the two regimes can be found in Exhibit 24. Equities outperformed government bonds over the full observation period, and it's interesting to see how dynamics changed between the quiet to the volatile periods. In the quiet period (Regime 1), equities outperformed bonds by around 4.6% quarterly, whereas in the volatile period (Regime 2), government bonds outperformed equities by more than 5%. The total return volatilities also jumped dramatically when the market switched from quiet to volatile periods. In addition, the correlation between equities and bonds was near zero during the quiet period but turned significantly negative (about –0.6) during the volatile period. Finally, we estimate that the low-volatility Regime 1 prevailed 62% of the time and the high-volatility Regime 2 prevailed 38% of the time.

Exhibit 23 US Equities and Government Bonds Return History and Identification of High-Volatility Regimes

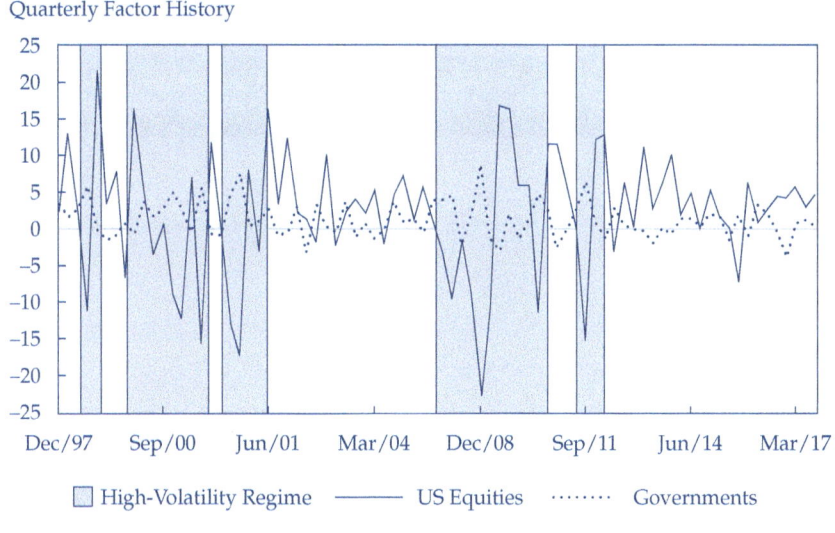

Source: Authors' calculations.

---

[11] The estimation process of such models is beyond the scope of this reading. Readers interested in additional details are referred to Hamilton (1989) and Kim and Nelson (1999).

Exhibit 24   Return Statistics (1997–2017)

	Equities	Government Bonds
Quarterly Average Return	2.1%	1.2%
Quarterly Return Volatility	8.5%	4.5%
Skewness	–0.5	0.6
Kurtosis	0.4	0.4
Average Return in Regime 1	5.1%	0.5%
Average Return in Regime 2	–3.1%	2.4%
Volatility in Regime 1	5.5%	1.9%
Volatility in Regime 2	13.7%	3.8%
Correlation in Regime 1		0.0
Correlation in Regime 2		–0.6

If we want to capture only skewness and fat tails in a simulation framework, we just need the normal distribution parameters of the distinct regimes and the overall state probabilities of either Regime 1 or Regime 2. Then, the analyst would generate normally distributed random scenarios based on the different means and covariances estimated under the two (or more) regimes with the appropriate frequency of the estimated probability of being the quiet or hectic regimes. This mixture of high- and low-volatility normal distributions would lead to an altogether skewed and fat-tailed distribution of asset class return or risk factor changes. In practice, some may build a more dynamic, multi-step simulation model for a longer time horizon, in which case it's also important to estimate the probability of switching from one regime to another.

Exhibit 25 shows histograms of equity returns, overlaid with the fitted normal distribution and the combined distributions from our regime-switching model. As the chart illustrates, the combination of two normal distributions improves the distribution fit and introduces some degree of skewness and fat-tail characteristics.

Exhibit 25   Normal and Fat-Tailed Distribution Fit for US Equity Quarterly Returns

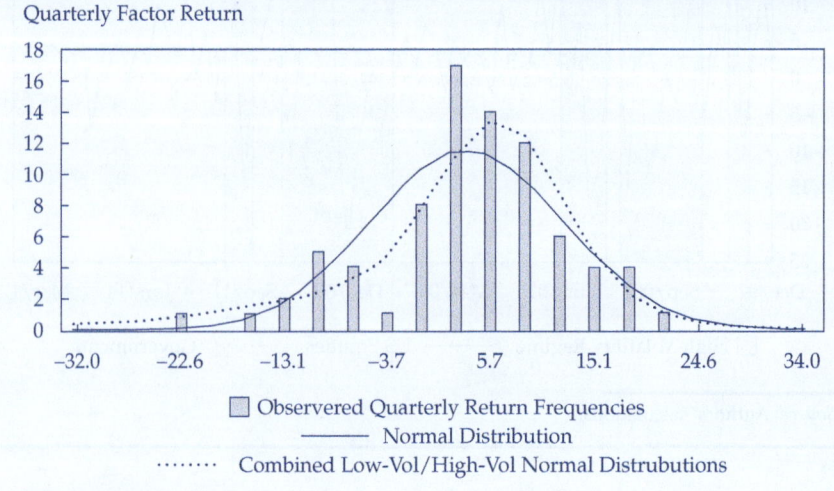

Source: Authors' calculations.

Several variations of regime-switching models are available. We have used a very basic set-up to illustrate the additional richness a regime-switching model can bring to the analysis. We could also apply a similar approach if we were to build asset classes using risk factors. We could overlay the non-normal distributions of the risk factors on the relevant asset class returns.[12]

10.2 Simulation for Long-Term Horizon Risk Assessment

We will now work through a practical application of Monte Carlo simulation in the context of asset allocation over a long time horizon. We simulate asset class returns in quarterly steps over a 10-year time horizon.[13] Such models exhibit some degree of mean-reversion and also capture dynamic interactions across risk factors or asset classes over multiple time periods.

The volatilities, correlations, and other parameters of the time series model are estimated based on the past 20 years of unsmoothed asset class return data. The expected returns for the selected asset classes (shown in Exhibit 26), however, are not based on historical average returns but are illustrative, forward-looking estimates. Note that these return expectations mostly assume passive investments in the specific asset class and don't include the possible value-added from (or lost through) active management. Hedge funds are the exception, of course, because by definition hedge funds are actively managed investment strategies rather than a true stand-alone asset class. The expected returns are also generally assumed to be net of fees to make them comparable across asset classes.

Asset class-level expected returns are critically important to an asset allocation exercise. Return expectations should be reflective of the current market conditions—including valuations, levels of interest rates, and spreads. Setting return expectations requires a combination of objective facts (e.g., the current yield and spread levels) and judgment (how risk factors and valuation ratios might change from the current levels over the relevant time horizon).

---

12 In this reading, we assume that various asset classes have constant risk factor sensitivities over time, an assumption that can be relaxed in practice. For example, Berkelaar, Kobor, and Kouwenberg (2009) present time-varying risk factors for various hedge fund strategies in a similar Monte Carlo simulation framework.
13 To ensure that we not only capture short-horizon risks but also properly assess long-term asset return behavior characteristics, we capture the linear interdependencies among multiple time series by working with a vector-autoregressive model.

Exhibit 26   Asset Class Expected Returns

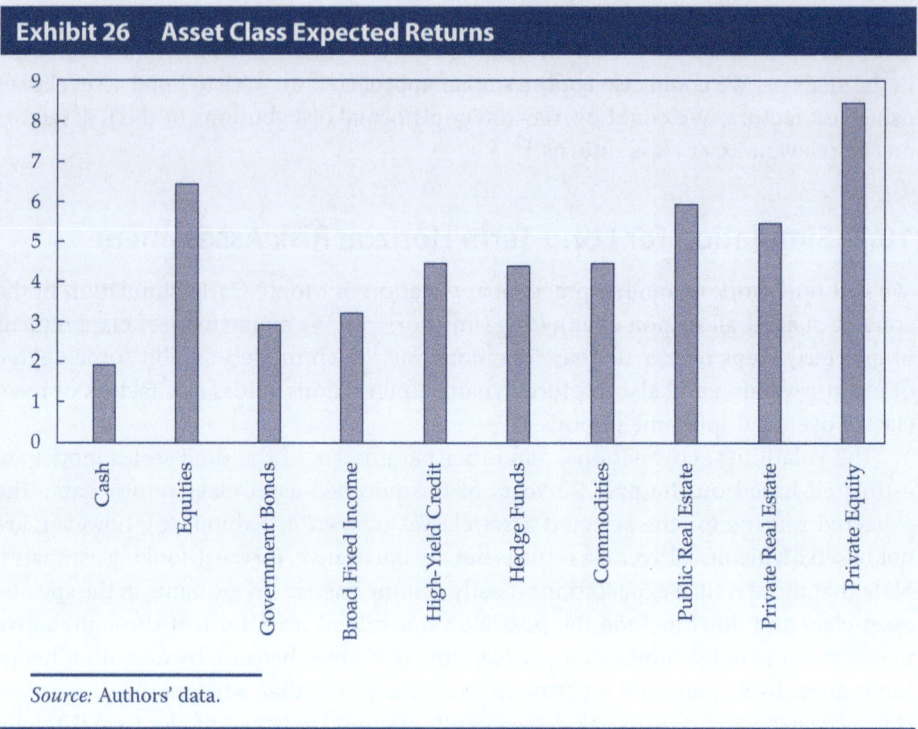

Source: Authors' data.

In this example, we compare three possible portfolios:

- A portfolio 100% invested in government bonds
- A portfolio allocated 50% to global public equities and 50% to broad fixed income
- A diversified "endowment portfolio" allocated 40% to global public equities, 15% to fixed income, 20% to broad hedge funds, 15% to private equity, 5% to private real estate, and 5% to commodities

Exhibit 27 shows the risk and return statistics for the three portfolios. VaR and CVaR downside risk measures focus over the shorter, quarterly, and 1-year time horizons. The worst drawdown and the cumulative annualized total return ranges are expressed over a 10-year time horizon.

Exhibit 27   Portfolio Risk and Return Estimates

	Government Bond Portfolio	50/50 Portfolio	Endowment Portfolio
Expected Geometric Return over 10 Years	2.3%	5.6%	7.0%
Annual Total Return Volatility	4.2%	6.6%	11.2%
95% VaR over Q/Q (quarter over quarter)	−3.1%	−2.9%	−4.6%
95% VaR over 1 Year	−5.2%	−4.2%	−9.1%
95% CVaR over Q/Q	−4.0%	−3.9%	−6.4%
95% CVaR over 1 Year	−6.9%	−6.6%	−13.1%
99% VaR over Q/Q	−4.5%	−4.6%	−7.5%
99% VaR over 1 Year	−7.9%	−8.1%	−15.6%
99% CVaR over Q/Q	−5.2%	−5.5%	−8.7%

Exhibit 27   (Continued)

	Government Bond Portfolio	50/50 Portfolio	Endowment Portfolio
99% CVaR over 1 Year	−9.2%	−10.3%	−18.7%
Worst Drawdown over 10 Years	−19.8%	−22.5%	−36.9%

10-Year Return Distribution	Government Bond Portfolio	50/50 Portfolio	Endowment Portfolio
5% Low	0.0%	2.3%	1.9%
25% Low	1.2%	4.2%	4.8%
50% (Median)	2.3%	5.6%	7.0%
75% High	3.1%	7.0%	9.1%
95% High	4.5%	9.0%	12.2%

From Exhibit 27, we see that the multi-asset endowment portfolio generates a significantly higher return than the portfolio exclusively invested in government bonds, albeit at much higher downside risk as measured by VaR, CVaR, or worst drawdown. This table alone, however, is insufficient to determine which investment alternative a particular investor should choose.

Consider the case of a university endowment fund. Let's assume that the investment objective is to support a 5% annual spending rate as well as to preserve the purchasing power of the asset base over the 10-year time horizon. We use the same simulation engine to generate the analytics of Exhibit 28. Here, we plot the expected cumulative total return within a +/− 1 standard deviation range together with the cumulative spending rate, as well as the spending rate augmented with inflation on a cumulative basis. The latter two variables represent the investment target, so we can meaningfully interpret the return potential of the two investment choices in the context of the investment objective. The 50% equities/50% government bond portfolio initially appeared to be a lower risk alternative in Exhibit 27, but Exhibit 28 shows that this choice is more likely to fall short of the return target, given that its median return of 5.6% is less than the nominal return target of approximately 7% (the 5% spending rate plus 2% inflation). At the same time, the endowment portfolio's 7% median return indicates that it would have a better chance of meeting the investment objective.

Exhibit 28 Cumulative Total Return Cones Simulated over a 10-Year Horizon

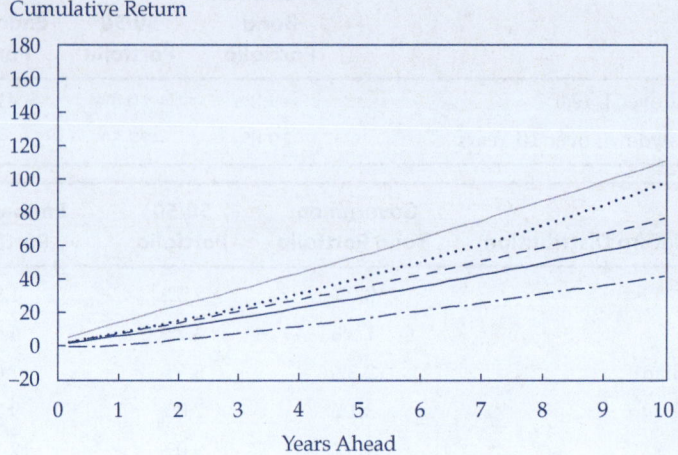

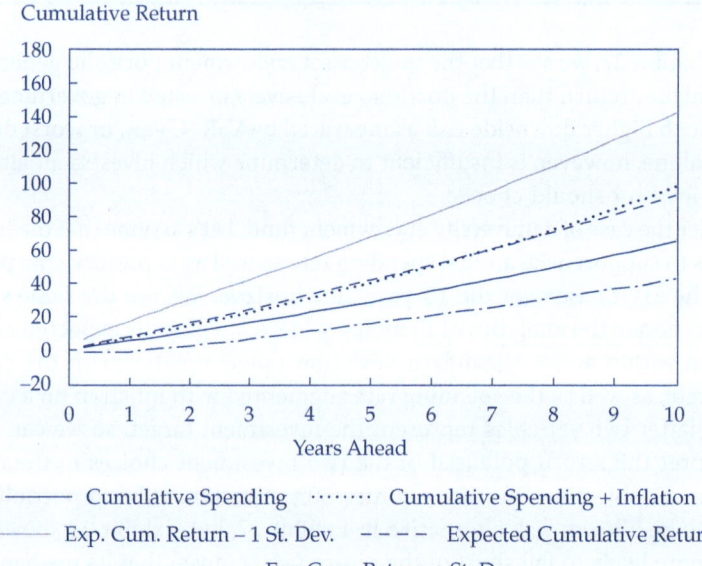

Exhibit 29 shows the probability of meeting the spending rate as well as the spending rate plus inflation at any point in time over the investment horizon. If risk is defined as the probability of falling short of meeting the return target (rather than the asset-only perspective of risk, volatility), the otherwise lower-risk 50% equities and 50% government bond portfolio becomes the higher risk alternative.

Exhibit 29 Estimated Probability of Achieving the Investment Goal

A.
Probability of meeting spending target

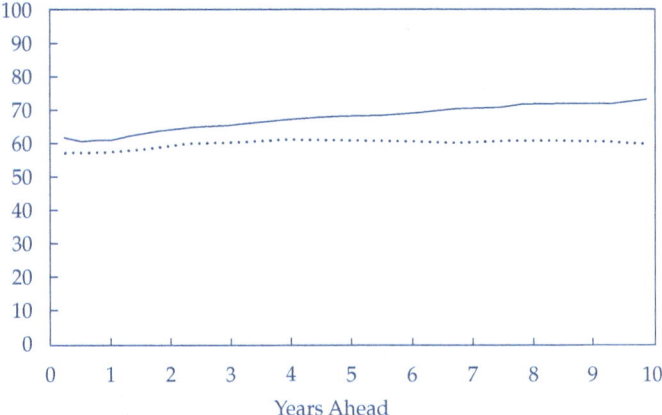

B.
Probability of meeting spending target plus inflation

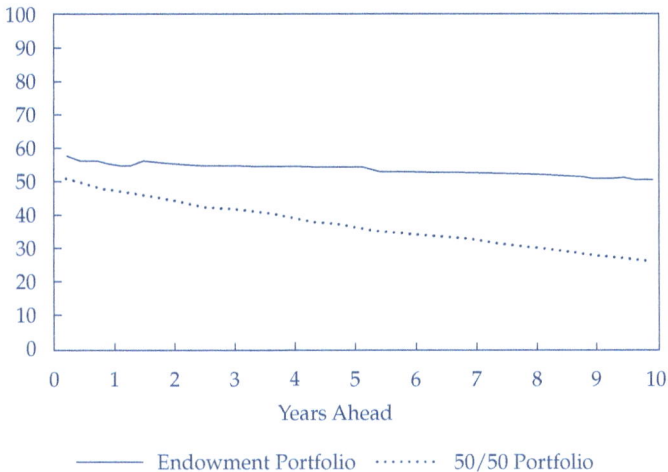

—— Endowment Portfolio ········ 50/50 Portfolio

PORTFOLIO OPTIMIZATION

11

f   discuss approaches to asset allocation to alternative investments;

Portfolio optimization for asset allocation has been covered in great detail in earlier readings. Here we focus on some special considerations for optimization in the context of alternative investments.

11.1 Mean–Variance Optimization without and with Constraints

We mentioned earlier that mean–variance optimization would likely over-allocate to alternative, mainly illiquid, asset classes given their higher expected returns and potentially underestimated risk. Some investors impose minimum and maximum constraints on various asset classes to compensate for this bias. Let's consider the ramifications of this approach.

Here, the input data for our optimization are comprised of the asset class expected returns depicted in Exhibit 26, while the covariance matrix is based on the unsmoothed asset class return history over the past 20 years. Exhibit 30 shows the optimized portfolio allocations generated by the mean–variance optimization without and with constraints. Each column in these bar charts represents an optimized portfolio allocation subject to a return target. The exhibit progresses from low-return targets on the left to high-return targets on the right. In total, we show 20 possible portfolio allocations first without and then with constraints.

By reviewing Panel B of Exhibit 30, we can see that the unconstrained portfolio allocations are dominated by cash and fixed income at the lower end of the risk spectrum, and private equity becomes the dominant asset class for higher risk portfolios. Optimization is quite sensitive to the input parameters: It's quite common to see allocations concentrated in a small number of asset classes. Thus, investors shouldn't take the unconstrained output as the "best" allocation. Small changes in the input variables could lead to large changes in the asset allocations.

Because investors would potentially reject the raw, concentrated output of unconstrained mean–variance optimization, we also ran a constrained optimization where we capped private equity and hedge fund allocations at 30% each, private real estate at 15%, and major public asset classes at 50% each. The resulting constrained allocations, shown in the Panel A of Exhibit 30, are less concentrated and appear to be more diversified.

Exhibit 31 depicts the mean–variance efficient frontiers corresponding to the optimized portfolio allocations of Exhibit 30. Note that both frontiers contain 20 dots, each representing an optimized portfolio. The numbers under each bar in Exhibit 30 identify the allocation associated with each of the dots on the efficient frontiers in Exhibit 31 (e.g., the allocation associated with portfolio 20 on the efficient frontier in Exhibit 31 is the one shown at the rightmost edge of Exhibit 30).

Portfolio Optimization

Exhibit 30 Unconstrained and Constrained Asset Allocations

A. Constrained Portfolios

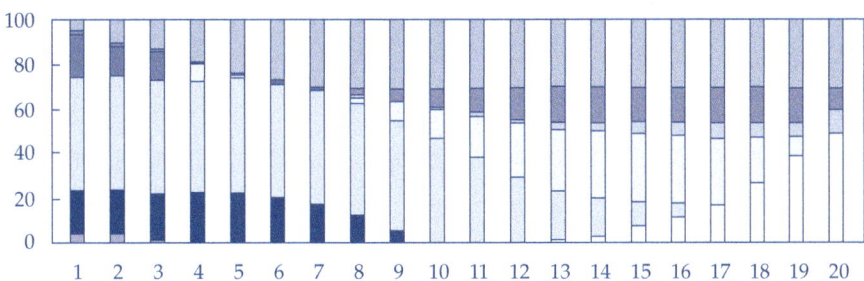

B. Unconstrained Portfolios

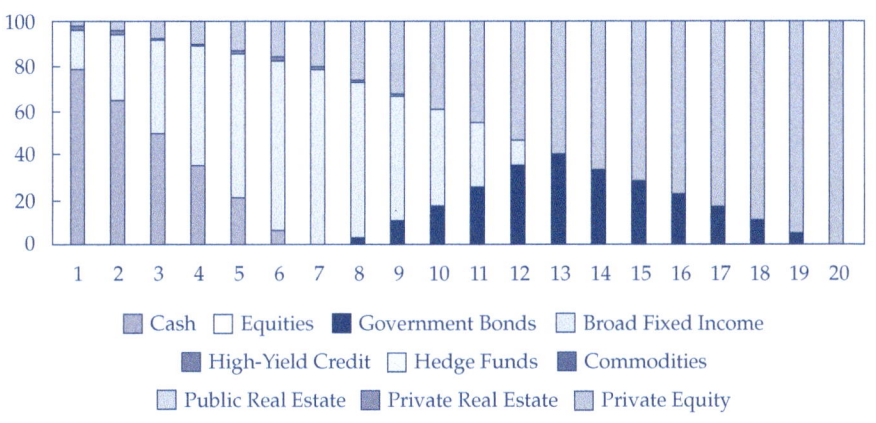

■ Cash □ Equities ■ Government Bonds □ Broad Fixed Income
■ High-Yield Credit □ Hedge Funds ■ Commodities
□ Public Real Estate ■ Private Real Estate □ Private Equity

Note that the constrained efficient frontier runs below its unconstrained peer (Exhibit 31). This is not unexpected, as we artificially prohibited the optimization from selecting the most efficient allocation it could get based on the available quantitative data.

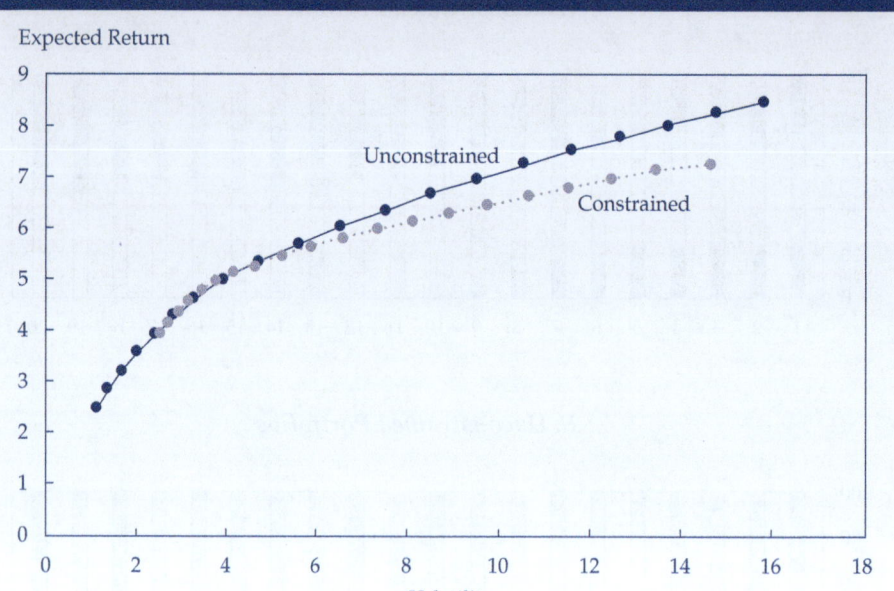

Exhibit 31 Unconstrained and Constrained Mean–Variance Efficient Frontiers

In practice, many investors are aware of the limits of the mean–variance framework—the possible underestimation of the true fundamental risks based on the reported returns of private investments—and they may also have in mind other constraints, such as capping illiquidity. Thus, introducing maximum and minimum constraints for certain asset classes may be a reasonable, although exogenous, adjustment to the quantitative optimization. However, not even constrained optimized allocations should be accepted without further scrutiny. In fact, similar volatility and expected return profiles can be achieved with a wide variety of asset allocations. So, although optimized portfolios may serve as analytical guidance, it's important to validate whether a change to an asset allocation policy results in a significant return increment and/or volatility reduction. Sometimes the results of a constrained optimization are largely driven by the constraints (especially if they are very tight). If that is the case, then the optimizer might not be able to perform its job due to the many (or very tight) constraints applied.

11.2 Mean–CVaR Optimization

Portfolio optimization can also improve the asset allocation decision through a risk management lens. An investor who is particularly concerned with the downside risk of a proposed asset allocation may choose to minimize the portfolio's CVaR rather than its volatility relative to a return target.[14] If the portfolio contains asset classes and investment strategies with negative skewness and long tails, the CVaR lens could materially alter the asset allocation decision. Minimizing CVaR subject to an expected return target is quantitatively much more complex than portfolio variance minimization: It requires a large number of historical or simulated return scenarios to properly incorporate potential tail risk into the optimization.[15]

---

[14] Because we are optimizing allocation to asset classes, the CVaR tail risk measure quantifies *systematic* asset class level risks. Individual asset managers or securities may impose additional idiosyncratic risk when the asset allocation is implemented in practice.

[15] Technical details are provided by Rockafellar and Uryasev (2000).

Portfolio Optimization

Our first illustration is applied to three hedge fund strategies: macro, equity market neutral, and long/short equity hedged. Our expected returns for the three strategies are 3.6%, 3.6%, and 6.0%, respectively. The observed return distribution for macro strategy is fairly normal, while equity market neutral exhibits negative skew and the highest kurtosis of these three strategies (see Exhibit 21).

Panels A and B of Exhibit 32 compare 20 possible portfolio allocations generated by the mean–variance and mean–CVaR optimizations, varying from low to high risk/return profiles. The allocation to long/short equity hedged (the black bar) is similar under both the MVO and CVaR approaches. The macro strategy receives a much higher allocation using the CVaR approach than it does using the MVO approach.

Exhibit 32   Hedge Fund Allocations

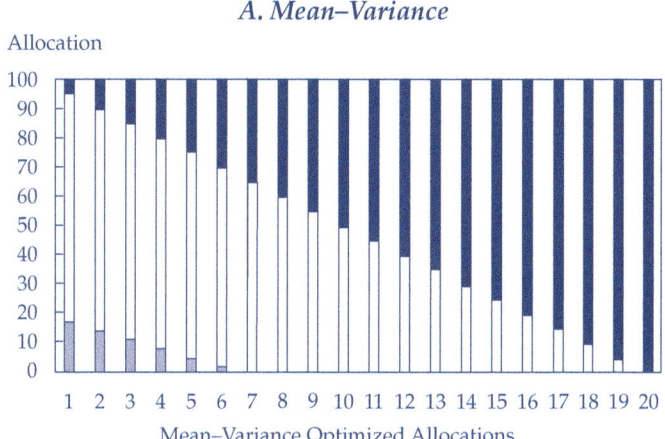

A. Mean–Variance

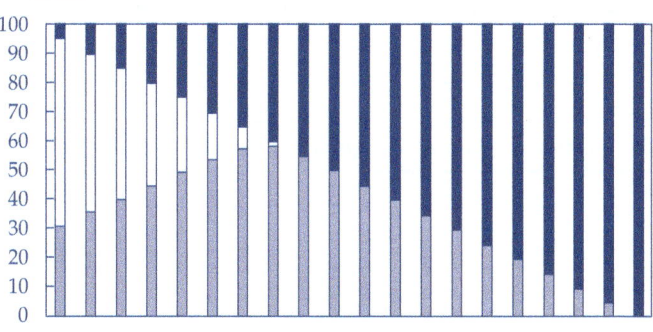

B. Mean–CVaR

☐ HF Macro   ☐ HF Equity Market-Neutral   ■ HF Equity Hedged

Exhibit 33 compares portfolio #12 from the mean–variance efficient frontier to portfolio #12 from the mean–CVaR efficient frontier. Both portfolios allocated 60% to the long/short equity strategy. Under the CVaR-optimization approach, the remaining 40% of the portfolio is invested in global macro. Under the MVO approach, the remaining 40% of the portfolio is invested in equity market-neutral.

Let's compare the portfolio volatilities and downside risk measures. The mean–CVaR portfolio has higher volatility (7.8% vs 7.3%) but lower tail risk (−6.8% vs −7.7%). Exhibit 33 also shows a third portfolio, which evenly *splits* the 40% not allocated to equity-hedged between global macro and equity market neutral. The volatility of this portfolio lies between the two optimal portfolios. Although nominally more diversified than either of the #12 portfolios from the optimization, its CVaR is worse than that of the mean–CVaR optimized portfolio (but still better than that of the MVO portfolio). An investor may have qualitative considerations that warrant including this more-diversified portfolio among the options to be evaluated.

Exhibit 33 Mean–Variance and Mean–CVaR Efficient Hedge Fund Allocations

	Asset Allocation			Portfolio Characteristics			
	Macro	Equity Market Neutral	Long/Short Equity	Expected Return	Volatility	95% VaR	95% CVaR
Mean–Variance Optimal	0.0%	40.0%	60.0%	5.0%	7.3%	−3.7%	−7.7%
Mean–CVaR Optimal	40.0%	0.0%	60.0%	5.0%	7.8%	−4.1%	−6.8%
Combination	20.0%	20.0%	60.0%	5.0%	7.5%	−3.7%	−7.3%

Exhibit 34 compares the optimal allocations of a broad asset class portfolio through the mean–variance and mean–CVaR lenses. In this example, the optimal allocations were selected subject to a 6.8% expected return target. Both approaches allocated a significant portion of the portfolio to private equity and hedge funds (30% each). A notable difference, however, is in the allocation to public and private real estate. Where the MVO approach allocated 22% to the combined real estate categories, the CVaR approach allocated nothing at all to either real estate category. We can identify the reason for this by referring back to Exhibit 21: The public and private real estate categories are characterized by 99% CVaRs of −40.2% and −27.9%, respectively.

Exhibit 34 Mean–Variance and Mean–CVaR Efficient Multi-Asset Portfolios

	Asset Allocation						Portfolio Characteristics		
	Equities	Govt Bonds	Hedge Funds	Public Real Estate	Private Real Estate	Private Equity	Expected Return	Volatility	99% CVaR
Mean–Variance Optimal	18%	0%	30%	7%	15%	30%	6.8%	11.5%	−20.7%
Mean–CVaR Optimal	34%	6%	30%	0%	0%	30%	6.8%	12.1%	−15.6%

EXAMPLE 6

Asset Allocation Recommendation

The CIO (chief investment officer) of the International University Endowment Fund (the Fund) is preparing for the upcoming investment committee (IC) meeting. The Fund's annual asset allocation review is on the agenda, and the CIO plans to propose a new strategic asset allocation for the Fund. Subject to prudent risk-taking, the recommended asset allocation should offer

- the highest expected return and
- the highest probability of achieving the long-term 5% real return target.

The inflation assumption is 2%.

In addition, the risk in the Fund is one factor that is considered when lenders assign a risk rating to the university. The university's primary lender has proposed a loan covenant that would trigger a re-evaluation of the university's creditworthiness if the Fund incurs a loss greater than 20% over any 1-year period.

The investment staff produced the following tables to help the CIO prepare for the meeting.

	Asset Allocation						
Alternative	Cash	Public Equity	Govt	Credit	Hedge Fund	Real Estate	Private Equity
A	5.0%	60.0%	30.0%	5.0%	0.0%	0.0%	0.0%
B	4.0%	50.0%	16.0%	5.0%	10.0%	5.0%	10.0%
C	2.0%	40.0%	8.0%	5.0%	18.0%	7.0%	20.0%
D	1.0%	30.0%	5.0%	4.0%	20.0%	10.0%	30.0%
E	2.0%	40.0%	3.0%	3.0%	15.0%	7.0%	30.0%
F	2.0%	50.0%	3.0%	0.0%	10.0%	5.0%	30.0%
G	1.0%	56.0%	3.0%	0.0%	10.0%	0.0%	30.0%

	Portfolio Characteristics						
					10-Year Horizon:		
Alternative	Expected Return	Volatility	1-Year 99% VaR	1-Year 99% CVaR	5th Percentile Return	95th Percentile Return	Probability of Meeting 5% Real Return	Probability of Purchasing Power Impairment
A	6.0%	9.0%	−12.4%	−15.0%	1.6%	10.5%	37.0%	7.1%
B	6.7%	10.3%	−14.6%	−17.3%	2.0%	11.4%	46.1%	4.3%
C	7.1%	11.1%	−15.8%	−18.8%	2.2%	12.2%	52.1%	3.2%
D	7.4%	11.5%	−16.3%	−19.4%	2.4%	12.6%	56.1%	2.5%
E	7.7%	12.3%	−17.4%	−20.6%	2.4%	13.2%	58.8%	2.8%
F	7.8%	13.0%	−18.5%	−21.8%	2.2%	13.7%	60.8%	3.6%
G	7.9%	13.5%	−19.3%	−22.7%	2.1%	14.1%	61.0%	4.0%

Notes:
- 1-year horizon 99% VaR: the lowest return over any 1-year period at a 99% confidence level (i.e., only a 1% chance to experience a total return below this threshold).
- 1-year horizon 99% CVaR: the expected return if the return falls below the 99% VaR threshold.
- 5th and 95th percentile annualized returns over a 10-year time horizon: a 90% chance that the annualized 10-year total return will fall between these two figures

(continued)

- probability of purchasing power impairment[16]: as defined by the IC, the probability of losing 40% of the endowment's purchasing power over 10 years after taking gifts to the endowment, spending from the endowment, and total return into account.

1 Which asset allocation is *most likely* to meet the committee's objective and constraints?

Solution to 1:

Portfolio D. Portfolios E, F, and G have 1-year, 99% CVaRs, which, if realized, would trigger the loan covenant. Portfolio D has the next highest probability of meeting the 5% real return target and the lowest probability of purchasing power impairment. Portfolios A, B, and C have lower probabilities of meeting the return targets and higher probabilities of purchasing power impairment.

12 RISK FACTOR-BASED OPTIMIZATION

f discuss approaches to asset allocation to alternative investments;

Increasingly, investors believe that viewing investment decisions through a risk factor lens (e.g., growth, inflation, credit risk) may improve the investment process. Separating fundamentally similar investments, like public and private equities, into distinct asset classes ignores the probability that both are exposed to the same risk factors. In this section, we will work through an asset allocation example using a risk factor lens.

Let's assume that an investor starts the asset allocation exercise by first allocating the overall risk budget across the main risk factors.[17] Instead of setting expectations for distinct asset classes, she may start thinking about the return expectations and correlation of the fundamental risk factors. Exhibit 35 shows her return expectations for the risk factors described in Exhibit 14. In this illustration, the global equity risk factor (a practical proxy for macroeconomic-oriented "growth") is expected to generate the highest return. She expects the duration and value factors to generate negative returns because stronger economic growth fueled by advances in technology would lead to rising rates and better returns for growth stocks. She is concerned about rising inflation, so she has assigned a positive expected return to the inflation factor.

---

16 Similar measures of risk are proposed by Swensen (2009) in the context of endowment funds.
17 Approaches to asset allocation and portfolio construction are expanding as the understanding of risk factors is increasing. A risk parity approach to asset allocation, for example, would allocate total risk in equal portion to the selected risk factors.

Risk Factor-Based Optimization

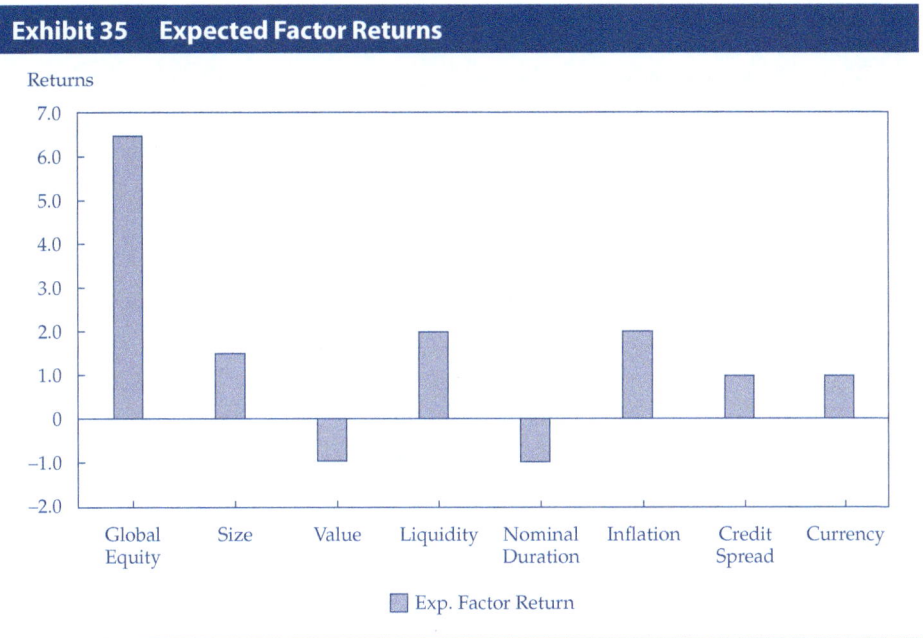

Exhibit 35   Expected Factor Returns

Using these returns and the historical factor volatilities and correlations, we can optimize the risk factor exposure by minimizing factor-implied risk subject to a total return target of 6.5%. The black bars in Exhibit 36 show these optimal factor exposures. Note that the target exposures of the value and nominal duration factors are positive, although the associated expected factor returns are negative. The model allocates to these factors for their diversification potential because they are negatively correlated with other risk factors. Duration and equity factors have a correlation of −0.6, whereas value and equity factors have a correlation of −0.3 based on the data used for this illustration.

We have established optimal risk factor exposures, so now we must implement this target using actual investments. Some investors may have access to only public market investments, while other investors may also have access to private illiquid investments. The gray and white bars in Exhibit 36 illustrate the two possible implementations of the target factor exposures. Portfolio 1 assumes the investor is limited to public market investments. Portfolio 2 uses both public market investments and private, illiquid investments. The portfolio allocation details are displayed in Exhibit 37.

Exhibit 36 Optimal Risk Factor Allocations and Associated Asset Class Portfolios

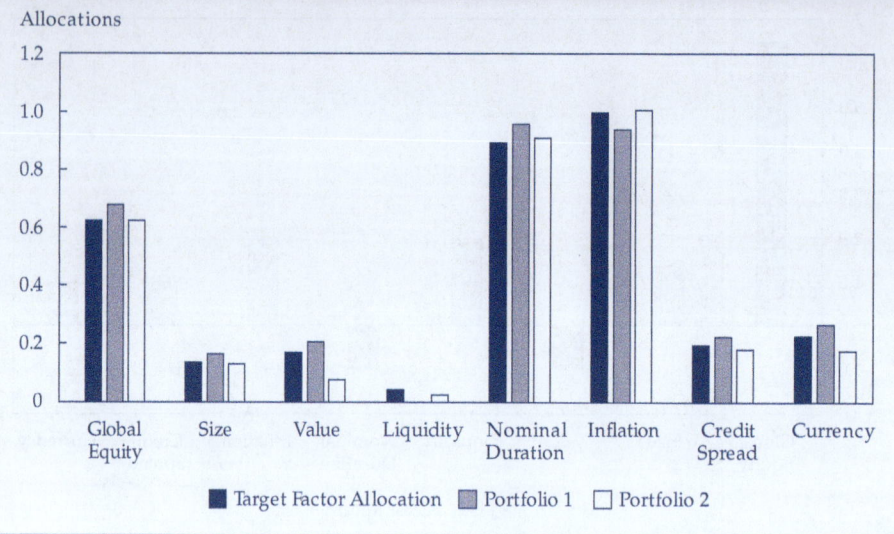

Exhibit 37 Asset Class Portfolios Designed Based on Optimal Risk Factor Allocations

	Portfolio 1	Portfolio 2
Domestic Equities; *Value Tilt*	21.0%	13.0%
Non-Domestic Developed Market Equities; *Value Tilt*	21.0%	13.0%
Foreign Emerging Market Equities	21.0%	12.0%
Government Bonds	0.0%	5.0%
Broad Fixed Income	10.0%	0.0%
High-Yield Credit	2.0%	3.0%
Inflation-Linked Bonds	7.0%	0.0%
Hedge Funds	15.0%	10.0%
Commodities	3.0%	4.0%
Public Real Estate	0.0%	12.0%
Private Real Estate	0.0%	13.0%
Private Equity	0.0%	15.0%
Total	**100.0%**	**100.0%**
Expected Return	6.2%	6.9%
Volatility	13.5%	13.2%

Even though they have similar factor exposures, you can see some significant differences in the asset class allocations of the two portfolios. Portfolio 1 allocates 63% to public equities, whereas Portfolio 2 allocates 35% to public equities plus 15% to private equity for its higher return potential. Portfolio 1 allocates 18% to alternatives (15% in hedge funds and 3% in commodities, two of the most liquid alternative asset classes), while Portfolio 2 has allocated 54% to alternatives (10% hedge funds, 4% commodities, 12% public real estate, 13% private real estate, and 15% private equity). Portfolio 1 achieves its inflation sensitivity by allocating to inflation-linked bonds

Risk Factor-Based Optimization

and commodities. Portfolio 2 achieves its desired exposure to the inflation factor through a combined allocation to real estate and commodities. The volatility of the two portfolios is similar, but Portfolio 2 is able to achieve a higher expected return given its ability to allocate to private equity.

Although a risk factor-driven approach is conceptually very elegant, we must mention a few caveats:

- While generally accepted asset class definitions provide a common language among the investment community, risk factors may be defined quite differently investor-to-investor. It's important to establish a common understanding of factor definitions and factor return expectations among the parties to an asset allocation exercise. This includes an agreement as to what financial instruments can be used to best match the factor exposures if they are not directly investable.

- Correlations among risk factors, just like correlations across asset classes, may dramatically shift under changing market conditions; thus, careful testing needs to be applied to understand how changing market conditions will affect the asset allocation.

- Some factor sensitivities are stable (like the nominal interest rate sensitivity of government bonds), while others are very unstable (like the inflation sensitivity of commodities). Factor sensitivities also need to be very carefully tested to validate whether the invested portfolio would truly deliver the desired factor exposures and not deliver unintended factor returns.

EXAMPLE 7

Selecting an Asset Allocation Approach

1. You have a new client who has unexpectedly inherited a substantial sum of money. The client is in his early 30s and newly married. He has no children and no other investible assets. What asset allocation approach is most suitable for this client?

2. Your client is a tax-exempt foundation that recently received a bequest doubling its assets to €200 million. There is an outside investment adviser but no dedicated investment staff; however, the six members of the investment committee (IC) are all wealthy, sophisticated investors in their own right. The IC conducts an asset allocation study every three years and reviews the asset allocation at its annual meeting. The current asset allocation is 30% equities, 20% fixed income, 25% private equity, and 25% real estate. Three percent of assets are paid out annually in grants; this expenditure is covered by an annuity purchased some years ago. The foundation's primary investment objective is to maximize returns subject to a maximum level of volatility. A secondary consideration is the desire to avoid a permanent loss of capital. What asset allocation approach is most suitable for this client?

Solution to 1:

Mean–variance optimization with Monte Carlo simulation is most appropriate for this client. He has limited investment expertise, so your first responsibility is to educate him with respect to such basic investment concepts as risk, return, and diversification. A simple MVO approach supplemented with Monte Carlo simulation to illustrate potential upside and downside of an asset allocation choice is mostly likely to serve the asset allocation and investment education needs.

> **Solution to 2:**
>
> Given the sophistication and investment objectives of the IC members, using a mean–CVaR optimization approach is appropriate to determine the asset allocation. This client has a more sophisticated understanding of risk and will appreciate the more nuanced view of risk offered by mean–CVaR optimization. Given the portfolio's exposure to alternative investments, the asset allocation decision will be enhanced by the more detailed picture of left-tail risk offered by CVaR optimization (the risk of permanent loss) relative to mean–variance optimization. The lack of permanent staff and a once-per-year meeting schedule suggest that a risk factor-based approach may not be appropriate.

13. LIQUIDITY PLANNING AND ACHIEVING AND MAINTAINING THE STRATEGIC ASSET ALLOCATION

g discuss the importance of liquidity planning in allocating to alternative investments;

Earlier, we addressed various aspects of liquidity associated with investing in alternative asset classes. In this section, we focus on multi-year horizon liquidity planning for private investments.

When managing portfolios that contain allocations to alternative investments, managing liquidity risk takes on critical importance. We need to ensure sufficient liquidity to meet interim obligations or goals, which might include:

- periodic payments to beneficiaries (e.g., a pension fund's retirement benefit payments or an endowment fund's distributions to support operating expenses);
- portfolio rebalancing or funding new asset manager mandates; or
- fulfilling a commitment made to a private investment fund when the general partner makes the capital call.

Alternative investments pose unique liquidity challenges that must be explicitly addressed before committing to an alternative investment program. Private investments—including private equity, private real estate, private real assets, and private credit—represent the most illiquid components of an investment portfolio. Private investments usually require a long-term commitment over an 8- to 15-year time horizon. An investor contributes capital over the first few years (the investment period) and receives distributions in the later years. Combined with the call down (or drawdown) structure of a private investment fund, this creates a need to model a hypothetical path to achieving and maintaining a diversified, fully-invested allocation to private investments. Here we will explore the challenges with private investment liquidity planning with three primary considerations:

1 How to achieve and maintain the desired allocation.
2 How to handle capital calls.
3 How to plan for the unexpected.

13.1 Achieving and Maintaining the Strategic Asset Allocation

Strategic planning is required to determine the necessary annual commitments an investor should make to reach and maintain the long-term target asset allocation. Large private investors often use a liquidity forecasting model for their private investment programs. Here, we illustrate one such model based on work published by Takahashi and Alexander (2001). We also discuss private investment commitment pacing as an application of this model. This model is only one possible way to forecast private investment cash flows; investors may develop their own model using their own assumptions and experience.

We will illustrate this model with a hypothetical capital commitment (CC) of £100 million to a fund with a contractual term (L) of 12 years.

We begin by modeling the capital contributions (C) to the fund. Certain assumptions must be made regarding the rate of contribution (RC). We'll assume that 25% is contributed in the first year and that 50% of the remaining commitments are contributed in each of the subsequent years:

Year 1: £100 million × 25% = £25 million

Year 2: (£100 million – £25 million) × 50% = £37.5 million

Year 3: (£100 million – £25 million – £37.5 million) × 50% = £18.75 million

and so on.

The capital contribution (C) in year t can be expressed with the following formula:

$$C_t = RC_t \times (CC - PIC_t) \tag{1}$$

where PIC denotes the already paid-in capital.

Alternatively, we can express this in words:

Capital Contribution = Rate of Contribution × (Capital Commitment – Paid-in-Capital)

In practice, the investment period is often limited to a defined number of years; also, not all of the committed capital may be called.

The next step is to estimate the periodic distribution paid to investors. Distributions (D) are a function of the net asset value (NAV). From one year to the next, the NAV rises as additional capital contributions are made and as underlying investments appreciate. NAV declines as distributions are made (or as assets are written down).

If the partnership investment develops as anticipated, then the fund's IRR would be equal to this rate.

To estimate the expected annual distribution payments, we need to make an assumption about the pattern of distributions. For example, an analyst may assume that the fund does not distribute any money in Year 1 or Year 2 but distributes 10% of the prevailing net asset value in Year 3, 20% in Year 4, 30% in Year 5, and 50% of the remaining balance in each of the remaining years. In the case of real estate funds, it is also possible that there is a pre-defined minimum annual distribution rate (called the "yield"). Once the annual rates of distribution are determined, the annual amount distributed is calculated by the following formula:

$$D_t = RD_t[NAV_{t-1} \times (1 + G)] \tag{2}$$

where

$$RD_t = (t/L)^B, \tag{3}$$

$$NAV_t = [NAV_{t-1} \times (1 + G)] + C_t - D_t \tag{4}$$

Again, in words:

Distributions at time t = Rate of Distribution at time t × [NAV at time t-1 × (1 + Growth Rate)], and

NAV at time t = prior NAV × (1 + Growth Rate) + Capital Contribution − Distributions

In Exhibit 38, we display the forecasted annual capital contributions, outstanding commitment forecast, distributions, NAV, and cumulative net cash flow for a private investment fund with a 12-year life. We assume that 25% of the committed capital is contributed in the first year and that 50% of the remaining commitments are contributed in each of the subsequent years. Using a bow (B) parameter of 2.5, we set the RD_t distribution rates such that the yearly distribution rates would increase fairly gradually. We assume a 13% growth rate from the investments in this fund.

Exhibit 38 Expected Annual Contribution, Outstanding Commitment, Rate of Distribution, Annual Distribution, NAV, and Net Cash Flow of a Hypothetical Private Investment Fund

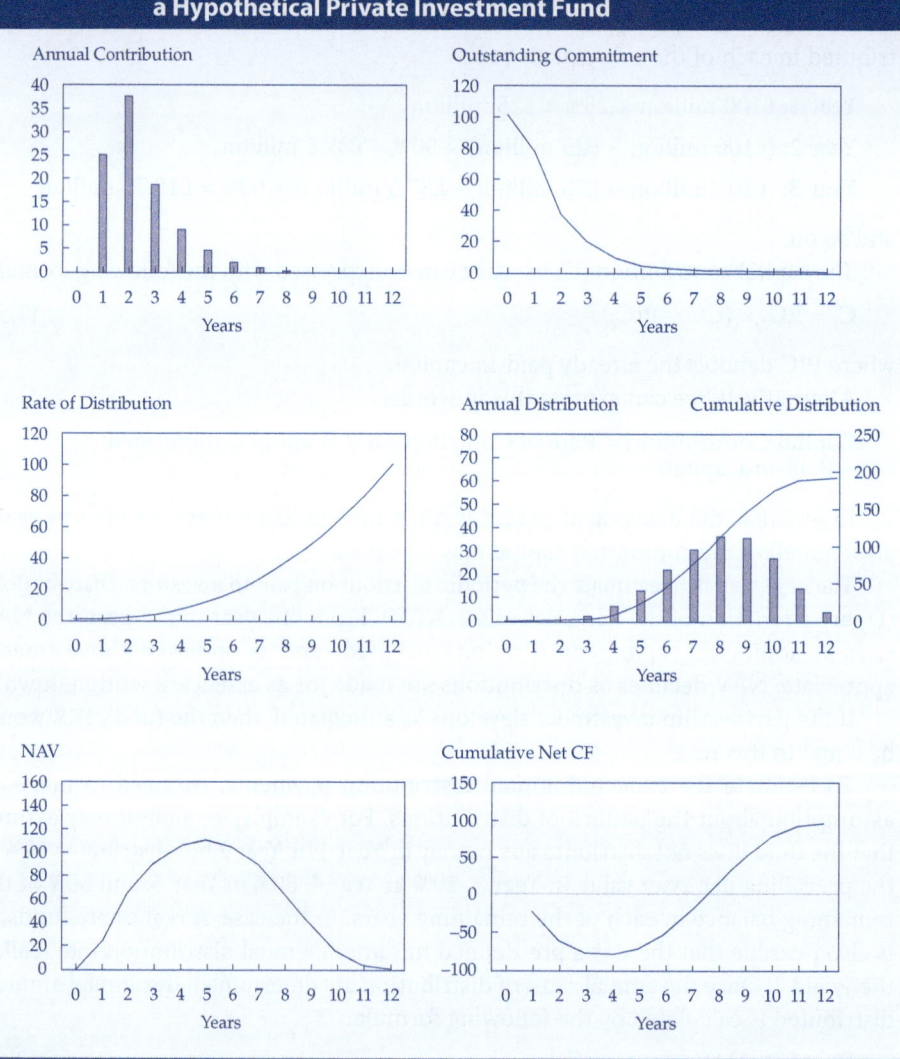

The corresponding annual RD_t rates are displayed in Exhibit 39.

Liquidity Planning and Achieving and Maintaining the Strategic Asset Allocation

Exhibit 39   Assumed Annual Distribution Rates (RD_t)

Year	1	2	3	4	5	6	7	8	9	10	11	12
Rate of Distribution	0%	1%	3%	6%	11%	18%	26%	36%	49%	63%	80%	100%

How does the shape of the expected rate of distribution influence NAV and the annual distribution amounts? For illustration purposes we can change our assumption of RD by setting the bow parameter (B) to 5.0, such that early year distribution rates are very low and start increasing in the second half of the fund's life. The new distribution rates are shown in Exhibit 40, and Exhibit 41 shows how distributions and the NAV would react to this change.

Exhibit 40   Alternative Assumed Annual Distribution Rates (RD_t)

Year	1	2	3	4	5	6	7	8	9	10	11	12
Rate of Distribution	0%	0%	0%	0%	1%	3%	7%	13%	24%	40%	65%	100%

Exhibit 41   Rate of Distribution, Expected Annual Distribution, NAV, and Cumulative Net Cash Flow with Back-Loaded Distributions

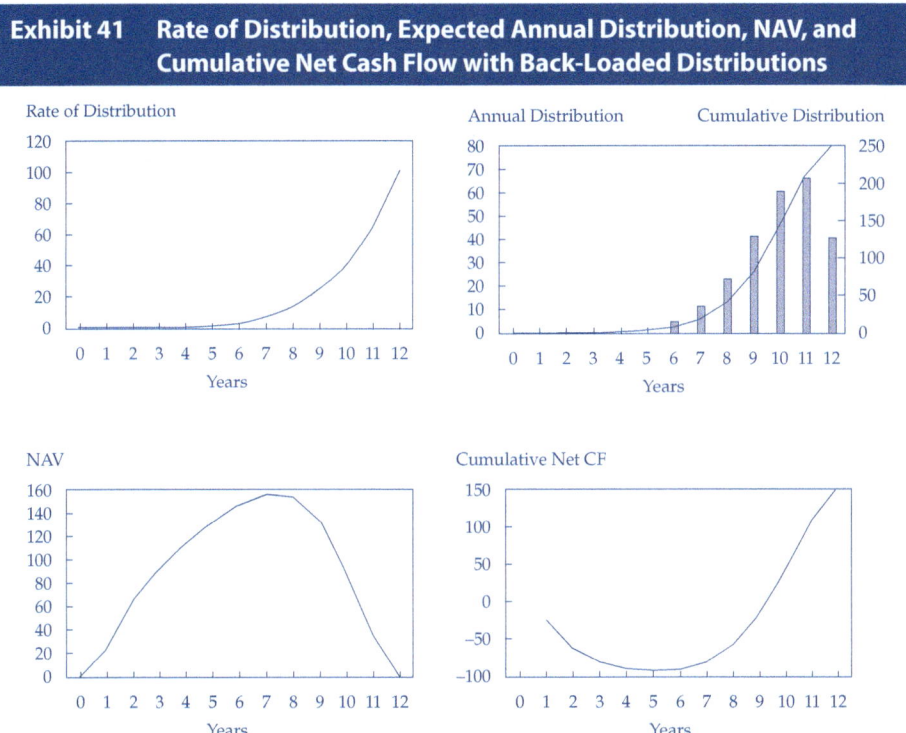

Although the annual capital contributions would not be affected, we can see that the lower distribution rate in the early years allows the NAV to grow higher. The cumulative net cash flow, however, would stay in the negative zone for a longer time.

> **EXAMPLE 8**
>
> **Liquidity Planning for Private Investments**
>
> 1 The NAV of an investor's share in a private renewable energy fund was €30 million at the end of 2020. All capital has been called. The investor expects a 20% distribution to be paid at the end of 2021. The expected growth rate is 12%. What is the expected NAV at year-end 2022?
>
> **Solution to 1:**
>
> The expected NAV at year-end 2022 is €30,105,600. The expected distribution at the end of 2021 is €6.72 million [(€30 million x 1.12) x 20%]. The NAV at year-end 2022 is therefore (€30 million x 1.12) × (1 − 0.20) x 1.12% = €30,105,600.

An important practical application of such models is to help determine the size of the annual commitment an investor needs to make to reach the target allocation of an asset class over the coming years (i.e., investment commitment pacing).

Assume that we manage an investment portfolio of £1 billion and that our strategic asset allocation target for private equities is 20%. We currently do not have any private equity investment in the portfolio. We also must project the growth of the aggregate investment portfolio, because we want to achieve the 20% allocation based on the expected *future* value of the portfolio and of the private equity investment, not today's value. We assume an aggregate portfolio growth rate of 6% per year, including both net contributions and investment returns.

With these assumptions, and the private investment cash flow and NAV forecasting model discussed previously, the investor can determine the annual commitments needed to reach the overall target allocation. By using the same cash flow forecasting parameters as for the analysis in Exhibit 38, we can see that a £100 million commitment would lead the NAV to peak at around £110 million five years from now. A rough approximation could be the following: In five years, the total portfolio size would be £1 billion × 1.06^5 ≈ £1.338 billion; so, at that point, the total private equity NAV should be approximately 20% × £1.338 billion=£268 million. Since we know that a £100 million commitment would lead to an NAV of £110 million in five years, we can extrapolate to arrive at the conclusion that a £243 million commitment today could achieve the goal.

However, this would result in a very concentrated private equity investment, with an NAV peaking in four to five years and then declining over the following years as distributions are made. A better practice is to spread commitments out over multiple years. A stable and disciplined multi-year commitment schedule leads to a more stable NAV size over time. It also achieves an important objective of diversifying exposure across vintage years. Thus, an investor can choose to commit a target amount of around £70 million per year over a period of four years (2017 through 2020) instead of concentrating the commitment in a single year. This schedule would bring the total private equity NAV to the target 20% level over five years. In Exhibit 42, we illustrate how the portfolio of private equity investments of different vintage years would build up over time. We also show how the total NAV would evolve beyond 2022 if no further capital commitment is made. As the chart suggests, the NAV would continue to grow through 2023 but would start to decline in later years as the 2017–2020 vintage private funds make distributions.

Liquidity Planning and Achieving and Maintaining the Strategic Asset Allocation

Exhibit 42 Commitment Pacing: Cumulative NAV of Private Equity Investments

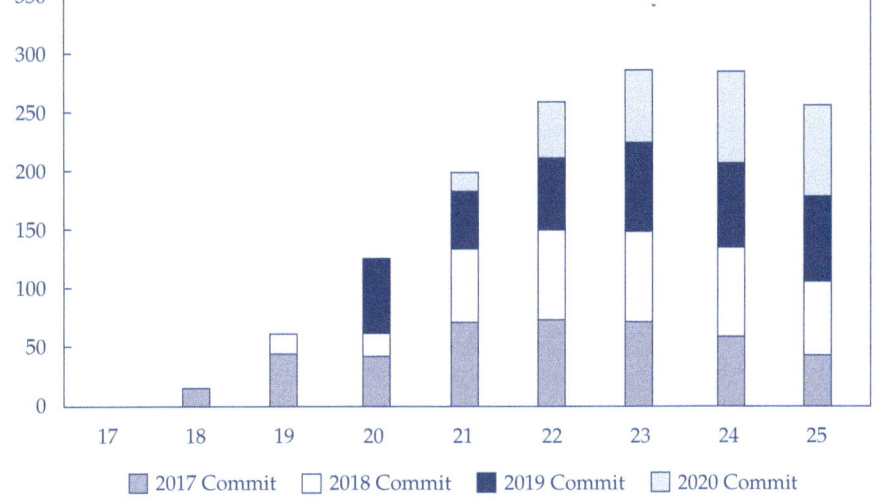

In Exhibit 43, we show how private equity investments would grow as a proportion of the overall investment portfolio. As in the previous chart, we extend the forecast beyond 2022 to show the proportion of private equity investments will start to decline without further capital commitments after 2020.

Exhibit 43 Commitment Pacing: Private Equity NAV as % of the Total Portfolio

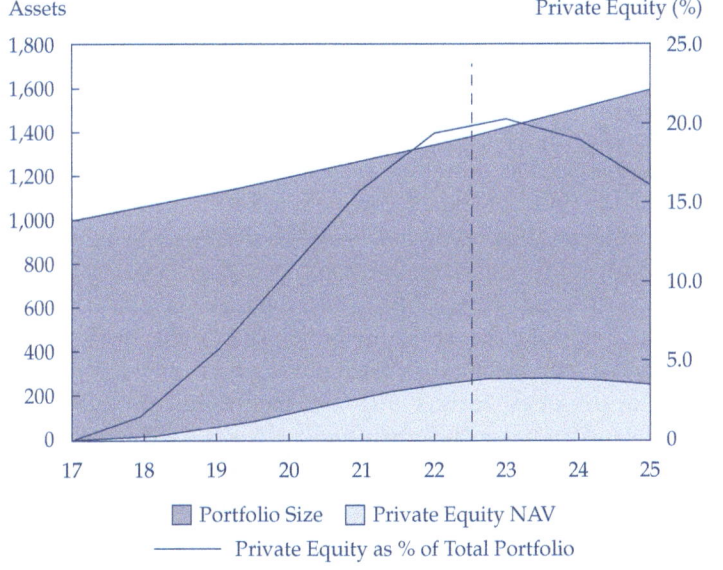

The investor must review her pacing model forecast periodically, updating it as needed based on the actual commitments and transactions that have occurred and refreshing the assumptions for the future. If the investor plans to maintain a 20%

allocation to private equity investments over the long run, she will clearly have to make ongoing commitments in the future, although at a slower pace once private equity is an established asset class in the portfolio.

To summarize, cash flow and pacing models enable investors to better manage their portfolio liquidity, set realistic annual commitment targets to reach the desired asset allocation, and manage portfolio beta in aggregate. Investors need to validate their model assumptions and evaluate how different parameter settings and liquidity stress scenarios could impact their investment portfolios.

14. MANAGING THE CAPITAL CALLS AND PREPARING FOR THE UNEXPECTED

g discuss the importance of liquidity planning in allocating to alternative investments;

The investor makes an up-front commitment of a certain dollar amount to a private investment fund, and the funds will typically be called (paid in) over a period of three to four years. In many cases, the general partner (GP) will never call the full amount of the capital commitment. The limited partner (LP) is obligated to pay the capital call in accordance with the terms agreed to with the GP, often within 30 days of receiving the call notification. However, it is not practical to keep all the committed (but not yet called) capital in liquid reserves given the opportunity cost of being out of the markets during the investment phase. Investors must develop a strategy for maintaining the asset allocation while waiting for the fund to become fully invested. Capital pending investment in a private equity fund is often invested in public equities as a proxy for private equities. A similar approach may be followed in the case of other private asset classes: The investor may consider high yield as a placeholder for pending private credit investments, REITs as a placeholder for private real estate investments, and energy stocks or commodity futures as a proxy for private real asset investments.

14.1 Preparing for the Unexpected

The liquidity-planning model described here addresses the key components of cash inflows and outflows, but the model results are clearly heavily dependent on the assumptions. The model parameters can be based purely on judgment, but a better practice would be to verify estimates and forecasts with a sample of representative private funds' historical experience. Obviously, the realized cash flows in the future are likely to differ from what the model predicted based on the assumed parameters. Thus, it is advisable to run the analysis using different sets of assumptions and under different scenarios. In a bear market, GPs may call capital at a higher pace and/or make distributions at a slower pace than had been expected. This suggests that in addition to the base case scenario planning, the analyst should develop an additional set of assumptions with faster capital calls and lower distribution rates.

If the fund is scheduled to begin liquidation when the investor's public market portfolio is performing poorly (as it did in the 2007–2008 period), it is likely that the GP will exercise his option to extend the fund life. If this happens, investors may find themselves with an asset allocation significantly different from target or being unable to meet the capital calls that were intended to be funded from the distributions. These contingencies should be modeled as part of stress testing the asset allocation.

Managing the Capital Calls and Preparing for the Unexpected

> **EXAMPLE 9**
>
> ### Private Investments, Asset Allocation, and Liquidity Planning
>
> The Endowment Fund of the University of Guitan (the Fund) has $750 million in assets. The investment committee (IC) adopted the following strategic asset allocation four years ago. Private investments are at the lower end of the permitted range. To reach the target allocation among private investments, the investment team has made several new commitments recently, and they expect capital calls over the coming year equal to approximately about 20% of the current private asset net asset value.
>
> | | Strategic Asset Allocation Target | Permitted Range | Current Asset Allocation (%) | Current Asset Allocation ($mil) |
> |---|---|---|---|---|
> | Cash | 2% | 0 to 5% | 3% | 22.5 |
> | Public Equities (including long/short equity) | 35% | 30 to 40% | 35% | 262.5 |
> | Government Bonds | 5% | 4 to 10% | 7% | 52.5 |
> | High-Yield Credit | 3% | 2 to 5% | 5% | 37.5 |
> | Hedge Funds (excluding long/short equity) | 20% | 17 to 23% | 23% | 172.5 |
> | Private Real Estate | 10% | 7 to 13% | 8% | 60.0 |
> | Private Real Assets | 5% | 3 to 7% | 4% | 30.0 |
> | Private Equity | 20% | 15 to 22% | 15% | 112.5 |
> | **Total** | | | | $750 mil |
> | Expected Return | 7.1% | | | |
> | Expected Volatility | 11.1% | | | |
> | 99% CVaR | −18.8% | | | |
> | Assumed Inflation Rate | 2% | | | |

The strategic asset allocation has a 52% probability of meeting the 5% real return target (4% spend rate, 1% principal growth, and 2% inflation).

At its last meeting, the endowment committee of the board approved a temporary increase in the spending rate, raising it from 4% to 5% for the next five years to support the university's efforts to reposition itself in the face of declining enrollments. The spending rate is calculated as a percentage of the Fund's trailing 5-year average value.

The CIO (chief investment officer) has produced a capital market outlook that will guide the fund's tactical asset allocation strategy for the next several quarters. Key elements of the outlook are:

- accommodative central bank policies are ending;
- equity valuation metrics have recently set new highs;
- the economic cycle is at or near its peak (i.e., there is a meaningful probability of rising inflation and a weaker economic environment over the next several quarters); and
- returns will quite likely be lower than what has been experienced over the past five years.

She also developed the following stress scenario based on her capital market outlook:

Return Stress Scenario	
Cash	2%
Public Equities (including l/s equity)	−30%
Government Bonds	−3%
High-Yield Credit	−10%
Hedge Funds (excluding l/s equity)	−8%
Private Real Estate	0%
Private Real Assets	10%
Private Equity	−10%

1. Identify and discuss the liquidity factors that the CIO should consider as she develops her portfolio positioning strategy for the next 12 to 24 months.

2. Recommend and justify a tactical asset allocation strategy for the Fund.

Solution to 1:

- Given the market outlook, it is reasonable to assume cash flows into the fund from existing private investments will be negligible.
- The fund has next-12-month liabilities as follows:
  - Approximately $37.5 million to the university ($750 million x 5%). This is a high (conservative) estimate based on an assumption that the trailing 5-year average Fund value is less than the current $750 million.
  - Approximately $40.5 million in capital calls from private investment commitments (equally allocated across private real estate, private real assets, and private equity

    [($60m + $30m + $112.5m) × 20%]
  - Total liabilities next 12 months = $78 million
- Sources of immediate liquidity:
  - Cash = $22.5 million
  - Government bonds = $52.5 million
  - $75.0 million in total (less than the $78 million liability)
- Other liquidity:
  - Public equities are at the midpoint of the permitted range. The allocation could be reduced from 35% to 30% and remain within the permitted range. This would free up $37.5 million ($750 million × 5%) for reinvestment in more-defensive asset classes or to meet anticipated liquidity needs. However, if the return scenario is realized (equities down 30%), then the equity allocation will fall below the 30% minimum and additional rebalancing will be required.
  - High-yield credit is at the upper end of the allowed range. The allocation could be reduced from the current 5% to 2% or 3%, freeing up an additional $15 to $22.5 million. The limited liquidity in high-yield bond markets may make this challenging.
  - The hedge fund allocation is at the upper end of the allowed range. The allocation could be reduced from the current 23% to something in the range of 17% to 20% (between the lower end of the band and the target allocation). However, given the required redemption notice

(generally 60 to 90 days in advance of the redemption date), if the market weakens the hedge funds might invoke any gates allowed for in their documents.

- Longer term, a temporary increase in the spending rate reduces the probability that the fund will meet its real return target. This objective would be further threatened if the inflation rate does rise as the CIO fears. The liquidity profile of the Fund's investments should prepare for the possibility that, in a bad year, they may be called upon to dip into capital to fund the spending obligation.

Solution to 2:

- The Fund should target the upper end of the ranges for cash and government bonds in light of the current high equity valuations, weakening economic outlook, and threat of rising inflation. Given rising inflation and interest rate concerns, she may also consider shortening the duration of the government bond portfolio.
- The higher cash and bond allocation will also provide the liquidity buffer needed to meet the Fund's liabilities. Additional cash might be justified to fund the known payouts.
- A high allocation to real estate could also be considered a defensive positioning, but the current 8% allocation may rise toward its 13% maximum, even without additional allocations, given the expected decline in the balance of the portfolio. In addition, tactical tilts in private asset classes are difficult to implement because it would take an extended time period to make new commitments and invest the additional capital.
- The allocations to public equites and hedge funds could be reduced to fund the increases in cash and government bonds.

The following table summarizes the proposed allocation and looks at the likely end-of-year allocations if events unfold as forecast.

	Allowed Ranges		Current Allocation	Proposed Allocation		Expected Return Next 12 Months	Allocation 12 Months Forward	
	Lower Limit	Upper Limit		%	$ (mil)		%	$ (mil)
Cash	0%	5%	3%	10%	75	2%		0*
Public Equities	30%	40%	35%	30%	225	−30%	25%	157.50
Government Bonds	4%	10%	7%	10%	75	−3%	12%	72.75
High-Yield Credit	2%	5%	5%	5%	37.5	−10%	5%	33.75
Hedge Funds	17%	23%	23%	17%	127.5	−8%	19%	117.30
Private Real Estate	7%	13%	8%	8%	60	0%	12%	72.00
Private Real Assets	3%	7%	4%	5%	37.5	10%	8%	48.75

(continued)

	Allowed Ranges		Current Allocation	Proposed Allocation		Expected Return Next 12 Months	Allocation 12 Months Forward	
	Lower Limit	Upper Limit		%	$ (mil)		%	$ (mil)
Private Equity	15%	22%	15%	15%	112.5	−10%	20%	123.75
Total				100%	$750.0		100%	$625.80

* Cash paid to fund liabilities ($37.5 million to the university and $40.5 million to fund private investment capital calls. Additional cash needs funded from government bond portfolio.

15 MONITORING THE INVESTMENT PROGRAM

h discuss considerations in monitoring alternative investment programs.

The monitoring of an alternative investment program is time and labor intensive. Data are hard to come by and are not standardized among managers or asset classes. The analyst must spend a good amount of time gathering data and ensuring that the analysis is comparable across managers and asset classes. It is incumbent on the investor to both monitor the managers *and* the alternative investment program's progress toward the goals that were the basis for the investment in these assets.

15.1 Overall Investment Program Monitoring

When an investor makes a strategic decision to invest in alternative assets, specific goals are typically associated with the alternative investment program—return enhancement, income, risk reduction, safety, or a combination of the four. The goals may vary by asset class. A real estate program, for example, might be undertaken with the objective of replacing a portion of the fixed-income allocation—providing yield or income but also providing some measure of growth and/or inflation protection. The real estate program should be monitored relative to those goals, not simply relative to a benchmark.

We know that an alternative investment program is likely to take a number of years to reach fully-invested status. Is it reasonable to defer an assessment of the program until that point? Probably not. The investor must monitor developments in the relevant markets to ensure that the fundamental thesis underlying the decision to invest remains intact. Continuing with our real estate analogy, if real estate cap rates[18] fall to never-before-seen lows, what are the implications for the real estate's ability to continue to fulfill its intended role in the portfolio? Or if the managers hired within the real estate allocation allocate more to commercial office properties than was anticipated, what are the implications for the ability of real estate to fulfill the income-oriented goal? Only by monitoring the development of the portfolio(s) will the investor be able to adjust course and ensure that the allocation remains on track to achieve the goals established at the outset.

---

[18] The ratio of net operating income (NOI) to property asset value (the inverse of price/earnings).

We also know that investor goals and objectives are subject to change. Perhaps a university experiences a persistent decline in enrollments and the endowment fund will be called upon to provide greater support to the university while it transitions to the new reality; what are the implications for a private equity program? Or what if the primary wage-earner in a two-parent household becomes critically ill; how might this affect the asset allocation? These types of events cannot be predicted, but it is important to continuously monitor the linkages between the asset allocation and the investor's goals, objectives, and circumstances. Particularly in the private markets—where changing course requires a long lead time and abruptly terminating an investment program can radically alter the risk and return profile of the portfolio—an early warning of an impending change can greatly improve the investor's ability to maintain the integrity of the investment program.

15.2 Performance Evaluation

Properly benchmarking an alternative investment strategy is a challenge that has important implications for judging the effectiveness of the alternative investment program. Many investors resort to custom index proxies (e.g., a static return premium over cash or equity index) or rely on peer group comparisons (e.g., Hedge Fund Research, Inc., Eurekahedge, Cambridge Private Equity Index). Both approaches have significant limitations.

Consider a private equity program benchmarked to the MSCI World Index plus 3%. This custom index may help frame the return expectation the investment committee holds with regard to its private equity assets, but it is unlikely to match the realized risk, return, and liquidity characteristics of the actual private equity program.

It is similarly challenging to develop a peer group representative of a manager's strategy given the high level of idiosyncratic risk inherent in most alternative investment funds. Existing providers follow vastly different rules in constructing these "benchmarks." They all have their own set of definitions (e.g., whether a fund is a credit fund or an event-driven fund), weighting methodology (asset weighted or equal weighted), method for dealing with potential survivorship bias, and other rules for inclusion (e.g., whether the fund is currently open or closed to new capital).

Exhibit 44 shows the returns from three different hedge fund index providers. An event driven fund that generated a 6% return over the relevant 5-year period might look attractive if evaluated relative to the Credit Suisse index, whereas it might look subpar if evaluated relative to the Eurekahedge index. Additionally, a manager's ranking within the peer group is affected as much by what *other* managers do as by his own actions. Clearly, peer group ranking is, at best, one small part of the overall benchmarking exercise.

Exhibit 44 The Trouble with Peer Groups

Strategy	Provider	3-Year Annualized Return (%)	5-Year Annualized Return (%)
		ending December 31, 2017	
Equity Hedge	HFRI	5.7	6.6
	Credit Suisse	4.3	7.1
	Eurekahedge	6.5	7.8
Event-Driven	HFRI	3.8	5.9
	Credit Suisse	0.8	3.7
	Eurekahedge	6.8	7.2

(continued)

Exhibit 44 (Continued)

Strategy	Provider	3-Year Annualized Return (%)	5-Year Annualized Return (%)
		ending December 31, 2017	
Global Macro	HFRI	0.6	0.7
	Credit Suisse	2.0	2.7
	Eurekahedge	–0.1	1.2

The timing and nature of reported alternative investment returns also pose challenges to monitoring the performance of alternative investment managers. For call-down strategies such as private equity, private real estate, and real assets, tracking and calculating performance might require different systems and methodologies. Private equity, credit, and real estate returns are typically reported using internal rates of return (IRRs) rather than time-weighted returns (TWR) as is common in the liquid asset classes. IRRs are sensitive to the timing of cash flows into and out of the fund. Two managers may have similar portfolios but very different return profiles depending on their particular capital call and distribution schedule. Investors have to be wise to the ways in which a manager can bias their reported IRR. Alternative metrics, such as multiple on invested capital (MOIC) have been developed to provide an additional frame of reference. (MOIC is a private equity measure that divides the current value of the underlying companies plus any distributions received by the total invested capital.)

Pricing issues also complicate performance evaluation of most alternative strategies. Stale pricing common in many alternative strategies can distort reported returns and the associated risk metrics. Betas, correlations, Sharpe ratios, and other measures must be interpreted with a healthy degree of skepticism.

Although performance measurement has its challenges with all asset classes, relying exclusively on any single measure with alternative investments increases the likelihood of inaccurate or misleading conclusions. With respect to the more illiquid investment strategies, judgment as to whether a given fund is meeting its investment objectives should be reserved until most or even all of the investments have been monetized, and capital has been returned to the investor. If capital is returned quickly (thereby possibly producing extraordinarily high IRRs), the investor may want to put greater emphasis on the MOIC measure. Similarly, funds that return capital more slowly than expected might want to put greater weight on the IRR measure. Even a fund with both a weak MOIC and a weak IRR need the measures to be put into context. An appropriate peer group analysis can help ascertain whether the "poor" performance was common across all funds of similar vintage (perhaps suggesting a poor investment climate) or whether it was specific to that fund. Likewise, a fund that posts strong performance may simply have benefited from an ideal investment period.

Perhaps the best way to gain performance insight beyond the numbers is to develop a qualitative understanding of the underlying assets. What are the manager's expectations at the time of acquisition? How does the manager plan to add value to the investment over the holding period? What is the manager's exit strategy for the investment? The investor can monitor how the investment develops relative to the initial thesis. This type of qualitative assessment can lead to a better understanding of whether the manager did well for the right reasons, whether the manager was wrong but for the right reasons, or whether the manager was just wrong.

15.3 Monitoring the Firm and the Investment Process

In addition to monitoring the portfolio, monitoring of the investment process and the investment management firm itself are particularly important in alternative investment structures where the manager cannot be terminated easily, and the assets transferred to another manager in which the investor has more confidence. What follows is a non-exhaustive list of issues that the investor will want to monitor:

- *Key person risk*: Most alternative investment strategies depend to a large extent on the skill of a few key investment professionals. These are what are known as "key persons." Key persons are typically specified in the fund documents, with certain rights allocated to the limited partners in the event a key person leaves the firm. It is important to ensure that these investment professionals remain actively involved in the investment process. There are also other employees of the investment manager whose departure may negatively affect the operation of the business or signal an underlying problem. If, for example, the chief operating officer or chief compliance officer leaves the firm, it is important to understand why and what effect it may have on the business. Finally, it is important to note that for quantitatively oriented strategies, key person risk is often reduced because the quantitative investment process remains in place even if a key person leaves.

- *Alignment of interests*: Alignment of interest issues range from the complexity of the organization, structure of management fees, compensation of the investment professionals, growth in assets under management (AUM), and the amount of capital the key professionals have committed to the funds that they are managing. The investor will want to verify that the money manager's interests remain closely aligned with their own. Has the manager withdrawn a significant portion of her own capital that had been invested alongside the limited partners? If so, why? Is the manager raising a new fund? If so, what safeguards are in place to ensure that the investment professionals are not unduly distracted with fundraising, firm administration, or unfairly concentrated on managing other funds? Is the opportunity set deep enough to support the additional capital being raised? Will the funds have shared ownership interest in a given asset? If so, what conflicts of interest may arise (e.g., the manager may earn an incentive fee in one fund if the asset is sold, while it may be in the best interest of the second fund to sell the asset at a later date).

- *Style drift*: Fund documents often give managers wide latitude as to their investment options and parameters, but it is incumbent on the investor to understand where the fund manager has a competitive advantage and skill and confirm that the investments being made are consistent with the manager's edge.

- *Risk management*: The investor should understand the manager's risk management philosophy and processes and periodically confirm that the fund is abiding by them. Where a fund makes extensive use of leverage, a robust risk management framework is essential.

- *Client/asset turnover*: A critical part of the ongoing due diligence process should include a review of clients and assets. A significant gain or drop in either may be a sign of an underlying problem. An unusual gain in assets could make it difficult for the investment professionals to invest in suitably attractive investments, potentially handicapping future performance. Conversely, significant client redemptions may force the money manager to sell attractive assets as he looks to raise cash. If this occurs during periods of market turmoil when liquidity in the market itself may be low, the manager may be forced to sell what he can rather than what he should in order to optimize performance. This could hurt the returns of non-redeeming clients and/or leave the remaining clients with illiquid holdings that might make it difficult for them to redeem in the future.

- *Client profile*: Investors will want to gauge the profile of the fund manager's other clients. Are the fund's other clients considered long-term investors, or do they have a history of redeeming at the first sign of trouble? Are they new to the alternative investment space and perhaps don't understand the nuances of the fund's strategy and risks? You may have a strong conviction in a money manager's skills, but the actions of others may affect your ability to reap the benefits of those skills. If too many of her other clients elect to redeem, the manager may invoke the gates allowed by the fund's documents or, at the extreme, liquidate the fund at what might be the worst possible moment. This was a common occurrence during 2008–2009, when investors sought to raise cash by redeeming from their more liquid fund managers. Even if a money manager weathers massive outflows, profitability and the ability to retain key talent may be at risk.

- *Service providers:* Investors will want to ensure that the fund manager has engaged independent and reputable third-party service providers, including administrators, custodians, and auditors. Although an investor may have performed extensive checks prior to investing, it is good practice to periodically verify that these relationships are intact and working well. If the service provider changes, the investor will want to understand *why.* Has the fund's AUM grown to a level that cannot be handled adequately by the current provider? Perhaps the service provider has chosen to terminate the relationship because of actions taken by the fund manager. Exploring the motivation behind a change in a service provider can uncover early warning flags deserving of further investigation.

EXAMPLE 10

Monitoring Alternative Investment Programs

1. The O'Hara family office determined that the illiquidity risk inherent in private investments is a risk that the family is ill-suited to bear. As a result, they decided several years ago to unwind their private equity program. There are still a few remaining assets in the portfolio. The CIO (chief investment officer) notices that the private equity portfolio has delivered outstanding performance lately, especially relative to other asset classes. He presents the data to his research staff and wants to revisit their decision to stop making new private equity investments. Explain why the investment results that prompted the CIO's comments should not be relied upon.

2. The ZeeZaw family office has been invested in the Warriors Fund, a relatively small distressed debt strategy, which has performed very well for a number of years. In a recent conversation with the portfolio manager, the CIO for ZeeZaw discovered that the Warriors fund will be receiving a significant investment from a large institution within the next few weeks. What are some of the risks that might develop with the Warriors Fund as a result of this new client? What are some other issues that the CIO might want to probe with the Warriors Fund?

Solution to 1:

With small, residual holdings, even a modest change in valuation can result in outsized returns; for example, a $2,000 investment that gets revalued to $3,000 would report a nominal return of 50%. The 50% return is not representative of private equity investment as a whole but is merely an artifact of the unwinding process. A more accurate picture of performance must consider the development of the fund IRR over time and consider other performance measures, such as the MOIC.

Solution to 2:

The CIO should investigate whether the fund manager is able to appropriately deploy this new capital consistent with the investment process and types of investments that contributed to the Warriors Fund success. Because the fund was relatively small, a very large influx of capital might force the portfolio manager to make larger investments than is optimal or more investments than they did before. Either change without the appropriate resources could undermine future success. Finally, a large influx of cash could dilute near-term performance, especially if the funds remain undeployed for a significant period of time.

SUMMARY

- Allocations to alternatives are believed to increase a portfolio's risk-adjusted return. An investment in alternatives typically fulfills one or more of four roles in an investor's portfolio: capital growth, income generation, risk diversification, and/or safety.
- Private equity investments are generally viewed as return enhancers in a portfolio of traditional assets.
- Long/short equity strategies are generally believed to deliver equity-like returns with less than full exposure to the equity premium. Short-biased equity strategies are expected to lower a portfolio's overall equity beta while producing some measure of alpha. Arbitrage and event-driven strategies are expected to provide equity-like returns with little to no correlation with traditional asset classes.
- Real assets (e.g., commodities, farmland, timber, energy, and infrastructure assets) are generally perceived to provide a hedge against inflation.
- Timber investments provide both growth and inflation-hedging properties.
- Commodities (e.g., metals, energy, livestock, and agricultural commodities) serve as a hedge against inflation and provide a differentiated source of alpha. Certain commodity investments serve as safe havens in times of crisis.
- Farmland investing may have a commodity-like profile or a commercial real-estate-like profile.
- Energy investments are generally considered a real asset as the investor owns the mineral rights to commodities that are correlated with inflation factors.
- Infrastructure investments tend to generate stable/modestly growing income and to have high correlation with overall inflation.

- Real estate strategies range from core to opportunistic and are believed to provide protection against unanticipated increases in inflation. Core real estate strategies are more income-oriented, while opportunistic strategies rely more heavily on capital appreciation.
- Bonds have been a more effective volatility mitigator than alternatives over shorter time horizons.
- The traditional approaches to defining asset classes are easy to communicate and implement. However, they tend to over-estimate portfolio diversification and obscure primary drivers of risk.
- Typical risk factors applied to alternative investments include equity, size, value, liquidity, duration, inflation, credit spread, and currency. A benefit of the risk factor approach is that every asset class can be described using the same framework.
- Risk factor-based approaches have certain limitations. A framework with too many factors is difficult to administer and interpret, but too small a set of risk factors may not accurately describe the characteristics of alternative asset classes. Risk factor sensitivities are highly sensitive to the historical look-back period.
- Investors with less than a 15-year investment horizon should generally avoid investments in private real estate, private real asset, and private equity funds.
- Investors must consider whether they have the necessary skills, expertise, and resources to build an alternative investment program internally. Investors without a strong governance program are less likely to develop a successful alternative investment program.
- Reporting for alternative funds is often less transparent than investors are accustomed to seeing on their stock and bond portfolios. For many illiquid strategies, reporting is often received well past typical monthly or quarter-end deadlines. Full, position-level transparency is rare in many alternative strategies.
- Three primary approaches are used to determine the desired allocation to the alternative asset classes:
  - Monte Carlo simulation may be used to generate return scenarios that relax the assumption of normally distributed returns.
  - Optimization techniques, which incorporate downside risk or take into account skew, may be used to enhance the asset allocation process.
  - Risk factor-based approaches to alternative asset allocation can be applied to develop more robust asset allocation proposals.
- Two key analytical challenges in modelling allocations to alternatives include stale and/or artificially smoothed returns and return distributions that exhibit significant skewness and fat tails (or excess kurtosis).
- Artificially smoothed returns can be detected by testing the return stream for serial correlation. The analyst needs to unsmooth the returns to get a more accurate representation of the risk and return characteristics of the asset class.
- Skewness and kurtosis can be dealt with by using empirically observed asset returns because they incorporate the actual distribution. Advanced mathematical or statistical models can also be used to capture the true behavior of alternative asset classes.
- Applications of Monte Carlo simulation in allocating to alternative investments include:

Summary

1. simulating skewed and fat-tailed financial variables by estimating the behavior of factors and/or assets in low-volatility regimes and high-volatility regimes, then generating scenarios using the different means and covariances estimated under the different regimes; and
2. simulating portfolio outcomes (+/− 1 standard deviation) to estimate the likelihood of falling short of the investment objectives.

- Unconstrained mean–variance optimization (MVO) often leads to portfolios dominated by cash and fixed income at the low-risk end of the spectrum and by private equity at the high-risk end of the spectrum. Some investors impose minimum and maximum constraints on asset classes. Slight changes in the input variables could lead to substantial changes in the asset allocations.
- Mean–CVaR optimization may be used to identify allocations that minimize downside risk rather than simply volatility.
- Investors may choose to optimize allocations to risk factors rather than asset classes. These allocations, however, must be implemented using asset classes. Portfolios with similar risk factor exposures can have vastly different asset allocations.
- Some caveats with respect to risk factor-based allocations are that investors may hold different definitions for a given risk factor, correlations among risk factors may shift under changing market conditions, and some factor sensitivities are very unstable.
- Cash flow and commitment-pacing models enable investors in private alternatives to better manage their portfolio liquidity and set realistic annual commitment targets to reach the desired asset allocation.
- An alternative investment program should be monitored relative to the goals established for the alternative investment program, not simply relative to a benchmark. The investor must monitor developments in the relevant markets to ensure that the fundamental thesis underlying the decision to invest remains intact.
- Two common benchmarking approaches to benchmarking alternative investments—custom index proxies and peer group comparisons—have significant limitations.
- IRRs are sensitive to the timing of cash flows into and out of the fund: Two managers may have similar portfolios but different return profiles depending on their capital call and distribution schedule.
- Pricing issues can distort reported returns and the associated risk metrics, such as betas, correlations, and Sharpe ratios.
- Monitoring of the firm and the investment process are particularly important in alternative investment structures where the manager cannot be terminated easily. Key elements to monitor include key person risk, alignment of interests, style drift, risk management, client/asset turnover, client profile, and service providers.

REFERENCES

Ang, A. 2011. "Illiquid Assets." *CFA Institute Conference Proceedings Quarterly* 28 (4).

Ang, A. 2014. *Asset Management: A Systematic Approach to Factor Investing*. New York: Oxford University Press.

Berkelaar, A. B., A. Kobor, and R. R. P. Kouwenberg. 2009. "Asset Allocation for Hedge Fund Strategies: How to Better Manage Tail Risk." In *The VaR Modeling Handbook: Practical Applications in Alternative Investing, Banking, Insurance, and Portfolio Management*, ed. Gregoriou, Greg N. New York: McGraw-Hill.

Cambridge Associates LLC. 2013. "*From Asset Allocation to Risk Allocation – The Risk Allocation Framework.*"

Getmansky, M., A. Lo, and I. Makarov. 2004. "An Econometric Model of Serial Correlation and Illiquidity in Hedge Fund Returns." *Journal of Financial Economics* 74 (3): 529–609.

Hamilton, J. D. 1989. "A New Approach to the Economic Analysis of Nonstationary Time Series and the Business Cycle." *Econometrica* 57 (2): 357–84.

Ivashina, Victoria, and Josh Lerner. 2018. "Looking for Alternatives: Pension Investments around the World, 2008 to 2017." Federal Reserve of Boston conference paper.

Kim, C., and C. R. Nelson. 1999. *State-Space Models with Regime Switching – Classical and Gibbs-Sampling Approaches and Applications*. Cambridge, MA: MIT Press.

Liu, Y., S. Sun, R. Huang, T. Tang, and X. Wu. Boston Consulting Group. March 2017. "*The Rise of Alternative Assets and Long-Term Investing.*"

Lo, A. 2002. "The Statistics of Sharpe Ratios." *Financial Analysts Journal* 58 (4): 36–52.

Naik, V., M. Devarajan, A. Nowobilski, S. Page, and N. Pedersen. 2016. *Factor Investing and Asset Allocation – A Business Cycle Perspective*. Charlottesville, VA: CFA Institute Research Foundation.

Rockafellar, R. T., and S. Uryasev. 2000. "Optimization of Conditional Value at Risk." *Journal of Risk* 2 (3): 21–42.

Rockafellar, R. T., and S. Uryasev. 2002. "Conditional Value at Risk for General Loss Distributions." *Journal of Banking & Finance* 26 (7): 1443–71.

Swensen, D. F. 2009. *Pioneering Portfolio Management: An Unconventional Approach to Institutional Investment*. New York: Free Press.

Takahashi, D., and S. Alexander. 2001. "*Illiquid Alternative Asset Fund Modeling.*" Yale School of Management (January).

PRACTICE PROBLEMS

The following information relates to Questions 1–8

Kevin Kroll is the chair of the investment committee responsible for the governance of the Shire Manufacturing Corporation (SMC) defined benefit pension plan. The pension fund is currently fully funded and has followed an asset mix of 60% public equities and 40% bonds since Kroll has been chair. Kroll meets with Mary Park, an actuarial and pension consultant, to discuss issues raised at the last committee meeting.

Kroll notes that the investment committee would like to explore the benefits of adding alternative investments to the pension plan's strategic asset allocation. Kroll states:

Statement 1   The committee would like to know which alternative asset would best mitigate the risks to the portfolio due to unexpected inflation and also have a relatively low correlation with public equities to provide diversification benefits.

The SMC pension plan has been able to fund the annual pension payments without any corporate contributions for a number of years. The committee is interested in potential changes to the asset mix that could increase the probability of achieving the long-term investment target return of 5.5% while maintaining the funded status of the plan. Park notes that fixed-income yields are expected to remain low for the foreseeable future. Kroll asks:

Statement 2   If the public equity allocation remains at 60%, is there a single asset class that could be used for the balance of the portfolio to achieve the greatest probability of maintaining the pension funding status over a long time horizon? Under this hypothetical scenario, the balance of the portfolio can be allocated to either bonds, hedge funds, or private equities.

Park confirms with Kroll that the committee has historically used a traditional approach to define the opportunity set based on distinct macroeconomic regimes, and she proposes that a risk-based approach might be a better method. Although the traditional approach is relatively powerful for its ability to handle liquidity and manager selection issues compared to a risk-based approach, they both acknowledge that a number of limitations are associated with the existing approach.

Park presents a report (Exhibit 1) that proposes a new strategic asset allocation for the pension plan. Kroll states that one of the concerns that the investment committee will have regarding the new allocation is that the pension fund needs to be able to fund an upcoming early retirement incentive program (ERIP) that SMC will be offering to its employees within the next two years. Employees who have reached the age of 55 and whose age added to the number of years of company service sum to 75 or more can retire 10 years early and receive the defined benefit pension normally payable at age 65.

Exhibit 1 Proposed Asset Allocation of SMC Defined Benefit Pension Plan

Asset Class	Public Equities	Broad Fixed Income	Private Equities	Hedge Funds	Public Real Estate	Total
Target	45%	25%	10%	10%	10%	100%
Range	35%–55%	15%–35%	0%–12%	0%–12%	0%–12%	–

Kroll and Park then discuss suitability considerations related to the allocation in Exhibit 1. Kroll understands that one of the drawbacks of including the proposed alternative asset classes is that daily reporting will no longer be available. Investment reports for alternatives will likely be received after monthly or quarter-end deadlines used for the plan's traditional investments. Park emphasizes that in a typical private equity structure, the pension fund makes a commitment of capital to a blind pool as part of the private investment partnership.

In order to explain the new strategic asset allocation to the investment committee, Kroll asks Park why a risk factor-based approach should be used rather than a mean–variance-optimization technique. Park makes the following statements:

Statement 3   Risk factor-based approaches to asset allocation produce more robust asset allocation proposals.

Statement 4   A mean–variance optimization typically overallocates to the private alternative asset classes due to stale pricing.

Park notes that the current macroeconomic environment could lead to a bear market within a few years. Kroll asks Park to discuss the potential impact on liquidity planning associated with the actions of the fund's general partners in the forecasted environment.

Kroll concludes the meeting by reviewing the information in Exhibit 2 pertaining to three potential private equity funds analyzed by Park. Park discloses the following due diligence findings from a recent manager search: Fund A retains administrators, custodians, and auditors with impeccable reputations; Fund B has achieved its performance in a manner that appears to conflict with its reported investment philosophy; and Fund C has recently experienced the loss of three key persons.

Exhibit 2 Potential Private Equity Funds, Internal Rate of Return (IRR)

Private Equity Fund	Fund A	Fund B	Fund C
5-year IRR	12.9%	13.2%	13.1%

1 Based on Statement 1, Park should recommend:
  A hedge funds.
  B private equities.
  C commodity futures.

2 In answering the question raised in Statement 2, Park would *most likely* recommend:
  A bonds.
  B hedge funds.

Practice Problems

    C private equities.

3 A limitation of the existing approach used by the committee to define the opportunity set is that it:

    A is difficult to communicate.

    B overestimates the portfolio diversification.

    C is sensitive to the historical look-back period.

4 Based on Exhibit 1 and the proposed asset allocation, the greatest risk associated with the ERIP is:

    A liability.

    B leverage.

    C liquidity.

5 The suitability concern discussed by Kroll and Park *most likely* deals with:

    A governance.

    B transparency.

    C investment horizon.

6 Which of Park's statements regarding the asset allocation approaches is correct?

    A Only Statement 3

    B Only Statement 4

    C Both Statement 3 and Statement 4

7 Based on the forecasted environment, liquidity planning should take into account that general partners may:

    A call capital at a slower pace.

    B make distributions at a faster pace.

    C exercise an option to extend the life of the fund.

8 Based on Exhibit 2 and Park's due diligence, the pension committee should consider investing in:

    A Fund A.

    B Fund B.

    C Fund C.

The following information relates to Questions 9–13

Eileen Gension is a portfolio manager for Zen-Alt Investment Consultants (Zen-Alt), which assists institutional investors with investing in alternative investments. Charles Smittand is an analyst at Zen-Alt and reports to Gension. Gension and Smittand discuss a new client, the Benziger University Endowment Fund (the fund), as well as a prospective client, the Opeptaja Pension Plan (the plan).

    The fund's current portfolio is invested primarily in public equities, with the remainder invested in fixed income. The fund's investment objective is to support a 6% annual spending rate and to preserve the purchasing power of the asset base over a 10-year time horizon. The fund also wants to invest in assets that provide the highest amount of diversification against its dominant equity risk. Gension considers potential alternative investment options that would best meet the fund's diversification strategy.

In preparation for the first meeting between Zen-Alt and the fund, Gension and Smittand discuss implementing a short-biased equity strategy within the fund. Smittand makes the following three statements regarding short-biased equity strategies:

Statement 1 Short-biased equity strategies generally provide alpha when used to diversify public equities.

Statement 2 Short-biased equity strategies are expected to provide a higher reduction in volatility than bonds over a long time horizon.

Statement 3 Short-biased equity strategies are expected to mitigate the risk of public equities by reducing the overall portfolio beta of the fund.

Gension directs Smittand to prepare asset allocation and portfolio characteristics data on three alternative portfolios. The fund's risk profile is one factor that potential lenders consider when assigning a risk rating to the university. A loan covenant with the university's primary lender states that a re-evaluation of the university's creditworthiness is triggered if the fund incurs a loss greater than 20% over any one-year period. Smittand states that the recommended asset allocation should achieve the following three goals, in order of priority and importance:

- Minimize the probability of triggering the primary lender's loan covenant.
- Minimize the probability of purchasing power impairment over a 10-year horizon.
- Maximize the probability of achieving a real return target of 6% over a 10-year horizon.

Smittand provides data for three alternative portfolios, which are presented in Exhibits 1 and 2.

Exhibit 1 Asset Allocation

Alternative Portfolio	Cash	Public Equity	Gov't.	Credit	Hedge Fund	Real Estate	Private Equity
A	4.0%	35.0%	6.0%	5.0%	20.0%	10.0%	20.0%
B	2.0%	40.0%	8.0%	3.0%	15.0%	7.0%	25.0%
C	1.0%	50.0%	3.0%	6.0%	10.0%	0.0%	30.0%

Exhibit 2 Portfolio Characteristics

Alternative Portfolio	1-Year 99% VaR	1-Year 99% CVaR	Probability of Meeting 6% Real Return (10-Year Horizon)	Probability of Purchasing Power Impairment (10-Year Horizon)
A	−16.3%	−19.4%	56.1%	2.5%
B	−17.4%	−20.6%	58.8%	2.8%
C	−19.3%	−22.7%	61.0%	4.0%

Notes:
- One-year horizon 99% VaR: the lowest return over any one-year period at a 99% confidence level

Practice Problems

> **Exhibit 2 (Continued)**
>
> - One-year horizon 99% CVaR: the expected return if the return falls below the 99% VaR threshold
> - Probability of purchasing power impairment: the probability of losing 40% of the fund's purchasing power over 10 years, after consideration of new gifts received by the fund, spending from the fund, and total returns

Gension next meets with the investment committee (IC) of the Opeptaja Pension Plan to discuss new opportunities in alternative investments. The plan is a $1 billion public pension fund that is required to provide detailed reports to the public and operates under specific government guidelines. The plan's IC adopted a formal investment policy that specifies an investment horizon of 20 years. The plan has a team of in-house analysts with significant experience in alternative investments.

During the meeting, the IC indicates that it is interested in investing in private real estate. Gension recommends a real estate investment managed by an experienced team with a proven track record. The investment will require multiple capital calls over the next few years. The IC proceeds to commit to the new real estate investment and seeks advice on liquidity planning related to the future capital calls.

9. Which asset class would *best* satisfy the Fund's diversification strategy?
   - A Private equity
   - B Private real estate
   - C Absolute return hedge fund

10. Which of Smittand's statements regarding short-biased equity strategies is *incorrect*?
    - A Statement 1
    - B Statement 2
    - C Statement 3

11. Based on Exhibit 2, which alternative portfolio should Gension recommend for the fund given Smittand's stated three goals?
    - A Portfolio A
    - B Portfolio B
    - C Portfolio C

12. Which of the following investor characteristics would *most likely* be a primary concern for the plan's IC with respect to investing in alternatives?
    - A Governance
    - B Transparency
    - C Investment horizon

13. With respect to liquidity planning relating to the plan's new real estate investment, Gension should recommend that the fund set aside appropriate funds and invest them in:
    - A 100% REITs.
    - B 100% cash equivalents.
    - C 80% cash equivalents and 20% REITs.

The following information relates to Questions 14–15

Ingerõria Greslö is an adviser with an investment management company and focuses on asset allocation for the company's high-net-worth investors. She prepares for a meeting with Maarten Pua, a new client who recently inherited a $10 million portfolio solely comprising public equities.

Greslö meets with Pua and proposes that she create a multi-asset portfolio by selling a portion of his equity holdings and investing the proceeds in another asset class. Greslö advises Pua that his investment objective should be to select an asset class that has a high potential to fulfill two functional roles: risk diversification and capital growth. Greslö suggests the following three asset classes:

- Public real estate
- Private real assets (timber)
- Equity long/short hedge funds

14 **Determine** which asset class is *most likely* to meet Pua's investment objective. **Justify** your response.

Determine which asset class is *most likely* to meet Pua's investment objective. (Circle one.)	**Justify** your response.
Public Real Estate	
Private Real Assets (Timber)	
Equity Long/Short Hedge Funds	

Five years after his first meeting with Pua, Greslö monitors a private real estate investment that Pua has held for one year. Until recently, the investment had been managed by a local real estate specialist who had a competitive advantage in this market; the specialist's strategy was to purchase distressed local residential housing properties, make strategic property improvements, and then sell them. Pua is one of several clients who have invested in this opportunity.

Greslö learns that the specialist recently retired and the investment is now managed by a national real estate company. The company has told investors that it now plans to invest throughout the region in both distressed housing and commercial properties. The company also lengthened the holding period for each investment property from the date of the initial capital call because of the complexity of the property renovations, and it altered the interim profit distribution targets.

15 **Discuss** the qualitative risk issues that have *most likely* materialized over the past year.

Practice Problems

The following information relates to Questions 16–18

The Ælfheah Group is a US-based company with a relatively small pension plan. Ælfheah's investment committee (IC), whose members collectively have a relatively basic understanding of the investment process, has agreed that Ælfheah is willing to accept modest returns while the IC gains a better understanding of the process Two key investment considerations for the IC are maintaining low overhead costs and minimizing taxes in the portfolio. Ælfheah has not been willing to incur the costs of in-house investment resources.

Qauhtèmoc Ng is the investment adviser for Ælfheah. He discusses with the IC its goal of diversifying Ælfheah's portfolio to include alternative assets. Ng suggests considering the following potential investment vehicles:

- Publicly traded US REIT
- Relative value hedge fund
- Tax-efficient angel investment

Ng explains that for the relative value hedge fund alternative, Ælfheah would be investing alongside tax-exempt investors.

16 **Determine** which of the potential investment vehicles *best* meets the investment considerations for Ælfheah. **Justify** your response. **Explain** for *each* investment not selected why the investment considerations are not met.

Determine which of the potential investment vehicles *best* meets the investment considerations for Ælfheah. (Circle one.)	**Justify** your response.	**Explain** for *each* investment not selected why the investment considerations are not met.
Publicly traded US REIT		
Relative value hedge fund		
Tax-efficient angel investment		

Ng and the IC review the optimal approach to determine the asset allocation for Ælfheah, including the traditional and risk-based approaches to defining the investment opportunity set.

17 **Determine** which approach to determine the asset allocation is *most appropriate* for Ælfheah. **Justify** your response.

Determine which approach to determine the asset allocation is *most appropriate* for Ælfheah. (Circle one.)	**Justify** your response.
Traditional	
Risk based	

The following year, Ng and the IC review the portfolio's performance. The IC has gained a better understanding of the investment process. The portfolio is meeting Ælfheah's liquidity needs, and Ng suggests that Ælfheah would benefit from diversifying into an additional alternative asset class. After discussing suitable investment vehicles for the proposed alternative asset class, Ng proposes the following three investment vehicles for further review:

- Funds of funds (FOFs)
- Separately managed accounts (SMAs)
- Undertakings for collective investment in transferable securities (UCITS)

18 **Determine** the investment vehicle that would be *most appropriate* for Ælfheah's proposed alternative asset class. **Justify** your response.

Determine the investment vehicle that would be *most appropriate* for Ælfheah's proposed alternative asset class. (Circle one.)	**Justify** your response.
FOFs	
SMAs	
UCITS	

The following information relates to Questions 19–20

Mbalenhle Calixto is a global institutional portfolio manager who prepares for an annual meeting with the investment committee (IC) of the Estevão University Endowment. The endowment has €450 million in assets, and the current asset allocation is 42% equities, 22% fixed income, 19% private equity, and 17% hedge funds.

The IC's primary investment objective is to maximize returns subject to a given level of volatility. A secondary objective is to avoid a permanent loss of capital, and the IC has indicated to Calixto its concern about left-tail risk. Calixto considers two asset allocation approaches for the endowment: mean–variance optimization (MVO) and mean–CVaR (conditional value at risk) optimization.

19 **Determine** the asset allocation approach that is *most suitable* for the Endowment. **Justify** your response.

Determine the asset allocation approach that is *most suitable* for the Endowment. (Circle one.)	**Justify** your response.
MVO	
Mean–CVaR optimization	

Calixto reviews the endowment's future liquidity requirements and analyzes one of its holdings in a private distressed debt fund. He notes the following about the fund:

- As of the most recent year end:
  - The NAV of the endowment's investment in the fund was €25,000,000.
  - All capital had been called.

Practice Problems

- At the end of the current year, Calixto expects a distribution of 18% to be paid.
- Calixto estimates an expected growth rate of 11% for the fund.

20 Calculate the expected NAV of the fund at the end of the current year.

SOLUTIONS

1. C is correct. Real assets (which include energy, infrastructure, timber, commodities, and farmland) are generally believed to mitigate the risks to the portfolio arising from unexpected inflation. Commodities act as a hedge against a core constituent of inflation measures. Rather than investing directly in the actual commodities, commodity futures may be incorporated using a managed futures strategy. In addition, the committee is looking for an asset class that has a low correlation with public equities, which will provide diversification benefits. Commodities are regarded as having much lower correlation coefficients with public equities than with private equities and hedge funds. Therefore, commodities will provide the greatest potential to fulfill the indicated role and to diversify public equities.

2. C is correct. When projecting expected returns, the order of returns from highest to lowest is typically regarded as private equities, hedge funds, bonds. Therefore, the probability of achieving the highest portfolio return while maintaining the funded status of the plan would require the use of private equities in conjunction with public equities. In addition, private equities have a high/strong potential to fulfill the role of capital growth. Fixed-income investments are expected to have a high/strong potential to fulfill the role of safety.

3. B is correct. A traditional approach has been used to define the opportunity set based on different macroeconomic conditions. The primary limitations of traditional approaches are that they overestimate the portfolio diversification and obscure the primary drivers of risk.

4. C is correct. With the introduction of the early retirement incentive plan (ERIP), the defined benefit pension plan will likely be called upon to make pension payments earlier than originally scheduled. As a result, the near term liquidity of the plan is the greatest risk arising from the addition of the alternative asset classes (e.g., private equities, hedge funds, and real estate). Investments in alternatives, such as private equities, can take upwards of five years to reach a full commitment and potentially another decade to unwind.

5. B is correct. The pension plan's investment in private equities via a blind pool presents the prospect that less than perfect transparency will be associated with the underlying holdings of the alternative asset manager. Capital is committed for an investment in a portfolio of assets that are not specified in advance. In addition, reporting for alternative funds is often less transparent than investors are accustomed to seeing on their stock and bond portfolios.

6. C is correct. Statement 3 is correct because risk factor-based approaches to asset allocation can be applied to develop more robust asset allocations. Statement 4 is correct because a mean–variance optimization typically over-allocates to the private alternative asset classes, partly because of underestimated risk due to stale pricing and the assumption that returns are normally distributed

7. C is correct. Park notes that the current macroeconomic environment could lead to a bear market within a few years. Liquidity planning should take into account that under a scenario in which public equities and fixed-income investments are expected to perform poorly, general partners may exercise an option to extend the life of the fund.

8. A is correct. Fund A should be selected based on both quantitative and qualitative factors. Fund A has a five-year IRR (12.9%) that is slightly lower than, but comparable to, both Fund B (13.2%) and Fund C (13.1%). Given the sensitivity

Solutions

to the timing of cash flows into and out of a fund associated with the IRR calculation, however, the final decision should not be based merely on quantitative returns. It is also important to monitor the investment process and the investment management firm itself, particularly in alternative investment structures. Considering the qualitative factors identified by Park, Fund A is the only fund with a strong, positive factor: It benefits from service providers (administrators, custodians, and auditors) with impeccable reputations. Fund B seems to be experiencing style drift, which suggests that the returns are not consistent with the manager's advertised investment edge (hence, a negative factor). Fund C has experienced the departure of key persons, which puts future fund returns in jeopardy (hence, a negative factor).

9 C is correct. An absolute return hedge fund has a greater potential to diversify the fund's dominant public equity risk than either private equity or private real estate. Absolute return hedge funds exhibit an equity beta that is often less than that of private equity or private real estate. Also, absolute return hedge funds tend to exhibit a high potential to diversify public equities, whereas equity long/short hedge funds exhibit a moderate potential to fulfill this role.

A is incorrect because although private equity provides moderate diversification against public equity, an absolute return hedge fund has a greater potential to do so. The primary advantage of private equity is capital growth.

B is incorrect because private real estate provides only moderate diversification against public equity, whereas absolute return hedge funds have a greater potential to do so. The primary advantage of private real estate is income generation.

10 B is correct. While bonds reduce the probability of achieving a target return over time, they have been more effective as a volatility mitigator than alternatives over an extended period of time.

A is incorrect because Statement 1 is correct. Short-biased strategies are expected to provide some measure of alpha in addition to lowering a portfolio's overall equity beta.

C is incorrect because Statement 3 is correct. Short-biased equity strategies help reduce an equity-dominated portfolio's overall beta. Short-biased strategies are believed to deliver equity-like returns with less-than-full exposure to the equity premium but with an additional source of return that might come from the manager's shorting of individual stocks.

11 A is correct. Among the three portfolios, Portfolio A minimizes the probability of triggering the primary lender's loan covenant, which is the highest-priority goal, because it has the lowest one-year 99% CVaR, −19.4%. Portfolio A also has the lowest probability of purchasing power impairment over a 10-year horizon (2.5%). While Portfolio A has the lowest probability of achieving a real return target of 6% over a 10-year horizon (56.1%), that is the least important goal to be met. Therefore, Gension should recommend Portfolio A for the fund.

B is incorrect because Portfolio B has a one-year 99% CVaR of −20.6%, which crosses the loan covenant threshold of a 20% loss. Portfolio A is the only one that satisfies the most important goal and is the portfolio least likely to trigger the loan covenant. Since Portfolio B does not achieve the most important goal of minimizing the probability of triggering the primary lender's loan covenant, Portfolio B should not be the recommended portfolio.

C is incorrect because despite the fact that Portfolio C has the highest probability of meeting the 6% real return over a 10-year horizon, 61.0%, it also has a one-year 99% CVaR of −22.7% and thus the highest probability of triggering the loan covenant. Portfolio A is the only one that satisfies the most important goal and is the portfolio least likely to trigger the loan covenant. Since Portfolio C does not achieve the most important goal of minimizing the probability of triggering the primary lender's loan covenant, Portfolio C should not be the recommended portfolio.

12 B is correct. As a public pension fund that is required to provide detailed reports to the public, a primary concern for the IC is transparency. Investors in alternative investments must be comfortable with less than 100% transparency in their holdings. Private equity funds often necessitate buying into a "blind pool." Although an investor can look at the assets acquired in a manager's previous funds, there is no assurance that future investments will exactly replicate the previous funds.

A is incorrect because the IC has a formal investment policy, as well as an in-house team with experience in alternatives and the knowledge and capacity to critically evaluate alternative investments.

C is incorrect because the IC has a long-term investment horizon. While investors with less than a 15-year horizon should generally avoid investing in alternatives, the IC has a 20-year investment horizon that should easily accommodate an investment in private equity.

13 A is correct. REITs are most appropriate for funds committed to private real estate investments since they will have the most similar return and risk characteristics and will help maintain the strategic asset allocation of the plan. Although cash equivalents have less volatility over a short-term horizon, they are less likely to meet the plan's long-term return objectives.

B is incorrect because the opportunity cost of being out of the markets over the next few years during the capital call period makes cash equivalents an inappropriate investment. Although cash equivalents have lower volatility, which is often desirable over a short-term period, they will not help the plan meet its long-term return objectives.

C is incorrect because, although REITs will have the return and risk characteristics most similar to private real estate, a 20% allocation is not large enough to achieve the plan's long-term return objectives. The 80% allocation to cash equivalents will greatly affect the return, making the plan less likely to meet the long-term return objectives.

14

Determine which asset class is most likely to meet Pua's investment objective. (Circle one.)	Justify your response.
Public Real Estate	• Timber exhibits a low correlation with public equities and can fulfill the functional role of risk diversification.
Private Real Assets (Timber)	• Timber provides high long-term returns and can fulfill the functional role of capital growth.
Equity Long/Short Hedge Funds	Private real assets (timber) is the asset class most likely to meet Pua's objective. Private real assets, such as timber, tend to exhibit a low correlation with public equities and therefore have a high potential to fulfill the functional role of risk diversification in Pua's current all-equity portfolio. In addition, timber has a high potential to fulfill the functional role of capital growth in the portfolio since growth is provided by the underlying biological growth of the tree as well as through appreciation in the underlying land value. Compared with timber, public real estate as an asset class would likely offer less opportunity for capital growth and lower diversification benefits. Also, equity long/short hedge funds as an asset class would provide a moderate degree of risk diversification in Pua's all-equity portfolio but do not carry significant capital growth potential.

15
- Pua's investment has been affected by key person risk as shown by the effect of the management change.

- Style drift has occurred as shown by the change from a local to a regional investment strategy and the expansion of the investment strategy to include commercial properties.

- The risk of the investment has changed owing to the added complexity of the property renovations.

- The longer holding periods and the change in interim profit distribution targets will affect this investment.

- Client/asset turnover following the management change may now affect the performance of the investment.

- The management change may alter the client profile, which could have a negative effect on investment performance.

Qualitative considerations can lead to a better understanding of the revised strategy for the investment and whether this investment remains suitable for Pua. Pua's investment has been affected by key person risk as shown by the management change from the local manager to a national company. Style drift has occurred as shown by the change from a local to a regional investment strategy and the expansion of the strategy to include commercial properties.

The risk of the investment has changed because of the added complexity of the renovations, and monitoring the company's risk management will be important for Greslö as she manages Pua's portfolio. Monitoring of the private real estate investment has revealed discrepancies in the new management strategy of the national company relative to the initial investment strategy of the local manager, including the longer holding periods and the changed interim profit distribution targets. Client/asset turnover following the management change may now significantly affect the performance of the investment. Finally, the change in management may alter the client profile, which could have a negative effect on investment performance.

16

Determine which of the potential investment vehicles *best* meets the investment considerations for Ælfheah. (Circle one.)	**Justify** your response.	**Explain** for *each* investment not selected why the investment considerations are not met.
Publicly traded US REIT	The publicly traded US REIT offers tax advantages to Ælfheah from the depreciation of its US real estate assets. The depreciation would help offset income received on those assets. In addition, the REIT would not require an in-house management team; thus, Ælfheah can maintain low overhead costs.	
Relative value hedge fund		The relative value hedge fund is unlikely to be a tax-efficient strategy for Ælfheah. This tax inefficiency is seen frequently with many hedge fund strategies, especially those funds and fund companies where tax-exempt investors dominate the client base. The fund manager may be insensitive to tax considerations for a taxable investor such as Ælfheah.
Tax-efficient angel investment		The tax-efficient angel investment is a specialized investment that will require a highly customized investment approach. Researching and managing this type of investment will require an in-house team to locate and supervise these more specialized investments. Adding these resources would increase overhead costs and violate the IC's investment consideration of maintaining low overhead costs.

17

Determine which approach to determine the asset allocation is *most appropriate* for Ælfheah. (Circle one.)	Justify your response.
Traditional	• The traditional approach is more appropriate since describing the roles of various asset classes is intuitive. • This approach will be easier for Ng to explain to the IC, whose members have only a basic understanding of the investment process. • This approach will make it easier to identify relevant mandates for the portfolio's alternative investments. • Since Ælfheah seeks to maintain low overhead costs, the risk-based approach would not be appropriate. The traditional approach is more appropriate for Ælfheah. The IC is less sophisticated in its understanding of alternative investments but may have some familiarity with the traditional asset class-based approach. Listing the roles of various asset classes will be more intuitive and easy for Ng to explain to the IC. The traditional approach has relevance for the IC's liquidity and operational considerations. This approach will make it easier to identify relevant mandates for the alternative investments in the portfolio. The traditional approach also will allow the IC to obtain a better understanding of how various asset classes behave so that Ng can tailor the asset allocation to address any concerns. The traditional approach will be easier to implement, and the IC does not want to add costly in-house resources, which would likely be necessary with the risk-based approach.
Risk based	

18

Determine the investment vehicle that would be *most appropriate* for Ælfheah's proposed alternative asset class. (Circle one.)	Justify your response.
FOFs SMAs UCITS	• An FOF would allow Ælfheah to co-invest with other investors in alternative investment opportunities for which Ælfheah might otherwise be too small to participate. • An in-house team would not be necessary to review and maintain an FOF, which uses an outside manager. • Ælfheah is unlikely to meet the very high minimum investment of an SMA, which may also require enhanced in-house investment resources. • Ælfheah does not need the higher liquidity of UCITS, which have a less attractive risk/return profile for Ælfheah's relatively small-sized portfolio. An FOF is the most appropriate investment vehicle for Ælfheah. This vehicle allows Ælfheah to co-invest alongside other investors in order to participate in alternative investment opportunities for which it would otherwise be too small to participate. An expert in-house team would not be necessary to review and maintain the types of investments in an FOF since this investment vehicle uses an outside manager. SMAs are available for certain large portfolios, such as those of large family offices or foundations, but it is unlikely that Ælfheah would meet the very high minimum investment requirement. This type of investment poses greater operational challenges for the investor; thus, an SMA may require enhanced in-house investment resources. UCITS are less appropriate for Ælfheah since the pension plan is a medium-sized (not small-sized) investor and its liquidity needs are being met. Ælfheah should instead invest in a vehicle that offers lower liquidity with a more attractive risk/return profile. Also, UCITS have regulatory restrictions that can make them more difficult for a fund manager to implement the desired investment strategy.

Solutions

19

Determine the asset allocation approach that is *most suitable* for the Endowment. (Circle one.)	Justify your response.
MVO	• Mean–CVaR will better address the IC's concern about left-tail risk (the risk of a permanent capital loss).
Mean–CVaR optimization	• If the portfolio contains asset classes and investment strategies with negative skewness and long tails, CVaR optimization could materially alter the asset allocation decision. Given the IC's investment objectives for the endowment, using a mean–CVaR optimization approach is more suitable for determining the asset allocation. The IC has 36% of its portfolio invested in alternative assets, 19% in private equity, and 17% in hedge funds. Thus, the IC has a more sophisticated understanding of risk and will appreciate the more nuanced view of risk offered by mean–CVaR optimization. The portfolio has exposure to alternative investments, and the IC is concerned about left-tail risk (the risk of a permanent loss of capital), as indicated to Calixto. Thus, the asset allocation decision will be enhanced by the more detailed understanding of left-tail risk offered by mean–CVaR optimization relative to MVO. MVO cannot easily accommodate the characteristics of most alternative investments. MVO characterizes an asset's risk using standard deviation. Standard deviation, a one-dimensional view of risk, is a poor representation of the risk characteristics of alternative investments for which asset returns may be not normally distributed. MVO typically over-allocates to alternative asset classes, partly because risk is underestimated because of stale or infrequent pricing and the underlying assumption that returns are normally distributed. An investor particularly concerned with the downside risk of a proposed asset allocation may choose to minimize the portfolio's CVaR rather than its volatility relative to a return target. If the portfolio contains asset classes and investment strategies with negative skewness and long tails, CVaR optimization could materially alter the asset allocation decision.

20 The expected NAV of the fund at the end of the current year is €25,258,050, calculated as follows:

First, the expected distribution at the end of the current year is calculated as

Expected distribution = [Prior-year NAV × (1 + Growth rate)] × (Distribution rate).

Expected distribution = [(€25,000,000 × 1.11) × 18%] = €4,995,000.

Therefore, the expected NAV of the fund at the end of the current year is

Expected NAV = [Prior-year NAV × (1 + Growth rate) + Capital contributions – Distributions] × (1 + Growth rate).

Expected NAV = [(€25,000,000 × 1.11) + 0 – €4,995,000] × 1.11 = €25,258,050.

PORTFOLIO MANAGEMENT
STUDY SESSION

10

Private Wealth Management (1)

This study session addresses the process of private wealth management and the construction of an investment policy statement (IPS) for the individual investor. The IPS is a blueprint for investing client assets. The IPS identifies the needs, goals, and risk tolerance of the investor, as well as constraints under which the investment portfolio must operate. The adviser then formulates an investment strategy to tax-efficiently reconcile these potentially conflicting requirements.

Taxes and regulations are important considerations for individual investors. Because taxes and regulations vary from locality to locality, tax-efficient strategies for portfolio construction and wealth transfer are necessarily specific to the locality in which the investor is taxed. The study session focuses on investment strategies applicable across a wide range of localities. Although illustrations of such strategies may be presented from a country-specific perspective, candidates should focus on the underlying investment principles and be able to apply them to other tax settings.

READING ASSIGNMENTS

Reading 21	Overview of Private Wealth Management by Christopher J. Sidoni, CFP, CFA, and Vineet Vohra, CFA
Reading 22	Topics in Private Wealth Management by Paul Bouchey, CFA, Helena Eaton, PhD, CFA, and Philip Marcovici

© 2021 CFA Insitute. All rights reserved.

READING 21

Overview of Private Wealth Management

by Christopher J. Sidoni, CFP, CFA, and Vineet Vohra, CFA

Christopher J. Sidoni, CFP, CFA, is at Gibson Capital, LLC (USA). Vineet Vohra, CFA, is at Cognasia Talent (Singapore and Hong Kong SAR).

LEARNING OUTCOMES

Mastery	The candidate should be able to:
☐	a. contrast private client and institutional client investment concerns;
☐	b. discuss information needed in advising private clients;
☐	c. identify tax considerations affecting a private client's investments;
☐	d. identify and formulate client goals based on client information;
☐	e. evaluate a private client's risk tolerance;
☐	f. describe technical and soft skills needed in advising private clients;
☐	g. evaluate capital sufficiency in relation to client goals;
☐	h. discuss the principles of retirement planning;
☐	i. discuss the parts of an investment policy statement (IPS) for a private client;
☐	j. prepare the investment objectives section of an IPS for a private client;
☐	k. evaluate and recommend improvements to an IPS for a private client;
☐	l. recommend and justify portfolio allocations and investments for a private client;
☐	m. describe effective practices in portfolio reporting and review;
☐	n. evaluate the success of an investment program for a private client;
☐	o. discuss ethical and compliance considerations in advising private clients;
☐	p. discuss how levels of service and range of solutions are related to different private clients.

© 2019 CFA Institute. All rights reserved.

1. INTRODUCTION AND PRIVATE CLIENTS VERSUS INSTITUTIONAL CLIENTS

a contrast private client and institutional client investment concerns;

Private wealth management refers to investment management and financial planning for individual investors. The private wealth sector has grown considerably as global wealth has increased and as individuals have taken on more of the responsibility for managing their own financial resources. Private wealth managers can help individual investors seek the benefits as well as navigate the complexities of financial markets.

This reading introduces candidates to the process of designing and executing an investment plan or strategy for the individual investor. We discuss the tools and techniques used by private wealth managers and how the wealth manager interacts with the client to serve the client's needs. Section 1 examines the key differences between private clients and institutional clients. In Section 2, we discuss how the wealth manager gains an understanding of the client and identifies key attributes of the client's financial situation that are relevant to the wealth management process. Sections 6 and 7 cover investment planning, including capital sufficiency and retirement planning. Section 8 discusses the investment policy statement, including its various underlying parts. Sections 10 and 11 analyze portfolio construction, portfolio reporting, and portfolio review. Finally, in Sections 13 and 14, we discuss the practice of private wealth management, including ethical considerations for private wealth managers, compliance considerations, and the various client segments that private wealth managers encounter.

Reflecting the variation in industry terms, we use the terms "private wealth managers," "wealth managers," and "advisors" interchangeably.[1] We also refer to "individual investors" as "private clients" or, simply, "clients." In practice, private wealth managers typically operate either independently or as representatives of organizations, such as wealth management firms, banks, and broker/dealers.

1.1 Private Clients versus Institutional Clients

Private clients include individuals and families seeking to invest their personal wealth. These clients are asset owners but typically retain private wealth managers to undertake investment responsibilities on their behalf. Private clients and institutional clients have different concerns, including the following:

- *Investment objectives*.[2] Private clients have diverse investment objectives, some of which may be broadly defined. By contrast, institutional investors tend to have specific, clearly defined investment objectives.

---

[1] It should also be noted that among client segments with high levels of wealth, the roles of wealth managers may vary.

[2] In practice, the terms "objectives" and "goals" are often used interchangeably. We also use them interchangeably in this reading.

Introduction and Private Clients Versus Institutional Clients

- *Constraints.* Private clients face constraints that differ from those of institutional clients, such as generally shorter time horizons, smaller portfolio sizes (less scale), and more significant tax considerations.
- *Other distinctions.* Institutional investors operate under a formal governance structure and often have a greater level of investment sophistication than many private clients. Behavioral issues may also be more prominent for private clients. In addition, while regulation is common to both private clients and institutional clients, the regulatory bodies and frameworks may differ.

1.1.1 Investment Objectives

Private clients have several potential investment objectives. Some common objectives include financial security during the client's retirement years, the ability to provide financial support to family members, and the funding of philanthropic goals. These objectives, however, may not be clearly defined or quantified. For example, a private client's goal may be to fund her retirement lifestyle, but she may not be able to quantify the annual cash flow requirement. She may be able to estimate what is required at the beginning of retirement but uncertain about how the required amount may fluctuate throughout retirement. A different client may wish to fund higher education expenses for his young children. However, he may not know how many of his children will attend a college or university, or what tuition and expenses will be.

Private client investment objectives often compete with one another and may change over time. Consider a business owner who wishes to fund a comfortable retirement for himself and also give generously to certain charities. An unexpected change in his business may shift his priorities considerably. For example, a business downturn may cause him to reduce his charitable goals or eliminate them completely. Conversely, a significant liquidity event, such as the sale of his business, may make a comfortable retirement virtually certain, causing the client to increase his charitable aspirations.

In contrast to private clients, institutional clients tend to have more clearly defined objectives, which are typically related to a specific liability stream. For example, the investment program of a pension plan is designed to meet its benefit obligation, while a university endowment allocates investments to achieve its spending policy. Unlike the objectives of private clients, the primary objectives of these institutional investors are unlikely to change materially over time.

1.1.2 Constraints

Private clients have unique constraints, resulting in investment strategies and approaches that are different from those of institutional clients. Such constraints include time horizon, scale, and taxes.

1.1.2.1 Time horizon In general, individual investors have a shorter time horizon than institutional investors, whose horizon is often theoretically infinite. With shorter time horizons, individual investors are typically more constrained than institutions with respect to risk taking and liquidity. Time horizons also depend on an investor's objectives. For example, individual investors may have different time horizons for different objectives, while institutional investors tend to have a single time horizon and a single investment objective.

1.1.2.2 Scale In general, individual investor portfolios tend to be smaller in size (or scale) than those of institutional investors. Because of this smaller portfolio size, many individual investors face limitations relating to certain asset classes, such as private equity and private real estate, which require a significant investment and would result in an imbalanced portfolio. As with time horizon, the size of private client portfolios can vary widely.

1.1.2.3 Taxes Taxes are a significant and complex consideration for many individual investors, and they vary by jurisdiction. The presence of taxes on investment income or on realized capital gains can impact such investment decisions as asset allocation and manager selection. Investment strategies that result in considerable taxable income may be more favored by a tax-exempt institution than by a taxable private client. Similarly, tax-efficient investments may be more attractive to taxable private clients. An example of a tax-efficient investment is a low-turnover common stock portfolio.

1.1.3 Other Distinctions

In addition to investment objectives and constraints, there are other key distinctions between private clients and institutional clients. Private clients have a less formal governance structure, are typically less sophisticated at investing, may operate under a different regulatory regime, and are more individually unique and complex. Because of these aspects, the personality profile, time allocation, and resource needs/constraints of a private wealth manager differ significantly from those of an institutional manager.

1.1.3.1 Investment Governance The investment governance model and the decision-making process for individual investors differ considerably from those of institutional investors. Institutional investors typically operate under a formal governance structure. This governance structure generally includes a board of directors and an investment committee, sometimes augmented by independent directors with investment expertise. The investment committee may consist of a subset of the board of directors, or the board may delegate this responsibility to an internal committee of staff members. The board and the investment committee play a key role in setting the investment strategy and monitoring investment performance.

By contrast, investment governance for individual investors tends to be less formal. The individual investor works with a private wealth manager to determine an appropriate investment policy. The investment policy is often described in an investment policy statement (which is discussed later in this reading) and typically grants implementation and reporting responsibilities to the wealth manager.

1.1.3.2 Investment Sophistication Institutional investors tend to have a higher degree of investment sophistication than the typical private investor as well as access to more investment resources. Unlike institutional clients, private clients do not normally benefit from the "checks and balances" of a formal investment governance framework. As a result, private clients can be more vulnerable to making "emotional" investment decisions.

1.1.3.3 Regulation In most countries, the regulatory environment is different for individual and institutional investors. In some cases, separate regulators focus on these two investor segments. For example, in the United States, the Securities and Exchange Commission (SEC) and state regulators oversee independent registered investment advisors (RIAs), while the Financial Industry Regulatory Authority (FINRA) covers those advisors who work for broker/dealer organizations. In other cases, the individual and institutional investor groups share a common regulator but are subject to different regulations. An example of this structure occurs in Singapore, where the Monetary Authority of Singapore (MAS) is the primary regulator of financial institutions, yet the MAS also regulates individual investors through its Financial Advisors Act (FAA). This shared regulatory structure also exists in several other countries, such as Australia, China, India, Indonesia, and Malaysia.

1.1.3.4 Uniqueness and Complexity One final difference between private and institutional clients relates to the uniqueness and complexity of individuals. Private clients with similar sets of financial considerations and objectives may nevertheless pursue different investment strategies. Multiple factors may influence each individual's preferences, needs, and concerns—notably, family background and upbringing, work history, sources of wealth, investment experience, groups of friends, and geographic location. Institutional clients with similar considerations and objectives may also follow different investment strategies, but this outcome is less likely with institutional clients than with private clients.

EXAMPLE 1

Private versus Institutional Clients

Garrett Jones, age 74, is a member of the investment committee for a local non-profit endowment. The endowment portfolio includes sizable allocations to less liquid and more volatile asset classes, such as hedge funds and private equity. Jones's personal portfolio, which is modest in size, contains no exposure to hedge funds or private equity. Jones asks his wealth manager about the lack of exposure to these asset classes.

Discuss why the wealth manager has likely not recommended investments in hedge funds and private equity to Jones.

Solution:

Jones's wealth manager has likely not recommended these investments because of certain private client constraints. First, as an individual investor, Jones likely has a shorter time horizon and/or greater liquidity needs than an institutional investor (such as the endowment for which Jones is a committee member). Second, the relatively small size of Jones's personal portfolio will most likely preclude investing in certain asset classes, such as hedge funds and private equity, which require a significant investment and would result in an imbalanced portfolio. Finally, Jones's personal tax considerations may make these investments relatively unattractive.

UNDERSTANDING PRIVATE CLIENTS: INFORMATION NEEDED IN ADVISING PRIVATE CLIENTS

2

- **b** discuss information needed in advising private clients;
- **c** identify tax considerations affecting a private client's investments;

Every new private client engagement begins with developing an understanding of the client. In this section, we begin with a discussion of the information needed in advising private clients and how wealth managers obtain this information. In addition, we discuss a process for formulating client goals, the evaluation of a private client's risk tolerance, and both the technical and "soft" skills needed to advise private clients.

2.1 Information Needed in Advising Private Clients

Wealth managers gather client information predominantly through conversations with clients and by reviewing various financial documents. In this section, we cover the relevant personal, financial, and other information needed in advising private clients.

2.1.1 Personal Information

The process of gathering personal information begins when the wealth manager first communicates with the individual investor. In introductory meetings or telephone calls, individuals typically learn about how wealth managers work with clients, the types of clients that they advise, their areas of expertise, and their fees for service. At the same time, wealth managers ask questions to learn more about prospective clients and what is important to them. While the main purpose of this first interaction is to determine mutual "fit, the introductory conversation often also provides valuable portfolio management information to both sides.

Once an individual becomes a private client, the wealth manager starts by learning about the client's family situation, including marital status, the number of children and grandchildren, and the ages of family members. In most jurisdictions, obtaining proof of client identification is required. For example, a copy of a passport may need to be obtained. The client's employment and career information is also important, as is a discussion about the client's future career, business, or retirement aspirations. In addition, wealth managers should assess the sources of a client's wealth. This information is not always evident from investment statements or reports. For example, a client who has gradually built her wealth through regular portfolio contributions over many years likely has significant experience with market volatility. She also may be able to articulate her emotional reactions (or lack thereof) to various market events. A different client who has relatively new wealth due to the sale of a business may not have this same experience or ability.

As part of the investment background conversation, the wealth manager should determine whether the client has an explicit return objective. Some clients have clear expectations for minimum absolute or relative return targets. Other clients are more concerned with meeting specific goals and may not have a particular return objective. Information about a client's investment preferences may also be generated through conversation with the wealth manager. For instance, liquidity preferences or a desire to consider environmental, social, and governance (ESG) issues in investments may surface in early conversations.

Finally, a detailed discussion of the client's financial objectives (often also referred to as "goals") and risk tolerance is part of the personal information gathering process. We discuss goals, objectives, and risk tolerance in more detail later in this reading.

2.1.2 Financial Information

It is important for wealth managers to understand the financial information of a private client. In many cases, private clients do not maintain and regularly update personal financial statements, such as a *personal balance sheet* (also known as a net worth statement) or a statement of cash flows. Therefore, one responsibility of the wealth manager is to piece together these financial statements for the client.

On a private client's personal balance sheet, assets typically include the following:

- Cash and deposit accounts
- Brokerage accounts
- Retirement accounts (e.g., employer-sponsored defined contribution plan accounts or the present value of defined benefit pensions)
- Other employee benefits, such as restricted stock or stock options
- Ownership interests (stock) in private businesses
- Cash-value life insurance[3]

---

[3] A cash-value life insurance policy involves a cash reserve in addition to protection for the death of an individual. This form of insurance usually combines life insurance with some type of cash accumulation vehicle.

- Real property, including residences, rental property, and land
- Other personal assets (e.g., automobiles, art, or jewelry)

Liabilities on a private client's balance sheet typically include the following:

- Consumer debt, such as credit card balances and loans outstanding
- Automobile loans
- Student loans
- Property-related loans, such as mortgages and home equity loans (or lines of credit)
- Margin debt in brokerage accounts

Clients provide information about their assets and liabilities to wealth managers through copies of statements and reports. A key challenge for wealth managers is that the information provided by clients may not be comprehensive. To fully understand a client's financial profile, a wealth manager needs to analyze and synthesize these statements and reports. Exhibit 1 shows a sample personal balance sheet for a fictitious married couple, Steven and Jenny MacAuley.

Exhibit 1   Sample Personal Balance Sheet

ASSETS		LIABILITIES	
Cash and Deposit Accounts		**Consumer Debt**	
Bank deposit account	EUR 40,000	Credit cards	EUR 30,000
Brokerage and Retirements Accounts		**Property-Related Loans**	
Individual account for Steven	EUR 850,000	Mortgage for personal residence	EUR 320,000
Individual account for Jenny	EUR 1,200,000	Mortgage for rental property 1	EUR 110,000
Retirement account for Steven	EUR 1,400,000	Mortgage for rental property 2	EUR 180,000
Private Investment			
Private stock for Jenny	EUR 2,000,000		
Real Property			
Personal residence	EUR 900,000		
Rental property 1	EUR 250,000		
Rental property 2	EUR 350,000		
Automobiles	EUR 75,000		
Other personal property	EUR 50,000		
Total Assets	EUR **7,115,000**	**Total Liabilities**	EUR **640,000**
		Total Net Worth	EUR **6,475,000**

Beyond assets and liabilities, cash flows are also highly relevant to a private client's financial situation. Sources of cash flows may include employment income, business profit distributions, government income benefits, pensions, annuity income, and portfolio income/distributions. A projection of the client's annual expenses is valuable even if clients do not maintain detailed expense information. In addition, the relevance of expense information varies by client. For example, consider a young, modestly affluent couple versus an older couple who possess wealth that is well beyond their needs. For the young couple, expense information is vital for the wealth manager in determining how much the couple can save toward their goals through improved budgeting. By contrast, obtaining detailed expense information is likely less important in the case of the older, wealthier couple, who are not as budget constrained.

2.1.3 Private Client Tax Considerations

A client's specific tax circumstances can be assessed from the client's tax returns. Tax returns, in particular, provide information that may not otherwise surface in conversations between the wealth manager and the client. In this section, we provide a basic overview of common types of taxes, discuss the global applicability of various tax types, and introduce basic tax strategies for private clients.

2.1.3.1 Common Tax Categories
Taxes for individuals vary by jurisdiction, although some categories are reasonably consistent globally:

- *Taxes on income.* These include taxes on salaries, interest, dividends, capital gains, and rental income.
- *Wealth-based taxes.* These include taxes on the holding of certain types of property (e.g., real estate) and taxes on the transfer of wealth (e.g., taxes on inheritance).
- *Taxes on consumption/spending.* These include sales taxes (i.e., taxes assessed on the final consumer of goods or services) and value-added taxes (i.e., taxes assessed in the intermediate steps of producing a good or service but ultimately paid by the final consumer).

Capital gains taxes are a good illustration of the variability and complexity of global taxes. For example, in Canada, only half of an individual's "net" capital gains (i.e., total capital gains minus total capital losses) are included in taxable income and are taxed at the client's top marginal rate (that is, the rate to be paid on additional income). In the United States and several other jurisdictions, gains on securities over short-term holding periods are taxed at the client's highest marginal income tax rate, while gains on securities over long-term holding periods are taxed at a "long-term" capital gains rate that is generally lower than the marginal income tax rate. India also distinguishes between long-term and short-term capital gains and has several additional considerations that relate to taxes on securities transactions.

2.1.3.2 Basic Tax Strategies
Taxes are normally reflected in a private client's financial plan and asset allocation decisions. While an in-depth discussion of tax strategies is beyond the scope of this reading, the following considerations are common to many clients:

- *Tax avoidance.* Individuals clearly prefer to avoid paying taxes, if possible. Tax avoidance should not be confused with illegal tax evasion. Some countries allow investors to contribute limited amounts to certain accounts that permit tax-free earnings and future withdrawals. Another example of tax avoidance involves various wealth transfer techniques. In a jurisdiction that permits limited amounts of gifts to be transferred without incurring gift taxes, the client can reduce the effects of an estate or inheritance tax both on the amount of the gift and on future capital appreciation.
- *Tax reduction.* Wealth managers typically seek opportunities to reduce the effect of taxes for private clients. For example, a wealth manager may recommend tax-exempt bonds that can produce a higher tax-adjusted return than taxable bonds. Or a wealth manager may recommend limiting exposure to asset classes with less favorable tax characteristics while increasing exposure to more tax-efficient asset classes.

- *Tax deferral.* By deferring the recognition of certain taxes until a later date, clients can benefit from compounding portfolio returns that are not diminished by periodic tax payments. Some investors in a progressive tax system (i.e., a system in which the tax rate increases as income increases) may also seek to defer taxes because they anticipate lower future tax rates. For example, a client with a high level of compensation (and a high marginal tax rate) during her working years may seek to defer taxes on investment income or gains until after retirement (assuming her marginal income tax rate will then be lower). Another example of a tax deferral strategy is limiting portfolio turnover and thus the realization of capital gains.

EXAMPLE 2

Basic Tax Strategies

Roseanna Rodriguez meets with her wealth manager, Raj Gupta, CFA, to discuss her investment strategy and financial plan. Gupta mentions the importance of tax strategies in Rodriguez's financial plan and makes three recommendations:

1. Invest in two different account types: (1) an account that permits both earnings and future withdrawals to be tax-free and (2) an account that permits earnings to accumulate tax-free but requires that taxes be paid when assets are withdrawn from the account.
2. Reduce exposure to an asset class with undesirable tax characteristics in favor of an asset class that is more tax-efficient.
3. Delay the sale of shares of a stock position until the year following retirement.

Identify the basic tax strategy (or strategies)—tax avoidance, tax reduction, or tax deferral—represented in each of the three recommendations.

Solution:

The first recommendation represents both tax avoidance and tax deferral. With the account that permits tax-free accumulation and distributions, Rodriguez would be avoiding taxes. With the account that permits tax-free accumulation but results in income taxes upon distribution, Rodriguez would be deferring taxes.

The second recommendation is an example of tax reduction because the recommended asset class would incur lower taxes. The third recommendation is an example of tax deferral and may also be an example of tax reduction if Rodriguez's tax rate declines after retirement.

2.1.4 Other Relevant Information

Private wealth managers typically gather other information from clients that is related to financial planning. For a client's estate plan (in applicable jurisdictions), the wealth manager obtains copies of relevant legal and governing documents, such as wills and trust documents. Wealth managers also obtain detailed information about the client's life insurance, disability insurance, excess liability coverage, and any other relevant insurance coverage.

We stated previously that private clients tend to have less formal governance models than institutional investors. As part of the information-gathering phase, wealth managers and clients typically establish decision-making parameters as part of investment governance. In fact, wealth managers have an opportunity to help *create* a governance model for clients. Wealth managers and clients normally agree on who can approve and/or change investment policies, who can authorize trading activity, and who can authorize money transfers. When advising couples, it is important to establish whether one individual will be the primary contact with the wealth manager and whether each individual is authorized to make decisions on behalf of the other. Clear guidelines on these issues can minimize the possibility of future misunderstandings or conflicts.

Wealth managers seek information regarding clients' service needs and expectations. For example, it is helpful for the wealth manager to describe her standard practices for portfolio reporting (i.e., frequency, format, information content, and delivery method) and discuss whether the client has reporting needs that differ from the wealth manager's standard practices. When clients expect to have regular cash flow activity, such as periodic withdrawals from their portfolio, the wealth manager should assist in creating an efficient and secure process for executing these transactions. Finally, some clients prefer that their wealth manager interact directly with their other service professionals, such as accountants and legal representatives. The wealth manager and the client should have a clear understanding of what information should and should not be shared with these parties.

3. CLIENT GOALS

d identify and formulate client goals based on client information;

As part of the information-gathering process, wealth managers help private clients formulate and prioritize their goals. These goals may relate to education, property, discretionary spending, gifts to loved ones, health care, or other significant financial considerations. Financial goals are not always apparent, defined, or measurable: they may be expressed by clients as wishes, desires, or aspirations. When goals are uncertain or ambiguous, wealth managers have an opportunity to help clients understand their true objectives, to assess trade-offs and issues with respect to goal prioritization, and to align the client's investment strategy accordingly. This section focuses on the two types of financial goals that are typical of private clients—planned goals and unplanned goals.

3.1 Planned Goals

Planned goals are those that can be reasonably estimated or quantified within an expected time horizon. The following are some examples of planned goals:

- *Retirement.* Maintaining a comfortable lifestyle beyond their working years is a goal for most clients.
- *Specific purchases.* Client goals may focus on specific purchases, which tend to be a function of the level of wealth and/or stage of life. For instance, younger clients or those with relatively low levels of wealth may wish to save for a primary residence. In contrast, older clients or those with more significant levels of wealth may plan for a second residence, a vacation property, or other luxury items (e.g., art or rare collectibles).
- *Education.* Clients often wish to fund their children's education. The amount of expenditure needed for education varies widely. In some locations, such as the United States, the increase in education costs has significantly exceeded the general rate of inflation. Foreign exchange risk may be a factor for clients whose children study abroad.

- *Family events.* Family events, such as weddings, can be significant expenditures for clients.
- *Wealth transfer.* Clients typically plan for their wealth to outlast their own lifetime. An inheritance for beneficiaries may be transferred when the client dies or, in some cases, during the client's lifetime. When clients have a definite amount that they wish to transfer, this goal may need to be prioritized over other goals.
- *Philanthropy.* Clients often wish to make charitable donations during or after their lifetime. This objective may depend on a client's wealth level and country/region.

3.2 Unplanned Goals

Unplanned goals are those related to unforeseen financial needs. These goals are typically more challenging than planned goals because of the difficulty of estimating the timing and the amount of funding needed. The following are some examples of unplanned goals:

- *Property repairs.* Although households may be insured against losses or catastrophes, clients may face additional spending needs if insurance does not fully cover such events. The timing of these potential obligations is often uncertain.
- *Medical expenses.* Private client households normally have medical insurance for illness or hospitalization, but health insurance may not cover all medical expenses. The potential for unexpected medical expenses varies significantly by country/region. As with education costs, increases in health care costs in some countries/regions have far exceeded the general rate of inflation. A related issue in some locations is the potential cost of elder care for oneself or one's family members.
- *Other unforeseen spending.* Beyond property repairs and medical expenses, various other unexpected events commonly occur in the lives of private clients that may require significant financial outlays.

3.3 The Wealth Manager's Role

Goals are among the more complex aspects of a client's financial profile. Because goals are often not clearly defined, wealth managers play a direct role in helping clients articulate these objectives. The following are some relevant considerations in client goal creation:

- *Goal quantification.* Sometimes clients do not have specific, quantifiable goals that wealth managers can analyze. For example, a young client may be unable to estimate her future retirement lifestyle needs, while another client's well-articulated retirement needs may not be realistic in the private manager's assessment. In both cases, the wealth manager has an opportunity to formulate specific client goals. The wealth manager can help the client quantify each goal and plan accordingly.
- *Goal prioritization.* Private clients tend to have multiple, sometimes competing, goals. For example, ensuring a more secure retirement may mean less funding for the education of a client's grandchildren. When clients have competing

priorities, wealth managers have an opportunity to help them decide what matters most. Goal prioritization depends on what is most important to the client, not necessarily which needs occur sooner in the client's investment horizon.

- *Goal changes.* Individual investors' circumstances may change for a variety of reasons. When these changes occur, wealth managers sometimes must help clients re-prioritize their financial goals and reassess their investment strategy. Identifying client goals is not a one-time task but rather a part of an ongoing dialogue between wealth manager and client.

Example 3 provides an illustration of client goals for a fictitious individual, C.Y. Lee.

EXAMPLE 3

Client Goals

Mr. C.Y. Lee is a managing director for the investment firm Acme & Bass, which is located in the Asia-Pacific region. Lee is 43 years old, is married, and has two children, ages 12 and 10. He and his family reside in a home that they own in Singapore. In a conversation with his wealth manager, Lee states that he wishes to fund the undergraduate tuition for his children to study abroad. Lee expects the tuition cost to be approximately £40,000 per year. Lee also wishes to fund his children's weddings at some point in the future. Because the education costs will occur in the next 5–10 years, Mr. Lee states that they are his top priority.

Lee anticipates working until age 65 and does not know how much he and his wife will need to fund their retirement lifestyle. He mentions his desire to purchase a flat in London and let (rent) it as part of their retirement plan. The flat would cost approximately £1.5 million. Lee is also concerned about the future health care expenses of his wife's parents and to what degree he and his wife may need to support them financially.

1 Identify Lee's planned goals.
2 Identify Lee's unplanned goals.
3 Discuss the issue of goal quantification for Lee.
4 Discuss the issue of goal prioritization for Lee.

Solution to 1:

Lee's planned goals are (a) funding his children's education; (b) funding his children's weddings; (c) funding his and his wife's retirement; and (d) purchasing and subsequently letting (renting) a flat in London.

Solution to 2:

Lee's unplanned goals relate to the future health care expenses of his wife's parents, as well as possible uninsured property repairs for the Lee's Singapore residence and, if purchased, their London flat.

Solution to 3:

Lee has quantified the education funding goal and the flat purchase. He and his wealth manager should work to estimate the cost of the weddings for Lee's children and the anticipated retirement lifestyle needs for Lee and his wife.

Solution to 4:

Lee states that his first priority is education funding for his children. However, the timing of a need should not be the sole determinant of goal priority. If funding their children's education costs will leave Lee and his wife unprepared for retirement, for example, they may wish to reevaluate their priorities.

PRIVATE CLIENT RISK TOLERANCE

e evaluate a private client's risk tolerance;

Evaluating a private client's risk tolerance is a key step in the information-gathering process. In practice, the term *risk tolerance* sometimes is used to describe a set of risk-related concepts. The following are some key terms used in this context:

- **Risk tolerance** refers to the level of risk an individual is willing and able to bear. Put another way, risk tolerance is the willingness to engage in a risky behavior in which possible outcomes can be negative. Risk tolerance is the inverse of **risk aversion**, which is the degree of an investor's *unwillingness* to take risk.

- **Risk capacity** is the ability to accept financial risk. The key difference between risk capacity and risk tolerance is that risk capacity is more objective in nature, while risk tolerance relates to an attitude. Risk capacity is determined by the client's wealth, income, investment time horizon, liquidity needs, and other relevant factors. Clients with greater risk capacity can tolerate greater financial losses without compromising current or future consumption goals.

- **Risk perception** is the subjective assessment of the risk involved in the outcome of an investment decision. Unlike risk tolerance, risk perception—how a client perceives the riskiness of an investment decision or the investment climate—depends on the circumstances involved. Consequently, a wealth manager can help shape a client's risk perception. Generally speaking, risk perception varies considerably among individuals.

4.1 Risk Tolerance Questionnaire

In practice, wealth managers often utilize questionnaires to assess clients' risk tolerance. The result of a risk tolerance questionnaire, typically a numerical score, is often used as an input in the investment planning process. Exhibit 2 provides some common types of questions that may be found on a risk tolerance questionnaire.

Exhibit 2

Sample Questions from a Risk Tolerance Questionnaire

1 When you make investment decisions, on which of the following do you tend to focus?
   - **a** Always on the potential for gain
   - **b** Usually on the potential for gain
   - **c** Always on the potential for loss
   - **d** Usually on the potential for loss

(continued)

> **Exhibit 2   (Continued)**
>
> 2   Compared to your friends and family, are you:
>   a   less willing to take risk?
>   b   equally willing to take risk?
>   c   more willing to take risk?
>
> 3   What potential percentage decline in your investment portfolio value over a one-year period are you willing to experience?
>   a   5%
>   b   10%
>   c   20%
>   d   30%
>   e   More than 30%
>
> 4   Which of the following statements best describes your attitude about the performance of your investment portfolio over the next year?
>   a   I can tolerate a substantial loss.
>   b   I can tolerate a loss.
>   c   I can tolerate a small loss.
>   d   I would have a hard time tolerating a loss of any magnitude.
>
> 5   Suppose that you have made an investment that, due to a sudden broad market decline, has declined in price by 25%. Which of the following actions would you take?
>   a   Sell all of the investment.
>   b   Sell a portion of the investment.
>   c   Hold the investment (take no action).
>   d   Buy more of the investment.
>
> 6   Suppose that you have access to two types of investments: one investment with low risk and low expected return and one with high risk and high expected return. Which of the following portfolio mixes would you select?
>   a   100% low risk/low return
>   b   75% low risk/low return and 25% high risk/high return
>   c   50% low risk/low return and 50% high risk/high return
>   d   25% low risk/low return and 75% high risk/high return
>   e   100% high risk/high return
>
> 7   Suppose that you are offered employment that involves the choice of a fixed salary, variable compensation that could be higher or lower than the fixed salary, or some mix of the two. Which of the following would you choose?
>   a   Entirely fixed salary
>   b   Mostly fixed salary
>   c   Entirely variable compensation
>   d   Mostly variable compensation
>   e   An equal mix of the two

Risk tolerance questionnaires are not perfect and it is unclear whether they are predictive of investor behavior. Recommending an investment or an asset allocation for a client based upon the questionnaire requires significant judgment on the part of a wealth manager. In fact, academic studies indicate a high degree of subjectivity in the client questionnaire approach. This subjectivity increases the potential for the wealth manager's own views on risk to become an influential factor in making investment decisions for a client. Other studies demonstrate how the structuring of questions affects investor responses. For example, presenting a loss in either percentage or dollar terms can lead to different responses from the same individual. Similarly, a question that involves a small dollar loss on a small portfolio may generate a different response than a question involving a large dollar loss on a large portfolio, even if the percentage losses are the same.

4.2 Risk Tolerance Conversation

As in the information-gathering process described earlier, conversations with the client can produce valuable insights into that individual's risk tolerance that may not be evident from a risk tolerance questionnaire or an assessment of personality type. These insights may include the following:

- The degree to which the client's financial decisions are influenced by friends or family members.
- The financial experiences that have shaped the client's perspective: For example, individuals who lived through deep recessions, even in childhood, may bring that perspective to present-day investment decisions.
- The client's past investment mistakes and successes.
- The client's accumulation of investment wealth—for example, whether the client achieved wealth through saving, inheritance, a liquidity event, or some combination thereof.
- The client's evaluation of investment risk—that is, whether the client thinks of investment losses in absolute or percentage terms.

Conversations about risk tolerance enable the wealth manager to educate a client about investment risk. For example, a wealth manager may demonstrate how certain risk factors (e.g., interest rate risk, credit risk, and equity risk) can produce incremental returns as well as incremental losses. As another example, a wealth manager may ask a client to select from a "menu" of portfolio options with a range of expected returns and degrees of volatility. The client's choice from this menu provides some information about the individual's risk tolerance.

4.3 Risk Tolerance with Multiple Goals

To this point, we have discussed a client's overall risk tolerance. Because clients often have multiple goals or objectives, their risk tolerance may vary for different goals. For example, a client may have a low risk tolerance with respect to near-term goals (such as education costs) but a higher risk tolerance when it comes to longer-term goals (such as retirement needs). A challenge for wealth managers in managing client relationships is to satisfactorily address potentially conflicting risk tolerance levels.

5. TECHNICAL AND SOFT SKILLS FOR WEALTH MANAGERS

f describe technical and soft skills needed in advising private clients;

Private wealth management resembles both an art and a science. That is, a wealth manager needs to have the professional aptitude to understand the client's financial goals, objectives, and constraints, as well as the financial acumen to recommend appropriate investments and portfolio management solutions. In short, wealth managers need both technical skills and non-technical ("soft") skills to succeed in their advisory roles.

5.1 Technical Skills

Technical skills represent the specialized knowledge and expertise necessary to provide investment advice to private clients. In some jurisdictions, regulators require minimum qualifications for technical skills among wealth managers. Examples of technical skills include the following:

- *Capital markets proficiency.* Private wealth management requires an understanding of capital market dynamics as part of helping clients achieve their financial goals. In most cases, wealth managers must have a broad understanding of capital markets and asset classes, as opposed to a specialist viewpoint. For example, a wealth manager will likely not have the same sector- or security-level expertise as an equity analyst who focuses on a specific industry.

- *Portfolio construction ability.* In conjunction with capital markets proficiency, private wealth managers need the ability to construct portfolios that are appropriate for each client's financial situation. This ability requires a deep understanding of asset class risks and returns; an awareness of the correlations among asset classes; and knowledge of investment vehicles, managers, products, and strategies for implementing a client's investment program.

- *Financial planning knowledge.* Wealth managers are typically not experts in specialized financial planning fields such as estate law, taxation, and insurance. However, these fields are highly relevant to the practice of wealth management. As a result, wealth managers who have a working knowledge of these related fields can add meaningful value for a client and can more effectively interact with the other professionals who serve that client.

- *Quantitative skills.* Given the need for investment analysis and portfolio construction, quantitative skills are critical for private wealth managers.

- *Technology skills.* Wealth managers use technology to manage client portfolios as well as improve efficiency in delivering advice and services. Examples of technology used by wealth managers include portfolio optimization software, simulation modeling tools, portfolio management software, portfolio accounting and performance reporting packages, and customer relationship management (CRM) software.

- *Language fluency.* In some situations, the ability to communicate in more than one language is a critical technical skill—for example, when a wealth manager has a multinational client base, manages cross-border transactions, or works in markets where more than one language is commonly spoken.

5.2 Soft Skills

Soft skills typically involve interpersonal relationships—that is, the ability to effectively interact with others. While soft skills are more qualitative and subjective than technical skills, they are critical nonetheless in the practice of private wealth management. Soft skills include the following:

- *Communication skills.* Because wealth managers interact extensively with clients, strong communication skills are essential. Communication skills begin with active listening when gathering client information. Effective verbal communication requires being able to ask the right questions as well as knowing *how* to ask questions. Meanwhile, effective written communication has become even more relevant with the increased use of email for communicating with clients. Presentation skills are commonly needed by wealth managers for engaging in group meetings and understanding the sophistication of the audience.

- *Social skills.* The ability to understand and relate to others and demonstrate empathy is a critical skill for wealth managers, particularly when "bad news" (e.g., poor investment performance) needs to be delivered to clients. Social skills also include the ability to read and interpret various non-verbal cues, such as body language.

- *Education and coaching skills.* An important role for a wealth manager is to educate and coach clients about investing and the wealth management process. Effective wealth managers are able to tailor this education and coaching to a client's level of sophistication.

- *Business development and sales skills.* Wealth managers often participate in or lead new business development for their firms or practices. Business development involves initiating contact with prospective clients (often called "prospects"), while the sales aspect involves successfully converting prospects into actual clients. Business development and sales entail several of the technical and soft skills previously mentioned. For example, wealth managers need to demonstrate capital markets and investment expertise while using effective communication and social skills.

EXAMPLE 4

Technical and Soft Skills

John Müller, CFA, a private wealth manager, recently received feedback from clients and colleagues as part of his performance review. Clients commented favorably on how Müller coordinates with external tax and legal professionals and on how well he listens to and understands his clients' needs. Colleagues remarked on Müller's broad knowledge of traditional and alternative asset classes and his ability to obtain new client engagements.

Describe which technical and soft skills Müller demonstrated as part of his performance review.

Solution:

In his performance review, Müller demonstrated the technical skills of capital markets proficiency and financial planning knowledge. Müller's capital markets proficiency was shown through his broad knowledge of traditional and alternative asset classes, while his financial planning knowledge was shown by his successful coordination with tax and legal professionals. In addition to technical skills, Müller demonstrated the soft skills of communication and business

> development and sales. Communication skills were shown by his ability to listen well and understand client needs, while business development and sales skills were shown by his record of obtaining new client engagements.

6. INVESTMENT PLANNING, AND CAPITAL SUFFICIENCY ANALYSIS

g evaluate capital sufficiency in relation to client goals;

After developing an understanding of their clients, wealth managers begin the process of helping clients meet their objectives. In this section, we discuss key investment planning concepts, such as capital sufficiency analysis, retirement planning, and the client's investment policy statement.

6.1 Capital Sufficiency Analysis

To meet their financial goals and objectives, clients must have sufficient capital or follow a plan that will likely result in sufficient capital. **Capital sufficiency analysis**, also known as **capital needs analysis**, is the process by which a wealth manager determines whether a client has, or is likely to accumulate, sufficient financial resources to meet his or her objectives.

6.1.1 Methods for Evaluating Capital Sufficiency

Two methods for evaluating capital sufficiency are deterministic forecasting and Monte Carlo simulation. Portfolio growth in a deterministic model occurs in a "straight-line" manner. For example, suppose a client's investment horizon is 15 years and the wealth manager has determined that the portfolio's likely compound annual return is 6%. In deterministic forecasting, the client is expected to achieve a 6% return in each of the 15 years in the analysis. While simple to understand, the deterministic method is typically unrealistic with respect to the variability in potential future outcomes.

By contrast, Monte Carlo simulation allows a wealth manager to model the uncertainty of several key variables and, therefore, the uncertainty or variability in the future outcome. Monte Carlo simulation generates random outcomes according to assumed probability distributions for these key variables. Instead of assuming, for instance, linear portfolio growth of 6% per year, Monte Carlo simulation would assume a simple average (arithmetic mean) return and a standard deviation of year-to-year returns for the portfolio. The portfolio's expected rate of return in a given year is determined randomly from this predefined distribution of possible returns. Monte Carlo simulation generates a large number of independent "trials," each of which represents one potential outcome for the client's investment horizon. By aggregating the outcomes of these various trials, the wealth manager is able to draw conclusions about the probability that the client will reach his or her objectives. It should be noted that such conclusions are sensitive to underlying assumptions, which may be subjective in nature.

6.1.2 Inputs to Capital Sufficiency Analysis

When using deterministic forecasting, the wealth manager must specify the following inputs: a portfolio return assumption, the current value of the portfolio, anticipated future contributions to the portfolio, and cash flows from the portfolio that represent client needs (according to the client's goals). As mentioned earlier, with Monte Carlo

Investment Planning, and Capital Sufficiency Analysis

simulation, the wealth manager assumes a simple average return and a standard deviation of returns for the portfolio, rather than determining an annual portfolio growth rate. Wealth managers should be cautious about using historical rates of return as inputs to either a deterministic forecast or a Monte Carlo simulation. Instead, forward-looking capital market assumptions should be the foundation for the analysis.

In some cases, the inputs to Monte Carlo simulation are more complex. Portfolio return is not the only input that can be made variable. Some Monte Carlo simulation software requires separate asset class assumptions—such as simple average return, standard deviation, and correlation with other portfolio asset classes—rather than assumptions at the overall portfolio level. Some software packages enable variability in the client's investment horizon, such as their life expectancy. Other common inputs to capital sufficiency analysis for private clients include taxes, inflation, and investment management fees.

6.1.3 Interpreting Monte Carlo Simulation Results

When performing a capital sufficiency analysis, one role of a wealth manager is to interpret the results for the client. Suppose a client is approaching retirement and wants to make sure that he does not run out of funds in his lifetime. The wealth manager uses the client's investment portfolio and assumptions about the client's expected retirement expenditures to run a Monte Carlo simulation that generates a thousand trials. The output for this fictitious portfolio is shown in Exhibit 3.

The table in Exhibit 3 illustrates portfolio values (adjusted for inflation) at specific time intervals and at certain percentiles of the thousand trials. The table also shows the percentage of trials at a given horizon in which the client successfully achieved her objective. For instance, after 10 years, a portfolio value of $765,821 at the 75th percentile indicates that in 75% of the trials, the portfolio value after 10 years *exceeded* $765,821. Similarly, over this same 10-year period, only 5% of trials resulted in a portfolio value that exceeded $3,519,828. "Successful Trials" at the bottom of the table indicates, for example, that after 20 years, 69% of the trials were successful; that is, the client failed to meet her objective in 31% of trials. The successful trials are those in which the client's portfolio value meets his objective, which is to have sufficient funds for his retirement (i.e., the client does not want to "run out of funds"). The percentage of successful trials is also known as the "probability of success." Wealth managers tend to guide clients toward a 75%–90% probability of success, although no industry standard range exists.

Exhibit 3 Monte Carlo Simulation Results

Percentile	Year 10 Portfolio Value	Year 15 Portfolio Value	Year 20 Portfolio Value
5th	$3,519,828	$3,651,264	$3,647,328
25th	$1,981,861	$1,698,449	$1,530,372
50th	$1,239,837	$843,820	$569,974
75th	$765,821	$305,126	($249,205)
95th	$197,179	($264,048)	($1,402,608)
Successful Trials	98%	88%	69%

When the probability of success falls below an acceptable range, potential solutions include the following:

- Increasing the amount of contributions toward a goal
- Reducing the goal amount
- Delaying the timing of a goal (e.g., retiring a few years later than originally planned)
- Adopting an investment strategy with higher *expected* returns, albeit within the client's acceptable risk tolerance and risk capacity

In light of these solutions, wealth managers should be careful about allowing capital sufficiency analysis to completely drive portfolio construction. For example, if a client's risk tolerance does not allow for an asset allocation with a higher expected return, adopting a higher-risk strategy may cause the client to abandon the strategy at a market extreme, thus undermining the portfolio's ability to meet the investor's objectives.

EXAMPLE 5

Monte Carlo Simulation

Reyansh and Pari Patel are saving to send their sons Rohan (age 4) and Vihaan (age 6) to college in the United States. Thus far, they have saved approximately $170,000. They will be able to save an additional $20,000 toward this goal in the next year and to increase the amount each year by 3% to address inflation. Current annual tuition costs are $40,000, and the Patels expect tuition to increase 6% annually.

The Patels' wealth manager, Sai Chhabra, CFA, uses a Monte Carlo simulation to calculate the probability of meeting the college tuition objective. The Monte Carlo simulation results are shown in Exhibit 4.

Exhibit 4 Monte Carlo Simulation Results

Percentile	Year 10 Portfolio Value	Year 15 Portfolio Value	Year 20 Portfolio Value
5th	$618,860	$608,445	$429,512
25th	$499,552	$409,753	$212,123
50th	$433,375	$309,823	$71,849
75th	$301,502	$219,852	($22,578)
95th	$213,121	$121,849	($79,845)
Successful Trials	100%	100%	67%

Discuss how the Patels might increase the probability of success in meeting their college tuition goal.

Solution:

To increase the probability of success in meeting their tuition goal, the Patels should consider three possible solutions:

1   Increase their annual contributions toward this goal.

2   Reduce the goal amount, perhaps by funding a portion of the tuition costs or by identifying schools with lower tuition costs.

3   Adopt an investment strategy with higher expected returns that is still within the Patels' acceptable risk tolerance and risk capacity.

A fourth possibility—delaying the timing of the goal—is not a practical solution, given the ages of the sons and when they intend to enter college.

RETIREMENT PLANNING

h   discuss the principles of retirement planning;

For many investors, funding their retirement lifestyle represents the largest and most important financial objective. Retirement planning has grown in significance as life expectancies have increased globally. In 1960, 65-year-old men in developed countries had a life expectancy of approximately 11 to 14 years, while 65-year-old women had a life expectancy of 14 to 16 years.[4] Since that time, the life expectancy of 65-year-old individuals (both men and women) has increased considerably. The increased emphasis on retirement planning has also been driven by a shift in the primary responsibility for funding retirement from employers and governments to individuals.

In this section, we discuss various principles of retirement planning, including the retirement stage of an individual's life, the analysis of retirement goals, and behavioral considerations for retired clients.

7.1 Retirement Stage of Life

A wealth manager's role in retirement planning includes assessing how much clients must save toward their retirement goals and helping clients determine at what age they will be financially prepared for retirement. Unlike institutional investors, which often have quantifiable liabilities, private clients may have difficulty estimating their future financial needs. Therefore, wealth managers have an opportunity to help shape clients' expectations about their future retirement lifestyle.

An overview of the following financial stages of life provides some context for our discussion of retirement planning:

- Education
- Early career
- Career development
- Peak accumulation
- Pre-retirement
- Early retirement
- Late retirement

---

4 These data were obtained from the Organisation for Economic Co-operation and Development (OECD).

During the education stage, an individual is typically developing human capital rather than financial capital. In this context, **human capital** is an implied asset that represents the net present value of an investor's future expected labor income, while **financial capital** represents the tangible and intangible assets (excluding human capital) owned by an individual or household. Individuals normally begin to accumulate assets for retirement in the early career stage. During this stage, individuals often have competing financial priorities, such as family needs, housing costs, and education. Retirement planning tends to take on greater importance as individuals move into the career development stage and, later, into the peak accumulation and pre-retirement stages. As individuals work and save money for retirement, they convert their human capital into financial capital. They also accumulate other financial benefits, such as pensions and government-provided retirement income, and they reduce non-retirement liabilities, such as mortgage loans and consumer debt.

In the early retirement stage, clients begin to draw from both financial resources and income sources for their retirement spending. Cash flows come from the client's investment portfolio as well as from pension income, government-provided retirement benefits, and if applicable, part-time or full-time employment.

In the late retirement stage, clients generally reduce expenditures on travel and leisure activities. Also during this stage, some individuals experience health issues that, in some countries, result in an increased burden on financial resources.

One of the wealth manager's roles in the early retirement and late retirement stages is determining a sustainable rate of distribution from the client's investment portfolio. This analysis is done on an ongoing basis to ensure that clients' financial resources will cover their remaining lifetime needs. That is, retirement planning does not begin or end with the client's retirement.

7.1.2 Analyzing Retirement Goals

Wealth managers may use several different methods to analyze a client's retirement goals. Three common methods—mortality tables, annuities, and Monte Carlo simulation—are discussed below.

7.1.2.1 Mortality Tables

A **mortality table** indicates individual life expectancies at specified ages. Wealth managers can use mortality tables to determine the probability that a client will live to a certain age; they can then estimate the client's anticipated retirement spending over his or her remaining lifespan.

Example 6 shows a sample mortality table. In the table, the plan year, client age, remaining life expectancy in years, and probability of surviving to a certain year are provided. This client is currently 72 years old and has a life expectancy of 12 years. The probability that he will survive to age 87 (i.e., 15 years from now) is 34%. The probability that he will survive to age 92 (i.e., 20 years from now) is 14%.

In practice, a wealth manager can use a mortality table to estimate the present value of a client's retirement spending needs by assigning associated probabilities to annual expected cash outflows.

EXAMPLE 6

Sample Mortality Table

Plan Year	Client Age	Life Expectancy	Survival Probability
0	72	12.0	100%
1	73	11.4	97%
2	74	10.8	93%

Plan Year	Client Age	Life Expectancy	Survival Probability
3	75	10.2	90%
4	76	9.7	86%
5	77	9.1	82%
6	78	8.6	77%
7	79	8.1	73%
8	80	7.6	68%
9	81	7.2	64%
10	82	6.7	59%
11	83	6.3	54%
12	84	5.8	49%
13	85	5.5	44%
14	86	5.1	39%
15	87	4.7	34%
16	88	4.4	29%
17	89	4.1	25%
18	90	3.8	21%
19	91	3.5	17%
20	92	3.3	14%

Source: Kitces and Hultstrom, "Joint Life Expectancy and Mortality Calculator." https://www.kitces.com/joint-life-expectancy-and-mortality-calculator/ (accessed September 14, 2018).

One potential drawback to using mortality tables is that an individual client's probability of living to a certain age may exceed that of the general population. Factors such as education level and access to quality health care tend to correlate with increased longevity. Therefore, the survival probabilities from an actuarial perspective may understate the true probability of a given client's living to a given age.

7.1.2.2 Annuities *Annuities* can be used to analyze a client's retirement goals. A relatively simple way of calculating the present value of a client's desired retirement spending is by pricing an annuity. Annuities provide a series of fixed payments, either for life or for a specified period, in exchange for a lump sum payment. Many types of annuities exist, some of which are quite complex. Two basic forms are the immediate annuity and the deferred annuity. With an **immediate annuity**, an individual (called the "annuitant") pays an initial lump sum, typically to an insurance company, in return for a guarantee of specified future monthly payments—beginning immediately—over a specified period of time. With a **deferred annuity**, the specified future monthly payments begin at a later date. Suppose a husband and wife, both age 65, wish to retire with $100,000 per year in inflation-adjusted income. An immediate fixed annuity with "100% survivor income" might cost the couple approximately $2,500,000. The percent of survivor determines how much of the original annual income amount will go to the surviving spouse after the death of the first spouse. In this example, in exchange for $2,500,000 today (i.e., present value), the insurance company promises to pay $100,000 per year, adjusted for inflation, through the lifetime of the surviving spouse.

Life annuities are those in which the income stream continues as long as the annuitant lives. Using mortality tables, a wealth manager calculates the client's retirement liability based upon the individual's life expectancy. If the client lives longer than the actuarial statistics assume, the client's actual retirement spending needs will exceed the amount that the wealth manager and client planned for. This scenario introduces **longevity risk**, which is the risk of outliving one's financial resources. Life annuities help to mitigate longevity risk.

7.1.2.3 Monte Carlo Simulation Revisited

Earlier, we discussed Monte Carlo simulation in the context of determining a client's capital sufficiency. Monte Carlo simulation can also be used to analyze a client's retirement goals. One advantage of Monte Carlo simulation is its applicability to the client's actual asset allocation. For instance, if a client does not intend to use annuities for retirement needs, then annuity pricing will not be useful in estimating the client's lifestyle needs. Instead, Monte Carlo simulation can be used to analyze the likelihood that the client's actual portfolio will meet anticipated retirement needs.

Another advantage of Monte Carlo simulation for retirement planning is its flexibility in modeling different scenarios and exploring issues that are important to clients. Typically, retirement goals are more complex than a fixed annual cash flow requirement. For instance, if a client wishes to determine the effect of a significant purchase/gift or large unforeseen expense, the wealth manager can model these scenarios with Monte Carlo simulation.

Wealth managers should be careful about the degree of precision that Monte Carlo simulation provides. Simulation modeling is only a method of estimation; it cannot predict the future. Moreover, the output from Monte Carlo simulation can be highly sensitive to small changes in input assumptions. This is especially true for the portfolio rate of return assumption. Finally, a typical Monte Carlo output includes the probability of reaching a goal (or goals) but not necessarily the "shortfall magnitude." Shortfall magnitude matters because if clients are at risk of not meeting their objectives, they can make adjustments. If the shortfall is severe, the necessary adjustment may be significant.

EXAMPLE 7

Retirement Planning

Emily Whitfield, CFA, is meeting with two different clients today, Sam and Rebecca, regarding their retirement plans. Sam is retiring soon. He wants to be certain to have €100,000 per year in income throughout retirement. Rebecca is interested in exploring several possible scenarios for her retirement, using assumptions that are specific to her actual portfolio.

Recommend the method of analyzing retirement goals that is most appropriate for each of these two clients.

Solution:

For Sam, annuities are most appropriate. The price of an annuity that produces €100,000 per year for life will determine how much Sam must have saved for retirement. For Rebecca, Monte Carlo simulation is most appropriate because she is interested in analyzing how different portfolio scenarios will affect her retirement plans.

7.1.3 Behavioral Considerations in Retirement Planning

Several behavioral considerations are relevant to retired clients and/or retirement planning. The following are some examples:

- *Heightened loss aversion.* Some studies suggest that retirees are much more loss-averse than younger investors. This observation has implications for clients' asset allocation through retirement and, therefore, for the return assumptions used in retirement planning.
- *Consumption gaps.* Due to loss aversion and uncertainty about future financial needs, many retirees spend less than economists would predict, resulting in a gap between actual and potential consumption.
- *The "annuity puzzle."* While annuities can help to mitigate longevity risk and, in some cases, may improve the probability of retirees meeting their spending objectives, individuals tend not to prefer to invest in annuities. This phenomenon is known as the "annuity puzzle." Explanations for the puzzle include investors' reluctance to give up hope of substantial lifestyle improvement, their dislike of losing control over the assets, and, in many cases, the high cost of annuities.
- *Preference for investment income over capital appreciation.* Behavioral economists have noted that individuals distinguish between income and capital when making spending choices. Evidence for this behavior includes the tendency of investors to spend dividend income rather than selling shares of securities and spending the proceeds. One possible explanation is that investors lack self-control with respect to spending. This theory suggests that spending only the income and not the principal is a self-control mechanism.

INVESTMENT POLICY STATEMENT   8

i. discuss the parts of an investment policy statement (IPS) for a private client;
j. prepare the investment objectives section of an IPS for a private client;
k. evaluate and recommend improvements to an IPS for a private client;

The **investment policy statement** (IPS) is a written planning document that describes a client's investment objectives and risk tolerance over a relevant time horizon, along with the constraints that apply to the client's portfolio. A wealth manager typically produces this document prior to constructing and implementing the client's investment portfolio. The IPS creates a link between the client's unique considerations and their strategic asset allocation. The IPS is also an operating manual, listing key ongoing management responsibilities. The client and wealth manager should review the IPS regularly and update it whenever changes occur either in the client's circumstances or in the capital markets environment that impact the client's investment strategy.

A well-constructed IPS has certain advantages for private clients. One advantage is that the IPS encourages investment discipline and reinforces the client's commitment to follow the strategy. This advantage is particularly important during adverse market conditions. A second advantage is that the IPS focuses on long-term goals rather than short-term performance. For the wealth manager, the IPS provides evidence of a professional, client-focused investment management process and the fulfillment of fiduciary responsibilities.

8.1 Parts of the Investment Policy Statement

The IPS includes the client's background and investment objectives, the key parameters of the investment program, the portfolio asset allocation, and some discussion of the duties and responsibilities of relevant parties. Topics addressed in most IPSs for private clients are discussed below.

8.1.1 *Background and Investment Objectives*

The client's background and investment objectives are critical parts of the IPS. Background items commonly include the client's name and age, as well as relevant personal and financial information. The wealth manager gains an understanding of the client's investment objectives during the information-gathering process. Common objectives include funding lifestyle needs during retirement, supporting family members, funding philanthropic activities, and meeting bequest goals. These examples typically represent ongoing objectives. By contrast, one-time objectives may include the purchase of a second home or a significant future travel expense. It is common for private clients to have multiple, competing objectives that they seek to achieve with the same portfolio.

Investment objectives should be detailed and quantified whenever possible. For instance, a client who is about to retire may seek to withdraw a specific amount each year that increases with the annual rate of inflation. A client also may have specific amounts in mind for future bequests or for charitable gifts. By comparison, oversimplified investment objectives such as "growth" or "growth and income" would not be sufficiently detailed.

Sometimes, clients have difficulty assigning specific amounts to future objectives. When this is the case, the wealth manager can create a more general objective, with the understanding that he will continue to work with the client to determine an achievable specific objective.

The wealth manager should also include in this section of the IPS other cash flows that are linked to investment objectives and that will therefore affect the capital sufficiency analysis. For instance, if a client intends to contribute additional amounts to her investment portfolio each year before subsequently beginning periodic withdrawals, the objective should reflect the expected contributions. Likewise, if the client anticipates that a significant liquidity event, such as the sale of a business, will be integral to meeting the investment objective, that information should be included in this section.

In a situation involving multiple objectives, the wealth manager should note which of the objectives is primary. For example, clients may wish to support their lifestyle needs through retirement while preserving an inheritance for their children. In this common example, the primary objective is the client's retirement security and the secondary objective is the inheritance for the children.

The investment objective, when linked to the client's asset allocation and the wealth manager's capital market assumptions, should provide the basic inputs to a capital sufficiency analysis. Whenever the capital sufficiency analysis does not support the investment objective, the wealth manager must work with the client to establish a revised objective that the manager judges to be achievable.

As part of the overall client background, the IPS should include the market value of the portfolio and of the accounts that make up the portfolio. The wealth manager should indicate the tax status of the account—that is, whether it is taxable, as in the case of an individual or joint account, or tax-deferred, as in the case of certain retirement plan accounts. When accounts are tax-deferred, the client pays tax on the distributions from the account rather than on the income generated by the investments. The background and investment objectives section should describe any other investment assets the client may have outside of the portfolio (e.g., accounts managed by another wealth manager) and any cash flows from external sources (e.g., pension income).

Investment Policy Statement

> **EXAMPLE 8**
>
> ## Background and Investment Objectives
>
> Huang Zhuo Wei, age 51, is a private investor in Singapore. Wei is an engineer by trade but has also been successful in real estate development. His portfolio consists of CNY 16.5 million in a liquid securities portfolio, including some common stock positions in which he has large embedded capital gains, and several real estate investments valued at approximately CNY 9 million (combined). He expects to make additional real estate investments in the coming years. He estimates that he can invest approximately CNY 330,000 per year, inflation-adjusted, in real estate until retirement. He has a much higher than average tolerance for volatility, and historically, his liquid portfolio has consisted mostly of large-cap stocks of technology companies. He has stated that his time horizon is 10 years, since he anticipates retiring in approximately 10 years. He estimates that he will need approximately CNY 1 million per year, inflation-adjusted, to support his lifestyle in retirement. He wishes to grow his investment resources and create a significant inheritance for his children.
>
> Discuss how Wei's wealth manager should create the investment objectives section of Wei's IPS.
>
> ## Solution:
>
> The purpose of this portfolio is to support Wei's lifestyle in retirement and to provide an inheritance for his children. Aside from the investment assets in his portfolio, Wei has private real estate investments valued at approximately CNY 9 million and is likely to add to this segment of his net worth over the next several years. Wei does not anticipate needing distributions from this portfolio for at least 10 years.
>
> Wei estimates an annual, inflation-adjusted lifestyle need of approximately CNY 1 million per year beginning at his retirement in 10 years. His cash needs will be satisfied in part through portfolio distributions and in part from his real estate portfolio. The wealth manager will continue to work with Wei to quantify his bequest objective and ensure that his portfolio distribution rate is sustainable throughout his retirement.

8.1.2 *Investment Parameters*

The investment parameters section of the IPS outlines important preferences that influence the client's investment program. Wealth managers may need to refine or customize these preferences to suit the particular client. Relevant components of investment parameters are discussed below.

8.1.2.1 Risk Tolerance In this part of the investment parameters section, the wealth manager indicates that she has considered the client's ability and willingness to withstand portfolio volatility. The process by which the wealth manager has assessed the client's risk tolerance is included here. For instance, if a risk tolerance questionnaire is used in the data-gathering process, the wealth manager may choose to include conclusions from the questionnaire.

8.1.2.2 Investment Time Horizon A client's investment horizon is indicated in this section, but often as a range rather than a specific number of years. If the wealth manager determines that the client has a long horizon, the IPS may state, for instance, that it "exceeds 15 years." By contrast, a short horizon may be described as "less than 10 years." Clients do not often indicate their own investment time horizons because they may misjudge the appropriate length. For example, married couples might underestimate their joint life expectancy. In general, the wealth manager should determine the investment time horizon in collaboration with the client. Because each goal may have a different time horizon, a client may have multiple time horizons (some of which may exceed the client's lifetime).

> **EXAMPLE 9**
>
> ### Investment Time Horizon
>
> In Example 8, Huang Zhuo Wei stated that his investment horizon is 10 years because he expects to retire at that point.
>
> Discuss how his wealth manager should reflect Wei's investment horizon in the IPS.
>
> **Solution:**
>
> Wei's true investment horizon is *through* retirement, a period that likely will be much longer than 10 years. His wealth manager should describe his time horizon as exceeding 10 years.

8.1.2.3 Asset Class Preferences The IPS should indicate the asset classes that will comprise a client's portfolio. Alternatively, the wealth manager may list the asset classes that the client has not approved. Some wealth managers include a short narrative about the importance of asset allocation and the process that the wealth manager used to educate the client about asset class risk and return characteristics. The narrative captures in written form the risk–return trade-off that the client explored with the wealth manager during the information-gathering process.

8.1.2.4 Other Investment Preferences Some clients have additional important investment preferences. One example relates to ESG investing, whereby a client may desire to invest in companies or sectors that are environmentally or socially focused. This section may contain a general comment about or specific criteria about for these ESG preferences.

Other investment preferences described in this section might be a "legacy" holding that the client wishes to retain or a non-recommended investment that the client wishes to make. For example, a client may choose to retain a common stock investment received via inheritance or maintain a position in company stock due to the nature of the client's employment.

8.1.2.5 Liquidity Preferences If the client has liquidity needs that are not established in the background and investment objectives section, those needs should be noted here. Some investors maintain a cash reserve in their portfolio, whereas other investors must initiate a portfolio distribution when they encounter an unanticipated cash need. Clients who require additional liquidity in their portfolios may instruct the wealth manager to maintain a specific cash balance in the portfolio.

If the client's liquidity preference constrains asset class selection decisions or implementation decisions, that constraint should be listed here. For example, if a client's liquidity needs dictate that entire portfolio can be sold relatively quickly and easily, illiquid asset classes such as private equity would likely not be part of the client's portfolio.

8.1.2.6 Constraints Some clients have constraints that restrict the wealth manager from implementing certain investments or strategies. For example, a client may be constrained by investment options in certain accounts, such as an employer-sponsored defined contribution retirement plan account. Another significant constraint can involve investments that have large unrealized capital gains and would create significant tax liabilities upon disposition. If a client has ESG-related constraints, such as prohibiting investment in certain sectors or individual securities, those constraints should appear in this section.

8.1.3 Portfolio Asset Allocation

This section contains the target allocation for each asset class in the client's portfolio. Wealth managers who use a strategic asset allocation approach typically define a target allocation for each asset class as well as upper and lower bounds. Wealth managers who use a tactical asset allocation approach may list asset class target "ranges" rather than specific target allocation percentages.

8.1.4 Portfolio Management

In this section of the IPS, the wealth manager discusses various issues involved in the ongoing management of the client portfolio. These issues may include the level of discretionary authority, how and when rebalancing activity will take place, and if relevant, tactical asset allocation changes within the client's portfolio.

8.1.4.1 Discretionary Authority The IPS indicates the degree of discretionary authority that the client has granted to the wealth manager. Discretionary authority refers to the ability of the wealth manager to act without having to obtain the client's approval. Full discretion means that the wealth manager is free to implement rebalancing trades and replace fund managers without prior client approval. If the client has given the wealth manager discretion over certain changes (e.g., rebalancing), this section of the IPS should reflect that arrangement. The wealth manager operating in a non-discretionary capacity makes recommendations to the client but is not able to implement a recommendation without client consent.

8.1.4.2 Rebalancing This section explains the wealth manager's rebalancing methodology. Some wealth managers use a "time-based" rebalancing policy, whereby client portfolios are rebalanced at a certain time interval (e.g., quarterly or annually) regardless of the difference between current asset class weights and target asset class weights. It is more common for wealth managers to use a "threshold-based" rebalancing policy, whereby the manager initiates rebalancing trades when asset class weights deviate from their target weights by a pre-specified percentage. The rebalancing section also sets expectations for how frequently the wealth manager reviews a client's portfolio for possible rebalancing opportunities.

8.1.4.3 Tactical Changes A wealth manager who periodically makes tactical changes (adjustments) to the client's asset allocation establishes the parameters for implementing such changes in this section of the IPS. If target allocation ranges have been established in the portfolio asset allocation section, this section indicates whether—as well as under what circumstances and to what degree—the wealth manager is permitted to go outside those ranges when executing a tactical change. Note that a wealth manager who uses only a strategic asset allocation approach would likely not include this section in the IPS.

8.1.4.4 Implementation This section includes information about the investment vehicles the wealth manager recommends to clients. Among the issues discussed here is whether the wealth manager recommends the exclusive use of third-party money managers, the exclusive use of proprietary investment offerings (those managed within the wealth manager's firm), or some combination of the two approaches. Also, this section indicates whether the wealth manager prefers to invest in mutual funds, exchange-traded funds (ETFs), or individual securities. A general discussion of the incremental cost of using third-party money managers is relevant here.

With respect to third-party managers, this section should include basic information about the wealth manager's due diligence process and how frequently it is performed. A more detailed option involves listing the quantitative screens used in the due diligence process and the qualitative criteria that influence the manager selection and retention decisions.

8.1.5 Duties and Responsibilities

This section discusses the wealth manager's overall responsibilities, including expectations about the ongoing review of a client's IPS.

8.1.5.1 Wealth Manager Responsibilities A list of responsibilities helps the client understand how the wealth manager operates in helping the client reach his investment objectives. The wealth manager typically addresses the following issues (where applicable):

- Developing an appropriate asset allocation
- Recommending or selecting investment options, such as pooled investment vehicles or individual securities
- Monitoring the asset allocation and rebalancing
- Using derivatives, leverage, short sales, and repurchase agreements (repos)
- Monitoring the costs associated with implementing the investment strategy
- Monitoring the activities of third-party service providers (e.g., asset managers and/or custodians)
- Drafting and maintaining the IPS
- Reporting of performance, including an indication of the base currency
- Reporting of taxes and financial statements
- Voting proxies
- Assisting with the preparation of agreements associated with private fund offerings

The wealth manager might also consider listing the responsibilities of third-party service providers. A custodian, for example, maintains segregated client accounts, values the investment assets, collects income, and settles transactions. Listing the custodian's responsibilities separately creates an opportunity to educate the client about this provider's distinct and important role.

8.1.5.2 IPS Review The wealth manager sets expectations for how frequently the client and wealth manager will review the IPS. As part of this review, it is important for the client to affirm that the investment objectives remain accurate. Likewise, it is important for the wealth manager to confirm that the strategy remains likely to meet those objectives.

8.1.6 IPS Appendix

The appendix includes additional details that typically change more frequently than the main portion of the IPS. Below are two examples of items that may be included in the appendix.

8.1.6.1 Modeled Portfolio Behavior Modeled portfolio behavior describes a range of possible performance outcomes over various holding periods and can provide more value to the client than merely stating the return objective or the "expected compound return." As part of this section, the wealth manager may provide a modeled distribution of returns at various percentile ranges. The median of the modeled return distribution may be termed the "modeled compound return." This approach also enables the wealth manager to present modeled portfolio downside risk (volatility), particularly for short periods, and to confirm that the client can withstand such an outcome.

8.1.6.2 Capital Market Expectations Capital market expectations include the wealth manager's modeled portfolio statistics—that is, the expected returns and standard deviations of asset classes, as well as modeled correlations between asset classes. Because clients sometimes confuse expected return (i.e., simple average return) with compound annual return, the wealth manager may consider including the modeled compound annual return for each asset class.

SAMPLE INVESTMENT POLICY STATEMENT

i. discuss the parts of an investment policy statement (IPS) for a private client;

j. prepare the investment objectives section of an IPS for a private client;

k. evaluate and recommend improvements to an IPS for a private client;

Exhibit 5 demonstrates a sample IPS for a fictitious private client couple, David and Amelia King. The Kings' wealth manager does not use a tactical asset allocation approach for the couple, so the section on tactical changes is not relevant in this case.

Exhibit 5 Sample Investment Policy Statement

Investment Policy Statement Prepared for David and Amelia King

Background and Investment Objectives

This Investment Policy Statement (IPS) is designed to assist David and Amelia in meeting their financial objectives. It contains a summation of their objectives and expectations, sets forth an investment structure for attaining these objectives, and outlines ongoing responsibilities.

The purpose of this portfolio is to support the continuation of David and Amelia's current lifestyle, provide for their family's needs, and fund their philanthropic objectives. Maintenance of their current lifestyle is their primary objective, followed by support for family members and charitable aspirations, in that order. To meet these objectives, they anticipate needing approximately $350,000 per year in inflation-adjusted portfolio distributions. In addition, they intend to purchase a second residence within the next two years. They expect the purchase price for the second residence to be approximately $1.5 million. David and Amelia have not articulated a specific dollar amount that they intend to leave to their children, nor a specific dollar amount that they wish to leave to charity at their death. The wealth manager will continue to work with them to quantify these objectives.

In establishing their asset allocation, David and Amelia have considered their current assets and expected cash needs. They are seeking to achieve a higher long-term rate of return and are willing to assume the associated portfolio volatility.

Portfolio Accounts

Taxable joint account for David and Amelia
Tax-deferred account for David

(continued)

Exhibit 5 (Continued)

Tax-deferred account for Amelia

Current Combined Market Value

$12,250,000

Investment Parameters

Risk Tolerance

The wealth manager has determined that David and Amelia are able and willing to withstand short- and intermediate-term portfolio volatility. They recognize and acknowledge the anticipated level of portfolio volatility associated with their asset allocation (as illustrated in the Modeled Portfolio Behavior section of the Appendix).

Investment Time Horizon

David and Amelia have an investment time horizon that exceeds 15 years.

Asset Class Preferences

The Kings and their wealth manager have selected the following asset classes:

- Short-term debt investments
- Intermediate-term bonds
- US stocks
- Non-US stocks
- Global real estate securities

Other Investment Preferences

The Kings wish to maintain their positions in Acme Manufacturing, Inc., which Amelia received through inheritance, and Artful Publishing, Ltd., which is her former employer. Neither position represents significant concentration risk in the context of their broader portfolio.

David has an interest in a private real estate limited partnership that invests primarily in office buildings throughout Asia. The wealth manager has taken this exposure into consideration in designing the broader asset allocation.

Liquidity Preferences

David and Amelia wish to maintain within their portfolio a minimum cash balance of $50,000. They typically maintain a more sizable cash balance at their primary bank.

Constraints

Amelia's position in Artful Publishing, Ltd., has significant embedded capital gains.

Portfolio Asset Allocation			
	Lower Rebalancing Limit	Strategic Allocation	Upper Rebalancing Limit
Short-term debt investments	8%	10%	12%
Intermediate-term bonds	16%	20%	24%

Sample Investment Policy Statement

Exhibit 5 (Continued)

	Lower Rebalancing Limit	Strategic Allocation	Upper Rebalancing Limit
US stocks	30%	35%	40%
Non-US stocks	20%	25%	30%
Global real estate securities	8%	10%	12%

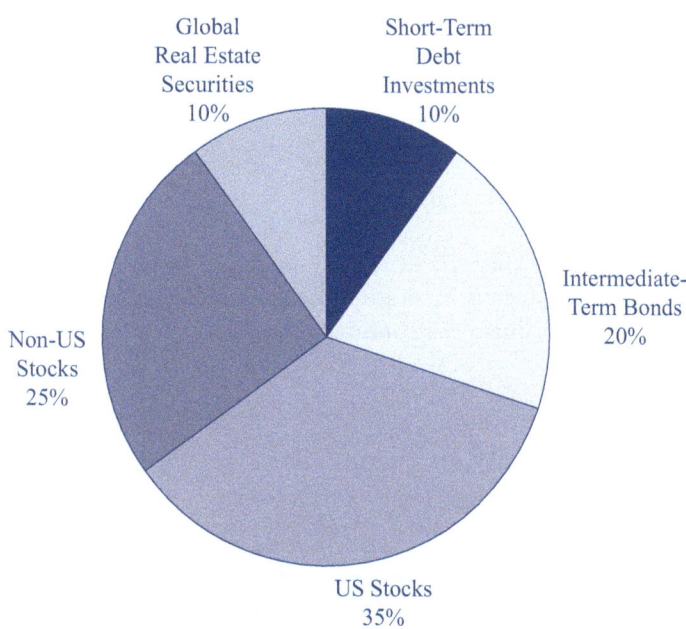

Portfolio Management

Discretionary Authority

The wealth manager will implement discretionary portfolio changes related to rebalancing the portfolio, investing new deposits, and generating liquidity to meet withdrawal requests.

The wealth manager will review with the client, prior to implementation, the addition of new positions or the elimination of existing positions.

Rebalancing

The wealth manager will review the portfolio on at least a monthly basis. Rebalancing will be determined by the lower and upper asset class limits set forth in the Portfolio Asset Allocation section of the IPS.

Implementation

To implement the investment strategy, the wealth manager will utilize third-party money managers via mutual funds, exchange-traded funds (ETFs), and separate accounts of individual securities. The wealth manager conducts a quarterly due diligence process to evaluate recommended managers as well as the universe of other available managers. This process involves quantitative risk and return comparisons to appropriate indexes and peer groups, as well as qualitative assessments of other factors that may impact a manager's ability to perform in the future. More information about this process is available at the client's request.

Duties and Responsibilities

Wealth Manager Responsibilities

The wealth manager is responsible for the following:

- Developing an appropriate asset allocation
- Selecting investment options
- Implementing the agreed-upon strategy
- Monitoring the asset allocation and rebalancing when necessary
- Monitoring the costs associated with implementing the investment strategy
- Monitoring the activities of other service vendors (e.g., custodians)
- Drafting and maintaining the IPS
- Performance reporting
- Tax and financial accounting reporting
- Proxy voting

IPS Review

The client will review this IPS at least annually to determine whether the investment objectives are still accurate. The wealth manager will review this IPS at least annually to evaluate the continued feasibility of achieving the client's investment objectives.

IPS Appendix

Modeled Portfolio Behavior[5]

Modeled Compound Return: 6.23%

Modeled Distribution of Returns					
Year	10th percentile	25th percentile	50th percentile	75th percentile	90th percentile
1	−10.45	−2.89	6.23	16.21	26.01
3	−3.75	0.86	6.23	11.88	17.24
5	−1.58	2.05	6.23	10.58	14.66
10	0.64	3.25	6.23	9.29	12.12
15	1.65	3.79	6.23	8.72	11.02
25	2.66	4.34	6.23	8.15	9.92

Portfolio downside risk, 1-year horizon:

- 25% likelihood of a return less than −2.89%
- 10% likelihood of a return less than −10.45%

Portfolio downside risk, 15-year horizon:

- 25% likelihood of a compound annual return less than 3.79%
- 10% likelihood of a compound annual return less than 1.65%

---

[5] The modeled returns and risk projections are based on forward-looking estimates and not on the past performance of specific funds or indexes. Modeled returns are before taxes and do not reflect investment management fees.

Capital Market Assumptions

Modeled Portfolio Statistics

	Expected Return (%)	Standard Deviation (%)	Modeled Compound Return (%)
Short-term debt investments	2.5	2.0	2.5
Intermediate-term bonds	3.5	8.0	3.2
US stocks	8.5	22.0	6.1
Non-US stocks	10.0	26.0	6.6
Global real estate securities	7.5	23.0	4.9

Modeled Correlations

		(1)	(2)	(3)	(4)	(5)
1	Short-term debt investments	1.00				
2	Intermediate-term bonds	0.79	1.00			
3	US stocks	−0.08	−0.03	1.00		
4	Non-US stocks	−0.29	−0.27	0.76	1.00	
5	Global real estate securities	−0.15	0.08	0.42	0.39	1.00

PORTFOLIO CONSTRUCTION AND ALLOCATION AND INVESTMENTS FOR PRIVATE WEALTH CLIENTS — 10

l. recommend and justify portfolio allocations and investments for a private client;

The practice of private wealth management involves aligning the unique attributes of the individual investor with the most appropriate investment plan and strategy. In prior sections, we discussed how wealth managers gather, synthesize, and analyze client information and goals/objectives. We now discuss the next phases of constructing the client's portfolio, monitoring the client's investment program, and reporting the portfolio to the client.

10.1 Portfolio Allocation and Investments for Private Wealth Clients

Once the client's IPS is developed, the next step is to implement the IPS through actionable investment advice. Portfolio construction, including asset and investment allocation, is a key aspect of this process. We first discuss two approaches to constructing a private client's portfolio—a traditional approach and a goals-based investing approach.

10.1.1 Portfolio Construction—Traditional Approach

Constructing portfolios for private clients involves several key steps:

- *Identify asset classes.* The wealth manager identifies the asset classes that may be appropriate for the client's portfolio. The identification of asset classes may vary by wealth manager. For instance, one wealth manager may designate "UK Equities" as an asset class, whereas another wealth manager may designate "UK Large-Capitalization Equities" and "UK Small-Capitalization Equities" as separate asset classes.

- *Develop capital market expectations.* The wealth manager considers the expected returns, standard deviations, and correlations of asset classes in relation to the client's investment horizon. Wealth managers typically update their capital market expectations according to changes in the financial market environment.

- *Determine portfolio allocations.* Wealth managers sometimes use mean–variance optimization to identify possible portfolio allocations that meet the client's return requirement and risk tolerance. Mean–variance optimization provides a framework for determining how much to allocate to each asset to maximize the expected return for an expected level of risk. The "optimal" portfolio for a given client is the portfolio that maximizes expected return given the client's degree of risk tolerance. Note that a client's optimal portfolio may contain allocations to certain asset classes that may be impractical or difficult for the client to maintain. Therefore, wealth managers generally apply asset class constraints in the optimization process. For example, the minimum and maximum thresholds for a given asset class might be 0% and 20%, respectively.

- *Assess constraints.* As we noted earlier in the reading, private clients often face certain constraints. For instance, suppose a client has a €5 million investment portfolio, with €2 million of the total portfolio invested in 14 individual stocks in Germany that have appreciated in value considerably. Selling these securities may be prohibitive due to potential taxes on any capital gains in the client's country of domicile. In this situation, the client's wealth manager may specify a minimum threshold for German equities to reflect the embedded capital gains. Another example of a constraint applies when a client owns a considerable amount of residential real estate. In this case, the client's wealth manager may limit the allocation to real estate investment trusts (REITs) in the client's investment portfolio.

- *Implement the portfolio.* At this stage, the wealth manager faces several decisions. One decision is the choice of active management or passive management (e.g., indexing) for each asset class. Once that decision is made, manager selection becomes an important consideration. Another decision for the wealth manager is which factors to recommend within a given asset class. Such factors may include "value" (value stocks over growth stocks) and "size" (small-capitalization stocks over large-capitalization stocks). Implementation also involves a decision to utilize individual securities or pooled vehicles, such as mutual funds and ETFs. Finally, the decision to apply currency hedging can be another important implementation decision.

- *Determine asset location.* When a client's portfolio comprises multiple accounts, the wealth manager must determine where to allocate the various asset classes and securities. This allocation decision is called **asset location**. Generally, tax considerations are a critical factor for asset location. If certain accounts offer unique tax benefits (e.g., tax deferral), the wealth manager will generally allocate to these accounts those investments that will likely produce a meaningful level of taxable income.

Portfolio Construction and Allocation and Investments for Private Wealth Clients

Example 10 demonstrates the portfolio construction process for a fictitious wealth manager and private client, ultimately resulting in a recommended allocation of the client's portfolio and underlying investments.

EXAMPLE 10

Portfolio Construction—Traditional Approach

Jonas Wilhelm, CFA, has just added a new private client. In Exhibit 6, Wilhelm identifies appropriate asset classes and develops capital market expectations for the new client's portfolio.

Exhibit 6 Asset Classes and Capital Market Expectations

Asset Class	Expected Return (%)	Standard Deviation (%)
Investment-grade bonds	3.0	3.0
High-yield bonds	4.5	8.0
European equities	9.0	18.0
Global (ex-European) equities	10.0	20.0
Real estate securities	8.5	18.0
Commodities	6.0	20.0

In determining portfolio allocations, Wilhelm developed a correlation matrix of these asset classes, as shown in Exhibit 7.

Exhibit 7 Asset Class Correlation Matrix

	IGB	HYB	EE	GEE	RE	COM
Investment-grade bonds (IGB)	1.00	0.84	−0.04	−0.01	0.14	0.02
High-yield bonds (HYB)	0.84	1.00	0.30	0.35	0.20	−0.04
European equities (EE)	−0.04	0.30	1.00	0.82	0.60	0.17
Global (ex-European) equities (GEE)	−0.01	0.35	0.82	1.00	0.52	0.36
Real estate securities (RE)	0.14	0.20	0.60	0.52	1.00	0.44
Commodities (COM)	0.02	−0.04	0.17	0.36	0.44	1.00

Based on a risk tolerance assessment, Wilhelm determines that the client can accept a portfolio standard deviation of return of approximately 10%. The client has a preference for European equities due to his familiarity with companies in Europe.

Wilhelm performs a mean–variance optimization that produces an optimal asset allocation. As shown in Exhibit 8, he modifies the portfolio allocation according to the client's preferences to arrive at a recommended allocation.

Exhibit 8 Portfolio Allocation

	Portfolio Allocation from Mean–Variance Optimization (%)	Portfolio Allocation Recommendation (%)
Investment-grade bonds (IGB)	30.92	34.00
High-yield bonds (HYB)	10.00	7.00
European equities (EE)	15.74	31.00
Global (ex-European) equities (GEE)	25.00	17.00
Real estate securities (RE)	15.00	8.00
Commodities (COM)	3.34	3.00
	100.00	100.00
Expected Return	6.77	6.69
Standard Deviation	10.00	10.00

10.1.2 *Portfolio Construction—Goals-Based Investing Approach*

With a **goals-based investing** approach, the wealth manager focuses on aligning investments with goals. That is, the manager identifies the client's goals and assigns the required funds to each goal. The manager then performs mean–variance optimization for each goal "portfolio" rather than at the overall portfolio level. Goal portfolios are optimized either to a stated maximum level of volatility or to a specified probability of success. Therefore, with goals-based investing, the allocation of the overall portfolio is a function of the respective allocations of the individual goal portfolios.

An advantage of the goals-based investing approach is that it may be easier for clients to express their risk tolerance on a goal-specific basis rather than at the overall portfolio level. A disadvantage is that the combination of goal portfolio allocations may not lead to optimal mean–variance efficiency for the entire portfolio. In other words, the aggregation of each goals-based portfolio allocation may not produce a total portfolio allocation that lies along the client's efficient frontier. Example 11 demonstrates how a wealth manager might allocate a client's portfolio using a goals-based investing approach.

It should be noted that the remaining steps of the portfolio construction process discussed previously—identifying asset classes, implementing the portfolio, and determining asset location—are the same for both the goals-based investing approach and the traditional approach.

EXAMPLE 11

Portfolio Allocation—Goals-Based Investing Approach

Using the information from Example 10, suppose that Jonas Wilhelm's client has two primary goals: (1) purchasing a ski cottage within the next 7 years and (2) supplementing his retirement income over the next 30 years. His total portfolio is valued at €3.1 million. The client will need approximately €500,000 for the ski cottage and desires low volatility for this goal.

If Wilhelm used a goals-based investing approach, his client's portfolio allocation might look like the example shown in Exhibit 9.

Exhibit 9 Portfolio Allocation—Goals-Based Investing

	Allocation in Ski Cottage Portfolio (%)	Allocation in Retirement Portfolio (%)	Aggregate Portfolio Allocation (%)
Investment-grade bonds (IGB)	70.00	27.00	34.00
High-yield bonds (HYB)	8.00	7.00	7.00
European equities (EE)	12.00	35.00	31.00
Global (ex-European) equities (GEE)	5.00	19.00	17.00
Real estate securities (RE)	3.00	9.00	8.00
Commodities (COM)	2.00	3.00	3.00
	100.00	100.00	100.00
Expected Return	4.42	7.12	6.69
Standard Deviation	4.56	11.15	10.00

The advantage of a goals-based approach in this case is that the client can express his expected return and risk tolerance with respect to the ski cottage goal.

PORTFOLIO REPORTING AND REVIEW

11

m   describe effective practices in portfolio reporting and review;

Portfolio reporting and portfolio review enable wealth managers to share information with clients, shape clients' expectations, and provide ongoing education. *Portfolio reporting* involves delivering information about their investment portfolio and performance in periodic physical or electronic mailings. *Portfolio review* refers to meetings or phone conversations between a wealth manager and a client to discuss the client's investment strategy. The key difference between portfolio reporting and portfolio review is that the wealth manager is more actively engaged with a review.

11.1 Portfolio Reporting

Typically, a portfolio report answers several questions, including, what is the portfolio asset allocation? how has the portfolio performed? and what transactions have occurred in the portfolio, such as contributions, withdrawals, interest/dividends, and capital appreciation? Accordingly, a portfolio report usually includes the following:

- A portfolio asset allocation report, which may reflect strategic asset allocation targets
- A performance summary report for the current (often year-to-date) period
- A detailed performance report, which may include asset class and/or individual security performance
- A historical performance report covering the period since the inception of the client's investment strategy
- A contribution and withdrawal report for the current period

- A purchase and sale report for the current period
- A currency exposure report detailing the effects of exchange rate fluctuations

A sample portfolio asset allocation report, performance summary report, and asset class performance report for the fictitious private client Hong Soo Wan are shown in Exhibit 10, Exhibit 11, and Exhibit 12, respectively.

Exhibit 10   Sample Portfolio Asset Allocation Report

Hong Soo Wan
Portfolio Asset Allocation Report
31 December 20XX

Asset Class	Market Value	Allocation	Target Allocation
Public fixed income	CNY 26,918,882	18.95%	20.00%
Private fixed income	CNY 4,109,563	2.89%	5.00%
Public equities	CNY 61,850,957	43.55%	41.00%
Private equities	CNY 18,233,357	12.84%	12.00%
Private real estate	CNY 21,008,677	14.79%	12.00%
Private natural resources	CNY 4,688,032	3.30%	5.00%
Hedge funds	CNY 5,222,597	3.68%	5.00%
Total Portfolio	CNY 142,032,065	100.00%	100.00%

Exhibit 11   Sample Performance Summary Report

Hong Soo Wan
Portfolio Summary Report
31 December 20XX

Beginning Portfolio Value	CNY 136,928,682
Contributions	CNY 0
Withdrawals	(CNY 2,130,481)
Interest and Dividends	CNY 2,840,641
Capital Appreciation	CNY 4,393,223
Ending Portfolio Value	CNY 142,032,065
Total Investment Gain	CNY 7,233,864
Time-Weighted Rate of Return	5.31%

Exhibit 12   Sample Asset Class Performance Report

Hong Soo Wan
Asset Class Performance Report
31 December 20XX

Exhibit 12 (Continued)

Asset Class	Allocation	Return for Period
Public fixed income	18.95%	2.71%
Private fixed income	2.89%	5.24%
Public equities	43.55%	5.72%
Private equities	12.84%	9.81%
Private real estate	14.79%	5.60%
Private natural resources	3.30%	(1.42%)
Hedge funds	3.68%	2.79%
Total Portfolio	100.00%	5.31%

For private clients, portfolio reports may lack some necessary context, such as commentary on recent economic and financial events or on the overall performance of asset classes. As a result, wealth managers often send an accompanying letter (or email) to clients with the portfolio report. This letter supplies some of the missing investment context and represents an opportunity for the wealth manager to provide education and advice.

Wealth managers often face an inherent conflict between the client's investment horizon, which may be decades in length, and the typical performance evaluation horizon, which may be one calendar quarter or one year. This horizon mismatch can potentially undermine long-term investment decision making. For instance, short-term volatility can be mistaken for signs that a client's long-term strategy is not effective. With the expanded use of technology by clients (e.g., electronic report delivery and instant access to portfolio information), it is increasingly critical for wealth managers to appropriately communicate performance information to clients and manage their expectations.

When goals-based investing is used, portfolio reporting may focus on the client's progress toward a goal (or goals) rather than on the (often short-term) performance of asset classes or individual securities. For example, if a client has two different portfolios dedicated to two separate goals, a wealth manager's report may include the progress toward each of the goals based upon a capital sufficiency analysis.

Benchmark reports are another component of portfolio reporting. In a typical benchmark report, a wealth manager states a client's performance by asset class relative to an appropriate asset class benchmark, as well as the client's overall portfolio performance relative to a blended benchmark (according to asset class weighting). An advantage of benchmark reporting is the additional context that it provides to clients.

EXAMPLE 12

Portfolio Reporting

Simon Crosby provides investment advice for clients in Canada. Each quarter, he sends his clients only a detailed list of all the investments in their portfolio. The list includes the acquisition cost, the acquisition date, and the current market value for each investment, as well as the percentage gain or loss on each investment relative to its cost.

Discuss how Crosby's reporting practice can be more effective.

> **Solution:**
>
> Crosby's reports do not enable his clients to determine their asset allocation or the performance of their overall portfolios. Crosby could address this issue by including a portfolio asset allocation report and a performance report. The current reporting structure also does not provide transaction details, such as portfolio contributions, withdrawals, interest/dividends, and capital appreciation, all of which could be provided by a portfolio summary report. Finally, Crosby's portfolio reporting can be improved by including market commentary, typically in a letter or email.

11.2 Portfolio Review

In comparison to portfolio reporting, portfolio reviews represent a higher level of engagement between the wealth manager and the client. Portfolio reviews provide an opportunity for the wealth manager to revisit the client's investment plan and reinforce the appropriateness of the strategy. The wealth manager can use these reviews to deepen the client's knowledge of the portfolio as well as to set and update expectations for the wealth manager's own responsibilities.

As part of the portfolio review, the wealth manager typically inquires about any changes in the client's objectives, risk tolerance, or time horizon. Changes in the client's employment, liquidity needs, family needs, external sources of cash flow, and estate planning can also result in changes to the client's investment strategy.

Another common aspect of a portfolio review is a comparison of the client's asset allocation to the target allocation. The following are some questions a wealth manager may consider: Should the portfolio be rebalanced? Are the client's asset class weights within the prescribed range for each asset class? Should there be any asset class adjustments? And what factors should influence tactical asset class positioning? Investment manager performance, relative to both applicable benchmarks and peers, is often discussed during portfolio reviews.

Wealth managers typically document the key points (or takeaways) from their portfolio reviews with clients. To maintain these notes, managers often use CRM software. Providing written communication to the client that reaffirms points from the meeting is also common practice. This communication can help avoid future misunderstandings and client disappointment.

12 EVALUATING THE SUCCESS OF AN INVESTMENT PROGRAM

- evaluate the success of an investment program for a private client;

Evaluating the success of an investment program in private wealth management is distinct from—and often more complex than—evaluating an investment program in the context of traditional asset (i.e., fund) management. For example, assume an asset management firm manages an emerging market stock fund. Evaluating the success of this fund would likely include comparing the fund's performance to that of an emerging market stock index over a representative holding period. The success or failure of this fund may be straightforward. In contrast, for private clients, portfolio performance, though important, is only part of the evaluation process.

12.1 Goal Achievement

A successful investment program for a private client is one that achieves the client's goals/objectives with an acceptable amount of risk. A private client's investment program is typically ongoing rather than short-term in nature. Therefore, the relevant question is not whether the investment strategy has succeeded for the client during a particular period, but whether the investment strategy remains likely to succeed in the future by achieving the client's longer-term goals. Capital sufficiency analysis, which we discussed earlier in the reading, is often used to determine whether the client remains likely to meet his or her objectives.

Another aspect of a successful investment program is that the client should remain likely to meet his or her objectives without meaningful adjustments to the plan. For instance, if clients must work for many years beyond their original intended retirement date or must drastically reduce their retirement lifestyle, the existing investment program has not achieved its original objective.

12.2 Process Consistency

Following a consistent process is crucial to ensuring the overall success of the client's investment program. The following are some points that wealth managers may consider in evaluating success:

- If the wealth manager selects third-party fund managers to implement the client's portfolio, how have the managers performed relative to their own benchmarks? When the wealth manager has recommended fund manager changes, have those changes improved or detracted from subsequent portfolio performance?
- Has the wealth manager followed the prescribed process for rebalancing the client's portfolio?
- Has the wealth manager taken steps to reduce costs in the client's portfolio? Is the wealth manager overlooking any opportunities to reduce fees and expenses?
- Has the wealth manager considered taxation issues in the client's portfolio?
- For clients with ESG preferences, has the wealth manager implemented the client's portfolio strategy accordingly?
- If the wealth manager uses tactical asset allocation, how has tactical positioning impacted the portfolio's performance?
- Is the wealth manager maintaining an ongoing dialogue with the client to assess potential changes in the client's goals, time horizon, risk tolerance, and other relevant factors?
- Where applicable, has the wealth manager coordinated the investment strategy with the client's estate plan and philanthropic objectives?

12.3 Portfolio Performance

Performance evaluation of a private client's portfolio can be expressed in either absolute or relative terms. An absolute performance benchmark might be inflation plus a fixed percentage or simply a fixed percentage return that relates to a client's capital sufficiency analysis. Generally, these absolute performance benchmarks apply to relatively long holding periods, such as five or more years.

To measure relative returns, a wealth manager compares the client's investment portfolio results to those of an appropriately weighted benchmark. Typically, the benchmark weights include both return and risk metrics. A more useful comparison for a private client's portfolio is the relative risk-adjusted return. It is also important to evaluate whether the portfolio's actual downside risk is consistent with the client's risk tolerance. Many private clients tend to compare their own portfolio's performance to the performance of the investments with which they are most familiar, such as their home country's stock index. This tendency is an important consideration for wealth managers in the portfolio construction process and when communicating performance to clients.

12.4 Definitions of Success

When the wealth manager and the client have different definitions of success for the client's investment program, the potential for client disappointment can increase. For example, the client's definition of success may be achieving superior relative returns or attaining a particular absolute return. However, the wealth manager's definition of success for the client may be achieving certain financial goals. It is good practice for both parties to agree on the definition of success in the early stages of the relationship. Generally speaking, it is the wealth manager's responsibility to initiate a conversation with a client about how the success of the investment program will be evaluated.

EXAMPLE 13

Evaluating the Success of an Investment Program

Oliver Wellesley, CFA, a wealth manager, is preparing to meet with a longtime client, Eva Smith, age 83. Wellesley and Smith began working together when Smith was 64 and preparing for her retirement. She has earned a 6.5% compound annual return with Wellesley as her wealth manager. This return is close to the annual return that Wellesley modeled in his capital sufficiency analysis of Smith's portfolio many years ago. Distributions from Smith's portfolio have adequately met her need for retirement income, which has always been her highest-priority goal. According to Wellesley's most recent capital sufficiency analysis, Smith's portfolio is very likely to meet her retirement income and estate bequest objectives in the future. However, Smith's investment return has trailed the weighted benchmark return by 0.40% since the portfolio's inception and has exhibited slightly more volatility than the benchmark. Smith recently reviewed her IPS and concluded that Wellesley has consistently followed the process outlined in the IPS.

Discuss how successful Smith's investment program has been under Wellesley's management.

Solution:

From the perspective of meeting goals/objectives, Smith's investment program has been successful. The strategy has met her retirement income needs, and Wellesley's capital sufficiency analysis suggests that she has a high probability of achieving future objectives (including ongoing retirement lifestyle goals and an estate bequest goal). Also, Wellesley has followed a consistent process, which is an indication of a successful investment program. However, if Smith and Wellesley agreed that outperforming a weighted benchmark was an important goal for her investment strategy, then the investment program has failed.

ETHICAL AND COMPLIANCE CONSIDERATIONS IN PRIVATE WEALTH MANAGEMENT

o discuss ethical and compliance considerations in advising private clients;

Like other investment practitioners, private wealth managers face many ethical and compliance issues. Some issues, however, are unique to the practice of private wealth management. In this section, we provide a brief overview of ethical and compliance considerations for private wealth managers. We then discuss the different client segments and service offerings within private wealth management.

13.1 Ethical Considerations

A starting point for ethical considerations in private wealth management is the CFA Institute Code of Ethics and Standards of Professional Conduct (Code and Standards). In this section, we discuss ethical considerations that are particularly relevant to private wealth management.

13.1.1 Fiduciary Duty and Suitability

In private wealth management, two primary ethical concepts are *fiduciary duty* and *suitability*. Fiduciary duty is the obligation to deliver a high standard of care when acting for the benefit of another party. Accordingly, private wealth managers are often said to be operating under a "fiduciary standard." Suitability is a key element of a wealth manager's fiduciary duty. According to the Code and Standards, when judging the suitability of a potential investment, the wealth manager should review many aspects of the client's knowledge, investing experience, and financial situation. The concepts of fiduciary duty and suitability are relevant to several components of the Code and Standards, including *Standard I(B): Independence and Objectivity*; *Standard III(A): Loyalty, Prudence, and Care*; *Standard III(C): Suitability*; and *Standard V(A): Diligence and Reasonable Basis*.

13.1.2 Know Your Customer (KYC)

The concept of "Know Your Customer" (KYC) applies globally in private wealth management. KYC requires wealth managers and their firms to obtain essential facts about every client for whom they open and maintain an account. These facts include the client's risk and return objectives and the origin of the client's wealth, which may help in identifying problems such as money laundering. KYC guidelines continue to evolve and can vary depending upon the country/region. The concept of KYC is relevant to *Standard III(C): Suitability* in the Code and Standards.

13.1.3 Confidentiality

Preserving client confidentiality is critical to maintaining trust in the relationship. Wealth managers typically possess highly personal and sensitive client information. This issue can be a particular challenge when a wealth manager advises multiple family members or advises clients who may know one or more of the wealth manager's other clients. Changes in electronic communication standards require wealth managers to have a thorough understanding of the confidentiality policies of their employers. Overall, the concept of confidentiality is relevant to *Standard III(E): Preservation of Confidentiality*.

13.1.4 Conflicts of Interest

The structure of wealth managers' revenue creates the potential for conflicts of interest. For example, when wealth managers earn commissions for recommending certain investment products, there may be an incentive to recommend only products that generate commissions (and perhaps those with the highest commissions). Conflicts of interest may also occur when wealth managers are subject to fee-based revenue models. For example, wealth managers who earn a percentage of the client's assets under management may have an incentive to recommend that the client not withdraw assets from the portfolio. The concept of conflicts of interest is relevant to *Standard I(B): Independence and Objectivity* and *Standard VI: Conflicts of Interest*.

> **EXAMPLE 14**
>
> ### Ethical Considerations in Private Wealth Management
>
> Shirley Marshall wants to purchase a new home. She asks her wealth manager whether she should (1) obtain a mortgage loan to acquire the home or (2) withdraw money from her portfolio to purchase the home with cash.
>
> Discuss potential ethical considerations for Marshall's wealth manager.
>
> **Solution:**
>
> A conflict of interest could exist if the wealth manager earns revenues based on a percentage of Marshall's assets under management. If Marshall elects to withdraw money from her portfolio to purchase the home, her assets under management with the wealth manager will decline (all other things being equal), resulting in a lower fee for the wealth manager. In this case, the wealth manager should analyze the decision objectively and disclose this potential conflict of interest to the client.

13.2 Compliance Considerations

Changes in the regulatory environment have relevance to private wealth management. Exhibit 13 summarizes some globally enacted regulations relating to compliance.

In the United States, two additional proposed regulations are relevant for wealth managers. Both the US Department of Labor Fiduciary Rule (Fiduciary Rule) and the Securities and Exchange Commission Best Interest Rule (Best Interest Rule) seek to enhance investor protection. The Fiduciary Rule would expand the definition of fiduciary to all professionals providing advice for retirement plans and IRAs (Individual Retirement Accounts). The Best Interest Rule would require a broker/dealer to act in the best interest of the investor and would restrict certain broker/dealers and their employees from using the term "advisor" or "adviser" as part of their title. As of the publication of this reading, neither of these rules has been enacted.

Exhibit 13 Key Compliance Regulations

Regulation	Summary
Markets in Financial Instruments Directive (MiFID II, European Union, 2018)	Designed to improve investor protection, market structure and transparency, firm governance, and external controls. Several of the investor protection provisions are of particular relevance to advisors. Investment advisors must demonstrate the suitability of their advice, including how it will meet client objectives, and must meet minimum levels of professional competence. Also, independent advisors and discretionary portfolio managers will no longer be permitted to receive commissions.
Common Reporting Standard (OECD Council/G20, 2014)	Requests that jurisdictions obtain information from their financial institutions and automatically exchange such information with other jurisdictions on an annual basis.
The Foreign Account Tax Compliance Act (FATCA, United States, 2010)	Enacted to prevent tax evasion by US individuals who hold "offshore" accounts and other financial assets. The rule requires non-US financial institutions to report information about financial accounts held by US taxpayers or by non-US entities in which US taxpayers hold a substantial ownership interest.

PRIVATE CLIENT SEGMENTS

14

p discuss how levels of service and range of solutions are related to different private clients.

The level of wealth varies considerably among private clients. Exhibit 14 provides a global breakdown of the number of adults within specific wealth ranges. Perhaps not surprisingly, the vast majority of individuals are in lower wealth ranges.

Exhibit 14 Private Wealth Composition

Wealth Range ($ millions)	Number of Adults Globally (millions)
0.1 – 1.0	391.0
1.0 – 5.0	31.4
5.0 – 10.0	3.0
10.0 – 50.0	1.5
> 50.0	0.1

Source: Credit Suisse (2017).

On a geographic basis, the majority of adults with wealth in the $100,000 to $1 million range are in Europe (37% of the total wealth range) and the Asia-Pacific region (36%). In higher ranges, notably among those with wealth exceeding $1 million, the number of adults is more concentrated in the United States. While the United States has the highest proportion in this wealth segment, growth in the number of millionaire investors has been faster in emerging market economies.

The variation in global wealth ranges has implications for the issues private clients face and the services they require. Accordingly, private wealth management firms typically organize their services depending on the private client segment(s) they serve. In this section, we discuss key client segments and the services and solutions that clients within these segments may desire.

14.1 Mass Affluent Segment

The mass affluent segment is generally focused on building their investment portfolio and may have financial planning needs (e.g., education funding, cash flow or budget management, and risk management). Risk management needs may relate to future sources of income and may result in the need for various forms of insurance. Older clients in this segment tend to have a focus on retirement planning and investing for a secure retirement.

In servicing the mass affluent segment, wealth managers do not typically customize their investment management approach for each client. This segment tends to have a higher number of clients per wealth manager and involves a greater use of technology in service delivery (i.e., information gathering, account establishment, and reporting). Revenue models in this segment range from a traditional brokerage model (whereby the client is charged a commission on investment transactions) to a fee-only model (whereby the client is charged a percentage of assets under management for discretionary portfolio management). **Discretionary portfolio management** refers to an arrangement in which the wealth manager has a client's pre-approval to execute investment decisions. This arrangement is similar to the concept of discretionary authority discussed earlier in the reading. By contrast, non-discretionary portfolio management refers to an arrangement in which the wealth manager makes recommendations to the client and seeks the client's approval prior to implementation.

14.2 High-Net-Worth Segment

Wealth managers that focus on the high-net-worth segment typically have a lower client-to-manager ratio than those that focus on the mass affluent segment. Also, wealth managers of high-net-worth clients tend to focus on customized investment management, tax planning, and wealth transfer issues (i.e., estate planning). Wealth transfer issues may lead to a longer investment time horizon and greater risk capacity (though not necessarily greater risk tolerance). The higher wealth levels of this segment may also lead to investment in less liquid asset classes and more sophisticated portfolios that require stronger product knowledge on the part of the wealth manager.

14.3 Ultra-High-Net-Worth Segment

The ultra-high-net-worth segment tends to have multi-generational time horizons, highly complex tax and estate-planning considerations, and a wider range of service needs. As a result, firms that represent this segment have relatively few clients per wealth manager.

Additional services may be provided to this segment, such as bill payment services, concierge services, travel planning, and advice on acquiring assets such as artwork or aircraft. Wealth managers focused on this segment often manage accounts for multiple family members and therefore also deal with family governance issues, such as preparing the client's heirs for the inheritance of substantial wealth. Wealth managers in this segment may assemble teams of service providers with specialized and complementary skills. For instance, firms may include specialized tax advisors, legal advisors, investment specialists, and a relationship manager (RM) as members of a client relationship team. Some ultra-high-net-worth individuals choose to hire these specialized experts to work exclusively for themselves and their family members. This arrangement is referred to as a "family office."

> **EXAMPLE 15**
>
> ### Client Segments
>
> Olivia and her husband, Charles, recently hired a new wealth manager because (1) their financial needs have changed and (2) they felt that their former wealth manager had far too many clients to provide them with customized service. Olivia and Charles are interested in more sophisticated tax planning and more exposure to alternative investments. They are still concerned about having sufficient assets for their lifetime, but they are much more confident than they were several years ago.
>
> Describe how Olivia and Charles shifted client segments upon the hiring of the new wealth manager.
>
> ### Solution:
>
> Prior to hiring the new wealth manager, Olivia and Charles were likely in the mass affluent segment, given their previous wealth manager's high number of clients and lack of customized service. As their financial needs changed and they desired more customized service, Olivia and Charles likely moved to the high-net-worth segment. Their new focus on tax planning and alternative investments is also evidence of a shift to the high-net-worth segment. Because the couple are still concerned about having sufficient assets for their lifetime, they likely are not in the ultra-high-net-worth category.

14.4 Robo-Advisors

Amid the rapid growth of financial technology, a trend in private wealth management is the robo-advisor. The term *robo-advisor* applies to wealth management service providers that have a primarily digital client interface and experience. Robo-advisors gather information—such as risk tolerance, time horizon, goals/objectives, assets, and liabilities—directly from the client via web-based questionnaires. Using mean–variance optimization or other techniques, the robo-advisor recommends a suitable asset allocation for the client and typically implements the investment strategy using exchange-traded funds or mutual funds. The processes that robo-advisors use in information gathering and portfolio optimization can be quite similar to those utilized by human advisors. However, the primary distinction is in the digital interface.

Robo-advisors monitor and manage client portfolios on an ongoing basis and periodically rebalance portfolios as needed. Robo-advisors also provide regular reporting to clients through online applications and may make human wealth managers available to handle certain client inquiries. Cost is a key factor that differentiates robo-advisors from human wealth managers. Robo-advisor services are generally available at a cost that is lower than the fees charged by traditional wealth management firms. Scalability of technology has enabled robo-advisors to service investors with relatively small portfolios.

Robo-advisors have expanded their services to various areas of private wealth management—for example, constructing ESG-related portfolios. Other robo-advisors have focused on investor behavior (e.g., encouraging saving or discouraging a reaction to declining securities prices), on factor investing, and on more sophisticated techniques to improve tax efficiency. While many robo-advisors compete directly with traditional wealth management firms, others have partnered with these firms. Such partnerships can enable firms to lower fees or to offer services to clients they might not otherwise have been able to serve.

SUMMARY

- Private clients and institutional clients have different concerns, primarily relating to investment objectives and constraints, investment governance, investment sophistication, regulation, and the uniqueness of individuals.
- Information needed in advising private clients includes personal information, financial information, and tax considerations.
- Basic tax strategies for private clients include tax avoidance, tax reduction, and tax deferral.
- A client's planned goals are those that can be reasonably estimated or quantified within an expected time horizon, such as retirement, specific purchases, education, family events, wealth transfer, and philanthropy.
- Unplanned goals are those related to unforeseen financial needs, such as property repairs and medical expenses.
- When establishing client goals, private wealth managers consider goal quantification, goal prioritization, and goal changes.
- Risk tolerance refers to the level of risk an individual is willing and able to bear. Risk tolerance is the inverse of risk aversion. Risk capacity is the ability to accept financial risk. Risk perception is an individual's subjective assessment of the risk involved in an investment decision's outcome.
- Wealth managers often utilize questionnaires to assess clients' risk tolerance. The result of a risk tolerance questionnaire, typically a numerical score, is often used as an input in the investment planning process.
- Wealth managers need both technical skills and non-technical ("soft") skills in their advisory roles. Technical skills include capital markets proficiency, portfolio construction ability, financial planning knowledge, quantitative skills, technology skills, and in some situations, foreign language fluency. Soft skills include communication skills, social skills, education/coaching skills, and business development and sales skills.
- Capital sufficiency analysis, also known as capital needs analysis, is the process by which a wealth manager determines whether a client has, or is likely to accumulate, sufficient financial resources to meet his or her objectives.
- Two methods for evaluating capital sufficiency are deterministic forecasting and Monte Carlo simulation.
- Wealth managers use several different methods to analyze a client's retirement goals, including mortality tables, annuities, and Monte Carlo simulation.
- An investment policy statement (IPS) for an individual includes the following parts: background and investment objective(s); investment parameters (risk tolerance and investment time horizon); asset class preferences; other investment

preferences (liquidity and constraints); portfolio asset allocation; portfolio management (discretionary authority, rebalancing, tactical changes, implementation); duties and responsibilities; and an appendix for additional details.

- Two primary approaches to constructing a client portfolio are a traditional approach and a goals-based investing approach.
- Portfolio reporting involves periodically providing clients with information about their investment portfolio and performance. Portfolio review refers to meetings or phone conversations between a wealth manager and a client to discuss the client's investment strategy. The key difference between portfolio reporting and portfolio review is that the wealth manager is more actively engaged in a review.
- The success of an investment program involves achieving client goals, following a consistent process, and realizing favorable portfolio performance.
- Ethical considerations for private wealth managers include "know your customer" (KYC), fiduciary duty and suitability, confidentiality, and conflicts of interest.
- Several global regulations have relevance for private wealth managers.
- Key private wealth segments include mass affluent, high net worth, and ultra high net worth.
- Robo-advisors have emerged in the mass affluent client segment. These advisors have a primarily digital client interface. Robo-advisor service providers generally charge lower fees than traditional wealth management firms. Scalability of technology has enabled robo-advisors to service investors with relatively small portfolios.

REFERENCES

Browning, Chris, Tuo Guo, Yanshan Cheng, and Michael Finke. 2016. "Spending in Retirement: Determining the Consumption Gap." *Journal of Financial Planning* 29 (2): 42–53.

Deloitte. "Tax Guides and Highlights." https://dits.deloitte.com/#TaxGuides (accessed as of September 2018).

Grable, John E. 2017. *Financial Risk Tolerance: A Psychometric Review. Research Foundation Briefs*. Charlottesville, VA: Research Foundation of CFA Institute.

Kitces, Michael, and David Hultstrom. "*Joint Life Expectancy and Mortality Calculator.*" https://www.kitces.com/joint-life-expectancy-and-mortality-calculator (accessed as of September 2018).

Klement, Joachim. 2015. *Investor Risk Profiling: An Overview. Research Foundation Briefs*. Charlottesville, VA: Research Foundation of CFA Institute.

KPMG. "*Individual Income Tax Rates Table.*" https://home.kpmg.com/xx/en/home/services/tax/tax-tools-and-resources/tax-rates-online/individual-income-tax-rates-table.html (accessed as of September 2018).

OECD. "*Information on Common Reporting Standard.*" Organisation for Economic Co-operation and Development. www.oecd.org/tax/automatic-exchange/common-reporting-standard (accessed as of September 2018).

OECD. "*Life Expectancy at 65.*" Organisation for Economic Co-operation and Development. https://data.oecd.org/healthstat/life-expectancy-at-65.htm (accessed as of September 2018).

Suisse, Credit. 2017. *Global Wealth Report 2017*. Credit Suisse Research Institute.

PRACTICE PROBLEMS

The following information relates to Questions 1–3

Henlopen McZhao is a private wealth manager. After a successful introductory meeting with Nescopeck Cree, she is meeting again with this new client to plan a wealth management strategy. McZhao seeks additional personal information from Cree.

McZhao learns that Cree is 45 years old and is currently employed as an attorney. Cree has a number of specific financial goals that he wishes to achieve in the future but has no particular return objective for his portfolio. Because he has been investing for 20 years, Cree is comfortable with moderate levels of market volatility. His employment provides for his current expenses, so Cree's liquidity requirements are minimal. Cree prefers to have his environmental and social concerns reflected in his investment choices.

1 **Discuss** additional personal information that McZhao should gather from Cree in order to properly advise this new client.

McZhao then focuses on Cree's financial goals:

- Cree wants to fund university expenses for his three children, with the first payment starting in 10 years. Cree does not know what to expect in terms of college costs.
- Cree plans to retire at age 62 and expects to need $80,000 per year to fund his retirement lifestyle. He is concerned that an increasing level of medical expenses for himself and his wife may reduce his financial assets.
- Cree expects to purchase an apartment building in three years and plans to use the rental income from this investment property to help fund his retirement needs.
- Cree's wife enjoys donating to philanthropic causes. She currently donates $10,000 per year, but by the time Cree retires, she hopes to increase this amount to $30,000 per year.
- Cree collects antique furniture and budgets $15,000 per year for additions to his collection. He mentions that this year's antique purchase will be his next large expense and currently has the highest priority of all his goals.

2 **Discuss** the issues relating to Cree's:
  i. goal quantification.
  ii. goal prioritization.

McZhao continues the discussion with Cree in order to evaluate his degree of risk tolerance associated with each of the following individual goals:

Practice Problems

Retirement:		Cree considers retirement a long-term goal and is willing to endure a 10% drop in expected retirement spending. However, he is very concerned with having sufficient funds to cover medical expenses.
Investment property:		Cree sees the investment property as a source of stable income, so it is very important to him to purchase the building. He realizes that maintenance and repair expenses will be necessary, and he also considers those very important.
Philanthropy:		Cree's wife strongly influences him to fund her philanthropic causes, and he wants to maintain some level of annual contribution. Cree believes that his wife would be willing to maintain her $10,000 per year contributions and not increase that amount.
Antique furniture:		Cree is willing to reduce or eliminate his spending on antique furniture.

3   **Determine** Cree's degree of risk tolerance associated with each of the following individual goals. **Justify** each response.

Determine Cree's degree of risk tolerance associated with each of the following individual goals. Justify each response.

Goal	Degree of Risk Tolerance	Justification
Retirement	Lower	
	Higher	
Investment Property	Lower	
	Higher	
Philanthropy	Lower	
	Higher	
Antique Furniture	Lower	
	Higher	

The following information relates to Questions 4–6

Sharfepto Zik, a private wealth manager, is meeting with a client, Garbanzo Patel, in order to create an investment policy statement (IPS) for Patel's upcoming retirement. Patel estimates that he will require €200,000 per year, with annual increases for inflation, during retirement. Patel's primary spending goals during retirement are to provide for his family's needs and maintain his retirement lifestyle. His secondary goals are to fund his philanthropic activities and leave a significant inheritance to his children.

During his retirement, Patel will receive union pension payments of €50,000 per year with annual increases for inflation. In his spare time, Patel runs a small business that provides him with an annual income of €120,000 and is valued at €1 million. He will continue running his business during retirement.

Patel holds a portfolio of securities valued at approximately €4 million. The portfolio primarily contains dividend-paying stocks and interest-bearing bonds. Patel has reinvested all these distributions back into his portfolio but anticipates that after retirement he may need to use some of the distributions to fund his expenses.

Patel plans to buy a vacation home in three years. His budget for the vacation home is approximately €1.4 million. Patel has not decided yet how he will fund this purchase.

4 **Prepare** the Investment Objectives section of Patel's IPS.

Patel has been working with Zik for 10 years. At the beginning of the 10-year period, Zik forecasted that the equities in Patel's portfolio would outperform their benchmark and that the bonds would match their benchmark. Now, at the end of the 10-year period, equities have outperformed the benchmark, but with higher volatility than the benchmark. In addition, the bonds in the portfolio matched their benchmark performance, but with lower volatility than the benchmark. However, returns and volatility are within IPS specifications for both equities and bonds.

Patel stated his goals to Zik at the beginning of the 10-year period and has not changed them. Patel's plan is to retire this year, and he wants to be able to support a specified annual spending level.

Zik's original capital sufficiency analysis modeled a 6% rate of return, and Patel's portfolio has earned slightly more than that over the 10-year period. Zik's most recent capital sufficiency analysis shows that the portfolio and strategy are very likely to meet Patel's needs as he transitions into retirement.

Zik has followed the guidelines stated in the original IPS in terms of rebalancing the portfolio, maintaining an ongoing dialog with Patel, and coordinating the strategy with Patel's retirement and philanthropic goals. Although fees have remained unchanged at 1%, Zik has been able to reduce expenses for equities by 20 bps and for bonds by 12 bps.

5 **Evaluate** the success of Zik's investment program for Patel in terms of:

   i. goal achievement.

   ii. process consistency.

   iii. portfolio performance.

After every regular monthly rebalancing, Zik sends an email to Patel with a portfolio report. Zik's portfolio report contains the following:

- An asset allocation report that reflects strategic asset allocation targets
- A detailed performance report that includes individual asset class and security performance
- A year-to-date performance summary report and a historical performance report starting from the inception of Patel's investment strategy

6 **Recommend** additional information that Zik could provide to enhance his portfolio reports for Patel.

Practice Problems

The following information relates to Questions 7 and 8

Val Sili, age 22, has just graduated from college and begins making ambitious future financial plans. The four stages of his plan are summarized below. Sili would like to have outside financial advice at each of these stages.

Stage 1—Age 22–26:	Sili plans to work as a software developer in a startup company, where he will earn both a salary and stock options. He will save as much as he can to invest, but his portfolio will be relatively small, and he will be willing to pay only low management fees. Sili would like to use a sophisticated mean–variance optimization technique for asset allocation, although he will limit his investments to exchange-traded funds and mutual funds.
Stage 2—Age 26–30:	Sili will have reached a more senior position in the company. He plans to have accumulated assets of $350,000, and his investment focus will be on building his portfolio. Sili will want help with his increasing financial planning needs and will be able to afford the fees of a professional wealth manager.
Stage 3—Age 30–36:	Sili plans to exercise his stock options to buy a large quantity of the company's stock at a price significantly below its market value. The proceeds should increase his portfolio value to $8 million. Sili will quit his job to start his own software company. Sili will be interested in more sophisticated investments with longer time horizons, greater risk, and less liquidity. He will also want specialized advisers for taxes, legal issues, and investment strategies.
Stage 4—After Age 36:	Sili will sell his software company for $200 million and retire. He will spend his retirement traveling on his private jet and collecting artwork for his collection; therefore, he will need advice on acquiring high-end assets. The substantial increase in the value of his investment portfolio will allow him to have a multi-generational time horizon. He will require a wider range of investment advisory services, including complex tax planning, estate planning, and bill payment services.

7 **Determine** the client segment or adviser type that is *most appropriate* for each stage of Sili's plan. **Justify** each response.

Determine the client segment or adviser type that is *most appropriate* for each stage of Sili's plan. Justify each response.

Stage 1—Age 22–26	Client Segment/Adviser Type:
	Justification:
Stage 2—Age 26–30	Client Segment/Adviser Type:
	Justification:
Stage 3—Age 30–36	Client Segment/Adviser Type:
	Justification:
Stage 4—After Age 36	Client Segment/Adviser Type:
	Justification:

Sili next uses three approaches to analyze his retirement goals:

Approach 1 Sili considers the probability that he will live to a certain age and then predicts his inflation-adjusted retirement spending according to the probability that he will still be living in a given year. This approach allows him to estimate the present value of his retirement spending needs by assigning associated probabilities to annual expected cash outflows.

Approach 2 Sili determines that he can specify his level of annual spending during retirement and that he can model that spending as a series of fixed payments. He calculates the present value of that series of payments as of the day of his retirement, resulting in the amount of money that he will need to fund his retirement goals.

Approach 3 Sili models the uncertainty of each key variable individually by assigning each one its own probability distribution and then generates a large number of random outcomes for each variable. He aggregates the outcomes to determine an overall probability of reaching his objectives. Sili sees this as a flexible approach that allows him to explore various scenarios, including unforeseen expenses.

8 **Identify** each approach that Sili uses to analyze his retirement goals. **Explain** each response.

Identify each approach that Sili uses to analyze his retirement goals. Explain each response.	
Approach 1	Identification:
	Explanation:
Approach 2	Identification:
	Explanation:
Approach 3	Identification:
	Explanation:

The following information relates to Questions 9–16

Noèmie Açor works for an international bank as a private wealth adviser. Açor speaks several regional languages in addition to her native language. She prepares for two client meetings next week. First, Açor will meet with Winifred Njau, who has recently retired. Njau has made a charitable pledge to a non-profit university endowment, the Udhamini Fund. Açor prepares a draft of the investment objectives section of an investment policy statement (IPS) for Njau using selected client information, which is presented in Exhibit 1.

Practice Problems

Exhibit 1	Selected Client Information Items for Njau
Liquidity needs	$500,000 charitable pledge to Udhamini payable in 15 years
Risk tolerance	Moderate
Asset allocation	40% equities and 60% fixed income

Açor's notes from her previous meeting with Njau indicate the following behavioral considerations related to Njau's retirement planning:

- Njau would like to increase her level of spending if supported by investment projections.
- Although Njau could pay a lump sum and receive a series of fixed payments, she prefers not to lose control over her assets.
- Njau understands the risk–return relationship and is willing to accept some short-term losses to achieve long-term growth.

Next, Açor reviews a recent risk tolerance questionnaire completed by Njau, which relates to overall portfolio risk. Açor focuses on the type of capital sufficiency analysis to perform for Njau. To determine the optimal allocation, Açor seeks to ensure that Njau's charitable pledge can be met and implements a goal-based investing approach. Açor runs a Monte Carlo simulation to determine the probability of success, which is the likelihood that Njau can meet her charitable pledge objective. The simulation results are presented in Exhibit 2.

Exhibit 2	Monte Carlo Simulation Results for Charitable Pledge (adjusted for inflation)		
	Year 10 Portfolio Value ($)	Year 15 Portfolio Value ($)	Year 20 Portfolio Value ($)
25th %	501,288	729,230	1,035,373
50th %	405,927	553,803	767,448
75th %	331,056	422,746	563,039

One week after this meeting, the bank sends a client satisfaction survey to Njau. In response to questions about Açor's soft skills and technical skills, Njau responds with the following comments:

Comment 1   Açor constructed a portfolio that is appropriate for my unique situation.

Comment 2   Açor spoke to me in my own regional language throughout the meeting.

Comment 3   Açor educated me about how my investments perform and affect my portfolio.

Açor's second meeting will be with Thanh Bañuq. Bañuq is Njau's nephew and serves on the board of directors of Udhamini. Açor obtained the essential facts about Bañuq when she opened his account, including his risk and return objectives and the origin of his wealth. In preparation for the meeting, Açor considers the high level of taxes that Bañuq pays. Açor will recommend changing the asset location of high-dividend-paying equities that Bañuq owns from a taxable account to a retirement account with tax-free earnings and withdrawals.

During their meeting, Açor and Bañuq discuss charitable pledges that Udhamini has recently received and the likelihood that Njau will meet her charitable pledge. Bañuq then asks Açor the following question:

"How might my investment objectives and constraints differ from those of a typical university endowment, such as Udhamini?"

The day after Açor's meeting with Bañuq, Açor realizes that her actions in the meeting may have raised an ethical concern.

9   Based on Exhibit 1, which of the following items is Açor *most likely* to include in the section of the IPS she is drafting for Njau?
    A   Moderate risk tolerance
    B   40% allocation to equities
    C $500,000 charitable pledge in 15 years

10 Based on Açor's notes from her previous meeting with Njau, the behavioral consideration exhibited by Njau is *most likely*:
    A   a consumption gap.
    B   the "annuity puzzle."
    C   heightened loss aversion.

11 Açor's portfolio allocation for Njau is *most likely* optimized on the basis of:
    A   a stated maximum level of volatility.
    B   total portfolio mean–variance efficiency.
    C   the results of the risk tolerance questionnaire.

12 Based on Exhibits 1 and 2, the probability that Njau will be able to meet her charitable goal is *closest* to:
    A   25%.
    B   50%.
    C   75%.

13 Which comment in Njau's response to the client satisfaction survey *best* describes a soft skill exhibited by Açor?
    A   Comment 1
    B   Comment 2
    C   Comment 3

14 Açor's recommendation regarding asset location in Bañuq's portfolio is *most likely* an example of tax:
    A   deferral.
    B   reduction.
    C   avoidance.

15 The *most appropriate* response to Bañuq's question is that he has:
    A   a shorter time horizon.
    B   less significant tax considerations.
    C   less diverse investment objectives.

16 The ethical concern that Açor *most likely* raised is:
    A   KYC.

Practice Problems

B suitability.
C confidentiality.

SOLUTIONS

1. McZhao should obtain the following additional personal information from Cree:
   - Family situation: Marital status, children and grandchildren, ages of family members
   - Identification: Copy of driver's license or passport
   - Additional career information: Future aspirations for career, business, and retirement
   - Investment background
   - More details on financial goals and risk tolerance

   McZhao has already learned about Cree's current employment, experience with market volatility, interest in meeting specific goals rather than a particular return objective, low current liquidity needs, and investment preferences based on his environmental and social concerns.

   Now that Cree has become a private client, a starting point of the relationship is for McZhao to learn about his client's family situation, such as marital status, children and grandchildren, and ages of family members. McZhao should also obtain proof of client identification (copy of driver's license or passport). Cree's employment and career information is important, as is discussion about his future career, business, and retirement aspirations.

   In addition, wealth managers should assess the client's investment background. As part of the investment background conversation, the wealth manager should determine whether the client has an explicit return objective or specific investment preferences. Finally, a detailed conversation about the client's financial objectives/goals and risk tolerance is part of the personal-information-gathering process.

2. With respect to goal quantification, Cree has quantified his retirement spending needs, the cost to maintain his antique purchases, and his wife's philanthropic support. McZhao should work with Cree to help estimate the costs for his children's university expenses and what he expects to pay for the investment property.

   With respect to goal prioritization, even though Cree believes that his highest priority is his next big expense ($15,000 for this year's additions to his antique collection), the timing of that expense should not be the sole determinant of its priority. McZhao needs to discuss with Cree which of his goals are most important. The purchases of expensive antiques and the large philanthropic contributions may adversely affect Cree's ability to fund his retirement lifestyle. Therefore, McZhao should help Cree consider reevaluating his priorities.

Solutions

3

Determine Cree's degree of risk tolerance associated with each of the following individual goals. Justify each response.

Goal	Degree of Risk Tolerance	Justification
Retirement	Lower / Higher	Retirement is a long-term goal. Cree is willing to incur a moderate drop in his planned expenses, so he likely has a higher risk tolerance for that goal. Cree is concerned about paying future medical expenses in retirement, and since his retirement is still 17 years in the future, he likely has a higher risk tolerance with the medical expenses goal.
Investment Property	Lower / Higher	Because the investment property is an important near-term goal, Cree likely has a lower risk tolerance with this goal. Similarly, he likely has a lower risk tolerance with the goal of funding maintenance and repairs for the property.
Philanthropy	Lower / Higher	Cree's wife's influence regarding their philanthropic giving makes Cree unwilling to stop his contributions completely, but he believes she will accept maintaining their contributions rather than increasing them substantially. As a result, Cree likely has a higher risk tolerance with this goal.
Antique Furniture	Lower / Higher	Cree is likely highly risk tolerant with his goal of purchasing antique furniture, because he is willing to cut that expense altogether.

4 Investment Objectives:

- Purpose: Support Patel's lifestyle in retirement (higher priority), provide for family's needs (higher priority), fund philanthropic activities (lower priority), provide inheritance for children (lower priority)
- Anticipated annual need: €200,000, with annual increases for inflation
- Annual need met with: Income from small business (approx. €120,000), pension (€50,000 with annual inflation increases), portfolio distributions
- Intent to purchase of €1.4 million vacation home in three years
- Zik should assist in quantifying philanthropic and bequest goals and determining how to fund the vacation home purchase.

The purpose of this portfolio is to support Garbanzo Patel's lifestyle in retirement, to provide for his family's needs, to fund his philanthropic activities, and to provide an inheritance for his children. Patel's primary objective is to provide for his family's needs and support his lifestyle during his retirement. The philanthropic and bequest objectives are lower priorities.

To meet all his objectives, Patel anticipates needing €200,000 per year, with annual increases for inflation. His cash needs will be primarily satisfied through income from his small business of approximately €120,000 per year and his union pension payments of €50,000 per year. The pension payments will increase annually for inflation. Any remaining cash needs will be satisfied by taking distributions from his portfolio.

Patel also intends to purchase a vacation home in three years and plans to pay approximately €1.4 million.

Patel has not articulated specific amounts for his philanthropic activities or his children's inheritances. Zik should work with Patel to quantify his philanthropic and bequest goals and to decide on the best way to fund the purchase of his vacation home.

5 By all three criteria, Zik has been successful.

   Goal achievement:
   - Patel's portfolio has achieved its goals with an acceptable amount of risk; its return and volatility have remained within the original IPS specifications.
   - The portfolio remains likely to succeed as an ongoing strategy, without meaningful adjustments to the plan; the most recent capital sufficiency analysis shows that the strategy is very likely to meet Patel's retirement needs.

   Process consistency:
   - Zik has followed the guidelines stated in the original IPS, has maintained an ongoing dialogue with Patel, has coordinated the strategy with Patel's retirement and philanthropic goals, and has even managed to reduce expenses.

   Portfolio performance (over the 10-year time horizon):
   - The equity portion of Patel's portfolio outperformed its benchmark but had higher volatility than the benchmark.
   - The bond portion of the portfolio matched its benchmark but had lower volatility than the benchmark.
   - The performance of both equities and bonds remained within the original IPS specifications.
   - For the overall portfolio, Zik targeted a 6% rate of return, and the portfolio has slightly exceeded that level over the period.

6 Zik's portfolio reporting can be made more effective by including the following items:
   - A transaction details report showing contributions, withdrawals, interest and dividends, and capital appreciation for the current period
   - A purchase and sale report for the current period
   - Currency exposure report detailing the effects of exchange rate fluctuations
   - A benchmark report that shows the performance of Patel's equity and bond portfolios relative to their respective benchmarks and the overall portfolio performance relative to a blended benchmark (based on weights that are appropriate for Patel's holdings)

- An accompanying letter that provides market commentary, investment context, education, and other advice

7

Determine the client segment or adviser type that is *most appropriate* for each stage of Sili's plan. Justify each response.

Stage 1— Age 22–26	Client Segment/Adviser Type:	Robo-Adviser (part of the mass affluent client segment)
	Justification:	Robo-advisers support advanced asset allocation techniques, implement typically with exchange-traded funds or mutual funds, and are lower-cost alternatives for relatively small portfolios. During this stage, Sili's portfolio will be relatively small and he will not be able to afford to pay the fees of a traditional wealth management firm. Yet he still wants to use sophisticated analysis for his investment planning. Robo-advisers are his most appropriate option. With their primarily digital client interface and experience, robo-advisers are designed to serve investors with relatively small portfolios at a lower cost than the fees charged by traditional wealth management firms. Robo-advisers enable their clients to use advanced techniques, such as mean–variance optimization, for determining asset allocations, and they implement their strategies typically with exchange-traded funds or mutual funds.
Stage 2— Age 26–30	Client Segment/Adviser Type:	Mass Affluent Segment
	Justification:	The mass affluent segment covers asset levels between $250,000 and $1 million and serves clients who are focused on building their portfolios and want help with financial planning needs. Now that Sili has a larger portfolio and is able to afford paying fees to a professional wealth manager, he belongs in the mass affluent client segment. With investment assets of $350,000, Sili's portfolio fits within the asset level range of this segment, typically $250,000–$1,000,000. Sili's characteristics during Stage 2 of being focused on building his portfolio and wanting help with his financial planning needs are typical of younger clients in the mass affluent segment.
Stage 3— Age 30–36	Client Segment/Adviser Type:	"Private Client" Range of High-Net-Worth Segment
	Justification:	The private client range in the high-net-worth segment covers asset levels between $1 million and $10 million and can provide a team of specialized advisers that supports more customized strategies for more sophisticated investments with longer time horizons, greater risk, and less liquidity. Sili's higher asset level of $8 million puts him in the range of the high-net-worth segment. This segment generally consists of clients with liquid investment assets ranging from $1 million to $50 million. Since this range is so wide, firms often focus on only a portion of the segment. A client such as Sili with assets between $1 million and $10 million falls within a range that is known in some geographic markets as the "private client" segment. Sili's interest in more sophisticated investments with longer time horizons, greater risk, and less liquidity requires a more customized strategy and stronger product knowledge from the wealth manager, and he is better served by a manager that specializes in high-net-worth clients than by a manager for the mass affluent segment. Also, with a wealth manager that specializes in high-net-worth clients, Sili will likely be served by a team of people with specialized and complementary skills, including tax advisers, legal advisers, investment specialists, and a relationship manager.

(continued)

Determine the client segment or adviser type that is *most appropriate* for each stage of Sili's plan. Justify each response.

Stage 4—After Age 36	Client Segment/Adviser Type:	Ultra-High-Net-Worth Segment
	Justification:	The ultra-high-net-worth segment covers asset levels over $50 million for clients with multi-generational time horizons and provides a wider range of services for complex tax situations, estate planning, bill payment, concierge services, travel planning, and advice on acquiring high-end assets.
		At this stage, Sili's portfolio value of $200 million puts him in the ultra-high-net-worth client segment, which handles clients with liquid investment assets exceeding approximately $50 million. As is characteristic of clients in this segment, Sili now has a multi-generational time horizon, highly complex tax and estate planning considerations, and a wider range of service needs. An ultra-high-net-worth adviser can assist Sili with bill payment services, concierge services, travel planning, and advice on acquiring such assets as artwork and aircraft.

8

Identify each approach that Sili uses to analyze his retirement goals. Explain each response.

Approach 1	Identification:	Mortality Tables
	Explanation:	A mortality table allows for estimating the present value of retirement spending needs by associating each outflow with a probability based on life expectancy.
		Sili uses a mortality table to determine the probability that he will live to a certain age. This information allows him to predict his anticipated inflation-adjusted retirement spending according to the probability that he will be living in a given year. A mortality table illustrates an individual's life expectancy at any given age. A wealth manager can use a mortality table to estimate the present value of a client's retirement spending needs by assigning associated probabilities to annual expected cash outflows.
Approach 2	Identification:	Annuity Method
	Explanation:	The calculated price of an annuity equals the present value of a series of future fixed outflows during retirement.
		A relatively simple way for Sili to calculate the present value of his desired retirement spending is by pricing an annuity. Annuities provide a series of fixed payments, either for life or for a specified period, in exchange for a lump sum payment.

Solutions

Identify each approach that Sili uses to analyze his retirement goals. Explain each response.

Approach 3	Identification:	Monte Carlo Simulation
	Explanation:	Monte Carlo simulation yields an overall probability of meeting retirement needs by aggregating the results of many trials of probability-based estimates of key variables, and it is a flexible approach for exploring different retirement scenarios.
		Monte Carlo simulation can analyze the likelihood of Sili's portfolio meeting his anticipated retirement needs. This simulation models the uncertainty of the key variables and the uncertainty or variability in the future outcome. A Monte Carlo simulation uses assumptions of probability distributions for the key variables and then runs a large number of independent trials that generate many random outcomes. These outcomes are then aggregated to determine the probability of Sili reaching his investment objectives.
		An advantage of Monte Carlo simulation for retirement planning is its flexibility in modeling and exploring different scenarios. Typically, retirement goals are more complex than a fixed, annual cash flow need. For instance, if Sili wishes to determine the effect of a significant purchase/gift or large unforeseen expenses, he can model these scenarios with a Monte Carlo simulation.

---

9 C is correct. Açor is preparing a draft of the investment objectives section of an IPS for Njau. Investment objectives include identifying funding needs and goals for the portfolio. So, Açor should include the $500,000 charitable pledge to Udhamini in 15 years in the investment objectives section of the IPS. Njau's goal is specific and is an important part of the investment objectives that will drive the preparation of the remainder of the IPS and the execution of the investment strategy.

10 B is correct. The "annuity puzzle" describes the phenomenon that retirees tend to avoid annuity investments, which may be appropriate to best help them reach their financial goals. An annuity provides a series of fixed payments, either for life or for a specified period, in exchange for a lump sum payment. Njau's reluctance to lose control over her assets by paying the lump sum in exchange for the fixed payments is one explanation for her reluctance, and she may also believe that an annuity would minimize the chance of a substantial improvement in her lifestyle.

11 A is correct. Açor uses the goal-based investing approach by allocating with a focus on Njau's charitable pledge to Udhamini. With this method, she seeks to optimize Njau's portfolio so that the pledge goal has a high probability of being met. Açor will set aside a required amount of funds to invest, and a mean–variance optimization will be run specifically for that portion of Njau's portfolio. The funds will be invested to a stated maximum level of volatility to meet the charitable need.

12 B is correct. The Monte Carlo simulation shows that Njau has a 50% probability of having an amount exceeding $553,803 in Year 15. Since Njau's charitable pledge goal to Udhamini is $500,000, she has a slightly greater than 50% probability of meeting or exceeding her charitable pledge goal in Year 15.

13 C is correct. Açor's ability to effectively educate Njau by showing Njau how her investments perform and affect her portfolio is a soft skill. Soft skills involve interpersonal relationships and include communication skills, social skills, education and coaching skills, and business development and sales skills.

14 C is correct. Changing the location of high-dividend-paying equities away from Bañuq's taxable account to a retirement account with tax-free earnings and future liquidity events is an example of a tax avoidance strategy. Implementing this asset location change will eliminate the taxes that Bañuq would have been required to pay on investment income and gains in this account.

15 A is correct. As a private client, Bañuq is more likely to have a shorter time horizon than that of Udhamini. Thus, Bañuq is likely to be more constrained with respect to risk taking and liquidity. A typical university endowment has a long time horizon, which can theoretically be infinite.

16 C is correct. The confidentiality standard is likely a concern because Açor may have shared confidential private information about Njau and her finances when she discussed Njau's charitable pledge with her nephew, Bañuq. Standard III(E): Preservation of Confidentiality obliges wealth managers who possess highly personal and sensitive client information to maintain confidentiality. Keeping confidential information private may be challenging for Açor since she manages the portfolios of both family members.

READING
22

Topics in Private Wealth Management

by Paul Bouchey, CFA, Helena Eaton, PhD, CFA, and Philip Marcovici

Paul Bouchey, CFA, is at Parametric Portfolio Associates, Seattle, WA, (USA). Helena Eaton, PhD, CFA, is at J.P. Morgan, London, (UK). Philip Marcovici is at Offices of Philip Marcovici, Hong Kong SAR, (China).

LEARNING OUTCOMES

Mastery	The candidate should be able to:
☐	a. compare taxation of income, wealth, and wealth transfers;
☐	b. describe global considerations of jurisdiction that are relevant to taxation;
☐	c. discuss and analyze the tax efficiency of investments;
☐	d. analyze the impact of taxes on capital accumulation and decumulation in taxable, tax-exempt, and tax-deferred accounts;
☐	e. explain portfolio tax management strategies and their application;
☐	f. discuss risk and tax objectives in managing concentrated single-asset positions;
☐	g. describe strategies for managing concentrated positions in public equities;
☐	h. describe strategies for managing concentrated positions in privately owned businesses and real estate;
☐	i. discuss objectives—tax and non-tax—in planning the transfer of wealth;
☐	j. discuss strategies for achieving estate, bequest, and lifetime gift objectives in common law and civil law regimes;
☐	k. describe considerations related to managing wealth across multiple generations.

Helena Eaton is a contributing author. Her contributions solely represent her views and should in no way be taken to reflect the views of JPMorgan Chase & Co.

Sections 9–11 of this reading draw from *Concentrated Single-Asset Positions* by Thomas J. Boczar, CFA, and Nischal Pai, CFA (©2013 CFA Institute). Sections 12–16 draw on *Estate Planning in a Global Context* by Stephen Horan, CFA, and Thomas Robinson, CFA (©2009 CFA Institute). While both have been extensively rewritten, we wish to acknowledge the previous authors' contributions.

© 2020 CFA Institute. All rights reserved.

1. INTRODUCTION

This reading focuses on three important areas of technical competency in the management of private client assets: the impact of taxes on wealth accumulation, the management of concentrated positions in public or private assets, and basic tools and techniques for preserving wealth through generations.

We begin with a discussion of taxes. Taxes are an important determinant of the taxable investor's final returns. While fees and trading costs have received a lot of attention in the press and academic spheres, the erosion of returns due to taxes can be much more significant.

Consider this scenario: After significant development and testing, your firm has just launched a new strategy that tactically shifts between different equity indexes. The backtests show significant alpha over most time horizons and especially strong performance during market downturns—a risk/return profile that should be highly attractive to your clients. You launch the strategy 1 January, and everyone is pleased with the performance in the first year. On 15 February of the following year, the founder of the firm receives a telephone call from the accountant for Charles and Ivy Lee, an important private client relationship. The accountant has been compiling the Lees' tax documents in preparation for filing the annual tax return. It seems that the trading activity inherent in your new strategy has generated a lot of capital gains, and the resulting tax bill is larger than the excess returns generated by your strategy!

This scenario is not uncommon. Because a significant proportion of actively managed assets is managed on behalf of tax-exempt institutions, such as retirement plans and sovereign wealth funds, strategies are often developed either without regard to taxes or with taxes as an afterthought and then applied—unsuccessfully—to taxable investors.

To illustrate the effect of taxes on wealth accumulation, let's examine a longer time horizon. The S&P 500 Index from 1 January 1990 through 30 June 2019 appreciated 7.5% per year, on average. With dividends reinvested and ignoring fees and transaction costs, the compound annual growth rate would have been 9.8%. If the Lees had invested $1 million on 1 January 1990, we would expect their portfolio to have grown to $16 million by the end of the nearly 30-year period. However, this is only true if the assets are not subject to taxation during the accumulation phase, as would be the case if they are held in a retirement account or a private family foundation. Exhibit 1 shows the growth of this hypothetical portfolio under several different tax assumptions.

If we assume the worst case, that both dividends and capital gains are taxed fully at a marginal tax rate of 50%, then the 9.8% compound annual growth rate would be cut roughly in half—to 5.0%. In other words, their $1 million would have only grown to $4 million after almost 30 years—only one-fourth of what the tax-exempt account realized. Clearly, taxes are an important investment consideration.

Fortunately, as a tax-aware practitioner, you may be able to use various tax-management techniques to reduce the tax drag. If capital gains and dividends are taxed at 25%, the final wealth of the taxable portfolio would have grown to $8 million. If capital gains taxes can be eliminated or deferred and only dividends are taxed at the 25% rate, then the $1 million would have grown to $13 million at the end of our horizon. It is still not as good as the tax-exempt case, but it is significantly better than our worst case.

Introduction

Exhibit 1 Growth of $1 million in the S&P 500 Index

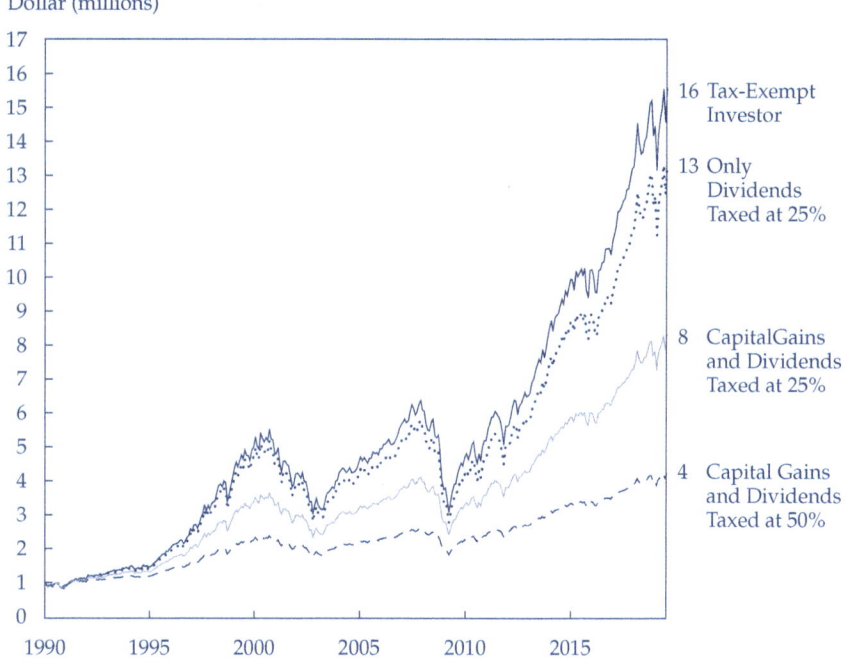

Notes: Growth of $1 million from January 1990 through June 2019 for the S&P 500 Index with dividends reinvested, ignoring fees and transaction costs. After-tax returns are computed in three ways: 1) Only dividends are taxed at 25%; 2) Dividends and capital gains are taxed at 25%; 3) Dividends and capital gains are taxed at 50%. In each month, we multiply the component of return by 1 minus the tax rate. For example, pre-tax returns of 10% and −10% would become 5% and −5% under a 50% tax rate. This calculation assumes that all capital gains and losses are realized each month and that when capital losses occur, there are sufficient capital gains from other investments so that the investor may deduct the losses in full. Essentially, the tax liability is deducted and the tax benefit added to the account as if it were a cash flow, thus reducing the magnitude and volatility of returns.
Sources: Authors' calculations using the S&P 500 Total Return Index and the S&P 500 Price Return Index. The after-tax return methodology follows Lucas and Sanz (2016).

Broadly speaking, a portfolio manager managing assets for a private client looks to maximize after-tax returns for a given level of risk. This reading lays the ground work for understanding how different types of taxes impact wealth accumulation. We review the general principles of taxation, how to measure tax efficiency, and how to reduce the impact of taxes on a portfolio.

Hopefully we've convinced you why it is important to manage your client's portfolio with taxes in mind. Tax considerations, however, are just one element of managing assets for private wealth clients. Suppose that only 50% of your private client's assets are invested in your tax-aware investment strategy. The other 50% of assets are tied up in a company that was the primary source of wealth creation for your client: Ivy Lee started a business in her early 20s that succeeded far beyond her initial expectations. While she has accumulated liquid assets outside of that business, a substantial portion of her net worth is held in company stock. From your earlier readings in the course of the CFA Program, you realize that this is a very risky position. Taken in the aggregate, her portfolio is undiversified; however, to sell the position outright would create an enormous tax liability or lead to a loss of control over the business she created. How, then, do you help the client achieve her goals? This reading discusses some practical tools that you can employ to manage the risk of this concentrated position.

Finally, Ivy and Charles want to maximize the likelihood that the strong financial foundation they have created will survive to provide support for their children's and grandchildren's future endeavors. Ivy has frequently heard the phrase "shirtsleeves to shirtsleeves in three generations," meaning that family wealth rarely survives beyond three generations. Some variation of that saying exists in many cultures. The Lees want your help to create a structure that will counter that conventional wisdom. While this reading won't make you an estate planning expert, it will prepare you to identify estate planning opportunities that may help the Lees achieve that goal and to work more effectively with the Lees' estate planning professionals toward that end.

2. GENERAL PRINCIPLES OF TAXATION: COMPONENTS OF RETURN AND TAX STATUS OF THE ACCOUNT

a compare taxation of income, wealth, and wealth transfers;

b describe global considerations of jurisdiction that are relevant to taxation;

In many countries, tax rates can exceed 50%, significantly eroding realized returns (capital gains, interest, and/or dividend income). An understanding of tax structures will improve the portfolio manager's decisions on behalf of the taxable client, decisions such as what asset classes and securities to invest in and when to realize gains and losses. (The readings on asset allocation address issues important to the taxable investor, including conducting an asset allocation study using after-tax returns and such pragmatic issues as the tax implications of rebalancing strategies. This reading does not revisit those issues; instead, it focuses on broader issues frequently faced by the private wealth adviser.) Three foundational elements of investment taxation should be considered when managing private wealth assets: 1) taxation of the components of return, 2) the tax status of the account, and 3) the jurisdiction that applies to the investor (and/or account). We address each of them, in turn.

2.1 Taxation of the Components of Return

Although the specifics of tax codes are country- and jurisdiction-specific, the following general categories of taxes are widely recognized:

- *Income Tax.* Income tax is calculated as a percentage of taxable income, often with different rates applied to various levels of income. Wages, rents, dividends, and interest earned are commonly treated as taxable income. Cross-border investments, common in the portfolios of many wealthy families, may also create taxable income in the investor's home country as well as in the country in which the investment is located.

- *Gains Tax.* Capital gains are the profits based on price appreciation that result from the sale of an asset, including financial assets. Gains are often distinguished from income and taxed at different rates.

- *Wealth or Property Tax.* A wealth or property tax most often refers to the taxation of real property (real estate) but may also apply to financial and other assets. Such taxes are generally assessed annually. Comprehensive wealth taxes apply in a limited number of countries but are increasingly being considered by other countries as a mechanism to raise revenue.

- *Stamp Duties.* A number of countries impose a tax on the purchase price of shares or real estate. Foreign investors may be subject to higher rates than domestic investors.
- *Wealth Transfer Tax.* A wealth transfer tax is assessed as assets are transferred from one owner to another using some mechanism other than an outright sale/purchase transaction. Examples of wealth transfer taxes include "estate" or "inheritance" taxes paid at the investor's death and "gift" taxes paid on transfers made during the investor's lifetime. In some cases, these taxes are the responsibility of the person transferring the asset; in other cases, these taxes are imposed on the recipient.

Therefore, investors pay taxes on what they *earn* (income and gains tax), what they *own* (wealth or property tax), what they *buy* (stamp duty tax), and what they *transfer* (gift and estate tax). The income and capital gains taxes are the ones that most directly affect the day-to-day portfolio management of private client assets. These taxes are briefly described next, along with some tax preferences frequently accorded to real estate investments.

2.1.1 Interest, Dividends, and Withholding Taxes

Most bonds, debt instruments, and interest-bearing accounts produce income in the form of interest payments. Many countries' tax codes create preferential treatment for some types of interest income. For example, in Italy interest income on government bonds is taxed at a lower rate. In the United States, income from state and local government bonds (municipal bonds) is often exempt from both federal and state income taxes; unless special provisions exist, interest is taxed at the ordinary income tax rate.

Double taxation is a term used to describe situations in which income is taxed twice. For example, corporate earnings are taxed at the company level and then that portion of earnings paid as dividends is taxed again at the investor level. Some countries mitigate the burden of double taxation of dividend income with specific exemptions or provisions in the tax code. Here are some examples:

- In Australia, if your personal tax rate is higher than the corporate tax rate, you will earn "franking" credits such that you only pay the difference between your personal tax rate and the corporate tax rate.
- In the United States, dividends from most domestic companies and qualifying foreign companies are taxed at a lower tax rate if you hold the stock for at least 60 days. (**Qualified dividends** are generally dividends from shares in domestic corporations and certain qualified foreign corporations which have been held for at least a specified minimum period of time—in the United States, 61 days for common stock, 91 days for preferred stock. The position must be unhedged.)

Portfolio managers investing on behalf of private clients must also consider the tax ramifications of cross-border investments. **Withholding taxes** are often imposed in the country in which the investment is made, most frequently on payments of interest, dividends and royalties. The income will be taxed in the country in which it was earned and may be taxed again in the home country of the investor. The taxing jurisdiction will withhold taxes on the *gross* income earned within the jurisdiction—without regard for offsetting investment expenses or losses that may be available from the taxpayer's other investment activities.

2.1.2 Capital Gains Taxes

To estimate the tax liability associated with a particular trade, we need to know the asset's **tax basis** and holding period. In many cases, the tax basis is the amount that was paid to acquire an asset, or its 'cost' basis. In the case of equities, this would be the share price multiplied by the number of shares plus commissions and other trading costs. Other assets, such as discount or premium bonds or REITs, may be subject to annual accounting adjustments to the tax basis.

The tax basis serves as the foundation for calculating a **capital gain or loss**, which equals the selling price (net of commissions and other trading costs) less the tax basis. Capital gains may be realized or unrealized capital gains. A realized capital gain is the profit "booked" when the asset is sold. An unrealized capital gain is the appreciation on an asset currently held in the portfolio. If an asset is sold at a loss, the loss may often be used to offset a realized capital gain.

There are circumstances where the tax basis may be other than the investor's actual cost basis. For example, in some countries, such as the United States, there is a basis "step-up" on death, meaning that someone who inherits an asset would have a tax basis equal to the fair market value of the asset on the date of death. No capital gains taxes are due as a result of this step-up in basis. Other countries have laws that lead to a step-up in tax basis upon death or upon a change in citizenship or residency, but the unrealized, embedded gains would be subject to tax.

Capital gains may also be short-term or long-term capital gains. The *holding period* is the length of time between the purchase and sale of an asset. Capital gains are generally taxed as income unless the asset is held longer than some minimum period specified by the tax laws of the relevant jurisdiction. Where such provisions exist, gains realized from assets held for the minimum period are taxed at a lower rate, called the *long-term capital gains* rate. Governments that apply lower tax rates to long-term gains create a tax incentive for long-term investors and a disincentive to speculative short-term trading. In these jurisdictions, stocks are generally more tax-efficient investments than taxable bonds since a significant portion of equity returns comes from tax-advantaged appreciation.

In some jurisdictions, there is a distinction between investment gains and trading gains. For example, in a jurisdiction where capital gains are tax-free or taxed at lower rates, the tax benefits may be lost if the investor is considered to be in the *business* of stock or real estate trading.

2.1.3 Real Estate Taxes

While many countries provide favorable tax treatment for an individual's principal residence—exempting capital gains arising from the sale of the residence—real estate *investments* are subject to a broader range of tax preferences. How the real estate is owned and financed will have a significant bearing on the after-tax returns generated by the investment.

Generally, jurisdictions tax the net income from a real estate investment, allowing such expenses as maintenance, interest, and depreciation to be deducted from gross income prior to calculating the tax liability. Where interest expenses are deductible, it may be attractive to finance a real estate purchase even if the investor has the funds necessary to pay the purchase price in full.

Depreciation expenses may also be deductible. For example, an investor buys a property in a jurisdiction that allows the investor to depreciate the property over 10 years. A portion of the purchase price of the building may be recorded as an expense during each year of ownership, reducing the investor's income tax liability. The depreciation expense is deducted from the investor's cost basis. These deductions are usually recaptured on a sale of the investment if the sales price exceeds the depreciated cost base of the asset involved.

In some countries, one real estate investment can be exchanged for another in a qualifying exchange, enabling the investor to defer capital gains taxes until the second property is sold.

2.2 The Tax Status of the Account

The tax status of the account will also factor into investment decisions for private clients. There are three principal types of accounts: taxable, tax-deferred, and tax-exempt. In a **taxable account**, the normal tax rules of the jurisdiction apply. For a **tax-deferred account**, investment and contributions may be made on a pre-tax basis and investment returns accumulate on a tax-deferred basis until funds are withdrawn, at which time they are taxed at ordinary income tax rates. In a **tax-exempt account**, no taxes are assessed during the investment, contribution, or withdrawal phase, nor are they assessed on investment returns. The tax status of an account is an important factor in understanding the tax implications of investment and wealth management decisions.

Pension funds, endowment funds, and foundations are generally *tax-exempt*. The retirement accounts of individuals are usually *tax-deferred*. In Australia, retirement superannuation plans are taxed but at a discounted rate relative to the individual investor rate. Exhibit 2 shows the tax status for different accounts by investor type.

Exhibit 2 Tax Status by Type of Investor and Account

Type of Investment Account	Typical Tax Status
Individual Investor	
Individual Brokerage Account	Taxable
Individual Retirement Account	Tax-deferred
Roth IRA (US)	Tax-exempt
Personal Trust	Taxable
Charitable Trust	Tax-exempt
Institutional Investor	
Foundation	Tax-exempt
Corporation	Taxable
Corporation – Nonprofit	Tax-exempt
Insurance Company	Taxable
Pension Fund	Tax-exempt
Superannuation Fund (Australia)	Taxable at a discounted rate
Endowment	Tax-exempt
Sovereign Wealth Fund	Tax-exempt

EXAMPLE 1 TAX CONSIDERATIONS FOR THE PRIVATE CLIENT

You are managing a portfolio for Hugh Jackson, a private wealth client. Just a few weeks remain in the tax year.

	Market Value	Unrealized Short-Term Gain	Realized Short-Term Gain	Unrealized Long-Term Gain	Realized Long-Term Gain	Year-to-Date Income (Dividends / Interest)
Domestic Equities	€8,000,000	−€500,000	€250,000	€2,500,000	€500,000	€120,000
Domestic Fixed Income	€5,000,000	0	0	€1,000,000	0	€150,000

(continued)

Income-Producing Real Estate	€1,000,000	0	0	€500,000	0	€60,000
Total	€14,000,000	–€500,000	€250,000	€4,000,000	€500,000	€330,000

1 Assuming this is a taxable account, what tax considerations are likely to influence your portfolio decisions?
2 If this were a tax-deferred retirement account and the client plans to take a €450,000 pre-tax withdrawal by year-end, how might the portfolio decisions be different?

Solution to 1:

- The client is subject to tax on the realized capital gains and income received year-to-date. (€250,000 + €500,000 + €330,000 = €1,080,000.)
- The dividend and interest income may be eligible for preferential tax treatment depending on the composition of the portfolio.
- The taxable component of the real estate income may be reduced through deductions of maintenance, interest, and depreciation.
- The €500,000 in short-term losses should be evaluated for possible sale prior to year-end. The losses could be used to offset the €250,000 in realized short-term gains and half of the realized long-term gains while raising the cash needed to fund the planned withdrawal.
- Any remaining long-term gain is subject to tax, typically at a rate lower than the investor's marginal income tax rate.

Solution to 2:

The client would be taxed only on the €450,000 withdrawal. The applicable tax rate is the client's marginal income tax rate. The distinctions between realized and unrealized capital gains and losses are irrelevant in a tax-deferred retirement portfolio.

3. THE JURISDICTION THAT APPLIES TO THE INVESTOR

c discuss and analyze the tax efficiency of investments;

Tax systems are used by governments to encourage or discourage certain activities (e.g., investing in domestic companies or saving for retirement). These incentives vary globally and can change as the needs and objectives of the government change. Rather than listing the specific rules for each country and jurisdiction, this reading provides a general framework to understand how different tax environments may affect clients. Private wealth advisers must become familiar with the tax provisions of each jurisdiction that affects their clients.

In general, the main types of tax systems we find internationally fall into three broad categories:

- Tax havens
- Territorial tax systems
- Worldwide tax systems, which may be based on either citizenship or residency

The Jurisdiction that Applies to the Investor

A **tax haven** is a country or independent area with no or very low tax rates for foreign investors. The Cayman Islands are a well-known tax haven—with no tax on income or capital gains, no tax on property holdings (other than on the transfer of a property to another individual or entity), and no corporate taxes. Similarly, the British Virgin Islands or The Bahamas do not tax income or capital gains. Russia and Saudi Arabia also have very low tax rates but aren't considered tax havens since the favorable tax treatment is reserved for residents.

Other jurisdictions operate **territorial tax systems**, where only locally-sourced income is taxed. For example, Hong Kong, a special administrative region of China, has much lower tax rates than the mainland and does not tax capital gains, dividends, or income earned outside of Hong Kong SAR. Examples of other territorial tax systems include the Philippines and Singapore.

Jurisdictions operating under a **worldwide tax system** tax all income regardless of its source. Examples are Switzerland, France, Germany, India, Canada, and Japan, among many other countries. Worldwide tax systems can give rise to double taxation as the country in which investments are made may impose taxes on this same income. This type of double taxation is often addressed through tax credits provided by the home country or through other forms of relief, such as tax treaties (i.e., bilateral agreements between countries).

Because countries operating under a worldwide tax system generally impose those taxes only on individuals considered to be residents of that country, residence rules become very important. Residence rules specify how much time a person can spend in a country without becoming a taxable resident. If an individual spends time in more than one country, tax treaties can play an important role in determining tax residence. Most tax treaties contain *tie-breaker* rules that prevent an individual from being considered a resident of more than one country at the same time.

The United States is one of the few countries that taxes citizens on a worldwide basis *regardless of residence*. As a result, US citizens living in Hong Kong SAR will be subject to US tax on their worldwide income, whereas Canadian citizens also living in Hong Kong SAR will not be taxed by Canada on income earned outside of Canada.

When working with wealthy families, it is essential to develop a full understanding of the tax jurisdictions that will affect investment and estate planning. It is not uncommon to have a client who is a citizen of one country, a resident of another, and who has investments (and heirs) in several others. A good rule of thumb is to start with the tax rules of the investor's home country. The home country rules may influence decisions on how to own assets in another country. The following example illustrates the various issues that must be addressed when considering cross-border investments for clients.

CONSIDERATIONS IN CROSS-BORDER INVESTING

Josie Boyd is a Hong Kong citizen living in Hong Kong SAR. She wants to invest in income-producing residential real estate in the United States. The ownership structure of an investment will have a material impact on its after-tax return. Consider the following:

- Hong Kong SAR operates under a territorial tax system; thus, it would not tax any income or gains arising from the US-located investment.

- The United States taxes investments in the United States regardless of the investor's citizenship or residence, taxing both income from the investment and any capital gain on a sale of an investment in which real estate is involved. The investment may also be subject to US estate and gift taxes. Depending on the location of the US investment, state taxation may come into play in addition to any federal tax obligation.

- Hong Kong SAR also has no inheritance or estate tax, so the only tax considerations to be addressed are those arising from the United States.

- If Josie owns the property directly in her name,
  - she may be subject to tax withholding on the gross rental income, with no opportunity to offset that income with investment expenses; and
  - there would be an estate tax payable upon her death, although the value of the estate would be reduced by any outstanding mortgage on the property.
- If Josie owns the property through a US corporation,
  - the US corporation could be owned by a non-US entity, either Josie herself or a non-US corporation, and investment expenses could be used to offset the rental income. Only the net income would be subject to withholding when it is paid to the non-US owner; and
  - at Josie's death,
    - the shares of the company either pass to Josie's heirs, or
    - if the company is liquidated, any gains on the property would be taxed at the corporate capital gains tax rate, which is higher than the capital gains tax rate for individuals. In addition, any retained earnings would be subject to withholding.
- If Josie owns the property through a non-US corporation,
  - the value of the asset would not be subject to US estate taxes at Josie's death: The shares of the company pass to Josie's beneficiaries, not the property itself, on her death. As a non-US company, it is not subject to US taxation. (This is not true in all countries, however.)

Clearly, the jurisdictional tax considerations are an integral part of any cross-border investment decision. While we used a corporation to illustrate some of the issues that might arise, corporations are not the only alternative, and for certain investments, they may be a poor choice. Trusts, private insurance companies, and private foundations are other alternative structures that can be used to maximize the after-tax return for private clients. The best solution is one tailored to the client's investment *and* estate planning objectives. An international tax specialist is needed to ensure that all relevant issues are considered in cross-border investment.

Exhibit 3 summarizes some relevant tax rates for the largest 25 jurisdictions by GDP as of 2018.

Exhibit 3   Top Marginal Tax Rates for Selected Jurisdictions, Largest 25 Jurisdictions by GDP

Income Tax Rate %

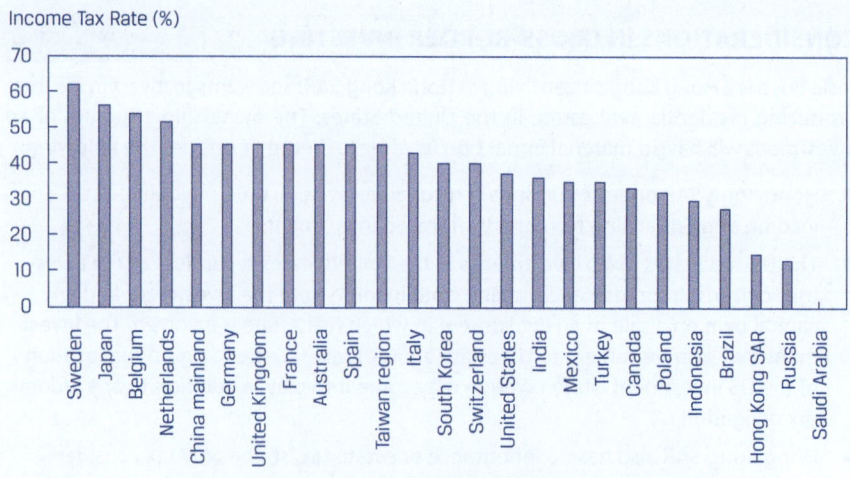

Exhibit 3   (Continued)

Capital Gains Tax Rate %

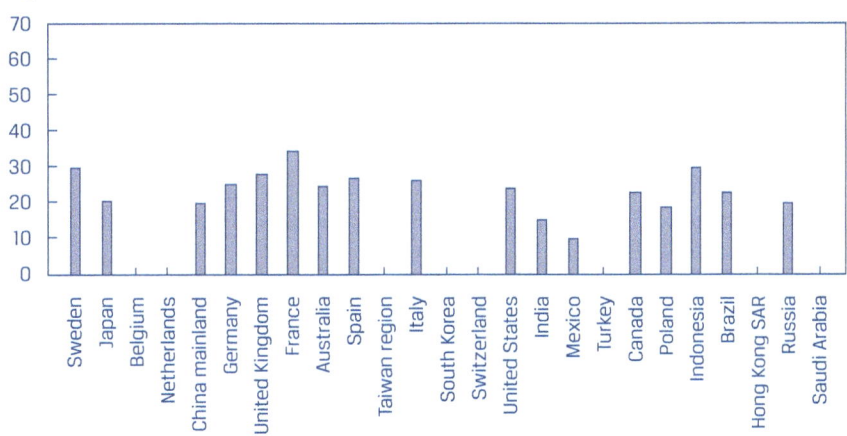

Estate Tax Rate %

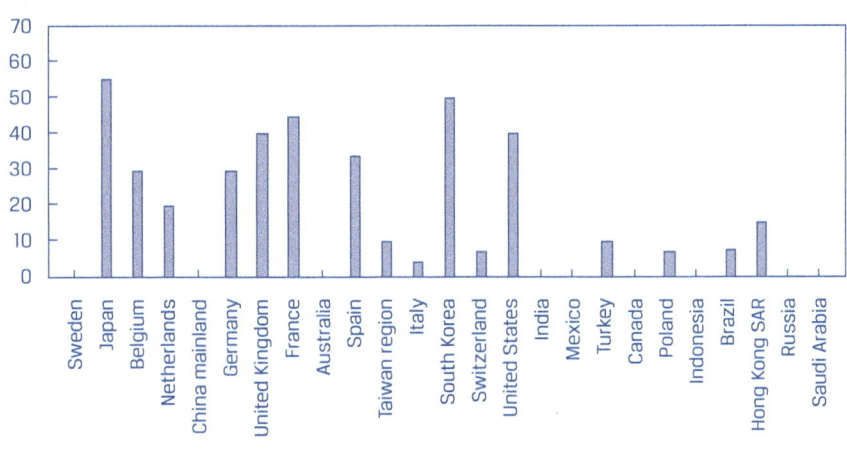

Note: Tax rates are as of 2018.
Sources: tradingeconomics.com and taxfoundation.org.

EXAMPLE 2   JURISDICTIONAL CONSIDERATIONS IN PORTFOLIO MANAGEMENT FOR PRIVATE CLIENTS

Franz Schmid is a portfolio manager for Global Wealth Advisors (GWA), an investment management firm focused on private clients. Franz manages diversified portfolios of stocks and bonds. GWA has recently been retained by two new clients—Valerie Low, based in Singapore, and David Muller, based in Switzerland. Each has a portfolio of CHF10 million held in a taxable account. Valerie and David have similar risk and return objectives, and each has agreed to an asset allocation of 50% domestic stocks and bonds (Singaporean and Swiss, respectively) and 50% US stocks and bonds. Singapore operates under a territorial tax regime. Switzerland operates under a worldwide tax regime. Based on the general principles of territorial and worldwide tax regimes, describe the implications of the two countries' tax regimes for each client's wealth management strategy.

Solution:

Franz must first determine the citizenship of each client to determine which tax rules must be considered in structuring the portfolio. He learns that they both are citizens of the country in which they currently reside.

Home Country Portfolios

Valerie Low. As a citizen and resident of Singapore, Valerie will be taxed only on income earned in Singapore. Because Singapore also exempts most dividends from Singapore companies and most domestic interest income from taxation, Franz's management of the Singaporean stock and bond portfolio will be unconstrained by tax considerations. His chief concern relates to the US taxation of the US stock and bond portfolio.

David Muller. As a citizen and resident of Switzerland, David will be subject to Swiss tax on all of his investments and US tax on his US investments. In broad terms, Switzerland taxes dividend and interest income but exempts individual investors' capital gains from taxation. Between local and federal taxes, David's dividend and interest income is likely to be taxed at a rate well over 40%. The portfolio Franz constructs for David will emphasize high-growth equities, where a large portion of the total return is derived from capital gains.

US Portfolios

Valerie Low. No tax treaty exists between Singapore and the United States, so the United States will impose a 30% withholding tax on gross dividends. Most interest income on government and corporate bonds is exempt from withholding, provided the investor supplies the issuer or corporate trustee proof of beneficial ownership. Because they are held by a non-US investor, any capital gains on the stocks and bonds in the US portfolio will not be taxed by the United States. The portfolio Franz develops for Valerie will emphasize fixed-income securities and high-growth, low-dividend equities.

David Muller. There is a tax treaty between Switzerland and the United States that will reduce the withholding rate on David's US dividends from 30% to 15%, a substantial savings. Thus, David's US equity portfolio may have a higher allocation to dividend-paying stocks than would Valerie's portfolio. Any capital gains on the stocks and bonds in the portfolio will not be taxed by the United States, and most interest income will be exempt from US taxation under the same rules applied in Valerie's circumstances.

Wealth and Estate Taxes

Valerie Low. Singapore has no estate tax, and there is no estate tax treaty between Singapore and the United States. The US estate tax applies to US stock holdings but not to holdings of qualifying corporate and government bonds. Therefore, Valerie's estate will be required to pay US estate taxes on her US stock investments. Franz may look to create a non-US company to hold Valerie's US stock investments.

David Muller. Switzerland's estate tax is relatively modest compared to the US estate tax rate. While there is an estate tax treaty between Switzerland and the United States, to obtain the estate tax exemption, David would have to disclose his entire net worth to the United States, something he is reluctant to do. Thus, David would like to consider the creation of a non-US company to hold his US investments. This is not a clear-cut solution for David, however. If the country in which this company is created does not have an income tax treaty with the United States, David's dividend income would be subject to the 30% withholding tax rate and capital gains realized within the company would be distributed to David as dividends, which are taxable in Switzerland. Short of pursuing other, more complex, options (e.g., a partnership or trust), David's best option appears to be direct ownership and full disclosure of his net worth.

INTERNATIONAL TRANSPARENCY, THE COMMON REPORTING STANDARD, AND FATCA

In the past, it was not uncommon for people investing on a cross-border basis to assume that their home country would not know about income generated outside that country. While not reporting the foreign income and assets to a home country with a worldwide tax system would have constituted illegal tax evasion, the existence of bank secrecy in such countries as Switzerland facilitated such wrongful activity. Today, substantial information exchange regimes are in operation, including the *automatic* information exchange under what is known as the Common Reporting Standard. Tax authorities have also increased their focus on the activities of those who enable tax evasion, such as banks and investment managers. Wealthy international families, with a growing awareness of these rules and of the significant penalties associated with tax evasion, are increasingly understanding the need for tax compliance. Thus, they are highly appreciative of investment management strategies that properly analyze tax exposures and make use of legal tax minimization opportunities.

Taxpaying obligations are also accompanied by reporting requirements internationally, and two major regulations are now in place to promote tax transparency and disclosure of beneficial ownership.

The Common Reporting Standard (CRS), also known as the Standard for Automatic Exchange of Financial Account Information, was developed by the OECD with G20 countries and is a reciprocal requirement for the automatic exchange of financial account information. As of April 2019, more than 100 jurisdictions have committed to implementing the Standard, including Switzerland and other financial centers.

FATCA, the Foreign Account Tax Compliance Act, is a US program designed to ensure that US taxpayers pay the appropriate taxes on wealth held outside the country. Financial institutions are required to report this information on US account holders. Failure to do so triggers a 30% withholding on all US income.

EXAMPLE 3 MAKING USE OF TAX TREATIES TO ENHANCE THE AFTER-TAX RETURN

Your client is a resident of Hong Kong SAR and is interested in adding "safe haven" assets to a portfolio. The client asked that you consider adding Swiss equites and bonds to the portfolio. (Switzerland has long been considered a "safe haven" for investors; it is at the center of Europe, has a stable political climate, and is economically integrated with most of the world.) After research, you have identified Swiss equities and bonds that you believe will fit with the client's investment profile.

You contemplate adding to the portfolio the following equities and bonds, with the following estimated returns:

Swiss equities: CHF200,000, producing annual dividends of CHF5,000 and projected annual appreciation of 5% (CHF10,000)

Swiss bonds: CHF200,000, producing annual interest payments of 3% (CHF6,000)

In your projections, you assume that the appreciation in the equities will be realized through a sale of the shares at year end. So, for your client the total return on the CHF400,000 portfolio will be:

Dividends: CHF5,000

Capital gains: CHF10,000

Interest income: CHF6,000

Total gross income, pre-tax: CHF21,000

Projected return: 5.25%

1 What questions do you need to ask your client in relation to tax matters, and what information regarding Hong Kong SAR and Swiss taxation do you need in order to determine the after-tax return?
2 How can returns on the portfolio be enhanced by focusing on tax treaties?

Solution to 1:

You need to confirm that the client is not a citizen or permanent resident of a jurisdiction that operates under a worldwide tax regime. (For example, US citizens and permanent residents are taxable in the United States even if not currently residing there.) You also need to confirm the Hong Kong SAR tax treatment of the Swiss portfolio. Here, your client confirms that under Hong Kong SAR tax law there is no Hong Kong SAR taxation on interest, dividends, or capital gains earned in relation to the contemplated Swiss investments.

You also need to understand the Swiss tax position. On review, you confirm with Swiss advisers that Swiss inheritance taxes would not apply to a non-Swiss investor (except on real estate) and that capital gains are tax-free. However, you also learn that Switzerland applies a 35% withholding tax on interest and dividends to foreign investors.

Thus, the after-tax return for your client is estimated as follows:

Total gross income, pre-tax: CHF21,000

35% Swiss withholding tax on CHF11,000 (dividends and interest): CHF3,850

After-tax income: CHF17,150

Projected after-tax return: 4.29% (CHF17,150/CHF400,000).

Solution to 2:

You check on whether a tax treaty exists between Hong Kong SAR, the place of residence of your client, and Switzerland, and you find that there is one. Under the treaty, a qualifying resident of Hong Kong SAR is entitled to a reduction in Swiss withholding taxes on both dividends and interest. In the case of dividends, the withholding rate is reduced from 35% to 10%; in the case of interest, the withholding rate is reduced from 35% to 0%.

Your calculation of the after-tax return is revised as follows:

Total gross income pre-tax: CHF21,000

10% Swiss withholding tax on CHF5,000 (dividends): CHF500

0% Swiss withholding tax on CHF6,000 (interest): CHF0

After-tax income: CHF20,500

Projected after-tax return: 5.13%

In order to recover the Swiss withholding tax, your client, with your help, would apply online to the Hong Kong SAR Inland Revenue Department for a Certificate of Resident Status and then submit it online to the Swiss Federal Tax Administration with details on the withholding tax imposed for the processing of the refund.

MEASURING TAX EFFICIENCY WITH AFTER-TAX RETURNS

d analyze the impact of taxes on capital accumulation and decumulation in taxable, tax-exempt, and tax-deferred accounts;

We've shown how taxes can materially affect an investor's net returns. Not only do they reduce the investor's return in the year they were paid, they also affect longer-term returns through the lost opportunity to compound gross returns over time. When managing portfolios for taxable investors, it is important to measure the tax efficiency of investments. We do this by quantifying the effects of taxation on returns. Calculating after-tax returns allows us to do a better job of selecting securities, managing trades, and evaluating the performance of portfolios. In this section, we discuss the "tax efficiency" of various asset classes and the calculation of after-tax returns.

4.1 Tax Efficiency of Various Asset Classes and Investment Strategies

A **tax-efficient strategy** is one that gives up very little of its return to the friction of taxes. Generally speaking, equity portfolios are often more tax efficient than strategies that rely on derivatives, real assets, or taxable fixed income. 1) Dividends on stocks often receive preferential tax treatment. 2) Capital gains are taxed less heavily than ordinary income in many jurisdictions. 3) The flexibility to manage the timing of the sell decisions gives asset managers an additional measure of control over the tax burden.

Alternative asset classes are favored by investors for their uncorrelated returns, but the tax considerations associated with these investments can be considerably more complicated than those associated with stocks and bonds. Real estate, timberland, and oil and gas partnerships often have their own tax rules. Market-neutral strategies typically employ leverage, short sales, convertible debt, options, futures contracts, and straddles. The tax rules around these instruments can be difficult to understand even for a tax expert. It is important to model these asset classes' contributions to portfolio risk and return on an after-tax, after-fee basis.

Within an asset class, the portfolio management process and style of investing can affect the tax efficiency of the portfolio. Generally speaking, higher-yield and higher-turnover strategies tend to be less tax efficient. However, the timing of the trading patterns is also an important factor. For example, momentum strategies, which tend to be high turnover strategies, are relatively tax efficient. They hold their winners and sell their losers—letting gains run and accelerating the realization of losses (which create a tax benefit, despite the tendency to have a higher turnover). On the other hand, value and small-cap strategies tend to be less tax efficient as they are likely to sell a security when it reaches a pre-determined target price and thus realize gains more frequently.

Using a "style box" approach to selecting managers can also create tax inefficiencies. A style box approach selects specialist managers to fill targeted large-cap, small-cap, value, growth, and alternative allocations within the equity portfolio. At the manager level, these style constraints force managers to realize gains if a security moves out of their style (or risk losing the account due to "style drift"). At the total fund level, rebalancing to the targeted style allocation can create additional taxable gains.

4.2 Calculating After-Tax Returns

To measure tax efficiency, we address the various return measures of interest to the private wealth manager:

- *After-tax holding period return*: Returns are adjusted for the tax liability generated in the period. There is an implicit, simplifying assumption that taxes are withdrawn from (or tax benefits deposited to) the account at the time the asset is sold. This measure allows an investor to judge the tax efficiency of an investment strategy, including how returns are affected by taxes on interest, dividends, and realized capital gains. After-tax holding period returns can be geometrically linked and annualized in the normal way.

- *After-tax post-liquidation return*: Post-liquidation returns assume that the portfolio is liquidated at the end of a hypothetical investment horizon—usually 1, 3, 5, and 10 years—and the taxes are paid on those gains. The post-liquidation measure allows an investor to consider the impact of the embedded tax liabilities (i.e., the unrealized capital gains) on ending wealth. This is especially useful in the evaluation of commingled funds, such as mutual funds.

- *After-tax excess returns*: Similar to regular returns, after-tax returns can be compared against a benchmark, helping an investor understand whether the tax drag is eroding the return benefits of a strategy.

- *Tax-efficiency ratio*: This ratio is the after-tax annualized total return divided by the pre-tax annualized total return. It helps to quickly sort managers by the efficiency of the product offering. When used in combination with the other measures, it is a useful tool to identify managers who can effectively manage taxable portfolios.

Each of these is discussed next.

4.2.1 After-Tax Holding Period Returns

The pre-tax holding period return, R, is calculated as the change in value (value − $value_0$) plus the income divided by the initial portfolio value:

$$R = \frac{(value - value_0) + income}{value_0} \tag{1}$$

The after-tax holding period return, R', modifies this formula to account for the tax liability created by the income received and capital gains realized in the period.

$$R' = \frac{(value - value_0) + income - tax}{value_0} \tag{2}$$

This is mathematically equivalent to:

$$R' = R - \frac{tax}{value_0}$$

The tax due in the period can be calculated by multiplying each component of realized return by the appropriate marginal tax rate. If we assume that there are a number of transactions (realized capital gains or losses, dividends, interest payments, etc.) that each produce a tax consequence and that the tax rate for a particular transaction i is denoted as t_i, then we can calculate the total tax for a portfolio in a given period as:

$$\text{tax} = \sum_{i=1}^{n} \text{transaction}_i \times t_i$$

If after-tax returns are calculated monthly, the cumulative after-tax return, R'_G, can be calculated by geometrically linking the monthly returns:

$$R'_G = \left[\left(1 + R'_1\right)\left(1 + R'_2\right)\ldots\left(1 + R'_n\right)\right]^{1/n} - 1$$

This equation is merely an *estimate* of how taxes can be expected to affect the compounding of the portfolio. It assumes that when capital losses are realized, sufficient capital gains from other investments exist so that the investor may deduct the losses in full. If there are no gains, the deductibility of investment losses can result in an after-tax return that is higher than the pre-tax return. The tax liability is deducted and the tax benefit is added to the account each period as if it were a cash flow, thus reducing the magnitude and volatility of returns. In practice, however, the intricacies of local laws and regulations mean that not all investors will receive full credit for the tax losses realized. Also, taxes are usually paid on an annual or quarterly basis rather than at the time of the taxable event and from an account other than the investment account (i.e., the investor's checking account). Thus, the taxable investment account is unlikely to compound at precisely the after-tax return rate.

APPROXIMATING MONTHLY AFTER-TAX RETURNS

In many organizations, pre-tax holding period returns are automatically calculated by the firm's accounting systems on a daily basis, while after-tax returns are only calculated monthly. If you want an intra-month after-tax return that accounts for any cash flows during the period, this can be done using the modified Dietz method. We show the calculation of after-tax returns using the modified Dietz method:

$$R' = R - \frac{\text{tax}}{\text{value}_0 + \sum_{j=1}^{N} C_j (N - j) / N}$$

where:

tax = cumulative tax liability for all transactions during the month
value_0 = initial value at the beginning of the month
C_j = cash flow on day j
N = number of calendar days in a month
$N - j$ = number of days from flow to end of month

If, for example,

- the initial value of the portfolio on 1 January is $500,000,
- a $3,500 dividend is received on 10 January,
- the dividend tax rate is 20%, and
- the monthly pre-tax total return for the portfolio is 2.50%,

then the after-tax return can be approximated as

$$2.50\% - \frac{0.20(3{,}500)}{500{,}000 + \frac{3{,}500(31-10)}{31}} = 2.36\%.$$

4.2.2 After-Tax Post-Liquidation Returns

When evaluating a mutual fund or other commingled vehicle as a potential investment, the taxable investor may need to consider the effect of unrealized capital gains embedded in the fund. One measure that can assist in the analysis is the **post-liquidation return**. The post-liquidation return assumes that all portfolio holdings are sold as of the end date of the analysis and that the resulting capital gains tax that would be due is deducted from the ending portfolio value. The US Securities and Exchange Commission requires that mutual funds report the post-liquidation return as well as an after-tax return calculated under an assumption that all income and capital gain distributions are taxed at the maximum federal rate at the time of distribution and that the after-tax portion of the dividend and interest income return is reinvested in the fund.

To calculate the post-liquidation return, R_{PL}, we must subtract the embedded tax liability at the end of the final period assuming that all remaining capital gains taxes are paid as they would be if the portfolio were liquidated.

$$R_{PL} = \left[\left(1 + R_1'\right)\left(1 + R_2'\right)\ldots\left(1 + R_n'\right) - \frac{\text{liquidation tax}}{\text{final value}}\right]^{1/n} - 1$$

where the liquidation tax is given by:

liquidation tax = (final value − tax basis) * capital gains tax rate.

These standardized calculations make comparing the tax efficiency of portfolios very straightforward.

EXAMPLE 4 CALCULATING THE POST-LIQUIDATION RETURN

A portfolio posts the following pre-tax and after-tax annual returns:

	Pre-Tax Return	After-Tax Return
Year 1	3.0%	2.5%
Year 2	10.0%	9.0%
Year 3	5.0%	4.2%
Year 4	−2.0%	−1.5%
Year 5	5.0%	4.4%
Cumulative Return	22.41%	19.72%
Annualized Return	4.13%	3.66%

Assume the portfolio has embedded gains equal to 10% of the ending value and must pay capital gains taxes at a 20% rate.

What is the annualized post-liquidation return over the 5-year period?

Solution:

To calculate the post-liquidation return, we must first calculate the ending portfolio value. Given the five annualized after-tax returns shown, the final after-tax portfolio value is calculated as follows:

(1 + 0.025)(1 + 0.09)(1 + 0.042)(1 − 0.015)(1 + 0.044) = 1.197.

The after-tax returns compounded in this way account for the tax on distributions and realized capital gains but do not account for any unrealized gains. The assumed tax liability from unrealized capital gains at liquidation is 2% of the final value (10% embedded gain times a 20% tax rate).

Therefore, the portfolio value net of the tax liability is 1.177:

$$1.197 - 0.02 = 1.177,$$

and the annualized post-liquidation return is 3.32%:

$$1.177^{(1/5)} - 1 = 3.32\%.$$

This compares to an annualized return for the non-taxable investor of 4.13%.

4.2.3 After-Tax Excess Returns

In an important article on tax management—"Is Your Alpha Big Enough to Cover Its Taxes?"—Jeffrey and Arnott (1993) showed that more than 85% of the active managers in their study underperformed the capitalization-weighted index fund on an after-tax basis. More recently, Sialm and Zhang (Forthcoming) found that, on average, high-tax bracket shareholders invested in equity mutual funds would have lost 108 basis points (bps) per year as a result of taxes due on investment income. This erosion of returns is similar in size to that created by fund expenses, a topic which has received much attention. Both papers confirm the widely-held belief that most mutual fund managers do not generate sufficient alpha to cover fees and taxes.

So, how do we measure the risk and return consequences of the tax management decisions? We use the **after-tax excess return**—the after-tax return of the portfolio, R', minus the after-tax return of the benchmark, B'. If the mandate is passive, the benchmark portfolio is an index. If the mandate is active, we might select an index as the benchmark *or* we could use a strategy benchmark—a model portfolio that represents the manager's stated investment approach. If we use an index as the benchmark, we are measuring whether the portfolio's excess return was sufficient to offset its tax burden. If we set the benchmark to be the model portfolio, we are measuring the implementation effects of tax management. In either case, the excess returns are calculated as follows:

x = pre-tax excess return = $R - B$, and

x' = after-tax excess return = $R' - B'$.

We use the following notation to measure the performance of a strategy on an after-tax basis:

R = portfolio pre-tax return
B = benchmark pre-tax return
R' and B' = after-tax returns for the portfolio and benchmark, respectively
x = pre-tax excess return
x' = after-tax excess return

The **tax alpha** isolates the benefit of tax management by subtracting the pre-tax excess return from the after-tax excess return:

α_{tax} = tax alpha = $x' - x$.

4.2.4 Tax-Efficiency Ratio

The **tax-efficiency ratio (TER)** is simply the after-tax return divided by the pre-tax return:

$$\text{TER} = \frac{R'}{R}$$

For example, if the total annualized return for a portfolio is 10% and the after-tax return is 8%, the tax-efficiency ratio would be 80% (= 0.08 / 0.10).

Exhibit 4 illustrates the extent to which the tax efficiency of even top-performing funds can vary. It plots the five-year pre-tax return of top-decile, no-load, small-cap mutual funds against their tax-efficiency ratios. The funds in this chart are all top-decile funds, having outperformed a majority of their peers over the five-year period. But this top-decile ranking is based on pre-tax returns. An important question for the private wealth investor is how much of that return do I get to keep? Ideally, you would want to focus on funds in the upper right-hand quadrant of the graph—the higher-returning, more-efficient funds. Most of the funds have a TER in the range of 70% to 75%, with annual returns of 10% to 10.5%. There are a few outliers, however. Fund A has a much higher pre-tax return than all of its peers. Its TER, though, is below the median TER of the group. Managers B and C have high TERs but returns that place them at the bottom of the group. Manager D is a negative outlier, with both returns and TER at the bottom of the group.

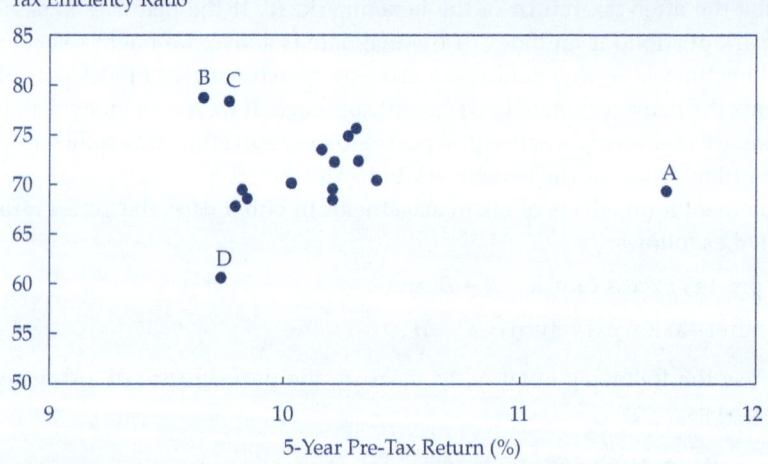

Exhibit 4 Comparing Managers Using Tax-Efficiency Ratios

The tax-efficiency ratio can help an analyst or portfolio manager understand which funds may be more appropriate for the taxable account of a private client. If the client's other investments generate tax losses, perhaps Manager A would be a good fit. While it is difficult to predict what the performance of these managers will be over the next five years, it is likely that their investment process will produce levels of tax efficiency similar to those that each has produced in the past.

Note that the tax-efficiency ratio is not as useful when returns are negative. For example, if a portfolio had a −10% pre-tax return and −12% after-tax return, the ratio would be 120% (−0.12/−0.10). We know, however, that this cannot be right; taxes are making the returns worse. Rather than relying on the TER, the analyst could choose to simply plot the after-tax returns versus pre-tax returns directly or look at other metrics, such as tax alpha, instead.

EXAMPLE 5 TAX AND THE CITY

Cary Broadshawl lives in New York City and holds a portfolio of stocks, bonds, and funds in a taxable brokerage account. The following table lists the federal and state tax rates that apply to her various investments. The marginal tax rate is the combined income tax rate—federal, state, and local—that applies to an incremental dollar of investment income that the investor earns. In this case, the highest marginal rate adds up to well over 50%, which is a difficult environment for an investor attempting to compound wealth over time.

Income Tax Rates by Jurisdiction	
US Federal income tax rate	37.00%
NY State income tax rate	8.82%
NY City income tax rate	3.88%
Federal net investment income (NII) tax rate	3.80%
Total tax rate on ordinary investment income	53.50%

Some asset classes qualify for preferential income tax rates.

Income Tax Rates by Asset	Tax Rate	Requirement
NY State municipal bond interest income	0.00%	For NY state residents
Out-of-state municipal bond interest income	12.70%	
Capital gains	36.50%	If held longer than 1 year
Qualified dividend income from stocks	36.50%	If held longer than 61 days
US Treasury interest income	40.80%	
Dividend income from REITs	43.50%	
Other fixed-income instruments	53.50%	
Non-qualified dividend income from stocks	53.50%	

Cary's adviser, Mr. Bigg, has constructed a diversified portfolio using mutual funds and exchange-traded funds. The following table highlights some characteristics of those funds, obtained from Mr. Bigg's data service provider.

	Annualized 5-Year Pre-Tax Return	5-Year Return after Taxes on Distributions	5-Year Post-Liquidation Return
Passive Equity ETF	10.85%	10.19%	8.71%
Active Equity Mutual Fund	12.05%	10.21%	9.05%
High-Yield Bond ETF	4.28%	1.72%	1.36%

Note: These returns are net of fund expenses and management fees.

Questions:

1. Calculate the tax-efficiency ratio for each of the funds in the table. Which of the funds is most tax efficient? Why are the other funds less tax efficient?

2. Mr. Bigg's data provider assumes the highest federal tax rates. How will the after-tax returns on the funds be affected by Cary's actual tax rates?

3. Cary bought 1,000 shares of Microsoft (MSFT) in her brokerage account for $130 per share at the beginning of the month and sold all 1,000 shares at the end of the month for $155 per share. She also received a dividend on MSFT of $0.50 per share during the month. Ignoring any transaction costs, what taxes are due?

4. Discuss the tax efficiency of Cary's MSFT investment. How could the tax efficiency have been improved?

5. Discuss the tax efficiency of this same trade assuming a sale price of $120 per share.

6. Cary's portfolio also holds several NY State tax-exempt municipal bonds. She plans to hold the bond to maturity. During the month, interest rates declined and the value of the bonds increased by 1%. While Cary didn't buy or sell during the month, she did receive 0.5% of the value of the bonds in interest payments. What are the pre-tax and after-tax returns of her NY state municipal bond portfolio?

Solution to 1:

- The tax-efficiency ratios for each of the funds are as follows:
    - Passive Equity ETF: 10.19/10.85 = 94%
    - Active Equity Mutual Fund: 10.21/12.05 = 85%
    - High-Yield Bond ETF: 1.72/4.28 = 40%
- The Passive Equity ETF is very tax efficient, as evidenced by its 94% tax-efficiency ratio. The after-tax return is only 0.66% lower than the pre-tax return over five years. The very low turnover in the passive portfolio produces little in the way of capital gains distributions. The tax drag from the ETF is largely due to the tax on dividend income. The post-liquidation returns are quite a bit lower but still tax efficient; in a passively managed portfolio, most shares are likely held long enough that the dividends qualify for preferential tax treatment. The capital gains are deferred (and the returns compounded) until Cary sells the ETF, and the gains on the sale of the ETF will qualify for the long-term capital gains tax rate.
- The Active Equity Mutual Fund has a higher pre-tax and after-tax return than the Passive Equity ETF but is less tax efficient as evidenced by its 85% tax-efficiency ratio. The after-tax return is 1.84% lower than the pre-tax return over five years. Ongoing capital gains, including the likelihood of some short-term gains, and dividend income on shares held for less than 61 days contribute to the lower tax-efficiency ratio. Still, on a post-liquidation basis, the active fund outperforms the passive fund by 34 basis points (9.05 – 8.71).
- The High-Yield Bond ETF is the least tax efficient. The after-tax return is 2.56% lower than the pre-tax returns. The tax-efficiency ratio is 40%, meaning that more than half of the compounded returns to this fund are paid in taxes. Interest income from high-yield bond investments receives no tax preferences. The after-tax return and post-liquidation returns are

Measuring Tax Efficiency with After-Tax Returns

very low in this case, making the High-Yield Bond ETF quite unattractive to a taxable investor, especially given that the fund is likely to have significantly higher risks than other investments.

Solution to 2:

- Because Cary lives in NY City, she is subject to state and local taxes as well as federal tax. Therefore, her actual after-tax returns are likely to be lower than the after-tax returns shown in in the table.

Solution to 3:

- Cary will realize a $25,000 capital gain on her sale of MSFT (1,000 shares × $25 gain per share). She will owe $13,375 in capital gains tax ($25,000 × 53.50% tax rate). Cary does not qualify for the long-term capital gains tax rate because she did not hold the stock for longer than a year.
- The $500 MSFT dividend received (1,000 shares × $0.50 per share) creates a $267.50 tax liability ($500 × 53.50% tax rate). Cary must pay the full tax rate because she did not hold the position for longer than 61 days to qualify for the preferential dividend tax rate.
- Her pre-tax return is 19.62%: (25,000 + 500) /130,000.
- Her after-tax return is 9.21%: [(25,000 + 500) − (500 × 0.535) − (25,000 × 0.535)]/130,000.

Solution to 4:

- This transaction was not very tax efficient, with a tax-efficiency ratio of 46% (9.12/19.62).
- The trading horizon of one month meant that Cary did not qualify for the lower tax rate on dividends and long-term capital gains.
- If Cary had held the stock for a year, then her transaction would have been much more tax efficient. Assuming she was still able to sell the stock for the same $155 per share after one year (and that she did not receive any further dividends), then her after-tax return would be 12.46%: [(25,000 + 500) − (500 × 0.365) − (25,000 × 0.365)]/130,000. The tax-efficiency ratio would be improved to 64% (12.46/19.62).

Solution to 5:

- If MSFT had fallen to $120 per share, then Cary's pre-tax return would be −7.31%: (−10,000 + 500)/130,000. She would realize a short-term capital loss of $10,000. This loss can be used to offset short-term gains that Cary realized at other times during the same tax year. The potential tax savings is $5,350 ($10,000 × 53.50%). Her after-tax return is −2.99% [(−10,000 + 500 − 500 × 0.535 + 10,000 × 0.535) / 130,000]. Yes, the after-tax return is higher than her pre-tax return. In estimating after-tax returns, we are most concerned with the portfolio impact. In this example, the transaction creates an economic benefit; the loss becomes smaller due to the potential tax savings, increasing the after-tax return.

Solution to 6:

- The pre-tax return of the municipal bond portfolio is 1.5% (1.0% gain + 0.5% interest).

- The after-tax return of the portfolio is 1.5%, the same as the pre-tax return. The capital gains are unrealized gains, and the interest income on New York municipal bonds is exempt from federal and state taxes.
- This is a very tax-efficient portfolio, with a tax-efficiency ratio of 100%. Cary plans to hold the bonds to maturity, so there are unlikely to be any capital gains realized from a sale prior to maturity. If she does sell the bonds prior to maturity, capital gains will likely qualify for the long-term capital gains tax rate. Also, the interest income is exempt from federal and state taxes.

5. TAXABLE, TAX-EXEMPT, AND TAX-DEFERRED ACCOUNTS: CAPITAL ACCUMULATION AND ASSET LOCATION

e   explain portfolio tax management strategies and their application;

We have shown how tax efficiency can be measured at the security and fund level, but tax considerations will also affect the client's financial plan, asset allocation strategy, and wealth transfer plan. Often clients will have a mixture of taxable, tax-deferred, and tax-exempt accounts. On the front end of the investment planning process, effective management must consider the interaction of the underlying investment strategy and the accounts in which it might be deployed. At the back end of the investment planning process (as the client approaches retirement and begins to spend down—decumulate—assets), there are additional opportunities to maximize the after-tax value of the client's assets.

Exhibit 5 shows various phases of developing and executing a financial plan and provides an example of tax-aware and tax-indifferent planning for each. While each investor faces unique circumstances that may affect strategy, the following table gives an idea of how taxes might change the planning process.

Exhibit 5   Examples of Tax-Aware Approaches to Planning

Strategic Decisions	Common Tax-Indifferent Approach	Tax-Aware Approach
Financial planning	Use pre-tax growth assumptions	Use after-tax growth assumptions for taxable accounts
Asset allocation	Use pre-tax return and volatility expectations	Use after-tax return and volatility expectations
Asset location	A single allocation across taxable and tax-deferred accounts	Tax-advantaged assets favored in the taxable account
Retirement income planning	Withdraw from retirement accounts first	Optimize withdrawals from taxable and tax-advantaged accounts
Charitable giving	Gift cash	Gift highly appreciated stock

In this section, we assess the effect of account type on capital accumulation, consider some of the issues related to the allocation of asset classes across a client's various accounts, and discuss tax-efficient decumulation and charitable giving strategies.

5.1 Capital Accumulation in Taxable, Tax-Deferred, and Tax-Exempt Accounts

The value of a tax-exempt account compounds in the usual way. For an annual return R over n years, the future value multiplier is given by:

$$FV = (1 + R)^n,$$

where n is the number of years.

The value of a taxable account compounds using the after-tax returns, R'. Compounding returns on an after-tax basis implicitly assumes that taxes on realized returns are paid (and tax credits received) each period. The tax payment is treated as a cash flow:

$$FV = (1 + R')^n.$$

The value of a tax-deferred account compounds using the pre-tax returns and pays tax only when assets are withdrawn from the account. (Withdrawals are taxed at the applicable income tax rates.) If we assume all the assets are withdrawn in a lump sum at the horizon and have a tax rate t, then

$$FV = (1 + R)^n(1 - t).$$

EXAMPLE 6 COMPARING ACCUMULATIONS IN DIFFERENT ACCOUNT TYPES

Chen Li lives in a tax jurisdiction with a flat tax rate of 20%, which applies to all types of income and capital gains. Assume that Li has the following account types:

Account 1: ¥1,000,000 invested in a taxable account earning 10%, taxed annually.

Account 2: ¥1,000,000 invested in a tax-deferred account earning 10%.

Account 3: ¥1,000,000 invested in a tax-exempt account earning 10%.

Compute the after-tax wealth for each account at the end of 20 years assuming the accounts are liquidated at the end of the horizon.

Solution:

Future value of taxable, tax-deferred, and tax-exempt accounts		
Account 1	**Account 2**	**Account 3**
¥4,660,957	¥5,382,000	¥6,727,500
FV = ¥1,000,000 [1 + 0.10(1 − 0.20)]^{20}	FV = ¥1,000,000 [(1 + 0.10)^{20}(1 − 0.20)]	FV = ¥1,000,000 (1 + 0.10)^{20}

5.2 Asset Location

A private wealth client typically has assets spread across taxable, tax-deferred, and tax-exempt portfolios. For these clients, asset allocation must not only consider the appropriate overall asset class mix but must also consider which asset classes are best suited to be held in which accounts. This is called **asset location**—the process for determining whether the assets will be held in a taxable, tax-deferred, or tax-exempt account. A general rule of thumb is to put tax-efficient assets in the taxable account and tax-inefficient assets in the tax-exempt or tax-deferred account. This is only a rule of thumb, however. While it suggests that taxable bonds should be held in a tax-exempt account and that equities (given the preferential tax rate applied to capital gains) should be held in the taxable account, investors with a long investment horizon or that have higher turnover equity strategies may find that putting equities in the tax-exempt account results in better after-tax returns.

Consider the following example. If the expected return for equities is 10% and for fixed income 6%, and if the asset allocation is 50% equity/50% fixed income, then we would expect a pre-tax 8% return. But for a taxable client, there are additional considerations. First, we should consider two additional asset classes: tax-exempt bonds and tax-managed equities. Tax-managed equities are more tax efficient than high-turnover equity strategies that do not consider taxes. Similarly, tax-exempt bonds are more tax efficient than regular bonds, although they typically have lower pre-tax return expectations. Exhibit 6 shows how the return expectations might change by asset class and account, assuming a 50% marginal tax rate on fixed income, 25% tax rate on equities, and 10% effective tax rate on tax-managed equities.

Exhibit 6 After-Tax Return Expectations by Asset Location

	Asset Location	
	Taxable Account	Tax-Exempt Account
Equity	7.5%	10%
Tax-Managed Equity	9%	10%
Fixed Income	3%	6%
Tax-Exempt Fixed Income	4%	4%

Exhibit 7 shows three potential asset location strategies. We assume the taxable and tax-exempt accounts each represent 50% of the client's total investment assets.

Exhibit 7 Maximizing the After-Tax Return of a Given Asset Allocation

Asset Class	Tax-Indifferent Allocation			Tax-Aware Allocation			Asset Location-Sensitive Allocation		
	Taxable Account	Tax-Exempt Account	Return Contrib.	Taxable Account	Tax-Exempt Account	Return Contrib.	Taxable Account	Tax-Exempt Account	Return Contrib.
Equity	25	25	4.38%	—	25	2.50%	—	—	—
Tax-Managed Equity	—	—	—	25	—	2.25%	50	—	4.50%
Fixed Income	25	25	2.25%	—	25	1.50%	—	50	3.00%

Exhibit 7 (Continued)

Asset Class	Tax-Indifferent Allocation			Tax-Aware Allocation			Asset Location-Sensitive Allocation		
	Taxable Account	Tax-Exempt Account	Return Contrib.	Taxable Account	Tax-Exempt Account	Return Contrib.	Taxable Account	Tax-Exempt Account	Return Contrib.
Tax-Exempt Bonds	—	—	—	25	—	1.00%	—	—	—
Total	50	50	**6.63%**	50	50	**7.25%**	50	50	**7.50%**

- The Tax-Indifferent strategy implements the same 50/50 strategy in each account.
- The Tax-Aware strategy replaces nominal equity and fixed-income assets in the taxable account with tax-managed equities and tax-exempt bonds.
- The Asset Location-sensitive strategy follows the rule "put tax-efficient assets (tax-managed equities) in the taxable account and tax-inefficient assets (fixed income) in the tax-exempt account."

The expected total after-tax returns for each strategy are 6.63%, 7.25%, and 7.50%, respectively. While the improvement in the annual return is small (87 basis points), that improvement compounds over time and can have a material impact on the client's wealth as the decumulation phase approaches.

An asset location strategy cannot be rigidly employed. The client may have a different goal and time horizon for each account type and may have multiple goals for the assets held within a single account. For example, a tax-efficient asset location strategy might suggest that the retirement savings account be allocated 100% to bonds while the taxable investment account is allocated 100% to tax-managed equities. If, however, a portion of the taxable account will be used in the next three years for the purchase of a vacation home, exposing these funds to the volatility of a 100% equity allocation may be unwise. Several quantitative tools are available to assist with after-tax portfolio optimization and rebalancing across account types.

EXAMPLE 7 ASSET LOCATION STRATEGY FOR CHARLES AND IVY LEE

- Charles Lee, 55 years old, has recently inherited $2,500,000 from his parents.
- Ivy Lee, 54 years old, will soon receive a $2,500,000 rollover from her company-sponsored retirement plan; this will be deposited in her tax-deferred retirement account.
- The Lees have agreed that they want to establish a $2,500,000 "angel" fund to make investments in small start-up companies, as they already have sufficient assets to fund their lifestyle needs. This angel investment, although technically equities, will be over-and-above the 60% allocated to equities in their core portfolio.
- The remaining $2,500,000 will be invested to maintain the 60/40 asset allocation using the same strategies employed for their other liquid assets.
- Their other investment assets are summarized as follows.

	Taxable Brokerage Account (tax basis)	Tax-Deferred Retirement Account	Other (tax basis)	Pre-Tax/After-Tax Return Expectation*
Passive Global Equity Fund		$3,000,000		7.0% / 7.0%
Passive Fixed Income (taxable)		2,000,000		3.0% / 3.0%
Active Global Equity Fund	$3,000,000 (2,500,000)			9.0% / 6.5%
Tax-Exempt Fixed Income	2,000,000 (1,800,000)			1.5% / 1.5%
Residential Real Estate			$3,000,000 (2,750,000)	n/a
Concentrated Equity Position			15,000,000 (4,000,000)	n/a
Total	$5,000,000	$5,000,000	$18,000,000	

*Assumed tax rates: 50% marginal income tax rate and 20% capital gains tax rate.

The Lees' adviser has warned them that while the average angel investor realizes 2.5x per dollar invested, more than half of all angel investments lead to a loss.

1. Which account would you recommend that the Lees use to fund their angel investments? Justify your response.
2. Of the four strategies currently employed in the Lees' accounts, which should the adviser recommend for the balance of the new money? Justify your response.

Solution to 1:

Charles' inheritance, which would be invested via the taxable brokerage account, should be used to make the angel investments. Held in the taxable account, the Lees can use any losses generated to offset gains elsewhere in the account. Over the long term, the Lees expect to realize significant capital gains on these investments. Held in the taxable account, these gains will be taxed at the 20% capital gains rate. If held in the tax-deferred retirement, the gains would be taxed at the 50% income tax rate as they are withdrawn.

Solution to 2:

Because Charles' inheritance is being used to make the angel investments, the $2,500,000 rollover from Ivy's company-sponsored retirement plan will need to be allocated among the existing investment strategies in a manner to maintain the 60/40 asset allocation. The rollover is in Ivy's tax-deferred retirement account. The most tax-efficient asset location strategy would place the equity investments in the brokerage account and the fixed-income allocation in the retirement account. This would allow the Lees to take full advantage of the more favorable tax rate on capital gains. With the new cash in Ivy's retirement account, the Lees will be able to rebalance their portfolio to achieve a more tax-efficient allocation.

- With $12,500,000 in financial assets (aside from the angel fund), the 60% equity allocation ($7,500,000) would be allotted first to the brokerage account. The brokerage account balance is $5,000,000; it should be

- invested completely in equities to achieve the desired 60/40 asset allocation. However, the tax-exempt fixed-income position has an embedded gain of $200,000 that would need to be realized to accomplish the rebalancing. The Lees' adviser will need to assess the merits of incurring the capital gains tax liability in order to reinvest in the higher-returning strategy. If losses can be realized elsewhere in the portfolio, they may be used to offset this gain.
- The choice between equity strategies in the brokerage account is less clear-cut. While the passive equity strategy is likely more tax efficient (capital gains are realized less frequently), the return expectation for the active strategy is 200 basis points higher. Other considerations, such as the desire to maintain a given tracking error relative to the benchmark, are likely to play a role in the selection of the most appropriate equity strategy. Also, the ability of the investment manager to employ tax management trading strategies is an important consideration.
- The remainder of the equity allocation ($2,500,000) would be achieved through the tax-deferred retirement account. The appropriate strategy is the Active Global Equity strategy, where its higher return (9% vs. the 7% expected return for the passive strategy) will compound tax-free over the Lees' long investment horizon.
- The 40% fixed-income allocation ($5,000,000) is achieved through the tax-deferred retirement account. The appropriate strategy is the Passive Fixed-Income (taxable) strategy.

The final asset allocation is shown in the following table:

	Taxable Brokerage Account	Tax-Deferred Retirement Account
Passive Global Equity Fund	$5,000,000	0
Active Global Equity Fund		$2,500,000
Total Equity		
Tax-Exempt Fixed Income		0
Passive Fixed Income (taxable)	0	5,000,000
Total Fixed Income	**$5,000,000**	**$7,500,000**

TAXABLE, TAX-EXEMPT, AND TAX-DEFERRED ACCOUNTS: DECUMULATION STRATEGIES AND CHARITABLE GIVING STRATEGIES

6

e explain portfolio tax management strategies and their application;

Investment advisers should work closely with the client's financial planner, estate planner, and tax attorney to make sure the investment program is aligned with the larger financial plan. Our discussion so far has focused on capital accumulation. In this section, we assume that clients have reached retirement age and will soon be using their retirement assets to support spending needs over their expected remaining lifetime. We examine a **tax-efficient decumulation strategy** for a retirement account.

Since retirement accounts are tax-exempt or tax-deferred, they compound at a higher rate than taxable accounts. A common rule of thumb suggests that it is better to make withdrawals from the taxable account first and allow the retirement account to continue to compound. Designing the most effective decumulation strategy may require a significant level of financial planning expertise.

In Exhibit 8, we show a simplified example of a tax-aware decumulation strategy using a taxable and a tax-exempt account. (Practically speaking, the tax-advantaged account is most likely a tax-deferred account, such as a retirement savings account. For this illustration, however, we assume that it is tax exempt). Each account has a beginning balance of $1,000,000. We assume a pre-tax rate of return of 10% for both accounts and a 25% effective tax rate on earnings in the taxable account, which equates to an after-tax rate of return of 7.5%. At the end of each year, the investor withdraws $200,000. The withdrawals are taken from the taxable account first, allowing the tax-exempt account to continue to compound at the higher effective rate. Once the taxable account is depleted, withdrawals are taken from the tax-exempt account. At the end of 10 years, the client has $1.80 million remaining. If the withdrawals are taken from the tax-exempt account first, as shown in Exhibit 9, the client will have only $1.48 million remaining at the end of 10 years.

Exhibit 8   Withdraw from Taxable Account First (Tax Aware)

Year	Withdrawal from Taxable Account	Withdrawal from Tax-Exempt Account	Year-End Taxable Account Balance	Year-End Tax-Exempt Account Balance
0			$1,000,000	$1,000,000
1	$200,000		875,000	1,100,000
2	200,000		740,625	1,210,000
3	200,000		596,172	1,331,000
4	200,000		440,885	1,464,100
5	200,000		273,951	1,610,510
6	200,000		94,497	1,771,561
7	101,585	$98,415		1,850,302
8		200,000		1,835,332
9		200,000		1,818,866
10		200,000		**$1,800,752**

Exhibit 9   Withdraw from Tax-Exempt Account First (Tax-Indifferent)

Year	Withdrawal from Taxable Account	Withdrawal from Tax-Exempt Account	Year-End Taxable Account Balance	Year-End Tax-Exempt Account Balance
0			$1,000,000	$1,000,000
1		$200,000	1,075,000	900,000
2		200,000	1,155,625	790,000
3		200,000	1,242,297	669,000

Exhibit 9   (Continued)

Year	Withdrawal from Taxable Account	Withdrawal from Tax-Exempt Account	Year-End Taxable Account Balance	Year-End Tax-Exempt Account Balance
4		200,000	1,335,469	535,900
5		200,000	1,435,629	389,490
6		200,000	1,543,302	228,439
7		200,000	1,659,049	51,283
8	$143,589	56,411	1,639,889	
9	200,000		1,562,880	
10	200,000		$ 1,480,097	

Under progressive tax regimes (jurisdictions where tax rates rise as the level of income rises), a more tax-efficient strategy may be to withdraw from the retirement account until the lowest tax brackets have been fully utilized. Any additional withdrawals would then be taken from the taxable account.

6.1 Tax Considerations in Charitable Giving

When the client's overall financial plan includes charitable giving, the source of the assets to be gifted should be approached strategically. In some jurisdictions, appreciated securities can be gifted to a qualified charity without triggering the capital gain. In these jurisdictions, gifting low-cost-basis assets from taxable accounts is preferred. The investor may receive a tax *benefit* (a tax deduction, reducing the overall tax liability) from the gift while simultaneously removing a future tax liability on the unrealized gain from the portfolio. Advisers and portfolio managers can help investors identify highly appreciated securities for gifting, thereby reducing the tax liability embedded in the portfolio.

EXAMPLE 8   IDENTIFYING ASSETS FOR CHARITABLE GIVING

Charles and Ivy Lee wish to give $750,000 to a local art museum. Ivy Lee has a concentrated holding of $15 million in appreciated company stock (with a tax basis of $4 million and $11 million in unrealized capital gains) that they would like to diversify over time. They also have a diversified portfolio of securities and a retirement account, as shown in Example 7. Their tax rate is 50% on income and 20% on realized capital gains. How should the Lees fund this charitable gift?

Solution:

The Lees should gift shares of the concentrated asset position. The museum, as a tax-exempt entity, can sell the shares without incurring a tax liability, and the Lees will reduce their exposure to the concentrated position. In many jurisdictions, the Lees will receive an income tax deduction, reducing their income tax liability by up to $375,000. Alternatively, the Lees might consider gifting appreciated assets from their brokerage account. However, the unrealized gains on the assets in this account are comparatively small and a larger financial advantage can be achieved by gifting part of the concentrated stock position.

7 TAX MANAGEMENT STRATEGIES AND BASIC TAX STRATEGIES

f   discuss risk and tax objectives in managing concentrated single-asset positions;

As the vast majority of professionally managed assets have historically been tax-exempt institutional portfolios, most investment theory and practice presume a pre-tax framework. The goal of this section is to give you an overview of tax management techniques so that when working with a taxable client you have the tools needed to understand and implement investment strategies efficiently.

> **TAX AVOIDANCE VS. TAX EVASION—ETHICAL AND LEGAL OBLIGATIONS**
>
> As fiduciaries, portfolio managers and advisers are obligated to invest efficiently and avoid unnecessary frictions. Taxes are one of the frictions to be managed, but there is a risk in being too clever when attempting to reduce that particular friction. Denis Healey, a former UK Chancellor of the Exchequer, is often quoted: "The difference between tax avoidance and tax evasion is the thickness of a prison wall."
>
> In 2010, the CEO of a hedge fund and private wealth management firm in Seattle ended up on the wrong side of that wall, setting up an offshore company to create tax losses its clients could then use to offset gains. However, the losing stocks didn't exist, and the offshore company had no employees and no earnings. The CEO of the firm and the tax attorney involved were both sentenced to six years in prison for the illegal tax scheme.
>
> Because usage of the terms likely differs from jurisdiction to jurisdiction, we will start by defining what we mean by "tax avoidance" and "tax evasion." The general principle is that **tax avoidance** is the legal activity of understanding the tax laws and finding approaches that avoid or minimize taxation. **Tax evasion** is the illegal concealment and non-payment of taxes that are otherwise due. If the primary purpose of the activity is to avoid paying tax and the activities are misleading or do not have merit in their own right, then the activity is likely unethical and may be illegal.
>
> The CFA Institute Code of Ethics and Standards of Professional Conduct require that CFA charterholders and candidates act with integrity, competence, diligence, respect, and in an ethical manner. Focusing on after-tax returns, minimizing unnecessary tax burdens, and being thoughtful about how taxation interacts with a portfolio are all elements of being a good steward of a client's assets. However, it is important to *never* be involved in helping a client disguise true ownership of assets or otherwise be involved in tax evasion. Charterholders and candidates must not engage in any professional conduct involving dishonesty, fraud, or deceit or commit any act that reflects adversely on their professional reputation, integrity, or competence.

7.1 Basic Portfolio Tax Management Strategies

Basic portfolio tax management strategies fall into two categories:

- Structuring a client's investments in a legitimate manner to reduce the amount of tax owed. Examples include:
    - holding assets in a tax-exempt account versus a taxable account;
    - investing in tax-exempt bonds instead of taxable bonds;
    - holding assets long enough to qualify for long-term capital gains treatment; and
    - holding dividend-paying stocks long enough to pay the more favorable tax rate.

- Deferring the recognition of certain taxable income until some future date, allowing investors to benefit from the compounding of pre-tax rather than after-tax portfolio returns. In a progressive tax system, investors may also benefit from deferring taxes to a future date if they anticipate their tax rate will be lower in retirement. Other examples of tax deferral strategies include:
  - limiting portfolio turnover and the consequent realization of capital gains and
  - selling securities at a loss to offset a realized capital gain (i.e., **tax loss harvesting**).

A frequent theme among these basic strategies is the holding period of an investment. Portfolio managers should be mindful of portfolio turnover and the timing of trades. Turnover is sometimes used as a proxy for tax efficiency. While low-turnover passive index funds tend to be more tax efficient than higher turnover active strategies, the relationship between turnover and tax efficiency is by no means straightforward. While it is true that turnover incurs transaction costs and can create a capital gains tax liability, turnover might also create tax benefits. Selling an asset at a loss can create a tax offset that can be applied to reduce capital gains taxes incurred in the current or even future tax periods (although, in some jurisdictions this type of trade is considered a wash sale and the tax offset is not allowed).

APPLICATION OF TAX MANAGEMENT STRATEGIES

f   discuss risk and tax objectives in managing concentrated single-asset positions;

A portfolio manager has to consider many things when implementing an investment strategy. Risks, returns, and costs are common concerns of all portfolio managers irrespective of whether the client is an institution or an individual. The manager of a private wealth portfolio is tasked with the additional complexity of minimizing the tax drag on returns. Here we take a closer look at several important topics for tax-aware portfolio management:

- selection of the investment vehicle (i.e., whether the assets are held in a partnership, fund, or separate account),
- tax lot accounting,
- tax loss harvesting,
- tax deferral, and
- quantitative tax management.

8.1 Investment Vehicles

As a private wealth manager, you may have the option of using commingled funds (e.g., mutual funds, UCITS, and partnerships), or the client portfolio may be a separately managed account in which the individual securities are owned directly. The structure of the investment vehicle in which the assets are held may affect the client's tax liability and the adviser's ability to manage the client portfolio in a tax-aware manner. When a portfolio has multiple owners, as in a partnership or fund, the tax consequences of the investment and trading activities are shared.

In a partnership, whether a hedge fund or private equity fund, the taxes are typically passed through to the underlying partners. Partnerships are an appealing tax structure since the fund itself operates free of taxation and distributions are typically classified as capital gains, not as ordinary income.

In a mutual fund, dividend and interest income is passed through to the underlying investors; thus, the investor is required to pay income taxes on that income in the year in which it was received. If the investor sells her mutual fund shares, she will be liable for any capital gains arising from the difference between the sale price and her tax basis. In addition, the investor may also be liable for capital gains taxes on transactions that take place *within* the fund. At the end of the year, the fund will issue a statement detailing the long- and short-term gains realized during the year. Investors must pay their proportionate share of the tax liability. The net asset value of the fund will be reduced by the amount of the capital gains distribution. This is true in the United States but is not true in all jurisdictions. In the United Kingdom, for example, investors are only liable for capital gains taxes at the time they sell their shares of the fund.

When new shareholders buy into the fund, they are also buying a share of the unrealized capital gains accrued in prior periods. These gains may become realized gains through the trading activity of the portfolio manager and through the redemption activity of other shareholders, creating a tax liability for investors who did not participate in the returns that created the gains. Let's illustrate this with a simple example.

> The JEMStone fund was launched in 20X0 with five investors and $5,000,000 in assets. Since that time, the assets in the fund have appreciated to $5,500,000. The embedded capital gain is $500,000. There has been no trading in the fund, and all the original investors hold their original shares. Each investor's tax basis is $1,000,000, and each investor's proportionate share of the fund is worth $1,100,000. The fund is open to new investors, and Mateo invests $1,100,000. The aggregate tax basis of the fund is now $6,100,000, and the net asset value of the fund is $6,600,000. Mateo owns one-sixth of the fund. His tax basis is $1,016,667. If the fund manager were to sell the underlying holdings, Mateo would receive a capital gains distribution of $83,333 on which he would be required to pay taxes, even though his investment has not appreciated. He effectively bought into some of the tax liability of the previous investors.

Mutual fund data providers calculate metrics like **Potential Capital Gain Exposure (PCGE)** to help investors determine whether a significant tax liability is embedded in a mutual fund. PCGE is an estimate of the percentage of a fund's assets that represents gains and measures how much the fund's assets have appreciated. It can be an indicator of possible future capital gain distributions.

PCGE = net gains (losses) / total net assets.

Some commingled structures are more tax efficient than others. Exchange-traded funds (ETFs), for example, can reduce any embedded capital gain tax liability by delivering low cost-basis holdings to trading partners as part of the share creation and redemption process for the fund. ETFs aren't sold directly to investors like mutual funds. Instead, ETF managers use banks and brokerage firms as intermediaries. These intermediaries deliver or receive baskets of portfolio stocks as part of the share creation and redemption process. Independent of inflows to and outflows from the fund, they will also deliver or receive these baskets of stock whenever the price of the fund deviates from its underlying value to generate an arbitrage profit. This arbitrage keeps the price of the fund in line with the net asset value of the fund while reducing

Application of Tax Management Strategies

any unrealized gain in the portfolio. In addition, ETF managers can choose which shares to include in the basket of stock delivered to the intermediary; to reduce any unrealized gain, they are likely to include the low-basis shares in that basket of stock.

Separately-managed accounts (SMAs) offer the most flexibility for tax management. The assets have only one owner, so portfolio decisions can be tailored to the tax situation of that specific investor. Losses that are realized within the SMA portfolio can be used to offset gains on assets held outside the SMA. In contrast, any losses within a mutual fund can only be used to offset gains realized within the fund and cannot be distributed to the shareholders. This makes the losses within a fund considerably less valuable to the taxable investor.

Exhibit 10 summarizes the tax characteristics of partnerships, mutual funds, ETFs, and separately-managed accounts.

Exhibit 10 Tax Characteristics of Investment Vehicles

Vehicle	Tax Characteristics
Partnership	Tax liabilities are passed through to partners.
Mutual fund	Tax liabilities are influenced by co-investors. For example, a redemption by one shareholder can trigger a capital gains tax liability for all shareholders.
Exchange-traded fund (ETF)	Tax liabilities can be reduced or eliminated through the creation and redemption process.
Separate account	Realized losses and gains can be aggregated across all of the client's accounts.

EXAMPLE 9 ESTIMATING THE FUTURE TAX EFFICIENCY OF MUTUAL FUNDS

Consider two mutual funds:

- Fund A started with $2 million in assets, experienced capital appreciation of $500,000, and distributed $100,000 of realized capital gains to shareholders.
- Fund B started with $2 million in assets, experienced capital appreciation of $100,000, and subsequently suffered a capital loss of $500,000.

What is the PCGE for each fund? What are the implications for a taxable investor?

Solution:

- Fund A has a PCGE of 16.7% (= the $400,000 gain remaining in the fund divided by total net assets of $2,400,000).
- Fund B has a PCGE of –25% (= the net –$400,000 loss divided by total net assets of $1,600,000).

- Fund B is more likely to be tax efficient going forward since it can use the losses in the portfolio to offset future realized gains.
- Fund A has net gains embedded in the portfolio. Managers can continue to hold the appreciated securities or sell them. If they sell a security at a gain, the fund must distribute the gains to shareholders that year. A high PCGE indicates the potential for capital gain distributions in the future.

8.2 Tax Loss Harvesting

The premise of **tax loss harvesting** is simple: Sell securities that are below their acquisition price in order to realize a loss that can be used to offset gains or other income. The rules vary by jurisdiction. Here is a sampling of rules around tax loss harvesting in a few jurisdictions:

- *Australia*—Trading for the sole purpose of realizing a tax benefit is not allowed. Each trade needs a non-tax motivation as its primary purpose. Tax management in the context of the overall investment strategy is allowed, but tax loss harvesting by itself is not.
- *Germany*—No limitations on tax loss harvesting trades.
- *United States*—A tax loss credit will be disallowed if you purchase the same, or a substantially identical, security within 30 days before or after the sale of the asset. This is the *wash sale rule*, and it applies across the taxpayer's accounts—including retirement accounts and in some cases even a spouse's account.

Effectively trading a portfolio to avoid short-term gains and harvest short-term losses is an important element of managing private client assets. All losses, whether long- or short-term, can be used to reduce current-year taxes. Most advisers and investors focus on these immediate and concrete dollar savings—for example, by making opportunistic loss harvesting trades during market corrections or at year end.

Central to tax loss harvesting is the concept of tax lot accounting. Typically, portfolio positions are built over time, with each purchase having its own tax basis. For example, a holding of 400 shares of Vodafone Group may be comprised of several tax lots, each with its own purchase date and tax basis. **Tax lot accounting**—keeping track of how much you paid for an investment and when you bought it—is crucial for understanding how much tax you might owe. An effective tax management program requires the portfolio accounting platform to keep track of this information.

The tax lot method is the rule for prioritizing the realization of losses and gains. The most common methods of tax lot accounting are first in, first out (*FIFO*); last in, first out (*LIFO*); and highest in, first out (*HIFO*). The *specified-lot method* (in which the portfolio manager identifies specifically which tax lot is to be traded) provides the most flexibility for ensuring a trade is tax efficient. If the investor does not specify which tax lot is to be sold at the time of the trade, the custodian will use its default rule for selecting tax lots for the calculation of gains. The default is typically FIFO. Given that equity markets generally appreciate through time, however, using FIFO means that the lowest tax basis shares are sold first—often making it the least tax-efficient option.

Tax lot accounting is not permitted in all jurisdictions. In Canada, for example, the cost basis used to determine gain or loss on any sale is the average acquisition cost of all lots in that security.

Application of Tax Management Strategies

EXAMPLE 10 TAX LOT SELECTION

Consider the shares of Vodafone stock depicted in Exhibit 11. The investor owns 400 shares, which have been acquired over time. There are four tax lots of 100 shares each. The investor wants to sell 100 shares.

1. What would be the tax liability associated with each of the tax lot accounting rules: FIFO, LIFO, and HIFO?
2. Which tax lot is the most tax efficient to sell?

Exhibit 11 Tax Lots for Stock with Price of $40, Assuming Current Date Is 1 July 20X9

Tax Lot Purchase Date	Shares	Acquisition Price	Gain (Loss)	Holding Period	Tax if Sold
A) 1 January 20X8	100	$30.00	$1,000	Long-term	$250
B) 1 June 20X8	100	$50.00	($1,000)	Long-term	($250)
C) 1 January 20X9	100	$48.00	($800)	Short-term	($400)
D) 1 June 20X9	100	$45.00	($500)	Short-term	($250)

Note: Assumes that the tax rate on long-term capital gains is 25% and short-term gains 50%.

Solution to 1:

- FIFO would select tax lot A, the earliest acquisition date. This results in a capital gain of $1,000 and a capital gains tax of $250.
- LIFO would choose tax lot D, the most recent acquisition date. This results in a capital loss of $500 and a $250 tax benefit, which could be used to offset short-term gain tax liabilities (or long-term gains) elsewhere in the client's portfolio.
- HIFO would choose tax lot B, the highest acquisition price. This results in a long-term loss of $1,000 and a $250 tax benefit, which could be used to offset short-term gain tax liabilities.

Solution to 2:

- In our example, the selection of tax lot C creates the most tax benefit—the largest short-term loss. HIFO is usually the most tax-efficient accounting methodology since selecting the tax lot with the highest acquisition price will usually produce the least capital gain or the deepest loss. In this case, however, tax lot B is a long-term lot and the tax benefit of a long-term loss is generally less than that of a short-term loss. None of the standard accounting methods would select tax lot C; the portfolio manager would need to specify the tax lot to be sold at the time of trading.

When managing a portfolio on behalf of a taxable client, it is important to ensure that the custodian is using the appropriate tax lot methodology. If the account is set up incorrectly, the tax-aware trades executed by the manager could be nullified by the custodian's accounting system.

Loss harvesting trades can create some difficulties in maintaining the desired portfolio exposures. To avoid the wash sale rule in the United States, you must hold cash or some other security for 31 days. Holding cash clearly leaves the portfolio underinvested and can create a drag on returns if the cash return is lower than the security. Managers will typically identify a replacement security to be held during the wash sale period to maintain a comparable portfolio exposure (e.g., buy Pepsi stock in lieu of Coca-Cola stock). Or, they will purchase an index or sector ETF. Another difficulty is that selling the placeholder and switching back to the original security after 31 days can create its own tax burden if a short-term capital gain is realized when the placeholder is sold.

Although a tax loss harvesting trade generates a loss to be used in the current tax year, recall that tax loss harvesting is a *tax-deferral* strategy. When you re-purchase the security after 31 days, you have re-established the position presumably with a lower tax basis, increasing the future capital gains tax liability.

8.3 Quantitative Tax Management

A core element of tax management is the ability to quantify and manage risk that is introduced as a result of the implementation of the portfolio. One common metric of risk versus a benchmark is tracking error. Quantitative methods can help the portfolio manager to optimize the portfolio for tax efficiency, and tracking error can be used to evaluate how much risk we are introducing by being tax aware.

Quantitative tax management uses a quantitative risk model to estimate the risks and correlations of each of the securities in the portfolio. The approach then uses the risk estimates from the model as an input to a portfolio optimization algorithm that:

- minimizes tracking error risk versus the index or model portfolio;
- maximizes realized losses;
- minimizes realized gains;
- minimizes trading costs; and
- satisfies any constraints, such as limits on security, industry, sector, and country weights as well as wash sale restrictions, turnover, and cash limits.

A quantitative approach to tax management can be used to minimize tax-drag and investment risk when onboarding a new client, in executing a loss harvesting strategy, and when delaying the realization of gains. Each of these is briefly discussed next.

Transitions: For an account funded with securities rather than cash, the portfolio manager must find a good trade-off between the tax cost of transitioning to the new portfolio and the risk of underperforming the new mandate if some of the appreciated securities continue to be held at an overweight in the portfolio. The goal of the quantitative model is to avoid realizing taxes at the time of inception by holding some of the existing securities but doing so in a risk-controlled way.

Tax-optimized loss harvesting: Instead of tax loss harvesting once a year, a portfolio manager can look for losses throughout the year, whenever they occur. Any investment management process, active or passive, can benefit from systematically monitoring the portfolio for tax opportunities. Where a country's rules nullify any tax benefits from trades undertaken for the sole purpose of realizing a tax benefit, losses arising from strategy-driven investment decisions can still be realized opportunistically. As securities are sold to realize a loss, replacement securities can be identified using a risk model and optimization algorithms to ensure that the desired portfolio exposures are maintained.

Gain-loss matching optimization: While you can avoid capital gains tax liabilities by never selling appreciated securities, this is likely to lead to a portfolio whose risk exposures are significantly out of balance. Portfolio managers can use a gain-loss

Application of Tax Management Strategies

matching optimization algorithm to balance the desire to avoid the realization of capital gains tax against the need to manage portfolio risk relative to the investor's benchmark or model portfolio.

EXAMPLE 11   TAX LOSS HARVESTING

Consider the following tax loss harvesting example. A $2 million portfolio has $365,000 in unrealized gains; $120,000 are short-term and $245,000 are long-term. There are also $48,000 of unrealized short-term losses. To determine the optimal trading strategy (i.e., how much gains and losses to realize), the portfolio manager will use the firm's algorithm and provide the inputs required by the framework just presented. Exhibit 12 shows the tax benefit generated for this portfolio trade.

Exhibit 12   Example of a Loss Harvesting Trade

	Pre-Trade Unrealized Gains and Losses	Post-Trade Unrealized Gains and Losses	Realized Gains and Losses
Short-Term Gains	$120,000	$120,000	$0
Long-Term Gains	$245,000	$242,000	$3,000
Short-Term Losses	($48,000)	($6,000)	($42,000)
Long-Term Losses	$0	$0	$0
Net Gain (Loss)			($39,000)
Tax Benefit			**$19,500**

Note: Assumes a 50% tax on short-term gains and a 25% tax on long-term gains.

The portfolio manager realized $42,000 of the $48,000 of short-term losses; there are $6,000 of unrealized short-term losses remaining. The portfolio manager also realized $3,000 of the $242,000 in long-term gains. The net realized loss from these trades is $39,000. This is a short-term loss (any loss remaining after netting retains its short-term or long-term character.) The loss can be used to offset $39,000 in gains elsewhere in the portfolio. Of course, it would be most advantageous to use the short-term loss to offset short-term gains, as these are taxed at a higher rate. The resulting tax savings would be $19,500 ($39,000 × 50% short-term gains tax rate). In a $2 million portfolio, this is equivalent to a nearly 100-basis point improvement in after-tax returns (19,500/2,000,000 = 0.975%).

In addition to the tax savings, the trade also resulted in risk-related improvements, such as reducing predicted tracking error and keeping country, sector, and other risk factor weights within bounds.

9 MANAGING CONCENTRATED PORTFOLIOS AND RISK AND TAX CONSIDERATIONS IN MANAGING CONCENTRATED SINGLE-ASSET POSITIONS

g describe strategies for managing concentrated positions in public equities;

Frequently, individuals' and families' wealth is concentrated in an asset or group of assets that has played a pivotal role in the creation of their wealth. Three major types of *concentrated positions* commonly encountered in managing private client assets are: (1) publicly traded stocks, (2) a privately-owned business, and (3) commercial or investment real estate.

Concentrated positions in public equity may derive from an initial public offering or the sale of a privately-owned business to a public company. Or, individuals may have worked at a publicly traded company, perhaps for many years, and received company stock as part of their compensation.

There is no universal agreement as to what constitutes a concentrated position; it frequently depends on the nature of the position. A 10% position in a small-cap stock might be considered a concentrated position. A 10% position in a liquid large-cap stock might be considered risky, but it likely doesn't meet the threshold of a "concentrated position" for the purposes of this discussion. In this reading, the term "concentrated position" is used to describe a holding that due to its low tax basis or personal association with the client inhibits the development of an efficient, diversified portfolio.

Advisers must be able to assist clients with decisions concerning such positions, including the risk and tax consequences associated with managing them. This section will discuss approaches to managing those concentrated positions.

9.1 Risk and Tax Considerations in Managing Concentrated Single-Asset Positions

We have identified four risk and tax-related considerations relevant to concentrated single-asset positions:

1. The company-specific risk inherent in the concentrated position
2. The reduction in portfolio efficiency resulting from the lack of diversification
3. The liquidity risk inherent in a privately-held or outsized publicly-held security
4. The risk of incurring an outsized tax bill that diminishes return if one were to sell part of the concentrated position in an attempt to reduce the other risks

Private companies tend to be smaller than public companies with all of the attendant risks of being a small company. They may have a more limited operating history or an undiversified business mix. They may have difficulty attracting high-quality management personnel due to the family ownership. Or, their access to financing may be more constrained than that of a public company. These risks, alone or in combination, typically make a concentrated position in a family-owned company much riskier than a similar-sized position in a publicly-traded company.

Whether the position is publicly-traded or privately-held, however, a concentrated position subjects the portfolio to a higher level of risk. A significant proportion of the client's wealth is exposed to the risk of adverse events affecting this company—either a company-specific event, such as an earnings shortfall, or an industry-specific event, such as changes in tariffs on imported materials. In the course of *building* wealth, adverse events pose unavoidable risk. However, once a certain level of wealth has been attained, the wealth owner's focus tends to shift toward maintaining that status. Private wealth managers must be able to counsel clients through this changing view of risk.

A portfolio with a concentrated position may also be subject to liquidity risk. Shares in a private company cannot be readily sold to meet unexpected expenses. If not subject to regulatory restrictions, a large position in a public company can be sold, although the sale is likely to incur higher transaction costs than a position of more moderate size. This lack of liquidity complicates the management of the remaining portfolio.

Lastly, concentrated positions frequently have a very low tax basis, having been held by the investor for a long time. Sale of all or a part of the position can trigger a significant tax liability.

While these and other considerations (notably, a client's emotional attachment to an asset that has been the foundation for financial success) make a simple sale problematic, the risk inherent in the position may outweigh the tax and liquidity issues.

9.1.1 Approaches to Managing the Risk of Concentrated Positions

Given the risks associated with holding a concentrated position, well-informed investors will seek to diversify these risks. Several different strategies might be considered depending on the facts and circumstance of the client's situation. The key factors to consider when selecting a strategy include the following:

- *Degree of concentration*—The larger the concentrated position is relative to the total portfolio, the more concerned an investor should be about the risks and the more urgent the need to address those risks.
- *Volatility and downside risk of the position*—The higher the risk associated with the position, the greater the benefit of diversification.
- *Tax basis* —The lower the tax basis, the higher the tax liability.
- *Liquidity* —The lower the liquidity, the more costly it will be to achieve the risk-reduction goal.
- *Tax rate of the investor*—The higher the tax rate, the higher the tax liability.
- *Time horizon of the investor*—A longer investment horizon gives the portfolio a better chance to offset any tax impact of a sale.
- *Restrictions on the investor*—If the investor is restricted from selling the asset through an employment or acquisition agreement, then a strategy other than an outright sale must be developed.
- *Emotional attachment and other non-financial considerations*—Often the concentrated position is the original source of wealth for the individual and/or family, so there is an emotional attachment that makes them reluctant to sell. Alternatively, an owner might wish to maintain voting control of the company or retain shares to signal a continued association with the company.

Several approaches can be used to mitigate the risks of a concentrated position. Each has different tax consequences:

1. *Sell and diversify*—The simplest (and often best) approach is to sell the concentrated position, pay the capital gains taxes, and re-invest the proceeds into a diversified portfolio.
2. *Staged diversification*—In some cases, timing risk is a concern. Selling in multiple tranches can at least partially mitigate the risk of inconvenient timing.

3   *Hedging and monetization strategies*—Several strategies using derivatives can be used to hedge the risk of a concentrated position. Once the position is hedged, monetization—such as a loan against the value of the concentrated position—provides owners with funds to spend or re-invest without triggering a taxable event.

4   *Tax-free exchanges*—In some jurisdictions, an investor may be able to exchange assets, replacing an illiquid private company position with publicly traded stock, without creating a taxable event. In the United States, a 1031 exchange allows you to sell a real estate asset and transfer the tax basis to another property purchased within a few months of the sale. Some exchange funds allow investors to pool their public stock positions with others to achieve diversification without triggering a tax event.

5   *Charitable giving strategies*—Charitable trusts, private foundations, and donor-advised funds (an investment account established for the sole purpose of supporting the donor's charitable giving) allow the asset to be transferred to a tax-exempt account in which it can be sold without incurring capital gains taxes. While the assets of private foundations and donor-advised funds can be used to fund only the client's philanthropic goals, the charitable trust can be structured to provide income to the client in the present with the assets fulfilling the philanthropic purpose in the future.

6   *Tax-avoidance and tax-deferral strategies*—In some jurisdictions, holding the position until death allows heirs to receive a step-up in basis (a new tax basis based on the value at the date of death) that will allow them to diversify the position and avoid capital gains taxes. Tax loss harvesting strategies that invest in a diversified equity portfolio and generate extra capital losses can be paired with a staged diversification strategy that matches gains with losses. This allows the client to spread out the tax burden over time, creating flexibility to defer some portion of the tax.

A variety of financial tools can be used to implement these approaches. For example, an investor can synthetically sell a stock by shorting the stock or using options, swaps, forwards, or futures. Although these actions produce a similar economic result, they may not be taxed similarly.

In the next sections, we review some of the more common strategies for managing concentrated positions. There are many variations on these, with different benefits depending on the jurisdiction and the investor. The range of alternatives is continuously changing as advisers innovate to capitalize on opportunities in new and existing regulations and as tax authorities seek to close unintended loopholes.

10   STRATEGIES FOR MANAGING CONCENTRATED POSITIONS IN PUBLIC EQUITIES

h   describe strategies for managing concentrated positions in privately owned businesses and real estate;

For the examples in this section, we will consider a client, Michael Stark, a US-based client who has $1,000,000 worth of Exxon stock that he received when he sold his company to Exxon. The restrictions on the sale of his stock recently have been lifted, so he is interested in exploring ways to reduce the risk of his concentrated position. The tax basis of his stock is approximately $100,000, or 10% of the current market value, and Michael is concerned about the tax implications of an outright sale. His tax rate on long-term capital gains is 25%. We will explore several strategies that could be used to help Michael achieve his risk-reduction goal. Managers will typically use more than one approach to managing a concentrated position. Strategy selection is dependent not only on the objective facts and circumstances of the concentrated position but also on clients' sophistication. Putting clients into a strategy that they don't understand often leads to unhappy clients.

10.1 Staged Diversification and Completion Portfolios

The simplest approach to managing the risk of a concentrated position is to sell it, pay the tax, and reinvest the proceeds in a diversified portfolio. Often the client wishes to sell the stock over the course of several years. This type of **staged diversification strategy** has the advantage of spreading the tax liability across multiple tax years, but it also extends the time that Michael will be overly exposed to Exxon. The proceeds from the stock sales can be used to fund a diversified portfolio. For example, an adviser might recommend selling part of the stock position and buying an ETF that tracks the broad market.

A more sophisticated approach is to construct a **completion portfolio**. A completion portfolio is an index-based portfolio that when added to the concentrated position creates an overall portfolio with exposures similar to the investor's benchmark. This technique uses a quantitative portfolio optimization process to select individual stocks or sector ETFs to form a portfolio that considers the remaining stock when evaluating the risk of the portfolio.

The completion portfolio can also be tax optimized on an ongoing basis as discussed in the section on "Quantitative Tax Management." The index-tracking completion portfolio is funded with the partial sale of the concentrated position. On an ongoing basis, the portfolio is rebalanced using a quantitative model. The model minimizes active risk versus the benchmark and maximizes the after-tax return of the portfolio—primarily by realizing more capital losses than gains. The losses realized in the diversified portfolio can be used to offset some of the gains realized by the sale of the concentrated stock. The process is designed to track a broad-based index on a pre-tax basis and outperform it on an after-tax basis.

Let's explore how this might work using Michael Stark's situation.

Michael owns $1 million in Exxon stock. While Exxon stock volatility has typically been less than many other US stocks, a major oil spill or other company scandal could easily put his wealth unnecessarily at risk.

An outright sale would trigger a realized gain of $900,000. Given his 25% tax rate, the tax liability would be $225,000. Michael wants to understand the trade-off between incurring the tax liability and his goal to create a more diversified equity portfolio that tracks the S&P 100. We can use an optimizer to evaluate the trade-offs between the tax liability and the tracking error relative to the benchmark. Our optimization objectives are to minimize the tax liability from selling Exxon and to minimize the tracking error to the S&P 100. These are competing objectives; fewer shares sold minimizes the tax liability but increases the tracking error. We use a fundamental risk model to estimate our risk versus the benchmark, in this case the S&P100 Index. The predicted tracking error for Exxon relative to this benchmark is 19.8%. (We are using tracking error to represent the risk of being undiversified relative to the benchmark.) Exhibit 13 shows the trade-off as we sell different proportions of Michael's Exxon stock and reinvest the proceeds into the S&P 100 Index.

Exhibit 13 Tax Liability vs. Tracking Error with Varying Levels of ExxonMobil (XOM) Exposure

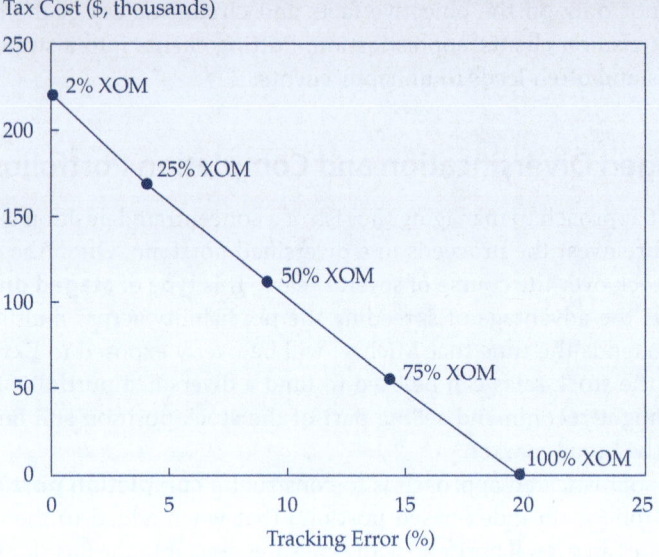

Note: Tracking error estimated using the MSCI Barra US risk model as of June 2019.

The final 2% of Michael's Exxon stock could be retained without negatively impacting tracking error because Exxon has a 2% weight in the index.

Michael will need to assess the expected trade-off between tax and risk to determine how much Exxon to sell. He might also stage the diversification over multiple tax years.

Using individual stocks to build out a completion portfolio has an advantage in that we can optimize the total portfolio to achieve desired factor exposures and tracking error targets. Whereas a broad-market ETF or mutual fund mirrors the entirety of the index (and likely includes Exxon), our completion portfolio can exclude Exxon or other stocks with a high correlation to the energy sector. The risk model considers Exxon to be 88% in the oil and gas industry and 12% in the chemicals industry. Thus, the completion portfolio should underweight oil, gas, and chemical companies relative to the index.

10.2 Tax-Optimized Equity Strategies—Equity Monetization, Collars, and Call Writing

Equity monetization refers to a group of strategies that allows investors to receive cash for their stock positions without an outright sale. These transactions are structured to avoid triggering the capital gains tax. In addition to avoiding the near-term tax liability, other factors might make this monetization strategy appealing. Investors may

- be subject to restrictions from the sale of the stock,
- not want to cede control of the voting rights, or
- want to keep the position but create short-term liquidity.

Monetization is a two-step process:

1. The first step is for the investor to hedge a large portion of the risk inherent in the concentrated position using a short sale, a total return swap, options, futures, or a forward sale contract. This may be straightforward for a large

public company with a liquid derivatives market that trades around the stock. It is likely to be more difficult or expensive for a smaller company with a thin derivatives market.

2   The second step is for the investor to borrow against the hedged position. In most instances, a high loan-to-value ratio can be achieved because the position is hedged. The loan proceeds are then invested in a diversified portfolio of other investments, thus reducing stock-specific risk of the portfolio significantly without triggering a capital gains tax.

A position can be hedged in a number of ways. You could sell the security short, sell a forward contract, or enter into a total return equity swap. In the reading "Risk Management Applications of Option Strategies," the concept of a *zero-cost collar* was introduced as a commonly used hedging strategy. When structuring a zero-cost (cashless) collar, the investor buys a put with a strike price at or slightly below the current price of the stock. The investor must pay the put premium to acquire the protection. The put will fully protect the investor from a loss should the stock price fall below the strike price (subject to the credit risk of the counterparty). Simultaneously, the investor sells a call with the same maturity with a strike price above the current price. The strike price is set at the level that brings in the amount required to pay for the put. The sale of the call finances the purchase of the put. Risk is reduced but not eliminated.

Historically, the concept of capital gain realization has been tied to the "sale or disposition" of appreciated securities. In the case of monetization transactions, no actual transaction has occurred in the appreciated securities themselves. The investor still owns the securities, and if the securities are viewed in isolation, the investor remains fully exposed to the risk of loss and opportunity for profit in the associated securities.

The critical question is whether an equity monetization strategy will be treated as a taxable event in a particular country. If the tax authorities of a country respect legal form over economic substance, equity monetization strategies should not trigger an immediate taxable event. However, in some jurisdictions the process of hedging the stock is likely to trigger a taxable event if the economic risks of holding the stock are completely eliminated. (In the United States, this is known as a *constructive sale*.) Hedges can be structured to retain some economic risk in the position and thus avoid triggering a taxable event.

Other tax considerations include the following:

- How are the gains and losses from unwinding the position treated? In jurisdictions that favor long-term gains with a lower tax rate, structures that result in long-term gains and short-term losses are preferred.
- Does the hedge affect the taxation of dividends received on the shares? In some jurisdictions, the call options could affect the taxation of the stock dividends. For example, in the United States, if call options sold on the stock are in-the-money or have expiration periods less than 30 days, dividends earned on the stock are taxed at the regular income tax rate instead of at the more favorable qualified dividend rate.

In some cases, a client may want to implement only the call selling program without any hedging or monetization. *Covered call writing* is often viewed as attractive if the owner believes the stock will trade in a range for the foreseeable future. For example, assume that Exxon is trading at $70 per share and that Stark is unwilling to sell any portion of his position at less than $80 per share. We could sell call options with a strike price of $80. If the shares appreciate to that level, the call will be exercised and we will deliver the shares at that price. But if the shares do not reach that level, Stark keeps the call premiums. Call writing can be a good substitute for a staged selling program. Perhaps the most significant benefit of implementing a covered call writing program, even if only on a portion of the position, is that it can psychologically prepare the owner to dispose of those shares.

EXAMPLE 12 HEDGING A CONCENTRATED EQUITY POSITION IN EXXON

Michael Stark is holding 15,000 shares of Exxon stock, which is currently trading at $70 per share. Assume that Michael is unwilling to sell any portion of his position at less than $80 per share but wants to protect his shares over the next year should the stock price crash. With the help of his adviser, Michael looks at two strategies: a covered call and a zero-cost collar:

- *Covered call:* Sell one-year call options with a strike price of $80 for a $5 per share premium.
- *Zero-cost collar:* Sell the same calls as in the covered call and use the proceeds to buy one-year put options with a $70 strike price.

Exhibit 14 shows the profit and loss for the collar and for a covered call (holding the stock and selling the call without buying the put protection).

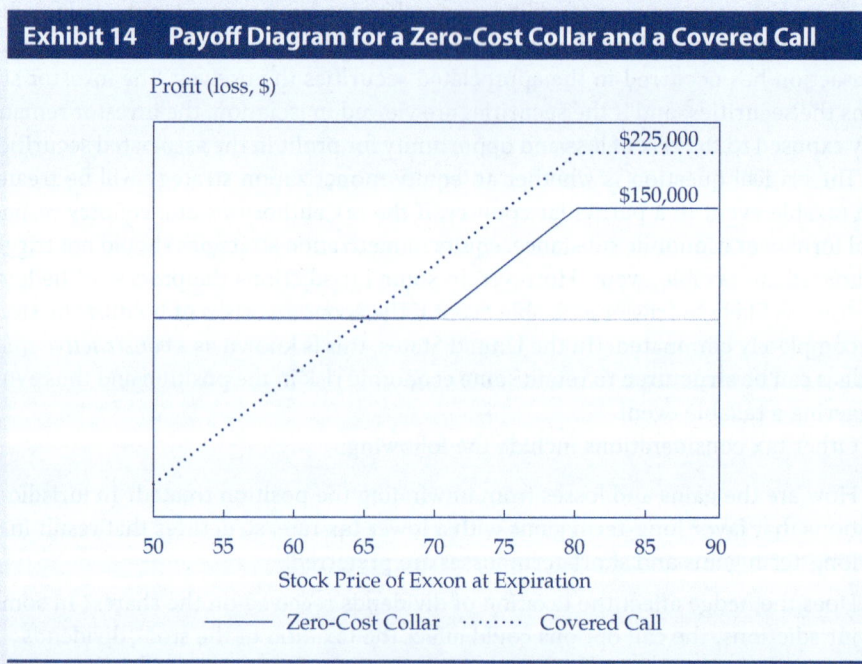

Exhibit 14 Payoff Diagram for a Zero-Cost Collar and a Covered Call

1. What is the maximum profit for the zero-cost collar? How much can Michael lose over the next year?
2. What are the pros and cons of a collar versus a covered call? What is the maximum profit for a covered call?
3. What are the tax consequences of opening the option positions?
4. What are the tax consequences at expiration?

Solution to 1:

Michael's maximum profit is capped at $150,000, and his losses are limited to zero. For example, if the stock price rallies to $90 per share at the expiration date, he is obliged to sell his shares at $80. With 15,000 shares, his profit is only

$150,000 instead of the $300,000 profit from just holding the stock. On the other hand, if the stock plunged to $50 his loss is zero since the protective put allows him to sell his shares at $70. If the stock price ends the year back where it started, at $70, his loss is still zero.

Solution to 2:

Both strategies forfeit any profits above the $80 price. The collar protects against downside risk and allows for monetization of the position through borrowing. The covered call has a maximum profit of $225,000. If Michael sells only a covered call, he would keep the $75,000 in call premiums.

Solution to 3:

- The premiums received on the short call are classified as a capital gain. The gain is not realized until the option expires or is bought back with an offset order. The holding period for the position is always considered to be short term since you "sell to open" and "buy to close" the position; thus, technically the purchase date and the closing date are the same day, even though the position may be open for a year or longer. If the call is sold deep in the money, the premiums would be very high, locking in the profit on the position. However, this is a very tax inefficient trade since an outright sell of the stock would qualify for the long-term tax rate of 25% but the call premium would be taxed at the much higher short-term gain rate.
- It is possible to bundle the collar into a single transaction to avoid tax on the call premiums. In this case, the tax would be zero because the net premium is zero.
- The call options could affect the taxation of the stock dividends.
- Perhaps most importantly, hedging the risk of the position could trigger a taxable event. If you no longer bear the risk of the investment, you have essentially sold the position. If the collar is constructed so that there is still some risk of loss, then the taxable event can be avoided.

Solution to 4:

Profits from the sale of the Exxon stock, including those shares called away by exercise of the call options, are treated as capital gains. If the stock was held for longer than a year, it qualifies for Michael's 25% long-term capital gain rate.

10.3 Tax-Free Exchanges

In some tax jurisdictions, a mechanism exists for accomplishing a tax-free exchange of a concentrated position. One mechanism in the United States is an **exchange fund**—a partnership in which each of the partners have each contributed low cost-basis stock to the fund. The partners then own a pro rata interest in the fund that holds a diversified pool of low-basis securities. Participating in the exchange fund is not considered a taxable event; the partners' tax basis in the partnership units remains the same as the tax basis of the stock each contributed. For tax purposes, each partner must remain in the fund for a minimum of seven years. When redeemed, the partner receives a basket of securities equal in value to the pro rata ownership in the fund.

Exchange funds have some limitations. First, the portfolio manager has discretion on whether to accept the shares and on the composition of the basket of shares distributed to partners when they withdraw. In addition, 20% of the portfolio must be "qualified assets," usually real estate investment trusts. The portfolio is often less diversified than a typical portfolio, and redemption fees may be required for early withdrawal.

Exhibit 15 assumes Michael invests in an exchange fund for seven years and then liquidates his portfolio. If the exchange fund provides the same return as the sell and diversify strategy (a big assumption), then the final liquidation value is higher for the exchange fund. This is another example of the benefit of tax deferral. Of course, the fund will charge management fees, which will reduce the benefit.

Exhibit 15   Exchange Fund Example

	Sell / Diversify	Exchange Fund
Market value	$1,000,000	$1,000,000
Tax basis	$100,000	$100,000
Capital gain	$900,000	
Tax on sale (at 25% rate)	$225,000	
Amount to invest	$775,000	$1,000,000
Market value in 7 years (10% return)	$1,510,256	$1,948,717
Tax basis	$775,000	$100,000
Capital gain	$735,256	$1,848,717
Tax on sale (at 25% rate)	$183,814	$462,179
Final Value	$1,326,442	$1,486,538

Note: Assumes a 25% tax rate and a 10% annual return for the exchange fund and the reinvestment portfolio of the diversification strategy.

10.4 Charitable Remainder Trust

Many estate planning techniques can be deployed to defray the risk associated with a concentrated position, especially if the investor has philanthropic goals. Exhibit 16 shows an example of a **charitable remainder trust**. In this structure, Michael would make an irrevocable donation of Exxon shares to a trust and receive a tax deduction for the gift. He would no longer have ownership of the assets. Within the trust, the shares could be sold and reinvested in a diversified portfolio without incurring a capital gain tax—since the charitable trust is exempt from taxes. The trust would provide income for the life of the named beneficiaries. (The beneficiaries would owe income tax on this income.) When the last-named beneficiary dies, any assets remaining in the trust would be distributed to the charity named in the trust.

Exhibit 16 Dynamics of a Charitable Remainder Trust

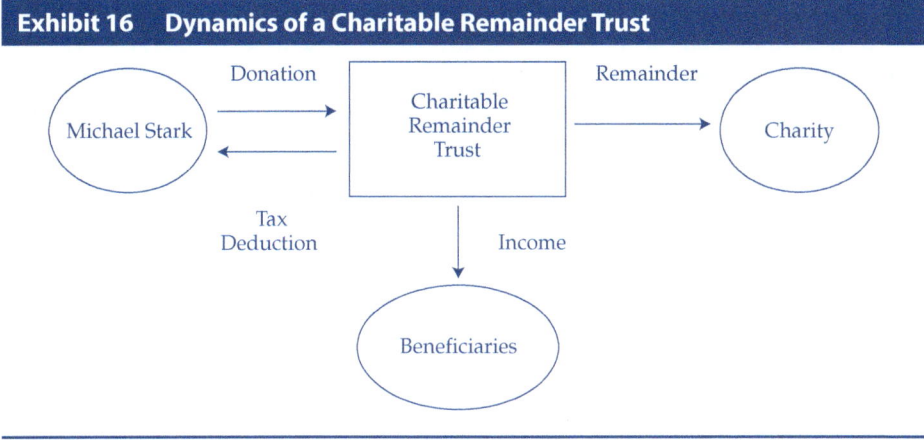

EXAMPLE 13 EXPLORING ALTERNATIVES TO SELLING

Michael Stark is reluctant to sell his shares of Exxon, primarily due to the large tax bill associated with a sale. What approaches to diversification would you discuss with Michael that do not involve the taxes from an outright sale of his stock?

Solution:

- *Covered Call Writing:* Out-of-the-money call options could be sold that would generate option premiums. While not an explicit diversification strategy, the cash generated by the options would somewhat reduce Michael's risk over time. If one of the options was exercised, Michael could buy shares on the open market to cover the option instead of delivering his company shares.
- *Equity Monetization:* Michael could construct a zero-cost collar or similar hedging strategy to reduce risk. A loan could then provide liquidity without realizing a taxable gain and without selling shares.
- *Exchange Fund:* Michael could deliver shares of stock to an exchange fund to get diversification without an outright sale.
- *Charitable Remainder Trust:* Michael could consult an estate planning attorney and devise a strategy for gifting shares to a charitable remainder trust.

STRATEGIES FOR MANAGING CONCENTRATED POSITIONS IN PRIVATELY OWNED BUSINESSES AND STRATEGIES FOR MANAGING CONCENTRATED POSITIONS IN REAL ESTATE

11

i. discuss objectives—tax and non-tax—in planning the transfer of wealth;

Business owners are often asset rich but cash poor, with most of their personal net worth tied up in their businesses. Generating liquidity can be difficult, can trigger a taxable event, and may result in the loss of control or dilution of the ownership stake. Strategies for business owners to generate full or partial liquidity include the following:

- Initial public offering (IPO)
- Sale to a third-party investor
- Sale to an insider
- Divestiture of non-core assets
- Personal line of credit against company shares
- Recapitalization
- Employee stock ownership plan

We next discuss some of the key strategies to free up capital short of an outright sale of the company.

11.1 Personal Line of Credit Secured by Company Shares

Owners might consider arranging a personal loan secured by their shares in the private company. If structured properly, this should not cause an immediate taxable event to the company or the owner. The transaction usually contains a "put" arrangement whereby the borrower can "put" the loan to the company as a source of repayment. This would likely be considered a taxable event to the business owner. The company can support this put obligation either through its existing credit arrangement or with a standby letter of credit issued for this specific purpose. While this effectively leverages the client's portfolio and the debt will eventually need to be repaid, until then owners have access to cash to diversify their concentration risk, avoid triggering a taxable event, and maintain ownership and control of the company. In most jurisdictions, the interest expense paid on the loan proceeds should be currently deductible for tax purposes.

11.2 Leveraged Recapitalization

A leveraged recapitalization is a strategy that is especially attractive to middle-market business owners who would like to reduce the risk of their wealth concentration and generate liquidity to diversify but who are not yet ready to exit entirely and have the desire to continue to grow their businesses. Typically, a private equity firm will invest equity and take partial ownership of the business. The private equity firm then provides or arranges debt with senior and mezzanine (subordinated) lenders. The owner receives cash for a portion of her stock and retains a minority ownership interest in the freshly capitalized entity. The owner is typically taxed currently on the cash received. If structured properly, a tax deferral is achieved on the stock rolled over into the newly capitalized company. The after-tax cash proceeds the investor receives could be deployed into other asset classes to help build a diversified portfolio.

11.3 Employee Stock Ownership Plan

In some countries, legislation allows business owners to sell some or all of their company shares to certain types of pension plans. For instance, in the United States an employee stock ownership plan (ESOP) is a type of pension plan that can be created by the company and is allowed to buy some or all of the owner's shares of company stock. In a version known as a leveraged ESOP, if the company has borrowing capacity the ESOP borrows funds (typically from a bank) to finance the purchase of the owner's shares.

Depending on the legal form of company structure, it may be possible to defer any capital gains tax on the shares sold to the ESOP. Using an ESOP, owners can partially diversify their holdings and overall portfolios while retaining control of the company and maintaining upside potential in the retained shares.

11.4 Strategies for Managing Concentrated Positions in Real Estate

Real estate often constitutes a significant portion of a client's net worth, and consequently, some real estate owners may be exposed to a significant degree of concentration risk and illiquidity. Property-specific risk is the non-systematic risk associated with owning a particular piece of real estate. It is the possibility that the value of the property might fall because of an event—perhaps an environmental liability or the bankruptcy of a major tenant—that affects that property but not the broader real estate market. Clients often underestimate those risks and thus overestimate the value of their properties. Like concentrated positions in public or private equity, real estate positions may have a very low tax basis and selling may trigger the recognition of a tax liability.

Owners of concentrated real estate positions seeking to monetize their real estate will frequently use various forms of debt and equity financing instead of an outright sale. Similar to private businesses, the primary strategies that real estate owners can use to monetize their properties include mortgage financing (recourse and non-recourse, fixed rate, or floating rate) and a charitable trust or donor-advised fund.

Many other real estate monetization techniques are unique to each tax jurisdiction. For example, many of today's public real estate investment trusts in the United States were created by property developers who gathered a number of their investments into a portfolio and then sold shares in that portfolio to the public.

11.5 Mortgage Financing

Besides an outright sale, which is the most common strategy, the use of mortgage financing is the next most common technique investors use to lower concentration in a particular property and generate liquidity to diversify asset portfolios without triggering a taxable event.

Consider an investor who owns a high-quality, income-producing property with a fair market value of $10 million. Suppose that the property has a tax cost basis close to zero. An outright sale of the property, given a capital gains tax rate of 25%, would result in the investor receiving $7.5 million in after-tax proceeds from the sale. The investor would not participate in any future appreciation.

As an alternative to an outright sale, the owner might obtain a loan against the property. He might choose a fixed-rate mortgage, setting the loan-to-value (LTV) ratio at the point where the net rental income generated from the property equaled the fixed mortgage payment (composed of interest expense and amortization of the loan principal). Assuming this cash flow-neutral LTV ratio is 75%, the investor could monetize $7.5 million of the real estate's value with no limitations on the use of the loan proceeds. The proceeds could be invested in a liquid, diversified portfolio of securities. The loan proceeds will not be taxed because they are not "income" for tax purposes. In addition, the net rental income derived from the property exactly covers the cost of servicing the debt and other expenses of the property, so the net income from the real estate is zero. Therefore, there are no income tax consequences from the transaction. While the investor maintains economic exposure to the asset, participating in any future appreciation, the overall portfolio is now leveraged 1.75:1 ($17,500,000/$10,000,000).

The investor might also choose an interest-only loan with a balloon payment, using the property as collateral. The loan proceeds *and* the rental income could be used to fund other investment activities.

Borrowing against appreciated, income-producing real estate, especially on a non-recourse basis (meaning that the lender's only recourse upon an event of default is to look to the property that was mortgaged to the lender), can be an attractive technique to effectively "realize" unrealized real estate gains. In lieu of selling the asset outright to realize the gain and trigger an immediate taxable event, the owner can often borrow against the property to access the same or a similar amount of proceeds that a sale would have generated but without paying any tax—and often with a net cost of carry close to zero—while capturing 100% of any increase in the property's value.

11.6 Real Estate Monetization for the Charitably Inclined—An Asset Location Strategy

A donor-advised fund (DAF) can also be used to monetize a concentrated position in real estate. We'll illustrate with an example. Jules Menendez wants to endow a named professorship at the university from which he graduated several years ago. The amount needed to fund the professorship is $3 million. He owns a rental property that is worth $2 million. The growth prospects for the property are less compelling than those of some other asset classes (e.g., publicly traded securities). He can contribute the property directly to a DAF and receive an immediate $2 million charitable contribution deduction. The property is then sold by the DAF and the proceeds invested in those more promising investments. No capital gains tax is due when the property is sold. (Nor are the accumulated depreciation deductions taken by the investor ever "recaptured.") The full $2 million is available to invest and manage. The assets grow tax free until grants are made. When the target of $3 million is reached, the DAF could then fund the professorship at Menendez's alma mater.

EXAMPLE 14 STRATEGIES FOR MANAGING CONCENTRATED POSITIONS IN PRIVATELY HELD BUSINESS AND REAL ESTATE

Emma Gagnon has built a successful chain of groceries stores of which she is majority owner. While she has accumulated some retirement assets via the company's various retirement and savings plans, 90% of her C$25,000,000 net worth is tied up in shares of the company she owns and unleveraged real estate that she leases to the stores. While she is only 50 years old and plans to continue growing the business, she is concerned that her eventual retirement is completely dependent upon the continued success of the business. Recommend two strategies that Emma might use to address this problem. Justify your response.

Solution:

Emma might consider a personal line of credit against a portion of her shares in the company. She can use the proceeds to build a diversified portfolio of assets that complements her exposure to the grocery business while maintaining her ownership position.

To free up capital tied up in the real estate she has leased to the stores, she could mortgage the properties. If the loans were non-recourse, they would effectively provide Emma with downside protection. The capital could be invested in a diversified portfolio unrelated to the grocery business.

DIRECTING AND TRANSFERRING WEALTH AND OBJECTIVES OF GIFT AND ESTATE PLANNING

j discuss strategies for achieving estate, bequest, and lifetime gift objectives in common law and civil law regimes;

The previous section dealt with the day-to-day practicalities of managing investment portfolios for private clients. To be an effective private wealth manager, however, you must have a basic understanding of the tools and techniques available to your clients seeking to preserve their wealth for future generations. While you will not be expected to structure these entities, you must have enough knowledge to identify when your client might want to engage with an estate planning specialist and will be managing assets located within the entity. This section covers the basics of estate planning, common estate planning strategies, and the "human" side of intergenerational wealth transfer. We also discuss typical approaches to asset protection, including reference to the minimization of political, litigation, and other risks.

12.1 Objectives of Gift and Estate Planning

At some stage, most wealthy individuals face the task of planning for the management of their assets beyond their own lifetimes. They may seek an effective way of transferring their assets to the next generation or donating assets to achieve charitable goals, either during their life or after death. We refer to this process as "gift and estate planning." An **estate** is all of the property a person owns or controls, which may consist of financial assets (e.g., bank accounts, stocks, bonds, business interests), tangible personal assets (e.g., artwork, collectibles, vehicles), immovable property (e.g., residential real estate, timber rights), and intellectual property (e.g., royalties). **Estate planning** is the process of preparing for the disposition of one's estate upon death and during one's lifetime. It usually requires the counsel of a variety of professionals, including financial, legal, and tax professionals.

Effective gift and estate planning should consider several objectives; the most important are described here:

- *Maintaining sufficient income and liquidity* to achieve desired lifestyle of the donors and beneficiaries as well as to pay any estate taxes due.

- *Deciding on control over the assets.* For example, clients may desire to pass the beneficial ownership to the next generation without giving them control over the investment and distribution of the assets. Or, when creating a charitable giving strategy, clients may desire to maintain some control over the specific charitable activities their money supports as opposed to simply giving money to charities.

- *Asset protection.* Certain estate planning vehicles, such as trusts, may protect assets from creditors by separating the settlor (the creator of the trust) and beneficiaries from the legal ownership of the assets. In some jurisdictions, trusts may be used for taking the assets outside of the forced heirship regime under which wealth owners have limited decision power over the disposition of their assets. **Forced heirship** is a requirement that a certain proportion of assets must pass to specified family members, such as a spouse and children. Those passing on wealth are therefore restricted in what they can pass on to non-family members. A forced heirship regime can be found mainly in the civil law countries, for example, Spain, France, and Switzerland. It does not apply in many common law countries, such as Canada, the United Kingdom, and the United States. Not all forced heirship jurisdictions are the same. In some cases, lifetime gifts are not covered; in others, they are. Some jurisdictions even allow the family to opt out of the forced heirship rules. Forced heirship also applies under Shari'a law, which is a religious law applicable to Muslim families. A number of countries in the Middle East, Africa, and Southeast Asia have Shari'a law as part of civil law.

> **CIVIL AND COMMON LAW REGIMES**
>
> Civil law, which is derived from Roman law, is the world's predominant legal system. It is based on fixed codes and statutes. In civil law states, judges apply general, abstract rules or concepts to particular cases. Common law systems, which usually trace their heritage to Britain, draw abstract rules from specific cases. In civil law systems, law is developed primarily through legislative statutes or executive action. In common law systems, law is developed primarily through decisions of the courts.

- *Transferring assets in a tax-aware manner.* The two main forms of taxes on wealth transfers correspond to the primary ways of transferring assets. Gifting assets during one's lifetime may, depending on the tax laws of the relevant country, be subject to a **gift tax**, and bequeathing assets upon one's death may be subject to an estate tax or an inheritance tax. In some jurisdictions, a **generation-skipping tax** may be levied if one generation is skipped when transferring the assets (e.g., the grandparents make gifts directly to their grandchildren, bypassing the parents). A generation-skipping transfer tax (GST tax) exists in the United States; the grandparent pays a 40% tax on assets transferred to the grandchildren in excess of the lifetime GST exclusion amount of $11.4 million (as of 2019).

- *Preservation of family wealth.* Setting up a family governance system alongside the estate planning process mitigates potential disputes among the family members, ensuring that they work together toward achieving jointly agreed upon investment and charitable goals. Family governance is a process for a family's collective communication and decision making. A good governance framework will serve current and future generations and should help to preserve and grow wealth across generations. Families often develop family constitutions designed to set out how governance will work for that family. While the family constitution is usually a non-binding document, the governance approach is made binding through the vehicles used in the succession plan, which might include trusts, foundations, life insurance, and companies.

- *Business succession.* Gift and estate planning helps the founder (or current generation of ownership) to pass control and beneficial ownership of the family business to the next generation. Additionally, the founder may face a choice between assigning managerial responsibilities to the outsider managers, keeping control of the business within the family, or even selling the business outright.

- *Achieving charitable goals.* Charitable giving to qualified charities or private foundations in most jurisdictions qualifies for gift tax or estate tax deduction or exemption, which leaves more capital to be deployed on charitable causes. If charitable giving is made during the donor's lifetime, it may also qualify for an income tax deduction. The creation of a private foundation may also serve to create a long-lasting family legacy around which subsequent generations can come to understand the family values.

ESTATE AND INHERITANCE TAX REGIMES

In general, the main difference between an **estate tax** and **inheritance tax** relates to who is responsible for paying it. An estate tax is levied on the total value of a deceased person's assets and paid out of the estate before any distributions to beneficiaries. An inheritance tax is paid by each individual beneficiary. Most jurisdictions only have one of these types of taxes. In the United Kingdom, for example, all taxes are paid at the donor/estate level. In the United States, there is an estate tax on the federal level, but the individual states may also levy estate and/or inheritance taxes.

Many jurisdictions have tax-free allowances that can be used for transferring assets under a certain threshold without paying an estate or inheritance tax.

Exhibit 17 shows some of the gift and estate tax regimes around the world. Be advised that the presentation of tax rates, exclusions, and payee are simplified for illustrative purposes. The actual tax laws are quite complex and cover many combinations of relationship and residency that are virtually impossible to summarize in any comprehensive fashion.

Exhibit 17 Estate and Inheritance Tax Rates for Selected Jurisdictions

Jurisdiction	Maximum Estate Tax Rate (%)	Allowances	Taxes Paid by:
Japan	55.0	Spousal exemption and up to ¥10 million per statutory heir	Beneficiary
Belgium	30.0[1]	Minor exemptions	Beneficiary
Netherlands	20.0[2]	Partner exemption of up to €650,913	Beneficiary
United Kingdom	40.0	Unlimited spousal or partner exemption	Estate
South Korea	50.0[3]	Spousal exemption of up to ₩3 billion; ₩50 million for a child of the deceased	Beneficiary
United States	40.0	First $11 million is exempt from taxation for citizens and domiciliaries. Unlimited spousal exemption for citizens and domiciliaries.	Estate

Note: Tax rates are as of 2018.
[1] For direct descendants. The maximum tax rate for other than direct descendants is 80%.
[2] For partner and children. Up to 40% for other persons.
[3] Higher for persons other than a son or daughter.
Source: EY 2019 Worldwide Estate and Inheritance Tax Guide (https://www.ey.com/gl/en/services/tax/worldwide-estate-and-inheritance-tax-guide---xmlqs?preview&XmlUrl=/ec1mages/taxguides/IEIT-2019/IEIT-US.xml).

Sound gift and estate planning will seek to fully utilize all tax-free gift allowances. In certain circumstances, it is financially advantageous to transfer an asset prior to death so the capital appreciation (and associated capital gains tax liability) accrues outside of the estate where it is likely to be less-heavily taxed. Many wealthy families often manage these tax considerations across multiple tax regimes. Often, wealthy individuals use for investment and estate planning purposes solutions (e.g., trusts, personal holding companies) registered in tax-light jurisdictions, such as Cayman Islands, The Bahamas, Bermuda, British Virgin Islands, Guernsey, Jersey, and Isle of Man. Each country has its own legislation in relation to personal holding companies (PHCs), which typically hold income-generating investment assets and are also known as controlled foreign corporations (CFCs). Shares of a PHC are often owned by individual family members or a family trust. Most countries are tightening their legislation related to moving assets to tax light jurisdictions with the aim to combat tax avoidance.

EXAMPLE 15 FORCED HEIRSHIP REGIME

Philippe and Helena Berelli and their two children live in a country with forced heirship laws that entitle a spouse to one-third of the total estate and the children to split one-third of the total estate. Suppose Philippe passes away today with a total estate of €800,000 and wishes to leave €300,000 to his surviving mother.

1. What is the minimum that Helena should receive?
2. What is the minimum amount the children should receive under forced heirship rules?
3. May Philippe bequeath €300,000 to his mother?

Solution to 1:

Under forced heirship rules, Helena is entitled to one-third of the total estate, or (1/3)(€800,000) = €266,667.

Solution to 2:

The children are collectively entitled to receive one-third of the total estate equal to €266,667, or €133,333 for each child.

Solution to 3:

Philippe is able to freely dispose of the remainder, which is €800,000 − €266,667 − €266,667 = €266,666. Therefore, Philippe is unable to bequeath €300,000 to his mother, but he may bequeath the remainder of €266,666.

The following vignette takes our private clients Ivy and Charles Lee and considers a set of estate planning objectives that would likely be relevant.

INVESTOR CASE FACTS: THE LEE FAMILY

Client: Ivy and Charles Lee. Ivy is a 54-year-old life sciences entrepreneur; she is the CEO of one privately-held life science enterprise and has significant ownership interests in two others. Charles is 55 years old and employed as an orthopedic surgeon. They have two children, aged 25 (Deborah) and 18 (David). Deborah is divorced and has a daughter with physical limitations. The Lees' total portfolio is $25 million, with $1 million in margin debt, plus residential real estate of $3 million, with $1 million in mortgage debt. David will soon begin studying at a four-year private university; the present value of the expected parental contribution is $250,000. The Lees desire to give a gift to a local art museum in five years. In present value terms, the gift is valued at $750,000.

From this brief description of the family circumstances, we can identify several possible estate planning objectives:

- *Business succession*—As the CEO of one privately held firm and with significant ownership interests in two others, Ivy's estate planning objectives should encompass a solution for the transfer of ownership, either to her heirs or to a third party. Similarly, Charles' orthopedic practice likely has embedded value beyond his role as a surgeon, and a plan should be devised to extract and transfer that value.

- *Asset protection*—Given Charles' profession as an orthopedic surgeon and Ivy's involvement with the evolving field of life sciences, it is likely that their assets may be vulnerable to claims from creditors (e.g., a medical malpractice award or a shareholder settlement in the event of firm failure).
- *Control*—Charles and Ivy would likely want to consider placing some controls on the management of their assets if they were both to die in the near term. Neither David nor Deborah appear likely to have sufficient experience or expertise to oversee a $25 million estate. In addition, Ivy and Charles may want to ensure that their granddaughter's medical, education, and other needs are taken care of irrespective of their daughter's future choices. Thus, they may seek a mechanism to segregate a portion of their assets to ensure the granddaughter's needs are looked after.
- *Charitable gift*—The planned gift to the museum offers an opportunity for tax and estate planning.
- *Tax awareness*—To maximize the value of assets that will be available to heirs and other beneficiaries at their death, the Lees will want to ensure that any estate plan that considers the taxes due during their lifetime and at their death.

13

GIFT AND ESTATE PLANNING STRATEGIES, INTRODUCTION TO ESTATE PLANNING: WILLS, PROBATE AND LEGAL SYSTEMS, AND LIFETIME GIFTS AND TESTAMENTARY BEQUESTS

j   discuss strategies for achieving estate, bequest, and lifetime gift objectives in common law and civil law regimes;

Having the right estate planning strategy is important to ensure smooth transition of wealth. The choice of gift and estate planning tools depends on the legal system as well as goals of each individual family. This section introduces the main concepts of estate planning, such as will, probate (the legal process for administering the will), and difference in approaches to wealth transfer in various legal systems. It also explains the main principles of using lifetime gifts and testamentary bequests (e.g., a transfer that is set out in an individual's last will) in wealth transfer. The most widely used estate planning tools, such as trusts, foundations, life insurance, and companies, are also discussed.

13.1 Introduction to Estate Planning: Wills, Probate, and Legal Systems

As discussed, an estate is all of the property a person owns or controls. **Estate planning** is the process of preparing for the disposition of one's estate upon death and during one's lifetime. The core document most closely associated with an estate plan is a will or testament. A **will (or testament)** outlines the rights others will have over one's property after death. A **testator** is the person who authored the will and whose property is disposed of according to the will. **Probate** is the legal process to confirm the validity of the will so that executors, heirs, and other interested parties can rely on its authenticity. Decedents without a valid will or with a will that does not dispose of their property are considered to have died **intestate**. In that case, a court will often decide on the disposition of assets under the intestacy laws of the applicable jurisdiction(s).

A country's legal system may constrain the ability of testators to freely dispose of their assets. The common law jurisdictions, such as the United Kingdom and the United States, generally allow testators freedom of disposition by will; that is, the right to use their own judgment regarding the rights others will have over their property after death.

Most civil law countries, however, place restrictions on testamentary disposition. Under forced heirship rules, for example, children have the right to a fixed share of a parent's estate. Wealthy individuals may attempt to move assets into an offshore trust governed by a different domicile to circumvent forced heirship rules. Or, they may attempt to reduce a forced heirship claim by gifting or donating assets to others during their lifetime to reduce the value of the final estate upon death.

Countries following **Shari'a**, the law of Islam, have substantial variation but are more like civil law systems, especially in regard to estate planning. Because Shari'a is not the law of the land in most countries, including some countries where a majority of the population is Muslim, those who wish to follow Islamic guidance on inheritance will want to do so through the making of a will as long as the contents of the will are not in conflict with the law of the specific jurisdiction.

A country's legal system defines which estate planning tools are available for the transfer of wealth. The legal concept of a trust, for example, is relatively unique to common law countries. A **trust** is a vehicle through which an individual (called a settlor) entrusts certain assets to a trustee (or trustees) who manages the assets for the benefit of assigned beneficiaries. A trust may be either a testamentary trust—a trust created through the testator's will—or a living or inter-vivos trust—a trust created during the settlor's lifetime. A trust is a legal relationship and not a legal person. A legal person is a person or organization that has legal rights and duties related to contracts, agreements, payments, transactions, obligations, and penalties (including the right to take legal action to enforce any related claims). The trust itself cannot hold assets, enter into contracts, or undertake other legal formalities. While assets may be placed "in trust," the legal owner of the assets is typically a trustee or a grantor depending on the type of trust. Some civil law countries may not recognize foreign trusts, and many civil law jurisdictions, including France and Germany, do not recognize trusts at all (though their tax laws do address the treatment of trusts). A *foundation*, unlike trusts, can hold assets in its own name. Foundations originated in civil law regimes as estate planning vehicles, and they are also available in some common law jurisdictions, predominantly used for similar purposes as charitable trusts.

13.2 Lifetime Gifts and Testamentary Bequests

Wealthy individuals can transfer their wealth by gifting it either during their lifetime or after death. In an estate planning context, lifetime gifts are sometimes referred to as lifetime gratuitous transfers, and they are made during the lifetime of the donor. The term "gratuitous" refers to a transfer made with purely donative intent—that is, without expectation of anything in exchange.[1] Gifts may or may not be taxed depending on the jurisdiction. In some civil law jurisdictions (e.g., France), tax-free allowances for lifetime gifts depend on the relationship between a beneficiary and a donor.

Bequeathing assets or transferring assets in some other way upon one's death is referred to as a **testamentary bequest** or a **testamentary gratuitous transfer**. From a recipient's perspective, it is called an inheritance. As discussed, taxes on wealth transfer may be applied to the transferor or the recipient. These taxes may be applied at a flat rate or based on a **progressive tax rate schedule**, where the tax rate increases as the

---

[1] "Gratuitous" means given freely and without obligation. It is a descendant of the Latin word "gratus," which means "pleasing" or "grateful."

amount of wealth transferred increases. Often the tax is applied after the deduction of a statutory allowance, described more fully later. The tax rate may also depend on the relationship between transferor and recipient. Transfers to spouses, for instance, are often tax exempt (e.g., in the United Kingdom, United States, and France).

Many jurisdictions establish periodic or lifetime allowances within which the gifts can be made without transfer tax. For example, UK taxpayers may make lifetime gifts up to £325,000 before inheritance tax is applied. In the United States, a donor's annual gift exclusions are limited to $15,000 per year, per donee (e.g., a parent may annually transfer $15,000 to each child or $30,000 from both parents). These amounts do not count toward the lifetime gift and estate tax exemption for citizens and domiciliaries ($22 million per couple as of 2019). There is no limit on the number of gift recipients. (These allowances are as of 2019 and are subject to change.) Other exclusions or relief may apply as well. It is common to be able to transfer some assets by gift in a tax-efficient manner.

EXAMPLE 16 UK INHERITANCE TAX EXAMPLE

Paul Dasani, a widower, passed away in May 2019. Dasani was a resident and domiciliary of the United Kingdom at the time of his death and had a total estate valued at £700,000. His children are the beneficiaries of the estate. The United Kingdom imposes an inheritance tax threshold on estates valued above £325,000 in 2019. The tax is payable by the trustee of the estate out of estate assets at a rate of 40% on the amount over the statutory allowance of £325,000.

What is the amount of inheritance tax payable?

Solution:

The inheritance tax is computed as:

Estate value	£700,000
Less threshold	(£325,000)
Excess	£375,000
Rate on excess	40%
Inheritance tax	£150,000

EXAMPLE 17 PROGRESSIVE ESTATE TAX EXAMPLE

Ya-wen Chao passed away in a jurisdiction with progressive estate tax rates as provided in the following table.

Taxable Estate (€)	Tax Rate (%)
Up to 600,000	2
600,001–1,500,000	4
1,500,001–3,000,000	7
3,000,001–4,500,000	11
4,500,001–6,000,000	15
6,000,001–10,000,000	20
10,000,001–15,000,000	26
15,000,001–40,000,000	33
40,000,001–100,000,000	41
Over 100,000,000	50

After all applicable exemptions, Chao had a taxable estate of €2,000,000. What is Chao's estate tax?

Solution:

The estate tax is computed as:

Tax on first 600,000 (2%) =	€12,000
Tax on next 900,000 (4%) =	36,000
Tax on remaining 500,000 (7%) =	35,000
Total estate tax =	€83,000

The choice between gifting assets during lifetime or after death depends on various considerations, including taxation system and expected return on the asset. Transferring assets during life using the tax-free allowances allows appreciation on gifted assets to be effectively transferred to the donee without gift or estate tax. Appreciation on the gifted asset is still subject to tax on investment returns (e.g., dividends and capital gains) whether it remains in the donor's estate or is transferred to a donee. But if the tax-free gift had not been made and had remained in the estate, the appreciation on it would have been subject to estate or inheritance tax. It is commonly believed that gifting assets that are expected to appreciate prior to death rather than transferring them after death is more tax efficient because the future estate tax liability will be greater. Depending on jurisdiction, there may be an economic difference between gifting during lifetime and testamentary transfer. In the United Kingdom, for example, a gift is not taxed but will be subject to inheritance tax if the donor passes away within seven years of the gift being made. In the United States, if a gift is made during the donor's lifetime, only the amount transferred is subject to gift tax; the taxes paid are independent of the gift (and effectively reduce the value of the donor's estate). If the transfer occurs at death, however, the entire estate is subject to estate tax and the amount available to transfer to the heirs is reduced. Here's a simple example to illustrate:

> Maria has an estate valued at $2,000,000. She lives in a jurisdiction with a unified gift and estate tax exemption of $1,000,000. The applicable estate tax rate is 40%. If, during her lifetime, she gifts $1,500,000 to her children, $500,000 is subject to tax. She pays the tax from her remaining assets and has $300,000 left after the payment of taxes. When she dies, she will owe an additional $120,000 in estate taxes and her children will receive an additional $180,000. In total, they will have received $1,680,000. If she waits until her death to transfer her assets to her children, her taxable estate will be $1,000,000 and the taxes due will be $400,000. The net assets available to her children will be $1,600,000.

Charitable gratuitous transfers. Most jurisdictions provide two forms of tax relief for wealth transfers to not-for-profit or charitable organizations. First, most charitable donations are not subject to a gift tax. Second, most jurisdictions permit income tax deductions for charitable donations. Therefore, families with philanthropic aspirations can transfer wealth very tax efficiently. Furthermore, if the family establishes its own charitable organization for the purpose of furthering its philanthropic objectives, investment returns on the assets transferred to the charity may compound tax free, increasing the amount of assets available to support the philanthropic objectives over the long term.

13.3 Efficiency of Lifetime Gifts versus Testamentary Bequests

In general, the relative after-tax value of a tax-free gift made during one's lifetime compared to a **bequest** that is transferred as part of a taxable estate can be expressed as the ratio of the future value of the gift to the future value of the bequest. The numerator is the future after-tax value of the tax-free gift. The denominator is the future after-tax value of a taxable transfer by bequest. The ratio is the relative value of making the tax-free gift compared to the bequest:

$$RV_{\text{Tax Free Gift}} = \frac{FV_{\text{Gift}}}{FV_{\text{Bequest}}}$$

The future value of the gift is a function of the expected pre-tax returns to the beneficiary, r_g, the effective tax rate on those returns, t_g, and the expected time until the donor's death, n:

$$FV_{\text{Gift}} = [1 + r_g(1 - t_g)]^n.$$

The future value of the bequest is a function of the expected pre-tax returns to the estate, r_e, the effective tax rate on those returns, t_e, the expected time until the donor's death, and the estate tax rate, T_e:

$$FV_{\text{Bequest}} = [1 + r_e(1 - t_e)]^n(1 - T_e).$$

Putting it all together, the relative value of the gift made during the donor's lifetime is:

$$RV_{\text{Tax Free Gift}} = \frac{FV_{\text{Gift}}}{FV_{\text{Bequest}}} = \frac{\left[1 + r_g(1 - t_g)\right]^n}{\left[1 + r_e(1 - t_e)\right]^n(1 - T_e)} \quad (3)$$

If the pre-tax return and effective tax rates are equal for both the recipient and donor, the relative value of the tax-free gift in Equation 3 reduces to $1/(1 - T_e)$. For example, consider the value of a €10,000 bequest in today's value subject to a 40% inheritance tax, netting €6,000 after tax. If the wealth is instead transferred as a tax-free gift without having to pay the 40% inheritance tax, the relative value of the tax-free gift is 1.67 times, or $1/(1 - 0.40)$, as great as the taxable bequest, or €10,000 versus €6,000.

In practice, the respective tax rates on returns will vary with each situation based on the tax status of the recipient and the tax status of the donor. In many cases, the tax rate of the recipient is likely to be lower than the tax rate of the donor; thus, a greater proportion of the return will compound over the investment horizon.

In jurisdictions that allow for tax-free gifts to be made during the grantor's lifetime without reducing the aggregate gift and estate tax exemption, individuals have the opportunity to transfer wealth without taxes each year. If these allowances or exclusions expire at the end of a tax year and do not accumulate over time, tax-free gifts not made in a particular tax year are lost opportunities to capture the benefits of tax management and greater compounding of returns. It is, therefore, often beneficial for a family with wealth transfer goals to commence an early gifting program, taking advantage of annual exclusions, where applicable.

Opportunities to add value may even exist when a lifetime gift is taxable. In general, the value of making taxable gifts, rather than leaving them in the estate to be taxed as a bequest, can be expressed as ratio of the *after-tax* future value of the gift and the bequest, Equation 3 can be modified to reflect the taxes payable on the gift, $(1 - T_g)$:

$$RV_{\text{Taxable Gift}} = \frac{FV_{\text{Gift}}}{FV_{\text{Bequest}}} = \frac{\left[1 + r_g(1 - t_g)\right]^n(1 - T_g)}{\left[1 + r_e(1 - t_e)\right]^n(1 - T_e)}$$

It is important to note that this model assumes that the gift tax is paid by the recipient rather than the donor.

For example, consider a family residing in Country A is contemplating a 30 million lifetime gratuitous transfer. In Country A, 18 million can be transferred free of tax, but the remaining 12 million transfer is subject to a 50% tax rate. The same 50% rate applies if the gift is delayed and transferred as a bequest, so no tax advantage related to differences between gift and estate tax rates exists. However, if the recipient of the 12 million gift had a lower marginal tax rate on investment returns (perhaps due to a progressive income tax schedule) of, say, 20% compared to the estate's marginal tax rate of, say, 50%, the gift can still create a tax advantage. Over a 10-year horizon, the advantage for locating an asset with an 8% pre-tax return with the donee rather than the donor would be equal to:

$$RV_{\text{Taxable Gift}} = \frac{[1 + 0.08(1 - 0.20)]^{10}(1 - 0.50)}{[1 + 0.08(1 - 0.50)]^{10}(1 - 0.50)} = \frac{0.9298}{0.7401} = 1.256.$$

That is, the lower 20% tax rate associated with the gift recipient will create 25.6% more wealth in 10 years than if the asset had remained in the estate and been taxed at 50% annually for 10 years.

EXAMPLE 18   GIFT AND ESTATE TAXES

Philippe Zachary is 50 years old and resides in one of the EU countries. He is working with his wealth manager to develop an estate planning strategy to transfer wealth to his second cousin, Étienne. Annual exclusions allow Philippe to make tax-free gifts of €20,000 per year, and gratuitous transfer tax liabilities are the responsibility of the recipient. Philippe notes that the relevant tax rate for bequests from the estate is likely to be 60%. He notes further, however, that gifts (in excess of the €20,000 exception mentioned) made prior to age 70 enjoy 50% relief of the normal estate tax of 60%, for an effective tax rate of 30%. In addition, Étienne enjoys a low tax rate of 20% on investment income because he has relatively low income. Philippe, on the other hand, is subject to a 48% tax rate on investment income. Philippe is considering gifting assets that are expected to earn a 6% return annually over the next 20 years.

1. Considering the first year's tax-free gift associated with the annual exclusion, how much of his estate will Philippe have transferred on an inflation-adjusted basis in 20 years without paying estate tax?

2. What is the relative value of the tax-free gift compared to the value of a bequest in 20 years?

3. Suppose Philippe wishes to make an additional gift that would be subject to gift tax. What would be the relative after-tax value of that taxable gift compared to a bequest 20 years later?

Solution to 1:

In 20 years, the future value (measured in real terms) equals €20,000 × [1 + 0.06(1 − 0.20)]^{20} = €51,080.56. Note that although the gift was not subject to a wealth transfer tax, its subsequent investment returns are nonetheless taxable at 20%.

Solution to 2:

The relative value of the tax-free gift compared to the bequest is:

$$RV_{\text{Tax Free Gift}} = \frac{[1 + 0.06(1 - 0.20)]^{20}}{[1 + 0.06(1 - 0.48)]^{20}(1 - 0.60)} = \frac{2.5540}{0.7395} = 3.45$$

The gift is substantially more tax efficient in this case for three reasons. First, the gift is tax free and the bequest is heavily taxed. Second, if Étienne receives the gift, subsequent investment returns will be taxed at a much lower rate than if it is kept inside the estate. Third, the difference has time to compound over a relatively long period of time since the time horizon is 20 years.

Solution to 3:

In this case, the recipient is responsible for paying the gift tax at 30%, or half of the 60% estate tax. The relative value of the tax-free gift compared to a bequest subject to inheritance tax is:

$$RV_{\text{Taxable Gift}} = \frac{[1 + 0.06(1 - 0.20)]^{20}(1 - 0.30)}{[1 + 0.06(1 - 0.48)]^{20}(1 - 0.60)} = \frac{1.7878}{0.7395} = 2.42.$$

Although the gift is taxed, the after-tax value of the gift relative to the bequest is still quite large because the gift tax rate is low and because the gift is located in a lightly taxed place (i.e., with Étienne) for a long period of time.

ESTATE PLANNING TOOLS: TRUSTS, FOUNDATIONS, LIFE INSURANCE, COMPANIES — 14

k describe considerations related to managing wealth across multiple generations.

The gratuitous transfers described are often implemented through structures that allow planning for taxes and produce a non-tax benefit. Common estate planning tools include, among others, trusts (a common law concept), foundations (a civil law concept), life insurance, and companies. The structure of each has implications for how assets are controlled, whether assets are protected from potential claims of future creditors, and how assets are taxed.

Trusts. A trust is an arrangement created by a *settlor* (sometimes called a grantor). The grantor transfers assets to the trust, naming a trustee. Depending on the type of trust and jurisdiction, the grantor can name as a trustee him/herself, another individual, or an institution (trust company). The trustee holds and manages the assets for the benefit of the beneficiaries. As a result, the beneficiaries are considered to be the beneficial, not legal, owners of the trust assets. (*Beneficial ownership* is a legal term that means that certain rights, such as the right to the income from the securities or the right to live in the house, belong to the beneficiary but that the title to the securities or the property are held by another person or entity.) The terms of the trust relationship and the principles used by the trustee to manage the assets and distributions to the beneficiaries are outlined in the trust document.

Trusts can be categorized in many ways, but two dimensions are particularly important in understanding their character. First, a trust can be either revocable or irrevocable. In a **revocable trust** arrangement, the settlor (the person whose assets are used to create the trust) retains the right to rescind the trust relationship and regain title to the trust assets. Under these circumstances, the settlor is generally considered to be the owner of the assets for tax purposes in most jurisdictions. As a result, the settlor is responsible for tax payments and reporting on the trust's investment returns. Additionally, the settlor's revocation power makes the trust assets vulnerable to the reach of creditors having claims against the settlor. Alternatively, where the settlor has no ability to revoke the trust relationship, the trust is characterized as an **irrevocable trust**. In an irrevocable trust structure, trustees may be responsible for tax payments and reporting in their capacity as owners of the trust assets for tax purposes. An irrevocable trust structure generally provides greater asset protection from claims against a settlor than a revocable trust.

Second, trusts can be structured to be either fixed or discretionary. Distributions to beneficiaries of a **fixed trust** are specified in the trust document to occur at certain times or in certain amounts. In contrast, if the trust document enables the trustee to determine whether and how much to distribute based on a beneficiary's general welfare, the trust would be called a **discretionary trust**. Under a discretionary trust, the beneficiaries have no legal right to income generated by the trust or to the assets in the trust itself. Therefore, the creditors of the beneficiaries cannot as easily reach the trust assets.

There are several main objectives for using a trust structure:

- *Control.* A common motivation for using a trust structure is to make resources available to beneficiaries without yielding complete control of those resources to them. For example, trusts can be used to provide resources to beneficiaries who may be unable or unwilling to manage the assets themselves—perhaps because they are young, immature, or disabled. Or, perhaps the settlor desires that the assets be used for particular purposes.

- *Asset protection.* In general, creditors are unable to reach assets that an individual does not own. As discussed, an irrevocable trust can protect assets from claims against the settlor and discretionary trusts can protect assets from claims against the beneficiaries. In community property jurisdictions (a marital property regime under which most property acquired by a spouse during a marriage is owned jointly by both spouses and is divided upon divorce, annulment, or the death of a spouse), trusts may also be used to ensure that ownership of a family business does not get diluted as a result of community property laws. Trusts can also be used to avoid probate.

- *Tax-related considerations.* Trusts can also be used for tax management purposes. For example, under a progressive tax rate regime, a wealthy individual's income may be taxed at relatively high rates. That individual might transfer assets to a trust where the income may be taxed at lower rates or where the income is paid to a beneficiary who is taxed at lower rates. Moreover, if an irrevocable trust is structured as discretionary, the trustee can manage distributions to a beneficiary in accordance with the beneficiary's tax situation. Alternatively, a settlor may create a trust in a jurisdiction with a low tax rate.

Foundations. A **foundation** is a legal entity available in certain jurisdictions. Foundations are typically set up to hold assets for a specific charitable purpose, such as to promote education or for philanthropy. When set up and funded by an individual or family and managed by its own directors, it is called a private foundation. The term family foundation usually refers to a private foundation where donors or members of the donors' family are actively involved.

Whereas a trust arrangement typically transfers decision-making authority to a trustee, a foundation allows the donor to retain control over the administration and decision making of the foundation. Depending on the jurisdiction, private foundations may be required to make certain minimum annual distributions; for example, in the United States, 5% of the foundation's prior year average net investment assets must

Estate Planning Tools: Trusts, Foundations, Life Insurance, Companies

be distributed each year. Among the benefits of foundations are a current income tax deduction for the value of assets transferred to the foundation, favorable tax treatment of investment returns, and protection of assets from estate tax. Like trusts, foundations survive the settlor and allow the settlor's wishes to be followed after the settlor's death. There is a growing trend of foundations being set up to employ charitable capital during a pre-defined number of years rather than in perpetuity.

Life insurance. Life insurance is another planning tool in which the policyholder transfers assets (called a premium) to an insurer who, in turn, has a contractual obligation to pay death benefit proceeds to the beneficiary named in the policy. As is the case with trusts, insurance can produce tax and estate planning benefits. Death benefit proceeds paid to life insurance beneficiaries are tax exempt in many jurisdictions, and in some cases, no tax-reporting consequences arise. In addition, premiums paid by the policyholder typically are neither part of the policyholder's taxable estate at the time of death nor subject to a gratuitous transfer tax. Life insurance can also be paired with trust structures to transfer assets to the beneficiaries outside of the probate process. For example, in the United Kingdom, if a trust that holds family assets buys a life insurance policy on the life of the settlor, the life insurance proceeds are not included in the estate of the settlor and proceeds will be paid directly to the beneficiaries without going through probate. This may provide a more favorable tax outcome—such as in India, which treats insurance proceeds more favorably than trust distributions.

Other forms of insurance can also be part of the "wealth planning toolbox." For example, some retirement insurance products, such as deferred variable annuities, can be part of the development of a tax-efficient asset protection and succession plan for a family.

Companies. Companies may also be a useful tool in which to place assets. For example, a **controlled foreign corporation (CFC)** is a company located outside a taxpayer's home country in which the taxpayer has a controlling interest as defined under the home country law. Depending on the jurisdiction, the taxes on income from assets in a CFC can be deferred until the earnings are distributed to shareholders or until the company is sold or shares otherwise disposed. Many countries have CFC rules designed to ensure that tax is ultimately paid in the home country of the beneficial owner.

EXAMPLE 19   ESTATE PLANNING FOR THE HARPER FAMILY

John Harper (56 years old) is a founder and CEO of a privately-owned supermarket chain recently valued by a financial consultant at $300 million. His wife, Breda Harper, is a 54-year-old housewife who took care of the family while John was building the business. The Harper family is based in a country with the common law regime. In addition to the business, John and Breda own commercial property, with an estimated value of $10,000,000, and a house. Most of the family wealth is concentrated in the family business and real estate. John and Breda have 3 children:

- James (35 years old) has been helping his father run the family business. At this stage, James intends to launch an online retail business of his own, which he would like to finance partially with a loan. James is married and has a 10-year-old daughter and a 12-year-old son.

- Nick (30 years old) is a young artist and currently relies on the family income to cover his living expenses. Nick has no financial knowledge and is not interested in investments. His father, John, would like to continue supporting Nick's lifestyle but would not be comfortable to let Nick manage his own funds. Nick is single.
- Ann (27 years old) is a pharmacist. She is married and has a 6-year-old daughter, who requires medical care, care that is financed from the income generated by the family business. Ann's husband works in corporate finance.

John intends to retire from running the family business and is thinking about passing the wealth to the next generations and creating a family legacy. After retirement, John and Breda would like to travel and support several philanthropic causes. They want to be actively involved in philanthropic activity and believe that their children and grandchildren should be involved in making philanthropic decisions as well.

1 Identify possible estate planning objectives of the Harper family.
2 Discuss estate planning strategies that can be employed to achieve each of the estate planning objectives you identified in response to question 1.

Solution to 1:

At least seven possible estate planning objectives are evident in the case facts presented:

- *Income and liquidity*—An estate planning solution should provide sufficient income to support the desired lifestyle of John and Breda, to cover medical care costs for Ann's daughter, to cover living expenses of other family members who rely on family income (Nick), and to cover any tax obligations related to wealth transfer.
- *Business succession*—John plans to retire, and the family needs to decide if the company will be run by a family member or an outsider. The family also needs to decide if the company remains in the family ownership or is sold to a third party.
- *Control over assets*—As John is not comfortable with Nick managing his own money, John needs an estate planning solution that will separate investment and income distribution decisions from the beneficial ownership. John would like to be actively involved in philanthropic decisions, thus he needs to maintain a certain degree of control over assets dedicated to philanthropy.
- *Transferring assets in a tax-aware manner*—An estate planning solution should be designed in a way that takes into account the jurisdiction-specific tax legislation.
- *Asset protection*—As James is planning to use a loan to set up his online retail business, protection of family assets from potential creditors may be one of the estate planning objectives.

- *Preservation of family wealth*—The Harper family consists of several generations (parents, children, grandchildren) who may have different goals and interests in relation to the family business. An estate planning solution should be developed in order to align interests of all family members while preserving family wealth.
- *Achieving charitable goals*—An estate planning solution should provide sufficient resources and instruments for achieving charitable goals of the family.

Solution to 2:

- *Income and liquidity*—The Harper family has several members who rely on the family income; thus, investment solutions should provide sufficient ongoing income in the long term. The following investment products should be considered: dividend paying equities, fixed income, or a combination of the two. Investment goals should be documented in the investment policy statement of the family alongside the risk and return objectives.
- *Business succession*—John is looking to retire. The main business succession options he has are as follows:
    - Keep both management and ownership of the business within the family. This might not be a plausible option, however, as the only person with the working knowledge of the business is James, who is planning to leave the family business and start his own firm.
    - Hire an external manager and keep the business in family ownership.
    - Sell the business fully or partially to a third party, or list its shares via an IPO.
- *Control over assets*—As John would like to provide for living expenses of his children and grandchildren but is not comfortable with giving some of them control over the investment and distribution decisions, a discretionary trust may be used, which gives trustees the power to decide on investments and distributions based on the circumstances of beneficiaries. It is important that John select a current and successor trustee in a way that avoids creating any tensions within the family. For example, John could name himself a trustee and select an institutional trustee as a successor to make sure that there is no conflict of interest among the family members.
- *Wealth transfer in a tax-aware manner*—John and Breda should take into account available tax-free allowances prescribed by law, such as spousal allowances or gifts to relatives. They should also consider if it makes sense to pass some assets to their grandchildren directly and what the tax implications would be, such as a generation-skipping tax. Founders should also consider if it makes sense to sell the business outright or put it into the trust for capital appreciation to occur outside of the estate.
- *Asset protection*—A trust structure can be used to protect the assets from creditors. An irrevocable trust can protect assets from claims against the settlor, and discretionary trusts can protect assets from claims against the beneficiaries.

- *Preservation of family wealth*—Creating a family governance system will help identify and align goals of various family members as well as smooth the process of wealth transfer to the next generation.
- *Charitable goals*—As John would like to be actively involved in decision-making related charitable activities and expressed desire to involve the next generations of his family, a private foundation is more suitable than gifting to charities. A private foundation allows the donor to make decisions on the causes to support and run various charitable projects. It also allows the family members to be involved. (In the United States, a donor-advised fund may also be an option.)

CROSS-BORDER ESTATE PLANNING

Cross-border families and cross-border investments require special care and coordination of advisers in more than one country. A trust established by a resident of one country may have beneficiaries not only in that country but also in other countries where children may be living. Sound estate planning must consider the rules of each jurisdiction. Similarly, cross-border asset ownership must be carefully considered. Consider investors located in Singapore and investing in US equities. While they may not be subject to worldwide estate and gift taxation (as they would be if they were citizens or residents of the United States), they *are* subject to US estate tax on assets located in the United States. And, unlike US citizens or residents who enjoy a significant estate tax exemption, non-US deceased receive minimal exemptions.

Occasionally, wealth or business owners will consider moving from one country to another, possibly even changing their citizenship. The change may be motivated by safety and political risk concerns, by tax considerations, or perhaps by estate planning considerations. An increasing number of countries (e.g., Japan, Canada, the United States, and many others) impose exit taxes on those giving up taxable residence. An exit tax often takes the form of a capital gains tax on unrealized capital gains accrued during the period in which the taxpayer was a tax resident of the country in question.

15. MANAGING WEALTH ACROSS GENERATIONS, GENERAL PRINCIPLES OF FAMILY GOVERNANCE, FAMILY CONFLICT RESOLUTION, AND FAMILY DYNAMICS IN THE CONTEXT OF BUSINESS EXIT

Modern wealthy families are often very large. In addition to the main wealth creator(s) or business founder(s), they may include numerous siblings, children with their families, grandchildren, etc. Families may face behavioral and emotional challenges, such as generational conflict, sibling rivalry, or other tensions, which may adversely impact decision making regarding the family business and transfer of wealth. When many stakeholders are involved, families may establish a system of family governance to ensure the effective generation, transition, preservation, and growth of wealth through time. According to Stalk and Foley (2012), the family-owned enterprise tends to decline by the third generation. The founder *creates wealth*, the second generation *maintains wealth*, and the third generation *depletes wealth*.

This is such a common phenomenon that many countries have a saying to capture the reality:

- "Shirtsleeves-to-shirtsleeves in three generations"
- "The father buys, the son builds, the grandchild sells, and his son begs"
- "Wealth never survives three generations"
- "From stables to stars to stables"

While 70% of family businesses fail or are sold before the second generation can take over their management, the decline in wealth across generations can generally be attributed to

- the dilution of wealth among a larger number of descendants,
- a lack of interest in the family business by younger generations, and/or
- a lack of education and planning by family members.

A strong family governance framework can mitigate some of these issues. The next section explains the concept of family governance, its purposes, and the associated governing bodies. We also address specific issues related to wealth transfer across generations in the families with wealth concentrated in a family business.

15.1 General Principles of Family Governance

Family governance is defined as a process for a family's collective communication and decision making designed to serve current and future generations. Family governance is based on the common values of the family, which are defined collectively by all members of the family, and is aimed at preserving and growing a family's wealth over a long period of time.

Family governance serves several purposes, such as:

- establishing principles for collaboration among family members,
- preserving and growing a family's wealth, and
- increasing human and financial capital across the generations.
- The family governance framework consists of formal legal documents, non-binding family agreements, and the list of goals and values defined collectively and agreed upon by the members of the family during the meetings.

Charles Collier, who served as the senior philanthropic adviser at Harvard University for 25 years, highlights several factors essential to effective family governance (see Collier 2012). These include the following:

- Focusing on the human, intellectual, and social capital of the family:
  - *Human capital*—the unique gifts and experiences of individual family members
  - *Intellectual capital*—the knowledge of family members outside of the family business
  - *Social capital*—the role of family members as philanthropists and leaders in their local communities
- Recognizing the importance of individual goals of each family member
- Improving communication within the family
- Defining a family's mission and vision
- Educating younger generations to master the competences and responsibilities that come with financial wealth

> **COMMON GOVERNANCE ENTITIES FOR HIGH-NET-WORTH FAMILIES**
>
> Families use a number of governing bodies for business decision making, investments administration, and philanthropy. These are the most common structures:
>
> - *The board of directors* is established when the family business reaches a mature stage and a larger decision-making body with addition of experienced outside experts is required. Adding external experts to the board of directors also helps mitigate an overconfidence bias, which may affect decisions of the founder in relation to expanding the business areas in which the founder has limited or no expertise. The board of directors consists of both family members (typically active in the business) and outside experts. The board of directors is responsible for establishing the direction and goals of the business and protects the interests of shareholders. Often, founders of family businesses establish an *advisory board* as a precursor to a full-fledged board of directors. This allows the founder to do a "trial run" to determine such considerations as board structure, composition, and governing policies as well as to become more acclimated to the idea of reporting to a board.
>
> - *The family council* consists of selected family members. The family council represents the family in dealing with the board of directors. The family constitution—which defines the operating principles of the family council, its composition, and responsibilities—is created in consultation with the entire family.
>
> - *The family assembly* is a forum gathering all family members. The assembly typically meets at least annually to discuss the business direction of the family-owned company. It serves the purpose of increasing transparency and preventing conflict among family members. It also creates a platform for using the human and intellectual capital of individual family members for the overall benefit of the family.
>
> - *The family office* fulfills the role of an investment and administrative center for the family; it is responsible for investment management, accounting, payroll, legal, concierge services, and financial matters.
>
> - *The family foundation* is a platform for focused philanthropy. It unites family members toward achieving common charitable goals.

A sound family governance system also serves to mitigate many of the behavioral biases that impede effective decision making. If established at an early stage and with all family members recognizing the importance of regular communication and collective decision making, it can be an effective value-added tool.

15.2 Family Conflict Resolution

Conflict resolution mechanisms are necessary in virtually all legal relationships and are commonly found in shareholder agreements and other documentation associated with shared ownership and investment. In the case of family businesses and wealth, addressing how conflicts will be resolved is also important. Conflict resolution can be particularly challenging in a family context.

For many wealth- and business-owning families, the starting point of conflict resolution procedures is the **family constitution**, typically a non-binding document that sets forth an agreed-upon set of rights, values, and responsibilities of the family members and other stakeholders. The approach to conflict resolution provided for in the family constitution can then become legally binding by being included in shareholder agreements, trust documentation, and in relation to family assets. While it is true that family constitutions and the governance approaches they provide are used only by families at the higher end of the wealth spectrum, the principles involved are relevant to all families. Merely thinking about possible conflicts and how they can be addressed is an important step in asset protection and succession planning.

15.3 Family Dynamics in the Context of Business Exit

Having a family business as the core of the family's wealth adds an additional layer of complexity. At some point, the founder must face the question of business succession planning: Will the management and ownership of the business be transitioned to a new generation within the family, or will the business be sold?

- *Transition of the business to the new generation.* Founders may allocate shares in the business to the new generation during their lifetime or after their death. The shares may be transferred directly or via trust. Control is an important decision the founders must make: Who will control the business after transition? A founder may choose to keep voting shares in order to retain power and operating control—transferring only non-voting shares to children in trust by gift or other methods. Alternatively, a founder may decide to pass voting shares to family members who are actively involved in the business and non-voting shares to family members who are not actively involved in the business.

As discussed earlier, the creation of governing bodies plays a crucial role in the smooth transition of the business across generations and its longevity. A board of directors with external members provides an independent perspective during the business transition and increases the chances of the business succeeding across generations. A family council with representation from each generation of the family helps to maintain communication between family members during the business transition. The family council also focuses on balancing liquidity needs of the family and capital needs of the business to ensure that the business remains competitive in the long run.

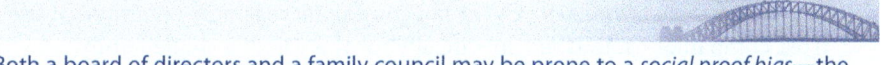

Both a board of directors and a family council may be prone to a *social proof bias*—the tendency for individuals to follow the judgment or endorsement of other members of the group without being fully aware of all the relevant facts.[2] One of the ways to mitigate the risk of a social proof bias is to ensure that the board of directors and family council include members with diverse skills and experience. The members should also actively contribute to the discussion by sharing information and knowledge on the topic.

- *Sale of the business.* Family businesses frequently have an emotional value to the founder(s) and family. Thus, when selling the business, the founder(s) may exhibit an *endowment bias*, overestimating the value of the business and refusing to accept the fact that it has weaknesses. This is likely to complicate sale negotiations. Private wealth advisers must manage the expectations of the founder to ensure smooth execution of the business sale.

---

[2] "Social proof," a term coined by Robert Cialdini in his 1984 book *Influence: The Psychology of Persuasion*, is also known as "informational social influence." It describes a psychological and social phenomenon wherein people who do not know what the proper behavior for a certain situation is will look to other people to imitate what they are doing and to provide guidance for their actions.

Exiting a family business involves far more than determining a fair value of the business. Other business, personal, family, and charitable goals are likely impacted by this significant transition. Capital gains and income taxes will be due upon sale. Cash flow needs post-sale may be affected, as will estate and charitable gifting strategies.

- *Considerations related to timing of business sale.* Many business owners will transfer actual ownership of the business to a trust or other vehicle well in advance of a potential business sale to remove any future appreciation from the estate of the business owner. A discount may be applied to the transfer value due to lack of control or lack of marketability, which may reduce the gift and estate tax liability.

- *Selection of trustees.* When using a trust as a wealth transfer vehicle, the founder must choose between an individual or corporate trustee unless co-trustees are used. Individual trustees who are close to the family may have good knowledge of the grantor and beneficiaries, including their values and aspirations. Institutional trustees may be better suited to ensure continuity for a multigenerational family and tend to have lower administration costs and broader skills and resources. The grantors may choose to divide responsibility, giving a non-trustee (e.g., a family member, adviser, or committee) some degree of control over the business strategy, investments, or distributions. The beneficiaries usually do not have direct access to trust assets; however, depending on the governing law and trust provisions, they may be able to participate in decision making in relation to trust administration or trustee succession. A good practice is to establish regular meetings that include trustees *and* beneficiaries to improve decision making in relation to assets held in the trust.

    The ability to replace a corporate trustee is important for multigenerational trusts. In some jurisdictions, a family council can directly control family trusts; in other jurisdictions, family councils may serve only as informal governing bodies.

    Private trust companies (PTCs) are becoming increasingly common. These are trust companies established specifically for the use of a single family.

- *Post-sale considerations.* The sale of the family business creates liquidity that can be used to establish a new business or a philanthropic entity. However, without advance planning, it may also result in the assets being dispersed among numerous family members, causing the business activity that brought family members together to disappear. With suitable structures put in place in advance (such as a family foundation or a donor-advised fund), the family may be united following the business exit by pursuing philanthropic goals. In this way, the family can increase its social capital, train the younger generations, and promote the family's values via impact investing. Founders who prefer to maintain control over distribution of the funds may specify the charitable causes that should be funded by the foundation or even provide a list of specific charities and funding amounts.

Irrespective of the chosen method for transferring wealth across generations, a robust system of family governance must be established to facilitate communication among the family members and a transparent decision-making process. Family governance helps to unite the family members around common business- or philanthropy-related goals and facilitates the preservation and growth of family wealth across generations.

> **EXAMPLE 20 ESTATE PLANNING FOR THE HARPER FAMILY (CONTINUED)**
>
> John Harper (from Example 19) has decided to continue managing the family business and keep it under family ownership for the next several years until a decision on business succession is made. He created $10,000,000 of liquidity by selling some commercial property. He plans to use this cash to build a portfolio of financial assets and start working toward achieving the family's charitable goals. John would like to set up a family governance structure to help transfer wealth to the next generations.
>
> Discuss the family governance bodies that would be appropriate for the Harper family.
>
> **Solution:**
>
> The Harper family should consider creating a corporate governance system, which includes the following governance bodies:
>
> - *Board of directors*—A board of directors with independent external members will help John to prepare for business succession and possible transition to an advisory role after retiring. The board of directors will also provide an external perspective on the future development of the business, potentially increasing the business value for a possible sale.
>
> - *Family council*—A family council should include members of the family who are best suited to represent the family in discussions with the board of directors. The council members should be elected by all family members. In the case of the Harper family, the family council may include James after he starts his own business, as he has a good knowledge of the family business. It might also include Ann's husband, who has knowledge of corporate finance.
>
> - *Family assembly*—A family assembly should consist of all family members and serve as a platform for defining family goals and values.
>
> - *Family office*—As John is looking to create an investment portfolio and start working on charitable goals, a family office will serve administrative, accounting, and other purposes.
>
> - *Family foundation*—John plans to be actively involved in charitable projects and would like to involve the members of his family; a private foundation is suitable for this purpose. The family foundation will help to unite family members around a common goal and develop the social capital of the family.

PLANNING FOR THE UNEXPECTED

Many other needs of wealth- and business-owning families come in to the tax minimization, asset protection, and estate planning picture. It is important to identify these needs and discuss them with the family.

It is usually possible to address a variety of needs within the same asset protection and estate planning structure. Interestingly, the greater number of needs that are addressed within the same trust, foundation, or other structure, the stronger the structure becomes. Many jurisdictions have general anti-avoidance rules that allow a tax authority to deny tax benefits if there is no commercial purpose to an arrangement other than to achieve tax benefits. For example, although a trust may be established in a manner that provides tax benefits, if it can be demonstrated that the main motive of the trust was to address succession issues or to protect against possible political risk, then the tax authorities will have a difficult time proving that tax avoidance was a primary objective.

16.1 Divorce

Marital laws vary from jurisdiction to jurisdiction, and a variety of rights are accorded to spouses. In some jurisdictions, rights arise only in relation to formal marriages. In other jurisdictions, long-term domestic arrangements may provide their own rights or rights equivalent to those that arise in a formal marriage.

On the dissolution of a marriage, financial arrangements between former spouses need to be agreed upon; if they are not, procedures are available to allow for the courts to intervene and make financial determinations. In the United Kingdom, for example, the general principle is that family assets are divided on a 50/50 basis on the dissolution of the marriage. While a court can deviate from this where it is considered to be fair and reasonable to do so, the even division of assets has made the United Kingdom an important location for divorces, particularly where a spouse is seeking to enforce claims against a former partner. (For example, a Saudi or Russian family may have a second home in the United Kingdom, which helps a spouse seeking to benefit from the UK approach to the division of family assets establish grounds for the application of UK law.)

An important consideration for wealth- and business-owning families is that matrimonial assets are not necessarily restricted to assets that may have been earned during the marriage. Inherited assets that are available to a spouse may be considered a part of family assets and are thus subject to a 50/50 division in the event of a divorce. While there are clearly good reasons why the United Kingdom and a number of other countries take similar approaches to the division of assets, this can have a significant impact on a family's objective to keep a family business within the family for multiple generations. Taking the risk of divorce into account is therefore critical, particularly given that in some countries as many as half of marriages end up in divorce. Trusts and other arrangements can provide protection for a family business depending on how they are structured and implemented.

In many countries, it is possible to have an agreement between a couple in relation to the financial arrangements governing their relationship, including the issue of divorce. Where such an arrangement is entered into before the marriage, this is usually known as a *pre-nuptial agreement*; where the arrangement is entered into after the marriage, this is usually known as a *post-nuptial* agreement. Even in countries where such agreements are not binding, they are often taken into account as guidance in the event of disputes on a divorce. And pre-nuptial agreements can be a good way to encourage open discussion about financial matters relevant to a marriage, which is often a good thing.

How and when pre-nuptial (and post-nuptial) agreements are discussed can be a very personal and sensitive issue. Many advisers recommend that the younger generation be guided from an early age on the benefits of pre-nuptial agreements. Some families, through the trust and other structures that are in place, require a pre-nuptial agreement as a condition of the benefit.

16.2 Incapacity

While it is very good news that people around the world are living longer given improvements in nutrition and medical care, living to 100 (as opposed to 75) has a major impact on thinking in relation to succession and related planning. For example, if a wealthy or business-owning individual dies at the age of 75, the children might be in their late 40s or early 50s, perhaps a sensible time to be inheriting from a parent. But what if the parent lives to 100? The children will likely be in their 60s, with limited opportunity to positively influence the family legacy.

Linked to this issue of increasing longevity is the sad reality that a variety of disabilities can arise when people live well into their 90s and over 100. Dementia is not uncommon in various forms, and good planning requires careful consideration early on of how the family and their assets can be well protected. Asking the many *what-ifs?* is an important step. What happens if the wealth owner becomes disabled? Who will make decisions? What if the wealth owner lives to 100? At what age should children have power over assets they inherit?

In the event of disability, decision making on both personal health-related issues and business issues may be accorded to a guardian. The procedures involved for appointing the guardian will vary from country to country. An unplanned transfer of decision-making authority carries with it two primary risks: 1) the process may take an extended period of time, during which the affairs of the wealth owner are left in limbo; 2) the person given decision-making authority may not be fully aware of the business and family situation. Disputes in relation to guardianship are very common, creating both bad feelings and delays that can be harmful to the family wealth and businesses.

Living wills and durable powers of attorney are among the tools available to wealth and business owners to address what can happen in the event of incapacity. A living will is a document that is used to convey people's wishes regarding medical care in the event they become incapacitated. The living will is generally legally binding. A durable power of attorney provides a third party with decision-making powers in areas specifically addressed by the power of attorney, which may include both financial and medical issues. The power of attorney is "durable" in that it continues to be effective even if the grantor becomes incapacitated. Trusts and other vehicles can also play a role if well thought through.

EXAMPLE 21   INCAPACITY PLANNING

Astrid is a widow and has been taking care of herself for many years. Retired, Astrid has a modest financial asset portfolio that she keeps an eye on, but she also relies on the input of her private wealth manager. Astrid is also the beneficiary of a life annuity that was set up by her now-deceased husband.

Astrid has two adult children, Frank and Edith. Edith has strong financial skills and is well-trusted by Astrid. Frank suffers from alcoholism and has been in and out of recovery. Astrid loves both her children and has supported Frank financially and emotionally. Frank is more than happy to have Edith handle financial matters.

Astrid holds a strong view that she does not want to be kept alive if she is permanently incapable of taking care of herself without dependence on life support. She has shared this view with her children, but Edith has always laughed and hugged Astrid—saying that if it was up to Edith, she would keep Astrid alive forever.

As Astrid turns 98, she develops dementia. Issues compound, Astrid's memory fades, and she requires constant care. Eventually she requires mechanical ventilation in order to remain alive.

1. What tools might Astrid have used to ensure that her medical and financial affairs are conducted smoothly?
2. What other eventualities are not covered by these tools?

Solution to 1:

A living will would allow Astrid to specify what types of medical treatment she would want in the event of incapacity. Because her daughter would "keep Astrid alive forever," a living will would allow health care providers to ensure Astrid's wishes are respected. It also relieves Edith of the psychological burden of terminating the medical measures that are keeping her mother alive. A durable power of attorney giving Edith authority to act on behalf of Astrid with respect to her financial affairs would ensure that Edith could assume those responsibilities without any delays and would also avoid any potential disagreements between Frank and Edith.

Solution to 2:

Astrid has not addressed what kind of financial support should be provided to Frank after her death. In the absence of a will, the rules of probate in her country of residence will determine how her assets are divided among her children. Given Frank's alcoholism, his share of the assets might quickly dwindle to nothing, leaving him with no source of financial support. Astrid might have created a trust to receive Frank's share of the inheritance, providing some reassurance that the assets would be spent wisely. She should carefully consider whether Edith is the appropriate trustee for this trust, as Edith may be conflicted about continuing to support Frank and his alcoholism.

SUMMARY

Even the best private wealth manager will never have all the answers. An effective private wealth manager will, however, be in a position to ask the right questions and consult the right experts to help clients navigate an increasingly complex world. This reading covers important points for managing assets on a tax-aware basis and managing concentrated positions in real estate and private and public equities. It also provides an overview of estate planning.

- Three foundational elements of investment taxation include: 1) taxation of the components of return, 2) the tax status of the account, and 3) the jurisdiction that applies to the investor (and/or account).
- Many countries' tax codes create preferential treatment for some types of dividend and interest income. Long-term capital gains are typically taxed at a lower rate than other forms of income.
- Income from real estate investments may be reduced by maintenance, interest, and depreciation expenses.
- Private clients often have a mix of taxable, tax-deferred, and tax-exempt investment accounts. Returns in tax-deferred and tax-exempt accounts compound using the pre-tax rate of return. Tax-deferred accounts pay tax only when assets are withdrawn from the account. Taxable accounts compound using the after-tax rate of return.
- Broadly speaking, countries may operate under one of three tax regimes: tax havens, territorial tax systems, and worldwide tax systems. A tax haven has no or very low tax rates for foreign investors. A territorial regime taxes only locally-sourced income. A worldwide tax regime taxes all income, regardless of its source.

Summary

- The Common Reporting Standard exists to ensure exchange of financial account information to combat tax evasion. The United States uses FATCA, the Foreign Account Tax Compliance Act, for the same purpose.
- Equity portfolios are often more tax efficient than strategies that rely on derivatives, real assets, or taxable fixed income. Higher-yield and higher-turnover strategies tend to be less tax efficient.
- The tax considerations associated with alternative asset classes are more complicated than those associated with stocks and bonds.
- Measures of tax efficiency include after-tax holding period return, annualized after-tax return, after-tax post-liquidation return, after-tax excess return, and the tax-efficiency ratio.
- Asset location is the process for determining which assets should be held in each type of account. A general rule of thumb is to put tax-efficient assets in the taxable account and tax-inefficient assets in the tax-exempt or tax-deferred account. The actual solution may differ depending on the strategy and the investor's horizon.
- It is typically better to make withdrawals from the taxable account first and then from the tax-deferred accounts. Under progressive tax regimes, it may be more tax efficient to withdraw from the retirement account first until the lowest tax brackets have been fully utilized.
- Tax avoidance is the legal activity of understanding the tax laws and finding approaches that avoid or minimize taxation. Tax evasion is the illegal concealment and non-payment of taxes that are otherwise due.
- Tax avoidance strategies include holding assets in a tax-exempt account versus a taxable account, investing in tax-exempt bonds instead of taxable bonds, holding assets long enough to qualify for long-term capital gains treatment, and holding dividend-paying stocks long enough to pay the more favorable tax rate. Tax-deferral strategies include limiting portfolio turnover and the consequent realization of capital gains and tax loss harvesting.
- The structure of the investment vehicle in which a client's assets are held may affect the tax liability and the adviser's ability to manage the client portfolio in a tax-aware manner. In a partnership, the income, realized capital gains, and realized capital losses are passed through to the investors, who are then responsible for any tax liability. In a mutual fund, the income and realized capital gains (but not losses) are passed through to the investors. The taxation of capital gains varies by jurisdiction.
- Potential capital gain exposure (PCGE) can be used to gauge the amount of tax liability embedded in a mutual fund.
- Exchange-traded funds are very tax efficient. Separately-managed accounts offer the most flexibility for tax management.
- Tax loss harvesting is a technique whereby the manager realizes a loss that can be used to offset gains or other income. Tax loss harvesting requires diligent tax lot accounting.
- Common methods of tax lot accounting are first in, first out (FIFO); last in, first out (LIFO); and highest in, first out (HIFO).
- A concentrated position subjects the portfolio to a higher level of risk, including unsystematic risk and liquidity risk. Approaches that can be used to mitigate the risks of a concentrated position include sell and diversify; staged diversification; hedging and monetization strategies; tax-free exchanges; tax-deferral strategies; and estate and tax planning strategies, such as charitable trusts, private foundations, and donor-advised funds.

- A completion portfolio is an index-based portfolio that when added to the concentrated position, creates an overall portfolio with exposures similar to the investor's benchmark.
- Equity monetization refers to a group of strategies that allows an investor to receive cash for a stock position without an outright sale. The investor can hedge a part of the position using a short sale, a total return swap, options, futures, or a forward sale contract and then borrow against the hedged position. The loan proceeds are then invested in a diversified portfolio of other investments.
- Donating the appreciated asset to a charitable remainder trust allows the shares to be sold without incurring a capital gains tax. The trust can then build a diversified portfolio to provide income for the life of the beneficiaries.
- Strategies to free up capital concentrated in a privately-owned business or real estate include a personal line of credit secured by company shares, leveraged recapitalization, an employee stock ownership plan, mortgage financing, and a charitable trust or donor-advised fund.
- Estate planning is the process of preparing for the disposition of one's estate upon death and during one's lifetime. Objectives of gift and estate planning include maintaining sufficient income and liquidity, achieving the clients' goals with respect to control over the assets, protection of the assets from creditors, minimization of tax liability, preservation of family wealth, business succession, and achieving charitable goals.
- An estate tax is the tax on the aggregate value of a deceased person's assets. It is paid out of the estate. An inheritance tax is paid by each individual beneficiary. A gift tax is paid on a transfer of money or property to another person without receiving at least equal value in return. Many jurisdictions have tax-free allowances that can be used for transferring assets under a certain threshold without paying an estate or inheritance tax.
- A will outlines the rights others will have over one's property after death. Probate is the legal process to confirm the validity of the will.
- Common law jurisdictions give owners the right to use their own judgment regarding the rights others will have over their property after death. Many civil law countries place restrictions on the disposition of an estate, typically giving certain relatives some minimum share of the assets.
- Common estate planning tools include trusts, foundations, life insurance, and companies. A trust is a legal relationship in which the trustee holds and manages the assets for the benefit of the beneficiaries. A trust can be either revocable or irrevocable. An irrevocable trust generally provides greater asset protection from creditors. A foundation is typically established to hold assets for a specific charitable purpose. The founder can exercise some control in the administration and decision making of the foundation.
- Life insurance and other forms of insurance can be used to accomplish estate planning objectives.
- Companies—specifically, a controlled foreign corporation—may allow the owner to defer taxes on income until the earnings are distributed to shareholders or until the company is sold or shares otherwise disposed.
- Family governance is a process for a family's collective communication and decision making designed to serve current and future generations. Good family governance establishes principles for collaboration among family members,

preserving and growing family's wealth, and increasing human and financial capital across the generations. A sound family governance system may mitigate many of the behavioral biases that impede effective decision making.

- Conflict resolution can be particularly challenging in a family context. A family constitution can help wealthy families anticipate possible conflicts and agree on a common set of rights, values, and responsibilities.
- Managing a concentrated position arising from a family business is more than just an investment issue. The private wealth adviser should be prepared to work with the client in succession planning and post-sale considerations, such as the loss of a key activity that united family members.
- Effective estate planning requires planning for the unexpected, including divorce and incapacity.

REFERENCES

Collier, Charles W. 2012. *Wealth in Families*. 3rd ed. Cambridge, MA: Harvard University Press.

Jeffrey, Robert H., and Robert D. Arnott. 1993. "Is Your Alpha Big Enough to Cover Its Taxes?" *Journal of Portfolio Management* 19 (3): 15–25.

Jennings, William W., Stephen M. Horan, and William Reichenstein. 2010. "*Private Wealth Management: A Review.*" Research Foundation Literature Reviews 5 (1).

Lucas, Stuart, and Alejandro Sanz. 2016. "Pick Your Battles: The Intersection of Investment Strategy, Tax, and Compounding Returns." *Journal of Wealth Management* 19 (2): 9–16.

Marcovici, Philip. 2016. *The Destructive Power of Family Wealth: A Guide to Succession Planning, Asset Protection, Taxation and Wealth Management*. Hoboken, NJ: John Wiley & Sons.

Sialm, Clemens, and Hanjiang Zhang.Forthcoming). "Tax-Efficient Asset Management: Evidence from Equity Mutual Funds." *Journal of Finance*.

Stalk, George, Jr, and Henry Foley. 2012. "Avoid the Traps That Can Destroy Family Businesses." *Harvard Business Review* 2012 (January–February). https://hbr.org/2012/01/avoid-the-traps-that-can-destroy-family-businesses

PRACTICE PROBLEMS

The following information relates to Questions 1–7

Jevan Chen is a tax adviser who provides tax-aware advice to various private clients. Two of Chen's clients are Sameeha Payne and Chaow Yoonim, who are US citizens and reside in the United States. A third client, LaShawna Kaminski, lives in a tax jurisdiction with a flat tax rate of 20%, which applies to all types of income and capital gains.

Payne is the founder and sole owner of Solar Falls Power, a privately held renewable energy company located in the United States. In addition to owning Solar Falls Power, Payne is also the sole owner of the property that the company uses as its headquarters. The vast majority of Payne's wealth is represented by these two assets. Payne's tax cost basis in each asset is close to zero.

Payne consults with Chen to develop a strategy to mitigate the risk associated with the two concentrated ownership positions. Payne's primary objective is to mitigate the concentration risk of both positions without triggering a taxable event while maintaining sole ownership. Payne's secondary objective is to monetize the property.

Payne is considering becoming a resident of Singapore, which operates under a territorial tax system, while maintaining her US citizenship. She contacts Chen to discuss tax implications related to the potential change in residency. She asks Chen the following tax-related question:

> As a US citizen, if I become a resident of Singapore, would I be taxed (1) only on income earned where I am a resident, (2) only on income earned where I am a citizen, or (3) on all income earned worldwide?

Chen next advises Yoonim, who recently inherited shares of Steelworq from a relative who passed away. Yoonim's deceased relative was a resident of the United States, which is a country that uses a "step-up" in basis at death. The deceased relative purchased the Steelworq shares 20 years ago for $14,900 (including commissions and other costs). At the time of the relative's death, the Steelworq shares had a market value of $200,000, and Yoonim recently sold the shares for $180,000. Yoonim's capital gains tax rate is 20%.

Yoonim seeks to diversify his portfolio by using the proceeds from the sale of Steelworq shares to invest in mutual funds. Yoonim's investment adviser identifies three mutual funds, and Yoonim asks Chen to determine which fund will be the most tax efficient going forward. Selected data for the three mutual funds is presented in Exhibit 1.

Exhibit 1   Selected Data on Mutual Funds A, B, and C

	Starting Assets	Gains	Capital Gains Distributions	Losses
Fund A	$3,000,000	$300,000	$400,000	—
Fund B	$4,000,000	$500,000	$300,000	$200,000
Fund C	$5,000,000	$700,000	—	$500,000

© 2020 CFA Institute. All rights Reserved.

Practice Problems

Yoonim next asks Chen to evaluate Mutual Fund D, which has an embedded gain of 5% of the ending portfolio value. Yoonim asks Chen to calculate a post-liquidation return over the most recent three-year period. Mutual Fund D exhibited after-tax returns of 7.0% in Year 1, 3.3% in Year 2, and 7.5% in Year 3, and capital gains are taxed at a 20% rate.

Finally, Chen turns his attention to Kaminski, who currently has $1 million invested in a tax-deferred account earning 7% per year. Kaminski will sell this investment at the end of five years, withdraw the proceeds from the sale in a lump sum, and use those proceeds to fund the purchase of a vacation home. Kaminski asks Chen to calculate the after-tax wealth that will be available in five years.

1. The risk mitigation strategy that would *most likely* allow Payne to achieve her primary objective with respect to the Solar Falls Power ownership position is to:
   A have Solar Falls Power conduct a leveraged recapitalization.
   B obtain a personal line of credit secured by Solar Falls Power shares.
   C establish a charitable remainder trust using Solar Falls Power shares.

2. A strategy that would *most likely* allow Payne to achieve both her primary and secondary objectives would be to:
   A contribute the property to a donor-advised fund.
   B obtain a fixed-rate mortgage against the property.
   C engage in a sale and leaseback transaction involving the property.

3. The *most appropriate* response to Payne's tax-related question is:
   A on all income earned worldwide.
   B only on income earned where Payne is a citizen.
   C only on income earned where Payne is a resident.

4. The tax liability on the sale of the Steelworq shares is:
   A −$4,000.
   B $0.
   C $33,020.

5. Based on Exhibit 1, the mutual fund *most likely* to be the most tax efficient going forward is:
   A Fund A.
   B Fund B.
   C Fund C.

6. The annualized after-tax post-liquidation return calculated by Chen is *closest* to:
   A 4.41%.
   B 5.62%.
   C 5.92%.

7. The after-tax wealth in Kaminski's tax-deferred account at the end of the five years will be *closest* to:
   A $1,122,041.
   B $1,313,166.
   C $1,402,552.

The following information relates to Questions 8–9

Private wealth manager Udaga Wacho is discussing a decumulation strategy with client Dogenza Ka. The strategy involves two of Ka's accounts, a taxable account and a tax-exempt account, and will allow Ka to withdraw $200,000 each year. Both accounts have a current balance of $1 million.

Ka asks Wacho if he should withdraw funds from the taxable account first until it is depleted prior to withdrawing from the tax-exempt account, or vice versa. Wacho reviews the accounts to make a recommendation; he assumes a fixed, pre-tax rate of return of 10% for both accounts and that earnings in the taxable account are taxed at a fixed effective rate of 25%. Wacho recommends that Ka withdraw funds from the taxable account first until it is depleted prior to withdrawing from the tax-exempt account.

8 **Discuss** why Wacho's recommended decumulation strategy is the more tax-efficient strategy.

Wacho and Ka next discuss tax loss harvesting and tax lot accounting for one of Ka's other accounts. Ka has recently built a position in shares of Hachiko Corporation; Ka's purchase history is presented in Exhibit 1.

Exhibit 1 Tax Lot Purchase History of Hachiko Corporation

Tax Lot	Shares	Purchase Date	Acquisition Price ($)
A	200	July 19, 20x2	122.00
B	200	Nov. 17, 20x2	135.00
C	200	May 9, 20x3	129.00

Today is 23 August 20x3, and Ka sells 200 shares. The current share price is $124.00. The tax rate for long-term holdings is 25%, and the tax rate for short-term holdings is 40%. A holding period of less than six months is considered short-term for tax purposes. Ka has chosen HIFO (highest in, first out) as his tax lot accounting method.

9 **Determine** the tax lot that would be *most* tax efficient to sell given Ka's chosen tax lot accounting method. **Calculate** the tax liability/benefit from the sale.

Determine the tax lot that would be *most* tax efficient to sell given Ka's chosen tax lot accounting method. (Circle one.)	Calculate the tax liability/benefit from the sale.
Tax Lot A	
Tax Lot B	
Tax Lot C	

Practice Problems

The following information relates to Questions 10–12

Tesando Omo is a highly successful entrepreneur. The software company that he started five years ago is now worth $200 million. It is a private company, and he is the controlling owner, with a 60% equity share. His only other investment is a position in the publicly traded shares of his previous employer, which he acquired by exercising stock options six years ago. This publicly traded share position has substantially increased in value and is now worth $36 million.

Omo recently sought financial advice from Umae Jing. After discussing Omo's personal situation and financial goals, Jing expresses concern about Omo's current portfolio and points out several important risk and tax-related considerations that are relevant to Omo's portfolio.

10 **Discuss** four important risk and tax-related considerations that are relevant to Omo's portfolio.

With most of Omo's personal net worth tied up in his software company, he is asset rich but cash poor. Jing suggests three possible strategies that Omo could use to generate liquidity from the software company:

Strategy 1: Personal loan secured by Omo's company's shares without a put arrangement

Strategy 2: Leveraged recapitalization

Strategy 3: Leveraged ESOP (employee stock ownership plan)

Omo tells Jing that his goals are to avoid an immediate taxable event for him or his company and to maintain his ownership and control of his company.

11 **Determine** the *most appropriate* strategy that can generate liquidity and accomplish Omo's goals. **Justify** your response.

Determine the *most appropriate* strategy that can generate liquidity and accomplish Omo's goals. (Circle one.)	**Justify** your response.
Strategy 1	
Strategy 2	
Strategy 3	

Jing asks Omo about his plans for the shares of his previous employer's company. Omo tells Jing that he would like to use the shares to fund charitable donations and to provide income for his children; however, he is concerned about adverse personal tax implications relating to those goals. Omo indicates that he is willing to cede control of the shares to meet these goals.

12 **Recommend** a strategy, alternative to an outright sale of the shares, that will satisfy Omo's goals and alleviate his concern.

The following information relates to Questions 13–14

Enlow Surgical is a medical practice specializing in plastic surgery. Dr. Tuscarora Enlow, a surgeon and sole owner of the business, meets with wealth manager Horphey Hinkle to discuss estate planning strategies.

Hinkle asks questions to learn about the medical practice. Enlow indicates that he founded the company 30 years ago and has built up a large customer base while investing in modern surgical equipment and surgery centers. In recent years, however, Enlow has had to frequently defend against malpractice lawsuits that target both the company's assets and his own personal assets.

Enlow's medical practice also employs Enlow's son, who is also a surgeon. Enlow tells Hinkle that he wants his son to benefit financially from the company's success, but he is reluctant to give his son control of the practice because of a lack of business acumen.

13 **Discuss** two estate planning objectives revealed in Hinkle's discussion with Enlow.

Enlow wants to transfer some of his wealth to his niece and nephew but isn't sure whether he should use lifetime gifts or testamentary bequests. The present value of the amount that he wants to transfer to each of them is $50,000.

Enlow's niece has a high income and is an aggressive and successful investor. Enlow's nephew, in contrast, has a low income and minimal interest in investing. Selected data for Enlow and his niece and nephew are presented in Exhibit 1.

Exhibit 1   Selected Data for Enlow and His Niece and Nephew

	Enlow	Enlow's Niece	Enlow's Nephew
Effective tax rate on investment returns	37%	52%	12%
Expected pre-tax returns	6%	9%	1%
Tax on gifts/inheritances	—	47%/47%	33%/39%
Statutory allowances on gifts/inheritances	—	$100,000 (gifts only)	None

Enlow asks Hinkle to advise him of the most tax-efficient way to make each wealth transfer. For the analysis, Hinkle assumes that the bequests, if chosen, would happen in 10 years.

14 **Recommend**, for both Enlow's niece and nephew, the *most* tax-efficient wealth transfer option (lifetime gift or testamentary bequest). **Show** your calculations.

Recommend, for goth Enlow's Niece and nephew, the *most* tax-efficient wealth transfer option (Circle one.)		**Show** your calculations.
Enlow's Niece	Lifetime gift	
	Testamentary bequest	
Enlow's Nephew	Lifetime gift	
	Testamentary bequest	

SOLUTIONS

1. B is correct. Payne can obtain a personal loan secured by her private company shares in Solar Falls Power to meet her primary objective of mitigating the concentration risk of both ownership positions without triggering a taxable event while maintaining sole ownership. One of the key benefits is that this type of borrowing should not cause an immediate taxable event. Although at some point the debt will need to be repaid, Payne would have access to cash to diversify her concentration risk while maintaining sole ownership of the company.

   A is incorrect because a leveraged recapitalization would not meet Payne's primary objective, since it would both trigger a taxable event and result in Payne not maintaining sole ownership of the company. In a typical leveraged recapitalization, a private equity firm provides or arranges debt with senior and mezzanine lenders. The owner of the privately owned business receives cash for a portion of her shares and retains a minority interest in the freshly capitalized entity. The owner is typically taxed currently on the cash received. If structured properly, a tax deferral is achieved on the stock rolled over into the newly capitalized company.

   C is incorrect because establishing a charitable remainder trust using Solar Falls Power shares would involve Payne donating her shares to a trust and receiving a tax deduction for the gift. However, this would result in Payne relinquishing sole ownership of Solar Falls Power, which would violate her primary objective to maintain sole ownership.

2. B is correct. Mortgage financing is a real estate monetization strategy that investors can use to reduce the concentration of a particular property and generate liquidity to diversify asset portfolios without triggering a taxable event or giving up sole ownership. Payne could monetize the property by obtaining a mortgage loan against the property, and the loan proceeds could then be reinvested in a diversified portfolio of securities.

   A is incorrect because in a donor-advised fund transaction, the property owner contributes the property to a donor-advised fund in exchange for a charitable contribution deduction. While this transaction would allow Payne to monetize the property with no tax liability, she would give up sole ownership of the property, and her primary objective includes maintaining sole ownership.

   C is incorrect because a sale and leaseback is a transaction in which the owner of a property sells the property to a new buyer and then immediately leases it back from the same buyer. The sale of the property would result in Payne having to pay significant capital gains taxes (her cost basis is close to zero) and no longer having sole ownership of the property. Therefore, a sale and leaseback transaction would not achieve Payne's objectives.

3. A is correct. If Payne becomes a resident of Singaporebut maintains her US citizenship, any income she receives worldwide will be subject to US tax, because the United States is one of the few countries that taxes citizens on a worldwide basis, regardless of residence.

4. A is correct. There is a tax loss of $4,000, representing a tax benefit, on Yoonim's sale of the Steelworq shares. In the United States, there is a basis "step-up" on death, meaning that someone who inherits an asset would have a tax basis equal to the fair market value of the asset on the date of death. Since

the Steelworq shares had a market value of $200,000 at the time of the relative's death and Yoonim sells the shares for $180,000, the tax liability on the sale of the Steelworq shares is calculated as:

Tax liability on sale of Steelworq shares = ($180,000 − $200,000) × 20% capital gains tax rate = −$4,000 (tax benefit).

5 A is correct. Fund A has a lower percent capital gain exposure (PCGE) than does Fund B or Fund C. PCGE is an estimate of the percentage of a fund's assets that represent gains and measures how much the fund's assets have appreciated. It can be an indicator of possible future capital gain distributions. PCGE can be used to gauge the amount of tax liability embedded in a mutual fund. The negative PCGE of Fund A implies that Fund A is more likely to be the most tax-efficient fund going forward, because it can use the embedded losses in its portfolio to offset future realized gains.

PCGE = Net gains (losses)/Total net assets.

$$\text{Fund A PCGE} = \frac{(\$300{,}000 - \$400{,}000)}{[\$3{,}000{,}000 + (\$300{,}000 - \$400{,}000)]} = -3.45\%.$$

$$\text{Fund B PCGE} = \frac{(\$500{,}000 - \$300{,}000 - \$200{,}000)}{[\$4{,}000{,}000 + (\$500{,}000 - \$300{,}000 - \$200{,}000)]} = 0.00\%.$$

$$\text{Fund C PCGE} = \frac{(\$700{,}000 - \$500{,}000)}{[\$5{,}000{,}000 + (\$700{,}000 - \$500{,}000)]} = 3.85\%.$$

6 B is correct. The annualized after-tax post-liquidation return is calculated as follows.

First, calculate the ending portfolio value. Given Fund D's after-tax returns over the past three years, the ending portfolio value is calculated as

Final after-tax portfolio value = (1 + 0.070) × (1 + 0.033) × (1 + 0.075) = 1.1882.

The after-tax returns compounded in this way account for the tax on distributions and realized capital gains but do not account for any unrealized capital gains. The assumed tax liability from capital gains at liquidation is 1.0% of the final value, which is the product of the 5% embedded gain and the 20% capital gains tax rate. The portfolio value net of the unrealized gains tax liability is given by subtracting the assumed tax liability from capital gains at liquidation from the final after-tax portfolio value:

Portfolio value net of the unrealized gains tax liability = 1.1882 − 0.01 = 1.1782.

Second, calculate the annualized post-liquidation return as follows:

$$1.1782^{\left(\frac{1}{3}\right)} - 1 = 5.62\%.$$

7 A is correct. The value of a tax-deferred account compounds using the pre-tax returns and pays tax only when assets are withdrawn from the account. Kaminski withdraws the proceeds at the end of her five-year holding period.

The value of the assets withdrawn from the tax-deferred account is calculated as follows:

$FV = PV \times (1 + R)^n \times (1 - t)$, where R is the portfolio pretax return.

$FV = \$1,000,000 \times (1 + 0.07)^5 \times (1 - 0.20)$.

$FV = \$1,122,041.38$.

8 Wacho's recommendation to withdraw funds from the taxable account first until it is depleted prior to withdrawing from the tax-exempt account is the more tax-efficient decumulation strategy. The tax-exempt account will compound at a higher rate (the pre-tax rate of 10%) than the taxable account (with an after-tax rate of 10% × (1 − 0.25) = 7.5%). With a fixed tax rate, it is optimal to make withdrawals from the taxable account first and allow the tax-exempt account to continue to compound. The two tables below demonstrate this outcome over the first 10 years: At the end of 10 years, the ending balance is larger under the tax-aware strategy ($1,800,752) than under the tax-indifferent strategy ($1,480,097).

Comparison of Decumulation Strategies (Values in $)

Year	Withdrawal from Taxable Account	Withdrawal from Tax-Exempt Account	Year-End Taxable Account Balance	Year-End Tax-Exempt Account Balance
A. Decumulation Strategy: Withdraw from Taxable Account First (Tax Aware)				
0	—	—	1,000,000	1,000,000
1	200,000	—	875,000	1,100,000
2	200,000	—	740,625	1,210,000
3	200,000	—	596,172	1,331,000
4	200,000	—	440,885	1,464,100
5	200,000	—	273,951	1,610,510
6	200,000	—	94,497	1,771,561
7	101,585	98,415	—	1,850,302
8	—	200,000	—	1,835,332
9	—	200,000	—	1,818,866
10	—	200,000	—	1,800,752
B. Decumulation Strategy: Withdraw from Tax-Exempt Account First (Tax Indifferent)				
0	—	—	1,000,000	1,000,000
1	—	200,000	1,075,000	900,000
2	—	200,000	1,155,625	790,000
3	—	200,000	1,242,297	669,000
4	—	200,000	1,335,469	535,900
5	—	200,000	1,435,629	389,490
6	—	200,000	1,543,302	228,439
7	—	200,000	1,659,049	51,283
8	143,589	56,411	1,639,889	—
9	200,000	—	1,562,880	—
10	200,000	—	1,480,097	—

9

Determine the tax lot that would be *most* tax efficient to sell given Ka's chosen tax lot accounting method. (Circle one.)	**Calculate** the tax liability/benefit from the sale.
Tax Lot A	The formula to calculate tax liability/benefit is:
Tax Lot B	Tax liability/Benefit = (Selling price − Acquisition price) × Tax rate × Number of shares.
	HIFO is usually the most tax-efficient accounting methodology—since selecting the tax lot with the highest acquisition price will usually produce the smallest capital gain or the largest loss. So, under HIFO, Tax Lot B would be chosen, with an acquisition price of $135.00. Given that the shares were held more than six months (acquired on 17 November 20x2, and the sale date is 23 August 20x3), the long-term tax rate of 25% is applicable.
Tax Lot C	Tax under HIFO = ($124 − #153) × 0.25 × 200 = −$550 (tax loss or benefit)

10 Omo's portfolio consists of two concentrated positions: his ownership share of his software company and his publicly traded shares in the company of his previous employer. As such, Omo's portfolio is not an efficient, diversified portfolio.

Four important risk and tax-related considerations that are relevant to Omo's portfolio are as follows:

1 The company-specific risk inherent in the concentrated positions
2 The reduction in portfolio efficiency resulting from the lack of diversification
3 The liquidity risk inherent in a privately held or outsized publicly held security
4 The risk of incurring an outsized tax bill that diminishes return if one were to sell part of the concentrated position in an attempt to reduce the other risks

Omo's software company is private and fairly small, with a valuation of $200 million. Private companies, such as Omo's software company, tend to be smaller than public companies and can possibly face some different risks compared to large companies, including a more limited operating history or an undiversified business mix, difficulty attracting high-quality management personnel, and more constraints on their access to financing. These risks, alone or in combination, make a concentrated position in a private company, such as Omo's software company, much riskier than a similar-sized position in a publicly traded company.

Regardless of whether Omo's investments are publicly traded or privately held, a concentrated position subjects the portfolio to a higher level of risk. Not only is Omo's portfolio unduly exposed to the risk of adverse events affecting his company; he will not be compensated for bearing specific or unsystematic risk—risk that can be diversified away. Thus, Omo's portfolio, with its concentrated positions, is likely an inefficient portfolio. The portfolio's risk-to-reward ratio is less than what could be achieved in the absence of the concentrated positions.

Omo's concentrated positions, particularly the shares in his software company, may also be subject to liquidity risk. Shares in a private company cannot be readily sold to meet unexpected expenses. This lack of liquidity complicates the management of the remaining portfolio. In contrast, since Omo's previous employer is a public company, its shares likely have less liquidity risk since they can be sold—though sales may be constrained by regulatory restrictions and sales of large positions may incur large transaction costs.

Concentrated positions frequently have a very low tax basis, sometimes having been held by the investor for a long time. Omo has owned his company from its very beginning and bought shares in his previous company six years ago, before a substantial appreciation in value. Though Omo's holding periods of five and six years aren't particularly long, both positions have grown significantly in value since inception. Sale of all or a part of these positions may trigger significant tax liabilities.

While these and other considerations (notably, Omo's possible emotional attachment to the company that has been the foundation of his financial success) make a simple sale problematic, the risk inherent in the position may outweigh the tax and liquidity issues.

11 Determine the *most appropriate* strategy that can generate liquidity and accomplish Omo's goals. (Circle one.)

	Justify your response.
Strategy 1	A personal loan secured by Omo's company's shares (Strategy 1) can generate liquidity and still satisfy all of Omo's goals. The loan would allow Omo to maintain his ownership and control of the company, and it has the advantage that it should not cause an immediate taxable event for the company or Omo if structured properly (without a put arrangement). Specifically, these loan transactions usually contain a "put" arrangement back to the company to make the lender comfortable—although such an arrangement would likely be considered a taxable event (Strategy 1 does not contain the put arrangement). Although at some point the debt will need to be repaid, Omo will have access to cash to diversify his concentration risk and will avoid triggering a taxable event. In most jurisdictions, the interest expense paid on the loan proceeds should be deductible for tax purposes. A leveraged recapitalization (Strategy 2) will not allow Omo to maintain his ownership and control of the company or avoid a taxable event. Typically, under a leveraged recapitalization, a private equity firm will invest equity and take partial ownership of the business. The private equity firm will then provide or arrange debt with senior and mezzanine (subordinated) lenders. Omo would receive cash for a portion of his stock and would retain a minority ownership interest in the freshly capitalized entity. Omo would likely be taxed currently on the cash received. If structured properly, a tax deferral will be achieved on the stock rolled over into the newly capitalized company. The after-tax cash proceeds that Omo receives could be deployed into other asset classes to help build a diversified portfolio, reducing Omo's risk of wealth concentration. A leveraged employee stock ownership plan (ESOP, Strategy 3) will not satisfy Omo's goal to maintain his ownership and control of the company but may allow him to avoid a taxable event. To implement an ESOP for his company, Omo would have to sell some or all of his shares to a pension plan that is created by the company. An ESOP that is leveraged would borrow funds (typically from a bank) to finance the purchase of Omo's shares. Depending on the legal form of company structure, it may be possible to defer any capital gains tax on the shares sold to the ESOP. Using an ESOP, Omo can partially diversify his holdings and diversify his overall portfolio while retaining control of the company and maintaining upside potential in the retained shares.
Strategy 2	
Strategy 3	

12 A charitable remainder trust will satisfy Omo's goals to use the shares to fund charitable donations and to provide income for his children, and it should alleviate his concern about adverse tax implications. With a charitable remainder trust, Omo would make an irrevocable donation of his shares to a trust and receive a tax deduction for the gift. He would no longer have ownership of the shares. Within the trust, the shares could be sold and reinvested in a diversified portfolio without incurring a capital gains tax—since the charitable trust is exempt from taxes. The trust would provide income for the life of its named beneficiaries (the beneficiaries would owe income tax on this income). When the last-named beneficiary dies, any assets remaining in the trust would be distributed to the charity named in the trust.

13 The discussion between Hinkle and Enlow reveals that Enlow should plan for the objectives of business control/succession and asset protection:

- Deciding on control over the assets/business succession: Although Enlow wants to pass the financial benefits from the business/medical practice on to his son, Enlow does not think his son has the business acumen to manage the practice. Enlow may want to consider assigning managerial responsibility to outside managers or selling the business outright to a third party.

- Asset protection: The frequency of malpractice lawsuits makes the assets of both the medical practice and Enlow's family vulnerable to claims from creditors. Certain estate planning vehicles, such as trusts, may protect assets from creditors by separating the creator of the trust and the beneficiaries from the legal ownership of the assets.

14 The formula for the relative after-tax value a lifetime gift compared to a testamentary bequest is

$$\mathrm{RV}_{Gift} = \frac{\mathrm{FV}_{Gift}}{\mathrm{FV}_{Bequest}} = \frac{\left[1 + r_g\left(1 - t_{ig}\right)\right]^n \left(1 - T_g\right)}{\left[1 + r_e\left(1 - t_{ie}\right)\right]^n \left(1 - T_e\right)}$$

Recommend, for goth Enlow's Niece and nephew, the *most* tax-efficient wealth transfer option (Circle one.)		Show your calculations.
Enlow's Niece	Lifetime gift	Enlow's niece has an annual exclusion of $100,000 before a gift tax applies. Since the gift is $50,000, less than the value of the exclusion, she would pay no gift tax. The relative value of transfers for Enlow's niece is $$RV_{Gift} = \frac{FV_{Gift}}{FV_{Bequest}} = \frac{[1+0.09(1-0.52)]^{10}(1-0.00)}{[1+0.06(1-0.37)]^{10}(1-0.47)}.$$ $$RV_{Gift} = \frac{FV_{Gift}}{FV_{Bequest}} = \frac{1.53}{0.77}.$$ $$RV_{Gift} = 1.99.$$ So, for the wealth transfer to Enlow's niece, making a lifetime gift is more tax efficient than a testamentary bequest. Transferring the $50,000 now would preserve almost two times more wealth after 10 years than if the money were transferred with a bequest in 10 yers. As shown above, the gift would allow Enlow's niece to receive 99% more wealth than via a bequest, even though the niece pays a higher tax on investment income (52%) than Enlow does (37%). The reasons for the superior tax efficiency of the gift are that (1) the niece expects a higher investment return (9%) than Enlow does (6%) and (2) the figt would not incur a transfer tax whereas a bequest would incur a transfer tax of 47%.
	Testamentary bequest	

Solutions

Enlow's Nephew	Lifetime gift / Testamentary bequest	The nephew has no annual exclusion, so he would have to pay transfer tax for the gift or inheritance. The relative value of transfers for Enlow's nephew is $$RV_{Gift} = \frac{FV_{Gift}}{FV_{Bequest}} = \frac{[1 + 0.01(1 - 0.12)]^{10}(1 - 0.33)}{[1 + 0.06(1 - 0.37)]^{10}(1 - 0.39)}.$$ $$RV_{Gift} = \frac{FV_{Gift}}{FV_{Bequest}} = \frac{0.73}{0.88}.$$ $$RV_{Gift} = 0.83.$$ For the wealth transfer to Enlow's nephew, a testamentary bequest is more tax efficient than making a lifetime gift. As shown above, after 10 years, the wealth from the gift transfer would only be 83% of the wealth the nephew would bet from a bequest in 10 years. The gift would transfer only 83% of the wealth that the bequest would transfer even though the nephew pays a much lower tax on investment income (12%) than Enlow pays (37%) and the applicable gift tax (33%) is lower than the inheritance tax (39%). The reason for the superior tax efficiency of the bequest is that Enlow expects a higher investment return (6%) than his nephew expects (1%).

PORTFOLIO MANAGEMENT
STUDY SESSION

11

Private Wealth Management (2)

The wealth of many individuals and families is often concentrated in a limited number of securities, business holdings, or real estate properties. The sale of concentrated positions to facilitate desired diversification may not be feasible or may create a substantial tax liability.

This study session examines the considerations and risks associated with concentrated single asset positions. Strategies for managing concentrated positions in publicly traded common shares, privately held businesses, and real estate are presented. Coverage on the dynamics of human and financial capital and the challenge of meeting financial goals throughout an investor's lifetime follows. The discussion specifically addresses investment strategies and financial products structured to mitigate the risk of not achieving these goals.

READING ASSIGNMENTS

Reading 23 Risk Management for Individuals
by David M. Blanchett, PhD, CFP, CFA, David M. Cordell, PhD, CFP, CFA, Michael S. Finke, PhD, and Thomas M. Idzorek, CFA

READING
23

Risk Management for Individuals

by David M. Blanchett, PhD, CFP, CFA, David M. Cordell, PhD, CFP, CFA, Michael S. Finke, PhD, and Thomas M. Idzorek, CFA

David M. Blanchett, PhD, CFP, CFA, is at Morningstar Investment Management LLC (USA). David M. Cordell, PhD, CFP, CFA, is at the University of Texas at Dallas (USA). Michael S. Finke, PhD, is at The American College (USA). Thomas M. Idzorek, CFA, is at Morningstar (USA).

LEARNING OUTCOMES

Mastery	The candidate should be able to:
☐	a. compare the characteristics of human capital and financial capital as components of an individual's total wealth;
☐	b. discuss the relationships among human capital, financial capital, and economic net worth;
☐	c. discuss the financial stages of life for an individual;
☐	d. describe an economic (holistic) balance sheet;
☐	e. discuss risks (earnings, premature death, longevity, property, liability, and health risks) in relation to human and financial capital;
☐	f. describe types of insurance relevant to personal financial planning;
☐	g. describe the basic elements of a life insurance policy and how insurers price a life insurance policy;
☐	h. discuss the use of annuities in personal financial planning;
☐	i. discuss the relative advantages and disadvantages of fixed and variable annuities;
☐	j. analyze and evaluate an insurance program;
☐	k. discuss how asset allocation policy may be influenced by the risk characteristics of human capital;
☐	l. recommend and justify appropriate strategies for asset allocation and risk reduction when given an investor profile of key inputs.

© 2016 CFA Institute. All rights reserved.

1. INTRODUCTION

Risk management for individuals is a key element of life-cycle finance, which recognizes that as investors age, the fundamental nature of their total wealth evolves, as do the risks that they face. **Life-cycle finance** is concerned with helping investors achieve their goals, including an adequate retirement income, by taking a holistic view of the individual's financial situation as he or she moves through life. Individuals are exposed to a range of risks over their lives: They may become disabled, suffer a prolonged illness, die prematurely, or outlive their resources. In addition, from an investment perspective, the assets of individuals could decline in value or provide an inadequate return in relation to financial needs and aspirations. All of these risks have two things in common: They are typically random, and they can result in financial hardship without an appropriate risk management strategy. Risk management for individuals is distinct from risk management for corporations given the distinctive characteristics of households, which include the finite and unknown lifespan of individuals, the frequent preference for stable spending among individuals, and the desire to pass on wealth to heirs (i.e., through bequests). To protect against unexpected financial hardships, risks must be identified, market and non-market solutions considered, and a plan developed and implemented. A well-constructed plan for risk management will involve the selection of financial products and investment strategies that fit an individual's financial goals and mitigate the risk of shortfalls.

In this reading, we provide an overview of the potential risks to an individual or household, an analysis of products and strategies that can protect against some of these risks, and a discussion regarding the selection of an appropriate product or strategy. Following the introduction, Section 2 provides an overview of human and financial capital. Sections 3–5 address the process of risk management, the financial stages of life for an individual, the economic (or holistic) balance sheet, and individual risks and risk exposures. Sections 6–10 discuss the types of products relevant to financial planning, including insurance and annuities. Sections 11–12 contain an insurance program case study and insights on implementing risk management solutions for individuals.

2. HUMAN CAPITAL, FINANCIAL CAPITAL, AND ECONOMIC NET WORTH

a compare the characteristics of human capital and financial capital as components of an individual's total wealth;

b discuss the relationships among human capital, financial capital, and economic net worth;

To better understand the financial health of an individual—and how to manage the risks faced by that individual—we can use an **economic balance sheet** (or **holistic balance sheet**). We discuss the economic balance sheet in more detail later in the reading, but it is important to note here that an individual's assets are made up of two primary components, **human capital** and **financial capital**, which present unique risk management challenges.

Ibbotson, Milevsky, Chen, and Zhu (2007) define human capital as the net present value of an investor's future expected labor income weighted by the probability of surviving to each future age. Financial capital includes the tangible and intangible assets (outside of human capital) owned by an individual or household. For example, a

Human Capital, Financial Capital, and Economic Net Worth

home, a car, stocks and bonds, a vested[1] retirement portfolio, and money in the bank are all examples of an individual's financial capital (or financial assets). In this section, both human capital and financial capital are explored in greater detail.

2.1 Human Capital

Advances in human capital theory have revolutionized how economists view the household risk management process. Conceptually, future wages or earnings can be thought of as analogous (in a rough sense) to future interest or dividend payments that flow from an individual's work-related skills, knowledge, experience, and other productive attributes that can be converted into wage income—or human capital. Because human capital provides a significant stream of income over decades, its present value is a significant part of most working households' total wealth portfolio. In fact, human capital is often the dominant asset on a household's economic balance sheet. From a risk management perspective, it is critical to understand the approximate total monetary value of an individual's human capital, the investment characteristics of the individual's human capital (i.e., whether the capital is more stock-like or bond-like), and how the approximate value of an individual's human capital relates to the value of the individual's financial capital. Here, we focus on estimating the approximate monetary value of an individual's human capital.

Given that future earnings for many workers are relatively stable over time, earnings can often be compared with the income one might receive from a bond. This analogy is useful because, similar to the way a financial analyst estimates the present value of a bond by discounting future cash flows, we can estimate human capital by discounting the expected future cash flows generated from wages or other income sources. Conceptually, individuals rent out or lease their human capital in the marketplace in exchange for an ongoing income that is a function of the state of the labor market. Some professions will receive a higher rental value (wage rate or salary) than others. Similarly, some professions will see their rental value fluctuate more with changes in the labor market environment.

Estimating the value of human capital is a complex process because the true value cannot be known. One simple approach is to use a discount rate that reflects the risk associated with the future cash flows (i.e., wages). Government employment and teaching are examples of professions that generally lead to relatively stable growth of future cash flows; in these cases, the human capital value would be estimated using a lower discount rate (to reflect the higher degree of certainty). Conversely, investment banking and racecar driving are examples of professions that may experience unstable and less secure future cash flows, so the value of human capital of investment bankers and racecar drivers would be based on a higher discount rate (to reflect the additional risk associated with their professions).

Equation 1 can be used to estimate the value of an individual's human capital today, at Time 0 (HC_0), where w_t is the income from employment in year t, r is the appropriate discount rate, and N is the length of working life in years. Working life

---

[1] Vesting refers to ownership of retirement or pension benefits. Once benefits are vested, they belong to the beneficiary. Benefits that are not fully vested can be forfeited or reduced if the individual does not meet future conditions (e.g., if the individual terminates employment before the required number of years of service to the organization).

typically ends at retirement, although it could also be based on the number of years an individual can potentially work (e.g., a 70-year-old may be retired but still have some remaining human capital that could be traded for income in the labor market):

$$HC_0 = \sum_{t=1}^{N} \frac{w_t}{(1+r)^t} \qquad (1)$$

This simple model in Equation 1 can be expanded using Equation 2, where we define the wage in time period t as a product of the wage in period $t - 1$ and the sum $(1 + g_t)$. That is, the wage in a given period is equal to the previous year's wage increased by g percent (the annual wage growth rate, in nominal terms). We can also modify the discount rate to be the sum of the nominal risk-free rate r_f and a risk adjustment y based on occupational income volatility. Similar to our example earlier contrasting the overall stability of labor income for government workers and teachers to that of investment bankers and racecar drivers, this adjustment recognizes the fact that the income from different professions can vary significantly. The risk adjustment should consider the inherent stability of the income stream as well as the possibility that the income stream will be interrupted by job loss, disability, or death that may be completely unrelated to the type of employment. Additionally, we incorporate mortality, where $p(s_t)$ is the probability of surviving to a given year (or age). Equation 1 uses a simplifying assumption that $p(s_t) = 1$ for each year until retirement (i.e., the individual will survive to retirement with certainty). Using these additional factors, Equation 2 can be restated as:

$$HC_0 = \sum_{t=1}^{N} \frac{p(s_t)w_{t-1}(1+g_t)}{(1+r_f+y)^t} \qquad (2)$$

EXAMPLE 1

Estimating Human Capital

Identify the key assumptions required to estimate an individual's human capital.

Solution:

Human capital can be calculated by using the following formula:

$$HC_0 = \sum_{t=1}^{N} \frac{p(s_t)w_{t-1}(1+g_t)}{(1+r_f+y)^t}$$

where

$p(s_t)$ = the probability of surviving to year (or age) t
w_t = the income from employment in period t
g_t = the annual wage growth rate
r_f = the nominal risk-free rate
y = risk premium associated with occupational income volatility
N = the length of working life in years

Estimating the Present Value of Human Capital

Using Equation 2, we briefly demonstrate how to estimate the present value of an individual's human capital. John Adam is 60 years old and plans on retiring in 5 years. Adam's annual wage is currently $50,000 and is expected to grow 2% per year. The risk-free rate is 4%. Adam works in a job with a moderate degree of occupational risk; therefore, we assume a risk adjustment based on occupational income volatility of 3%. There is a 99% probability that Adam survives the first year, a 98% probability that he survives the second year, and probabilities of 98%, 97%, and 96% for the following years, respectively. Given this information and using Equation 2, what is the present value of Adam's human capital?

Risk-free rate	= 4%
Income volatility adjustment	= 3%
Total discount rate	= 7%

Year	Wages (2% annual growth)	Present Value of Wages[a]	Probability of Survival	Probability Weighted Wages[b]
1	$51,000	$47,664	99%	$47,187
2	$52,020	$45,436	98%	$44,527
3	$53,060	$43,313	98%	$42,447
4	$54,122	$41,289	97%	$40,050
5	$55,204	$39,360	96%	$37,786
		Total value of human capital		**$211,997**

[a] This column illustrates "Wages" discounted by 7% as indicated by the discount rate shown. For example: $47,664 = $51,000/1.07; $45,436 = $52,020/1.07^2; and so on.
[b] The calculation for this column is as follows: $47,187 = $47,664 × 99%. A similar calculation is used for the following years.

How would the estimated value of Adam's human capital change if the wage growth rate were changed to 0%, the risk-free rate decreased to 2%, and the risk adjustment for occupational income volatility also decreased to 2% (using the same base wage and mortality estimates)?

Risk-free rate	= 2%
Income volatility adjustment	= 2%
Total discount rate	= 4%

Year	Wages (No Growth)	Present Value of Wages	Probability of Survival	Probability Weighted Wages
1	$50,000	$48,077	99%	$47,596
2	$50,000	$46,228	98%	$45,303
3	$50,000	$44,450	98%	$43,561
4	$50,000	$42,740	97%	$41,458
5	$50,000	$41,096	96%	$39,453

(continued)

Year	Wages (No Growth)	Present Value of Wages	Probability of Survival	Probability Weighted Wages
		Total value of human capital		$217,371

Reality is typically more complicated than models. Growth rates, nominal risk-free rates, risk adjustments, and mortality are not easily estimated. Additionally, wages do not tend to increase at a constant rate over an individual's lifetime, mortality and disability risk can reduce the value of human capital, and the average growth rate within occupations or even within the overall economy is unknown. In other words, the future payout on human capital, like the future payout on many financial assets, is uncertain. The potential loss of human capital, particularly early in the life cycle, represents an important risk that must be considered. Life and disability insurance, which we discuss later in the reading, are examples of financial instruments that can be used to protect against a random loss in household earnings. As human capital diminishes later in the life cycle, other risks that threaten financial capital and increase spending needs rise in importance. Accordingly, strategies that reduce investment risk and protect against long-term health care expenses and long-life spending needs increase in importance.

Viewing human capital as an asset with its own risk and return characteristics allows us to develop a holistic investment strategy that includes tangible and intangible assets. A total wealth perspective combines human capital with financial capital and incorporates the concept of life-cycle planning (also discussed later) to develop a strategy that maximizes household welfare.

2.2 Financial Capital

Financial capital can be subdivided into various components besides tangible and intangible, such as personal assets and investment assets. Investment assets can be further differentiated into many subtypes with distinctive marketability, tax, and standalone risk characteristics. The relationships between the value of the various components of an individual's financial capital and the value of his or her human capital are important in investment and risk management decision making.

The approach used in financial accounting provides an excellent template for classifying the different financial assets owned by an investor. In financial accounting, the balance sheet includes a summary of all the assets owned by an entity, whether an individual or organization, at a given point in time. Assets are defined broadly as either current or non-current. Current assets are expected to be consumed over the following year; money in a checking account, for example, would be considered a current asset. For an individual, non-current assets—that is, all assets not classified as current assets—include such items as automobiles, real estate, and investments (such as stocks and bonds). Non-current assets differ for a company because they include such items as property, plant, and equipment, as well as intangible assets, such as goodwill.

The financial accounting approach to segmenting assets has important implications when assessing an individual's financial capital because different assets have different roles and each may be exposed to various types of risk. Broadly speaking, an individual's assets can be described as "personal" assets or "investment" assets; personal assets are consumed whereas investment assets are held for their potential to increase in value and fund future consumption. Some assets, such as real estate, can act as both a personal asset (shelter, as an alternative to renting) and an investment asset (to help fund retirement) for an individual.

> **EXAMPLE 2**
>
> ### Comparing Financial and Human Capital
>
> Describe human capital and financial capital.
>
> ### Solution:
>
> Human capital is commonly defined as the mortality-weighted net present value of an individual's future expected labor income. Financial capital includes the tangible and intangible assets (outside of human capital) owned by an individual or household. For example, a home, a car, stocks, bonds, a vested retirement portfolio, and money in the bank are all examples of an individual's financial capital (or financial assets).

2.2.1 Personal Assets

Personal assets are assets an individual consumes (or uses) in some form in the course of his or her life. Such assets may include automobiles, clothes, furniture, and even a personal residence. In many cases, personal assets are not expected to appreciate in value, and they are often worth more to the individual than their current fair market value.

As mentioned earlier, some assets, like real estate, could be considered a "mixed" asset with both personal and investment characteristics. Another potential example of a mixed asset is collectibles (such as jewelry, wine, stamps, and artwork), which will be discussed separately in a later section. Mixed assets can be especially desirable because they enable individuals to derive satisfaction (i.e., utility) from their current value as well as having the potential to increase in value over time.

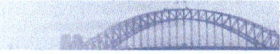

Classifying Private Accrued Defined Benefits and Government Retirement Benefits

When separating an individual's total wealth into human capital and financial capital, accrued defined benefits from private pension and government retirement plans—such as the Canada Pension Plan and Old Age Security Pension, the Age Pension in Australia, the mandatory state pension in Germany, and Social Security in the United States—can potentially be classified as either human capital or financial capital. Some practitioners note that accrued defined benefits and government pension benefits are typically a form of deferred labor income, and thus, they prefer to classify these benefits as human capital. Others find it more intuitive to think of accrued defined benefits and social security as a form of human capital that has been converted into a financial asset. In this reading, we classify accrued defined benefits and government pension benefits as components of financial capital.

2.2.2 Investment Assets

Investment assets are the components of an individual's wealth that are often the easiest to identify and typically receive the majority of the attention from financial planners and investment professionals. Investment assets extend beyond relatively tangible investment assets (such as a liquid portfolio) to include less tangible assets (such as an accrued defined benefit pension).

One criterion for subdividing investment assets is marketability, which describes how easy it is to trade an asset. We subdivide marketable assets into publicly traded and non-publicly traded segments, and we define non-marketable assets as those without any ready market (e.g., human capital).

Traditional portfolio construction generally focuses entirely on publicly traded marketable assets, like stocks and bonds, with optimization determining the weights allocated to marketable assets. This approach often ignores the existence of marketable assets that are not publicly traded as well as other non-marketable assets "owned" by the individual (e.g., human capital). In reality, each asset has important risk characteristics that should be considered. In the absence of a generalized framework that can estimate the risk and return of all of the components of an individual's total wealth and their correlations, one must understand the inherent risk and return characteristics of the non-marketable assets and make informed judgments when constructing a holistic portfolio. We will explore this concept more fully later in the reading.

2.2.3 Publicly Traded Marketable Assets

Traditional balance sheets tend to emphasize publicly traded marketable assets because their value and risk characteristics are generally easier to estimate than those of non-publicly traded assets. Publicly traded marketable assets include money market instruments, bonds, and common and preferred equity.

2.2.4 Non-Publicly Traded Marketable Assets

Non-publicly traded marketable assets include real estate, some types of annuities, cash-value life insurance, business assets, and collectibles.

2.2.4.1 Real Estate Real estate—or direct real estate, as it is sometimes called to distinguish it from real estate investment trusts (REITs)—is typically among the largest assets owned by an individual. In many countries, home ownership is common, although the level of home ownership varies materially by country. For example, in Germany, approximately half of households own a home, whereas in China, the number is closer to 90%. To purchase a home, many individuals obtain a mortgage loan. It is common for the home buyer to contribute some percentage of the home's value (e.g., 20%) as a down payment to mitigate some of the risk to the lender. The term of the mortgage loan can vary (e.g., 15 years, 30 years), as can the mortgage's interest rate (which can be either fixed or floating). Mortgage payments are often the largest fixed obligation of homeowners, especially during the early years of a mortgage loan. Mortgages present a unique risk for homeowners because they create a leveraged exposure in a home. For example, a 20% down payment (80% mortgage loan) implies that for any given change in the value of the home, the change in the equity (value less the mortgage loan) of the home will be five times greater than the change in the value of the home. Mortgage loans are either recourse or non-recourse, and the status varies by region. With recourse mortgages, if the borrower defaults on the mortgage, the lender has the right to recover from the borrower any amount due on the loan, whereas non-recourse loans prevent the lender from recovering any further amount from the borrower. Non-recourse loans are thus riskier for lenders because the only available collateral for the loan is the home. As a result, non-recourse loans generally have higher interest rates and/or higher borrower credit standards than recourse loans.

2.2.4.2 Annuities Annuities are effectively a private defined benefit pension for which an insurance company has guaranteed, or will guarantee, income for life or over some fixed period for the beneficiary (called the annuitant). The estimated balance sheet value of an annuity is comparable to that of a defined benefit pension with a discount for potential insolvency risk, which is difficult to eliminate through diversification or a market hedge. Annuities will be discussed in more detail later in the reading.

2.2.4.3 Cash-Value Life Insurance A variety of types of life insurance are available, including cash-value life insurance, for which the policy not only provides protection upon a death but also contains some type of cash reserve. This form of insurance usually combines life insurance protection with some type of cash accumulation vehicle. Some insurance policies allow the purchaser to invest in relatively aggressive investments, such as equities, although more conservative investments, such as bonds, are generally more common. Life insurance products will also be discussed at greater length later in the reading.

2.2.4.4 Business Assets Business assets can represent a significant portion of the total wealth of an individual, especially a self-employed individual. A variety of unique considerations are involved in investing for business owners because their total capital may be very closely tied to the overall performance of the business (i.e., if the business does poorly, it affects not only the value of the business, but also the owner's earnings as well). The value of business assets may best be estimated through recent sales of comparable private businesses within the same industry—often as a multiple of net income or net income with various adjustments (e.g., EBITDA). The value of business assets may vary based on market conditions and will often correlate with other financial assets within a household portfolio. This potential correlation is an important consideration in the risk management process for individuals, particularly small business owners.

2.2.4.5 Collectibles Collectibles include such items as stamps, paintings, wine, and precious metals (e.g., coins). The value of these assets is often set by auction markets or specialized dealers and involves substantial transaction costs. Collectibles may also provide a flow of utility for the owner. For example, in addition to benefiting from the potential price increase of a painting, the owner is able to display the painting in his or her home and view it daily.

2.2.5 Non-Marketable Assets

The most significant non-marketable financial assets are pensions, whether from a private employer or from a governmental organization. In this section, we consider both types of pensions.

2.2.5.1 Employer Pension Plans (Vested) There are a variety of retirement plan types across the globe. These accounts can generally be described as either employee-directed savings plans, in which contribution amounts and investments are controlled by the individual (and not guaranteed), or traditional pension plans, which guarantee some level of retirement benefits, typically based on past wages. We include only vested pension benefits as financial assets, because unvested pension benefits are typically contingent on future work and are thus considered to be part of human capital.

The value of a vested traditional defined benefit pension from an employer can be estimated by determining the mortality-weighted net present value of future benefits. The mortality-weighted net present value at Time 0 (now), $mNPV_0$, can be estimated using Equation 3, which is reasonably equivalent to Equation 1. Equation 3 is based on the future expected vested benefit (b_t), the probability of surviving until year t [$p(s_t)$], and a discount rate (r). The discount rate should vary based on the relative riskiness of the future expected benefit payment—that is, the rate will be higher for riskier future benefit payments—and should reflect whether the benefit is in nominal or real terms:

$$mNPV_0 = \sum_{t=1}^{N} \frac{p(s_t)b_t}{(1+r)^t} \quad (3)$$

Estimating an appropriate discount rate to use in valuing a pension can be quite complex, although it is generally less complex than estimating the discount rate to use in valuing an individual's human capital. There are a number of factors to consider in determining the pension discount rate. As a starting point, one should consider the health of the plan (e.g., its funding status, where the value of the plan's liability is estimated using an appropriate market-based discount rate), the credit quality of the sponsoring company, and any additional credit support. If the company in question has long-term bonds, the yield on the bonds can provide a proxy for an appropriate discount rate. As one example of credit support, the Pension Protection Fund (PPF) was established in the United Kingdom as part of the Pensions Act 2004 to guarantee continued payment of most UK defined benefit pension plans should the employer become insolvent. The existence of PPF insurance helps to decrease the payout risk (and accompanying discount rate) for eligible UK pension plans.

2.2.5.2 Government Pensions Government pensions are similar to employer pension plans but are generally more secure (in those countries with a high degree of creditworthiness). As with employer pension plans, the vested or accrued benefit amount can be estimated by calculating the mortality-weighted net present value. Given the guaranteed nature of these benefits, government pensions can be considered relatively bond-like. For example, in the United States, retiree government pension benefits (called Social Security retirement benefits) can be thought of as a government bond with benefits indexed to inflation (because Social Security retirement benefits usually increase annually based on inflation). This inflation adjustment is consistent with securities called Treasury Inflation-Protected Securities (TIPS).

Regardless of the domicile, one should consider the financial health of the government entity sponsoring the defined benefit plan as well as the legal framework and any accompanying political risk at the country level.

2.2.6 Account Type

Financial capital is often held in account types that have different tax attributes. Although these account types (and the potential tax benefits surrounding them) vary materially by country, the accounts can generally be described as taxable, tax-deferred, or non-taxable. A taxable account is one for which taxes are due annually on the realized gains, dividends, and/or interest income. A tax-deferred account is one for which taxes on any gains are deferred until some future date, such as when a withdrawal is made from the account. A non-taxable account is one for which taxes are never due, no matter how much the account grows.

2.3 Economic Net Worth

An individual's *net worth* consists of the difference between traditional assets and liabilities that are reasonably simple to measure, such as investment assets, real estate, and mortgages. **Economic net worth**, however, extends net worth to include claims to future assets that can be used for consumption, such as human capital and the present value of pension benefits. When we refer to economic net worth in this reading, we refer to the more holistic accounting of resources that can be used to fund future consumption for the purpose of financial planning over the life cycle.

A FRAMEWORK FOR INDIVIDUAL RISK MANAGEMENT

c discuss the financial stages of life for an individual;

This section contains an overview of the important considerations when developing an effective risk management plan for an individual. First, a risk management strategy for individuals is introduced. Next, the primary financial stages of the life of an individual are discussed. We then incorporate the human capital and financial capital concepts developed in Section 2 into an individual's economic (or holistic) balance sheet, explaining how key components of that balance sheet develop over time. Finally, we identify some of the primary risks to an individual and how they evolve during an individual's lifetime.

3.1 The Risk Management Strategy for Individuals

In general, *risk management* for individuals is the process of identifying threats to the value of household assets and developing an appropriate strategy for dealing with these risks. The risk management strategy provides a framework that allows a household to decide when to avoid, reduce, transfer, or self-insure those risks. There are typically four key steps in the risk management process:

1. Specify the objective.
2. Identify risks.
3. Evaluate risks and select appropriate methods to manage the risks.
4. Monitor outcomes and risk exposures and make appropriate adjustments in methods.

3.1.1 Specify the Objective

The overarching objective of individual risk management is to maximize household welfare through an appropriate balance of risk and safety. Risk represents a possible decrease in future spending caused by unexpected events, such as a market crash, a physical disability, the premature death of a primary earner, or health care expenses. As with investments, this objective is achieved by deciding how much risk a household is willing to bear in order to achieve its long-run spending goals.

3.1.2 Identify Risks

Households face a significant number of risks, including earnings, premature death, longevity, property, liability, and health risks. These risks will be discussed at length in subsequent sections. Each of these risks is associated with a potential loss of financial and/or human capital, and individuals should address each of them to determine how best to address the possibility of loss.

3.1.3 Evaluate Risks and Select Appropriate Methods to Manage the Risks

The existence of a risk exposure does not necessarily require the purchase of an insurance product. The appropriate risk management strategy considers the magnitude of the risk and the range of options available to address that risk. Section 11 will explain the choice among the four techniques of risk avoidance, risk reduction, risk transfer, and risk retention. *Risk avoidance* involves avoiding a risk altogether. For example, one way to avoid the risk to human and financial capital from riding a motorcycle is to simply not own or ride one. *Risk reduction* involves mitigating a risk by reducing its impact on an individual's welfare, either by lowering the likelihood that it will occur or by decreasing the magnitude of loss (for example, by wearing a helmet when riding a motorcycle). *Risk transfer* involves transferring the risk: The use of insurance and annuities to transfer risk to insurers will be discussed later in the reading. *Risk retention* involves retaining a risk and thus maintaining the ability to finance the cost of losses; when funds are set aside to meet potential losses, the individual is said to *self-insure*.

3.1.4 Monitor Outcomes and Risk Exposures and Make Appropriate Adjustments in Methods

Once the appropriate risk management method has been selected, risks must be monitored and updated as the household moves through its life cycle. It is advisable to annually review an insurance/risk management program, including all the ongoing risk exposures and risk management methods. As an individual's goals and personal and financial situation change, these changes will affect risk exposures and optimal risk management strategies. In addition to an annual review, every life change—such as a birth, marriage, inheritance, job change, relocation, divorce, or death—should trigger a review of the risk management plan.

3.2 Financial Stages of Life

Individuals tend to follow a predictable pattern during their lifetimes: They invest in education early in life, embark on a career, start families, accumulate assets, fund growing household expenses, transition into retirement, and ultimately pass on wealth through bequests. In each of these life-cycle stages, the household faces unique goals and risks that require appropriate investment and risk management strategies.

Defining financial stages of life in clear and concise terms does pose a challenge because all individuals are different; however, financial stages are a useful construct when thinking about risk management and the optimal forms of insurance and other products to consider at different ages. Therefore, we divide the financial stages of life for adults into the following seven periods:

- Education phase
- Early career
- Career development
- Peak accumulation
- Pre-retirement
- Early retirement
- Late retirement

3.2.1 Education Phase

The education phase occurs while an individual is investing in knowledge (or human capital) through either formal education or skill development. In theory, the education phase could begin as early as when an individual starts primary school, but this phase typically involves the period when the individual starts developing more specific human capital by attending college or trade school or undertaking an apprenticeship. In some cases, an individual in the education phase may be largely financially dependent on his or her parents or guardians and have little, if any, accumulated financial capital. There is generally little focus on savings or risk management at this point; however, some individuals in this phase may already have families and could benefit from products, such as life insurance, that hedge against the risk of losing human capital.

3.2.2 Early Career

The early career phase normally begins when an individual has completed his or her education and enters the workforce. This stage may begin as early as age 18 (16 in some countries) or as late as the late 20s (or even early 30s), depending on the level of education attained, and generally lasts into the mid-30s. During this period, the individual often marries, perhaps has young children, may purchase a home, and usually begins to save for their children's college expenses. Sometimes, a career-related relocation occurs that could have negative short-term financial implications. Significant family and housing expenses may not allow for much retirement savings. Insurance may be especially valuable during this phase because human capital represents such a large proportion of total wealth and family members are highly dependent on the human capital of one or two individuals to fund expected future consumption.

3.2.3 Career Development

The career development phase normally occurs during the 35–50 age range and is often a time of specific skill development within a given field, upward career mobility, and income growth. This phase often includes accumulation for the children's college educations as well as expenditures for college. Concern intensifies about retirement income planning and financial independence. Higher earners will begin building wealth beyond education and retirement objectives and may make large purchases, such as a vacation home, or travel extensively. Retirement saving tends to increase at a more rapid pace during this phase compared with the early career phase.

3.2.4 Peak Accumulation

In the peak accumulation phase, generally during the ages of 51–60, most people either have reached or are moving toward maximum earnings and have the greatest opportunity for wealth accumulation. This phase may include accumulating funds for other goals and objectives, but it is usually a continuation of retirement income planning, coordination of employee benefits with investment and retirement strategies, and travel. Investors following a life-cycle portfolio strategy will begin to reduce investment risk to emphasize income production for retirement (particularly near the end of this period) and become increasingly concerned about minimizing taxes, given higher levels of wealth and income. There is also potentially more career risk in this phase because if an individual were to lose his or her job, it might be relatively difficult for that individual to find another job with similar pay.

3.2.5 Pre-retirement

The pre-retirement phase consists of the few years preceding the planned retirement age, and it typically represents an individual's maximum career income. Many people in this phase continue to restructure their portfolios to reduce risk and may consider investments that are less volatile. There is further emphasis on tax planning, including the ramifications of retirement plan distribution options.

3.2.6 Early Retirement

The early retirement phase in the cycle is generally defined as the first 10 years of retirement and, for successful investors, often represents a period of comfortable income and sufficient assets to meet expenses. For individuals who are forced to retire because of injury or unemployment, this time may be one of shifting expectations and may involve changing to a lifestyle more commensurate with the individual's savings. This is generally the most active period of retirement and is when an individual is less likely to suffer from cognitive or mobility limitations. The primary objective of the retiree is to use resources to produce activities that provide enjoyment. Some retirees seek a new career, and many will look for a job (part time or full time) that has less stress. It is important to note that upon entering retirement, the need for asset growth does not disappear. For many households, the length of retirement could exceed two decades; given this potential horizon, it is important to continue taking an appropriate level of investment risk in retirees' portfolios.

3.2.7 Late Retirement

The late retirement phase is especially unpredictable because the exact length of retirement is unknown. This uncertainty about longevity for a specific individual is known as longevity risk, which is the risk that an individual outlives his or her financial resources in retirement. Physical activity typically declines during this phase, as does mobility. Although many individuals live comfortably and are in good health until their final days, others experience a long series of physical problems that can deplete financial asset reserves. Cognitive decline can present a risk of financial mistakes, which may be hedged through the participation of a trusted financial adviser or through the use of annuities. Annuities will be discussed in more detail later in the reading.

Two additional concerns may be appropriate to any financial stage. First, depending on the family situation, the need to provide for long-term health care may become apparent. Second, some people may need to devote resources to care for parents or a disabled child for an extended period of time.

EXAMPLE 3

Financial Stages of Life

From a personal financial planning standpoint, what are typical characteristics of someone in the "peak accumulation" phase?

Solution:

An individual in the peak accumulation phase of the life cycle would typically have the following characteristics:

- Approximate age of 51–60
- Maximum earnings and opportunity for wealth accumulation
- Increased interest in retirement income planning
- Greater emphasis on stability and less emphasis on growth in the investment portfolio
- Greater concern about tax strategies
- Increased concern about losing employment because it may be more difficult to find new employment

---

4 THE INDIVIDUAL BALANCE SHEET

d   describe an economic (holistic) balance sheet;

A traditional balance sheet includes assets and liabilities that are usually easy to quantify. Our purpose in developing an individual balance sheet is to more comprehensively represent the assets available to fund life-cycle consumption and for wealth preservation and transfer bequests. The primary value of a balance sheet in this context is to illustrate the magnitude of risk exposures for an individual. This perspective is particularly important for individuals who are in life-cycle stages during which human capital is a significant share of overall wealth and for individuals who hold claims on pension assets that grow in value later in the life cycle.

In this section, we attempt to provide a more complete picture of an investor's wealth through the use of an economic balance sheet (or holistic balance sheet), which we initially mentioned in Section 2. Such a balance sheet provides a useful overview of the individual's total wealth portfolio, supplementing traditional balance sheet assets with human capital and pension wealth and expanding liabilities to include consumption and bequest goals. These additional liabilities are important because they often represent leverage created in order to gain access to assets, such as the cost of education to create human capital. They also represent regular payment obligations that may influence the optimal amount of portfolio liquidity and investment risk. Human capital and pension wealth are important because they represent expected income flows that can be drawn on to fund future consumption.

4.1 Traditional Balance Sheet

The simplest balance sheet for an individual investor includes recognizable marketable assets and liabilities. Assets include any type of investment portfolio, retirement portfolio (or plan), real estate, and other tangible and intangible items of value. Liabilities include mortgage debt, credit card debt, auto loans, business debt, and student loans. An example of a simple balance sheet (or statement of net worth) is shown in Exhibit 1, where the assets are netted against the liabilities to determine the net worth of the individual.

Exhibit 1   Traditional Balance Sheet as of 31 December 2014

Assets		Liabilities	
Liquid Assets		**Short-Term Liabilities**	
Checking account	€35,000	Credit card debt	€25,000
Certificates of deposit	€100,000	Total short-term liabilities	€25,000
Total liquid assets	€135,000		
Investment Assets		**Long-Term Liabilities**	
Taxable account	€750,000	Car loan*	€25,000
Retirement plan	€600,000	Home mortgage	€500,000
Cash value of life insurance	€25,000	Home equity loan	€90,000
Total investment assets	€1,375,000	Total long-term liabilities	€615,000
Personal Property			
House	€2,200,000		
Cars	€160,000		
House contents	€150,000		
Total personal property	€2,510,000		
Total Assets	€4,020,000	Total Liabilities	€640,000

(continued)

Exhibit 1	(Continued)		
Assets		Liabilities	
		Net Worth	€3,380,000

Note: A portion of the car loan would likely be short term, but to simplify, we included the entire loan as a long-term liability.

The net value of an asset, or its equity, is calculated by subtracting liabilities associated with that asset from the gross value. For example, an individual may own a home worth £1 million, but if that individual has a £900,000 mortgage, the equity in the home would be only £100,000 (ignoring any additional intangible benefits associated with home ownership).

It should be noted that this traditional balance sheet includes those assets that can be valued easily but ignores other individual assets that are material, such as human capital and pension benefits. For individuals in the earlier life-cycle stages, human capital is larger than other assets on the balance sheet. For those who are eligible to receive a guaranteed retirement income stream, the present value of these assets is significant and can be of great value to older individuals. Although non-marketable and difficult to value precisely, human capital and retirement benefits are extremely important when planning the optimal use of assets and the repayment of liabilities over a life cycle.

4.2 Economic (Holistic) Balance Sheet

The primary goal of an economic (holistic) balance sheet is to arrive at an accurate depiction of an individual's overall financial health by accounting for the present value of all available marketable and non-marketable assets as well as all liabilities. This view allows an individual to map out the optimal level of future consumption and non-consumption goals (such as bequests or other transfers) given the resources that exist today and those that are expected in the future. Although a traditional balance sheet provides information about marketable assets that exist today, it offers limited insight into how these assets should be used to maximize the expected lifetime satisfaction of the individual (a concept economists call "utility"). An economic balance sheet allows an individual to anticipate how available resources can be used to fund consumption over the remaining lifetime.

Exhibit 2 provides a simplified example of an economic balance sheet, which is an expanded version of the traditional balance sheet in Exhibit 1. The traditional assets and liabilities are condensed from the traditional balance sheet in Exhibit 1, with the present value of human capital and pensions added as assets and the present value of lifetime consumption and bequests added as liabilities. For further simplification purposes, we assume that all the assets and liabilities in Exhibit 1 are already calculated at their present value.

Exhibit 2	Economic (Holistic) Balance Sheet as of 31 December 2014		
Assets		**Liabilities**	
Financial capital	€4,020,000	Debts	€640,000
Liquid assets		Credit card debt	
Investment assets		Car loan	

Exhibit 2 (Continued)

Assets		Liabilities	
Personal property		Home mortgage	
		Home equity loan	
Human capital	€1,400,000	Lifetime consumption needs (present value)	€4,200,000
Pension value	€500,000		
		Bequests	€400,000
Total Assets	€5,920,000	Total Liabilities	€5,240,000
		Economic Net Worth	€680,000

An economic balance sheet that includes the present value of non-marketable assets (e.g., human capital and pensions) and liabilities (e.g., consumption needs and bequests) provides a much more accurate baseline from which to maximize the expected utility of future consumption. Assessing pension and human capital value can also be useful when setting consumption or bequest goals because these assessments provide a more accurate estimation of the future trade-offs an individual will make. Younger households with greater human capital, in addition to spending more to protect the value of this human capital early in the life cycle, will be able to plan for more generous retirement savings goals than households with comparatively lower human capital.

The total economic wealth of an individual changes throughout his or her lifetime, as do the underlying assets that make up that wealth. The total economic wealth of younger individuals is typically dominated by the value of their human capital because younger individuals have not had as much time to save and accumulate financial wealth. As individuals grow older, they are likely to save some of their earnings and will accumulate financial capital. The total value of human capital and the total value of financial capital tend to be inversely related over time as individuals attempt to smooth consumption through borrowing, saving, and eventual spending. When human capital is depleted, an absence of financial capital would result in no wealth to fund an individual's consumption needs. Although some people may live with family or friends at older ages out of necessity, most would prefer to have financial independence in retirement—something that typically requires individuals to save throughout their prime working years.

Although the economic net worth in the hypothetical economic balance sheet was equal to €680,000, it is possible for an individual to have either a surplus or a shortfall. For example, if the individual is not saving enough to adequately fund the lifestyle he or she will want at retirement, that individual may have a shortfall. Alternatively, if the individual is saving more than enough to fund lifestyle needs and has no bequest goals, he or she may have a surplus. In either case, an economic balance sheet provides some perspective about the overall financial situation of an individual based on his or her holistic wealth.

> **EXAMPLE 4**
>
> ### Traditional vs. Economic Balance Sheet
>
> Contrast a traditional balance sheet with an economic balance sheet.
>
> **Solution:**
>
> A traditional balance sheet includes assets and liabilities that are generally relatively easy to quantify. An economic balance sheet provides a useful overview of one's total wealth portfolio by supplementing traditional balance sheet assets with human capital and pension wealth and including additional liabilities, such as consumption and bequest goals.

4.3 Changes in Economic Net Worth

To provide some context for how the relative value of various household assets changes over a lifetime, we will use the hypothetical example of a British individual at age 25. This 25-year-old is assumed to make £40,000 a year in after-tax income. Over his or her lifetime, real wages are expected to grow at a constant rate of 1% per year, the annual savings rate is 10%, the nominal discount rate is 8%, and the rate of expected inflation is 3%. The value of human capital is estimated using Equation 2. Financial capital at age 25 is assumed to be £10,000, and it is expected to grow at an annual real rate of return of 3% per year. The assumed need from the portfolio is £20,000 for the first year of retirement (age 65) and is increased annually by inflation throughout retirement.

We further assume that at age 30 the individual purchases a home that costs £100,000 in today's currency. The home is purchased with a 10% down payment (which comes from financial capital), with the remainder financed by a 30-year mortgage at a fixed nominal interest rate of 5%. The real growth rate of the value of the home is assumed to be 1%. Total pension benefits of £20,000 per year (in today's currency, at age 25) are assumed to commence at age 65, and the real discount rate for pension retirement benefits is 5%. We assume the benefits are accrued throughout the employment of the individual.

Exhibit 3 shows the values of the assets in the individual's economic balance sheet and how they are expected to change over time. To simplify the concept, we demonstrate graphically how the sample inputs reflect the allocation in the exhibit.

The Individual Balance Sheet

Exhibit 3 Life-Cycle Economic Balance Sheet Allocation

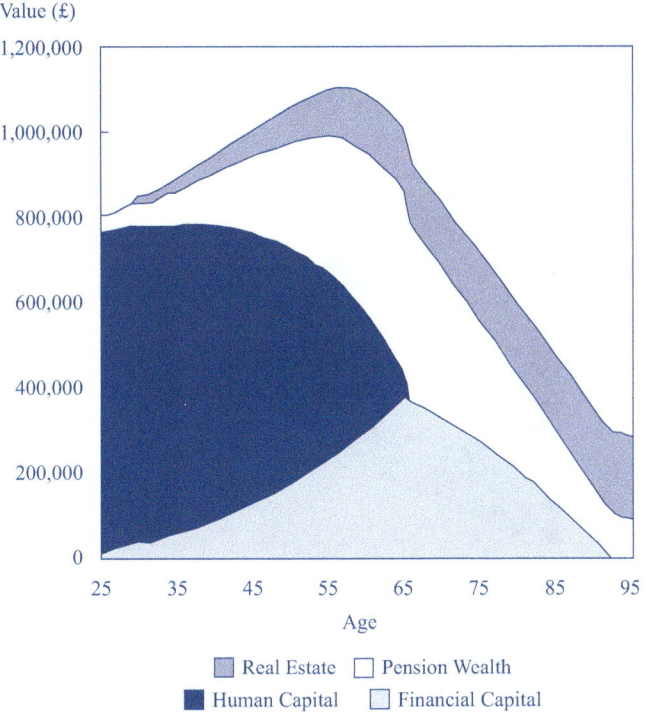

Traditional balance sheet assets, such as investments in marketable securities, real estate, and businesses, vary in importance from one life-cycle stage to the next. In general, tangible assets, such as real estate and personal goods, which provide great value to a young family, dominate a household's portfolio early in the life cycle. As households age, they accumulate financial assets that must be managed efficiently to provide the greatest expected later-life consumption for the amount of risk the household is willing to take. Non-traditional balance sheet assets, such as employer pensions, increase in importance later in the life cycle, providing an important source of stable consumption and affecting the optimal allocation of securities within an investment portfolio. To illustrate, Exhibit 4 provides the relative weights for the various assets included in Exhibit 3.

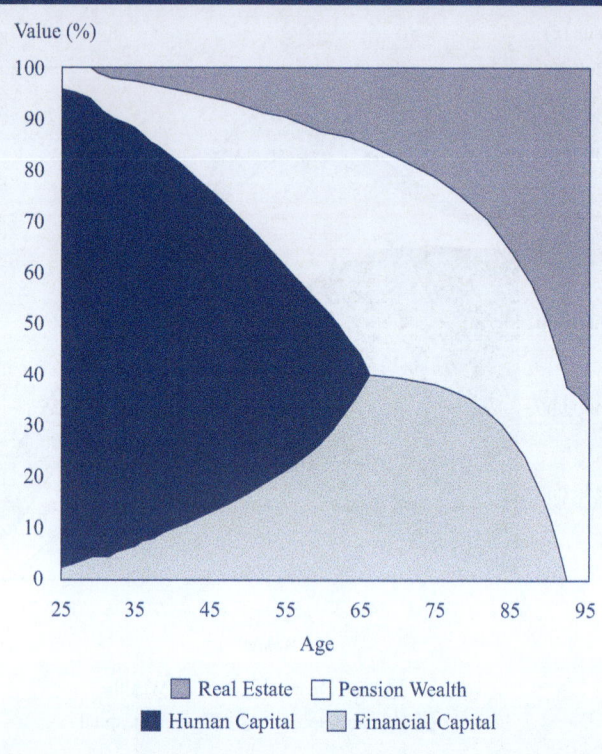

Exhibit 4 Relative Weights of Economic Balance Sheet Allocation

In Exhibit 4, we see that for the typical individual, an investment portfolio represents a significant portion of wealth at age 65 but is still less than 50% of the total economic wealth when home equity, pension wealth, and human capital are also considered. As that individual proceeds through his or her retirement years and funds consumption, the relative share of the investment portfolio declines. In the early retirement stage, total economic wealth is dominated by pension wealth (i.e., the remaining mortality-weighted net present value of benefits) and the value of real estate (i.e., the individual's personal residence). For wealthier individuals, the value of defined benefit pension wealth will likely represent a low percentage of the total wealth portfolio in retirement. To the extent that defined benefit pension wealth has very low credit risk (for example, because of the low default probability of National Insurance in the United Kingdom), a retiree's optimal investment portfolio allocation will be affected. As discussed earlier, one must consider the financial health of both the plan and the sponsor providing the defined benefit pension.

In a related manner, a 65-year-old with £2 million in pension wealth will have a higher level of expected remaining lifetime consumption than a retiree with £1 million in pension wealth and the same traditional balance sheet net worth. Both individuals will need to consider means to safeguard the value of the pension wealth as part of the financial planning process. For example, a pension from a private employer may be subject to company-specific risk. The risk of employer insolvency might be hedged in financial markets by positions in securities and derivatives (if available) that have a negative correlation with the value of the company. As mentioned previously, guarantees of benefit payments may exist, such as the Pension Protection Fund in the United Kingdom that protects many private defined benefit schemes.

The allocation of the different asset types will affect the optimal financial asset allocation decision. A 45-year-old individual in Germany with €1 million in human capital and €500,000 in investment assets should invest differently than a 45-year-old with €3 million in human capital and an identical €500,000 in investment assets. The volatility in the investment portfolio of the individual with lower human capital will have a much greater impact on variation in expected consumption if both individuals have a 40-year planning horizon. Assume that the first 45-year-old with €1.5 million in combined human and financial capital expects to spend approximately €38,000 each year until age 85. The other 45-year-old with €3.5 million in economic net worth expects to spend €88,000 each year. All else being equal, a 40% loss in the first individual's portfolio (0.4 × €500,000 = €200,000) will lead to a 13.2% loss in expected spending per year [(€200,000/40 years)/€38,000] whereas a 40% investment loss to the second individual's portfolio will lead only to a 5.7% decrease in expected consumption [(€200,000/40 years)/€88,000]. For this reason, portfolio recommendations will be less conservative for the investor with high human capital than for the investor with low human capital if both have the same level of risk tolerance.

EXAMPLE 5

Changes in Human and Financial Capital

Describe how the relative values of human capital and financial capital change over an individual's lifetime.

Solution:

The total value of human capital and the total value of financial capital tend to be inversely related over time as individuals attempt to smooth consumption through borrowing, saving, and eventual spending. When human capital becomes depleted, without financial capital, an individual will have no wealth to fund his or her lifestyle. Human capital is generally largest for a younger individual, whereas financial capital is generally largest when an individual first retires.

INDIVIDUAL RISK EXPOSURES

e discuss risks (earnings, premature death, longevity, property, liability, and health risks) in relation to human and financial capital;

Managing risks to financial and human capital is an essential part of the household financial planning process. In this section, we provide an overview of the risks faced by individuals and discuss how they relate to human and financial capital. In future sections, we introduce financial products that could be used to manage many of these risks.

5.1 Earnings Risk

Earnings risk, within the context of personal risk management, refers to the risks associated with the earning potential of an individual—that is, events that could negatively affect the individual's human and financial capital. As noted previously, health issues can affect earnings, and some health risks are a function of the occupation itself. For example, a construction worker is likely to face higher health-related earnings risk than the average worker. Aside from health issues, unemployment and underemployment represent major factors in earnings risk. Sometimes, an employee's job performance or a poor "fit" may lead to job loss, but many people find themselves without a job through no fault of their own.

The risk associated with unemployment for reasons other than disability is rather difficult to characterize. In some cases, such as government employees and union members with seniority, the likelihood of unemployment may be very low. Smaller, younger companies may be riskier employers because of dynamic business conditions or cash flow issues. But even large, well-established companies have been known to go out of business or to close unprofitable divisions or locations. In such cases, even an offer to transfer to another location may be undesirable for someone late in his or her working life, for someone with a working spouse and/or children in school, or for someone who strongly prefers to remain in the same location for a variety of other reasons. Some industries are cyclical and are prone to layoffs, whereas other industries are subject to competitive pressures that may lead to permanent terminations. Self-employed individuals and even some professionals are prone to variability in their earnings. Of course, the cost is the loss or reduction of earnings and may also include the loss of employer contributions to one's retirement fund as well as other benefit programs. A lengthy period of unemployment may itself create more risk because employers are sometimes hesitant to hire people who have been out of work for an extended period of time. If the individual finally finds a job, it may be at a dramatically lower compensation level.

Obviously, the loss of income represents a reduction in both human and financial capital, and this reduction is exacerbated if job opportunities are few, especially in a poor economy or in a region or industry that is particularly affected. For individuals who lose a job as they approach retirement age, it could be very difficult to find another job, even if there are regulations against age discrimination. Aside from the stress on the family budget, unemployment can be psychologically devastating to the individual and his or her family. With earnings risk, as well as health risk (which is discussed in further detail later), an implication in estimating the total value of human capital is that individuals who work in dangerous occupations or in jobs that have a high likelihood of variability or disruption in earnings have either lower future expected earnings or a higher discount rate or both. Financial capital may also be affected by earnings risk because assets will be needed to make up for any loss of income. Furthermore, there may be a need to seek additional training or education to acquire requisite skills, and this retooling can be very expensive.

5.2 Premature Death Risk

The term **premature death risk**, which is sometimes referred to as mortality risk, relates to the death of an individual earlier than anticipated whose future earnings, or human capital, were expected to help pay for financial needs and aspirations of the individual's family. These needs include funding day-to-day living expenses, such as food, housing, and transportation, as well as paying off debts, saving for a child's education, and providing for a comfortable retirement for the surviving spouse. An individual's death may also lead to a reduction in the income of the surviving spouse because some family responsibilities of the deceased individual must now be performed by the surviving spouse (assuming the spouse does not remarry). For a young family, the effect can be especially tragic because the increase in household lifestyle that might have accompanied the career of the deceased may never occur (again, if there is no remarriage).

A risk to consumption needs also occurs if a non-earning member of the family dies. The loss can be estimated as the discounted value of the services provided by the deceased family member plus any out-of-pocket death expenses. If a household's primary caregiver dies, the rest of the family can help with that member's responsibilities, but often additional, paid help is required to replace the primary caregiver's duties.

Individual Risk Exposures

This scenario will mean a dramatic change in lifestyle, compounding the incalculable emotional effect of the death. It could even have a negative impact on the career of the surviving spouse, who may feel drained by the added responsibilities.

Besides the obvious reduction in human capital that the death of an income earner represents, there are also effects on financial capital. Death expenses (including funeral and burial), transition expenses, estate settlement expenses, and the possible need for training or education for the surviving spouse are among the financial costs that may be incurred.

5.3 Longevity Risk

Longevity risk within the context of financial planning relates to the uncertainty surrounding how long retirement will last and specifically the risks associated with living to an advanced age in retirement (e.g., age 100). An extended retirement period may deplete the retiree's resources to the point at which income and financial assets are insufficient to meet post-retirement consumption needs. A common question posed to financial planners is, "How much money do I need to have when I retire?" The answer is dependent on the lifespan of the individual, and longevity is a key variable that can only, at best, be estimated. Other important variables include the nominal rate of return on the portfolio, the rate of inflation, additional sources of income (and whether those sources are adjusted for inflation), and the level of spending. Determining how large a fund an individual will actually have at retirement depends on the amount and timing of contributions, the nominal rate of return, and the amount of time until retirement.

When calculating the sum needed at retirement, financial planners often run a Monte Carlo simulation that is based on an assumed asset allocation to calculate the probability that the funds will last for a specified number of years. Another approach for the time variable is to use a mortality table, adjust for health factors, and add years to be conservative. For example, Friedrich is retiring at age 65, and the mortality tables in his country indicate that a 65-year-old man has an expected lifespan of 20 years. But Friedrich is healthy, exercises regularly, eats well, and has had annual physical examinations, and his parents lived until their late 80s, which was past life expectancy at that time. Friedrich might assume that his retirement will last only 20 years (his life expectancy), but the mortality tables indicate a 50% chance that he will live beyond the forecasted period, which is why it is common to add years to be conservative (e.g., plan for retirement to last 30 years, or until age 95). The decision regarding the additional number of years is obviously subjective. The only way to minimize the likelihood of living beyond the forecasted retirement period would be to use extremely advanced ages (e.g., age 110).

Longevity risk can have a significant impact on the lifestyle of an individual. Even in countries that provide significant pension benefits, income may be inadequate to support the hoped-for lifestyle, and insufficient assets may exacerbate the situation. Making matters worse, many pension programs do not consider inflation. Furthermore, some pension programs, even those sponsored by governmental entities, are unlikely to have sufficient assets to pay future expected liabilities without significant changes to the pension structure. Relying on a pension thus entails its own set of risks.

Longevity risk affects human capital in the sense that an individual who is concerned about "living too long" may choose to work longer than someone else might. Indeed, all else being equal, the person who is concerned about outliving his or her money and who intends to work longer has more human capital, but at the possible expense of a less desirable (i.e., longer) retirement stage.

5.4 Property Risk

Property risk relates to the possibility that a person's property may be damaged, destroyed, stolen, or lost. There are, of course, many different possible events relating to property risk. A house may catch fire, an automobile may be involved in a collision or be damaged in a hailstorm, or a valuable necklace may be lost. In the context of property risk, *direct loss* refers to the monetary value of the loss associated with the property itself. For example, a house fire may cause €50,000 of damage. If the repair process requires that the family live elsewhere while the damage is repaired, the expenses incurred are considered an *indirect loss*. If the family is renting a room to a boarder, the income lost during construction would also be considered an indirect loss. Similarly, if a driver damages his or her automobile by running into a curb, the damage to the automobile is a direct loss and the cost of renting a replacement automobile is an indirect loss.

Because property represents a financial asset, property risk is normally considered to be associated with a potential loss of financial capital. But property used in a business to create income is rightfully considered in a discussion of human capital. That is, this type of business property can be considered a tool that helps drive future earnings, and to the extent that such property is at risk, human capital is also at risk. Business owners should be especially conscious of the fact that in the absence of insurance or other risk management techniques, both financial and human capital is at risk.

5.5 Liability Risk

Liability risk refers to the possibility that an individual or household may be held legally liable for the financial costs associated with property damage or physical injury. In general, one may be *liable* if because of one's action—or inaction when one is legally responsible for taking action—bodily injury, property damage, or other loss is incurred by another person or entity.

For individuals, the most common cause of legal liability involves driving an automobile. An automobile accident may cause bodily injury leading to medical costs, lost income, and even the necessity for long-term care. For the vast majority of people, the potential liability of a major automobile accident exceeds not only their financial capital but also their human capital as well. For example, in some jurisdictions, a liability judgment may result in the confiscation (often termed garnishing) of the wages or other income of the person found liable. Note, though, that the person who is found liable—for example, in an automobile accident—may also have suffered an injury that may affect the individual's financial and/or human capital.

As an example of liability risk, assume that a driver causes an automobile accident in which a passenger in the other car is injured and the other driver's automobile is heavily damaged. In many jurisdictions, the individual who caused the accident is deemed responsible for the repair or replacement of the damaged automobile and the medical expenses and lost income of the victim. As another example, in many countries, a homeowner or even an apartment renter may be deemed legally liable for an accident that causes injury or property damage to a visitor. For example, a guest may accidentally slip on some steps, be seriously injured by the fall, and become incapable of gainful employment. Even if the visitor was careless, laws may specify that the owner or renter of the property is liable.

5.6 Health Risk

Health risk refers to the risks and implications associated with illness or injury. Direct costs associated with illness or injury may include coinsurance, copayments, and deductibles associated with diagnostics, treatments, and procedures. In the context of health insurance, the term *coinsurance* means that the insured must share some of the costs of the specific health care provided. For example, an insurance company may be obligated to pay 80% of the cost of a medical procedure and require that the insured pay the other 20%. *Copayments* refer to the requirement that the insured pay a specified amount of money for a medical service, typically treatment by a physician. For example, a copayment, or "copay," of US$30 may be required for a visit to a primary care physician and US$45 may be required for a visit to a specialist. The remainder of the actual expense is paid by the insurance company. A *deductible* is an amount that the insured is required to spend on health care approved by the insurance company during the plan year before the insurance company pays for anything. For example, there may be a US$500 deductible per person and a US$1,500 total deductible for a family. Insurance companies contend that coinsurance, copayments, and deductibles discourage frivolous use of the health care system, thereby keeping insurance premiums lower.

In some countries, health care costs for individuals can be significant. Obviously, the risk associated with these costs varies considerably both across and within countries and must be considered as a risk to financial capital. Health factors typically have a significant impact on the premiums individuals pay for life, disability, and long-term care insurance.

Health risks manifest themselves in different ways over the life cycle and can have significant implications for human capital as well as for financial capital. For example, if a worker becomes disabled as a result of an accident or health incident, he or she may be unable to work while health expenses are incurred, resulting in a loss to both current assets and future earnings. The impact of a negative health event on human capital can be approximated by using the discounted cash flow framework and estimating the decline in projected cash flows along with an increase in the discount rate arising from increased earnings uncertainty. Illness and injury can also obviously have an adverse impact on life expectancy, potentially resulting in death before planned retirement. Furthermore, health issues involving non-earning members of the family can also be costly. There may be a need for special medical services, housing improvements, specialized vehicles, and other health-related expenses. In the case of the special needs of a child, the financial obligation could continue well beyond the parents' working lives, or even their actual lives.

Although long-term care is a part of the national health care system in some countries, such as Germany and Japan, in others, such as the United States, the cost of long-term care can represent a significant burden on financial capital. In countries where long-term care expenses are incurred by the individual, policies that provide insurance to protect against the cost of long-term care should be considered. Long-term care insurance is designed to cover a portion of the cost of necessities, such as home care, assisted living facilities, and nursing homes.

The risk and cost of long-term care may be considered both a health issue and an issue of insufficient assets at an advanced age—the latter being a component of the aforementioned longevity risk. The risks may also go beyond the immediate family unit. For example, one may have a parent who is not financially capable of paying for long-term care. An added risk is that inflation in long-term care costs (i.e., medical costs) has historically been higher than base inflation.

EXAMPLE 6

Individual Risk Exposures (1)

Describe premature death risk with respect to financial and human capital.

> **Solution:**
> Within a personal financial planning context, premature death means that an individual dies before fully providing for his or her financial needs (and, if applicable, those of the family). By definition, at that point human capital is eliminated because the deceased individual can no longer generate income. To a lesser degree, there may also be an impact on financial capital. In addition to expenses associated with a funeral and burial, there may be a need for significant transitional funds or even a requirement to settle certain debts or business obligations upon the individual's death. Funds may also be required for education and/or training of the surviving spouse to generate income.

EXAMPLE 7

Individual Risk Exposures (2)

Describe longevity risk within the context of personal financial planning, and explain how it relates to human and financial capital.

Solution:

Longevity risk refers to the possibility that an individual may live long enough to deplete his or her resources—to outlive one's money. Longevity risk relates primarily to financial capital—that is, spending one's retirement portfolio. But there is also an aspect of human capital in that one may address longevity risk, in part, by retiring later, thus expanding one's retirement portfolio and reducing the number of years to draw it down while increasing one's human capital.

6   LIFE INSURANCE: USES, TYPES AND ELEMENTS

f   describe types of insurance relevant to personal financial planning;
g   describe the basic elements of a life insurance policy and how insurers price a life insurance policy;

An individual's balance sheet provides a comprehensive overview of the asset categories held to fund current and future spending. Each of these categories involves some risk of a random loss. Managing these risks involves assessing possible loss exposures and considering market and non-market solutions to both address the possibility of and reduce the magnitude of a loss. We review the range of products that can be used to reduce these risks and present a strategy for analyzing the value of possible treatment options.

What are the consequences of risk? Effective risk management for individuals addresses the trade-offs between expected total wealth and security. Individual life-cycle planning involves assessing expected available resources and planning an optimal earning and spending path over a lifetime. But life does not always unfold as expected. A negative event can threaten the value of assets, and a loss in this value will cause total wealth (and expected future consumption) to fall. For each risk exposure, a solution exists to manage that risk exposure, whether through an altered portfolio allocation, a change in behavior, or the purchase of financial and/or insurance products. Each of these solutions involves a cost that generally results in a lower expected level of consumption over time. Shifting assets from risky to risk-free securities results in the loss of a risk premium. In the case of financial products, purchasing insurance trades a reduction in expected lifetime consumption for an increase in the stability of expected spending after a loss. In this section, we discuss the various types of insurance that individuals may use in financial planning. We then turn our attention to annuities, another financial product available to individuals.

6.1 Life Insurance

Life insurance protects against the loss of human capital for those who depend on an individual's future earnings. In this section, we provide an overview of the key uses of life insurance, the primary types of life insurance, the basic elements of a life insurance policy, how a life insurance policy is priced, and how to determine the appropriate amount of life insurance to purchase, if any.

6.1.1 *Uses of Life Insurance*

Life insurance provides a hedge against the risk of the premature death of an earner. A family's need for life insurance is related to the risk of the loss of the future earning power of an individual less the expected future spending of that individual. In each case, the risk associated with premature death can be mitigated by transferring the risk to a third party (i.e., by purchasing life insurance). The optimal amount of insurance to purchase is a function of both the expenses of the insurance hedge and the magnitude of the difference in expected lifetime utility with and without that family member.

Life insurance can also be an important estate-planning tool. A life insurance policy can provide immediate liquidity to a beneficiary without the delay involved in the legal process of settling an estate (i.e., distributing assets to beneficiaries) following the death of an individual. This liquidity can be particularly valuable if the estate contains illiquid assets or assets that are difficult to separate and distribute equitably among heirs.

Another possible use of life insurance is as a tax-sheltered savings instrument, notably in the United States. As mentioned previously in this reading, cash-value policies invest a portion of the premium in a tax-advantaged account that represents the difference between the current cost of providing insurance coverage and the premium. The mortality charge is the cost of providing life insurance, which increases with age (as does mortality risk). As mortality risk increases, the accumulated excess premium can be used to pay the increasingly higher costs of providing insurance protection. These excess premiums can be invested in a variety of instruments that can grow over time sheltered from taxation and can eventually be cashed out without paying for older-age life insurance protection.

6.1.2 *Types of Life Insurance*

There are two main types of life insurance: temporary and permanent. For the purposes of this reading, both types of life insurance are assumed to be non-cancelable: The policy lapses only at the end of the term (for temporary life insurance) or upon death (for permanent life insurance).

Temporary life insurance provides insurance for a certain period of time specified at purchase. This type of coverage is commonly referred to as "term" life insurance. If the individual survives until the end of the period (e.g., 20 years), the policy will terminate unless it can be automatically renewed. Generally, premiums for term life insurance either remain level over the insured period (e.g., 20 years) or increase over the period as mortality risk increases. The cost of term insurance is less than that of permanent insurance, and the cost per year is less for shorter insured periods (e.g., 10 years versus 20 years), again because of increasing mortality risk.

Permanent life insurance provides lifetime coverage, assuming the premiums are paid over the entire period. Policy premiums for permanent life insurance are usually fixed, and there is generally some underlying cash value associated with a permanent insurance policy. There are several types of permanent life insurance that vary by region. Here, we will discuss the two most common types of permanent life insurance: *whole life insurance* and *universal life insurance*.

Whole life insurance remains in force for an insured's entire life (hence the name). Whole life insurance generally requires regular, ongoing fixed premiums, which are typically paid annually, although monthly, quarterly, and semiannual payment options also exist. Failure to pay premiums can result in the lapse of the insurance policy. There is generally a cash value associated with a whole life insurance policy that may be accessed if the insured chooses to do so. The non-cancelability of whole life insurance can make this type of policy appealing to purchase at younger ages, when an individual is typically healthier. Whole life insurance policies can be participating or non-participating. Participating life insurance policies allow potential growth at a higher rate than the guaranteed value, based on the profits of the insurance company. A non-participating policy is one with fixed values: The benefits will not change based on the profits and experience of the insurance company. Universal life insurance is constructed to provide more flexibility than whole life insurance. The policy owner, generally the insured, has the ability to pay higher or lower premium payments and often has more options for investing the cash value. The insurance will stay in force as long as the premiums paid or the cash value is enough to cover the policy expenses of the provider.

Many permanent life insurance policies have a "non-forfeiture clause," whereby the policy owner has the option to receive some portion of the benefits if premium payments are missed (i.e., before the policy lapses). The scenarios permitted by a non-forfeiture clause generally include a cash surrender option (whereby the existing cash value is paid out), a reduced paid-up option (whereby the cash value is used to purchase a single-premium whole life insurance policy), and an extended term option (whereby the cash value is used to purchase a term insurance policy, generally with the same face value as the previous policy).

In addition, a number of potential "riders" can be added to both temporary and permanent life insurance policies. Riders are modifications that add some risk mitigation beyond the basic policy. One example of a common rider is an "accidental death" rider (also referred to as accidental death and dismemberment, or AD&D), which increases the payout if the insured dies or becomes dismembered from an accident. Other common riders include an accelerated death benefit (which may allow insured parties who have been diagnosed as terminally ill to collect all or part of the death benefit while they are still alive), guaranteed insurability (which allows the owner to purchase more insurance in the future at certain predefined intervals), and a waiver of premium (whereby future premiums are waived if the insured becomes disabled). The value of the rider will depend on the level of protection against an unexpected decline in consumption not otherwise provided by a basic policy. An additional way for life insurance policyholders to access the value of the policy is the option to sell the policy to a third party, which is often called a viatical settlement. After purchasing the policy, the third party becomes responsible for paying the premiums and will receive the death benefit when the insured dies.

6.1.3 Basic Elements of a Life Insurance Policy

The basic elements of a life insurance policy include

- the term and type of the policy (e.g., a 20-year temporary insurance policy),
- the amount of benefits (e.g., £100,000),

- limitations under which the death benefit could be withheld (e.g., if death is by suicide within two years of issuance),
- the contestability period (the period during which the insurance company can investigate and deny claims),
- the identity (name, age, gender) of the insured
- the policy owner,
- the beneficiary or beneficiaries,
- the premium schedule (the amount and frequency of premiums due), and
- modifications to coverage in any riders to the policy.

In addition, for a life insurance policy to be valid, the policy owner generally needs to have an insurable interest in the life of the insured. Thus, the presence of an insurable interest is a basic element of an insurance policy as well.

The insured, the policy owner, the beneficiary (or beneficiaries), and the insurer are the four primary parties involved in any life insurance policy. The insured is the individual whose death triggers the insurance payment. The policy owner is the person who owns the life insurance policy and is responsible for paying premiums. The beneficiary is the individual (or entity) who will receive the proceeds from the life insurance policy when the insured passes away. The actual beneficiary of a jointly owned life insurance policy may be determined by the order of death of the prospective beneficiaries (e.g., a husband and a wife). Lastly, the insurer is the insurance company that writes the policy and is responsible for paying the death benefit. The amount payable to the beneficiary is typically referred to as the "face value" of the life insurance policy.

For most life insurance policies, the policy owner and the insured are the same person. In certain instances, however, a policy owner may choose to obtain insurance to protect against a loss in economic value from the death of another individual. For example, as part of a divorce, one ex-spouse may purchase life insurance on the other ex-spouse. Similarly, a business may purchase life insurance on a key executive under the assumption that the business would be negatively affected by that executive's death.

When the insured is not the policy owner, the policy owner must have an "insurable interest" in the life of the insured. Insurable interest prevents individuals from gambling on the lives of strangers and removes any incentive to hasten the insured person's demise. An insurable interest means that the policy owner must derive some type of benefit from the continued survival of the individual that would be negatively affected should that individual pass away. For example, a spouse has an insurable interest because he or she relies on the income or household services of the other spouse. A business has an insurable interest in key executives who are essential to the ongoing operations of the business.

Life insurance benefits are payable to the beneficiary upon the death of the insured. Usually, some form of documentation or proof of death is required by the life insurance company, such as a death certificate, before benefits are paid to the beneficiary. Death benefits from a life insurance policy can be paid in various forms, such as a lump sum or an annuity, although lump sums are generally more common.

There may be certain situations in which a life insurance company would not be required to pay a benefit. For example, if the insured commits suicide within some predetermined period after purchasing the policy (e.g., two years), or if the insured made material misrepresentations relating to his or her health and/or financial condition during the application process, benefits may not be payable. There is often a maximum contestability period during which the insurer has a legal right to contest the death benefit, after which the insurer cannot deny the claim even if it involves suicide and/or material misstatement.

> **EXAMPLE 8**
>
> ### Elements of a Life Insurance Policy
>
> Describe the concept of insurable interest for life insurance.
>
> **Solution:**
>
> An insurable interest means that the policy owner must derive some type of benefit from the continued survival of the insured that would be negatively affected should the insured pass away. For example, an individual may rely on a spouse for his or her financial well-being. If the spouse dies, income is no longer generated, leading to financial problems. Another example is a business that may have an insurable interest in a key employee who generates large sales volumes. The purpose of an insurable interest is to prevent individuals from gambling on the lives of others or from having a financial reason to arrange the death of the insured.

7. LIFE INSURANCE - PRICING, POLICY COST COMPARISON AND DETERMINING AMOUNT NEEDED

g describe the basic elements of a life insurance policy and how insurers price a life insurance policy;

There are a number of factors that determine how an insurer prices life insurance, and there are many different types of life insurance policies. Although the details of the actuarial calculations are beyond the scope of this reading, it is useful to understand the basic concepts of life insurance pricing.

In general, there are three key considerations in the pricing of life insurance: mortality expectations, a discount rate, and loading.

7.1 Mortality Expectations

One of the most important factors in determining the price for life insurance is the expected mortality of the insured individual (i.e., how long the person is expected to live). Actuaries at insurance companies estimate mortality based on both historical data and future mortality expectations. Generally speaking, life expectancies in most regions of the world have been increasing. Certain attributes, such as age and gender, are obvious factors in evaluating life expectancy. Whether the applicant is a smoker (or has other health risks) is another important factor because smoking is associated with deadly diseases. Exhibit 5 shows an example of the probability of men and women (both smokers and non-smokers) dying at various ages, although these numbers will vary considerably in different countries.

Rather than use a generalized mortality table, life insurance company actuaries typically make adjustments to consider additional factors. The underwriting process serves to categorize applicants according to their perceived riskiness, consistent with the actuaries' specifications. The resulting customized tables consider applicants' health history, particularly conditions that are associated with shorter-than-average life expectancy, such as cancer and heart disease. If an applicant's parents or siblings died at a relatively early age from certain diseases, that applicant may be considered a bigger risk. Excess weight is another health issue leading to shorter life expectancies. Certain activities, such as scuba diving and flying personal aircraft, are deemed to increase mortality risk also. All of these underwriting factors can be collected on a typical life insurance application, and the salesperson who gathers this information can be considered the first level of the underwriting process.

For larger policies, insurance companies may require a physical examination, performed by an insurer-paid nurse or physician, and the examination could include blood pressure, cholesterol and other blood analysis, an electrocardiogram, and other tests. All of these factors can be used to categorize applicants in tables that discriminate among standard risks, preferred (lower) risks, and high risks, and the cost to the insured can vary considerably. Of course, some people have a sufficient number of factors, or serious-enough factors, to make them uninsurable. This underwriting process reduces the likelihood of *adverse selection*. Adverse selection refers to the fact that individuals who know that they have higher-than-average risk are more likely to apply for life insurance. Unless the insurance company performs its underwriting well, mortality experience can be worse than projected.

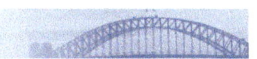

The Probability of Dying at Certain Ages

Exhibit 5 provides information about the mortality (i.e., the probability of dying) for males and females at different ages.[2] The cost of life insurance is based on the probability that the insured will die during the duration of the policy. The table helps demonstrate why younger (versus older) individuals, females (versus males), and non-smokers (versus smokers) tend to pay less for life insurance—the expected probability of dying in a given year is lower.

Exhibit 5 Mortality of Males and Females at Certain Ages

	Male			Female		
Age	Composite	Non-Smoker	Smoker	Composite	Non-Smoker	Smoker
35	0.14%	0.09%	0.14%	0.08%	0.07%	0.10%
40	0.21%	0.15%	0.24%	0.12%	0.10%	0.17%
45	0.26%	0.19%	0.35%	0.14%	0.11%	0.23%
50	0.30%	0.23%	0.48%	0.21%	0.15%	0.37%
55	0.42%	0.35%	0.74%	0.32%	0.25%	0.60%
60	0.67%	0.50%	1.21%	0.52%	0.37%	1.00%
65	1.12%	0.84%	2.08%	0.88%	0.59%	1.66%
70	1.81%	1.40%	3.35%	1.48%	0.95%	2.61%
75	3.18%	2.58%	5.34%	2.45%	1.71%	3.93%
80	5.38%	4.65%	7.56%	4.23%	3.33%	6.27%
85	9.71%	8.80%	11.75%	7.77%	6.54%	10.74%
90	17.41%	16.55%	19.04%	13.79%	12.27%	17.34%
95	25.49%	25.16%	26.09%	21.96%	20.82%	24.65%

---

[2] Data are based on the American Academy of Actuaries' 2017 Commissioners Standard Ordinary (CSO) Tables. https://www.soa.org/experience-studies/2015/2017-cso-tables/ accessed 21 November 2018

> **EXAMPLE 9**
>
> **Mortality Expectations**
>
> If a given male and female are the same age and have equivalent health profiles, evaluate which one should expect to pay more for life insurance.
>
> **Solution:**
>
> A key pricing component of life insurance is expected mortality. From Exhibit 5, one can see that the chance of death for females across the age spectrum is less than it is for males of the same age. Therefore, all else being equal, females should expect to pay less than males for the equivalent life insurance.

7.2 Calculation of the Net Premium and Gross Premium

The *net premium* of a life insurance policy represents the discounted value of the future death benefit. To illustrate a simplified calculation of the net premium, we will consider the example of a one-year, non-renewable term life insurance policy with a death benefit of US$100,000 for Ramon, a 40-year-old non-smoking male. The insurance company insures thousands of people with characteristics like Ramon's. Thus, the life insurance company will experience a predictable distribution of death benefit payments in a given year, although it does not know who among its customers will die during that year.

Premiums are collected at the beginning of the year, and for simplicity, we will assume that death benefit payments occur at the end of the year. As shown in Exhibit 5, and in the absence of other underwriting information, Ramon has a probability of 0.15% of dying within the year. Although the life insurance company will pay a death benefit of either US$100,000 or US$0, we can calculate an expected outflow at the end of the year of US$150, which equals (0.0015 × US$100,000) + (0.9985 × US$0). Finally, a discount rate, or interest factor, representing an assumption of the insurance company's return on its portfolio, is applied to the expected outflow. Assuming a 5.5% rate, US$150 is discounted by one year to a present value of US$142.18 (US$150/1.055), which is the net premium.

As mentioned previously, life insurance companies typically offer level term policies, under which the insured can pay equal annual premiums for a specified number of years—for example, a five-year level term policy. The calculation still requires discounting expected future death benefit payments back to the present, but we must also consider the fact that the individuals who die within the five-year period will not be paying premiums for the remaining outstanding term.

To determine what the insurance company would actually charge Ramon for the one-year policy, the insurer must consider other factors to calculate the *gross premium*. The gross premium adds a *load* to the net premium, allowing for expenses and a projected profit for the insurance company.

Expenses are incurred by the insurer for both writing a life insurance policy and managing it on an ongoing basis. Expenses associated with writing a life insurance policy include the costs of the underwriting process, which potentially include a sales commission to the agent who sold the policy and the cost of a physical exam. Ongoing expenses include overhead and administrative expenses associated with monitoring the policy, ensuring that premiums are paid on a timely basis, and verifying a potential death claim. Furthermore, most companies provide a low percentage "renewal commission" for the first years of the policy, which encourages the agent to provide needed advice to the policy owner and to try to keep the policy owner from terminating the policy.

Life insurers can be divided into two groups—stock companies and mutual companies. Stock companies are similar to other corporations in that they are owned by shareholders, have a profit motive, and are expected to provide a return to those shareholders. Within the constraints of supply and demand for their product, stock life insurance companies add a projected profit as a part of the load in pricing their policies. In contrast, mutual companies are owned by the policy owners themselves and there is no profit motive. Mutual companies typically charge a gross premium that is somewhat higher than the net premium plus expenses, even though mutual companies do not have profits per se. Then, if mortality experience, expenses, and/or investment returns are better than projected, the amount by which the gross premium exceeds the net premium plus expenses may be paid back to the policy owners as a policy dividend, which is considered a return of premium to the policy owner rather than income.

Premiums for level term policies are higher than those for annually renewable (one-year) policies in the early years. But premiums are lower in the later years of the policies—most notably for longer periods, such as a 20-year level term—because annually renewable term policies often have rapidly increasing premiums. As can be seen in Exhibit 5 earlier in this section, mortality rates begin accelerating rather quickly after age 40. Life insurers sometimes offer low initial rates on annually renewable policies with the expectation that many purchasers of these policies will simply pay the increasing premiums.

Some consumers buy an annually renewable term policy with the intention of taking advantage of the "loss-leader" pricing in the early years and then, when rates rise too much, switching to another company that has a lower premium at the newly attained age. Unfortunately, there is risk in this strategy in that a health issue or accident could make that individual uninsurable, leaving him or her with an annually renewable policy that has an escalating premium.

EXAMPLE 10

Life Insurance Pricing

Discuss the three most relevant elements of life insurance pricing.

Solution:

The three most relevant considerations in pricing life insurance are mortality expectations, the discount rate, and loading.

- Mortality expectations: The insurer is concerned about the probability that the insured will die within the term of the policy. Actuaries evaluate mortality expectations based on historical experience, considering such factors as age and gender, the longevity of parents, blood pressure, cholesterol, whether the insured is a smoker, and whether the insured has had any diseases or injuries that are likely to lead to death during the policy term.

- Discount rate: A discount rate, or interest factor, representing an assumption of the insurance company's return on its portfolio, is applied to the expected outflow.

- Loading: After calculating the net premium for a policy, which may be considered the pure price of the insurance, the insurance company adjusts the premium upward to allow for expenses and profit. This adjustment is the load, and the process is called loading.

7.3 Cash Values and Policy Reserves

As noted earlier, although initial premiums are higher, whole life policies offer the advantage of level premiums and an accumulation of cash value within the policy that (1) can be withdrawn by the policy owner when the policy endows (or matures) or when he or she terminates the policy or (2) can be borrowed as a loan while keeping the policy in force. These cash values build up very slowly in the early years, during which the company is making up for its expenses. For example, just the first-year commission on a whole life policy could be equivalent to 100% of the first-year premium; thus, the company is "in the hole" for the first few years and trying to recover the initial expenses. The commissions decline in subsequent early years as the effort required by a sales agent to service the policy is reduced.

Exhibit 6 shows a representation of the build-up of cash value within a whole life policy that endows at a specified age, perhaps age 100. It is important to recognize the interrelationship of the following amounts:

- The premium stays constant.
- The face value stays constant.
- The cash value increases.
- The insurance value decreases.

Essentially, as cash values increase and the insurance value decreases, the ongoing premium is paying for less and less life insurance.

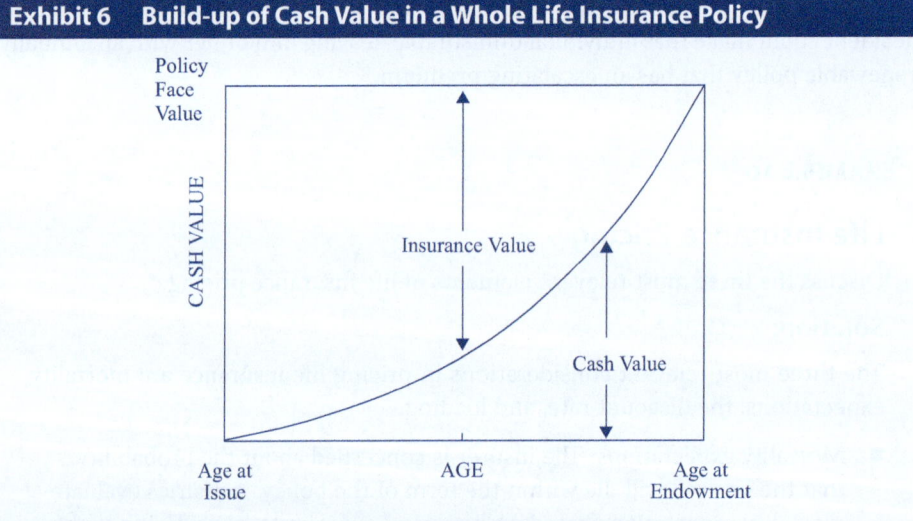

Exhibit 6 Build-up of Cash Value in a Whole Life Insurance Policy

To the extent that the life insurance is intended to replace human capital, it may become unnecessary after the individual's working years are finished. Enough financial capital may have been accrued to make even the immediate death expenses payable from other funds without the need for life insurance. The existence of increasing cash values within a policy adds another dimension to the decision whether to terminate a policy.

Note also that life insurers are typically required by regulators to maintain *policy reserves*, which are a liability on the insurance company's balance sheet. Policy reserves become especially important for whole life policies. With a whole life policy, the insurance company specifies an age at which the policy's face value will be paid as an endowment to the policy owner if the insured person has not died by that time. The insurance company must accumulate reserves during the life of the policy to be able to make that payment. The policy reserve can be defined as follows: Policy reserve = Present value of future benefits − Present value of future net premiums. From the equation, we can infer that as the insured person gets older, the present value of the future death benefit (or the cash value that could be withdrawn) gets larger. At the same time, the present value of the future net premiums gets smaller because fewer premiums remain. Thus, the policy reserves must grow larger over time until, at the time of endowment, the reserves equal the present value of the future benefits. (See Rejda and McNamara 2014, p. 272.)

7.4 Consumer Comparisons of Life Insurance Costs

It may seem easy to compare the cost of two different policies of equal size by simply looking at the first year's premiums. Although this may be the case with term policies, comparing the cost of two whole life insurance policies is much more complex because, for example, one policy may have larger premiums but also faster growth of cash values.

Consumer and/or governmental organizations may provide comparisons of policies from various life insurance companies based on projected data, including assumptions about future dividends and cash values. In many jurisdictions, regulations require that life insurance companies provide consumers with cost data that consider the time value of money and assume a specified number of years. The two most popular indexes for comparison are the *net payment cost index* and the *surrender cost index*, both of which calculate a cost per year per thousand dollars of life insurance coverage under different sets of assumptions. Both methods assume a specific time period, such as 20 years, and a specific compounding discount rate, such as 5%.

The net payment cost index assumes that the insured person will die at the end of a specified period, such as 20 years. Calculation of the net payment cost index includes the following steps:

A Calculate the future value of an annuity due of an amount equal to the premium, compounded at a 5% discount rate for 20 years. An annuity due—an annuity for which the premium payment is received at the beginning of the period (versus an ordinary annuity, for which the premium payment is received at the end of the period)—is used because premiums are paid at the beginning of the period.

B Calculate the future value of an ordinary annuity of an amount equal to the projected annual dividend (if any), compounded at 5% for 20 years. An ordinary annuity is used because dividend payments are made at the end of the period.

C Subtract B from A to get the 20-year insurance cost.

D Calculate the payments for a 20-year annuity due with a future value equal to C and a discount rate of 5%. This amount is the interest-adjusted cost per year. Again, an annuity due is used because premium payments occur at the beginning of the year.

E Divide by the number of thousand dollars of face value.

The surrender cost index assumes that the policy will be surrendered at the end of the period and that the policy owner will receive the projected cash value. Calculation of the surrender cost index includes the following steps:

A Calculate the future value of an annuity due of an amount equal to the premium, compounded at 5% for 20 years. We use an annuity due here for the same reason indicated for the net payment cost index.

B Calculate the future value of an ordinary annuity of an amount equal to the projected annual dividend (if any), compounded at 5% for 20 years. We use an ordinary annuity here for the same reason indicated for the net payment cost index.

C Subtract B and the Year 20 projected cash value from A to get the 20-year insurance cost.

D Calculate the payments for a 20-year annuity due with a future value equal to C and a discount rate of 5%. This amount is the interest-adjusted cost per year.

E Divide by the number of thousand dollars of face value.

For example, a US$100,000 face value whole life policy has an annual premium of US$2,000, paid at the beginning of the year. Policy dividends of US$500 per year are anticipated, payable at year-end. A cash value of US$22,500 is projected for the end of Year 20.

Net Payment Cost Index Calculation

Future value of premiums (annuity due): US$2,000 annual payment, 20 years, 5%	US$69,439
Future value of dividends (ordinary annuity): US$500 annual payment, 20 years, 5%	−16,533
20-year insurance cost	US$52,906
Annual payments for 20-year insurance cost (annuity due): 20 years, 5%	1,524
Divide by US$ thousands of face value	÷ 100
Net Payment Cost Index, cost per US$ thousand per year	US$15.24

Surrender Cost Index Calculation

Future value of premiums (annuity due): US$2,000 annual payment, 20 years, 5%	US$69,439
Future value of dividends (ordinary annuity): US$500 annual payment, 20 years, 5%	−16,533
20-year cash value (given above)	−22,500
20-year insurance cost	US$30,406
Annual payments for 20-year insurance cost (annuity due): 20 years, 5%	876
Divide by US$ thousands of face value	÷ 100
Surrender Cost Index, cost per US$ thousand per year	US$8.76

The major benefit of these indexes is the ease of comparing policies of the same type. Generally speaking, the lower the index value is, the better the value. However, policies do not always perform as projected. If the insurance company's actual return, expense, and/or mortality experiences are worse than projected, the *ex post* indexes could be larger.

Calculating Life Insurance Needs

Two distinctly different methods are commonly used to calculate the amount of life insurance needed. The *human life value* method is consistent with the concept of human capital. It involves replacing the estimated net contribution to family finances that the insured would generate if that individual did not die during his or her projected earning life. In general, this calculation involves estimating future income that would be generated by the insured, offset by incremental expenses that would be attributable to the insured. The net amounts in each year are then discounted back to the present to calculate the amount of insurance needed. An amount may be added to cover so-called "final expenses," such as funeral and other death expenses.

The *needs analysis* method, as the name implies, is concerned with meeting the financial needs of the family. Needs analysis typically involves estimating living expenses for survivors for an appropriate amount of time, typically until adulthood for surviving children and to projected life expectancy for a surviving spouse. Also included are education costs, final expenses, and any other special expenses. These amounts are discounted back to the present to calculate the total funds needed. Any assets available are subtracted, and the amount remaining is the life insurance needed.

Both the human life value and needs analysis methods are demonstrated in detail in Section 7.5.

7.5 How Much Life Insurance Does One Need?

The optimal amount of life insurance for an individual will vary based on a number of factors. Some individuals with no dependents or bequest goals may not need any insurance, whereas an individual with young children and a non-working spouse may need a significant amount of life insurance. In this section, we outline some of the key considerations to use when determining how much life insurance to purchase.

The primary purpose of life insurance is to replace the present value of future earnings. A 65-year-old individual without children will experience an emotional loss from the premature death of a spouse, as well as some additional short-term expenses, but the economic loss will be modest (or even negative if expected spending needs fall in retirement). Other reasons to consider life insurance include the following:

- *Immediate financial expenses:* These include direct costs associated with death, such as funeral and legal expenses. Although the costs associated vary by region, funerals can be expensive and represent a potentially sizable financial burden on the family. Additional immediate financial expenses could include covering the short-term loss of wages.

- *Legacy goals:* In addition to income replacement, an individual may use life insurance to achieve certain legacy goals. These can include gifts to charities, bequests to family members, and estate planning.

To calculate the amount of insurance needed, one should estimate the amount of money needed to restore the present value of expected earnings that would have occurred if the earner remained alive. Because the purpose of life insurance is to smooth consumption by preventing a drop in spending from an unexpected premature death, the value of life insurance should be equal to the difference in household spending with and without the human capital of the earner. An accurate calculation will adjust household spending needs downward to compensate for the reduction in household size, in addition to estimating the present value of the expected human capital of the insured. The cost of the insurance is obviously an important consideration as well.

Another important consideration when purchasing life insurance is the insurance company's ability to meet its financial obligations. Company financial strength is evaluated by various rating agencies and is important because it provides an indication of the ability of the insurer to meet its obligations and to weather adverse market conditions.

> **EXAMPLE 11**
>
> ### Appropriateness of Life Insurance
>
> Consider two potential life insurance candidates: (1) a 40-year-old doctor who is married with two young children, substantial student loans, and sizable earnings; and (2) a 35-year-old single person with a moderate amount of financial wealth. Based on the information presented, which person would be a more appropriate candidate for life insurance and why?
>
> ### Solution:
>
> The first individual is a much more appropriate candidate for life insurance. Given that the doctor has substantial debt and high earnings, the value of this individual's earnings potential (human capital) is significant. Likewise, with two young children, there is a high dependence on future earnings, representing another reason the earnings potential should be hedged with life insurance. In contrast, the 35-year-old does not have any beneficiaries that would need to be supported. But the younger individual may want to consider purchasing insurance while he or she is still insurable.

8. OTHER TYPES OF INSURANCE

f   describe types of insurance relevant to personal financial planning;

Disability income insurance is designed to mitigate earnings risk as a result of a disability, which refers to the risk that an individual becomes less than fully employed because of a physical injury, disease, or other impairment. Many disabilities for gainfully employed individuals are relatively short rather than lifelong, but the financial disaster associated with the possibility of a lifelong disability can be addressed in a comprehensive risk management plan.

What is meant by disability? The definition of disability used by insurance providers typically specifies one of the following:

- Inability to perform the important duties of one's regular occupation
- Inability to perform the important duties of any occupation for which one is suited by education and experience
- Inability to perform the duties of any occupation

Consider a surgeon who loses the use of his or her dominant hand in an accident. By the first definition, this individual would likely be deemed fully disabled. By the second definition, this individual might be able to work as a general practitioner physician. By the third definition above, as long as the individual was able to be employed (e.g., as a professor at a medical school), he or she might not be considered disabled. For most people, especially professionals with specialized skills, policies that use the first definition are best, even though they are more expensive. In general, a disability income insurance policy will specify that some percentage of the difference between the pre-injury income and the post-injury income would be paid to the insured.

As with all insurance policies, disability income insurance policy standards vary widely in different jurisdictions and even for different companies. For most policies, the premium is fixed and based on the age of the insured at the time of policy issue, and the policies are underwritten for the health and occupation of the insured. Disability income coverage is available both through individual policies and through many employers. Disability income policies usually include provisions for partial and residual disability. Partial disability means that although the insured cannot perform all the duties of his or her occupation, the individual can perform enough to remain employed, albeit at a lower income. Partial disability provisions pay a reduced benefit, providing a financial incentive for the insured to get back to work as soon as possible. Residual disability refers to the possibility that although the insured can perform all the duties of his or her occupation, the individual cannot earn as much money as before. Consider the surgeon who can still perform operations but because of a back injury cannot perform as many surgeries per day as before the injury. The reduction in income would be addressed by the residual disability benefit, which is smaller than the benefit for full disability.

Typically, insurers will cover compensation only up to specific amounts. Furthermore, they will insure only up to a specific percentage of compensation, perhaps 60%–80%, for two reasons. First, if the insured becomes disabled, other expenses decrease, such as certain payroll taxes, commuting costs, clothing, and food; thus, full replacement is not necessary. Second, there is a greater chance for fraudulent claims if the disability income payments are close to the normal compensation.

Other aspects of disability income insurance include the following:

- The *benefit period* specifies how long payments will be made. A specified number of years may be stated in the policy, but typically, the benefit period lasts until normal retirement age, which varies globally between approximately 55 and 70. The age limit discourages the filing of fraudulent claims intended to substitute disability benefits for retirement income. Usually, a minimum number of years of benefits, perhaps five, is specified in case the individual should become disabled within that many years of the specified age. For example, a 62-year-old who becomes disabled would receive benefits to age 67. This provision encourages individuals to maintain their policies all the way to retirement.

- The *elimination period*, or *waiting period*, specifies the number of days the insured must be disabled before payments begin being made. Naturally, the shorter the elimination period, the higher the premiums. A typical elimination period for policies in the United States is 90 days.

- The *rehabilitation clause* provides payments for physical therapy and related services to help the disabled person rejoin the workforce as soon as possible.

- The *waiver of premium* clause specifies that premiums need not be paid if the insured becomes disabled, and it often includes a reimbursement of premiums during the elimination period.

- The *option to purchase additional insurance rider* allows the insured to increase coverage without further proof of insurability, albeit at the rate appropriate for the insured's current age.

- A *non-cancelable and guaranteed renewable* policy guarantees that the policy will be renewed annually as long as premiums are paid and that there will be no changes to premiums or promised disability benefits until, usually, age 65. Even if employment income declines during the working life, the monthly benefit will remain at the level specified in the policy.

- A *non-cancelable* policy cannot be canceled as long as premiums are paid, but the insurer can increase premiums for the entire underwriting class that includes the insured. This version is less expensive than a non-cancelable and guaranteed renewable policy, but one should be aware that insurance companies with significant loss experience are likely to raise rates.
- Inflation adjustments to benefits may be provided by a *cost of living rider*, which will adjust benefits with an accepted index or by a specified percentage per year.

Note that, as with virtually all insurance types, any provision in a disability insurance policy that appears advantageous to the insured party will likely increase the premium.

8.1 Property Insurance

Property insurance is used by individuals to manage property risk, which was discussed earlier in the reading. Although property insurance coverage applies to a multitude of situations, for most individuals, the primary areas to cover are the home/residence and the automobile.

8.1.1 Homeowner's Insurance

With regard to a residence, homeowner's insurance is designed to address risks associated with home ownership as well as risks associated with personal property and liability. Renter's insurance is similar to homeowner's insurance but without coverage on the structure. Property insurance protects the insured in case of loss related to his or her property. As we discussed earlier, there are, of course, many different possible events relating to property risk, such as a house fire, an automobile collision, a stolen television, or a lost necklace.

Homeowner's policies may be specified as "all-risks," which means that all risks are included except those specified, or as "named-risks," which means that only those risks specifically listed are covered. All-risks policies are generally more costly. Homeowner's insurance may also be available in either of two versions, based on the way a claim is settled. A policy based on *replacement cost* will reimburse the insured person for the amount required to repair a damaged item or replace a lost, destroyed, or stolen item with a new item of similar quality at current prices. A policy based on *actual cash value* will reimburse the insured person for the replacement cost less depreciation. The replacement cost version is a more expensive policy.

As mentioned earlier in the reading, a *deductible* is the amount of a loss that must be absorbed by the policy owner before the insurance company will make any payment. Deductibles represent a form of active risk retention. If the homeowner's policy has a US$1,000 deductible and there is hail damage of $10,000, the homeowner must pay the first $1,000 and the insurance company would be liable for the remaining $9,000. Deductibles ensure that the homeowner retains some responsibility (and risk) associated with a loss.

As part of their business models, insurance companies price their policies to encourage the use of higher deductibles. For the consumer, this means that a cost–benefit analysis should be performed when determining the optimal deductible level because a larger deductible likely means a lower insurance premium. Imagine that a policy with a $1,000 deductible for a given property has an annual premium of $2,000 and a policy with a $500 deductible has an annual premium of $2,100. The consumer should recognize that selecting the second policy means essentially paying $100 more for a $1,000 insurance policy that has a $500 deductible. An alternative way of looking at it is to ask whether it is worth $100 to insure the second $500 of loss.

Some individuals underinsure their homes to save money, but they do so at their own risk. If a potential loss could exceed the amount of insurance, that individual is retaining risk of that excess amount, either consciously or unconsciously. For individuals who have significant wealth, whose home is a relatively small percentage of their net worth, and who have adequate liquidity, it may make sense to self-insure these types of risks (i.e., maintain only a limited amount of homeowner's insurance or own a policy with a very high deductible).

Mortgage lenders typically require that the homeowner carry enough insurance that if the mortgagor dies, a total loss would trigger payment of an amount at least equal to the outstanding mortgage. Because mortgage balances typically decline over time, insurance contracts covering the outstanding mortgage can be purchased with a decreasing face value and decreasing premiums.

Insurance companies have a different interest from that of mortgage lenders. They want the house to be insured for its full value—less the value of the land because the land will not be destroyed—or at least a high percentage of full value. Premiums are calculated based on this assumption. Although the insurance company is obligated to pay only the face value of the policy in the case of a total loss, it is at a disadvantage if partial losses occur.

Consider a $500,000 (replacement cost) home that, because inflation in home prices has been ignored, is insured for only $250,000. In the absence of other contractual restrictions, if the house sustains $250,000 of damage in a fire, the insurance company would have to pay the entire face value of the policy even though the house sustained only a 50% loss. From the company's standpoint, it should have been receiving the larger premiums for a $500,000 house to pay $250,000 for a 50% loss.

To offset this dilemma, losses are reimbursed at a lower rate if the home is underinsured. It is common for an insurance company to reduce payments if the home is insured for less than 80% of its replacement cost.

Homeowners' liability risks are typically addressed within the insurance policy on the home. That is, there is a provision in the policy for liability coverage for a specified amount in case, for example, a visitor is injured in an accident at the home. This coverage excludes professional liability, such as physicians' malpractice insurance, and business liability, which should be covered with separate policies. The homeowner's policy also excludes liability resulting from intentional acts—for example, throwing a chair through a neighbor's window.

Aside from purchasing homeowner's insurance, one can address homeowner risk through other risk management techniques. The following are some examples:

- Risk of theft of valuable financial documents can be avoided by storing them in a bank's safe deposit box.
- Risk of overall theft can be reduced through the use of high-quality locks, alarms, and surveillance systems.
- Risk of loss or corruption of electronic data can be avoided by storing backups offsite.
- Risk of damage to electronic equipment from a power surge can be reduced by installing surge protectors.
- Risk of loss from fire can be reduced through the use of fire-resistant building materials—and through the easy availability of fire extinguishers.

8.1.2 Automobile Insurance

Automobile property risk can also be addressed through various risk management methods. For example, one might avoid driving in inclement weather conditions. One might require passengers to wear seat belts, reducing their likelihood of injury. One might use common, frequently promoted safe driving techniques or even take alternate routes that are less risky. If buying a new car, one might consider a vehicle with a backup camera and lane-change warning system.

Automobile insurance rates are primarily based on the value of the automobile and the primary operator's age and driving record. Other factors are also included but vary considerably among jurisdictions. Coverages for damage to the automobile are typically divided into two parts. *Collision coverage* is for damage from an accident, and *comprehensive coverage* is for damage from other sources, such as glass breakage, hail, and theft. There may also be coverage available in case one's automobile is damaged by an uninsured or underinsured driver, as well as medical coverage for passengers in the insured's automobile. Insurance companies normally insure automobiles only up to the cost of replacing the automobile with one of the same make and model and in the same condition. If the cost to repair the automobile exceeds its actual cash value, the insurance company typically reimburses only the amount of the actual cash value.

As with homeowner's insurance, automobile owners typically retain some risk through the use of deductibles or by avoiding collision and comprehensive coverage. Again, selecting the amount of the deductible or rejecting property coverage involves a simple cost–benefit analysis. If the individual is able to bear the wealth risk and to afford repairs or a new car if damage occurs, then risk retention will increase expected wealth over time.

Liability associated with automobiles is typically covered under the same policy, with specified limits for bodily injury and property damage. In most countries, some level of third-party coverage is mandatory and additional insurance may be purchased to increase the level of protection. Liability limits often vary for different types of loss—for example, higher limits to cover the costs of physical injury and separate limits to cover the loss of property. If actual liability in an accident exceeds these amounts, the automobile owner is responsible for the remainder.

8.2 Health/Medical Insurance

Any discussion of **health insurance** is highly dependent on the country of residence. In certain countries, health care is governmentally funded and there is no private health insurance. In others, there is a two-tiered system, with governmental coverage for everyone and upgraded coverage for additional payments.

In the United States, one type of insurance approach is called an *indemnity plan*, which allows the insured to go to essentially any medical service provider, but the insured must pay a specified percentage of the "reasonable and customary" fees. Another type of plan is a *preferred provider organization* (PPO), which is a large network of physicians and other medical service providers that charge lower prices to individuals within the plan than to individuals who obtain care on their own. A third type of plan is a *health maintenance organization* (HMO), which allows office visits at no, or very little, cost to encourage individuals to seek help for small medical problems before they become more serious.

Comprehensive major medical insurance covers the vast majority of health care expenses, such as physicians' fees, surgical fees, hospitalization, laboratory fees, x-rays, magnetic resonance imaging (MRIs), and most other expenses that are "reasonable and customary" and part of generally accepted medical care. Aside from the premiums for the actual coverage, major medical insurance includes several other provisions that can substantially influence the total financial outlay. Below are some of the key terms of most health (medical) insurance plans:

- *Deductibles* refer to the amount of health care expenses that the insured person must pay in a year before any expense reimbursement is paid by the insurance company.
- *Coinsurance* specifies the percentage of any expense that the insurance company will pay, often 80%, with the insured person responsible for the remainder.

- *Copayments* are fixed payments that the insured must make for a particular service, such as a doctor's office visit.
- *Maximum out-of-pocket expense* refers to the total amount of expenses incurred within a year beyond which the insurance company pays 100%. It is often expressed in terms of an individual maximum and a family maximum. This concept is often referred to as a stop-loss limit.
- *Maximum yearly benefit* refers to the maximum amount that the insurance company will pay in a year.
- *Maximum lifetime benefit* refers to the maximum amount that the insurance company will pay over an individual's lifetime.
- *Preexisting conditions* refer to health conditions that the insured had when applying for insurance. They may or may not be covered by the insurance company, depending on the policy, laws, and regulations.
- *Preadmission certification* refers to a requirement that the insured receive approval from the insurer before a scheduled (non-emergency) hospital stay or treatment.

Of course, the cost of a plan will be affected by the degree of inclusion and specified value of the preceding provisions. Besides the cost of the plan, health insurance purchasers should be concerned about the breadth and quality of the network of physicians and hospitals available to insured individuals.

8.3 Liability Insurance

To manage liability risk, individuals often obtain **liability insurance**. It is possible that the amount of liability coverage in the homeowner's and automobile insurance policies is less than one thinks is appropriate. In that case, it is reasonable to purchase a *personal umbrella liability insurance* policy. This type of policy has specified limits but pays claims only if the liability limit of the homeowner's or automobile policy is exceeded. For example, consider an individual whose automobile policy specifies a property damage liability limit of US$100,000 and who has an umbrella policy with a liability limit of US$1 million. If that individual is responsible for an automobile accident that causes US$300,000 of damage, the automobile policy would pay the first US$100,000 and the umbrella policy would pay the remaining US$200,000. Umbrella policies are relatively inexpensive.

It is common for people to think of liability insurance coverage in terms of protecting one's own financial assets. Some jurisdictions may specify exempt property—one's home or retirement savings, for example—that cannot be seized in the case that liability for an accident exceeds the amount of insurance coverage. Thus, one might ask oneself, "What is the worst thing that could happen to me in case of an extremely large liability judgment?" But if the goal is to indemnify the injured party—that is, to make the injured party "whole" financially—the amount of insurance purchased should be based on the potential financial catastrophe that could face an injured party.

8.4 Other Types of Insurance

Other types of risks may be present, depending on the individual's situation. For example, when purchasing a home, many individuals purchase *title insurance* (and in some jurisdictions, it is required). The purpose of title insurance is to make sure that ownership of the property is not in doubt. Personal watercraft and trailers may require a separate insurance policy or an endorsement, which is a form of insurance coverage added to an existing policy to cover risks that are not otherwise included in that policy. Again, appropriate levels of risk avoidance, reduction, prevention, and retention will depend on the situation and the size and probability of the potential loss.

One may consider service contracts when purchasing an automobile, home appliance, or other sizable product to avoid repair costs. These types of pseudo-insurance are profit centers for the companies selling them and are often relatively expensive for consumers, partly because of a lack of competition. For example, at the time of purchase of an automobile, one may be offered the opportunity to purchase an extended warranty at the same time from the automobile dealer. There is limited opportunity for price shopping, and the price of the service contract can usually be rolled into the automobile loan. Under these circumstances, the automobile dealer can charge a high rate to the disadvantage of the purchaser. Note that even this type of contract typically involves a deductible.

9. ANNUITIES: TYPES, STRUCTURE AND CLASSIFICATION

h discuss the use of annuities in personal financial planning;

Individuals have a finite but unknown lifespan. The efficient allocation of financial resources across an unknown lifespan is a planning challenge because consumption smoothing requires the allocation of available financial resources across an expected time frame. Humans may plan to spread their resources based on an average lifetime, but this strategy exposes them to the risk of outliving their assets in old age. One efficient strategy is to pool the risk of an unknown lifespan across individuals through the use of an annuity.

Annuities have existed in a variety of forms for thousands of years. The Romans sold a financial instrument called an "annua" that returned a fixed yearly payment, either for life or for a specified period, in return for a lump sum payment. Even today, annuities remain popular risk management tools, especially for older individuals and retirees who want to mitigate the risk associated with outliving their assets (i.e., longevity risk). Annuities are generally purchased from an insurance company; however, government pensions and payouts from employer pension plans are also technically annuities.

Annuities have become increasingly complex over time, and various types exist. With an **immediate annuity**, an amount of money is paid to the insurance company in return for a guarantee of specified future monthly payments over a specified period of time, either a number of years or the life of the insured, who is called the *annuitant*. A **deferred annuity** allows an individual to purchase an income stream to begin at a later date. We further discuss various forms of immediate and deferred annuities in the following sections.

The annuity payment guaranteed by the insurance company is most directly based on the amount of money tendered, the age and gender of the annuitant, and the insurance company's required rate of return (including its cost of funds and its expense and profit factors). Although life insurance helps provide financial protection in case the insured "dies too soon," immediate life annuities provide financial protection in case the insured "lives too long."

In this section, we discuss some of the key aspects of annuities, such as the parties to an annuity contract, the different types of annuities that exist, payout methods, annuity taxation, and the appropriateness of annuities for individuals. We conclude with an overview of how annuities can benefit retirees and provide a framework that explains which retirees may benefit the most from an annuity.

9.1 Parties to an Annuity Contract

There are four primary parties to an annuity contract: the insurer, the annuitant, the contract owner, and the beneficiary. The insurer—generally an insurance company—is the entity that is licensed to sell the annuity. The annuitant is the person who receives the benefits. The contract owner is the individual who purchases the annuity and is typically the annuitant. In some instances, the contract owner and the annuitant may be different: For example, if the annuity is purchased by a company for a retiring employee, then the company is the contract owner and the employee is the annuitant. Lastly, the beneficiary is an individual or entity that will receive any proceeds upon the death of the annuitant. For contracts like a plain vanilla single-premium annuity, there may not be any death benefit; however, with variable annuities and annuities with some kind of minimum guaranteed payment period (e.g., 10 years), often referred to as a "period certain" option, there may be some residual value once the annuitant passes away.

9.2 Classification of Annuities

There are a variety of ways to classify annuities. The two most critical dimensions that help distinguish the primary types of annuities are (1) deferred versus immediate and (2) fixed versus variable. We will expand on these types shortly, but briefly, deferred annuities provide income that begins at a future date after the initial purchase of the annuity. In some cases, the original investment may retain some liquidity prior to initiation of annuity payments if the purchaser retains the right to sell the deferred annuity. In contrast, with immediate payout annuities—or single-premium immediate annuities (SPIAs), as they are often called—the individual permanently exchanges a lump sum for a contract that promises to pay the annuitant an income for life. For both deferred and immediate annuities, the annuity can be invested in what is termed a "fixed" account or a "variable" account.

Many other versions of annuities are available to meet different needs. For example, a *joint life annuity* is based on the expected lifespans of two annuitants, usually husband and wife, and payments are made as long as at least one of the two is alive. All else equal, the monthly payment is lower for this type of annuity because adding a second annuitant extends the payment timespan.

9.2.1 *Deferred Variable Annuities*

In its most basic form, a deferred variable annuity is similar to a mutual fund, although it is structured as an insurance contract and typically sold by someone licensed to sell insurance products. With most deferred variable annuities, there is a menu of potential investment options from which an individual can choose. Typical investment options might include a pre-determined target risk asset allocation consisting of a diversified mix of securities managed by multiple investment managers. Many of the investment managers replicate popular mutual fund strategies for the annuity separate account. Compared with traditional investment programs (e.g., mutual funds), these annuities can be more expensive for investors, and the number of investment fund options within the programs may be limited.

Deferred variable annuity contracts may include a death benefit. A typical death benefit guarantees that the beneficiary named in the contract will receive the entire amount used to purchase the annuity—a feature that has value to the beneficiary only if the individual dies when the value of the contract is less than the initial investment. Like all features of deferred annuities, the death benefit creates a risk for the issuing insurance company. To offset this risk, the insurance company charges a fee. As with mutual funds, individuals maintain control of their money through the right to exit (or sell) the contract, although there can be considerable surrender charges for withdrawing one's money. Also, similar to mutual funds, a deferred variable annuity does not guarantee lifetime income unless the individual (1) adds an additional feature (a contract rider) or (2) annuitizes the contract by converting the value of the deferred variable annuity into an immediate payout annuity. It is worth noting that relatively few deferred variable annuity investors end up "annuitizing."

Adding a guaranteed minimum withdrawal benefit for life rider to a deferred variable annuity can create a guaranteed income stream for life for the investor. The typical guaranteed minimum withdrawal benefit for life promises to pay the individual a fixed percentage (e.g., 4%) of the initial investment value as long as he or she lives. Each payment is subtracted from the current value of the deferred variable annuity contract. If the markets continue to perform well, the initial investment value may not be depleted, and any remaining value will go to the investor's beneficiaries. In a down market, the investment value may be depleted. If this is the case, the insurance company is contractually obligated to continue to pay the investor the guaranteed minimum benefit as long as the investor is alive.

9.2.2 Deferred Fixed Annuities

Deferred fixed annuities provide an annuity payout that begins at some future date. For each dollar invested, the insurance company will tell the investor how much income he or she will receive when annuity payments commence at a specified age in the future. It costs considerably less for a 30-year-old to purchase a dollar of income for life starting at age 65 than it does for a 55-year-old to purchase a dollar of income for life starting at age 65. At any point prior to annuitization (i.e., conversion of the investment into an annuity), the investor can cash out and receive the economic value of the accumulated purchases less any applicable surrender charges, in which case the annuity contract is terminated. Once in retirement, the individual has two options: (1) cash out or (2) begin withdrawing the accumulated funds. In either case, the "economic value" of the accumulated purchases is annuitized, converting the deferred fixed annuity into an immediate fixed. In contrast to deferred variable annuities, which most investors choose not to annuitize, most deferred fixed annuities are eventually annuitized.

9.2.3 Immediate Variable Annuities

With an immediate variable annuity, the individual permanently exchanges a lump sum for an annuity contract that promises to pay the annuitant an income for life. As the name suggests, the amount of the payments varies over time based on the performance of the portfolios that the assets are invested in. A common feature that can be added to an immediate variable annuity for an additional cost is an income floor that protects the annuitant in the event of a down market.

9.2.4 Immediate Fixed Annuities

With immediate fixed annuities, the most common and most utilized type of annuity, an individual trades a sum of money today for a promised income benefit for as long as he or she is alive. The "income yield" for an immediate fixed annuity is the total amount of ongoing annual income received as a percentage of the initial purchase price. For example, if an individual purchases an immediate fixed annuity for $100,000 and in exchange receives a guarantee to be paid $8,000 per year for as long as the individual is alive, the income yield for the annuity would be 8%.

The income yield for immediate fixed annuities, or any type of annuity, varies based on a number of factors. One key factor is the age of the insured individual (or individuals). Exhibit 7 contains the payout rates for two different immediate annuity types: a life-only annuity (which pays benefits only as long as the individual is alive, with no residual benefits) and a life annuity with a 10-year certain payment (whereby benefits are guaranteed to last for at least 10 years). Quotes are included for three different types of annuitants: male, female, and joint (a couple). (The couple consists of a male and a female assumed to be the same age, and the survivor benefit is 100% of the primary benefit; that is, the benefit stays the same as long as either of the couple survives.)

Exhibit 7   An Example of Annual Payouts as a Percentage of Initial Premium

	Life Only				Life with 10-Year Period Certain		
Age	Male	Female	Joint	Age	Male	Female	Joint
60	6.28%	5.87%	5.51%	60	6.15%	5.86%	5.42%
65	7.02	6.47	5.96	65	6.75	6.32	5.88
70	8.04	7.31	6.65	70	7.46	7.01	6.59
75	9.53	8.73	7.68	75	8.33	7.93	7.45
80	11.90	10.87	9.35	80	9.30	8.96	8.51
85	15.17	14.27	11.70	85	10.08	9.95	9.45
90	20.10	19.34	14.51	90	10.66	10.49	9.86

Source: www.immediateannuities.com (retrieved December 2014).

There are a number of important takeaways from Exhibit 7. First, the payouts (i.e., income yields) are higher when expected remaining longevity is shorter. For example, a male of 85 will receive a higher income yield than a male of 65 because the older male has a shorter life expectancy. A 65-year-old female will have a smaller payout than a 65-year-old male because females have a longer average life expectancy than males. The income yield is determined by estimating the average longevity of a given annuitant pool. A shorter average payment period will mean higher income for the older annuitants in the pool.

Another takeaway from the table is that the inclusion of a period certain (or return-of-premium feature) will reduce the payout, but to varying degrees. For example, adding the 10-year period certain has a relatively small effect on the income yield for a 60-year-old male (which decreases from 6.28% to 6.15%), but it has a significantly greater impact for the 90-year-old male (whose payout rate decreases from 20.10% to 10.66%). Again, this difference is based on life expectancies. The probability of a 60-year-old male dying in the first 10 years is much smaller than the probability of a 90-year-old male dying over the next 10 years, so the payouts are adjusted accordingly. An individual who is concerned with lifetime income maximization is likely better off not adding any type of rider that includes a residual benefit; however, such a rider may be desirable if an individual has competing goals of generating lifetime income and providing some residual wealth for heirs.

In addition to mortality, another key variable that affects annuity pricing is the expected return the insurance company can earn on premiums. Because insurance companies tend to invest conservatively, the available yield on bonds provides a relatively good proxy, at least from a historical perspective, for how payout rates change over time. When current yields on bonds are lower than historical bond yields and life expectancies are increasing, payouts on annuities will be relatively low by historical standards. Low annuity yields may discourage many individuals from buying annuities if they believe that yields will eventually go back up. In reality, however, lower annuity payout rates simply reflect the increasing cost of hedging longevity risk using available investments.

9.2.5 Advanced Life Deferred Annuities

The final type of annuity that we discuss is a hybrid of a deferred fixed annuity and an immediate fixed annuity. This so-called *advanced life deferred annuity* (ALDA) is often referred to as pure longevity insurance. Although it might sound a bit contradictory, ALDAs are deferred immediate payout annuities. Similar to an immediate fixed annuity, an ALDA involves the permanent exchange of a lump sum for an insurance contract that promises to pay an income. However, in contrast to an immediate payout annuity, for which the payments begin immediately, an ALDA's payments begin later in life—for example, when the individual turns 80 or 85.

Given that a specific monthly benefit may not begin until age 85, a deferred immediate life annuity would clearly cost less to purchase than a regular immediate life annuity. We note three reasons for this lower cost. First, because payments on the deferred annuity begin so far in the future, the insurance company has ample time to earn money on the amount tendered. Second, life expectancy for an 85-year-old is much shorter than for a 65-year-old, so the number of payments made will be fewer. Third, it is quite possible that the annuitant may actually die before any payments are made. For a relatively small premium, longevity insurance can provide additional security and can supplement income in later years.

EXAMPLE 12

Comparing Annuities

Compare fixed immediate annuities and variable immediate annuities.

Solution:

Both fixed and variable immediate annuities represent an irrevocable exchange of money for an insurance contract (the annuity contract). With a fixed immediate annuity, payments are "fixed" in either nominal terms or, in some cases, real terms, providing certainty about payment streams. With both fixed and variable immediate annuities, a common feature is a "period certain," whereby the payments continue to a designated beneficiary for a specified period, typically 10 years.

10. ANNUITIES: ADVANTAGES AND DISADVANTAGES OF FIXED AND VARIABLE ANNUITIES

h   discuss the use of annuities in personal financial planning;
i   discuss the relative advantages and disadvantages of fixed and variable annuities;

In this section, we discuss the relative advantages and disadvantages of both fixed and variable annuities. As a reminder, fixed annuities provide a benefit that is fixed (or known) for life, whereas variable annuities have a benefit that can change over time and that benefit is generally based on the performance of some underlying portfolio or investment. When selecting between fixed and variable annuities, there are a number of important considerations.

10.1 Volatility of Benefit Amount

The most obvious difference between fixed and variable annuities is the type of benefit. Fixed annuities provide a constant income stream that is guaranteed not to change, whereas the income from a variable annuity could change considerably depending on the terms of the annuity payout. Retirees seeking a high level of assurance with respect to benefit payouts are likely better served by a fixed annuity, or a variable annuity that limits the possible change in the benefit over time. Retirees who are risk tolerant may be more interested in a variable annuity. If a retiree is willing to adjust his or her spending over time, that individual may be able to increase the amount spent each year by selecting a variable annuity for which the payment is linked to a risky portfolio of assets.

10.2 Flexibility

The flexibility of an annuity varies materially with the type of annuity and its individual features. For example, an individual who purchases an immediate fixed annuity has effectively traded some amount of wealth for a guarantee of income for life. In most situations, this exchange is irrevocable: The individual who purchased the immediate fixed annuity cannot "undo" the transaction and request the original purchase amount back. The fact that these annuities are irrevocable makes sense from the insurer's perspective because (in theory) if given the option, every individual would request the initial premium back.

Variable annuity payments are typically tied to the performance of an underlying subaccount. This subaccount can often be withdrawn by the annuitant, subject to limitations. Therefore, variable annuities can provide the annuitant with guaranteed income for life as well as the flexibility to access the funds should he or she (or they) need to do so. There may be penalties associated with withdrawing funds from a variable annuity, and in some cases, withdrawals may not be allowed (e.g., in the case of an immediate variable annuity).

10.3 Future Market Expectations

A fixed annuity locks the annuitant into a portfolio of bond-like assets at whatever rate of return exists at the time of purchase. This scenario creates some interest rate risk because the value of these underlying securities will fall if interest rates rise.

If the annuitant assumes that interest rates will vary over time, he or she may be tempted to delay annuitization until interest rates rise. This delay, however, will reduce expected consumption during the delay period because the annuitant receives only market returns on investment assets and no mortality credits. Mortality credits, which will be discussed at greater length shortly, are effectively the difference between the future payout one would receive without pooling one's investments and the future payout one receives when the investment pool includes individuals who have already passed away. Delay of annuitization may also expose the annuitant to the risk that life expectancies will systematically increase during the delay period, which would increase the cost of annuitization (i.e., decrease future potential available payouts). Annuitizing earlier allows the annuitant to hedge the risk of a large increase in future longevity for a population.

Variable annuities allow an annuitant to accept some variation in payments in return for the possibility of higher future payments if the market performs well. Because most retirees will rationally accept some market risk with their investment portfolio, this option allows individuals to increase their retirement income efficiency by benefiting from both a mortality credit and a risk premium. The benefit of accepting market risk varies by type of annuity, and many variable annuity features limit the potential growth in income payments in future time periods. Variable annuities without growth-limiting features, such as minimum income guarantees, are most likely to provide a future income that outpaces inflation on average.

10.4 Fees

The fees associated with variable annuities tend to be higher than those for fixed annuities. These higher fees come from a variety of factors but are primarily attributable to the costs of hedging market risk, administrative expenses, and reduced price competition. Evidence suggests that the price of insurance products is significantly affected by price competition, and immediate fixed annuities are much easier for a consumer to compare (the consumer will simply select the highest annuity payment for the amount he or she will spend). The opaque pricing of variable annuities can reduce price competition if consumers are unable to easily compare the relative efficiency of product characteristics. A thorough price analysis may require weighing the possible added costs of opaque variable annuity features—perhaps using analytical tools to help assess these costs—against the benefits of a potentially higher return.

10.5 Inflation Concerns

Inflation can have a significant negative impact on the real income received from a fixed annuity. For example, if annual inflation averages 3%, after approximately 24 years, the income would be worth approximately half as much as it was worth when the annuity began. In their purest form, fixed annuities are nominal and will not change with inflation; however, it is possible to create a partial inflation hedge by having benefits "step up" some predetermined amount each year (e.g., 3%). Although this adjustment is not a perfect inflation hedge, it does provide a mechanism to ensure that payments increase over time. There are a number of variable annuities (and riders on fixed annuities) that allow the payments to increase or decrease based on changes in inflation. An individual interested in guaranteeing some lifetime level of income that changes with inflation may find these types of policies or riders valuable.

10.6 Payout Methods

The payout methods available from an annuity are similar regardless of whether the annuity is fixed or variable. In certain instances, the annuitant is unable to choose the payout method, especially with some types of government pensions, but there is generally some level of choice when purchasing a private annuity from an insurance company. The primary payout methods were discussed previously but are summarized again here:

- *Life annuity:* Payments are made for the entire life of the annuitant and cease at his or her death.
- *Period-certain annuity:* Payments are made for a specified number of periods without regard to the lifespan or expected lifespan of the annuitant.

- *Life annuity with period certain:* This payment type combines the features associated with a life annuity and a period-certain annuity, so payments are made for the entire life of the annuitant but are guaranteed for a minimum number of years even if the annuitant dies. The most common length of the period certain is 10 years. For example, if the annuitant dies after 6 years, a life annuity with 10 years period certain will make payments to the annuitant's beneficiary for the remaining 4 years and then cease.
- *Life annuity with refund:* This type is similar to a life annuity with period certain, but instead of guaranteeing payments for life or for a certain number of years, a life annuity with refund guarantees that the annuitant (or the beneficiary) will receive payments equal to the total amount paid into the contract, which is equal to the initial investment amount less fees.
- *Joint life annuity:* With a life annuity on two or more individuals, such as a husband and a wife, payments continue until both members are no longer living. For example, a married couple may purchase an immediate annuity that pays a monthly benefit as long as either one of them is alive. The contract states the benefit that the survivor will receive, which can be as much as 100% of the primary benefit or a smaller amount, such as 50% or 75% of the full benefit. The annuity payments cease when the survivor passes away.

It is important to note that the payout methods are not mutually exclusive. In theory, one could combine each of the different methods into a single annuity. Annuity payments can also be made at different frequencies, such as monthly, quarterly, or annually, although monthly payments are generally the most common. It is also possible to include riders or other methods that specify how the benefit may change over time. For example, it is possible to purchase an annuity for which the payment increases by some fixed percentage (or amount) each year.

10.7 Annuity Benefit Taxation

In some locations, annuities can offer attractive tax benefits, such as tax-deferred growth. For example, in the United States, the growth in an annuity is taxed only when the individual receives income from the annuity. This presents an opportunity for tax-deferred growth, especially for someone who purchases the annuity at a relatively young age or has exhausted other tax-sheltering alternatives. The actual taxation of the benefits varies considerably by type of annuity but is generally based on some average of the difference between the amount paid for the annuity and the benefits received.

The actual method of taxation varies materially by country, and before purchasing an annuity or recommending an annuity for a client, one should become familiar with the applicable tax consequences or consult a local expert on annuity taxation. In general, the potential for tax deferral, combined with a high marginal tax rate on alternative investments, may make annuities attractive for retirees.

10.8 Appropriateness of Annuities

When creating an income stream from a pool of assets, each retiree has a choice. The individual can choose either to receive periodic withdrawals from an investment portfolio (i.e., not annuitize) or to purchase an annuity (i.e., annuitize). This decision is obviously based on a variety of factors and preferences. When discussing the potential benefits of annuitizing, it is important to understand the concept of mortality credits (which we briefly mentioned earlier). Each payment received by the annuitant is a combination of principal, interest, and mortality credits. Mortality credits are the benefits that survivors receive from those individuals in the mortality pool who have already passed away. It is possible to demonstrate this effect visually using a chart (see Exhibit 8).

In Exhibit 8, we show an example of mortality credits for US male individuals, using male mortality rates based on the Society of Actuaries' 2012 Individual Annuity Reserve Table and an interest rate of 3%. We also assume that the individual receives US$70 of annual income for life for an approximate initial cost of US$1,000. Given these assumptions, the annual benefit payment can be decomposed into three parts: interest (based on the remaining assets from the initial investment minus benefits paid), return of premium, and mortality credits.

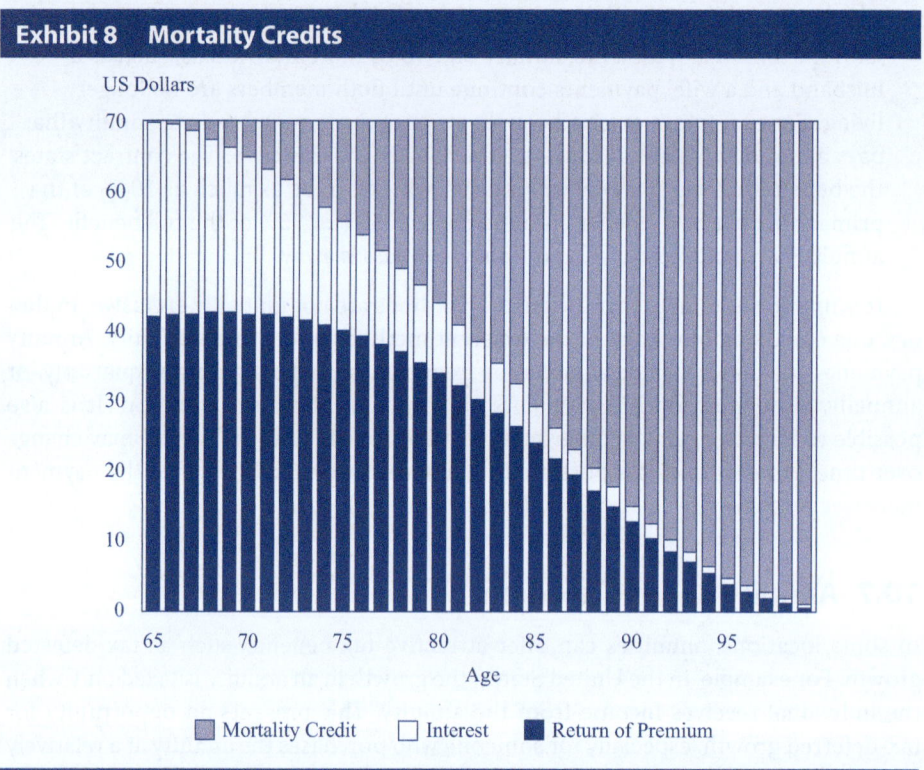

Exhibit 8   Mortality Credits

An individual who self-insures longevity risk would receive only (approximately) the interest and return-of-premium portions of Exhibit 8. The additional mortality credits arise because some individuals will pass away early, thereby subsidizing the future benefits of those individuals who are still alive. In this way, an individual can receive more income and additional certainty from purchasing an annuity. However, this certainty comes at a cost because the expected benefits of an annuity are generally not positive. Annuities are a form of insurance, and most forms of insurance, by definition, do not (and should not) have a positive expected value because it would imply that the insurance company lost money on the average policy sold. Moreover, it would likely not be advantageous to purchase an annuity from an insurance company that lost money on the average policy sold because that company would likely eventually go out of business and no longer be able to fund future expected benefit payments.

Therefore, an individual who purchases an annuity is acquiring the benefit of certainty regarding lifetime income in exchange for accepting lower potential wealth at death, as well as lower lifetime income depending on the cost of the annuity. This perspective can be used to create a "retirement income efficient frontier" whereby the decision of how much to annuitize is based on an individual's preference for wealth maximization and aversion to running out of money. This concept is similar to the traditional Markowitz (1952) efficient frontier; but for the retirement income efficient frontier, wealth replaces expected returns on the vertical axis and shortfall risk (which is defined approximately as the risk associated with running out of money over one's lifetime) replaces standard deviation on the horizontal axis. The exact definitions of "wealth" and "shortfall risk" (as well as the terms themselves) have varied across literature but still tend to be relatively consistent. The concept of the retirement income efficient frontier, which is displayed visually in Exhibit 9, is derived from Chen and Milevsky (2003), among others.

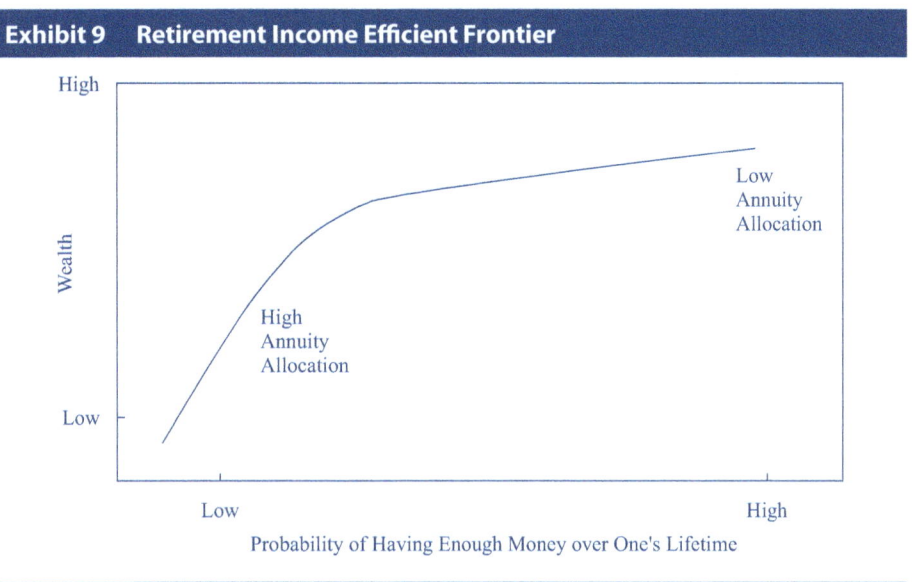

Exhibit 9   Retirement Income Efficient Frontier

Certain factors can generally be expected to affect a retiree's demand for annuities, either positively or negatively. For example, the following factors would generally suggest increased demand for an annuity:

- Longer-than-average life expectancy
- Greater preference for lifetime income
- Less concern for leaving money to heirs
- More conservative investing preferences (i.e., greater risk aversion)
- Lower guaranteed income from other sources (such as pensions)

The broad international shift away from defined benefit plans and toward defined contribution plans has increased the demand for annuities. Therefore, it is important to have an understanding of annuities and which individuals they are most likely to benefit.

RISK MANAGEMENT IMPLEMENTATION: DETERMINING THE OPTIMAL STRATEGY AND CASE ANALYSIS

11

j   analyze and evaluate an insurance program;

A variety of factors need to be considered when implementing an optimal risk management strategy for an individual or a household. In this section, we will indicate how human capital affects the asset allocation decision, provide a case study analyzing and critiquing an insurance program, and present appropriate strategies for asset allocation and risk reduction for a given investor.

11.1 Determining the Optimal Risk Management Strategy

As with portfolio selection, the decision to retain risk or to manage risk through insurance or annuities is determined by a household's risk tolerance. At the same level of wealth, a more risk-tolerant household will prefer to retain more risk—either through higher insurance deductibles or by simply buying little or no insurance—than a less risk-tolerant household. Additionally, the amount of overhead and administrative expenses built into the cost of the insurance (the load) will vary by product.

If an individual decides not to insure a risk exposure, he or she may still choose to moderate the impact of a potential loss. The term *loss control* refers to efforts to reduce or eliminate the costs associated with risks. There are three general approaches to loss control. *Risk avoidance* is the purest form of loss control. That is, one can remove the possibility that an event involving loss will occur. For example, one may avoid the risk of loss of a collector car or piece of jewelry by selling the asset. This strategy can be particularly appealing if the asset is no longer providing significant utility, or if the magnitude of the risk exposure rises because of price appreciation. Two other types of loss control are *loss prevention* and *loss reduction*. Loss prevention is the process of taking actions to reduce the probability that a loss event will occur. For example, installing a security system reduces the probability of a break-in that could lead to a loss by theft. Operating an automobile that has a backup camera reduces the probability of causing property damage or personal injury when the automobile is backing up. Installing a swimming pool alarm reduces the probability that a child will drown. Loss reduction is the process of seeking to reduce the size of a loss if a loss event occurs. For example, maintaining a high-quality fire extinguisher in the kitchen may allow a homeowner to contain a fire that would otherwise cause extreme damage. Unlike the loss prevention examples, the fire extinguisher does not reduce the likelihood of the loss event.

As initially discussed in Section 3.1.3, in addition to risk avoidance and risk reduction, individuals can also manage risk through the techniques of *risk transfer* and *risk retention*. Although risk transfer generally involves insurance or annuities, individuals can also use *non-insurance risk transfers* in many situations, and these usually take the form of contracts. For example, an apartment renter may select a long-term lease to lock in the amount of the monthly rent for a longer time during a period of inflation, thus transferring the risk of increased rent to the landlord, who then must absorb the opportunity cost. Incorporation of an individual's business provides a non-insurance risk transfer in many countries. By incorporating, the individual shields his or her personal financial assets from any legal judgment in which the business is found to be at fault.

A systematic risk management approach would be to consider the optimal strategy for each risk exposure. Some guidelines are helpful in deciding when it is appropriate to accept (retain) risk, when it is best to reduce the potential magnitude (or severity) of the risk, and when it makes sense to transfer risk. Small-magnitude risks below a risk retention limit should be retained (i.e., self-insured) and the magnitude/severity reduced to the point where the expected cost is equal to the expected benefit. For example, installing a high-quality fire-rated roof on a house may reduce both the probability of a fire (e.g., from sparks from a house fire next door) and the potential damage from a fire. However, the cost of installing a new, expensive roof may be too high to be justified. In this case, the large-magnitude potential loss from fire can be transferred through property insurance and a deductible can be used to set the optimal amount of risk retention.

A common risk management approach is summarized in Exhibit 10.

Exhibit 10   Risk Management Techniques

Loss characteristics	High frequency	Low frequency
High severity	Risk avoidance	Risk transfer
Low severity	Risk reduction	Risk retention

An insurance product can provide indemnification by ensuring that there will be no (or minimal) loss in economic net worth. For example, an insurance claim will provide reimbursement of flood damage to a $20,000 vehicle if the household has a comprehensive insurance policy. If not, the household risks reducing its economic net worth by the size of the loss exposure. Indemnification in life insurance can be more complex. A human life value analysis seeks to replace the loss in human capital. A needs analysis estimates the present value of future consumption that would need to be replaced if the income of a primary earner were lost.

EXAMPLE 13

Risk Management Strategy

Describe *loss control* in risk management.

Solution:

Loss control refers to efforts to reduce or eliminate costs associated with risks. A simple method of loss control is to avoid risks (risk avoidance)—for example, by not engaging in high-risk hobbies, such as rock climbing. Another approach to loss control is loss prevention, in which one attempts to reduce the likelihood of a risky event. For example, one may install an alarm system to discourage burglars. Loss reduction refers to approaches that attempt to minimize the size of the loss if a risky event does occur. For example, an airbag in an automobile does not reduce the likelihood of an accident, but it may reduce the seriousness of injuries sustained by those involved in an accident.

11.2 Analyzing an Insurance Program

This section provides a case study of how one might analyze an individual's insurance needs and design an insurance program. In this case, Jacques and Marion Perrier are 40 years old and 38 years old, respectively. They have two children: Henri, age 8, and Émilie, age 6. Jacques is a manager of technical services for a large corporation and earns €100,000 per year. Marion works part-time as a nurse, earning €20,000 after tax per year but plans to return to full-time work in 10 years, when Émilie turns 16. Marion expects that, with adjusted market conditions and after 10 years of inflation, she will earn €60,000 after tax per year as a full-time nurse at that time. Jacques and Marion are in excellent health and maintain a lifestyle that is well within their income.

The family lives in the city in a comfortable condominium that they bought for €250,000 five years ago and that is currently valued at €300,000. They owe €190,000 on a mortgage that still has 25 years to maturity. Although both Jacques and Marion take public transportation to work, they have an automobile, which is 10 years old but in excellent condition with relatively few kilometers of use. Jacques and Marion intend to live in the condominium at least until Jacques's planned retirement at age 60. At that time, they will decide whether to remain in the condominium or move to the small town nearby where Jacques grew up.

Four years ago, when his parents died, Jacques inherited the moderately sized but attractive home where he grew up. It was worth €150,000 at the time and has increased in value to €165,000 (a 10% increase during this period). For two years, the family tried to use the house as a weekend retreat, but they discovered that their children's activities and the desire to go to different places caused them to use the house infrequently. For the past two years, they have rented the house to a middle-aged couple who have no children. There is no debt on the house, and the rent is enough to pay for taxes and other expenses and to generate positive cash flow that Jacques and Marion are using for family vacations.

Both of Jacques's parents died at age 70. Marion's father died at age 80. Her mother, Françoise, is in good health at age 72, and women in her family have generally lived to very old ages. Françoise has a pension but does not have much in assets.

11.2.1 Current Insurance Plan

Life Insurance. Jacques bought a whole life insurance policy with a death benefit of €200,000 when Henri was born. Jacques is the insured, and his estate is the beneficiary. His employer also provides a €50,000 term life insurance policy that names Marion as the beneficiary. There is no life insurance on Marion.

Health Insurance. The family is covered by a national health insurance plan.

Disability Insurance. Jacques's employer provides short-term disability payments for up to six months. As a part-time employee, Marion has no disability benefits.

Long-Term Care Insurance. Elderly individuals in Jacques and Marion's country are eligible for long-term care at a cost equal to 75% of their pension benefits.

Property Insurance. The exterior of the condominium is insured through the condominium owners' association. The insured value is increased annually to consider current market and replacement values. Jacques and Marion have a property insurance policy on the contents of their condominium for €20,000. Jacques's parents insured the house for €100,000 15 years ago. They never increased the coverage, and Jacques has maintained the same policy. The automobile has coverage for liability and collision, as well as comprehensive coverage.

Data Summary

- Jacques: age 40; €100,000 annual earnings; €200,000 whole life insurance policy; €50,000 term life insurance policy
- Marion: age 38; €20,000 annual earnings after tax; no life insurance
- Children: Henri, age 8, and Émilie, age 6
- Condominium: €300,000 current value; €190,000 25-year remaining mortgage; exterior of building fully insured; contents insured for €20,000
- Rental home: €165,000 current value; no mortgage; insured for €100,000

11.2.2 Program Review

Life Insurance. As we discussed earlier, two approaches are commonly used in calculating life insurance needs. The first is the human life value method, which estimates the present value of earnings that must be replaced. As we will demonstrate, the human life value method indicates that Jacques should purchase approximately €1.11 million of additional life insurance. The second approach is the needs analysis method, which estimates the financial needs of dependents. As we will also demonstrate, the needs analysis method indicates that Jacques should purchase approximately €1.25 million of additional life insurance.

Of course, there is no absolute when calculating life insurance needs because there are so many variables and uncertainties. However, in this case, the two methods generate relatively close numbers. To augment Jacques's current life insurance program, he should purchase at least €1 million in additional term life insurance, but €1.25 million would be more desirable.

Although an annually renewable term policy will be less expensive, a 20-year level term policy should be considered. At the end of 20 years, Jacques will be nearing the end of his working career and the children will be fully grown. Jacques and Marion will have accumulated a high enough level of savings that income replacement will be unnecessary. At that time, the term policy can be allowed to lapse and the €200,000 whole life policy can be retained.

Whole life coverage like Jacques's current policy is relatively expensive, but the pricing and cash build-up at this point in the policy's life indicate that it is probably wise not to replace the policy with term coverage now. Even though life insurance rates have fallen as life expectancies have lengthened and competition has increased, the decline is probably not enough to offset the advantages of the whole life policy at this point. In addition to providing life insurance coverage, the policy's cash-value buildup can be considered a conservative part of the asset allocation of the retirement portfolio.

Marion should be named as the primary beneficiary on the new policy, with Henri and Émilie as secondary beneficiaries, although countries may differ on the exact approach for designating a beneficiary who is a minor. It may be advisable to name a custodian and/or create a trust for Henri and Émilie until they reach adulthood. The old policy should be changed to include these beneficiary designations as well. Making death benefits payable to the estate, as is the case currently on the whole life policy, can make receipt of payments much slower and may subject benefits to greater taxation.

Although Marion's income is modest, her death would cause a financial burden in terms of both lost income and added expenses to replace her family and household responsibilities. Furthermore, her income will increase when she returns to full-time work in 10 years, and financial responsibility for the children will still exist at that time. At Marion's current age and with her excellent health, and because she is female, life insurance rates are very low. However, it is possible that a health issue or accident could cause her rate to increase or even make her uninsurable. Given the complexity of Marion's situation, it is difficult to calculate a recommendation for the amount of life insurance needed.

Life insurance companies typically offer lower rates for larger amounts of coverage in a series of steps. For example, the price per €1,000 of coverage may decrease at €100,000, €250,000, €500,000, and €1,000,000 of coverage. But companies are hesitant to underwrite policies that are large relative to the insured's human life value, or the discounted value of future earnings. A €250,000 policy would take advantage of the price break but would be relatively large for Marion's current income. Still, it is justifiable based on her future employment plan. Purchasing a policy of this size will provide adequate protection for the 10 years until she goes back to work full time, and at that point the children will be more independent, reducing the need for life insurance. As with Jacques, a 20-year level term policy is reasonable.

Life Insurance Needs For Jacques and Marion

As mentioned previously, the *human life value* method is consistent with the concept of human capital and involves replacing the estimated net contributions to family finances that Jacques would generate if he did not die during his projected earning life. Calculating these contributions involves the following steps:

- Start with the actual pre-tax compensation that Jacques would receive from employment: €100,000.

- Adjust for income taxation, and here we assume a 30% rate: €100,000 – €30,000 = €70,000 post-tax compensation.

- Adjust for family expenses attributable to Jacques that will not exist after his death, such as his transportation, travel, clothing, food, entertainment, and insurance premiums. Here, we assume those expenses to be €20,000. So €70,000 – €20,000 = €50,000 income after expenses.

- Add the value of any non-taxable employee benefits that the family will no longer receive, such as employer contributions to retirement plans, which we assume to be €15,000: €50,000 + €15,000 = €65,000.

- Estimate the amount of pre-tax income needed to replace that income on an after-tax basis. Note that the rate of taxation of annual income generated from life insurance proceeds may be different from the rate of taxation of Jacques's employment income, and marginal rates may be lower for lower incomes. Here, we assume a 20% tax rate: €65,000/(1 – t) = €65,000/(1 – 0.20) = €81,250.

- We then apply an annual growth rate, assumed here to be 3%, to consider the effects of inflation and career advancement over the full 20 years until retirement.

- Finally, we discount all the future cash flows back to the present at an appropriate rate, assumed here to be 5%.

Assuming the lost income replacement would be needed by Jacques's family immediately, the human life value calculation can be solved as the present value of an annuity due with growing payments (a so-called "growing annuity due"). Using calculator keystrokes for an annuity due with level payments, the growth of payments can be incorporated by adjusting the discount rate to account for the growth rate of earnings. The adjusted rate i can be calculated as follows:[3] [(1 + Discount rate)/(1 + Growth rate)] – 1, or (1.05/1.03) – 1 = 1.94%. Thus,

- set the calculator for beginning-of-period payments;
- $n = 20$ (the number of years until retirement);
- payment = €81,250; and
- $i = 1.94\%$.

Solving for the present value of an annuity due, the human life value method recommends €1,362,203 of life insurance for Jacques. Because Jacques already has €250,000 of life insurance, he should purchase an additional €1,112,203, according to this method. This amount would likely be rounded to €1.1 million.

---

[3] Most individuals' situations would call for a discount rate that is higher than the inflation rate. If that is not the case, or if future cash flows are not projected to grow at a constant rate, the present value can be calculated in the typical manner as the present value of a series of unequal payments.

As discussed earlier, the *needs analysis* method is concerned with meeting the financial needs of the family rather than replacing human capital. Needs analysis typically includes the following steps, which are presented in greater detail in Exhibit 11:

- Estimate the amount of cash that will be needed upon the death of the insured person. This amount will include final expenses (funeral and burial) as well as any taxes that may be payable. It is also common to pay off all debt (including mortgages) and to fully fund future education costs. An emergency fund should be created.
- Estimate the capital needed to fund family living expenses. This calculation requires discounting estimated living expenses (i.e., calculating the present value of future cash flow needs) during multiple time frames, typically as follows:
    - Estimate the surviving spouse's living expense needs, assumed here to continue for 52 years, until Marion is 90 years old. Note that when the mortgage and other debts are paid off, living expenses are lower.
    - Estimate the children's living expense needs, assumed here to continue until they are 22 years old. This amount does not include the education fund.
    - Include an additional amount for extra expenses during a transition period after Jacques's death, perhaps covering two years. In general, this period recognizes that there may be some contractual obligations, such as a car lease, that may not terminate upon a person's death.
    - Consider Marion's future income (earnings). Note, however, that Marion may prefer not to go back to work full time as soon as planned because of the extra responsibilities of being a single parent. She may even choose to resign from her part-time job.
- Calculate total needs as the sum of cash needs and capital needs.
- Calculate total capital available, which may include cash/savings, retirement benefits, life insurance, rental property, and other assets.
- Calculate the life insurance need as the difference between the total financial needs and the total capital available.

Exhibit 11 is a representation of a needs analysis for Jacques.

Exhibit 11 Financial Needs: Life Insurance Worksheet

Cash Needs	Euro (€)
Final expenses	10,000
Taxes payable	5,000
Mortgage retirement	190,000
Other debt	10,000
Education fund	200,000
Emergency fund	30,000
Total cash needs	445,000

Capital Needs [present value of annuity due: growth rate = 3%, discount rate = 5%, adjusted rate (as above) = 1.94%]

Marion's living expenses (60,000/year for 52 years)	1,991,941
Children's living expenses:	
Henri (10,000/year for 14 years)	123,934
Émilie (10,000/year for 16 years)	139,071
Transition period needs (10,000/year for 2 years)	19,810
Less Marion's income:	
Until Émilie is 16 (20,000/year for 10 years)	–183,713

(continued)

Exhibit 11 (Continued)

Cash Needs	Euro (€)
Age 48–60 (60,000/year for 12 years)	–398,565[a]
Total capital needs	1,692,478
Total Financial Needs	**2,137,478**
Capital Available	
Cash and savings	30,000
Vested retirement accounts—present value	200,000
Life insurance	250,000
Rental property	165,000
Total capital available	645,000
Life insurance need (Total financial needs less total capital available)	**1,492,478**

[a] Calculated in two steps: (1) Compute the amount needed in 10 years, when Marion will begin earning €60,000 per year. Assuming 12 years of earnings from age 48 to age 60, a 3% annual growth in earnings, and a 5% discount rate (1.94% adjusted discount rate), a present value of an annuity due calculation shows that €649,220 will be needed in 10 years. (2) Discount the €649,220 back to the present—10 years at the unadjusted discount rate of 5%—for a total of €398,565. The discount rate is not adjusted during this period because there are no payments to which a growth rate would be applied. We simply discount a future value to the present.

This amount of life insurance under the needs analysis method would likely be rounded to €1.5 million—considerably higher than the €1.11 million calculated earlier using the human life value method. The amount of life insurance selected may depend on which method seems to be more relevant to the family situation. One may view the two values as a reasonable range and use the larger number, the smaller number, or perhaps an average of the two. In many cases, selection of an amount may be further affected by "breakpoints" in the insurance company's premium schedule. The premium rate may decline when insurance coverage reaches, for example, €250,000, €500,000, and €1,000,000.

As a final note, consider that if Jacques dies prematurely, there will be an increased need for life insurance for Marion while Henri and Émilie are still children.

11.2.3 Recommendations

Health Insurance. Although the Perrier family is covered by national health insurance, they may want to seek private health insurance. In many countries, this type of coverage provides quicker treatment, a wider choice of physicians, and a higher standard of care.

Disability Insurance. Both Jacques and Marion should consider long-term disability income insurance that guarantees the option to purchase additional coverage without underwriting. This type of policy would allow them to increase coverage as their incomes increase. They should look for "own occupation" coverage that specifies that they would be considered disabled if they could no longer perform the duties of their current positions. They should also select a benefit period that extends at least until their respective retirement ages, possibly age 65. For Jacques, a relatively long, 180-day elimination period would coordinate well with his company's short-term disability plan and would save money. Marion should consider a shorter elimination period, perhaps 90 days, because she has no short-term coverage. Both should choose an option that allows increased coverage based on inflation.

Taxation should be considered in purchasing a disability income policy. In some jurisdictions, premium payments may be deductible for income tax purposes but benefits are taxed. In others, it may make a difference whether the policy is purchased individually or through the employer. In any case, the amount of the benefit selected should be sufficient to replace income, net of any tax advantages and reduction of expenses. Most insurance companies do not like to sell policies with benefits that represent more than 70%–80% of an individual's income (less for high-income individuals) because high percentages create a moral hazard, in that the insured may decide that declaring a disability would give him or her a larger net income without the need to work.

Long-Term Care Insurance. Although the Perriers' country provides some degree of long-term care assistance, it is possible that the facilities available are not of the standard that would satisfy them. Furthermore, the pricing structure appears to strongly favor individuals with limited income. The Perriers should consider long-term care insurance for themselves, especially if there is a coordination provision with the national plan. At their current ages, rates would be reasonable and would be locked in at the time the policy is purchased. Although stays in long-term care facilities are typically shorter than five years, it would be prudent to purchase a policy that does not have a time limit. Most policies have benefits that are based on a specified amount of money per day. The amount selected should be appropriate for the local cost structure, and the Perriers should pay the extra premium required to receive an automatic inflation adjustment, both before and after any claim.

Long-term care insurance may also be appropriate for Marion's mother, especially because women in her family tend to have long lives. This coverage will be more expensive at her age, but it would alleviate the potential need for care in the home, which would probably be provided by Marion. To avoid the financial and psychological stress of providing home care, a long-term care policy would be useful.

Property Insurance. Jacques and Marion should check to make sure that the condominium association's insurance coverage is sufficient for the structure. They should also determine whether that policy provides any coverage for contents and, if so, to what extent. It is likely that the condominium association's coverage for contents, if any, is modest, and Jacques and Marion undoubtedly have personal property worth far more than the €20,000 of coverage in their personal policy.

The Perriers should make a thorough valuation of their personal property, even though this is a cumbersome task, and make sure they have or obtain a sufficient amount of coverage. A prudent approach that helps avoid insurance claim problems is to make a written and/or photographic inventory of all contents and improvements within the condominium. Any personal property that has specified limits within their policy should be appraised and scheduled. For example, an expensive necklace should be taken to a jeweler for a formal appraisal, after which the necklace should be added to the insurance policy, which will likely require a higher premium. A copy of the appraisal and inventory should be provided to the insurance company, and another copy should be kept off site in case of a disaster in their condominium.

Property insurance on the house should be reviewed. It appears that the amount of coverage is far less than appropriate. Furthermore, it is not clear whether the transfer of ownership of the property is properly noted on the policy. In the case of a claim, Jacques and Marion may have to deal with legal issues in order to collect. Even if the property ownership issue is clarified, it is likely that the house is insured as the Perrier's residence or secondary residence. However, it is now a rental house, and it requires a different insurance policy. They should also determine whether the rental house's contents are included in the policy. Because they probably are not, it would be worthwhile to explain to the renters that they should obtain their own insurance on the contents (their property). This step is especially important because the Perriers could be considered liable for any loss of the renters' property if, for example, there is a fire caused by faulty wiring.

With regard to auto insurance, the Perriers should make sure that they have substantial liability insurance coverage, especially because it appears that they will have substantial assets to protect. However, they may want to consider whether collision and comprehensive coverage are cost effective for a 10-year-old automobile. Because they seem to drive relatively little, it may make sense to self-insure.

With sufficient liability coverage on the condominium and the auto, the Perriers may qualify for umbrella liability insurance. They should consider this relatively inexpensive coverage to provide additional liability protection relating to the auto and condominium. As a nurse, Marion may want to consider professional liability insurance if it is not provided by her employer. If either Jacques or Marion serves on any type of board of directors of a corporation, public service, or other entity, they should make sure that that entity provides appropriate liability coverage for its directors.

Longevity Insurance. Marion's mother may be an excellent candidate for longevity insurance. As noted earlier, longevity insurance is typically structured as a life annuity with payments beginning at some future date, such as age 85. Because it is not underwritten, it is generally a poor choice for someone whose life expectancy is shorter than average for his or her age and a good choice for someone whose life expectancy is longer than average, as is the case with Marion's mother. The annuity payments would not start for more than a decade, but they would offer additional income in her later years and help combat inflation, and the cost would be relatively low. Longevity insurance may be viewed as a complement to or even a partial substitute for long-term care insurance. A cost–benefit analysis of the available options should be performed to ensure that the policy selected best matches the goals and financial resources of the household.

12 THE EFFECT OF HUMAN CAPITAL ON ASSET ALLOCATION AND RISK REDUCTION

k discuss how asset allocation policy may be influenced by the risk characteristics of human capital;

l recommend and justify appropriate strategies for asset allocation and risk reduction when given an investor profile of key inputs.

There are two primary ways to consider how the different subcomponents of an individual's total economic wealth should affect portfolio construction. The first is asset allocation, which includes the overall allocation to risky assets. The second is the underlying asset classes, such as stocks and bonds, selected by the individual. For example, an individual who works in a risky profession that has a high correlation with the stock market might first choose a less aggressive portfolio (e.g., with a lower allocation to stocks than the average person of the same age). Next, the investor would select which individual stocks and bonds (or asset classes) to hold to minimize the overall risk of the portfolio within a total wealth framework.

For many people and for many occupations, human capital is generally considered to be a relatively bond-like asset. For example, dividend growth in the S&P 500 Index exhibited a quarterly volatility of 16.4% from first quarter 1948 to fourth quarter 2013, whereas wage growth volatility was closer to 2.5% over the same period.[4]

---

[4] Based on data obtained from the US Bureau of Economic Analysis.

Among individuals, occupation can have a large impact on the degree of wage growth volatility. For example, Oyer (2008) found that stock market conditions can have a strong impact on the lifetime earnings of MBA students. Asset performance that is strongly correlated with the lifetime earnings of a worker will provide less hedging benefit because the assets magnify, rather than reduce, variability in consumption.

EXAMPLE 14

Human Capital and Asset Allocation (1)

The riskiness of human capital, as well as that of other assets, should affect the allocation of an individual's financial capital. Consider three investors: George, John, and Sam. Each investor owns only two assets—human capital and financial capital—and wants his total wealth (i.e., human capital plus financial capital) to have a 45% stock allocation. If human capital is assumed to be 30% stock-like, what is the optimal allocation for the financial capital of George, John, and Sam?

Person	Human Capital (HC)	Financial Capital (FC)	Total Wealth (TW)
George	$500,000	$150,000	$650,000
John	$800,000	$300,000	$1,100,000
Sam	$150,000	$150,000	$300,000

Solution:

The allocation is as follows:

Person	(A) TW × 45% Target Equity	(B) HC × 30% HC Equity	(C) (A) − (B) FC Equity	(D) (C)/FC FC Equity Allocation %
George	$292,500	$150,000	$142,500	95.00%
John	$495,000	$240,000	$255,000	85.00%
Sam	$135,000	$45,000	$90,000	60.00%

Even within an occupation, each individual has different human capital risks. For example, two people may have the exact same job, but because of random market forces, one could lose his or her job and be unable to find suitable reemployment for an extended period of time. Many financial services workers lost their jobs during the global financial crisis of 2008–2009, and many who became unemployed have been forced to change careers given the lack of available openings. This outcome could have a significant impact on their long-term human capital. Alternatively, a person may have a health shock that seriously reduces their ability to rent his or her human capital for the same wage rate as before. Health shocks that meet the threshold of disability may be partially hedged through the insurance market, and the impact of job loss can be partially hedged through unemployment insurance. Most human capital volatility (other than premature death), however, is difficult to hedge through the insurance market.

If both spouses are employed, this may reduce the overall riskiness of the household's human capital. Each spouse provides his or her own income, each with its own risks, but unless the human capital of the two spouses is highly correlated (e.g., if they are both employed in the same family business), their combined human capital will benefit from diversification. An individual who receives income from numerous sources—such as salaries from different jobs, as well as dividends, interest, and so on—must consider the characteristics of his or her total compensation.

A lower-earning partner may also have a more risky human capital value if the higher-earning partner is tied to a specific geographic location. In the event of a job loss, this household may suffer a more significant decline in human capital value than a household in which both partners are able to move to a location where they can maximize their wage rate. The human capital of a less mobile household will have a lower present value and greater volatility. If human capital is very employer-specific (if the individual would have trouble earning the same wage from a different employer), then it is also less valuable and more risky. A household with a non-working spouse may be in a less vulnerable position than a single-person household if the non-working spouse can exercise the option to rejoin the workforce if the primary earner suffers an unexpected loss in earnings.

Most of the wealth an investor holds outside the investment portfolio (e.g., human capital and defined benefit pensions) tends to be relatively conservative in nature (i.e., more bond-like than stock-like). After an optimal investment policy is determined that establishes a target mix of risky and risk-free assets based on risk tolerance, the total wealth asset allocation should be adjusted as the value of the assets changes over time. For example, younger investors should likely allocate more of their investment portfolio to stocks because the value of human capital (which is bond-like) is highest early in the life cycle. Conversely, older investors should shift more of their wealth toward bonds because their bond-like human capital is gradually depleted as they approach retirement. This investment strategy is consistent with such life-cycle investments as target-date funds (in which the target date is the expected retirement date of the individual), which gradually increase the allocation to bonds as investors get closer to retirement.

The economic (holistic) balance sheet discussed earlier in the reading considers the current value of marketable and non-marketable assets. However, this type of balance sheet does not consider the stochastic nature of each individual asset or how the value of one asset rises and falls with respect to other assets within the portfolio over time. It also does not consider the relative liquidity of each asset category, which can be particularly important when there are limited financial instruments that can be used, for example, to borrow against the value of a pension. The allocation for the financial portfolio should be coordinated with the risk associated with the non-marketable assets in an investor's portfolio, such as human capital. Using this perspective, the financial portfolio can be considered a completion or hedge portfolio, because it is invested in such a way as to optimize the overall risk characteristics of an individual's total wealth.

Human capital is a unique asset class in a number of ways. First, it can require a continued investment in knowledge and skills to maintain or increase its value. Some professions are more risky than others and will provide either greater income variance or income that is more strongly correlated with systematic risks (i.e., will rise and fall with economic cycles). Some forms of human capital are more vulnerable to disability risks or premature death. A precision welder may earn the same income as an accountant, but the welder may be more vulnerable to an injury that would sharply reduce the value of that human capital. Human capital is also more illiquid, and there are limited financial instruments available that can be used to effectively borrow against expected human capital when earnings fall below a desired level of consumption. Some occupations will have an earnings path that is likely to keep pace with inflation, whereas other occupations will not. Employees in some occupations may have invested in human capital that allows them to be very productive in a specific role for their employer. This heavy investment in employer-specific human capital may not easily be rented to another employer for the same wage rate. This places the employee at greater risk of future income volatility. Many who enjoyed steady income growth in the past—for example, mortgage brokers in the United States during the 2000s—were not fully aware of their own human capital risk. Similarly, individuals who work in the real estate industry should likely seek to underweight real estate assets in their portfolios to reduce exposure to real estate from a total wealth perspective. This diversification may be a challenge for those who carry optimistic beliefs about the future growth of their own industry, but history shows that few industries are immune to market shocks.

EXAMPLE 15

Human Capital and Asset Allocation (2)

Describe how investment strategies can be modified to account for human capital risk.

Solution:

Investment assets may be strongly or weakly correlated with the human capital value of a worker. The overall volatility of one's economic balance sheet can be reduced by selecting assets that correlate weakly (or even negatively) with human capital. Sector investments may be particularly valuable if they are not a complement to the industry that employs the primary earner. Workers with more volatile assets may also prefer more liquid investments.

EXAMPLE 16

Human Capital and Asset Allocation (3)

Compare investment planning for a young family with investment planning for a newly retired couple.

Solution:

A younger household will hold most of its wealth in human capital. For most households, human capital is a bond-like asset that returns a relatively stable income over time. This fact increases the optimal allocation to risky assets within the investment portfolio for younger households. For a newly retired couple, the value of human capital declines relative to the value of the investment portfolio. To balance the total risk of the older household's portfolio, investment portfolio risk should be reduced because investment assets are a larger share of the economic balance sheet (ignoring the impact of charitable bequests and other obligations).

12.1 Asset Allocation and Risk Reduction

An individual or household manages wealth risk mainly to smooth spending over time. A strategy that combines appropriate investments with insurance products, or other risk management tools, can be used to provide the highest level of spending for the level of risk the individual or household is willing to take. Each household will have its own risks and preferences that determine which strategy makes sense.

Investment risk, property risk, and human capital risk can be either idiosyncratic or systematic. Idiosyncratic risks include the risks of a specific occupation, the risk of living a very long life or experiencing a long-term illness, and the risk of premature death or loss of property. Within a total wealth framework, idiosyncratic human capital risks are reduced through investment portfolio strategies and/or through insurance (or annuity) products. Pooling risk allows a household to efficiently reduce idiosyncratic risk. Systematic risks affect all households. For example, a diversified investment portfolio of risky assets will be exposed to the systematic risk that the overall market will fall in value. Earnings can also be affected by systematic risk through a recession or slow economic growth. A cure for cancer might increase overall longevity, placing all households at greater risk of outliving their assets.

The first step in creating strategies for asset allocation and risk reduction is to identify idiosyncratic risk exposures that can be efficiently reduced through diversification or hedging. A young doctor with two children and a lower-earning spouse bears a number of idiosyncratic risks. First, the couple's investment portfolio should be well diversified and not highly correlated with the doctor's income. Second, the household's largest asset, its human capital, could be diminished or lost through disability or premature death. Life insurance and disability insurance provide a hedge that pools idiosyncratic human capital risk. Medical malpractice insurance provides protection against idiosyncratic liability risk. In general, hedging these risks trades a small drop in expected wealth for an increase in the likelihood of smooth spending.

Young households may have additional liquidity constraints that will affect recommended products. A doctor who expects his or her earnings to rise sharply and who has high current expenses may choose to defer retirement saving for a few years. This individual should not, however, avoid paying premiums on insurance used to hedge the value of human capital. Term life insurance can provide ample coverage at a modest price, and the household may consider a longer elimination period on disability insurance to fit the cost into the current budget. The investment portfolio allocation may be of little consequence because the value of the total wealth portfolio consists almost entirely of human capital. Instead, investments may be selected to increase liquidity that can be used to protect current consumption from any short-term income shock.

A 60-year-old couple nearing retirement with grown, independent children and a large investment portfolio will face a different set of risks. Although their combined income may be higher than that of the young doctor, the value of their human capital is far less if they plan to retire in five years. Therefore, for the older couple, risks to the investment portfolio are far more relevant than human capital risks. Life insurance may have value only as a means of covering estate planning and liquidity needs. Disability insurance can likely be dropped. Health and liability remain significant idiosyncratic risk exposures that can be efficiently reduced through health, long-term care, and liability insurance. Home equity can be protected through property insurance; the risk of idiosyncratic regional real estate price variation should also be considered. The couple's risk of outliving their assets can be protected through the purchase of annuities. Market risk can be particularly important because, compared with a younger household, the older couple's investments are a far larger share of total household wealth. An older household may have fewer liquidity constraints and thus more flexibility to retain risks—for example, through higher insurance deductibles and longer elimination periods on long-term care insurance. This older household may also choose to retain the majority of property risk. A rational increase in risk retention can be combined with a reduction in portfolio risk to achieve an efficient balance of total wealth risk. The household will receive a higher expected return (equal to the insurance load) from accepting greater insurable risk while simultaneously reducing the expected return on the investment portfolio by increasing the share of safe assets.

Human capital risks are correlated with market returns and can be at least partially hedged through holistic portfolio construction. Consider a 50-year-old couple, Jennifer and Wade. Jennifer earns US$75,000 a year working as a tenured college professor, and Wade earns US$100,000 selling drilling parts to the oil industry. Jennifer participates in the state public employee pension system, which is currently in good enough financial condition to cover promised benefits for the next 40 years. Wade has US$300,000 saved in a 401(k), half in employer stock. Both are eligible to receive Social Security benefits.

Wade works in a cyclical industry and will see high variability in income but a modest covariance of earnings with the performance of the overall stock market. Although Wade's income today is higher than Jennifer's income, the difference in the present value of their human capital will not be that great. Wade's income is more volatile because it rests largely on the strength of the domestic oil industry. Jennifer may apply a discount rate equivalent to that of current state government bonds because her salary is unlikely to change and her salary risk is comparable to the state's ability to pay general obligation debts. The discount rate on Wade's income may be placed above the historical equity premium because his human capital risk is not easily diversified and is more volatile than the market in general.

To preserve consumption if Wade is laid off for a period of time, the couple should consider holding a significant amount of assets in marketable securities that can be easily liquidated to fund short-term spending needs. These types of assets include money market accounts and short-term government bonds, which can be easily traded in the secondary market. Investment assets held in taxable accounts can be accessed for emergency spending in the event of long-term unemployment. The combination of Jennifer's stable salary and Wade's volatile income allows the couple to take on greater risk than if they lived on Wade's income alone. If Wade and Jennifer have an average level of investment risk tolerance, then they should invest in a mix of stocks and bonds, each within the most tax-efficient account, to create a balanced portfolio appropriate to the couple's risk preferences and the risk of the remainder of the total wealth portfolio.

Wade's more risky human capital is highly correlated with the overall economy, although as previously mentioned, his wages are likely not strongly correlated with the equity market in general. A more efficient investment portfolio will provide a partial hedge against Wade's idiosyncratic human capital risk. The obvious first step would be to sell Wade's investments in employer stock. This may be complicated by restrictions on selling the stock or even Wade's subjective opinion of the potential value of his employer's stock. If Wade is restricted from selling his company stock, an adviser might suggest put options to hedge this risk. To balance the risk to Wade's human capital, the retirement portfolio should overweight sector funds that are either uncorrelated or negatively correlated with the oil industry. Sectors, such as transportation, that perform well when oil prices fall will provide some buffer against fluctuations in the value of Wade's human capital.

The value of Jennifer's pension will likely be a significant share of the couple's total wealth. Discounted at a modest bond rate of comparable duration to the expected pension payments, the value of her pension likely exceeds the US$300,000 that John has saved in his 401(k). If her pension were less secure, which can be estimated based on the percentage of future obligations that can be funded from current assets, then the pension would be discounted at a higher rate. Jennifer's pension can be viewed as a forced savings plan with a promised stable future payout that is comparable to a bond. If the discounted value is estimated to be US$500,000, then this portion of the total portfolio will be characterized as a bond-like asset. Couples with significant pension assets can accept greater risk in the rest of their investment portfolio because poor risky asset performance has less of an impact on future spending when the bulk of consumption will be funded from stable pension income. Wade can take greater risk in his 401(k) because the couple will be able to rely on Jennifer's pension. Note that although it is often difficult to consider, the possibility of divorce should also affect recommendations if pension assets are not allocated to the other spouse. For example, couples may want to hold greater liquidity, and spouses with defined contribution savings or more volatile human capital may choose to take less investment risk.

> **EXAMPLE 17**
>
> **Asset Allocation and Risk Reduction**
>
> Consider two 35-year-old couples, each of which earns a combined US$150,000 per year. One couple consists of an individual who is employed as a petroleum engineer and a non-working spouse. The other couple consists of two high school teachers. Compare asset allocation and risk reduction strategies for each couple.
>
> **Solution:**
>
> The human capital value of the couple consisting of the petroleum engineer and the non-working spouse is likely lower than the combined human capital value of the high school teachers, although the combined lifetime cumulative wages of the teachers is likely lower than those of the engineer and the spouse. Earnings for the engineer are highly correlated with oil prices, and either rising or falling prices will affect the household's available income in the future. The impact of a disability on employability may be more severe for the engineer than for a teacher. The engineer should thus likely consider a less risky portfolio and should overweight securities that have a low correlation with oil prices. Conversely, the teachers should select a riskier portfolio as a result of their higher human capital and low correlation with individual market sectors.

SUMMARY

The risk management process for individuals is complex given the variety of potential risks that may be experienced over the life cycle and the differences that exist across households. In this reading, key concepts related to risk management and individuals include the following:

- The two primary asset types for most individuals can be described broadly as human capital and financial capital. Human capital is the net present value of the individual's future expected labor income, whereas financial capital consists of assets currently owned by the individual and can include such items as a bank account, individual securities, pooled funds, a retirement account, and a home.
- Economic net worth is an extension of traditional balance sheet net worth that includes claims to future assets that can be used for consumption, such as human capital, as well as the present value of pension benefits.
- There are typically four key steps in the risk management process for individuals: Specify the objective, identify risks, evaluate risks and select appropriate methods to manage the risks, and monitor outcomes and risk exposures and make appropriate adjustments in methods.
- The financial stages of life for adults can be categorized in the following seven periods: education phase, early career, career development, peak accumulation, pre-retirement, early retirement, and late retirement.
- The primary goal of an economic (holistic) balance sheet is to arrive at an accurate depiction of an individual's overall financial health by accounting for the present value of all available marketable and non-marketable assets, as

Summary

well as all liabilities. An economic (holistic) balance sheet includes traditional assets and liabilities, as well as human capital and pension value, as assets and includes consumption and bequests as liabilities.

- The total economic wealth of an individual changes throughout his or her lifetime, as do the underlying assets that make up that wealth. The total economic wealth of younger individuals is typically dominated by the value of their human capital. As individuals age, earnings will accumulate, increasing financial capital.

- Earnings risk refers to the risks associated with the earnings potential of an individual—that is, events that could negatively affect someone's human and financial capital.

- Premature death risk relates to the death of an individual, such as a family member, whose future earnings (human capital) were expected to help pay for the financial needs and aspirations of the family.

- Longevity risk is the risk of reaching an age at which one's income and financial assets are insufficient to provide adequate support.

- Property risk relates to the possibility that one's property may be damaged, destroyed, stolen, or lost. There are different types of property insurance, depending on the asset, such as automobile insurance and homeowner's insurance.

- Liability risk refers to the possibility that an individual or other entity may be held legally liable for the financial costs of property damage or physical injury.

- Health risk refers to the risks and implications associated with illness or injury. Health risks manifest themselves in different ways over the life cycle and can have significant implications for human capital.

- The primary purpose of life insurance is to help replace the economic value of an individual to a family or a business in the event of that individual's death. The family's need for life insurance is related to the potential loss associated with the future earnings power of that individual.

- The two main types of life insurance are temporary and permanent. Temporary life insurance, or term life insurance, provides insurance for a certain period of time specified at purchase, whereas permanent insurance, or whole life insurance, is used to provide lifetime coverage, assuming the premiums are paid over the entire period.

- Fixed annuities provide a benefit that is fixed (or known) for life, whereas variable annuities have a benefit that can change over time and that is generally based on the performance of some underlying portfolio or investment. When selecting between fixed and variable annuities, there are a number of important considerations, such as the volatility of the benefit, flexibility, future market expectations, fees, and inflation concerns.

- Among the factors that would likely increase demand for an annuity are the following: longer-than-average life expectancy, greater preference for lifetime income, less concern for leaving money to heirs, more conservative investing preferences, and lower guaranteed income from other sources (such as pensions).

- Techniques for managing a risk include risk avoidance, risk reduction, risk transfer, and risk retention. The most appropriate choice among these techniques often is related to consideration of the frequency and severity of losses associated with the risk.

- The decision to retain risk or buy insurance is determined by a household's risk tolerance. At the same level of wealth, a more risk-tolerant household will prefer to retain more risk, either through higher insurance deductibles or by simply not buying insurance, than will a less risk-tolerant household. Insurance products that have a higher load will encourage a household to retain more risk.

- An individual's total economic wealth affects portfolio construction through asset allocation, which includes the overall allocation to risky assets, as well as the underlying asset classes, such as stocks and bonds, selected by the individual.

- Investment risk, property risk, and human capital risk can be either idiosyncratic or systematic. Examples of idiosyncratic risks include the risks of a specific occupation, the risk of living a very long life or experiencing a long-term illness, and the risk of premature death or loss of property. Systematic risks affect all households.

REFERENCES

Chen, Peng, and Moshe A. Milevsky. 2003. "Merging Asset Allocation and Longevity Insurance: An Optimal Perspective on Payout Annuities." *Journal of Financial Planning*, vol. 16, no. 6 (June): 52–62.

Ibbotson, Roger G., Moshe A. Milevsky, Peng Chen, and Kevin X. Zhu. 2007. *Lifetime Financial Advice: Human Capital, Asset Allocation, and Insurance*. Charlottesville, VA: Research Foundation of CFA Institute.

Markowitz, Harry. 1952. "Portfolio Selection." *Journal of Finance*, vol. 7, no. 1 (March): 77–91.

Oyer, Paul. 2008. "The Making of an Investment Banker: Stock Market Shocks, Career Choice, and Lifetime Income." *Journal of Finance*, vol. 63, no. 6 (December): 2601–2628.

Rejda, George E., and Michael J. McNamara. 2014. *Principles of Risk Management and Insurance*, 12th ed. Upper Saddle River, NJ: Prentice Hall.

PRACTICE PROBLEMS

The following information relates to Questions 1–8

Richard Lansky is an insurance and wealth adviser for individuals. Lansky's first meeting of the day is with Gregory Zavris, age 27, a new client who works as a journalist. Gregory's only asset is $5,000 in savings; he has $67,000 in liabilities. During the conversation, Lansky describes the concepts of financial capital and human capital, as well as the components of economic and traditional balance sheets. Gregory asks Lansky:

> On which balance sheet are my future earnings reflected?

Gregory does not have medical insurance. He asks Lansky for advice regarding a policy that potentially would allow him to avoid paying for office visits related to minor medical problems.

In the afternoon, Lansky meets with Gregory's parents, Molly and Kirk, ages 53 and 60. Molly is a tenured university professor and provides consulting services to local businesses. Kirk is a senior manager for an investment bank. Lansky determines that Molly's income is more stable than Kirk's.

Kirk and Molly discuss estate planning, and Lansky recommends a whole life insurance policy on Kirk's life, with Molly responsible for paying the premiums. In the event of Kirk's death, Gregory would be entitled to the proceeds from the policy. Lansky explains that one feature of the policy provides for a portion of the benefits to be paid even if a premium payment is late or missed.

Molly tells Lansky that she has recently been reading about annuities and would like to clarify her understanding. Molly makes the following statements.

Statement 1   Both deferred and immediate annuities provide the same flexibility concerning access to invested funds.

Statement 2   The income yield for a given amount invested in a life-only immediate annuity is higher for an older person than for a younger person.

At the end of the consultation, Molly asks Lansky for advice regarding her retired aunt, Rose Gabriel, age 69. Molly believes that Gabriel's life annuity and pension benefits will provide enough income to meet her customary lifestyle needs. Gabriel lives in her mortgage-free home; her medical insurance plan covers basic health care expenses. Women in Gabriel's family generally have long life spans but often experience chronic health problems requiring extended nursing at home. Therefore, Molly is concerned that medical expenses might exceed Gabriel's net worth during her final years.

1   Gregory's human capital is:
    A   lower than his financial capital.
    B   equal to his financial capital.
    C   higher than his financial capital.

2   The *most* appropriate response to Gregory's balance sheet question is:
    A   the economic balance sheet only.
    B   the traditional balance sheet only.

C both the economic and the traditional balance sheets.

3 Given Gregory's policy preference, which type of medical insurance should Lansky recommend?
   A Indemnity plan
   B Preferred provider plan
   C Health maintenance organization plan

4 In estimating Molly's human capital value, Lansky should apply an income volatility adjustment that is:
   A less than Kirk's.
   B the same as Kirk's.
   C greater than Kirk's.

5 Regarding the whole life insurance policy recommended by Lansky, Kirk would be the:
   A owner.
   B insured.
   C beneficiary.

6 The whole life insurance policy feature described by Lansky is a:
   A non-forfeiture clause.
   B waiver-of-premium rider.
   C guaranteed insurability rider.

7 Which of Molly's statements about annuities is/are correct?
   A Statement 1 only
   B Statement 2 only
   C Both Statement 1 and Statement 2

8 The type of insurance that will *best* address Molly's concern about Gabriel is:
   A disability insurance.
   B longevity insurance.
   C long-term care insurance.

The following information relates to Questions 9–15

Henri Blanc is a financial adviser serving high-net-worth individuals in the United States. Alphonse Perrin, age 55, meets with Blanc for advice about coordinating his employee benefits with his investment and retirement planning strategies.

Perrin has adopted a life-cycle portfolio strategy and plans to retire in 10 years. Recently, he received a promotion and $50,000 salary increase to manage a regional distribution center for a national retail firm. Perrin's spending needs are currently less than his annual income, and he has no debt. His investment assets consist of $2,000,000 in marketable securities (90% equity/10% fixed income) and a vineyard with winery valued at $1,500,000.

Blanc leads Perrin through a discussion of the differences between his financial capital and his human capital, as well as between his traditional balance sheet and his economic balance sheet. Perrin is vested in a defined benefit pension plan based

Practice Problems

on years of service and prior salary levels. Future benefits will vest annually based on his new salary. Perrin makes the following statements regarding his understanding of pension benefits.

Statement 1   Unvested pension benefits should be classified as human capital.

Statement 2   Vested pension benefits should not be classified as financial capital until payments begin.

Perrin asks Blanc to compare his traditional and economic balance sheets. Blanc calculates that the sum of the present values of Perrin's consumption goals and bequests exceeds that of his unvested pension benefits and future earnings.

Perrin tells Blanc that he expects a slower rate of growth in the US economy. Perrin expresses the following concerns to Blanc.

Concern 1   Holding all else equal, I wonder what the effect will be on my human capital if the nominal risk-free rate declines?

Concern 2   My employer projects a slower rate of sales growth in my region; therefore, I am anxious about losing my job.

Perrin is a widower with three adult children who live independently. Perrin's oldest son wishes to inherit the vineyard; the two other children do not want to be involved. Perrin would like to accommodate his children's wishes; however, he wants each child to inherit equal value from his estate. Blanc explains potential uses of life insurance to Perrin and suggests that one of these uses best meets Perrin's immediate needs.

Perrin expresses a preference for a life insurance policy that provides a range of investment options. Perrin selects a policy and asks Blanc to calculate the net payment cost index (per $1,000 of face value, per year), using a life expectancy of 20 years and a discount rate of 5%. Table 1 provides information about Perrin's policy.

Table 1 Perrin's Life Insurance Policy	
Face value	$500,000
Annual premium (paid at beginning of the year)	$12,000
Policy dividends anticipated per year (paid at end of the year)	$2,000
Cash value projected at the end of 20 years	$47,000

9 Which of Perrin's statements regarding his pension is/are correct?
   A   Statement 1 only
   B   Statement 2 only
   C   Both Statement 1 and Statement 2

10 Blanc's calculations show that Perrin's economic net worth is:
   A   less than his net worth.
   B   equal to his net worth.
   C   greater than his net worth.

11 In response to Perrin's Concern #1, human capital will *most likely*:
   A   decrease.
   B   remain the same.
   C   increase.

12 Perrin's Concern #2 identifies a risk related to:
   A   human capital only.

B   financial capital only.
   C   both human and financial capital.

13 Which of the following uses of life insurance *best* meets Perrin's immediate needs?
   A   Provides estate liquidity
   B   Acts as a tax-sheltered savings instrument
   C   Replaces lost earning power for dependents

14 The type of life insurance *most appropriate* for Perrin is:
   A   term.
   B   universal.
   C   whole life.

15 The net payment cost index that Blanc should calculate is *closest* to:
   A $17.48.
   B $20.00.
   C $20.19.

The following information relates to Questions 16–23

Adrian and Olivia Barksdale live in Australia with their 16-year-old twins. Adrian, 47, works in a highly cyclical industry as an engineering manager at a bauxite mine. Olivia, 46, is an accountant. The Barksdales are saving for their retirement and college funding for both children. Adrian's annual salary is A$190,000; Olivia's annual salary is A$85,000. The family's living expenses are currently A$95,000 per year.

Both Adrian and Olivia plan to work 18 more years, and they depend on their combined income and savings to fund their goals. The Barksdales' new financial adviser, Duncan Smith, recommends an appropriate disability insurance policy to cover Adrian, given his large salary. Because he has a highly specialized job, Adrian is willing to pay for the most comprehensive policy available.

Smith is also concerned about the Barksdales' existing life insurance coverage. Currently, the Barksdales have a term life policy insuring Adrian with a death benefit of A$100,000. Smith assesses the family's insurance needs in the event Adrian were to die this year. To do so, Smith uses the needs analysis method based on the financial data presented in Exhibit 1 and the following assumptions:

- The discount rate is 6.0%, and the tax rate is 30%.
- Salary and living expenses grow at 3.5% annually.
- Salary and living expenses occur at the beginning of each year.
- The following assumptions apply in the event of Adrian's death:
  - Olivia will continue to work until retirement;
  - Family living expenses will decline by $30,000 per year;
  - Olivia's projected living expense will be $50,000 per year for 44 years; and
  - The children's projected living expenses will be $15,000 per year for 6 years.

Practice Problems

Exhibit 1   Barksdale Family Financial Needs Worksheet

Cash Needs	AUD (A$)
Final expenses and taxes payable	20,000
Mortgage retirement	400,000
Education fund	300,000
Emergency fund	30,000
Total cash needs	750,000
Capital Available	
Cash and investments	900,000
Adrian: Life insurance	100,000
Total capital available	1,000,000

Next, Smith discusses the advantages and disadvantages of annuities. The Barksdales are interested in purchasing an annuity that offers the following characteristics:

- a payout that begins at retirement,
- the ability to invest in a menu of investment options, and
- a payout that continues as long as either Olivia or Adrian is living.

Olivia's mother, Sarah Brown, is also a client of Smith. She is age 75 and retired, and she needs a known income stream to assist her with current and future expenses. Brown's parents both lived longer than average, and she is concerned about outliving her assets. Smith recommends an annuity.

The Barksdales also worry about longevity risk given their family history and healthy lifestyle. Both spouses want an annuity for their later years (beginning in 40 years) that will ensure the greatest supplemental, level income stream relative to the cost. The Barksdales are willing to forgo the right to cash out the policy.

Smith turns to a discussion about the Barksdales' investment portfolio and how total economic wealth (human capital plus financial capital) might affect asset allocation decisions. The Barksdales' human capital is valued at $2.9 million and estimated to be 35% equity-like. Smith determines that an overall target allocation of 40% equity is appropriate for the Barksdales' total assets on the economic balance sheet.

Smith makes two recommendations regarding the Barksdales' investment portfolio.

Recommendation 1   The portfolio should have lower risk than a portfolio for similar investors in the same lifestyle stage.

Recommendation 2   The portfolio should underweight securities having a high correlation with bauxite demand.

16 Based on Adrian's job and salary, the *most appropriate* disability policy would define disability as the inability to perform duties of:

   A any occupation.

   B Adrian's regular occupation.

   C any occupation for which Adrian is suited by education and experience.

17 Based on the given assumptions and the data in Exhibit 1, the additional amount of life insurance coverage needed is *closest* to:

   A A$0.

   B A$331,267.

    C A$2,078,101.

18 Based on the Barksdales' annuity preferences, which type of annuity should they purchase?
    A Deferred fixed
    B Deferred variable
    C Immediate variable

19 Based on the Barksdales' annuity preferences, which annuity payout method should they choose?
    A Joint life annuity
    B Life annuity with refund
    C Life annuity with period certain

20 Based on Brown's goals and concerns, which type of annuity should Smith recommend for her?
    A Deferred fixed
    B Immediate fixed
    C Immediate variable

21 Which type of annuity *best* satisfies the Barksdales' desire for supplemental income in their later years?
    A Deferred fixed
    B Deferred variable
    C Advanced life deferred

22 Based on Exhibit 1, and meeting the Barksdales' target equity allocation for total economic wealth, the financial capital equity allocation should be *closest* to:
    A 35.0%.
    B 54.5%.
    C 56.1%.

23 Which of Smith's recommendations regarding the Barksdales' investment portfolio is/are correct?
    A Recommendation 1 only
    B Recommendation 2 only
    C Both Recommendation 1 and Recommendation 2

SOLUTIONS

1. C is correct. Gregory is in the early career stage of life, and human capital represents a large proportion of his total wealth. Gregory is relatively young; therefore, the present value of his expected earnings implies positive human capital. Furthermore, Gregory's savings are rather low, so his financial capital is small. Consequently, his human capital is greater than his financial capital.

2. A is correct. The present value of expected future earnings is reflected on an economic balance sheet but not on a traditional balance sheet.

3. C is correct. A health maintenance organization plan is a type of medical insurance that allows office visits at no, or very little, cost. Gregory would like to avoid paying for office visits related to minor medical problems; hence this alternative is the most appropriate.

4. A is correct. The income volatility adjustment reflects the fact that income from different professions can vary significantly. Molly works in an industry that has low correlation with the capital markets; she also earns income from an additional source. Kirk works in an industry that has high correlation with capital markets, and so he might experience higher income variability than Molly. Consequently, in estimating Molly's human capital, the income volatility adjustment for Molly should be lower than Kirk's.

5. B is correct. The policy would be on Kirk's life; his death would trigger the insurance payment. Therefore, Kirk would be the insured.

6. A is correct. The whole life insurance policy feature described is a non-forfeiture clause, whereby there is the option to receive some portion of the benefits if premium payments are missed (i.e., before the policy lapses).

7. B is correct. Statement 2 is correct because, all else equal, the income yield is higher when expected longevity is shorter; therefore, the income yield will be higher for an older person.

8. C is correct. Molly is concerned about a potential late-life medical condition that may require extended home care for Gabriel. Long-term care insurance is designed to cover a portion of the cost of home care, assisted living facilities, and/or nursing home expense. Gabriel has enough resources to cover her living expenditures, but her medical insurance might be insufficient to cover the costs of extended home care, medicine, or hospital stays. Consequently, long-term care insurance is the most appropriate insurance choice given Gabriel's situation.

9. A is correct. Unvested pension benefits are typically contingent on future work and are thus considered to be part of human capital. Statement #2 is incorrect: vested pension benefits can be considered components of financial capital.

10. A is correct. Economic net worth is calculated as follows:

    Economic net worth = Net worth from the traditional balance sheet + (Present value of future earnings + Present value of unvested pension benefits) − (Present value of consumption goals + Present value of bequests)

    Perrin's economic net worth is less than his net worth because the sum of the present values of consumption and bequests is greater than the sum of the present values of future earnings and unvested pensions.

11 C is correct. Human capital, HC_0, is calculated as follows:

$$HC_0 = \sum_{t=1}^{N} \frac{p(s_t)w_{t-1}(1+g_t)}{(1+r_f+y)^t}$$

Holding all else equal as Perrin directs, a reduction in the nominal risk-free rate, r_f, would decrease the total discount rate, thus increasing the present value of human capital.

12 C is correct. The projected slowdown in his employer's sales growth may result in Perrin's unemployment, indicating that he may be subject to earnings risk. Human capital would be reduced by the loss of future earnings and halt accrual of pension benefits at Perrin's present employer. Financial capital could also be affected because assets may need to be sold to make up for any loss of income.

13 A is correct. Life insurance best meets Perrin's immediate need for estate liquidity. A life insurance policy can provide liquidity without the delay involved in the legal process of settling the estate. This liquidity can be particularly valuable if the estate contains illiquid assets or assets that are difficult to separate and distribute equitably among heirs. Currently, it would be difficult to separate and equitably distribute Perrin's financial assets to his three children such that the oldest son inherits the vineyard and winery while keeping the other two children uninvolved because the business is worth more than one-third of Perrin's investment assets. The problem of separating and equitably distributing the estate exists presently regardless of the value of Perrin's personal property.

14 B is correct. Perrin's estate distribution plan indicates a need for estate liquidity funded by permanent insurance that can remain in force until his death. Perrin prefers a policy that offers a range of investment options. Universal life is thus most appropriate because it is a form of permanent insurance that can remain in force until Perrin's death and typically has more options for investing the cash value than do whole life policies.

15 C is correct. The net payment cost index assumes that the insured will die at the end of a specified period—in this case, the given life expectancy of 20 years. Calculating the net payment cost index includes the following steps.

Future value of premiums (annuity due, 5%, 20 years)	$416,631.02

Financial calculator operations:

N = 20, I = 5, PV = 0, PMT = –12,000, mode = begin: FV → 416,631.02

Future value of dividends (ordinary annuity, 5%, 20 years)	($66,131.91)

N = 20, I = 5, PV = 0, PMT = 2,000, mode = end: FV → –66,131.91

20-Year insurance cost	$350,499.11
Annual payments for insurance cost (annuity due, 5%, 20 years)	($10,095.24)

N = 20, I = 5, PV = 0, FV = 350,499.11, mode = begin: PMT → –10,095.24

Net payment cost index ($10,095.24/500)	($20.19)

16 B is correct. The most comprehensive policy would define disability as the inability to perform Adrian's regular occupation. For professionals with specialized skills, policies that use regular occupation are generally preferred even though they are more expensive. Mr. Barksdale works in a specialized, high-paying occupation, and the family depends on his income.

17 B is correct. The additional amount of life insurance coverage needed is calculated as the difference between the family's total financial needs and total capital available.

Total financial needs are calculated as follows.

Cash Needs	AUD (A$)
Final expenses and taxes	20,000
Mortgage retirement	400,000
Education fund	300,000
Emergency fund	30,000
Total cash needs	750,000

Capital Needs	Present Value
Olivia's living expenses, 44 years	1,377,175
Children's living expenses, 6 years	84,848
(Olivia's income, 18 years)	−880,756
Total capital needs	581,267
Total financial needs	**1,331,267**

Capital needs are determined as the present value of an annuity due: growth rate = 3.5%, discount rate = 6.0%. Growth of payments is incorporated by adjusting the discount rate to account for the growth rate of earnings. As long as the discount rate is larger than the growth rate, the adjusted rate i can be calculated as follows: [(1 + Discount rate)/(1 + Growth rate)] − 1, or i = (1.06/1.035) − 1 = 2.42%.

The present value of Olivia's living expenses is calculated as follows:

PMT = −$50,000; i = 2.42%, n = 44. Set for payments at beginning of year. PV = $1,377,175.

The present value of the children's living expenses is calculated as follows:

PMT = −15,000; i = 2.42%, n = 6. Set for payments at beginning of year. PV = $84,848.

The present value of Olivia's income is calculated as follows:

PMT = −$85,000 × (1− Tax rate); PMT = $85,000 × 0.70 = 59,500; i = 2.42%, n = 18. Set for payments at beginning of year. PV = −$880,756.

Total capital needs are calculated as follows:

$1,377,175 + $84,848 − $880,756 = $581,267. Adding this amount to total cash needs of $750,000 results in total financial needs of $1,331,267.

The total capital available is calculated as follows.

Capital Available	AUD (A$)
Cash and investments	900,000
Current life insurance	100,000
Total capital available	1,000,000

The additional life insurance need is calculated as follows.

Total financial needs	1,331,267
Total capital available	1,000,000
Life insurance shortfall (excess)	331,267

18 B is correct. The Barksdales want an annuity with a deferred payout (beginning at retirement) and an ability to invest in a diversified mix of securities. Most deferred variable annuities offer a diversified menu of potential investment options, whereas a fixed annuity locks the annuitant into a portfolio of bond-like assets at whatever rate of return exists at the time of purchase.

19 A is correct. A joint life annuity best addresses the Barksdales' goal of receiving a payout as long as either of them is alive. Under a joint life annuity, two or more individuals, such as a husband and a wife, receive payments until all beneficiaries die.

20 B is correct. With immediate fixed annuities, Brown will trade a sum of money today for a promised income benefit for as long as she is alive. Brown is already age 75 and is concerned about longevity risk; she wants a known income stream currently and in the future. Therefore, an immediate fixed annuity is the most appropriate choice.

21 C is correct. In contrast to an immediate payout annuity, an advanced life deferred annuity's (ALDA's) payments begin later in life—for example, when the individual turns 80 or 85. An ALDA would provide the greatest supplemental level income relative to the cost because the payments are made far in the future, life expectancy is shorter when the payments begin, and some policyholders will die without receiving payments.

22 C is correct. The equity allocation of the Barksdale's financial capital is calculated as follows:

Total economic wealth = Human capital + Financial capital = $2,900,000 + $900,000 = $3,800,000.

Target equity allocation of total economic wealth = $3,800,000 × 40% = $1,520,000

Human capital equity allocation = $2,900,000 × 35% = $1,015,000

Financial capital equity allocation = $1,520,000 − $1,015,000 = $505,000

% Financial capital equity allocation = Financial equity allocation/Total financial capital
= $505,000/$900,000
= 0.5611, or 56.1%

23 C is correct. People with higher risk and potential volatility in income (human capital) should take on lower risk in their investment portfolios. Adrian's income is more than two-thirds of the household total and is somewhat volatile because of cyclical demand for his employer's product. Additionally, because income is tied to a particular industry or sector, the Barksdales should underweight securities having a high correlation with bauxite demand.

Glossary

Absolute return benchmark A minimum target return that an investment manager is expected to beat.

Accounting defeasance Also called in-substance defeasance, accounting defeasance is a way of extinguishing a debt obligation by setting aside sufficient high-quality securities to repay the liability.

Accumulation phase Phase where the government predominantly contributes to a sovereign wealth pension reserve fund.

Active management A portfolio management approach that allows risk factor mismatches relative to a benchmark index causing potentially significant return differences between the active portfolio and the underlying benchmark.

Active return Portfolio return minus benchmark return.

Active risk The annualized standard deviation of active returns, also referred to as *tracking error* (also sometimes called *tracking risk*).

Active risk budgeting Risk budgeting that concerns active risk (risk relative to a portfolio's benchmark).

Active share A measure of how similar a portfolio is to its benchmark. A manager who precisely replicates the benchmark will have an Active Share of zero; a manager with no holdings in common with the benchmark will have an Active Share of one.

Activist short selling A hedge fund strategy in which the manager takes a short position in a given security and then publicly presents his/her research backing the short thesis.

After-tax excess return Calculated as the after-tax return of the portfolio minus the after-tax return of the associated benchmark portfolio.

Agency trade A trade in which the broker is engaged to find the other side of the trade, acting as an agent. In doing so, the broker does not assume any risk for the trade.

Alpha decay In a trading context, alpha decay is the erosion or deterioration in short term alpha after the investment decision has been made.

Alternative trading systems (ATS) Non-exchange trading venues that bring together buyers and sellers to find transaction counterparties. Also called *multilateral trading facilities (MTF)*.

Anchoring and adjustment An information-processing bias in which the use of a psychological heuristic influences the way people estimate probabilities.

Anchoring and adjustment bias An information-processing bias in which the use of a psychological heuristic influences the way people estimate probabilities.

Anomalies Apparent deviations from market efficiency.

Arithmetic attribution An attribution approach which explains the arithmetic difference between the portfolio return and its benchmark return. The single-period attribution effects sum to the excess return, however, when combining multiple periods, the sub-period attribution effects will not sum to the excess return.

Arrival price In a trading context, the arrival price is the security price at the time the order was released to the market for execution.

Asset location The type of account an asset is held within, e.g., taxable or tax deferred.

Asset-only With respect to asset allocation, an approach that focuses directly on the characteristics of the assets without explicitly modeling the liabilities.

Asset swap spread (ASW) The spread over MRR on an interest rate swap for the remaining life of the bond that is equivalent to the bond's fixed coupon.

Asset swaps Convert a bond's fixed coupon to MRR plus (or minus) a spread.

Authorized participants Institutional investors who create and redeem ETF shares using an OTC primary market with an ETF sponsor.

Availability bias An information-processing bias in which people take a heuristic approach to estimating the probability of an outcome based on how easily the outcome comes to mind.

Back-fill bias The distortion in index or peer group data which results when returns are reported to a database only after they are known to be good returns.

Barbell A fixed-income investment strategy combining short- and long-term bond positions.

Base With respect to a foreign exchange quotation of the price of one unit of a currency, the currency referred to in "one unit of a currency."

Base-rate neglect A type of representativeness bias in which the base rate or probability of the categorization is not adequately considered.

Basis risk The risk resulting from using a hedging instrument that is imperfectly matched to the investment being hedged; in general, the risk that the basis will change in an unpredictable way.

Bear flattening A decrease in the yield spread between long- and short-term maturities across the yield curve, which is largely driven by a rise in short-term bond yields-to-maturity.

Bear spread An option strategy that becomes more valuable when the price of the underlying asset declines, so requires buying one option and writing another with a *lower* exercise price. A put bear spread involves buying a put with a higher exercise price and selling a put with a lower exercise price. A bear spread can also be executed with calls.

Bear steepening An increase in the yield spread between long- and short-term maturities across the yield curve, which is largely driven by a rise in long-term bond yields-to-maturity.

Behavioral finance macro A focus on market level behavior that considers market anomalies that distinguish markets from the efficient markets of traditional finance.

Behavioral finance micro A focus on individual level behavior that examines the behavioral biases that distinguish individual investors from the rational decision makers of traditional finance.

Bequest The transferring, or bequeathing, of assets in some other way upon a person's death. Also referred to as a testamentary bequest or testamentary gratuitous transfer.

Best-in-class An ESG implementation approach that seeks to identify the most favorable companies and sectors based on ESG considerations. Also called *positive screening*.

Bid price In a price quotation, the price at which the party making the quotation is willing to buy a specified quantity of an asset or security.

Breadth The number of truly independent decisions made each year.

Buffering Establishing ranges around breakpoints that define whether a stock belongs in one index or another.

Bull flattening A decrease in the yield spread between long- and short-term maturities across the yield curve, which is largely driven by a decline in long-term bond yields-to-maturity.

Bull spread An option strategy that becomes more valuable when the price of the underlying asset rises, so requires buying one option and writing another with a *higher* exercise price. A call bull spread involves buying a call with a lower exercise price and selling a call with a higher exercise price. A bull spread can also be executed with puts.

Bull steepening An increase in the yield spread between long- and short-term maturities across the yield curve, which is largely driven by a decline in short-term bond yields-to-maturity.

Bullet A fixed-income investment strategy that focuses on the intermediate term (or "belly") of the yield curve.

Business cycle Fluctuations in GDP in relation to long-term trend growth, usually lasting 9-11 years.

Butterfly spread A measure of yield curve shape or curvature equal to double the intermediate yield-to-maturity less the sum of short- and long-term yields-to-maturity.

Butterfly strategy A common yield curve shape strategy that combines a long or short bullet position with a barbell portfolio in the opposite direction to capitalize on expected yield curve shape changes.

Calendar rebalancing Rebalancing a portfolio to target weights on a periodic basis; for example, monthly, quarterly, semiannually, or annually.

Calendar spread A strategy in which one sells an option and buys the same type of option but with different expiration dates, on the same underlying asset and with the same strike. When the investor buys the more distant (near-term) call and sells the near-term (more distant) call, it is a long (short) calendar spread.

Canada model Characterized by a high allocation to alternatives. Unlike the endowment model, however, the Canada model relies more on internally managed assets. The innovative features of the Canada model are the: a) reference portfolio, b) total portfolio approach, and c) active management.

Capital gain or loss For tax purposes equals the selling price (net of commissions and other trading costs) of the asset less its tax basis.

Capital market expectations (CME) Expectations concerning the risk and return prospects of asset classes.

Capital needs analysis See *capital sufficiency analysis*.

Capital sufficiency analysis The process by which a wealth manager determines whether a client has, or is likely to accumulate, sufficient financial resources to meet his or her objectives; also known as *capital needs analysis*.

Capture ratio A measure of the manager's gain or loss relative to the gain or loss of the benchmark.

Carhart model A four factor model used in performance attribution. The four factors are: market (RMRF), size (SMB), value (HML), and momentum (WML).

Carry trade A trading strategy that involves buying a security and financing it at a rate that is lower than the yield on that security.

Carry trade across currencies A strategy seeking to benefit from a positive interest rate differential across currencies by combining a short position (or borrowing) in a low-yielding currency and a long position (or lending) in a high-yielding currency.

Cash drag Tracking error caused by temporarily uninvested cash.

Cash flow matching Immunization approach that attempts to ensure that all future liability payouts are matched precisely by cash flows from bonds or fixed-income derivatives.

Cash-secured put An option strategy involving the writing of a put option and simultaneously depositing an amount of money equal to the exercise price into a designated account (this strategy is also called a fiduciary put).

CDS curve Plot of CDS spreads across maturities for a single reference entity or group of reference entities in an index.

Cell approach See *stratified sampling*.

Charitable gratuitous transfers Asset transfers to not-for-profit or charitable organizations. In most jurisdictions charitable donations are not subject to a gift tax and most jurisdictions permit income tax deductions for charitable donations.

Charitable remainder trust A trust setup to provide income for the life of named-beneficiaries. When the last named-beneficiary dies any remaining assets in this trust are distributed to the charity named in the trust, hence the term *charitable remainder* trust.

Closet indexer A fund that advertises itself as being actively managed but is substantially similar to an index fund in its exposures.

Cognitive cost The effort involved in processing new information and updating beliefs.

Cognitive dissonance The mental discomfort that occurs when new information conflicts with previously held beliefs or cognitions.

Cognitive errors Behavioral biases resulting from faulty reasoning; cognitive errors stem from basic statistical, information processing, or memory errors.

Collar An option position in which the investor is long shares of stock and then buys a put with an exercise price below the current stock price and writes a call with an exercise price above the current stock price. Collars allow a shareholder to acquire downside protection through a protective put but reduce the cash outlay by writing a covered call.

Completion overlay A type of overlay that addresses an indexed portfolio that has diverged from its proper exposure.

Completion portfolio Is an index-based portfolio that when added to a given concentrated asset position creates an overall portfolio with exposures similar to the investor's benchmark.

Conditional value at risk (CVaR) Also known as expected loss The average portfolio loss over a specific time period conditional on that loss exceeding the value at risk (VaR) threshold.

Confirmation bias A belief perseverance bias in which people tend to look for and notice what confirms their beliefs, to ignore or undervalue what contradicts their beliefs, and to misinterpret information as support for their beliefs.

Conjunction fallacy An inappropriate combining of probabilities of independent events to support a belief. In fact, the probability of two independent events occurring in conjunction is never greater than the probability of either event occurring alone; the probability of two independent events occurring together is equal to the multiplication of the probabilities of the independent events.

Conservatism bias A belief perseverance bias in which people maintain their prior views or forecasts by inadequately incorporating new information.

Contingent immunization Hybrid approach that combines immunization with an active management approach when the asset portfolio's value exceeds the present value of the liability portfolio.

Controlled foreign corporation (CFC) A company located outside a taxpayer's home country in which the taxpayer has a controlling interest as defined under the home country law.

Covered call An option strategy in which a long position in an asset is combined with a short position in a call on that asset.

Covered interest rate parity The relationship among the spot exchange rate, the forward exchange rate, and the interest rate in two currencies that ensures that the return on a hedged (i.e., covered) foreign risk-free investment is the same as the return on a domestic risk-free investment. Also called *interest rate parity*.

Credit cycle The expansion and contraction of credit over the business cycle, which translates into asset price changes based on default and recovery expectations across maturities and rating categories.

Credit default swap (CDS) basis Yield spread on a bond, as compared to CDS spread of same tenor.

Credit loss rate The realized percentage of par value lost to default for a group of bonds equal to the bonds' default rate multiplied by the loss severity.

Credit migration The change in a bond's credit rating over a certain period.

Credit valuation adjustment (CVA) The present value of credit risk for a loan, bond, or derivative obligation.

Cross-currency basis swap An interest rate swap involving the periodic exchange of floating payments in one currency for another based upon respective market reference rates with an initial and final exchange of notional principal.

Cross hedge A hedge involving a hedging instrument that is imperfectly correlated with the asset being hedged; an example is hedging a bond investment with futures on a non-identical bond.

Cross-sectional consistency A feature of expectations setting which means that estimates for all classes reflect the same underlying assumptions and are generated with methodologies that reflect or preserve important relationships among the asset classes, such as strong correlations. It is the internal consistency across asset classes.

Cross-sectional momentum A managed futures trend following strategy implemented with a cross-section of assets (within an asset class) by going long those that are rising in price the most and by shorting those that are falling the most. This approach generally results in holding a net zero (market-neutral) position and works well when a market's out- or underperformance is a reliable predictor of its future performance.

Currency overlay A type of overlay that helps hedge the returns of securities held in foreign currency back to the home country's currency.

Currency overlay programs A currency overlay program is a program to manage a portfolio's currency exposures for the case in which those exposures are managed separately from the management of the portfolio itself.

Custom security-based benchmark Benchmark that is custom built to accurately reflect the investment discipline of a particular investment manager. Also called a *strategy benchmark* because it reflects a manager's particular strategy.

Decision price In a trading context, the decision price is the security price at the time the investment decision was made.

Decision-reversal risk The risk of reversing a chosen course of action at the point of maximum loss.

Decumulation phase Phase where the government predominantly withdraws from a sovereign wealth pension reserve fund.

Dedicated short-selling A hedge fund strategy in which the manager takes short-only positions in equities deemed to be expensively priced versus their deteriorating fundamental situations. Short exposures may vary only in terms of portfolio sizing by, at times, holding higher levels of cash.

Default intensity POD over a specified time period in a reduced form credit model.

Default risk Likelihood that a borrower will default or fail to meet its obligation to make full and timely payments of principal and interest according to the terms of a debt obligation.

Deferred annuity An annuity that enables an individual to purchase an income stream that will begin at a later date.

Defined benefit A retirement plan in which a plan sponsor commits to paying a specified retirement benefit.

Defined contribution A retirement plan in which contributions are defined but the ultimate retirement benefit is not specified or guaranteed by the plan sponsor.

Delay cost The (trading related) cost associated with not submitting the order to the market in a timely manner.

Delta The change in an option's price in response to a change in price of the underlying, all else equal.

Delta hedging Hedging that involves matching the price response of the position being hedged over a narrow range of prices.

Demand deposits Accounts that can be drawn upon regularly and without notice. This category includes checking accounts and certain savings accounts that are often accessible through online banks or automated teller machines (ATMs).

Diffusion index An index that measures how many indicators are pointing up and how many are pointing down.

Direct market access (DMA) Access in which market participants can transact orders directly with the order book of an exchange using a broker's exchange connectivity.

Disability income insurance A type of insurance designed to mitigate earnings risk as a result of a disability in which an individual becomes less than fully employed.

Discount margin The discount (or required) margin is the yield spread versus the MRR such that the FRN is priced at par on a rate reset date.

Discretionary portfolio management An arrangement in which a wealth manager has a client's pre-approval to execute investment decisions.

Discretionary trust A trust that enables the trustee to determine whether and how much to distribute based on a beneficiary's general welfare.

Disposition effect As a result of loss aversion, an emotional bias whereby investors are reluctant to dispose of losers. This results in an inefficient and gradual adjustment to deterioration in fundamental value.

Dividend capture A trading strategy whereby an equity portfolio manager purchases stocks just before their ex-dividend dates, holds these stocks through the ex-dividend date to earn the right to receive the dividend, and subsequently sells the shares.

Domestic asset An asset that trades in the investor's domestic currency (or home currency).

Domestic currency The currency of the investor, i.e., the currency in which he or she typically makes consumption purchases, e.g., the Swiss franc for an investor domiciled in Switzerland.

Domestic-currency return A rate of return stated in domestic currency terms from the perspective of the investor; reflects both the foreign-currency return on an asset as well as percentage movement in the spot exchange rate between the domestic and foreign currencies.

Double taxation A term used to describe situations in which income is taxed twice. For example, when corporate earnings are taxed at the company level and then that portion of earnings paid as dividends is taxed again at the investor level.

Drawdown A decline in value (represented by a series of negative returns only) following a peak fund valuation.

Drawdown duration The total time from the start of the drawdown until the cumulative drawdown recovers to zero.

Due diligence Investigation and analysis in support of an investment action, decision, or recommendation.

Duration matching Immunization approach based on the duration of assets and liabilities. Ideally, the liabilities being matched (the liability portfolio) and the portfolio of assets (the bond portfolio) should be affected similarly by a change in interest rates.

Duration times spread Weighting of spread duration by credit spread in order to incorporate the empirical observation that spread changes for lower-rated bonds tend to be consistent on a percentage, rather than absolute, basis.

Duration Times Spread (DTS) Weighting of spread duration by credit spread to incorporate the empirical observation that spread changes for lower-rated bonds tend to be consistent on a percentage rather than absolute basis.

Dynamic asset allocation A strategy incorporating deviations from the strategic asset allocation that are motivated by longer-term valuation signals or economic views than usually associated with tactical asset allocation.

Dynamic hedge A hedge requiring adjustment as the price of the hedged asset changes.

Earnings risk The risk associated with the earning potential of an individual.

Econometrics The application of quantitative modeling and analysis grounded in economic theory to the analysis of economic data.

Economic balance sheet A balance sheet that provides an individual's total wealth portfolio, supplementing traditional balance sheet assets with human capital and pension wealth, and expanding liabilities to include consumption and bequest goals. Also known as *holistic balance sheet*.

Economic indicators Economic statistics provided by government and established private organizations that contain information on an economy's recent past activity or its current or future position in the business cycle.

Economic net worth The difference between an individual's assets and liabilities; extends traditional financial assets and liabilities to include human capital and future consumption needs.

Effective federal funds (FFE) rate The fed funds rate actually transacted between depository institutions, not the Fed's target federal funds rate.

Emotional biases Behavioral biases resulting from reasoning influenced by feelings; emotional biases stem from impulse or intuition.

Empirical duration Estimation of the price-yield relationship using historical bond market data in statistical models.

Endowment bias An emotional bias in which people value an asset more when they hold rights to it than when they do not.

Endowment model Characterized by a high allocation to alternative investments (private investments and hedge funds), significant active management, and externally managed assets.

Enhanced indexing approach Maintains a close link to the benchmark but attempts to generate a modest amount of outperformance relative to the benchmark.

Enhanced indexing strategy Method investors use to match an underlying market index in which the investor purchases fewer securities than the full set of index constituents but matches primary risk factors reflected in the index.

Equity monetization A group of strategies that allow investors to receive cash for their concentrated stock positions without an outright sale. These transactions are structured to avoid triggering the capital gains tax.

Estate Consists of all of the property a person owns or controls, which may consist of financial assets (e.g., bank accounts, stocks, bonds, business interests), tangible personal assets (e.g., artwork, collectibles, vehicles), immovable property (e.g., residential real estate, timber rights), and intellectual property (e.g., royalties).

Estate planning The process of preparing for the disposition of one's estate upon death and during one's lifetime.

Estate tax Levied on the total value of a deceased person's assets and paid out of the estate before any distributions to beneficiaries.

Evaluated pricing See *matrix pricing*.

Excess return Used in various senses appropriate to context: 1) The difference between the portfolio return and the benchmark return; 2) The return in excess of the risk-free rate.

Excess spread Credit spread return measure that incorporates both changes in spread and expected credit losses for a given period.

Exchange fund A partnership in which each of the partners have each contributed low cost-basis stock to the fund. Used in the United Sates as a mechanism to achieve a tax-free exchange of a concentrated asset position.

Execution cost The difference between the (trading related) cost of the real portfolio and the paper portfolio, based on shares and prices transacted.

Exhaustive   An index construction strategy that selects every constituent of a universe.

Expected shortfall   The average loss conditional on exceeding the VaR cutoff; sometimes referred to as *conditional VaR* or *expected tail loss*.

Expected tail loss   See *expected shortfall*.

Extended portfolio assets and liabilities   Assets and liabilities beyond those shown on a conventional balance sheet that are relevant in making asset allocation decisions; an example of an extended asset is human capital.

Factor-model-based benchmarks   Benchmarks constructed by examining a portfolio's sensitivity to a set of factors, such as the return for a broad market index, company earnings growth, industry, or financial leverage.

Family constitution   Typically a non-binding document that sets forth an agreed-upon set of rights, values, and responsibilities of the family members and other stakeholders. Used by many wealth- and business-owning families as the starting point of conflict resolution procedures.

Family governance   The process for a family's collective communication and decision making designed to serve current and future generations based on the common values of the family.

Financial capital   The tangible and intangible assets (excluding human capital) owned by an individual or household.

Fixed trust   Distributions to beneficiaries of a fixed trust are specified in the trust document to occur at certain times or in certain amounts.

Forced heirship   Is the requirement that a certain proportion of assets must pass to specified family members, such as a spouse and children.

Foreign assets   Assets denominated in currencies other than the investor's home currency.

Foreign currency   Currency that is not the currency in which an investor makes consumption purchases, e.g., the US dollar from the perspective of a Swiss investor.

Foreign-currency return   The return of the foreign asset measured in foreign-currency terms.

Forward rate bias   An empirically observed divergence from interest rate parity conditions that active investors seek to benefit from by borrowing in a lower-yield currency and investing in a higher-yield currency.

Foundation   A legal entity available in certain jurisdictions. Foundations are typically set up to hold assets for a specific charitable purpose, such as to promote education or for philanthropy. When set up and funded by an individual or family and managed by its own directors, it is called a *private foundation*. The term *family foundation* usually refers to a private foundation where donors or members of the donors' family are actively involved.

Framing   An information-processing bias in which a person answers a question differently based on the way in which it is asked (framed).

Framing bias   An information-processing bias in which a person answers a question differently based on the way in which it is asked (framed).

Fulcrum securities   Partially-in-the-money claims (not expected to be repaid in full) whose holders end up owning the reorganized company in a corporate reorganization situation.

Full replication approach   When every issue in an index is represented in the portfolio, and each portfolio position has approximately the same weight in the fund as in the index.

Fund-of-funds   A fund of hedge funds in which the fund-of-funds manager allocates capital to separate, underlying hedge funds (e.g., single manager and/or multi-manager funds) that themselves run a range of different strategies.

Funding currencies   The low-yield currencies in which borrowing occurs in a carry trade.

G-spread   Yield spread for a fixed-rate bond over a government benchmark.

Gamblers' fallacy   A misunderstanding of probabilities in which people wrongly project reversal to a long-term mean.

Gamma   The change in an option's delta for a change in price of the underlying, all else equal.

General account   Account holding assets to fund future liabilities from traditional life insurance and fixed annuities, the products in which the insurer bears all the risks—particularly mortality risk and longevity risk.

Generation-skipping tax   Taxes levied in some jurisdictions on asset transfers (gifts) that skip one generation such as when a grandparent transfers asset s to their grandchildren. (see related Gift Tax).

Gift tax   Depending on the tax laws of the country, assets gifted by one person to another during the giftor's lifetime may be subject to a gift tax.

Goals-based   With respect to asset allocation or investing, an approach that focuses on achieving an investor's goals (for example, related to supporting lifestyle needs or aspirations) based typically on constructing sub-portfolios aligned with those goals.

Goals-based investing   An investment industry term for approaches to investing for individuals and families focused on aligning investments with goals (parallel to liability-driven investing for institutional investors).

Green bonds   Fixed-income instruments issued by private or public sector borrowers that directly fund ESG initiatives.

Grinold–Kroner model   An expression for the expected return on a share as the sum of an expected income return, an expected nominal earnings growth return, and an expected repricing return.

Halo effect   An emotional bias that extends a favorable evaluation of some characteristics to other characteristics.

Hard-catalyst event-driven approach   An event-driven approach in which investments are made in reaction to an already announced corporate event (mergers and acquisitions, bankruptcies, share issuances, buybacks, capital restructurings, re-organizations, accounting changes) in which security prices related to the event have yet to fully converge.

Hazard rate   The conditional POD, or the likelihood that default will occur given that it has not already occurred in a prior period.

Health insurance   A type of insurance used to cover health care and medical costs.

Health risk   The risk associated with illness or injury.

Hedge ratio   The relationship of the quantity of an asset being hedged to the quantity of the derivative used for hedging.

Herding   When a group of investors trade on the same side of the market in the same securities, or when investors ignore their own private information and act as other investors do.

High-water mark   A specified net asset value level that a fund must exceed before performance fees are paid to the hedge fund manager.

Hindsight bias   A bias with selective perception and retention aspects in which people may see past events as having been predictable and reasonable to expect.

Holdings-based attribution A "buy and hold" attribution approach which calculates the return of portfolio and benchmark components based upon the price and foreign exchange rate changes applied to daily snapshots of portfolio holdings.

Holdings-based style analysis A bottom-up style analysis that estimates the risk exposures from the actual securities held in the portfolio at a point in time.

Holistic balance sheet See *economic balance sheet*.

Home bias A preference for securities listed on the exchanges of one's home country.

Home-country bias The favoring of domestic over non-domestic investments relative to global market value weights.

Home currency See *domestic currency*.

Human capital An implied asset; the net present value of an investor's future expected labor income weighted by the probability of surviving to each future age. Also called *net employment capital*.

I-spread (interpolated spread) Yield spread measure using swaps or constant maturity Treasury YTMs as a benchmark.

Illusion of control A bias in which people tend to believe that they can control or influence outcomes when, in fact, they cannot. Illusion of knowledge and self-attribution biases contribute to the overconfidence bias.

Illusion of control bias A bias in which people tend to believe that they can control or influence outcomes when, in fact, they cannot. Illusion of knowledge and self-attribution biases contribute to the overconfidence bias.

Immediate annuity An annuity that provides a guarantee of specified future monthly payments over a specified period of time.

Immunization An asset/liability management approach that structures investments in bonds to match (offset) liabilities' weighted-average duration; a type of dedication strategy.

Impact investing Investment approach that seeks to achieve targeted social or environmental objectives along with measurable financial returns through engagement with a company or by direct investment in projects or companies.

Implementation shortfall (IS) The difference between the return for a notional or paper portfolio, where all transactions are assumed to take place at the manager's decision price, and the portfolio's actual return, which reflects realized transactions, including all fees and costs.

Implied volatility The outlook for the future volatility of the underlying asset's price. It is the value (i.e., standard deviation of underlying's returns) that equates the model (e.g., Black–Scholes–Merton model) price of an option to its market price.

Implied volatility surface A three-dimensional plot, for put and call options on the same underlying asset, of days to expiration (x-axis), option strike prices (y-axis), and implied volatilities (z-axis). It simultaneously shows the volatility skew (or smile) and the term structure of implied volatility.

Incremental VaR (or partial VaR) The change in the minimum portfolio loss expected to occur over a given time period at a specific confidence level resulting from increasing or decreasing a portfolio position.

Information coefficient Formally defined as the correlation between forecast return and actual return. In essence, it measures the effectiveness of investment insight.

Inheritance tax Paid by each individual beneficiary of a deceased person's estate on the value of the benefit the individual received from the estate.

Input uncertainty Uncertainty concerning whether the inputs are correct.

Interaction effect The attribution effect resulting from the interaction of the allocation and selection decisions.

Intertemporal consistency A feature of expectations setting which means that estimates for an asset class over different horizons reflect the same assumptions with respect to the potential paths of returns over time. It is the internal consistency over various time horizons.

Intestate A person who dies without a valid will or with a will that does not dispose of their property are considered to have died intestate.

Intrinsic value The difference between the spot exchange rate and the strike price of a currency option.

Investment currencies The high-yielding currencies in a carry trade.

Investment policy statement A written planning document that describes a client's investment objectives and risk tolerance over a relevant time horizon, along with the constraints that apply to the client's portfolio.

Investment style A natural grouping of investment disciplines that has some predictive power in explaining the future dispersion of returns across portfolios.

Irrevocable trust The person whose assets are used to create the trust gives up the right to rescind the trust relationship and regain title to the trust assets.

Key person risk The risk that results from over-reliance on an individual or individuals whose departure would negatively affect an investment manager.

Key rate duration A method of measuring interest rate sensitivities of a fixed-income instrument or portfolio to shifts in key points along the yield curve.

Knock-in/knock-out Features of a vanilla option that is created (or ceases to exist) when the spot exchange rate touches a pre-specified level.

Leading economic indicators A set of economic variables whose values vary with the business cycle but at a fairly consistent time interval before a turn in the business cycle.

Liability-based mandates Mandates managed to match or cover expected liability payments (future cash outflows) with future projected cash inflows.

Liability-driven investing An investment industry term that generally encompasses asset allocation that is focused on funding an investor's liabilities in institutional contexts.

Liability driven investing (LDI) model In the LDI model, the primary investment objective is to generate returns sufficient to cover liabilities, with a focus on maximizing expected surplus return (excess return of assets over liabilities) and managing surplus volatility.

Liability glide path A specification of desired proportions of liability-hedging assets and return-seeking assets and the duration of the liability hedge as funded status changes and contributions are made.

Liability insurance A type of insurance used to manage liability risk.

Liability-relative With respect to asset allocation, an approach that focuses directly only on funding liabilities as an investment objective.

Liability risk The possibility that an individual or household may be held legally liable for the financial costs associated with property damage or physical injury.

Life-cycle finance A concept in finance that recognizes as an investor ages, the fundamental nature of wealth and risk evolves.

Life insurance A type of insurance that protects against the loss of human capital for those who depend on an individual's future earnings.

Life settlement The sale of a life insurance contract to a third party. The valuation of a life settlement typically requires detailed biometric analysis of the individual policyholder and an understanding of actuarial analysis.

Limited-life foundations A type of foundation where founders seek to maintain control of spending while they (or their immediate heirs) are still alive.

Liquidity budget The portfolio allocations (or weightings) considered acceptable for the liquidity categories in the liquidity classification schedule (or time-to-cash table).

Liquidity classification schedule A liquidity management classification (or table) that defines portfolio liquidity "buckets" or categories based on the estimated time it would take to convert assets in that particular category into cash.

Longevity risk The risk of outliving one's financial resources.

Loss-aversion bias A bias in which people tend to strongly prefer avoiding losses as opposed to achieving gains.

Loss severity Also known as loss given default (LGD). The amount of loss if a default occurs, usually expressed as a percentage of annual terms.

Macro attribution Attribution at the sponsor level.

Manager peer group See *manager universe*.

Manager universe A broad group of managers with similar investment disciplines. Also called *manager peer group*.

Matrix pricing An approach for estimating the prices of thinly traded securities based on the prices of securities with similar attributions, such as similar credit rating, maturity, or economic sector. Also called *evaluated pricing*.

Matrix pricing (or evaluated pricing) Methodology for pricing infrequently traded bonds using bonds from similar issuers and actively traded government benchmarks to establish a bond's fair value.

Mental accounting bias An information-processing bias in which people treat one sum of money differently from another equal-sized sum based on which mental account the money is assigned to.

Micro attribution Attribution at the portfolio manager level.

Minimum-variance hedge ratio A mathematical approach to determining the optimal cross hedging ratio.

Mission-related investing Aims to direct a significant portion of assets in excess of annual grants into projects promoting a foundation's mission.

Model uncertainty Uncertainty as to whether a selected model is correct.

Mortality table A table that indicates individual life expectancies at specified ages.

Multi-class trading An equity market-neutral strategy that capitalizes on misalignment in prices and involves buying and selling different classes of shares of the same company, such as voting and non-voting shares.

Multi-manager fund Can be of two types—one is a multi-strategy fund in which teams of portfolio managers trade and invest in multiple different strategies within the same fund; the second type is a fund of hedge funds (or fund-of-funds) in which the manager allocates capital to separate, underlying hedge funds that themselves run a range of different strategies.

Multi-strategy fund A fund in which teams of portfolio managers trade and invest in multiple different strategies within the same fund.

Multilateral trading facilities (MTF) See *Alternative trading systems (ATS)*.

Negative butterfly An increase in the butterfly spread due to lower short- and long-term yields-to-maturity and a higher intermediate yield-to-maturity.

Negative screening An ESG implementation approach that excludes certain sectors or companies that deviate from an investor's accepted standards.

Non-deliverable forwards Forward contracts that are cash settled (in the non-controlled currency of the currency pair) rather than physically settled (the controlled currency is neither delivered nor received).

Nonstationarity A characteristic of series of data whose properties, such as mean and variance, are not constant through time. When analyzing historical data it means that different parts of a data series reflect different underlying statistical properties.

Norway model Characterized by an almost exclusive reliance on public equities and fixed income (the traditional 60/40 equity/bond model falls under the Norway model), with largely passively managed assets and with very little to no allocation to alternative investments.

OAS duration The change in bond price for a given change in OAS.

Offer price The price at which a counterparty is willing to sell one unit of the base currency.

Opportunity cost The (trading related) cost associated with not being able to transact the entire order at the decision price.

Option-adjusted spread (OAS) A generalization of the Z-spread yield spread calculation that incorporates bond option pricing based on assumed interest rate volatility.

Optional stock dividends A type of dividend in which shareholders may elect to receive either cash or new shares.

Options on bond futures contracts Instruments that involve the right, but not the obligation, to enter into a bond futures contract at a pre-determined strike (bond price) on a future date in exchange for an up-front premium.

Overbought When a market has trended too far in one direction and is vulnerable to a trend reversal, or correction.

Overconfidence bias A bias in which people demonstrate unwarranted faith in their own intuitive reasoning, judgments, and/or cognitive abilities.

Overlay A derivative position (or positions) used to adjust a pre-existing portfolio closer to its objectives.

Oversold The opposite of overbought; see *overbought*.

Packeting Splitting stock positions into multiple parts.

Pairs trading An equity market-neutral strategy that capitalizes on the misalignment in prices of pairs of similar under- and overvalued equities. The expectation is the differential valuations or trading relationships will revert to their long-term mean values or their fundamentally-correct trading relationships, with the long position rising and the short position declining in value.

Parameter uncertainty Uncertainty arising because a quantitative model's parameters are estimated with error.

Participant/cohort option Pools the DC plan member with a cohort that has a similar target retirement date.

Participant-switching life-cycle options Automatically switch DC plan members into a more conservative asset mix as their age increases. There may be several automatic de-risking switches at different age targets.

Passive investment In the fixed-income context, it is investment that seeks to mimic the prevailing characteristics of the overall investments available in terms of credit quality, type of borrower, maturity, and duration rather than express a specific market view.

Passive management A buy-and-hold approach to investing in which an investor does not make portfolio changes based upon short-term expectations of changing market or security performance.

Percent-range rebalancing An approach to rebalancing that involves setting rebalancing thresholds or trigger points, stated as a percentage of the portfolio's value, around target values.

Performance attribution Attribution, including return attribution and risk attribution; often used as a synonym for return attribution.

Permanent life insurance A type of life insurance that provides lifetime coverage.

Portfolio overlay An array of derivative positions managed separately from the securities portfolio to achieve overall intended portfolio characteristics.

Position delta The overall or portfolio delta. For example, the position delta of a covered call, consisting of long 100 shares and short one at-the-money call, is +50 (= +100 for the shares and -50 for the short ATM call).

Positive butterfly A decrease in the butterfly spread due to higher short- and long-term yields-to-maturity and a lower intermediate yield-to-maturity.

Positive screening An ESG implementation approach that seeks to identify the most favorable companies and sectors based on ESG considerations. Also called *best-in-class*.

Post-liquidation return Calculates the return assuming that all portfolio holdings are sold as of the end date of the analysis and that the resulting capital gains tax that would be due is deducted from the ending portfolio value.

Potential capital gain exposure (PCGE) Is an estimate of the percentage of a fund's assets that represents gains and measures how much the fund's assets have appreciated. It can be an indicator of possible future capital gain distributions.

Premature death risk The risk of an individual dying earlier than anticipated; sometimes referred to as *mortality risk*.

Present value of distribution of cash flows methodology Method used to address a portfolio's sensitivity to rate changes along the yield curve. This approach seeks to approximate and match the yield curve risk of an index over discrete time periods.

Principal trade A trade in which the market maker or dealer becomes a disclosed counterparty and assumes risk for the trade by transacting the security for their own account. Also called *broker risk trades*.

Probability of default The likelihood that a borrower defaults or fails to meet its obligation to make full and timely payments of principal and interest.

Probate The legal process to confirm the validity of the will so that executors, heirs, and other interested parties can rely on its authenticity.

Program trading A strategy of buying or selling many stocks simultaneously.

Progressive tax rate schedule A tax regime in which the tax rate increases as the amount of income or wealth being taxed increases.

Property insurance A type of insurance used by individuals to manage property risk.

Property risk The possibility that a person's property may be damaged, destroyed, stolen, or lost.

Protective put An option strategy in which a long position in an asset is combined with a long position in a put on that asset.

Pure indexing Attempts to replicate a bond index as closely as possible, targeting zero active return and zero active risk.

Put spread A strategy used to reduce the upfront cost of buying a protective put, it involves buying a put option and writing another put option.

Qualified dividends Generally dividends from shares in domestic corporations and certain qualified foreign corporations which have been held for at least a specified minimum period of time.

Quantitative market-neutral An approach to building market-neutral portfolios in which large numbers of securities are traded and positions are adjusted on a daily or even an hourly basis using algorithm-based models.

Quoted margin The yield spread over the MRR established upon issuance of an FRN to compensate investors for assuming an issuer's credit risk.

Re-base With reference to index construction, to change the time period used as the base of the index.

Realized volatility Historical volatility, the square root of the realized variance of returns, which is a measure of the range of past price outcomes for the underlying asset.

Rebalancing In the context of asset allocation, a discipline for adjusting the portfolio to align with the strategic asset allocation.

Rebalancing overlay A type of overlay that addresses a portfolio's need to sell certain constituent securities and buy others.

Rebalancing range A range of values for asset class weights defined by trigger points above and below target weights, such that if the portfolio value passes through a trigger point, rebalancing occurs. Also known as a corridor.

Rebate rate The portion of the collateral earnings rate that is repaid to the security borrower by the security lender.

Reduced form credit models Credit models that solve for default probability over a specific time period using observable company-specific variables such as financial ratios and macroeconomic variables.

Reduced-form models Models that use economic theory and other factors such as prior research output to describe hypothesized relationships. Can be described as more compact representations of underlying structural models. Evaluate endogenous variables in terms of observable exogenous variables.

Regime The governing set of relationships (between variables) that stem from technological, political, legal, and regulatory environments. Changes in such environments or policy stances can be described as changes in regime.

Regret The feeling that an opportunity has been missed; typically an expression of *hindsight bias*.

Regret-aversion bias An emotional bias in which people tend to avoid making decisions that will result in action out of fear that the decision will turn out poorly.

Relative value A concept that describes the selection of the most attractive individual securities to populate the portfolio with, using ranking and comparing.

Relative value volatility arbitrage A volatility trading strategy that aims to source and buy cheap volatility and sell more expensive volatility while netting out the time decay aspects normally associated with options portfolios.

Relative VaR The minimum portfolio loss expected to occur over a given time period at a specific confidence level based on a portfolio containing active positions minus benchmark holdings.

Repo rate The interest rate on a repurchase agreement.

Representativeness bias A belief perseverance bias in which people tend to classify new information based on past experiences and classifications.

Repurchase agreements In repurchase agreements, or *repos*, a security owner agrees to sell a security for a specific cash amount while simultaneously agreeing to repurchase the security at a specified future date (typically one day later) and price.

Request for quote (RFQ) A non-binding quote provided by a market maker or dealer to a potential buyer or seller upon request. Commonly used in fixed income markets these quotes are only valid at the time they are provided.

Reserve portfolio The component of an insurer's general account that is subject to specific regulatory requirements and is intended to ensure the company's ability to meet its policy liabilities. The assets in the reserve portfolio are managed conservatively and must be highly liquid and low risk.

Resistance levels Price points on dealers' order boards where one would expect to see a clustering of offers.

Return attribution A set of techniques used to identify the sources of the excess return of a portfolio against its benchmark.

Returns-based attribution An attribution approach that uses only the total portfolio returns over a period to identify the components of the investment process that have generated the returns. The Brinson–Hood–Beebower approach is a returns-based attribution approach.

Returns-based benchmarks Benchmarks constructed by examining a portfolio's sensitivity to a set of factors, such as the returns for various style indexes (e.g., small-cap value, small-cap growth, large-cap value, and large-cap growth).

Returns-based style analysis A top-down style analysis that involves estimating the sensitivities of a portfolio to security market indexes.

Reverse repos Repurchase agreements from the standpoint of the lender.

Revocable trust The person whose assets are used to create the trust retains the right to rescind the trust relationship and regain title to the trust assets.

Risk attribution The analysis of the sources of risk.

Risk aversion The degree of an investor's unwillingness to take risk; the inverse of risk tolerance.

Risk budgeting The establishment of objectives for individuals, groups, or divisions of an organization that takes into account the allocation of an acceptable level of risk.

Risk capacity The ability to accept financial risk.

Risk perception The subjective assessment of the risk involved in the outcome of an investment decision.

Risk premium An extra return expected by investors for bearing some specified risk.

Risk reversal A strategy used to profit from the existence of an implied volatility skew and from changes in its shape over time. A combination of long (short) calls and short (long) puts on the same underlying with the same expiration is a long (short) risk reversal.

Risk tolerance The capacity to accept risk; the level of risk an investor (or organization) is willing and able to bear.

Sample-size neglect A type of representativeness bias in which financial market participants incorrectly assume that small sample sizes are representative of populations (or "real" data).

Scenario analysis What-if analysis that involves changing multiple assumptions at the same time in order to evaluate the change in an investment's value.

Seagull spread An extension of the risk reversal foreign exchange option strategy that limits downside risk.

Securities lending A form of collateralized lending that may be used to generate income for portfolios.

Selective An index construction methodology that targets only those securities with certain characteristics.

Self-attribution bias A bias in which people take personal credit for successes and attribute failures to external factors outside the individual's control.

Self-control bias A bias in which people fail to act in pursuit of their long-term, overarching goals because of a lack of self-discipline.

Separate accounts Accounts holding assets to fund future liabilities from variable life insurance and variable annuities, the products in which customers make investment decisions from a menu of options and themselves bear investment risk.

Sharpe ratio The average return in excess of the risk-free rate divided by the standard deviation of return; a measure of the average excess return earned per unit of standard deviation of return. Also known as the *reward-to-variability ratio*.

Short-biased A hedge fund strategy in which the manager uses a less extreme version of dedicated short-selling. It involves searching for opportunities to sell expensively priced equities, but short exposure may be balanced with some modest value-oriented, or index-oriented, long exposure.

Shortfall probability The probability of failing to meet a specific liability or goal.

Shrinkage estimation Estimation that involves taking a weighted average of a historical estimate of a parameter and some other parameter estimate, where the weights reflect the analyst's relative belief in the estimates.

Single-manager fund A fund in which one portfolio manager or team of portfolio managers invests in one strategy or style.

Smart beta Involves the use of transparent, rules-based strategies as a basis for investment decisions.

Smart order routers (SOR) Smart systems used to electronically route small orders to the best markets for execution based on order type and prevailing market conditions.

Social proof A bias in which individuals tend to follow the beliefs of a group.

Soft-catalyst event-driven approach An event-driven approach in which investments are made proactively in anticipation of a corporate event (mergers and acquisitions, bankruptcies, share issuances, buybacks, capital restructurings, re-organizations, accounting changes) that has yet to occur.

Special dividends A dividend paid by a company that does not pay dividends on a regular schedule, or a dividend that supplements regular cash dividends with an extra payment.

Spread duration The change in bond price for a given change in yield spread. Also referred to as *OAS duration* when the option-adjusted spread (OAS) is the yield measure used.

Staged diversification strategy The simplest approach to managing the risk of a concentrated position involves selling the concentrated position over some period of time, paying associated tax, and reinvesting the proceeds in a diversified portfolio.

Static hedge A hedge that is not sensitive to changes in the price of the asset hedged.

Status quo bias An emotional bias in which people do nothing (i.e., maintain the "status quo") instead of making a change.

Stock lending Securities lending involving the transfer of equities.

Stop-losses A trading order that sets a selling price below the current market price with a goal of protecting profits or preventing further losses.

Stops Stop-loss orders involve leaving bids or offers away from the current market price to be filled if the market reaches those levels.

Straddle An option combination in which one buys *both* puts and calls, with the same exercise price and same expiration date, on the same underlying asset. In contrast to this long straddle, if someone *writes* both options, it is a short straddle.

Strangle A variation on a straddle in which the put and call have different exercise prices; if the put and call are held long, it is a long strangle; if they are held short, it is a short strangle.

Stratified sampling A sampling method that guarantees that subpopulations of interest are represented in the sample. Also called *representative sampling* or *cell approach*.

Structural credit models Credit models that apply market-based variables to estimate the value of an issuer's assets and the volatility of asset value.

Structural models Models that specify functional relationships among variables based on economic theory. The functional form and parameters of these models are derived from the underlying theory. They may include unobservable parameters.

Structural risk Risk that arises from portfolio design, particularly the choice of the portfolio allocations.

Stub trading An equity market-neutral strategy that capitalizes on misalignment in prices and entails buying and selling stock of a parent company and its subsidiaries, typically weighted by the percentage ownership of the parent company in the subsidiaries.

Support levels Price points on dealers' order boards where one would expect to see a clustering of bids.

Surplus The difference between the value of assets and the present value of liabilities. With respect to an insurance company, the net difference between the total assets and total liabilities (equivalent to policyholders' surplus for a mutual insurance company and stockholders' equity for a stock company).

Surplus portfolio The component of an insurer's general account that is intended to realize higher expected returns than the reserve portfolio and so can assume some liquidity risk. Surplus portfolio assets are often managed aggressively with exposure to alternative assets.

Survivorship bias Bias that arises in a data series when managers with poor track records exit the business and are dropped from the database whereas managers with good records remain; when a data series of a given date reflects only entitites that have survived to that date.

Swaption This instrument grants a party the right, but not the obligation, to enter into an interest rate swap at a pre-determined strike (fixed swap rate) on a future date in exchange for an up-front premium.

Synthetic long forward position The combination of a long call and a short put with identical strike price and expiration, traded at the same time on the same underlying.

Synthetic short forward position The combination of a short call and a long put at the same strike price and maturity (traded at the same time on the same underlying).

Tactical asset allocation Asset allocation that involves making short-term adjustments to asset class weights based on short-term predictions of relative performance among asset classes.

Tax alpha Calculated by subtracting the pre-tax excess return from the after-tax excess return, the tax alpha isolates the benefit of tax management of the portfolio.

Tax avoidance The legal activity of understanding the tax laws and finding approaches that avoid or minimize taxation.

Tax basis In many cases, the tax basis is the amount that was paid to acquire an asset, or its 'cost' basis, and serves as the foundation for calculating a capital gain or loss.

Tax-deferred account An account where investments and contributions may be made on a pre-tax basis and investment returns accumulate on a tax-deferred basis until funds are withdrawn, at which time they are taxed at ordinary income tax rates.

Tax-efficiency ratio (TER) Is calculated as the after-tax return divided by the pre-tax return. It is used to understand if a fund is appropriate for the taxable account of a client.

Tax-efficient decumulation strategy Is the process of taking into account the tax considerations involved in deploying retirement assets to support spending needs over a client's remaining lifetime during retirement.

Tax-efficient strategy An investment strategy that is designed to give up very little of its return to taxes.

Tax evasion The illegal concealment and non-payment of taxes that are otherwise due.

Tax-exempt account An account on which no taxes are assessed during the investment, contribution, or withdrawal phase, nor are they assessed on investment returns.

Tax haven A country or independent area with no or very low tax rates for foreign investors.

Tax loss harvesting Selling securities at a loss to offset a realized capital gain or other income. The rules for what can be done vary by jurisdiction.

Tax lot accounting Important in tax loss harvesting strategies to identify the cost of securities sold from a portfolio that has been built up over time with purchases and sales over time. Tax lot accounting keeps track of how much was paid for an investment and when it was purchased for the portfolio. Not allowed in all jurisdictions.

Taxable account An account on which the normal tax rules of the jurisdiction apply to investments and contributions.

Taylor rule A rule linking a central bank's target short-term interest rate to the rate of growth of the economy and inflation.

Temporary life insurance A type of life insurance that covers a certain period of time, specified at purchase. Commonly referred to as "term" life insurance.

Term deposits Interest-bearing accounts that have a specified maturity date. This category includes savings accounts and certificates of deposit (CDs).

Term structure of volatility The plot of implied volatility (*y*-axis) against option maturity (*x*-axis) for options with the same strike price on the same underlying. Typically, implied volatility is not constant across different maturities – rather, it is often in contango, meaning that the implied volatilities for longer-term options are higher than for near-term ones.

Territorial tax systems Jurisdictions operate where only locally-sourced income is taxed.

Testamentary bequest See *Bequest*.

Testamentary gratuitous transfer See *Bequest*.

Testator The person who authored the will and whose property is disposed of according to the will.

Thematic investing An investment approach that focuses on companies within a specific sector or following a specific theme, such as energy efficiency or climate change.

Theta The daily change in an option's price, all else equal. Theta measures the sensitivity of the option's price to the passage of time, known as time decay.

Time deposits Interest-bearing accounts that have a specified maturity date. This category includes savings accounts and certificates of deposit (CDs).

Time-series estimation Estimators that are based on lagged values of the variable being forecast; often consist of lagged values of other selected variables.

Time-series momentum A managed futures trend following strategy in which managers go long assets that are rising in price and go short assets that are falling in price. The manager trades on an absolute basis, so be net long or net short depending on the current price trend of an asset. This approach works best when an asset's own past returns are a good predictor of its future returns.

Time-to-cash table See *liquidity classification schedule*.

Time value The difference between the market price of an option and its intrinsic value, determined by the uncertainty of the underlying over the remaining life of the option.

Total factor productivity A variable which accounts for that part of *Y* not directly accounted for by the levels of the production factors (*K* and *L*).

Total return payer Party responsible for paying the reference obligation cash flows and return to the receiver but that is also compensated by the receiver for any depreciation in the index or default losses incurred by the portfolio.

Total return receiver Receives both the cash flows from the underlying index and any appreciation in the index over the period in exchange for paying the MRR plus a predetermined spread.

Total return swap A swap in which one party agrees to pay the total return on a security. Often used as a credit derivative, in which the underlying is a bond.

Tracking error The standard deviation of the differences between a portfolio's returns and its benchmark's returns; a synonym of active risk. Also called *tracking risk*.

Tracking risk The standard deviation of the differences between a portfolio's returns and its benchmark's returns; a synonym of active risk. Also called *tracking error*.

Trade urgency A reference to how quickly or slowly an order is executed over the trading time horizon.

Transactions-based attribution An attribution approach that captures the impact of intra-day trades and exogenous events such as a significant class action settlement.

Transfer coefficient The ability to translate portfolio insights into investment decisions without constraint.

Trigger points In the context of portfolio rebalancing, the endpoints of a rebalancing range (corridor).

Trust A legal is a vehicle through which an individual (called a settlor) entrusts certain assets to a trustee (or trustees) who manages the assets for the benefit of assigned beneficiaries. A trust may be either a testamentary trust—a trust created through the testator's will—or a living or inter-vivos trust—a trust created during the settlor's lifetime.

Uncovered interest rate parity The proposition that the expected return on an uncovered (i.e., unhedged) foreign currency (risk-free) investment should equal the return on a comparable domestic currency investment.

Unsmoothing An adjustment to the reported return series if serial correlation is detected. Various approaches are available to unsmooth a return series.

Value at risk (VaR) A measure of the minimum portfolio loss expected to occur over a given time period at a specific confidence level.

Variance notional The notional amount of a variance swap; it equals vega notional divided by two times the volatility strike price [i.e., (vega notional)/(2 × volatility strike)].

Vega The change in an option's price for a change in volatility of the underlying, all else equal.

Vega notional The trade size for a variance swap, which represents the average profit and loss of the variance swap for a 1% change in volatility from the strike.

Vesting A term indicating that employees only become eligible to receive a pension after meeting certain criteria, typically a minimum number of years of service.

Volatility clustering The tendency for large (small) swings in prices to be followed by large (small) swings of random direction.

Volatility skew The skewed plot (of implied volatility (*y*-axis) against strike price (*x*-axis) for options on the same underlying with the same expiration) that occurs when the implied volatility increases for OTM puts and decreases for OTM calls, as the strike price moves away from the current price.

Volatility smile The U-shaped plot (of implied volatility (*y*-axis) against strike price (*x*-axis) for options on the same underlying with the same expiration) that occurs when the implied volatilities priced into both OTM puts and calls trade at a premium to implied volatilities of ATM options.

Will (or Testament) A document that outlines the rights others will have over one's property after death.

Withholding taxes Taxes imposed on income in the country in which an investment is made without regard for offsetting investment expenses or losses that may be available from the taxpayer's other investment activities.

Worldwide tax system Jurisdictions that tax all income regardless of its source.

Yield spread The simple difference between a bond's YTM and the YTM of an on-the-run government bond of similar maturity.

Z-score Credit risk model that uses financial ratios and market-based information weighted by coefficients to create a composite score used to classify firms based on the likelihood of financial distress.

Zero-discount margin (Z-DM) A yield spread calculation for FRNs that incorporates forward MRR.

Zero-volatility spread (Z-spread) Constant yield spread over a government (or interest rate swap) spot curve.